Sisson's
Word and Expression
Locater

By the same author

SISSON'S SYNONYMS:
AN UNABRIDGED SYNONYM & RELATED-TERMS LOCATER

THE UNABRIDGED CROSSWORD PUZZLE DICTIONARY

Sisson's

Word and Expression Locater

A. F. Sisson

Parker Publishing Company, Inc.
West Nyack, N.Y.

Thirty-third Printing.....October 1983

Library of Congress Catalog Card Number: 66-10390
Printed in the United States of America

How to Use This Book

This volume is a type of thesaurus, containing a most complete word and expression index and the more important synonyms or words of related connotation. It is thus an *index verborum* and a *synonymicon.* In fact, it is an index to the unabridged dictionary and to other sources of the more obscure and unusual words and phrases useful in English construction. It may seem paradoxical that there should be a need for a word index, since all standard dictionaries have their items arranged in alphabetical order. Nevertheless, a person may be unable to locate a word or expression unless he has a reasonable idea of the spelling of the word, or unless he can remember at least the initial portion of the expression he wishes to use.

Suppose one cannot recall the Latin expression meaning "there is no accounting for tastes." In this book, such expression (*de gustibus non est disputandum*) will be found, together with a French phrase of similar meaning, indexed under "taste." A person may wish to know the term for the religious ascetic who sits and gazes at his navel, or the name of this practice. Both can be located in this book under "navel," whereas unless one knows "hesychast," "omphalopsychite," or "omphaloskepsis" he would be unlikely to find these words in a dictionary. Perhaps one may want the name of the primitive practice of making a small crude model of a person who is to be harmed by sticking the model with pins or otherwise mistreating it. This word cannot be found under "model" or "magic" in any dictionary or other word book, but it can in this volume, which also contains hundreds of words and expressions that *cannot* be found in the unabridged dictionary.

Other unusual words made easy to locate include that for hater of tobacco smoke (misocapnist, **q.v. under** "tobacco"); mania for holding public office (empleomania, **indexed under** "public"); a novel, often biographical, developing a character from childhood to maturity (entwicklungsroman, **listed under** "novel"); computing time by counting tree rings (dendrochronology, **q.v. under** "time" **and** "tree"); having beautiful and shapely buttocks (callipygian, **indexed under** "buttocks"); pretentious use of recondite words and phrases (lexiphanicism, **see under** "word"); use of long words such as these (sesquipedalianism **or** polysyllabism, **also indexed under** "word"); an uncontrollable obsession for words (verbo-onomatomania, **see under** "word"); stretching when drowsy upon awakening (pandiculation, **q.v. under** "stretching"); a description of rivers (potamography, **listed under** "river"); the right of the strongest (*le droit du plus fort,* **see** "strong"); practice of transposition of letters, words, etc., in reading or writing (metathesis **or** strephosymbolia, **q.v. under** "letter," "transposition" **or** "word"); unintentional repetition of letters or words (dittography, **see under** "repetition"); an unconscious use of a word or words other than that intended (heterophemy **or** *lapsus linguae,* **see under** ("word"); speech that puts one asleep (*discours as-*

soupissant, **indexed under** "speech") ; an insignificant anonymous writer (anonymuncule, **listed under** "writer") ; a person who is self-taught (autodidact, **see under** "self") ; a supplement to a book containing matters not included in the text (paralipomena, **q.v. under** "supplement") ; a novel with real persons, events, etc., disguised (*roman à clef,* **listed under** "novel") ; a person who is mentally defective but brilliant in some field (idiot savant, **listed under** "person") ; false and spurious writings (anagignoskomena, apocrypha, **or** pseudepigrapha, **q.v. under** "falsely" **or** "writing") ; use of a man's name by a woman writer, as George Eliot (pseudandry, **listed under** "name" **or** "writer") ; use of a woman's name by a man writer (pseudogyny, **similarly listed**) ; complete works of a writer (*opera omnia,* **q.v. under** "writer") ; mania for writing (*cacoethes scribendi* **or** *furor scribendi,* **listed under** "writing") ; a pompous person (Aldibrontiphoscophornio, **indexed under** "person") ; and thousands of others.

From the foregoing, it will be observed that this book enables one not only to locate, from the thought involved, unusual and unfamiliar terminology, but also to help recall to mind a word or phrase which may have been temporarily forgotten. It is thus a locater, an aid to memory (*aide-memoire* **which expression will be found under** "memory"), and an aid to vocabulary enhancement.

This is, in some respects, a dictionary in reverse. Instead of supplying the meaning of a word, it furnishes the word from its meaning. As an indication of its comprehensiveness, one need only to examine such entries as "word" (136 entries and 309 definitions), "person" (137 entries and 413 definitions) ; "stubborn" (56 synonyms or related meanings), and such other items as "fear," "food," "knowledge," "language," "name," "self," "time," to name only a few.

Sisson's Word and Expression Locater has been prepared for persons who seek to express their thoughts with precision and effectiveness, and who desire to have access to an alphabetized listing of words and phrases useful in their work or studies. Business executives, advertising copywriters, authors, journalists, and others who prepare literature for public perusal will find among the synonyms and related terms a wellspring of variable choices to overcome bromidic and stereotypical words and expressions so often encountered, thus making it possible to add scintillation and a cachet of originality to their literary efforts. For example, in this book one finds after the entry "attractive" (with cross-reference to "alluring") the following choices: arresting, beguiling, bewitching, bonny, captivating, Circean, comely decorative, decorous, enticing, fascinating, intriguing, magnetic, mesmeric, personable, persuasive, prepossessing, psychagogic and seductive. Many other classifications are even more extensive, there being 56 synonyms for "stubborn" 34 for "change," 34 for "secret," 26 for "trick," and 23 for "gaiety" to cite but a few.

This volume will be of invaluable assistance to college and high-school students in the preparation of term papers, theses, and other monographs, or as a vocabulary builder. Any educated adult who wishes to enhance his vocabulary, or to locate a word or expression which has escaped his memory, will find this book very useful.

How to Use This Book

Many ordinary words, those a person of average schooling would be presumed to know, have not been included, nor is the book loaded with scientific or technical terms, there being listed only those which have some general application. In this way, and in many other respects, it differs from all previous synonymicons, thesauri, word finders, and other books dealing with vocabulary

All polysyllabic words found in English writing are not in this book. For example, the following are taken from *Gargantua* by Rabelais, Chapter XV:

disincornifistibulated his nether shoulder blade

morrambouzevezengouzequoquemorgasacbaquevezinemaffreliding my poor eyes

mocrocastebezasteverestegrigeligoscopapopondrillated us in all our upper members

trepignemanpenillorifrizonoufresterfumbledtumbled and squeezed her.

And from Shakespeare's *Love's Labor Lost* (Act V, Scene I): honorificabilitudinitatibus.

I have made a careful edit of the manuscript copy of *Sisson's Word and Expression Locater* by Dr. A. F. Sisson, and I should like to say that I have been deeply impressed by the contents of this most remarkable book. In my forty-one years as a teacher of English language and literature at the University of Maryland, I have examined many books dealing with vocabulary and linguistic studies and with words and their ways and uses in the development of the English language, and I can certify that no book with which I am familiar shows as much thoroughness and as much real scholarship as the *Word and Expression Locater.*

Any person interested in expanding his vocabulary or in finding unusual expressions for familiar and trite terminology is certain to be rewarded by referring to this remarkable text. Teachers, editors, critics, linguists and especially writers of scholarly texts should own and use Dr. A. F. Sisson's *Word and Expression Locater.* Its use is certain to be rewarding.

SUSAN E. HARMAN, Ph. D.
Professor Emeritus
English Language and Literature
University of Maryland

Explanation of Abbreviations and Signs Used in This Book

Phrases and expressions relating to aspects of subject words appear in italics under subject words. For example, *great* and *lack of* and *one having great diversity of* are indexed under ABILITY, with definitions provided.

a. .... adjective
abb. .... abbreviated
acct. .... account
adv. .... adverb
bet. .... between
cond. ...... condition
conj. .... conjunction
dir. .... direction
esp. .... especially
fem. .... feminine *or* female
int. .... interjection
lit. .... literature *or* literary
misc. ...... miscellaneous
mus. .... music *or* musical
n. .... noun
opp. .... opposite
part. .... particularly
pert. .... pertaining
pl. .... plural
prep. .... preposition
q.v. ...... which see
rel. .... relating *or* relative
sing. .... singular
usu. .... usually
v. .... verb
w/o. .... without

A

ABANDON: **v.** abdicate; abjure; apostatize; jettison; recant; relinquish; renounce; repudiate; surcease; surrender; vacate; **n.** ABANDONMENT: abdication; abjuration; apostasy; defection; recantation; relinquishment; renunciation; **a.** ABANDONED: apostate; apostatic; derelict; renunciative; renunciatory

ABASH: **v.** chagrin; daunt; discomfit; discompose; disconcert; humble; humiliate; mortify; **n.** ABASHMENT: **(see** "embarrassment") humiliation; mortification

ABBREVIATE: **v.** abridge; curtail; diminish; epitomize; synopsize; truncate; **n.** ABBREVIATION: **see** "summary"

ABDOMEN: **n.** paunch; pleon; tharm; venter
contents of: **n.** viscus; **(pl.** viscera); **a.** alvine; c(o)eliac; intestinal; splanchnic; visceral
having large: **a.** abdominous; ventripotent
pain in (esp. stomach): **n.** gastralgia
pert. to: **a.** abdominous; alvine; c(o)eliac; intestinal; splanchnic; visceral

ABERRATION: **see** "deviation"

ABET: **v.** advocate; countenance; espouse; foment; instigate; sanction; subscribe; subsidize; succor; **a. (see** "aiding") adjuvant; ancillary; contributory; subsidiary; **n.** ABETMENT: **(see** "help") adjuvancy; **n.** ABETTOR: **see** "accessory"

ABHORRENCE, *object or person of:* **n.** abomination; *bête noire;* execration; odium

ABILITY **(or** ABILITIES): **n.** adroitness; (ambi)dexterity; aptitude; attainment; caliber; capability; capacity; competence; *dynamis;* dynamism; endowment; faculty; ingeniosity; ingenuity; panurgy; potency; proficiency; talent; versatility
great: **n.** expertise; virtuosity
lack of: **n.** incapacitation; incompetence
one having great diversity of: **(see** *"jack-of-all-trades"*) **n.** Proteus; **n.** (ambi)dexterity

ABJECT: **(see** "base") **a.** contemptible; despicable; grovel(l)ing; ignoble

ABLE: **(see** "competent") **a.** dextrous; ingenious; proficient; versatile

ABNORMAL: **a.** aberrant; adventitious; anomalistic; anomalous; atypical; bizarre; eccentric; exceptional; extraordinary; grotesque; heteroclite; heterodox; idiosyncratic; pathological; phenomenal; preternatural; prodigious; supernatural; teratogenic; unconventional; unorthodox; **n.** ABNORMALITY: aberration; anomalism; anomaly; deviant; deviate; foible; heterodox(y); idiosyncrasy; imperfection; irregularity; macula; mannerism; phenomenality; phenom(enon); singularity; stigma
person or thing: **n.** aberrant; anomaly; atypical; deviant; deviate; heteroclite; heterodox; mutation; phenomenality; phenom(enon); prodigy; *rara avis;* sport

ABODE: **(see** "house") **n.** aerie; caravansary; domicile; habitat(ion); hearthstone; ingleside; rookery; xenodochium; **a.** domiciliary

ABOLISH: **(see** "eliminate") **v.** abrogate; annihilate; deracinate; disestablish; eradicate; expunge; exterminate; extirpate; invalidate; vitiate

ABOMINABLE: **see** "accursed"

ABOUT: **prep.** anent; *circa; circiter; in re*
-face: **(see** "reversal") **n.** *volte-face*

ABOVE: **a.** superior; superadjacent; supernal
as: **adv.** *ut supra*
being or coming from: **a.** celestial; supernal
-board: **adv.** *cartes sur table*
mentioned, where: **adv.** *ubi supra*

ABRADE: **see** "annoy"

ABREAST: **see** "up-to-date"

ABRIDGE: **see** "abbreviate" **and** "abstract"

ABRIDGEMENT: **(see** "summary") **n.** *précis;* schema

ABRUPT: **(see** 'rude") **a.** brusque; impetuous; instantaneous; precipitant; precipitate; precipitous; staccato; subitaneous; tumultuous; unceremonious; **n.** ABRUPTNESS: **(see** "haste") brusqueness; brusquerie; impetuosity; impulsivity; instantaneity; precipitancy

ABSENCE: **n.** absentation
during: **adv.** *durante absentia*
in: **adv.** *in absentia*
of mind: **see** "absent-mindedness"
to be conspicuous by: **adv.** *briller par son absence*

ABSENT: **a.** absentaneous; abstracted
in state of being: **adv.** *in absentia*
-minded: **a.** abstracted; distrait; distraught; inattentive; oblivious; preoccupied
-mindness: **n.** *absence d'esprit;* abstraction; heedlessness; preoccupation; reverie

ABSOLUTE: **(see** "inclusive" **and** "out-and-out") **a.** arbitrary; arrant; authentic; authoritative; autocratic; categorical; despotic; exhaustive; imprescriptible; inalienable; indefeasible; indubitable; invincible; irrefutable; mathematical; official; peremptory; plenary; plenipotent(ial); plenipotentiary; *pur et simple;* sweeping; thorough-going; unalienable; unequivocal; unmitigated; unqualified; unquestionable; unswerving; wholehearted
possession or control: **n.** monopolization; monopoly; **a.** monopolistic
rule: **n.** tyrannis; tyranny; **a.** tyrannic(al)

ABSORB: **v.** assimilate; consume; engulf; imbibe; incorporate; osmose; metabolize; monopolize; **a.** ABSORBENT: assimilative; assimilatory; bibulous; imbibitional; monopolistic; osmotic

ABSORPTION: **n.** assimilation; bibulosity; consumption; inbibition; incorporation; metabolism; monopolization; osmosis
agent increasing: **n.** absorbefacient
not capable of: **a.** inabsorbable

ABSTRACT: **v.** **(see** "remove") abridge; condense; epitomize; purloin; **a.** abstruse; acroamatic; esoteric; hermetic(al); inconcrete; incorporeal; metaphysical; nebulous; recondite; stratospheric(al); supernatural; theoretical; transcendental; **n.** abbrieviature; abridgement; capsulation; compendium; conspectus; epitome; lexicon; *precis; résumé;* summary; syllabus; synopsis
entity (as "whiteness" or "virtue"): **n.** abstractum; (**pl.** abstracta); subsistent
in the: **adv.** *in abstracta*
quality or state of being: **n.** transcendentality
rel. to or dealing w/ the: **a.** nomothetic; theoretic(al)
scheme or plan: **n.** architectonic(s)

ABSTRACTED: **see** "absent-minded"

ABSTRACTION: **n.** abbreviature; abridgement; abstrusity; immateriality; incorporeality; incorporeity; nebulosity
mental: **n.** brown study; cogitation; lucubration; preoccupation; reverie

ABSTRUSE: **see** "abstract" **and** "abstraction"
something which is, or quality of being: **n.** abstrusity; immateriality; incorporeality; incorporeity; nebulosity; profundity

ABSURD: **(see** "funny") **a.** ad absurdum; asinine; baroque; bizarre; chimerical; daedalic; egregious; fantastic; fatuous; grotesque; impracticable; inane; infeasible; insuperable; laputan; ludicrous; macaronic; monstrous; preposterous; ridiculous; unbelievable; unrealistic
too (absurd) for belief: **adv.** *ab absurdo; ad absurdum*

ABSURDITY: **n.** asininity; *bêtise;* bizarrerie; grotesqueness; grotesquerie; inanity; incredibility; ineptitude; irrationality; *non sequitur;* ridiculosity; **a.** **see** "absurd"

imaginary creature regarded as absolute (absurdity) : **n.** coquecigrue
proof of opposite by showing: **n.** *reductio ad absurdum*
argument by this method: **n.** apagoge; **a.** apagogic(al)
stupid: **n.** maggotry
to the point of: **adv.** *ad absurdum*

ABUNDANCE: **n.** affluence; amplitude; copiosity; copiousness; cornucopia; lavishness; luxuriance; magnitude; opulence; opulency; plen(t)itude; pleonasm; plethora; prodigality; profusion; repletion; satiety; sumptuosity; superfluity; **a.** ABUNDANT: abounding; affluent; ample; copious; cornucopian; exhaustless; exuberant; feracious; inexhaustible; lavish; lush; luxuriant; opulent; plenteous; plen(t)itudinous; plethoric; profuse; prolific; replete; teeming
of words: **n.** affluence; circumlocution; *copia verborum;* facundity; loquaciousness; loquacity; periphrasis; tautology

ABUSE: (**see** "censure") **v.** blaspheme; defame; disparage; malign; maltreat; revile; traduce; vituperate; **n.** (**see** "sassiness") abusiveness; animadversion; billingsgate; calumny; castigation; condemnation; contumely; defamation; excoriation; execration; expostulation; humiliation; infamy; maltreatment; objurgation; obloquy; philippic; reprehension; scurrility; villification; vituperation
language of: **n.** billingsgate; vituperation

ABUSIVE: **a.** captious; castigatory; caustic; censorious; clamorous; condemnatory; contemptuous; contumelious; damnatory; defamatory; denunciatory; despicable; disparaging; infamous; malign; objurgatory; opprobrious; reproachful; reprobative; sarcastic; sardonic; satirical; scurrilous; trenchant; vituperative; vituperous
and loud: **a.** scurrilous; thersitical
speech or writing: **n.** diatribe; jeremiad; philippic; tirade

ACADEMIC: **a.** collegiate; conjectural; didactic; doctrinaire; doctrinal; hypothetical; literary; pedantic; Platonic; postulatory; propaedeutic(al); quodlibetic(al); scholarly; scholastic; speculative; suppositional; supposititious; theoretical
environment: **n.** academe; academia
expression: **n.** scholasm

ACCENT: **n.** cadence; emphasis; ictus; inflection; intonation; stress

ACCEPT · *as own or as equal, or give full validity to:* **v.** nostrificate; **n.** nostrification
for want of anything better: **adv.** *faute de mieux;* **n.** Hobson's choice

ACCEPTED: (**see** "conventional") **a.** according to Hoyle; canonical; conformable; orthodox; prevalent, sanctioned; traditional; **n.** ACCEPTANCE: acceptation; canonicity; orthodoxy
in social usage: **a.** *comme il faut*
moral standards or behavior: **n. pl.** (the) amenities; canons of propriety; (the) civilities; convenances; conventions; (the) proprieties
standards, conforming to: (**see** "proper" **and** "standards") **a.** canonical; ethical; orthodox

ACCESS: **n.** approach; channel; *entrée*

ACCESSORY: (**see** "adjunct") **n.** accomplice; addendum; appurtenance; auxiliary; coadjutor; collaborator; collaborateur; colleague; complementary; confederate; *confrère;* incidental; satellite; subordinate; succenturiate; **a.** (**see** "subsidiary") auxiliary; complementary; incidental; succenturiate
in crime: **n.** confederate; *particeps criminis; socius criminis*
something which is: **n.** appurtenance; parergon; (pl. parerga); satellite

ACCIDENT: **n.** calamity; casualty; contingency; contretemps; fortuity; inadvertence; inadvertency; misadventure; mischance; mishap
inevitable or unavoidable: **n.** act of God; *casus fortuitus; force majeure; vis major*
loss from: **n.** *damnum fatale*
unlucky: **n.** contretemps

ACCIDENTAL: (**see** "involuntary") **a.** adjective; adventitious; casual; contingent; extraneous; fortuitous; inadvertent; incidental; serendipitous; unfortunate; unintentional; unmotivated; unpremeditated; untoward; unwitting
discovery: **n.** serendipity; **a.** serendipitous
quality or state of being: **n.** accidentality; extraneity; fortuity; inadvertency

ACCLAIM: (see "honor" and "fame") n. *éclat;* homage; plaudit

ACCLIMATE: see "accustom"

ACCOMMODATE: see "adapt"

ACCOMPANIMENT: n. circumstantiality; collaboration; complement; concomitance; Comitancy; concomitant; corollary; obbligato
w/o musical: a. or adv. *a capella*

ACCOMPANYING: (see "at same time" and "secondary") a. adventitious; circumstantial; concomitant; incidental

ACCOMPLICE: see "accessory"

ACCOMPLISH: (see "complete") v. actualize; consummate; effectuate; execute; fulfill; implement; perpetrate; realize; a. (see "done") implementary

ACCOMPLISHMENT: n. achievement; actuality; actualization; consummation; effectuation; entelechy; fulfillment; implementation; realization; talent
one's special: n. forte; *métier; tour de force*

ACCORD: (see "agreement") n. assonance; compatibility; congruity; consentience; consonance; correspondence; harmony; unanimity; unity
in: a. concordant; consentaneous; consentient; consonant; *en rapport;* harmonious; unanimous

ACCORDING *to custom:* adv. *ad usum* (abb. ad us.); *comme il faut; ex more*
to rule: adv. *ad amussim; ad usum* (abb. ad us.); *en règle;* a. consuetudinary; conventional; *de règle; de rigueur; selon les règles;* traditional
to value: adv. *ad valorem*

ACCUMULATE: v. agglutinate; aggregate; conglomerate; pyramid; n. ACCUMULATION: accretion; acervation; agglutination; aggregation; cache; congeries; conglomeration; incrustation; pyramid; superfetation; a. ACCUMULATIVE: accumulatable; augmentative; cumulative; pyramidal

ACCURATE: (see "correct" and "precise") a. authentic; authoritative; authorized; definitive; trustworthy; unflattering; veracious; n. ACCURACY: authenticity; correctitude; correctness; definitude; exactitude; fidelity; punctuality; veracity

ACCURSED: (see "bad") a. abominable; detestable; execrable; inimical; maledictive; maledictory; malefic
greed of gold: n. *auri sacra fames*

ACCUSATION: n. arraignment; ascription; attribution; crimination; delation; denouncement; impeachment; imputation; incrimination; inculpation
central part of: n. gravaman
counter: n. recrimination; v. recriminate; a. recriminative; recriminatory

ACCUSE: v. impeach; impute; (in)criminate; inculpate; indict; reproach; a. ACCUSATORY: accusative; imputable; imputational; (in)criminative; inculpative; inculpatory

ACCUSER: n. accusant; (fem. accusatrix); delator; denunciator; informer; plaintiff; prosecutor

ACCUSTOM: v. acclimate; acclimatize; discipline; familiarize; habituate; inure; naturalize; orientate; season; n. acclimation; acclimatization; habituation; inurement; orientation

ACID: a. acescent; acidulated; acidulent; acidulous; acrimonious; caustic; corrosive; penetrating; trenchant; vinegary; n. ACIDITY: acerbity; acor, acrimony; causticity
containing or yielding: a. acidiferous
convert into: v. acidify; n. acidification

ACME: n. apex; apogee; climacteric; climacterium; climax; consummation; culmination; meridian; *nec plus ultra;* pinnacle; sublimity; ultimate; vertex; zenith; a. (see "greatest") climacteric

ACQUAINTED: (see "familiar") a. *au courant; au fait;* cognizant; (con)versant

ACQUIRE: see "get"

ACQUITTAL: n. absolution; deliverance; emancipation; exculpation; justification; vindication; a. absolutory; justificatory; vindicatory

ACRIMONY: **n.** acerbity; acridity; asperity; causticity; irascibility; malevolence; virulence

ACT(S): (**see** "action") **n.** exploit; gest(e); gymnastic(s); gyration; performance; **v.** function; officiate; operate
bold: **n.** bravura; (**pl.** audacities)
caught in the: **adv.** *in actu; in flagrante delicto;* red-handed
courteous or graceful: **n. pl.** civilities; convenances; (the) amenities; (the) proprieties; urbanities
evil or unlawful: **n.** felony; malefaction; malfeasance; misdemeanor; **a.** felonious; malfeasant
interval or short program bet.: **n.** *entr'acte*
justified by result: **n.** *exitus acta probat*
"of God": **n.** *casus fortuitus; force majeure; vis major*
pathological repetition of those of others: **n.** echopraxia
thoughtless: **n.** *étourderie*

ACTING *for a principal:* **a.** delegated; substitutionary; vicarious; **n.** *locum tenems*
or actors, pert. to: **a.** histrionic(al); (melo)dramatic; operatic; theatrical; tragicomic; **n.** histrionic; theatricality; (**pl.** histrionics; theatrics)
second-rate (playing to audience): **n.** cabotinage; theatricality

ACTION(S): (**see** "act(s)" **and** "conduct") **n.** accomplishment; achievement; liveliness; sprightliness; vivacity
initiator of: **see** "stimulator"
not free (theory): **n.** determinism; fatalism; predestination
out of (action): **adv.** *hors de combat;* **a.** emerited; emeritus; superannuated
ready for: **a.** *en garde*
remote, or w/o contact: **n.** *actio ad distans*
repetition, pathological, of those of others: **n.** echomimia; echopraxia
shameless or vainglorious: **n. pl.** heroics; histrionics; theatricalities; theatrics
sudden and successful: (**see** "stroke") **n.** coup
symbolic: **n.** charade

ACTIVATOR: **see** "stimulator"

ACTIVE: (**see** "busy") **a.** animated; athletic; dynamic(al); indefatigable; kinetic; operose; sedulous; spirited; sprite; sthenic; vivacious

ACTIVITY: (**see** "energy") **n.** agility; animation; celerity; gambit; liveliness; nimbleness; operosity; ploy; pursuit; sprightliness; vivacity
center of: **n.** tempest; vortex
feverish: **n.** alarums and excursions
muscular, abnormally increased: **n.** hyperkinesia; **a.** hyperkinetic

ACTOR(S): (**see** "acting") **n.** barnstormer; facient; histrio(n); participant; thespian; tragedian; (**fem.** tragedienne); trouper; (**pl.** *corps dramatique; dramatis personae; personae*)
beginner (fem.): **n.** ingenue; soubrette
extra, or w/ small part: **n.** supernumerary
goddess of: **n.** Minerva
leading or star: **n.** protagonist; (**fem.** *première*)
next to star: **n.** deuteragonist
of third importance in play: **n.** tritagonist
pert. to: **see under** "acting"
silent: **n.** *persona muta*

ACTRESS, *young:* **n.** ingenue; soubrette

ACTUAL: (**see** "real") **a.** authentic; concrete; *de facto;* existent; legitimate; official; substantial; unadulterated; veritable
assume to be or treat as: **v.** hypostatize

ACTUALITY: (**see** "accomplishment") **n.** entity; existent; objectivity, verity
complete: **n.** entelechy; *factum est; fait accompli*

ACUTE: **a.** critical; crucial; discerning; exigent; extreme; penetrating; penetrative; poignant; trenchant

ADAGE: (**see** "maxim") **n.** aphorism; apothegm; bromide; saw; truism; **a.** aphoristic; apothegmatic(al); bromidic

ADAPT: (**see** "accustom") **v.** acclimate; acclimatize; accommodate; conform; habituate; harmonize; naturalize; orientate; reconcile; **a.** ADAPTABLE: (**see** "teachable") adaptational; amenable; flexuous; labile; malleable; plastic; tractable
to a situation: **v.** temporize; **n.** conformation; habituation; inurement; orientation; temporization

ADAPTATION: **n.** accommodation; adjustment; conformation; habituation; inurement; lability; orientation
as lit. or mus. work: **n.** rifacimento
to situation or environment: **see under** "adapt"

ADD: **v.** aggrandize; aggravate; augment; enhance; exacerbate; intensify; introduce; magnify; (super)impose; **a.** ADDED: **see** "additional"

ADDICT: **n.** buff; devotee; enthusiast; habituate; *habitué*

ADDITION: **n.** accessory; addendum; additament; adjunct(ion); ap(p)anage; appendage; augmentation; (super)imposition; **a.** ADDITIONAL: (**see** "supplementary") **n.** *au reste*
gradual: **n.** accrescence; accretion; agglutination; concretion

ADDRESS: (**see** "skill") **n.** adroitness; bearing; deportment; dexterity; ingenuity
in speech or writing: (**see** "speech") **n.** allocution; apostrophe; salutation; **a.** apostrophic; salutational; salutatory; **v.** apostrophize
to person usu. not present, or to something personified for rhetorical purpose: **n.** apostrophe; **v.** apostrophize

ADEQUATE: (**see** "equivalent") **a.** condign; commensurate; competent; **n.** ADEQUACY: abundance; adequation; amplitude; competence; competency; copiosity; copiousness; equivalence; plentitude; sufficiency

ADHERE: **v.** (ag)glutinate; cohere; persevere; **n.** ADHERENT: **see** "follower"; **a.** adhesive; agglutinative; cohesive; glutinous; mucillaginous; tenacious; viscid; viscous
closely (*adhering*): **a.** adhesive; cohesive; osculant; tenacious

ADJACENT (or ADJOINING): **a.** abutting; co(n)terminous; contiguous; juxtaposed; juxtapositional; limitrophe; satellite; tangent; **n.** ADJACENCY: contiguity; immediacy; tangency

ADJOURNMENT, *final:* **adv.** *sine die*

ADJUNCT: (**see** "accessory") **n.** addendum; additament; ap(p)anage; appendage; appurtenance; auxiliary; endowment; perquisite

ADJUST: (**see** "adapt") **v.** accommodate; concinnate; equalize; equate; harmonize; methodize; pacify; rectify; resolve; synchronize; systematize; **a.** ADJUSTABLE: adaptable; adjustmental; amenable; fictile; malleable; modificatory; modulatory; plastic; pliable; **n.** ADJUSTABLITY: adaptability; amenability; modulability; plasticity

ADJUSTMENT: **n.** acclimation; acclimatization; accommodation; concinnity; equilibration; equilibrium; harmonization; orientation; synchronization
to line of sight: **n.** collimation; **v.** collimate

ADMIRE: **v.** adulate; apotheosize; canonize; deify; eulogize; idolize; panegyrize; venerate; **n.** ADMIRATION: adoration; adulation; approbation; canonization; deification; idolatry; idolization; **a.** ADMIRING: adulatory; complimentary; encomiastic; eulogistic; idolatric; idolatrous; laudatory; panegyrical

ADMIT: **v.** acknowledge; acquiesce; adhibit; concede; divulge; intromit; **n.** ADMITTANCE (**or** ADMISSION): acknowledg(e)ment; acquiescence; concession; *entrée;* intromission; reception

ADO: (**see** "commotion" **and** "turmoil") **n.** agitation; brouhaha; coil; hullabaloo; imbroglio

ADORN: **v.** bedizen; caparison; diamondize; embellish; enrich; garnish; lard; **n.** ADORNMENT: bedizenment; caparison; *drap d'or;* embellishment; garnishment; ornamentation

ADROIT: (**see** "skillful") **a.** dexterous; **n.** ADROITNESS: address; dexterity; *savoir-faire*

ADULTERY: **n.** infidelity; unfaithfulness

ADULT(HOOD): **n.** majority; maturity
approaching: **a.** maturescent; **n.** maturation; maturescence
garment to symbolize (*anc. Rome*): **n.** *toga virilis*
maintaining stable social conds. among (*adults*): **n.** homeostasis

rites at attaining (*Heb.*): **n.** bar mitzvah; (**fem.** bath [or bas] mitzvah)

ADVANCE: **v.** aggrandize; aggravate; augment; enhance; escalate; exacerbate; graduate; progress; **n.** ADVANCEMENT: aggrandizement; aggravation; anabasis; augmentation; development; enhancement; escalation; evolution; exacerbation; graduation; overture; preferment; progression; tender
sensational: **n.** breakthrough

ADVANTAGE: **n.** opportunity; precedence; preference; preferment; superiority; **a.** ADVANTAGEOUS: (**see** "beneficial") auspicious; expedient; opportune; preferent(ial); profitable; propitious; remunerative; strategic(al); strategetic; tactical

ADVENTURE: **n.** escapade; gambade; gambado; gest(e); ploy; **a.** ADVENTUROUS (**or** ADVENTURESOME): cavalier; Icarian; incautious; picaresque; precarious; precipitate; quixotic; risky; speculative; temerarious; uncalculating; venturesome

ADVERSARY: **n.** antagonist; competitor; disputant; opponent

ADVERSE: (**see** "stubborn") **a.** adversative; antagonistic; antipathetic(al); antipathic; antithetical; calamitous; counteractive; deplorable; derogatory; detrimental; disadvantageous; disparaging; inimical; ominous; portentous; prejudicial; repellant; repugnant; repulsive; sinister; unpropitious; untoward

ADVERSITY, *friends proved by: amici probantur rebus adversis*

ADVERTISE: **v.** disseminate; exploit; promulgate; publicize; ventilate; **n.** ADVERTISING: dissemination; exploitation; promotion; promulgation; propaganda; publicity; **a.** exploitative; promotional; propagandistic

ADVICE: **n.** adhortation; admonition; counsel; exhortation; expostulation; intelligence; recommendation; **a. see** "advisable" **and** "advisory"
willing to follow: **a.** amenable; cordial; docile; facile; fictile; genial; gracious; **n.** amenability; docility; malleability; plasticity; tractability

ADVISABLE: **a.** expedient; opportune; politic; provident; prudent(ial); seemly

ADVISER, *disinterested:* **n.** *amicus curiae* (friend of the court)
woman: **n.** Egeria

ADVISORY: **a.** admonitory; consultative; consultatory; (ex)hortative; (ex)hortatory; expedient; expostulatory; recommendatory

ADVOCACY: **n.** commendation; desiration; espousal; patronage; subscription

ADVOCATE: (**see** "agent") **n.** barrister; champion; counselor; exemplifier; exponent; hierophant; paladin; paraclete; paranymph; partisan; propugnator; protagonist; **v.** commend; desiderate; espouse
devil's: **n.** *advocatus diaboli*
leading: **n.** hierophant

AFFABLE: (**see** "courteous") **a.** benign; complacent; complaisant; conversable; cordial; gallant; gracious; hospitable; ingratiating; suave; urbane

AFFECTATION: (**see** "pretense") **n.** artificiality; hypocrisy; mannerism; *minauderie;* pietism; pretension
esp. in language: **n.** grandiloquence; preciosity

AFFECTED: **a.** affectational; artificial; *distingué;* histrionic; hypocritical; (melo)-dramatic; pedantic; pietistic; *précieuse; précieux;* pretentious; puritanical; staged; theatrical
or artificial style in lang.: **n.** euphuism; grandiloquence; preciosity; **a.** aureate; euphuistic(al); grandiloquent
person: **n.** *poseur;* (**fem.** *poseuse*); *précieuse*

AFFIRM: **v.** asseverate; confirm; predicate; ratify; validate; **n.** AFFIRMATION: asseveration; declaration; predication; ratification; validation

AFFIRMATIVE: **a.** declarative; positive
implication: **n.** negative pregnant

AFFLICTION: (**see** "disease") **n.** anguish; calamity; plague; scourge; tribulation; visitation

AFFRONT: **n.** humiliation; indignity; provocation

to position or authority: **n.** *infra dignitatem* (**abb.** infra dig.) ; *lese majesty*

AFRAID: (**see** "timid") **a.** apprehensive; awestricken; timorous

AFRESH: **adv.** *de integro; de novo*

AFTER: **a.** posteriad; posterior; postlimin(i)ary; subsequent; succedent
death: **a.** posthumous; post-mortem
me (or us) the flood: après moi (**or** *nous) le déluge*
meals: **a.** postprandial
sadness, gladness: post nubila, jubila
this: **adv.** *post hoc*
this, therefore because of this: **adv.** *post hoc, ergo propter hoc*
-word: **n.** epilogue

AFTERNOON, *pert. to:* **a.** postmeridian; post meridiem

AGAIN: **see** "afresh"

AGAINST: **see** "opposed"

AGE: (**see** "aged") **v.** decline; maturate; mature; mellow; senesce; **n.** caducity; decrepitude; dotage; longevity; maturation; primogeniture; saeculum; senescence; senility; seniority; *siècle;* superannuation
advanced: **n.** (anec)dotage; caducity; senectude; superannuation
evidence of by tone or coating: **n.** patina
old: **see under** "old"
old, study of: **see under** "aged"
respect for: **n.** veneration
under legal: **n.** infancy; juniority; nonage

AGED: (**see** "old") **a.** aet.; aetat.; anile; antediluvian; antiquated; decrepit; Nestorian; patriarchal; senescent; superannuated; venerable
government by: **n.** gerontocracy
love of or attraction to: **n.** gerontophilia; **a.** gerontophilic
middle-: **see** "middle"
study of diseases and problems of: **n.** geriatrics; gerontology; nostology
worship of: **see under** "old"

AGENT: (**see** "advocate") **n.** dragoman; facient; factor; factotum; fiduciary; mandatary; minister; plenipotentiary; proxy; representative
joint: **n.** coefficient
secret: **n.** (agent) provocateur
w/ or by authority of an: **adv.** by proxy; *per procuration; per procurantionem*

AGGRAVATE: **v.** aggrandize; enhance; exacerbate; exaggerate; exasperate; infuriate; intensify; irritate; magnify; provoke; stimulate; **a.** AGGRAVATING: **see** "annoying"; **n.** AGGRAVATION: exacerbation; exacerbescence; infuriation; provocation; vexation

AGGRESSIVE: (**see** "hostile") **a.** assertive; bellicose; belligerent; combative; contentious; enterprising; gladiatorial; martial; militant; provocative; pugilistic; pugnacious; self-asserting; taurine; truculent; warlike; **n.** AGGRESSIVENESS: (**see** "hostility") bellicosity; belligerency; combativeness; pugnacity; truculency

AGILE: (**see** "brisk") **a.** acrobatic; adroit; lissome

AGILITY, *mental or physical:* **n.** address; adeptness; adroitness; dexterity; legerity; lissomeness

AGITATED: **a.** activated; cyclonic; demoniacal; distracted; febrile; fervid; feverish; foaming; fuming; maniac(al); overwrought; perturbed; seething; tumultuary

AGITATION: (**see** "ado") **n.** chemistry; hatemongering; instigation; jactation; jactitation; perturbation; turmoil

AGITATOR: (**see** "stimulator") **n.** (agent) provocateur; firebrand; hatemonger; hothead; hotspur; incendiary; instigator; prompter

AGO: **see** "aged" **and** "old"

AGOG: **see** "eager"

AGONY: (**see** "anguish" **and** "distress") **n.** *angoisse;* excruciation; travail; tribulation
scene or occasion of: **n.** Gethsemane

AGREE: **v.** coincide; correspond; harmonize; homologate; synchronize; syncretize; **a.** AGREED: *d'accord; en rapport;* **n.** see "agreement"

AGREEABLE: (**see** "pleasing") **a.** apolaustic; appetizing; compatible; com-

plaisant; concordant; congruous; consentaneous; consentient; consistent; consonant; delectable; dulcet; gemutlich; halcyon; harmonious; palatable; plausible; sapid; savory
and disagreeable, rel. to both: **a.** algedonic

AGREEABLENESS: **n.** agreeability; amenity; compatibility; complaisance; congeniality; delectation; docility; tractability; unanimity

AGREEING: **a.** acquiescent; assentatious; consentaneous; consentient; *d'accord; en rapport;* unanimous; **adv.** *una voce*
in rate or speed: **n.** synchroneity; synchronicity; synchronism; **a.** synchronous; **v.** synchronize

AGREEMENT: **n.** assentation; assonance; commensality; communion; concord(ance); congeniality; congruence; congruity; consentience; consonance; correspondence; *entente;* harmony; rapport; solidarity; unanimity
as bet. states: **n.** *entente*
friendly: **n.** *entente cordiale*

AGRICULTURE: **n.** agronomics; agronomy; geoponics; horticulture; husbandry; **a.** AGRICULTURAL: agrarian; agrestic; agronomical; horticultural
goddess of: **n.** Ceres

AHEAD: **see** "premature"
of times: **n.** *avant-garde; avant-gardism; avant-gardist(e)*; vanguard(ism)

AID(E): (**see** "accessory," "assistant" **and** "helper") **n.** adjuvant; adminicle; ancillary; coadjutor; cohort; facilitation; handmaid(en); secours; **v.** (**see** "help") succor
financial: **n.** endowment; largess(e); subvention

AIDING: (**see** "supplemental") **a.** accessory; adjuvant; adminicular; benevolent; contributory; ministrant; subsidiary

AIM: (**see** "purpose") **n.** ambition; aspiration; intendment; philosophy; significance
having a purposeful: **a.** tendentious

AIMLESS: **a.** capricious; chaotic; desultory; haphazard; indiscriminate; random; tumultuary; unpremeditated; **n.** AIMLESSNESS: (**see** "idleness" **and** "idling") indirection

AIR: (**see** "atmosphere") **v.** publicize; ventilate; **n.** aura; demeanor; deportment; mien; nimbus; (**pl.**) *minauderie*
bad or contaminated: **n.** miasma; **a.** miasmic
containing or conveying: **a.** aeriferous; pneumatic
expired in breathing: **n.** exhalation; expiration; flatus
in open: **a.** *à la belle étiole; al fresco;* hypaethral; *sub Jove;* upaithric
letting or sucking in: **n.** implosion; **a.** implosive
originating in: **a.** atmogenic
pert. to, moved or worked by: **a.** pneumatic
w/ superior or condescending: **a.** or **adv.** *de haut en bas*

AIRTIGHT: **a.** hermetic(al); impenetrable; impervious

AIRY: **a.** aerial; animated; atmospheric; blithesome; buoyant; debonair; ethereal; frolicsome; riant; sprightly; vivacious; zephyrean; zephyrous; **n.** AIRINESS: aeriality; buoyancy; ethereality; sprightliness

AKIN: (**see** "related") **a.** affiliated; agnate; cognate; collateral; congeneric; consanguineous; fraternal; germane; propinquitous; **n.** agnation; consanguinity; propinquity

ALARM: (**see** "apprehension") **n.** tocsin

ALCOHOL: **n.** *aqua vitae;* ethanol; ethyl hydroxide; (**pl.** ardent spirits; spiritous liquors)
pert. to: **a.** bacchanalian; spiritous; vinic; vinous; **n.** spirituosity
total abstinence fr.: **n.** nephalism; nephalist; teetotaler; teetotalism; teetotalist

ALCOHOLIC: **n.** (**see** "drunkard") bacchanalian; bacchante; dipsomaniac; dramdrinker; oenophilist; winebibber; **a.** intoxicating; liquorish; liquorous; liquory; spiritous; vinic; vinous

ALCOHOLISM: **n.** bibacity; bibation; bibulosity; crapulence; dipsomania; ebriosity; inebriation; inebriety; insobriety; intemperance; oenophlygia; temulence; winebibbing

pert. to: (**see** "drunken") **a.** dipsomaniacal

ALERT: **see** "prompt," "observant" **and** "watchful"

ALIEN: (**see** "foreign") **a.** adventitious; contradictory; estranged; extraneous; extrinsic; impertinent; inappropriate; inconsistent; irrelevant; unsympathetic; **n.** auslander; outlander; tramontane

resident: **n.** peregrine

to: **prep.** *dehors*

ALIGN: (**see** "adjust") **v.** collimate; hierarchize; regiment; **n.** ALIGNMENT: collimation; hierarchization; regimentation

ALIKE: (**see** "uniform") **a.** analogical; analogous; congruent; homogeneous; homologous; homonymous; parallel; synonymous; **n.** ALIKENESS: **see** "uniformity"

in form and size: **a.** congruent; homomorphic

in nature or character: **a.** concordant; unisonant; unisonous

ALIVE: **a.** animated; pullulant; spirited; teeming; vital; vivacious

ALL: **adv.** *in toto;* **n.** (**see** "allness") totality

-comprehensive: **a.** encyclopedic(al); omnigenous; unabridged; universal; **n.** mutuality; omneity; omnitude; totality; unanimity; universality

-creating: **a.** omnific; omnificent; **n.** omnificence

-devouring: **a.** omniverous

-inclusive: (**see** "universal") **a.** (en)-cyclopedic(al); omniferous; omnivorous; **n.** catholicity; catholicon; comprehensibility; comprehensiveness; universality

is vanity: **n.** *omnia vanitas*

-knowing: **a.** omniscient; pansophic(al); **n.** omniscience; pansophism

-or-nothing: **adv.** *tout bien ou rien*

-powerful: (**see** "almighty") **a.** multipotent; omnipotent; **n.** omnipotence

-present: **a.** omnipresent; ubiquitous; **n.** omnipresence; ubiquity

-seeing: **a.** panoptic

taking or occupying (all): **a.** monopolistic; **n.** monopolization; monopoly

the more: **adv.** *a fortiori*

the world: **n.** *tout le monde*

together: (**see** "unanimous") **adv.** *en masse;* holus-bolus

ALLEGIANCE: **see** "loyalty"

ALLEGORY: (**see** "fable") **n.** apologue; symbolization; **a.** ALLEGORICAL: parabolic(al)

make into: **v.** allegorize; **n.** allegorization

ALLIANCE: (**see** "union") **n.** affinity; confederation; consociation; consortion; consortium; monopolization; monopoly

ALLIED: **a.** agnate; analogous; cognate

ALLNESS: **n.** catholicity; entirety; omneity; omnitude; totality; universality

ALLOT: **v.** allocate; apportion; appropriate; parcel; ration

ALLOW: **v.** acknowledge; acquiesce; authorize; concede; countenance; empower; franchise; sanction; suffer; **a.** ALLOWED (**or** ALLOWABLE): (*see* "permissive") authorized; dispensable; franchised; legitimate; licensed; licit

graciously: **v.** vouchsafe

not (allowable): **a.** impermissible; **n.** impermissibility

ALLOWANCE: **n.** authorization; complement; emolument; honorarium; indulgence; mileage; permission; perquisite; sanction; stipend(ium); sufferance; tolerance; **a.** stipendiary

additional, as for injured feelings: **n.** solatium

with some: **adv.** *cum grano salis*

ALLUDE: **see** "hint"

ALLURE: **v.** beckon; beguile; cajole; captivate; enamor; ensorcel(l); enthral(l); entice; fascinate; instigate; inveigle; mesmerize; prompt; provoke; seduce; stimulate; tantalize; **n.** ALLUREMENT: blandishment(s); cajolery; persuasion

ALLURING: **a.** *aguichant;* (**fem.** *aguichante*); arresting; captivating; Circean; enticing; fascinating; magnetic; mesmeric; persuasive; provocative; seductive; sirenic(al); tantalizing; tempting

appeal: **n.** siren song

ALLUSION: (**see** "hint") **n.** inference; innuendo; intimation

ALLY: **see** "assistant"

ALMIGHTY: **a.** multipotent; omnipotent; puissant; **n.** ALMIGHTINESS: omnipotence; puissance
ruler: **n.** Pantocrator

ALMOST: (**see** "near") **adv.** quasi

ALONE: (**see** "aloof") **a.** exclusive; immanent; incomparable; individual; isolated; lorn; sequestered; solitary; solus; unaccompanied; un(at)tended; unique
abnormal fear of being: **n.** autophobia; monophobia
all (alone): **adv.** *tout seul;* (**fem.** *toute seule*)
capable of standing, as sentence structure or logical idea: **a.** categorematic
not capable of: **a.** syncategorematic
one who enjoys being: (**see** "hermit") **n.** solitudinarian

ALONGSIDE: **a.** attingent; contiguous; juxtaposed; tangent
to place: **v.** appose; collocate; juxtapose; **n.** collocation; juxtaposition

ALOOF: (**see** "alone") **a.** cautious; circumspect; delitescent; detached; indifferent; remote; secluded; sequestered; unsociable; **n.** ALOOFNESS: delitescence; delitescency; detachment; indifference; remoteness

ALOUD: **adv.** *à haute voix;* audible

ALPHABET: **n.pl.** rudiments
book of the: **n.** abecedarium; primer
learner or student of: **n.** alphabetarian
pert. to: **a.** abecedarian; alphabetical; alphabetiform; rudimentary
teacher of: **n.** abecedarian

ALPHABETICAL *order, in:* (**see** "order") **adv.** *alphabétiquement; par ordre alphabétique*
order, initial letters of poem or writing in: **n.** abecedarius

ALTER: (**see** "change") **v.** castrate; commute; diversify; emasculate; metamorphose; metastasize, modulate; spay; swerve; tamper; transfigure; transform; transmogrify; transmute; **n.** ALTERATION: conversion; deformation; deviation; diversion; emendation; metastasis; modulation; (per)mutation; reciprocity; transfiguration; transformation; transmogrification; transmutation; **a.** ALTERATIVE: emendatory

ALTERCATION: **see** "quarrel"

ALTERNATIVE: (**see** "choice") **n.** alternant; horns of a dilemma; option; preference; **a.** alternant; oscillative; reciprocative; synal(l)agmatic

ALTITUDE: **n.** elevation; loftiness; stature
pert. to or at greatest: (**see** "acme") **a.** altitudinous; culminant

ALTOGETHER: **adv.** collectively; *en banc; en bloc; en masse; en toto; tout ensemble;* unanimously

ALTRUISTIC: **see** "unselfish"

ALWAYS: (**see** "everlasting") **adv.** habitually; *in adfinitum; in aeternum; in perpetuity; in perpetuum; in saecula saeculorum;* invariably; perpetually; unceasingly; uniformly

AMASS: **see** "accumulate"

AMATEUR: (**see** "devotee") **n.** catechumen(ate); dilettante; initiate; neophyte; novice; proselyte; tyro; votary; **a.** AMATEURISH: dilettantish; non-professional

AMATIVE: **a.** affectionate; amatory; amorous; anacreontic; enamored; erotic; fervent; impassioned; **n.** amorosity; amorousness

AMAZE: (**see** "astonish") **v.** flabbergast; paralyze; petrify; **n.** AMAZEMENT: astonishment; consternation; perturbation; petrifaction; stupefaction; **a.** AMAZING: astonishing; astounding; incredible; ineffable; monstrous; portentous; preposterous; prodigious; stupendous; unspeakable

AMBIGUITY: (**see** "doubt") **n.** amphibology; double entendre; double entente; dubiosity; paradox

AMBIGUOUS: (**see** "vague") **a.** amphibolic; amphibological; amphibolous; cabalistic; Delphian; Delphic; dubious; enigmatic(al); equivocal; homonymous;

indeterminate; obscure; paradoxical; sibylline; unintelligible
construction or phrase: **n.** amphibologism; amphibology; verbal fallacy

AMBITION: **n.** aspiration; initiation; initiative; intendment; **a.** AMBITIOUS: ardent; aspirant; aspiring; elaborate; emulous; extensive; fervent; impetuous; pretentious (**see** "showy"); rapacious; sedulous; solicitous

AMENDS, *make or making:* **v.** expiate; rectify; redress; **a.** compensative; compensatory; expiatory; reparative; **n.** atonement; expiation; indemnity; redress; reparation; retribution

AMENITIES: **see** "proprieties"

AMIABLE: (**see** "affable") **a.** benignant; complaisant; cordial; gracious; hospitable; indulgent; neighborly; obliging; winsome

AMONG *other persons:* **adv.** *inter alios*
other things: **adv.** *inter alia*
ourselves: **adv.** *entre nous; inter nos*

AMOROUS: **see** "amative" **and** "loving"

AMOUNT: (**see** "sum") **n.** aggregate; amplitude; magnitude; portion; quantum; (**pl.** quanta); totality

AMPLE: **a.** boundless; capacious; commodious; copious; expansive; prolix; replete; spacious; verbose; voluminous

AMUSE: **v.** beguile; divert; entertain; recreate; tit(t)ivate; **n.** AMUSEMENT: distraction; diversion; divertissement; entertainment; facetiosity; joviality; recreation; tit(t)ivation; **a.** AMUSING: diverting; divertive; entertaining; facetious; farcical; jocose; jocular; ludicrous; recreative; risible; whimsical

ANAL *region:* **n.** breech; perineum; podex; pudendum

ANALOGOUS: (**see** "alike" **and** "similar") **a.** homeopathic; homogeneous; synonymous

ANALYSIS: **n.** anatomy; critique; exegesis; exposition; hermeneutics; interpretation; synopsis; titration
by separation: **n.** dialysis; **a.** dialytic

ANALYZE: **v.** anatomize; dissect; parse; **a.** ANALYTIC(AL): exegetic(al); expositive; expository; hermeneutic; interpretative

ANATOMICAL *material, substance or tissue:* **n.** substantia

ANATOMY: **n.** anthropotomy
specialist in (anatomist): **n.** anthropotomist

ANCESTOR(S): **n.** antecedent; ascendant; forebear; forefather; forerunner; precursor; primogenitor; procreator; progenitor; (**fem.** progenitress; progenitrix); prototype
after the manner of one's: **adv.** *more majorum*
from many: **a. or n.** polyphyletic
from single: **a. or n.** monophyletic
having same: **a.** agnate; cognate; consanguineous
immediate: **n.** ascendant
in direct line: **n.** progenitor
list or record of: **n.** genealogy; pedigree
resemblance to remote: **n.** atavism; **a.** atavistic
veneration or worship of: **n.** ancestor cult; manism; **a.** manistic
worship of spirits of: **n.** manism; **a.** manistic

ANCESTRAL: (**see** "hereditary") **a.** ancestorial; primogenitive; progenitorial

ANCESTRY: **n.** extraction; genealogy; lineage; paternity; pedigree; stemma
pert. to: **a.** ancestral; ancestorial; atavic; atavistic; genealogical; hereditary; progenitive; progenitorial

ANCHOR *of hope:* **n.** *anchora spei*
of salvation or safety: **n.** *anchora salutis*

ANCIENT: (**see** "aged" **and** "old") **a.** antediluvial; antediluvian; antemundane; antiquated; antique; archaic; archaistic; immemorable; immemorial; Neanderthal(ian); Ogygian; paleolithic; paleozoic; patriarchial; preadamite; prehistoric; primeval; protohistoric; venerable; **n.** ANCIENTNESS: ancientry; antiquity; venerability
one attached to opns. or practices of the: **n.** antiquarian
worship of what is: **n.** archaeolatry; archaicism; archaism

writing(s): **n.** or **a.** cuneiform; hieroglyphic

AND *elsewhere:* **adv.** *et alii* (**abb.** *et al*)
others: **adv.** *et alii* (**abb.** *et al*)
so forth: **adv.** *et cetera* (**abb.** etc.); *und so weiter* (**abb.** u.s.w.)
symbol for (&): **n.** ampersand
the following: **adv.** *et sequens* (**abb.** *et seq.*); (**pl.** *et sequentes; et sequentia*)

ANEMIA: **n.** emptiness; lifelessness
in young: **n.** chlorosis
local area: **n.** ischemia

ANEW: **adv.** *de novo; de integro*

ANGELIC: **a.** beatific; celestial; cherubic; heavenly; saintly; seraphic; sublime

ANGELS *and saints, homage to:* **n.** dulia
belief concerning: **n.** angeology

ANGER: (**see** "fury") **n.** acrimony; animosity; animus; asperity; choler; dudgeon; ebullition; exasperation; incensement; indignation; irascibility; malice; malignity; petulance; pique; resentment; turbulence; vexation; virulence; umbrage; **a.** ANGRY: (**see** "mad") acrimonious; choleric; indignant; iracund; irascible; irate; ireful; piqued; provoked; rancorous; wrathful
tending to incite: **a.** ignescent; incendiary; inflammatory; phlogistic; provocative; seditious; **v.** alienate; inflame; pique; provoke
will or powerful force (angry), effect or expression of: **n.** *terribilita*

ANGERED, *easily:* (**see** "contentious" **and** "hostile") **a.** choleric; iracund; irascible

ANGLES, *having equal:* **a.** equiangular; isagonal; isagonic
having many: **a.** mult(i)angular

ANGUISH: (**see** "distress") **n.** affliction; *angoisse;* angst; bereavement; consternation; (ex)cruciation; travail
place of: **n.** Gethsemane

ANIMAL(S): **n.** mammal(i)an; quadruped; vertebrate; (**pl.** animalia; mammalia; vertebrata); **a.** carnal; gross; mammalian; mammality; zoological
abnormal fear of: **n.** zoophobia
and plant life, regional: **n.** biota; fauna and flora
and plants, science of development of: **n.** biology; **a.** biological
and plants, science of distribution of: **n.** biogeography
behavior, study of: **n.** ethology; **n.** ethologist; **a.** ethological
caused by or associated w/: **a.** mammalogical; zoogenic; zoogenous; zoological
characteristics, attribute to inanimate objects: **n.** animalism; animism; theriomorphism
characteristics, attribute to man: **n.** theriomorphism
fond of: **n.** philotherianism; **a.** philotherian; zoophilic; zoophilous
form, having: **a.** theriomorphic; zoomorphic; **n.** theriomorph
form, symbolic, in art or lit.: **n.** zoomorphism; **a.** zoomorphic; **v.** zoomorphize
happier than humans, theory: **n.** animalitarianism
human characteristics attributed to: **n.** anthropomorphism; anthropopathism; **a.** anthropomorphic; anthropopathic
life: **n.** fauna
loving of: **a.** philotherian; zoophilic; zoophilous
nature: **n.** animality; mammality
object shaped like: **n.** theriomorph; theriomorphic; **a.** theriomorphism
of or rel. to: **a.** animalic; animalistic; mammalian; zoic; zoological; **n.** animality; mammality
state of being an (or animal life): **n.** animality; mammality
study of: **n.** zoology
very small: **n.** animalcule; animalculum; (**pl.** animalcula; animalculae)
Wild, utilization or exploitation of: **n.** besticulture; domestication

ANIMATE: (**see** "incite") **v.** ensoul; invigorate; motivate; prompt; quicken; suscitate; vitalize; vivificate; vivify; **a.** ANIMATED: **see** "lively"

ANIMATION: **n.** ebullience; effervescence; exhilaration; exuberance; intoxication; invigoration; liveliness; sprightliness; suscitation; vivacity; vivaciousness
suspended: **n.** anabiosis; catalepsy; hibernation; **a.** cataleptic

ANIMATING *and stirring, as a song:* **a.** proceleusmatic

ANNIHILATE: (**see** "abolish") **v.** decimate; demolish; deracinate; eradicate; expunge; exterminate; extinguish; extirpate; obliterate; pulverize

ANNOTATION(S): **n.** scholium; (**pl.** scholia)
marginal: **n.** postil; scholium; (**pl.** marginalia; scholia)

ANNOTATOR: **n.** glossarist; scholiast; **a.** scholiast

ANNOUNCEMENT: **n.** annunciation; declamation; manifesto; proclamation; pronunciation; **a.** declamatory; proclamatory

ANNOUNCING: **a.** annunciatory; declamatory; declaratory; enunciative; proclamatory; pronunciative

ANNOY: **v.** abrade; chafe; discomfit; discommode; disconcert; gall; harass; importune; molest; pique; provoke; **n.** ANNOYANCE: discomfiture; harassment; irritation; molestation; nuisance; pique; provocation; umbrage; vexation; **a.** ANNOYING: abhorrent; aggravating; calamitous; discommodious; disconcerting; execrable; excruciating; galling; invidious; mortifying; nettlesome; pestiferous; pestilent; plaguing; provocative; repellant; repulsive

ANNUAL: **a.** etesian
state of occurring (*annually*): **n.** annularity

ANNUL: **v.** abrogate; countermand; disclaim; neutralize; nullify; obliterate; quash; recant; repeal; rescind; revoke; **a.** ANNULLING: recissory; revocative; revocatory; **n.** ANNULMENT: abrogation; cassation; defeasance; disaffirmance; disaffirmation; nullification; recision; rescission; revocation
not capable of (*annulment*): **a.** inalienable; indefeasible

ANOINTING, *act of:* **n.** unction

ANOMALOUS: **see** "abnormal"

ANOTHER *self:* **n.** alter ego

ANSWER: (**see** "reply") **v.** rejoin; replicate; respond; retort; **n.** antiphon; counterstatement; rebuttal; rejoinder; replication; *réplique;* response; responsion; retort
negative: **n.** negation

ANTAGONISM: (**see** "hostility") **n.** antipathy; friction; **a.** ANTAGONISTIC: (**see** "contrary") ambivalent; dissident; dissonant; inimical; schizoid

ANTICIPATION: **see** "expectation"; **a.** ANTICIPATORY: intuitive; prevenient
of needs of others: **n.** *prévenance;* prevenience

ANTICLIMAX: **n.** bathos; disappointment; **a.** ANTICLIMACTICAL: bathetic

ANTS, *family of:* **n.pl.** formicidae
feeding on: **a.** formicivorous
study of: **n.** myrmecology
study of, specialist in: **n.** formicologist; myrmecologist

ANXIETY: (**see** "uneasiness") **n.** angst; anxiousness; apprehension; disquiet(ude); dyspathy; dysphoria; inquietude; malaise; solicitude; trepidation; uneasiness
generalized or indefinite: **n.** dysphoria; panophobia

ANXIOUS: (**see** "impatient") **a.** apprehensive; expectant; solicitous; solicitudinous
care or desire: **n.** solicitude; **a.** solicitous; solicitudinous

APART: **see** "alone" **and** "aloof"

APATHETIC: **a.** adiaphorous; *blasé; dégagé;* detached; dispirited; hebetudinous; impassive; imperturbable; impervious; indifferent; insipid; lackadaisical; languid; languorous; Laodicean; lethargic; pachydermatous; phlegmatic; pococurante; spiritless; stoical; supine; torpid; unenthusiastic; unfeeling
person: **n.** Laodicean; pococurante

APATHY: (**see** "inaction") **n.** acedia; adiaphoria; anhedonia; detachment; doldrums; hebetude; immobility; impassiveness; impassivity; inappetency; indifference; inertia; inertness; lackadaisy; languor; lassitude; lethargy; listlessness; *minauderie;* nonchalance; phlegm; stoicism; supineness; supinity; tenuity; torpor; unconcern; unfeelingness
religious: **n.** adiaphoria; adiaphorism;

adiaphorist; Laodicean; **a.** adiaphoristic; adiaphorous; Laodicean

APE *or monkey:* **n.** anthropoid; primate; simian; **a.** anthropoidal; simian; simious
resembling: **a.** pithecomorphic; **n.** simianity
study of: **n.** pithecology

APERTURE: (**see** "opening") **n.** fenestration; orifice; os; ostiole
having wide or spreading: **a.** patulous

APEX: **n.** acme; apogee; cacumen; culmination; meridian; perihelion; pinnacle; sublimity; zenith

APOLOGY: **n.** apologia; **a.** APOLOGETIC: excusatory
for error: **n.** *amende honorable*
formal: **n.** apologetic
one who makes: **n.** apologete; apologist

APOSTLE: (**see** "follower") **n.** disciple; harbinger; messenger

APPARATUS: **n.** armamentarium; mechanism; (**pl.** accoutrements; appurtenances; armamentaria; *matériel;* paraphernalia)

APPAREL: **see** "clothing"
showy or sumptuous: **n.** caparison

APPARENT: (**see** "evident") **a.** conspicuous; demonstrable; discernible; exoteric; explicit; illusory; indubitable; manifest; obvious; ostensible; ostensive; palpable; patent; perceivable; perceptible; phanic; presumable; presumptive; *prima facie;* seeming; self-evident; unconcealed; unobstructed

APPEAL: **n.** attraction; attractiveness; enchantment; entreaty; imploration; invocation; popularity; supplication; **a.** APPEALING: (**see** "alluring") invocative; invocatory; provocative; provocatory; supplicative
alluring: **n.** siren song; **a.** Circean; sirenic(al)
to ignorance of facts: **n. or adv.** (*argumentum*) *ad ignorantiam*
to mind or reason: **a.** cogent; compelling; convincing; **n.** cogency
to modesty: **n. or adv.** (*argumentum*) *ad verecundiam*
to penalties: **n. or adv.** (*argumentum*) *ad baculum*
to pity or compassion: **n. or adv.** (*argumentum*) *ad misericordiam*
to please the crowd: **n. or adv.** (*argumentum*) *ad capitandum* (*vulgus*)
to popular passion and prejudice: **n. or adv.** (*argumentum*) *ad populum*
to prejudices: **n. or adv.** (*argumentum*) *ad hominem*
to reason: **n.** *argumentum;* argumentation
to selfish interests: **n. or adv.** (*argumentum*) *ad hominem*
to the people: **n. or adv.** (*argumentum*) *ad populum*
to the purse: **n. or adv.** (*argumentum*) *ad crumenam*
to the rod: **n. or adv.** (*argumentum*) *ad baculum*

APPEAR: (**see** "emerge") **v.** materialize; **a. see** "apparent" **and** "seeming"

APPEARANCE: (**see** "aspect") **n.** attendance; color; debut; debutant(e); development; habitus; manifestation; ostent; perspective; phantasmagoria; phenomenon; prospect; semblance; simulacrum
bodily: **n.** countenance; feature; habitus; lineament; mien; profile; physiognomy; physique; visage
do not trust: **adv.** *ne fronti credi*
general or external: **n.** facies; superficies
having diseased: **a.** cachectic; cadaverous; scrofulous
trust not overmuch to: **adv.** *nimium ne credi colori*
ungainly: **n.** angularity

APPEARING: **see** "apparent" **and** "seeming"

APPEASE: **v.** allay; alleviate; assuage; conciliate; dulcify; lenify; mitigate; moderate; mollify; propitiate; soothe; temper; tranquilize; **a.** APPEASING: (**see** "peaceful") expiatory; mitigatory; piacular; propitiative; propritiatory; **n.** APPEASEMENT: atonement; conciliation; expiation; mitigation; pacification; propitiation

APPEASED, *incapable of being:* **a.** avenging; immitigable; implacable; inappeasable; inflexible; intractable; irreconcilable; rancorous; relentless; remorseless; ruthless; unappeasable; unassuageable; unmitigable; untamable; unyielding; vindicative

APPENDAGES, *having:* **a.** appendiculate(d)

APPETITE: (**see** "taste") **n.** appetition; edacity; orexis; voracity
appealing to the: **see** "appetizing"
causing loss of (as drug. etc.): **a.** anorexigenic; **n.** anorexia; anorexic
depraved or perverted: **n.** allotriogeustia; allotriophagia; geophagy; parorexia
excessive or abnormal: **n.** (**see** "glutton") acoria; ad(d)ephagia; bulimia; gluttony; gulosity; hyperorexia; phagomania; polyphagia; **a.** (**see** "gluttonous") bulimic; polyphagous
increasing: (**see** "appetizing") **a.** orexigenic
lack or loss of: **n.** anorexia; inappetence; **a.** anore(c)tic; anorexic
person devoted to gratification of: **n.** bon vivant; epicure; gastronome(r); gourmet; hedonist; sybarite; **a.** epicurean; hedonistic; Sybaritic; **n.** hedonics; hedonism
pleasures of: **n. pl.** *abdominis voluptates*
rel. to: **a.** appetible; appetitive; epithumetic; orectic
sensual or sexual: (**see** "sensual") **n.** concupiscence; **a.** concupiscent; concupiscible; epithumetic
stimulator of: (**see** "appetizer") **n.** or **a.** apertive
without: (**see** "lack or loss of" *above*) **a.** anorectic

APPETIZER: **n.** *apéritif;* apertive; *canapé; hors d'oeuvre*

APPETIZING: **a.** ambrosial; appetible; appetitious; appetitive; delectable; gustable; gustatory; gustful; luscious; nectareous; orexigenic; palatable; piquant; sapid; saporous; savory; toothsome; **n.** sapidity; sapor; saporosity; piquance; piquancy

APPLAUD, *one hired to:* **n.** claqueur
persons hired to: **n.** claque

APPLAUSE: (**see** *"approval"*) **n.** acclamation; commendation; *éclat;* encomium; eulogy; laudation; plaudit; **a.** commendatory; laudatory; plauditory
eagerness for: **n.** captation; esurience

APPLES, *of or rel. to:* **a.** pomaceous

APPLICABLE: **a.** adaptable; apposite; appropriate; commensurate; congruent; germane; pertinent; proportional

APPOINTMENT: **n.** consultation; engagement; rendezvous; tryst; (**pl.** accoutrements)
secret: **n.** assignation; rendezvous; tryst

APPORTION: **v.** admeasure; allocate; appropriate; mete; parcel; ration; **n.** APPORTIONMENT: appropriation

APPRECIABLE: **a.** measurable; palpable; perceptible; ponderable; recognizable

APPREHENDED, *not readily:* **a.** impalpable

APPREHENSION: **n.** cognition; cognizance; disquiet(ude); foreboding; forewarning; inquietude; intellection; misgiving; perception; prehension; premonition; presentiment; understanding; **a.** APPREHENSIVE: anticipative; conscious; discerning; knowing; premonitory; presentient
instantaneous: **n.** intuition; **a.** intuitional; intuitive

APPROPRIATE: (**see** "apportion") **v.** accroach; arrogate; commandeer; confiscate; impound; preempt; sequester; **a.** apposite; apropos; *comme il faut;* concordant; condign; decorous; felicitous; germane; idoneous; opportune; pertinent; seemly; **n.** APPROPRIATENESS: (**see** "fitness") apropostity; idoneity; relativity
yet untrue: **a.** *ben trovato*

APPROVAL: (**see** "applause") **n.** acclaim; acclamation; accolade; accreditation; approbation; bravissimo; bravo; commendation; *éclat;* endorsement; imprimatur; plaudit; ratification; ratihabition; sanction; subscription; sufferage; sufferance; unanimity
expressive of: **a.** acclamatory; adulatory; affirmatory; approbatory; commendable; commendatory; laudable; laudatory; plauditory; sanctionative; **adv.** *à la bonne heure*
sign or mark of: **n.** cachet; *forensis strepitus* (clamor of the forum); hallmark; imprimatur

APPROVE: **v.** accredit; approbate; commend; compliment; endorse; homologate; ratify; sanctify; sanction; subscribe
not (approved): **see** "unauthorized"

APPROXIMATION: (**see** "nearness") **n.** *circa*

APT: (see "appropriate" and "knowing") **a.** apropos; decorous; poignant; seemly; **n.** APTNESS: appropriateness; aproposity; towardliness
expression: (see "witticism") **n.** bijouterie; *bon mot;* epigram

ARBITRARY: (see "arrogant") **a.** absolutist(ic); bigoted; capricious; captious; despotic; determinate; dogmatic; imperious; inexorable; positive; preferential; thetic(al); tyrannical
statement(s): **n.** dictum; (pl. dicta); dogmatism; *ipse dixit;* ipsedixism

ARCH: **a.** picaresque; roguish; **n.** arcuation; concameration; incurvation

ARCHDEACON, *like a:* **a.** archidiaconal

ARCHED: **a.** archated; arcuated; cambered; concamerated
body: **n.** opisthotonos

ARCHER: **n.** sagittarius; sagittary; toxophilite; **n.** ARCHERY: toxophily
pert. to (or archery): **a.** toxophilite; toxophilitic

ARCHITECTURAL *figure:* **n.** *antic (grotesque)*; caratid (fem.); telamon (male)

ARCHITECT(URE), *pert. to:* **a.** (archi)tectonic

ARDENT: (see "eager") **a.** crusading; devoted; dithyrambic; ebullient; enraptured; enthusiastic; evangelical; evangelistic; fervent; glowing; igneus; impassioned; passionate, (per)fervid; plutonic; rapturous; volcanic

ARDOR: (see "zeal") **n.** calenture; ebullience; ebulliency; ebullition; *empressement;* enthusiasm; fervidity; fervor; fidelity; incalescence; intensity; loyalty; passion; rapture
increasing in: **a.** incalescent

ARDUOUS: (see "laborious") **a.** exacting; rigorous; strenuous; **n.** strenuosity

AREA: (see "region") **n.** arena; environment; environ(s); milieu
containing things of obscure classification: **n.** penumbra
occurring or taking place in same: **a.** sympatric

ARGUE: **v.** contend; ergotize; expostulate; maintain
for argument's sake: **v.** ratiocinate; **n.** ratiocination; speciosity

ARGUMENT: (see "appeal" and "reasoning") **n.** argumentation; argumentum; (pl. argumenta); dialectic(s); disputation; enthymeme; expostulation; polemic; quodlibet; syllogism; **a.** see "argumentative"
art of: **n.** dialectic(s); forensic(s); polemic(s)
by induction: see "induction"
clever and plausible but fallacious: **n.** casuistry; philosophism; pilpul; sophism; sophistry; speciosity; **a.** casuistic; quodlibetic; specious; sophistical
hater or hatred of: **n.** misologist; misology; **a.** misopolemical
last or final: **n.** *ultimo ratio*
on subtle or debatable point: **n.** quodlibet; **a.** quodlibetic

ARGUMENTATIVE: **a.** agonistic; contentious; controversial; debatable; dialectic; discursory; disputatious; disputative; eristic; forensic; polemic(al); presumptive

ARGUMENTUM: see "appeal"

ARID: (see "dry") **a.** anhydrous; jejune; monotonous; sterile; unproductive

ARISING: **a.** ascendant; assurgent; emergent
spontaneously: **a.** abiogenic; idiogenetic; idiopathic
unexpectantly: **a.** or **n.** emergent

ARISTOCRAT: (see "elite") **n.** *bas bleu;* Brahmin; grand signeur; grandee; patrician (pl. aristoi)

ARISTOCRATIC: **a.** hierarchic(al); patrician
class: **n.pl.** aristoi; **n.** patriciate

ARISTOTLE('S) *dictum:* **n.** *dictum de omni et nullo* (what may be affirmed or denied of a class may be affirmed or denied of every member thereof)
follower of: **n.** Aristotelian; Peripatetic; Peripateticism; **a.** Peripatetic

ARM(S): **n.** accouterment(s); armament(s); armamentarium; arsenal; ord-

nance; tentacles; weaponry; (**pl.** armamentaria; *matériel*); **a.** tentacular
by force of: **adv.** *vi et armis*
call to: aux armes!
having: **a.** brachiate; tentaculate
w/ open: **adv.** *à bras ouverts*

ARMOR, *complete suit of:* **n.** panoply

ARMPIT: **n.** axilla; (**pl.** axillae)

AROUND: **prep.** *circa; circiter;* **adv.** approximately

AROUSE: (**see** "incite") **v.** fillip; stimulate; **a.** AROUSING: (**see** "stimulating") galvanic

ARRANGE: **v.** alphabetize; catalogue; categorize; classify; collate; collicate; compartmentalize; concinnate; dispose; improvisate; improvise; marshal; methodize; mobilize; orchestrate; predetermine; synthesize; systematize; tabulate
for: **v.** bespeak

ARRANGED: **a.** alphabetized; categorized; compartmentalized; concinnate; orchestrated; schematic; stratified; synthesized; systematized; tabulated
in layers or strata: **a.** stratose

ARRANGEMENT: (**see** "plan") **n.** collation; collocation; combination; concinnity; contrivance; disposition; improvisation; permutation
clear: **n.** *lucidus ordo*
in layers, classes, castes, etc.: **n.** compartmentalization; hierarchization; stratification; **a.** stratose
of parts to form lit. style: **n.** concinnity
systematic: **n.** alphabetization; categorization; orchestration; schema; (**pl.** schemata); subordination; **a.** (**see** "arranged") schematic

ARRAY: (**see** "arrange" **and** "adorn") **v.** marshal; **n.** ARRAY(MENT): battery; display; gamut; rainbow; spectrum
complete or magnificent: **n.** panoply

ARREST: **v.** apprehend; restrain; retard; thwart; **n.** arrestation; arrestment

ARROGANCE: **n.** audacity; effrontery; haughtiness; hauteur; hubris; insolence; lordliness; presumption; superbity; **a.** ARROGANT: (**see** "haughty") audacious; autocratic; cavalier; commanding; compelling; dictatorial; dogmatic; domineering; fastuous; hubristic; imperative; imperious; impudent; lordly; magisterial; masterful; misproud, overbearing; preemptory

ARROWHEAD, *shaped like:* **a.** sagitatte

ART(S): (**see** "skill") **n.** (a)esthetic(s); dexterity; expertise; finesse; techne; virtuosity
early work of: **n.** incunabulum
for art's sake: **adv.** *ars gratia artis*
four liberal: **n.** quadrivium
goddess of: **n.** Athena; Muse
irrationality in: **n.** Dadism; Dadist
is long, life is short: ars longa, vita brevis
lost: **n.pl.** *artes perditae*
morbid or scandalous creation in: **n.** *fleur du mal*
one having taste for: **n.** connoisseur; esthete; virtuoso
patron or benefactor of: **n.** Maecenas
pert. to: **a.** (a)esthetic(al); artistic
the fine: **n.** *beaux-arts*
three liberal: **n.** trivium
work of: **n.** *objet d'art; ouvrage d'art*

ARTERIES, *hardening of:* **n.** arteriosclerosis; **a.** arteriosclerotic

ARTFUL: **see** "crafty"

ARTIFICE: (**see** "deception" **and** "trick") **n.** astucity; astuteness; contrivance; finesse; gambit; imposture; ingenuity; intrigue; inventiveness; machination; maneuver; stratagem; subterfuge; subtlety

ARTIFICIAL: (**see** "false") **a.** affected; artifactitious; Brummagem; conventional(ized); counterfeit; ersatz; fabricated; factitious; feigned; fictitious; histrionic; melodramatic; *papier-mâché;* postiche; pseudo; shallow; simulated; spurious; supposititious; synthetic(al); theatrical; **n.** ARTIFICIALITY: affectation; artifact; simulation; theatricality
limb or other body substitute: **n.** prosthesis; **a.** prosthetic
to make: **v.** artificialize

ARTIFICIALLY *made or produced:* **a.** (arti)factitious; ersatz; *papier-mâché;* synthetic; (**n.pl.** *fructus industriales*)

ARTIST, *greatest work of:* **n.** *chef-d'oeuvre; magnum opus;* maestro; *meisterwerk; pièce de résistance*
studio of: **n.** atelier

ARTISTIC: **a.** (a)esthetic(al); Bohemian; **n.** (a)estheticism; Bohemianism

ARTLESS: **a.** candid; ignorant; inartistic; *ingénu;* ingenuous; naive; unaffected; unauspicious; uncultured; unskillful; unsophisticated; **n.** ARTLESSNESS; *naïveté;* simplicity; unsophistication

AS *above:* **adv.** *ut supra* (**abb.** u.s.)
below: **adv.** *ut infra* (**abb.** u.i.)
circumstances require: **adv.** *pro re nata* (**abb.** p.r.n.)
far as this: **adv.** *quod hoc*
if: **adv.** qua; quasi
(*in the capacity of*): **adv.** qua
it should be: **adv.** *comme il faut*
occasion requires, or need occurs: **see** "circumstances require" *above*
usual: **adv.** *à l'ordinaire; comme à l'ordinaire; comme d'ordinaire*

ASCENDANCY: (**see** "prevalence") **n.** paramountcy; precedence; sovereignty; supremacy

ASCETIC: **n.** anchoret; anchorite; ascesis; Essene; heautontimorumenas; hermit; recluse; sabbatarian; Simeon Stylites; solitudinarian; **a.** austere; Essenic; Essenian; self-denying; self-disciplined; self-mortifying
extreme: **n.pl.** Cathari; perfecti
practice: **n.** ascesis; asceticism; austerity; self-denial; self-discipline; self-mortification

ASCRIBE: **v.** accredit; arrogate; attribute; impute

ASEXUAL *reproduction:* **n.** abiogenesis; agamogenesis; parthenogenesis; **a.** abiogenetic(al); agamic; agamous

ASHES, *like or color of* (*ashen*): **a.** cineraceous; cinerous

ASIDE: **adv.** *en aparté*

ASLEEP: **a.** comatose; dormant; hypnotic; inactive; latent; lethargic; quiescent; somniferous; somnolent; torpescent; **n.** see "sleep"
cond. of limb due to pressure: **n.** obdormition

ASPECT(S): **n.** angle; countenance; facet; ostent; semblance
general or external: **n.** facies; habitus; mien; physique; superficies (**also pl.**)
having many: **a.** heterogeneous; multifarious; multiphasic; multivarious; omnifarious

ASPERSE: **see** "slander"

ASPIRIN: **n.** acetylsalicylic acid

ASS *at the lyre:* **n.** *asinus ad lyram*

ASSAIL: **v.** censure; **n.** ASSAILMENT: castigation; oppugnation

ASSEMBLE: **v.** categorize; collimate; conglomerate; congregate; convene; convoke; correlate; muster; rendezvous; synthesize; **n.** ASSEMBLAGE: agglomeration; aggregation; conglomeration; convocation; ensemble

ASSENT: **v.** accede; acquiesce; sanction; **n.** ASSENTATION: acquiescence; approbation; concurrence; sanction; **a.** ASSENTATIOUS: acquiescent; approbative; compliant

ASSERTION: **see** "statement"

ASSERTIVE: (**see** "positive") **a.** affirmative; articulate; declaratory; peremptory; pronunciative

ASSETS *on hand:* **n.pl.** *valeurs disponibles*

ASSIGNEE: **n.** cessionary

ASSIGNMENT: **n.** allotment; appointment; appropriation; assignation; designation

ASSIST: **see** "help"; **n.** ASSISTANCE; (**see** "aid[e]") abetment; coadjuvancy; cooperation; encouragement; furtherance; patronage; secours; subvention; succor

ASSISTANT: (**see** "helper") **n.** abettor; acolyte; adjutant; adjuvant; aide-de-camp; ancillary; associate; auxiliary; coadjutor; confederate; *confrère; collaborateur;* collaborator; colleague; handmaid(en); subaltern(ate); subordinate;

subsidiary; (**fem.** coadjutress; coadjutrix)
in religious ceremony: **n.** acolyte

ASSOCIATE(S): (**see** "assistant") **n.** affiliate; affiliation; *confrère;* cohort; colleague; companion; concomitant; consort; socius; supporter; **v.** affiliate; fraternize
close: **n.** *alter ego;* compeer
group of: **n.** claque; clique; mieny
in crime: **n.** accessory; *particeps criminis; socius criminis*

ASSOCIATED: **a.** affiliated; appendant; corollary

ASSOCIATION: (**see** "alliance" **and** "brotherhood") **n.** companionship; congress; conjunction; consortium; fraternity; partnership
existence in: **n.** concomitance; concomitancy; **a.** concomitant
for common or mutually pleasing purposes: **n.** comity
harmful: **n.** antibiosis; **a.** inimical

ASSORTED: **a.** heterogeneous; miscellaneous; **n.** ASSORTMENT: (**see** "variety") heterogeneity; hodgepodge; miscellaneity; miscellany; (**pl.** miscellanea); multiformity; olla-podrida

ASSUAGE: **see** "ease"

ASSUME: **v.** appropriate; arrogate; ascribe; attribute; conjecture; hypothecate; hypothesize; posit; postulate; presume; theorize; undertake; **a.** ASSUMED: academic; appropriated; assumptious; assumptive; conjectural; counterfeit; factitious; feigned; fictitious; gratuitous; hypothesized; hypothetical; inferred; postulated; postulatory; simulated; *soi-disant;* speculated; speculative; spurious; supposititious; theoretical; usurped; **adv.** *sub silentio*

ASSUMPTION: **n.** adoption; appropriation; arrogance; hypothesis; incorporation; postulate; postulation; (**pl.** postulata); presumption; supposition; susception
basic: **n.** constantation
involving: **a.** hypothetical; officious; postulatory; presumptuous; supposititious

ASSURANCE: **n.** arrogance; audacity; certitude; confidence; effrontery; guarantee: impudence; infallibility; self-possession; *savoir faire;* self-reliance; surety
lack of: **n.** inferiority complex; timidity
with: **n.** *à plomb;* aplomb; certitude; confidence; self-possession

ASSUREDLY: **adv.** certes; indubitably; verily

ASTONISH: **v.** affright; astound; amaze; flabbergast; paralyze; petrify; **n.** ASTONISHMENT: amazement; petrifaction; petrification

ASTONISHING *occurrence:* **n.** *coup de foudre*

ASTRAY: (**see** "roaming") **a.** *dépaysé*

ASTRONOMY, *muse of:* **n.** Urania

ASYLUM: **see** "sanctuary"

AT *any price:* **adv.** *à tout prix*
first sight or view: **a.** *prima facie*
full length: **a.** *in extenso*
hand: **a.** calamitous; imminent; impending; threatening; **n.** immanence
home: **a.** or **adv.** *en famille*
last: **adv.** *en fin;* ultimately
once, all: **adv.** *tout à coup;* holus-bolus
pleasure: **adv.** *a bene placito; ad libitum* (**abb.** ad lib.); *à volonté*
random: **adv.** *à l'abandon; à tort et à travers;* **a.** stochastic
same time: **a.** conjugate; contemporaneous; contemporary; simultaneous; synchronic(al); synchronous; **adv.** or **a.** *pari passu;* **n.** contemporaneity; simultaneity
this time: **adv.** *hoc tempore*
whatever the cost: **adv.** *à tout prix*
will: (**see** "at random" *above*) **adv.** *ad arbitrium; à discrétion*

ATHLETE: **n.** gladiator
weaned from another school: **n.** or **v.** proselyte

ATHLETICS, *intense interest or participation in:* **n.** athleticism

ATMOSPHERE: (**see** "air") **n.** aura; decor; environment; fascination; glamor; nimbus; ornamentation
encompassing or pervading: **n.** ambiance; ambience; ambiente; **a.** ambient
heavy or pervasive; **n.** miasma; **a.** miasmal; miasmatic; miasmic; noxious

originating in: **a.** atmogenic
outer layers of, in order: **n.** stratosphere; ionosphere; mesosphere; exosphere
unhealthful: **see** "heavy" *above*

ATOMIC: **a.** Democritean; infinitesimal; molecular

ATONE: **v.** expiate; harmonize; reconcile; **a.** expiatory; piacular; propitiative; propitiatory; **n.** ATONEMENT: expiation; propitiation; reconciliation; satisfaction
incapable of being (atoned): **a.** inexpiable
means of (atonement): **n.** expiation; purgatory

ATTACK: (**see** "criticize") **v.** assail; bombard; **n.** ambuscade; assailment; oppugnation
adapted for: **a.** expugnatory
bitter or violent: **n.** denunciation; diatribe; invective; philippic; tirade; vituperation; **a.** denunciatory; invective; vituperative; **v.** inveigh
literary: **n.** *coup de plume*
nervous: **n.** *une attaque de nerfs*
not open to: **a.** impregnable; indubitable; inexpugnable; invincible; irrefutable
open to: **a.** exposed; expugnable; surmountable; vincible; vulnerable
person rather than issue(s): **adv.** *(argumentum) ad hominem*
(rape or attempted rape): **n.** indecent assault
ready for: **adv.** *en garde*
sudden: **n.** coup; paroxysm; seizure; **a.** paroxysmal
sudden surprise: **n.** *coup d'état; coup de main*
verbal: **n.** polemic; tirade

ATTAIN: **see** "get"; ATTAINMENT: **see** "endowment"

ATTEMPT: (**see** "endeavor") **v. or n.** essay; **n.** conatus; undertaking
act of making: **n.** conation; endeavor; **a.** conative
at first: **n.** *coup d'essai*

ATTENDANT(S): **n.** accompaniment; appendant; auxiliary; concomitant; corollary; entourage; retinue
loyal: **n.** hireling; mercenary; minion; myrmidon
uniformed: **n.** chasseur

ATTENTION(S): (**see** "diligence" **and** "heed") **n.** advertence; advertency; application; assiduity; (**pl.** assiduities); attentiveness; circumspection; concentration; consideration; diligence; intendence; perception; **a. see** "attentive"
draw to: **see** "allure"
drawing away from: **a.** digressive; distractive; diversionary
lack of: **n.** detachment; ignoration; inattention; laches
little: **n.pl.** assiduities; *petits soins*
paying of no: **see** "lack of" *above*

ATTENTIVE: **a.** advertent; assiduous; circumspect; diligent; heedful; inspective; perceptive; sedulous; **a. or adv.** *arrectis aribus*
to needs of others: **n.** complaisance; *prévenance;* prevenience

ATTIRE: (**see** "dress") **n.** accoutrement(s); array; caparison; equipage; habiliment; (in)vestment; toilette; vesture
formal or fashionable: **n.** toilette
of office: **n.pl.** pontificalibus

ATTITUDE: (**see** "behavior") **n.** attitudinization; disposition; posture
strike an: **v.** attitudinize; **a.** attitudinal; *n.* attitudinarianism
one who does: **n.** attitudinarian

ATTORNEY: **n.** barrister; counselor; solicitor
w/o help of: **adv.** *in propria persona*

ATTRACT: **v. see** "allure"; **a.** ATTRACTIVE: (**see** "alluring") arresting; beguiling; bewitching; bonny; captivating; Circean; comely; decorative; decorous; enticing; fascinating; intriguing; magnetic; mesmeric; personable; persuasive; prepossessing; psychagogic; seductive; **n.** ATTRACTION: **see** "appeal"

ATTRIBUTE: (**see** "characteristic") **n.** ap(p)anage; appendage; cachet; endowment; essence; perquisite; property; proprium; quality

AUCTION, *act of offering for sale or bidding at:* **n.** licitation

AUDACITY: (**see** "gall") **n.** arrogance; effrontery; hubris; impertinence; impetuosity; intrepidity; temerity

AUDIENCE, *playing to the:* **n.** cabotinage; Sardoodledom; theatricality

AUGMENT: (**see** "increase") **v.** aggrandize; enhance; exacerbate

AUGUR: (**see** "foretell") **v.** auspicate; **a.** auspicatory

AUSPICES: (**see** "protection") **n.** (a)egis; patronage; tutelage
under bad: **adv. or n.** *malis avibus*
under better: **adv. or n.** *melioribus auspiciis*
under good: **adv. or n.** *bonis avibus*

AUSTERE: (**see** "strict") **a.** acrimonious; ascetic; Draconian; extortionate; imperative; inexorable; inflexible; inquisitorial; obdurate; procrustean; rigorous; ruthless; Spartan(ic); stringent; uncompromising; unembellished; unrelenting; **n.** AUSTERITY: ascesis; inflexibility; Spartanism; stringency
person: **see** "disciplinarian"

AUTHENTIC: (**see** "authoritative") **a.** authorized; *bona fide;* legitimate; official; original; trustworthy; veritable

AUTHOR(S): (**see** "authorship" **and** "writer") **n.** ancestor; creator; originator; procreator; **a.** auctorial; authorial
complete works of an: **n.pl.** *opera omnia*
in handwriting of: **a.** holographic; onomastic; **n.** holograph
insignificant anonymous: **n.** anonymuncule
unknown: **n.** anonym(e); pseudonym; **a.** anonymous; pseudonymous; **n.** pseudonymity
written by several: a. polygraphic

AUTHORITARIAN: (**see** "dictatorial") **a.** autocratic; hierarchic(al); totalitarian; **n.** autocrat; despot; tyrant

AUTHORITATIVE: **a.** absolute; apostolic(al); authentic; canonical; cathedral; cathedratic; certified; classic; conclusive; convincing; dictatorial; documented; dogmatic; *ex cathedra;* magistral; magisterial; magistratical; official; orthodox; pompous; peremptory; **n.** AUTHORITATIVENESS: apostolicity; officiality; orthodoxy
group or tribunal: **n.** areophagus; areophagite; **a.** areophagitic; **n.** apostolicism
passage (in writing[s]): **n.** *locus classicus*
pronouncement, saying, etc.: **n.** allocution; dictum

AUTHORIZED: **see** "authoritative"

AUTHORITY: **n.** ascendency; authorization; autonomy; canonicity; dominion; influence; jurisdiction; magisteriality; officiality; prerogative; sovereignty; suzerainty
assume exaggerated: **v.** pontificate
beyond prescribed or permitted: **adv.** *ultra vires*
blind submission to: **n.** authoritarianism
by what?: **adv.** *quo warranto?*
exceeding legal or proper: **adv.** *ultra vires*
full: (**see** "unlimited" *below*) **a. or n.** *carte blanche;* **adv.** *pleno jure*
of another, subject to: **a.** *aleni juris*
of office, etc.: **n.** attribution; **a.** attributive
on any subject: **n.** pundit
range or limit of: **n.** dominion; jurisdiction; purview
to transact business: **n.** plenipotence; **a.** plenipotent
unlimited: **n.** *carte blanche; lettre de cache;* multipotence; omnipotence; **adv.** *pleno jure*
unlimited, having: **a.** multipotent; omnipotent; plenipotent(iary)
with: **see** "authoritative"
within prescribed or permitted: **adv.** *intra vires*
w/o prescribed or permitted: **adv.** *ultra vires*

AUTHORSHIP: **n.** instigation; paternity
study of writing(s) to determine authenticity of: **n.** bibliotics

AUTOBIOGRAPHY: (**see** "biography") **n.pl.** anamnesis; memoirs; recollections; reminiscences

AUTOCRATIC: **see** "authoritarian"

AUTOMATIC: (**see** "involuntary") **a.** automatous; mechanical; reflex; self-regulating; spontaneous; **n.** AUTOMATION: automatism; mechanization; spontaneity
to make: **v.** automate; automatize; mechanize; robotize

AUTOMATON: **n.** android; golem; robot

AUXILIARY: (**see** "assistant") **n.** adjunct; adminicle; **a.** (**see** "subsidiary") adminicular; supplementary
as in sentence construction: **a.** syncategorematic; synsemantic

AVAILABLE: **a.** accessible; attainable; dispensable; expendable; obtainable; remittable; utilizable

AVARICE: **n.** covetousness; cupidity; greediness; parsimony; rapaciousness; rapacity; venality

AVENGER *of wrong:* **n.** Nemesis; *vindex injuriae*

AVERSE: **see** "unwilling"

AVERSION: (**see** "dislike) **n.** animosity; antipathy; reluctation; repugnance; revulsion; unwillingness; **a.** AVERSIVE: reluctant; repugnant; repulsive
having natural or constitutional: **a.** antipathetic(al); antipathic
special: **n.** *bête noire*
to society: **n.** anthropophobia; apanthropia; apanthropy; **a.** anthropohobic; apanthropic

AVOID: **v.** abjure; bypass; eschew; evade; sidestep; **n.** AVOIDANCE: abjuration; annulment; eschewal; evasion

AVOWEDLY: **adv.** *ex professo*

AWAKENING: **n.** burgeoning; disenchantment; disillusionment; quickening; realization; recognition

AWARD: **v.** adjudge; apportion; bestow; **n.** accolade; guerdon
highest: **n.** *cordon bleu; grand prix*

AWARE: (**see** "knowing) **a.** apprised; cognizant; conscious; mindful; observant; sensible; sensitive; sentient; vigilant; watchful; **n.** AWARENESS: apprehension; cognition; cognizance; consciousness; discernment; insight; intuition; observation; orientation; perception; percipience; sentience; sentiency; vigilance
capable of being: **a.** cognizable; cognoscible; cognoscitative

AWE-*inspiring:* **a.** august; awesome; doughty; formidable; illustrious; redoubtable
religious: **n.** (the) numinous

AWFUL: (**see** "outrageous") **a.** appalling; awe-inspiring; awesome; ghastly; horrendous; horrific; indescribable; ineffable; ominous; portentous; redoubtable

AWKWARD: (**see** "clumsy") **a.** bungling; elephantine; gauche; inapt; inept; inexpert; infelicitous; inopportune; loutish; lumbering; maladroit; ponderous; uncouth; ungainly; unwield(l)y
incident: **n.** contretemps; gaucherie

AWKWARDNESS: **n.** clumsiness; embarrassment; gaucherie; inaptitude; inelegance; ineptitude; maladroitness
of manner(s): **n.** gaucherie; rusticity

AXIOM: **n.** **see** "maxim"; **a.** AXIOMATIC: (**see** "self-evident") aphoristic; hypothetico-deductive; postulational

B

BABBLE: **n.** babblement; bavardage; galimatias; gibberish; harangue; jargon; stultiloquence; stultiloquy; **a.** stultiloquent(ial)

BABY-*talk:* **n.** hypocorism; **n. or a.** hypocoristic

BACHELOR: **n.** agamist; celibate; coelebs; misogynist; **n.** BACHELORHOOD: bachelorism; celibacy; **a.** agamous; celibatarian

BACK: (**see** "support") **n.** dorsum; posteriority; tergum; **a.** dorsal; posterior; tergal
bending: **n.** retroflexion
farthest: **a.** posteriormost
lying on: a. supine; **n.** decubation; dorsal decubitus; reclination; recumbency; supinity
out: **v.** renege
turning: **a.** recessive; regressive; retrocessive; retrogradatory; retrograde; retroverse; **n.** recession; recidivism; regression; retrocession; retrogradation; retrogression; retroversion; reversion

BACKGROUND: **n.** heredity; history; lineage; milieu; *mise-en-scène;* pedigree
pert. to: **a.** circumstantial; employmental; environmental; situational

BACKER: (**see** "supporter") **n.** abettor; cohort; colleague; constituent; corroborator

BACKSLIDE: **v.** recidivate; regress; relapse; renege; retrogress; **n.** recidivation; recidivism; retrogression

BACKSLIDER: **n.** apostate; recidivant; recidivist; renegade; turncoat

BACKWARD: **a.** *à reculons;* backwoodsy; behindhand; diffident; reactionary; reluctant; unprogressive; **n.** BACKWARDNESS: barbarism; barbarity; regression; retrocession; retrogradation; retrogression

BACKWARDS, *moving or directed:* **a.** *à reculons;* retrograde; **n.** retrogression
name written: **n.** ananym
sentence or word reading same as forward: **n.** palindrome

BACTERIA, *agent destroying:* **a. or n.** antibiotic; antiseptic

BAD: (**see** "adverse" **and** "wicked") **a.** abominable; base; damnable; deficient; delinquent; delitescent; demeritorious; despicable; detestable; dilapidated; disagreeable; diseased; disobedient; displeasing; egregious; execrable; faulty; flagrant; harmful; intractable; malignant; mischievous; notorious; pernicious; regrettable; sinister; substandard; unhealthy; viperous
because prohibited or unlawful: **adv. or n.** *malum prohibitum*
blood: **n.** *mauvais sang*
boy or person: (**see** "person, base and despicable") **n.** *enfant terrible*
custom or habit: **n.** cacoethes
faith, in: **adv.** *malâ fide*
in itself, or inherently: **adv. or n.** *malum in se*
manner, in a: **adv.** *malo modo*
mood, in a: **see** "irritable"
situation: **n.** *mauvais pas;* plight
smelling: **see** "stinking"
taste: **n.** *mauvais goût;* **a.** egregious
-tempered: **see** "irritable"
-tempered person: n. curmudgeon

BADNESS: **n.** abomination; depravity; malevolence; malignancy; sinisterity; virulence

BAFFLE: **v.** checkmate; circumvent; counteract; disconcert; frustrate; obfuscate;

thwart; **a.** BAFFLED: nonplussed; perplexed; **n.** BAFFLEMENT: confusion; obfuscation; perplexity; **a.** BAFFLING: enigmatic(al); inexplicable; obfuscatory; obscure

BAGGAGE (**see** "equipment") **n.** luggage; (**pl.** impedimenta)

BAILOR: **n.** adpromissor

BALANCE: **v.** equalize; equate; equilibrate; equilibrize; equiponderate; librate; neutralize; stabilize; **n.** composure; equanimity; equilibrium; equipoise; equipollence; equiponderance; equiponderation; harmony; libration; poise; proportion; serenity; stability; stabilization; symmetry
lack of: **n.** astasia; disequilibration; disequilibrium; imbalance; instability
mental: **n.** composure; equanimity; homeostasis; serenity; **a.** Apollonian; Apollonistic; Apollonic; equanimous
serving to: **a.** compensative; compensatory; equipollent; equiponderant
with: **adv.** *aequo animo*

BALANCED: (**see** "level") **a.** Apollonian; equalized; harmonious; neutralized; stabilized

BALANCING: **a.** compensative; compensatory; equilibrant; (equi)libratory; equipollent; equiponderant; isonomic

BALD: **a.** alopecic; epilated; glabrate; glabrescent; glabrous; outright; palpable; patent; unadorned; undisguised
head, or bald-headed person: **n.** pilgarlic

BALDNESS: **n.** acomia; alopecia; atrichia; atrichosis; calvities; phalacrosis
front of head: **n.** anaphalantiasis

BALK: **v.** demur; frustrate; impede; thwart; **n.** demur; hindrance; **a.** BALKY: (**see** "contrary") recalcitrant; restive

BALL, *formed into or shaped like:* **a.** conglobate; conglomerate; globular; orbicular; spheroid(al); **n.** conglomeration; spheroid; **v.** conglobe

BALLET, *art of:* **n.** choreography; **a.** choreographic(al)
dancer, esp. a star (fem.): **n.** *coryphée*
rel. to or suitable for: **a.** balletic
teacher: **n.** choreographer

BALMY: **a.** anodyne; anodynous; aromatic; balsamic; favonian; lenitive; mitigative; temperate

BAN: **v.** anathematize; execrate; interdict; prohibit; proscribe; **n.** anathema; execration; interdiction; prohibition; proscription; **a.** interdictive; interdictory; proscribed; proscriptive
temporary: **n.** armistice; moratorium

BANAL: (**see** "trite") **a.** asinine; insipid; pedestrian; platitudinous; **n.** BANALITY: pedestrianism

BANISH: **v.** deport; dispossess; eject; exile; expatriate; extradite; ostracize; proscribe; relegate; **n.** BANISHMENT: expatriation; expulsion; extradition; ostracism; relegation

BANKRUPT: (**see** "poor") a. depleted; deprived; destitute; exhausted; impecunious; impoverished; insolvent; **n.** BANKRUPTCY: depletion; destitution; impoverishment; insolvency

BANNED, *list of what is:* (**see under** "book(s)") **n.** *index expurgatorius*

BANNER, *of battle, or one inspiring devotion:* **n.** oriflame
symbolical: **n.** labrum

BANQUET: **n.** convivium; symposium
pert. to: **a.** convivial; epulary; festive

BANQUETER: **n.** symposiarch; symposiast

BANTER: **n.** asteism; badinage; persiflage; raillery; sarcasm; **v.** persiflate
one who engages in: **n.** persifleur; railleur

BAPTISM, *spiritual:* **n.** consolamentum

BARBARIC: (**see** "cruel" **and** "wild") **a.** atrocious; barbaresque; barbarous; feral; ferocious; inhuman; philistinic; philistinish; procrustean; tramontane; tyrannical; uncivilized; **n.** BARBARITY: barbarousness; barbarism; ferity; inhumanity; philistinism; savagery

BARE: (**see** "naked") **a.** exposed; manifest; minimum
to lay: **v.** denude; denudate; **a.** denudate; denudative; **n.** denudation

BARGAIN: (**see** "barter") **v.** haggle; negotiate
at a: **adv.** *à bon marché; à vil prix* (dirt cheap)

BARK, *remove:* (**see** "peel") **v.** decorticate; **n.** decortication

BARREL, *shaped like:* **a.** doliform

BARREN: **a.** acarpous; fruitless; hardscrabble; immature; infecund; infertile; inhospitable; jejune; juvenile; nonparous; nulliparous; sterile; unfructuous; unfruitful; unprofitable; **n.** BARRENNESS: desolation; infecundity; infertility; sterility

BARTENDER(ING): **n.** mixologist; mixology

BARTER: (**see** "bargain") **v.** commute; reciprocate; **n.** commutation; *quid pro quo*

BASE: (**see** "wicked") **a.** contemptible; counterfeit; degenerate; degraded; degrading; despicable; dishonorable; ignoble; infamous; inferior; low-minded; mean-spirited; menial; plebeian; proletarian; substratal; substrative; unworthy; **n.** foundation; fundament(um); groundwork; pedestal; plinth; principium; substratum
attached at: **a.** sessile
of operations; **n.** *pou sto*
particularly military: **n.** *point d'appui*
rel. to or situated at: **a.** basal; basic; basilar; fundamental

BASENESS: (**see** "wickedness") **n.** degeneration; degradation; turpitude

BASHFUL: (**see** "shy") **a.** coy; Daphnean; demure; diffident; self-conscious; timorous; verecund; **n.** BASHFULNESS: coyness; diffidence; *mauvaise honte;* timidity; timorousness; verecundity

BASIC: **a.** abecedarian; abecedary; alkaline; basal; basilar; canonical; constitutional; elementary; essential; fundamental; indispensable; ingrained; inherent; innate; intrinsic; irreducible; orthodox; primary; primitive; primeval; substrate; **adv.** BASICALLY: *au fond;* essentially; fundamentally; intrinsically; **n.** BASICNESS: essentiality; fundamentality; primality; quintessence; ultimacy
law: **n.** canon; constitution; decalogue; magna c(h)arta
principle: **n.** fundament(um); postulate; tenet

BASIS: (**see** "base") **n.** authority; foundation; frame of reference; fundament(um); philosophy; *point d'appui; pou sto;* principium; theory

BASK *in sun:* **v.** apricate; **n.** aprication

BASTARD: **n.** *filius nullis; filius populi;* hybrid; illegitimate; mongrel; **a.** counterfeit; debased; illegitimate; sinister; spurious
fact or cond. of being: **n.** bar sinister

BAT: **n.** chiropter; *fledermaus;* Vespertilio; (**pl.** Vespertilionidae); **a.** chiropteran; vespertilian; vesptertine

BATH(S): **n.** ablution; balneation; , **n.** BATHING: balneology; **a.** ablutionary; balneal; balneary
treatment by: **n.** balneo-therapeutics; balneo-therapy; hydrotherapy

BATTLE: **n.** collision; conflict; encounter; engagement; skirmish
flag or standard: **n.** oriflamme
great and decisive: **n.** Armageddon

BATTLEFIELD: **n.** aceldama; Armageddon; battleground

BAUBLE: **see** "trifle"

BE *what you seem to be: esto quod esse videris*

BEAK: (**see** "nose") **n.** proboscis
hooked type: **a.** aduncous; aquiline

BEAN, *pert. to or like:* **a.** fabaceous
shaped like: **a.** fabiform

BEAR *or bear family, pert. to:* **a.** arctoid; (**pl.** arctoidea); ursine

BEARD(S), *cultivation or growing of:* **n.** pogonotrophy
study of or treatise on: **n.** pogonology
trimming: **n.** pogonotomy

BEARDED: **a.** aristate; awned; barbate; pogoniate

BEARING: **n.** address; application; behavior; carriage; démarche; demeanor;

deportment; direction; mien; poise; posture; prestance; purport; relation; significance
live beings: **a.** proligerous; viviparous
noble: **n.** *démarche noble*

BEARINGS, *loss of:* **n.** disorientation

BEAST: (**see** "animal") **n.** behemoth; quadruped
one believing himself to be (mental disorder): **n.** lycanthropy; zoanthropia; zoanthropy

BEAT: (**see** "accent") **n.** arsis; ictus; intonation; palpitation; pulsation; thesis
as w/ stick: **v.** castigate; cudgel; flagellate; fustigate; lambaste
or stress, recurring: **n.** ictus; vespertili
rapidly: **v.** palpitate; **a.** palpitant; **n.** palpitation; tachycardia (*heart*)

BEAUTIFUL: (**see** "attractive") **a.** (a)esthetic(al); beauteous; captivating; comely; delectable; excellent; *fait a peindre;* pulchritudinous; tempean
form: **n.** *belle tournure*
love of the: **n.** (a)esthetics; philocaly; **a.** (a)esthetic(al); philocalic

BEAUTY: (**see** "glory") **n.** beauteousness; comeliness; excellence; felinity; magnificence; pulchritude; radiance; splendor; symmetry; **v.** BEAUTIFY: (**see** "adorn") adonize; embellish
and art, pert to: **a.** (a)esthetic(al); artistic
goddess of: **n.** Aphrodite; Venus
ideal or perfect: **n.** *beau idéal; beauté achevée, une beauté accomplie*
paragon of: **n.** phoenix
physical: **n.** comeliness; pulchritude; **a.** comely; pulchritudinous
place of great natural (beauty) or charm: **n.** Tempe; **a.** tempean
science of: **n.** (a)esthetics
worshipper of: **n.** (a)esthete; connoisseur

BECAUSE *of this:* **adv.** *propter hoc*

BECKON: **see** "allure"

BECLOUD (or BEDIM): **see** "obscure"

BED: **n.** foundation; framework; matrix
-chamber, small: **n.** cubiculum
-wetting: **n.** nocturnal enuresis

BEDECK: (**see** "adorn") **v.** caparison; lard

BEFORE: (**see** "previous") **prep.** awaiting; confronting; **adv.** anterior
as: **adv.** *sicut ante; status quo ante*
feeling of having been somewhere (before): **n.** *déjà vu(e)*; paramnesia
going: (**see** "preliminary") **a.** antecedent; antecedental; premundane; **n. see** "forerunner"
state of being; **n.** antecedence; anteriority; precedence; **a.** antecedaneous; antecedent; anterior; precedent; premundane; prevenient

BEG: (**see** "beseech" **and** "pray") **v.** adjure; importune; solicit

BEGET: **v.** procreate; (pro)generate; propagate; reproduce; **n.** BEGETTING: procreation; **a.** procreant; procreative; reproductive

BEGGAR: **n.** cadger; gaberlunzie; mendicant; pariah; petitioner; suppliant; **a.** BEGGARLY: contemptible; sordid; tatterdemalion

BEGGING: **a.** beseeching; importunate; mendicant; precative; precatory; soliciting; solicitous; supplicatory; **n.** mendicancy; mendicity
the question (assuming what is to be proved): **n.** *petitio principii*

BEGIN: **v.** actuate; generate; germinate; inaugurate; initiate; institute; motivate; originate; **n.** BEGINNER: (**see** "learner") abecedarian; actuator; amateur; apprentice; catalyst; catechumen; founder; neophyte; novice; novitiate; originator; postulate

BEGINNING: (**see** "origin") **n.** actuation; commencement; exordium; foundation; genesis; impulsion; inauguration; inception; incipience; incipiency; inconabulum; (**pl.** inconabula); initiation; investiture; nascency; *premier pas;* primordium; principium; **a.** aborning; alpha; catechumenical; elementary; embryonic; genetic; germinal; inchoate; incipient; inconabular; *in fieri;* initiatory; nascent; parturient; primitive; primordial; rudimentary
and end: **n.** alpha and omega
existing at or from the: **a. or adv.** *ab inconabulis; ab initio; ab initium;* aboriginal; primordial; **adv.** *ab ovo*

having no: **adv.** *ab aeterno*
in the: **adv.** *in principio*
just: **a.** inchoate; inchoative; potential; **n.** inchoation; nascency
to end, from: **adv.** *ab ovo usque ad mala*
to form: **a.** aborning; nascent; parturient; **n.** nascency

BEHAVIOR: (**see** "conduct") **n.** attitude; bearing; comportment; demeanor; deportment; discipline; ergasia; manner; mien
artificial: **n.** affectation; theatricality; (**pl.** dramatics; histrionics; hysterics; pathetics; sentimentalities; theatrics)
asocial or antisocial: **n.** sociopath(y); **a.** sociopathic
authority on rules of: **n.** *arbiter-elegantiae; arbiter elegantiarum*
bad: (**see** "misconduct") **n.** beastliness; bestiality
bold or licentious: **n.** *grivoiserie;* **a.** *grivois*
childish or infantile: **n.** immaturity; infantility; puerilism; puerility; **a.** infantile; infantilistic
coarse: (**see** "coarseness") **n.** buffoonery
conforming to proper: **see** "standards"
courteous: **n.** benignity; civility; congeniality; cordiality; graciosity
during good: **adv.** *ad vitam aut culpam; quamdiu se bene gesserit*
extravagant or conspicuous: (**see** "artificial" *above*) **n.** baboonery; buffoonery; exhibitionism; theatricality; theatrics; **a.** exhibitionistic(al); theatrical
false: **see** "artificial" *above*
good: **see** "courteous" *above*
influencing by suggesting desirable life goals: **n.** psychagogy; **a.** psychagogic
lofty: **n.** dramatism; theatricality; (**pl.** theatrics)
not conforming to proper: **see** "improper"
one w/ disordered toward other people: **n.** (constitutional) psychopath
science or study of: **n.** behaviorism; ethics; ethology; psychology; **a.** ethological
violent: **a.** manic(al); rampageous; riotous

BEHEAD: **v.** decapitate; guillotine; obtruncate

BEHIND: **n.** *derrière;* gluteus; podex; posterior; **a. or adv.** *en arrière*
force acting from: **n.** *vis a tergo*
from: **adv.** *a tergo;* **a.** posterior

BEING(S): (**see** "existence" **and** "human") **n.** actuality; bios; ens; entity; esse; existent; **a.or adv.** *in esse*
description of nature of: **n.** ontography
for the time (being): **a. or adv.** *ad hoc; pro tem(pore)*
of Beings (supreme): **n.** *Ens Entium*
physical: **see under** "existence"
rel. to: **a.** *ontic; ontological*
science dealing w/ nature of: **n.** metaphysics; ontology; **a.** ontological
small: **n.** animalcule; inchling

BELCH: **v.** eruct(ate); **n.** eructation

BELIEF(S): **n.** acceptation; conviction; credence; creed; doctrine; *idée fixe;* persuasion; philosophy; principle; profession; sentiment; tenet
abandon: **v.** apostatize; **n.** apostasy; apostate
erroneous: **n.** pseudodoxy
in facts only: **n.** materialism; positivism
in one's self: **n.** egoism; solipsism
one holding no particular: **see under** "creed"
reconciliation or union of conflicting: **n.** syncretism; **a.** syncretic; syncretistic; **v.** syncretize
semi-mystical surrounding person or object: **n.** mystique
worthiness of: **see** "believable"

BELIEVABLE: **a.** credible; creditable; plausible; trustworthy; **n.** BELIEVABILITY: credibility; plausibility; trustworthiness

BELIEVER *in all religions:* **n.** omnist

BELITTLE: **v.** debase; decry; defame; denigrate; depreciate; disparage; minimize; stigmatize; vilify; villipend; **a.** BELITTLING: denigratory; depreciatory; derogative; derogatory; minimizing; villipending; **n.** BELITTLEMENT: denigration; derogation; disparagement; minimization; stigmatization

BELL(S), *art of ringing:* **n.** campanology
shaped like: **a.** campaniform; campanular; campanulate
small tinkling: **n.** tintinnabulum; (**pl.** tintinnabula)
sound of: **n.** tintinnabulation; **a.** tintinnabular
study of, or making: **n.** campanology

BELLIGERENT: (see "hostile") **a.** bellicose; umbrageous; **n.** bashi-bazouk

BELLOWING: **a.** mugient; vociferating; vociferous

BELLY: **see** "abdomen"
dance: **n.** *danse du ventre*

BELONG: **v.** appertain; inhere; **a.** appurtenant; **n.** appurtenance; appurtenant

BELOW: **adv.** inferior; nether; subalternate; subjacent; suboptimal; subordinate; substrative; underlying
as: **adv.** *ut infra*

BEND: **v.** arcuate; circumflex; deflect; incurve; replicate; **n.** arcuation; circumflexion; flexure; flexuosity; incurvation; (in)curvature; sinuosity; tortuosity; **a.** see "bent"

BENEATH, *to place:* **v.** infrapose; **n.** infraposition

BENEFACTOR: **n.** donor; grantor; patron; philanthropist; Prometheus; Samaritan
generous: **n.** Maecenas; **n.** Maecenasship: Maecenatism

BENEFICIAL: (see "advantageous") **a.** benefic; opportune; rewarding; salubrious; salutary; sanative

BENEFICIARY: **n.** cestui; donee; legatee

BENEFICIENT: (see "charitable") **a.** benevolent; munificient; salubrious; salutary

BENEFIT: **n.** advantage; benefaction; benefice; beneficience; benevolence; blessing
for whose?: **adv.** *cui bono?*
of clergy; **n.** *beneficium clericale*

BENEVOLENT: **see** "charitable"

BENT: **a.** arcuate; circumflex; determined; flexuous; geniculate; incurvate; pronate; resolved; **n.** (see "inclination") affectation; disposition; penchant; tendency
backwards, as the body: **n.** opisthotonos; retroflexion; **a.** opisthotonic

BERATE: (see "scold") **v.** castigate; chide; execrate; objurgate; reprove; vituperate; **a.** castigatory; execratory; objurgatory; **n.** execration; objurgation; vituperation

BESEECH: (see "pray") **v.** entreat; impetrate; implore; importune; obsecrate; obtest; solicit; supplicate; **a.** BESEECHING: imploratory; importunate; precative; precatory; solicitous; **n.** imploration; obtestation; solicitation

BESIDE: **see** "alongside"

BESIEGE: (see "surround") **v:** beleaguer

BEST, *all is for the:* **a.** Panglossian
cond. or fact of being: **n.** optimity; optimum; preeminent; preeminence; superiority; **a.** optimum; *par excellence;* superordinary; superordinate
make (best) of: **v.** optimize
-man: **n.** *garçon d'honneur;* paranymph
the, or the very: (see "choice") **n.** *crème de la crème; nec plus supra; nec plus ultra;* **adv. or a.** *par excellence;* **adv.** preeminent; supereminent

BETRAYAL: **n.** apostasy; duplicity; perfidy; prodition; treachery; treason; triplicity
of trust: **n.** perfidy; prodition; seduction; **a.** perfidious; treacherous

BETRAYER: **n.** apostate; recreant; traitor

BETROTHAL: **n.** affiance; engagement; espousal; troth; **pl.** sponsalia

BETS, *series of:* **n.** parlay

BETTER, *for want of anything:* **n.** *faute de mieux;* Hobson's choice
quality or cond. of being: **n.** meliority; optimity; **a.** optimum; superordinary; superordinate
so much the: **adv.** *tant mieux*
to make or become: **v.** (a)meliorate; **a.** meliorative; **n.** melioration

BETTERMENT *of society by improving health conds., etc.:* **n.** meliorism

BETWEEN: **a.** interjacent; intermediate; intervening; **n.** interjacency
ourselves: **adv.** *entre nous; inter nous*
three: **adv.** *à trois*
two: **adv.** *à deux*
two fires: **adv.** *entre deux feux*

two points or events: **a.** intermediary; intermediate; intervenient; intervening; parenthetical

BEVERAGE: **n.** draught; libation; potable; potation

BEWAIL: **v.** bemoan; deplore; lament; **a.** deprecable; lamentable; plangorous; **n.** BEWAILMENT: deploration; deprecation; lamentation

BEWARE: **adv.** *prenez garde*

BEWILDER: **v.** astonish; astound; bemuse; electrify; flabbergast; metagrobolize; obfuscate; perplex; **a.** BEWILDERED: (**see** "confused") bemused; *désorienté;* disconnected; distraught; electrified; *éperdu;* thunderstruck; **n.** BEWILDERMENT: (**see** "confusion") disorientation; embranglement; obfuscation; perplexity

BEWITCH: (**see** "enchant") **v.** captivate; ensorcel(l); exorcise; fascinate

BIAS: **n.** inclination; partiality; *parti pris;* predilection; prejudice; prepossession; tendency; **a.** BIASED: diagonal; oblique; opinionated; prejudiced; prejudicial; slanting; tendentious

BIBLE, *adherence to letter of:* **n.** Biblicism; Biblicist; fundamentalism
books not recognized: **n.pl.** apocrypha; anagignoskomena
books recognized as authoritative (N. Test.): **n.pl.** homolog(o)umena; **a.** protocanonical
pert. to: **a.** biblical; scriptural; **n.** biblicality; scripturality
student of: **n.** Biblicist; Biblist
worship of: **n.** Bibliolatry

BIG: (**see** "huge") **a.** preeminent; pregnant; pretentious
-bellied: **a.** abdominous; ventripotent
-bug: (**see** "person, important") **n.** bigwig; celebrity; cynosure; grandee; luminary; magnate; magnifico; notability; panjandrum; personage
-headed: (**see** "conceited") **a.** megacephalic; megacephalous

BIGOT: **see** "person, narrow-minded"; **a.** BIGOTED: (**see** "narrow-minded") inegalitarian; **n.** BIGOTRY: fanaticism; intolerance; (pen)insularity; provincialism; sectarianism; sectionalism

BILATERAL: **a.** bipartisan; reciprocal; synal(l)agamatic; **n.** BILATERALITY: bipartisanship; duality

BILK: (**see** "cheat") **v.** disappoint; frustrate; swindle

BILL *having multiple purposes:* **n.** omnibus (bill)

BIND: **v.** colligate; constrain; contract; ligate; restrain; restrict; shackle
something which (binds): **n.** ligation; ligature; linchpin

BINDING: **a.** astrictive; (a)stringent; indissoluble; obligatory; **n.** astriction; astrictive; colligation; contraction; ligation; ligature; stringency
by, or as if by, oath or covenant: **n.** objurgation; **a.** sacramental

BIOGRAPHICAL *novel, developing character fr. child to adulthood:* **n.** entwicklungsroman
sketches, collection or production of: **n.** prosopography

BIOGRAPHY: **n.** anemnesis; *curriculum vitae;* memoir(s); personalia; prosopography; reminiscence(s)
short: **n.** profile

BIOLOGICAL *development:* **n.** ontology; **a.** ontological

BIOLOGICALLY *defective or deficient:* **a.** dysgenic

BIRD(S), *collector of eggs:* **n.** oologist; oology
loving or fond of: **a.** ornithophilous
of a region or area: **n.** avifauna; ornithofauna
pert. to: **a.** avian; ornithic; ornithoid
rearing and care of: **n.** aviculture
study of: **n.** ornithology
-watching: **n.** ornithoscopy

BIRTH: **n.** accouchement; ancestry; confinement; debut; embarcation; extraction; genesis; geniture; inauguration; inchoation; insipience; lineage; nativity; procreation
about to give, or giving: **a.** aborning; *in statu nascendi;* parturient
after (subsequent to): **a.** postnatal; postpartum

asst. at: **n.** accoucher; midwife; obstetrician; (**fem.** accoucheuse; midwife)
at moment of: **a.** or **adv.** aborning; **a.** parturient; **n.** parturition
before: **a.** antemundane; antenatal; antepartum; prenatal; **adv.** *in utero*
bringing forth young by: **a.** parturient; proligerous; viviparous; **n.** viviparity
bringing forth young by eggs: **a.** oviparous; ovoviparous; **n.** oviparity; ovoviparity
existing from or before: **a.** congenital; connatal; connate; familial; genetous; hereditary; inherent; innate; primeval
giving to live beings: **see** "bringing forth young by" *above*
illegitimate: **n.** bar sinister
land of one's: **n.** *natale solum*
occurring at or about time of: **a.** aborning; parturient; perinatal
of gentle: **a.** gentilitial; gentilitious; **n.** gentility; gentry
pert. to: **a.** aborning; natal; parturient
rate of: **n.** natality
resident of place or region of: **n.** sedens
room set apart for, as in hosp.: **n.** natuary

BIRTHDAY, *pert. to:* **a.** genethliac(al)
poem: **n.** genethliacon

BISEXUAL: **a.** androgynous; hermaphroditic(al); **n.** androgyne; hermaphrodite; **n.** BISEXUALITY: androgyneity; androgyny; hermaphroditism

BIT: **n.** driblet; granule; minimum; minum; modicum; morceau; morsel; smack; tincture; tinge

BITING: (**see** "sarcastic") **a.** acidulous; acrid; acrimonious; caustic; censorious; corrosive; incisive; mordacious; mordant; piquant; poignant; vinegary
of nails: **n.** onychophagia; onychophagy; phaneromania
remarks: **n.** causticity; mordacity; spinosity

BITTER: (**see** "sarcastic") **a.** acrimonious; caustic; determined; distasteful; grievous; poignant; relentless; unpalatable; unsavory; vehement; **n.** BITTERNESS: acerbity; acridity; acrimony; poignancy
in temperament: (**see** "biting") **a.** acerb(ic); **n.** acerbity
something which is: **n.** wormwood (**or** gall and wormwood)

BIZARRE: (**see** "odd") **a.** atypical; baroque; chimerical; daedal(ic); daedalian; fantastic; grotesque; **n. see** "oddity"
quality: **n.** bizarrerie

BLACK: **a.** atramental; atramentous; discreditable; dishonorable; nigrescent; swart; **n.** BLACKNESS: nigrescence; nigritude
beast (figurative): **n.** *bête noir*
magic: **n.** necromancy; sorcery
sheep (figurative): (**see** "scamp") **n.** *mauvais sujet*

BLACKEN: **v.** nigrify; **a.** BLACKISH: nigrescent; nigricant
name of: **v.** defame; denigrate; depreciate; disparage; revile; sully; vilify; vilipend; **n.** denigration; vilification; **a.** denigratory

BLACKHEAD: **n.** comedo

BLACKMAIL: **n.** chantage

BLAME: **v.** accuse; animadvert; censure; condemn; criticize; impute; incriminate; inculpate; reprehend; reprimand; reproach; reprove; upbraid; **n.** animadversion; culpa(bility); obloquy; onus; reprehension; **a.** BLAMABLE (**or** BLAMEWORTHY): (**see** "guilty") censurable; condemnatory; culpable; demeritorious; peccable; reprehensible; reprovable
free from: **v.** absolve; exculpate; exonerate; vindicate; **n.** exculpation; exoneration; vindication; **a.** exculpable; exculpatory

BLAMELESS: (**see** "innocent") **a.** impeccable; impeccant; inculpable; irreproachable; unimpeachable; **n.** BLAMELESSNESS: impeccability

BLAND: (**see** "soothing") **a.** affable; anodyne; anodynic; anodynous; benign; complaisant; favonian; halcyon; ingratiating; lenient; suave; tasteless; unconcerned; unperturbed; urbane

BLARE: **see** "fanfare"

BLAZING: **see** "fiery"

BLEACH: **v.** achromatize; decolorize; etiolate
from lack of sun or light: **v**: etiolate; **n.** etiolation

BLEEDING, *hereditary disease of:* **n.** hemophilia; hemophiliac

BLEMISH: **n.** cloud; imperfection; macula(tion); stigma

BLEND: **v.** amalgamate; coalesce; harmonize; inosculate; **n.** amalgamation; coalescence; tincture

BLESS: **v.** consecrate; macarize; sanctify; **a.** BLESSING: benedictory; invocatory; macarian; **n.** (**see** "approval") beatitude; benediction; benison; felicitation; invocation

BLESSED *are the peacemakers:* **adv.** *beati pacifici*

BLIND: **a.** amaurotic; **adv.** BLINDLY: *à tâtons*
-alley: **n.** cul-de-sac; deadlock; impasse
drive or impulse: **n.** ate
envy is: invidia est caeca
partially: **a.** purblind; **n.** hemianopsia

BLINDNESS: **n.** ablepsia; amaurosis; anopsia; cecity
night-: **n.** nyctalopia
one-sided: **n.** homonymous hemianopsia
study of: **n.** typhlology

BLINK: **v.** nict(it)ate; twinkle; **n.** nictitation

BLISS: (**see** "happiness") **n.** beatitude; ecstasy; elysium; felicity; paradise; transport; **a.** BLISSFUL: beatific; beatified; ecstatic; Edenic; elysian; enchanted; felicific; felicitous; halcyon; paradisiacal; rapturous; transported
consummate: **n.** beatitude; **a.** beatific

BLOCK: **v.** impede; obstruct; occlude; oppilate; **n.** hindrance; impediment; occlusion; oppilation; **a.** impedimental; occlusive

BLOOD: **n.** consanguinity; gore; lineage; **a.** BLOODY: gory, merciless; murderous; sanguinary
bad: **n.** *mauvais sang*
color of: **a.** sanguine(ous)
feeding on: **a.** hematophagous; sanguinivorous; sanguivorous
having excess of: **a.** plethoric; **n.** plethora
impurity of: **n.** acatharsia; septicemia
not of pure: (**see** "half-breed") **a.** unpedigreed
of, containing, or tinged w/: **a.** sanguinolent
-pressure instrument; **n.** sphygmomanometer
supply, local, temp. lack of: **n.** ischemia; **a.** ischemic
-thirsty: **a.** murderous; sanguinary; sanguineous; **n.** acharnement

BLOODSHED, *place of:* **n.** Aceldama; Armageddon

BLOOM: **v.** burgeon; effloresce; flourish; **n.** burgeoning; (ef)florescence; heyday; maturescence
full: **n.** anthesis; maturescence

BLOOMING: **a.** burgeoning; (ef)florescent; (ef)floriferous; prosperous
again: **a.** recrudescent; remontant

BLOTCH: **a.** imperfection; macula(tion); **a.** macular; maculate

BLOW: **v.** bluster; fulminate; squander; **n.** assault; calamity; concussion; coup; impact; trauma(tism)
knockdown: **n.** recumbentibus
physical or mental: **n.** trauma(tism); **a.** traumatic; **v.** traumatize
taking effect elsewhere: **n.** contrecoup
without a: **adv.** *sine ictu*

BLUE: **a.** depressed; melancholy; puritanical; unpromising; **n.** "BLUES": despondency; doldrum(s); megrim(s); melancholy
deep clear: **a.** cerulean
ribbon (highest distinction): **n.** *cordon bleu; grand prix*

BLUENESS *of skin:* **n.** cyanosis; **a.** cyanotic

BLUESTOCKING: **n.** *bas bleu;* (**fem.** *femme savante*)

BLUNDER: **v.** botch; bungle; mismanage; **n.** (**see** "stupidity") *faux pas; gaffe;* parapraxia; parapraxis
in speech: **n.** parapraxia; solecism; **a.** solecistic(al)
social: **n.** *faux pas; gaffe;* solecism

BLUNT: (**see** "frank") **v.** anesthesize; hebetate; narcotize; **a.** brusque; hebetate;

insensible; insensitive; obtund; obtuse; unceremonious; untactful; **n.** BLUNTNESS: brusquerie; hebetude; insensibility; obtusity

BLUSH: **n.** erubescence; rubedo; **a.** erubescent

BLUSTER: **see** "boast" **and** "swagger;" **n.** BLUSTERER: (**see** "boaster") swashbuckler

BOARDER: **n.** *pensionnaire*

BOAST: (**see** "swagger") **v.** bluster; flaunt; flourish; gasconade; preen; rodomontade; swashbuckle; **n.** BOASTER: braggadocio; braggart; bravado; cockalorum; fanfaron; gasconade; hector; jackanapes; megalomaniac; rodomont; Scaramouche; swashbuckler; **n.** BOASTING: (**see** "bombast") fanfaronade; jactitation; pomposity; rodomontade; vainglory; vaporing

BOASTFUL: **a.** bombastic; braggadocian; grandiose; grandiloquent; magniloquent; ostentatious; pompous; rodomontade; sonorous; swashbuckling; thrasonic(al); vainglorious; vaporing; vaunting
person: **see** "boaster"
talk, speech or action: **n.** bravado; cockalorum; fanfaronade; gasconade; rodomontade

BOAT-SHAPED: **a.** navicular

BODY: **n.** cadaver; corpus; quantum; (**pl.** quanta); substance; substantiality; torso; **a.** BODILY: constitutional; corpor(e)al; incarnate; physical; somantic
abnormal cond. of: **n.** dyscrasia; pathology
and mind, rel. to: **a.** psychosomatic
and soul: **n.** *corpus et âme*
build: (**see** "type" **below**) **n.** habitus; physique
cavity, opening of: **n.** introitus; os
dead: **n.** cadaver; corpse
discharge(s): **see** "excrement(s)"
form into: **v.** corporify; embody; incarnate
freed from the: **a.** disincarnate
having a: **a.** corporality; corporeity; incarnate; materiality
having abnormally large: **a.** macrosomatic; macrosomatous; **n.** macrosomia
having small: **a.** microsomatic; microsomatous
human: **n.** tenement
movement, pert. to: **a.** gestic
originating within: **a.** autogenic; autogenous; endogenous; psychogenic; psychosomatic; physiogenic; somatogenic
originating w/o: **a.** exogenous; heterogeneous
pert. to: **a.** constitutional; corpor(e)al; musculo-skeletal; physical; somatic; **n.** somatization
preoccupied with the: **n.** physicality
sensations, recognition of location of: **n.** stereognosis; topognosis; **a.** stereognostic
sensations, rel. to: **a.** somesthetic
type, human:
light or asthenic: **a.** ectomorphic; leptosome; **n.** ectomorph; hyperontomorph; leptosome
muscular or athletic: **a.** eumorphic; mesomorphic; **n.** mesomorph
short, broad, round: **a.** endomorphic, pyknic; **n.** endomorph; pyknic
thick, robust, powerful: **n.** meso-ontomorph

BOG: **n.** morass; quagmire; **a.** quaggy

BOGUS: (**see** "sham") **a.** artificial; Brummagem; counterfeit; factitious; fraudulent; spurious

BOIL (*sore*): **n.** furuncule; **a.** furuncular; (**n.pl.** furunculosis)

BOILING: **a.** ebullient; effervescent; seething; torrid; **n.** ebullition; effervescence

BOISTEROUS: (**see** "noisy") **a.** brawling; disorderly; raucus; robustious; robustuous; roisterous; termagant; truculent; tumultuous; **n.** BOISTEROUSNESS: raucity; raucousness

BOLD: (**see** "brave") **a.** adventurous; (ad)venturesome; arrogant; audacious; chivalrous; courageous; doughty; enterprising; harageous; impertinent; impudent; intrepid; malapert; presumptuous; prominent; resolute; valiant; **adv.** *con bravura;* **n.** BOLDNESS: assumption; audacity; doughtiness; effrontery; impudence; intrepidity; pertness; presumption; temerity
attempt: **n.** bravura
or courageous when drunk: **a.** pot-valiant

showy type of (boldness): **n.** bravado; **a.** doughty; vainglorious

BOMBAST: **n.** balderdash; braggadocio; fustian; gasconade; grandiloquence; magniloquence; pomposity; rhapsody; rodomontade; tumidity; turgescence; turgidity; tympany; **a.** BOMBASTIC: (**see** "boastful") fustian; grandiloquent; grandiose; *guindé;* inflated; magniloquent; pompous; tumescent; tumid; turgescent; turgid; vainglorious
in speech or writing: **n.** fustian; gasconade; grandiloquence; grandiosity; magniloquence; rodomontade; **a.** (**see** "rhetorical") declamatory; fustian; grandiloquent; grandiose; stilted

BOND(S): **n.** collateral; covenant; debenture; liaison; ligation; ligature; obligation; nexus; recognizance; shackle
of matrimony: **n.** *vinculum matrimonii*
strong or inextricable: **n.** Gordian knot; **a.** Gordian

BONE(S), *growth on:* **n.** exostosis
pert. to or resembling: **a.** osseous
place for: **n.** charnel house; ossuary
union of two: **n.** ankylosis; synostosis; **a.** ankylotic

BONFIRE: **n.** *feu de joie*

BONUS: **n.** cumshaw; dividend; lagniappe

BOOBS, *class of persons considered:* **n.** booboisie

BOOK(S), *binder of:* **n.** bibliopegist; **a.** bibliopegistic(al)
catalogue of: **n.** bibliotheca
censorship of: **see** "list of banned or proscribed" **below**
collecting, esp. rare: **n.** bibliomania
collection: **n.** bibliotheca
collector: **n.** bibliophile; **a.** bibliophilic
dealer: **n.** bibliopole; bibliopolist
destroyer or mutilator of: **n.** biblioclast
edition containing variant readings of the text: **n.** variorum (edition)
extreme preoccupation w/: **n.** bibliomania
first edition: **n.** princeps
guide or travel: **n.** Baedeker
hater or hatred of: **n.** biliophobe; bibliophobia
history and science of: **n.** bibliology
hoarder: **n.** bibliotaph(e); **a.** bibliotaphic
license to print: **n.** imprimatur
list of banned or proscribed: **n.** *index expurgatorius;* (**pl.** *index expurgatorii*); *index librorum prohibitorum*
love or lover of: **n.** bibliolater; bibliomania; bibliomaniac; bibliophage; bibliophile; bibliophilism; bibliophilist; bibliophily; philobiblist
mania for acquiring: **n.** bibliomania
of no interest of worth: **n.pl.** *biblia abiblia*
one having great knowledge of: **n.** bibliognost; **a.** bibliognostic
printed before 1501: **n.** incunabulum
production of: **n.** bibliogony
reference: (**see** "handbook") **n.** manual; promptuary; *vade mecum*
second-hand dealer in: **n.** *bouquiniste*
seller, esp. rare: **n.** bibliopole; bibliopoly; **a.** bibliopolic
series of five: **n.** pentalogy
of four: **n.** tetrad; tetralogy
of three: **n.** triad; trilogy
stealer of: **n.** biblioklept
strange or unusual: **n.pl.** curiosa; erotica; facetiae
unknown writer of: **n.** anonym(e)
-worm: **n.** bibliophage; *helluo librorum;* **a.** bibliophagous
worship or worshipper: **n.** bibliolatry; Bibliolatry (Bible); bibliolater; Bibliolater (Bible); **a.** bibliolatrous

BOOKCASE: **n.** bibliotheca

BOOKISH: **a.** bibliognostic; erudite; pedantic; scholastic; **n.** bibliognost

BOOKLET: **n.** brochure; monograph; pamphlet

BOON: **a.** convivial; intimate; jovial; merry
companion: **n.** alter ego; *bon camarade*

BOOR: **n.** bromide; bumpkin; churl; clodhopper; dullard; grobian; yokel; **a.** BOORISH: (**see** "rude") churlish; clownish; gauche; loutish; **n.** BOORISHNESS: gaucherie; grobianism; rudeness; rusticity

BORDER: (**see** "boundary") **n.** confine; extremity; margin; periphery; verge
have a distinct: **a.** discrete; limbate
situated on (border) or frontier: **a.** limitrophe

BORDERLINE: **a.** dubious; intermediate; liminal; limitrophe; marginal; peripheral; questionable; **n. see** "boundary"

BOREDOM: **n.** ennui; tedium; wearisomeness; **a.** BORED: *ennuyé;* (**fem.** *ennuyée*); **adv.** *ad nauseam*

BORING: **see** "dull" **and** "tiresome"

BORN *after father's death:* **a.** posthumous
being (born) or produced: **a.** aborning; *in statu nascendi;* nascent; parturient; **n.** nascency; parturition

BORROWING *makes sorrowing: borgen macht sorgen*

BOTHER: **see** "annoy"

BOUNCE: **v.** rebound; resile; ricochet; **a.** resilient; *n.* resilience; resiliency; ricochet

BOUND(S): (**see** "leap," "restrain" **and** "scope") **n.** ambit; circumscription; environs; precinct; **v.** circumscribe; confine; delineate; embosom; encompass
by a single: **a. or adv.** *per saltum*
keep within: **adv.** *sevare modum*

BOUNDARY: **n.** circumference; confines; perimeter; periphery; terminal; termination; terminus; **a.** circumferential
having common: **a.** conterminal; conterminous; contiguous; **n.** contiguity
line: **n.** perimeter; periphery

BOUNDED: **a.** circumscribed; finite; limited; **n.** finitude

BOUNDLESS: (**see** "eternal") **a.** illimitable; immeasurable; impenetrable; inexhaustible; infinite; limitless; measureless; unbounded; uncircumscribed; unfathomable; **n.** BOUNDLESSNESS: illimitability; infinitude; infinity

BOW, *with humiliation or penance:* **v.** go to Canossa

BOWELS, *act of relieving:* **n.** cacation; defecation; excretion
excretion from: **see** "feces"
remove: **v.** disembowel; eviscerate; exenterate
rumbling of: **n.** borborygmus; crepitation; flatus; **a.** borborygmic

BOXER: **n.** pugilist
clumsy: **n.** stumblebum

BOXING: **n.** pugilism; **a.** pugilant; pugilistic
rules of: **n.** Marquis of Queensberry
world of: **n.** fistiana; pugilism

BOY *kept for sexual purposes:* **n.** catamite; pathic

BOYISH: **a.** ephebic; immature; juvenile; puerile; youthful; **n.** BOYISHNESS: juvenility; puerilism; puerility

BRACELET, *of or like:* **a.** armillary

BRACING: **a.** invigorating; roborant; salubrious; tonic, vigorous; zestful

BRAG: (**see** "boast") **v.** gasconade; **n.** (**see** "boaster") braggadoccio; fanfaron; rodomontade; **n.** Scaramouche; BRAGGING: **see** "boasting"

BRAIN: **n.** cerebrum; encephalon; intellect; intelligence; psyche; sensorium
action: (**see** "thought") **n.** cerebration
having very small: **a.** micrencephalous; **n.** micrencephaly

BRAINY: **see** "intellectual"

BRAN, *of or like:* **a.** furfuraceous

BRANCH(ES): **n.** arborization; bifurcation; divarication; divergence; ramification; ramus; **v.** arborize; (bi)furcate; divaricate; diverge; ramify; subdivide
comprised of more than two: **a.** polychotomous
having many small: **a.** ramulose
having two: **a.** biramose; biramous
producing: **a.** sarmentose; sarmentous

BRANCHING: **a.** bifurcate(d); biramose; biramous; cladose; divergent; radial; radiating; ramose; ramous
in all directions: **a.** radial; radiating; ramifying; tentacular

BRANDY: **n.** *eau de vie*

BRASH: **see** "reckless"

BRASS: **n.** audacity; effrontery; hubris; impertinence; impudence; insolence; presumption; temerity; **a. see** "brazen"

BRAVADO: (see "swagger") **n.** panache

BRAVE: (see "bold") **a.** audacious; cavalier; chivalresque; chivalric; chivalrous; courageous; dauntless; doughty; fortitudinous; heroic; intrepid; martial; resolute; Spartan(ic); undaunted; valiant; valorous; **v.** beard; challenge; defy
and gallant man, as one who liberates victims of tyranny: **n.** pimpernel
fortune favors the: **adv.** *fortes fortuna (ad) juvat*

BRAVERY: **n.** audacity; bravado; chivalry; dauntlessness; derring-do; doughtiness; fortitude; gallantry; hardihood; intrepidity; intrepidness; prowess; temerity; valiancy; valor
show of: **n.** bravado; bravura; panache; swagger; verve

BRAWL: **n.** altercation; brannigan; brouhaha; contention; controversy; disputation; dissention; donny-brook; fracas; tumult; wrangle

BRAZEN: (see "shameless") **a.** arrogant; audacious; brassy; clangorous; gaudy; hubristic; presumptuous; unscrupulous

BREACH: **n.** abruption; (ab)scission; crevasse; desuetude; dissension; hiatus; infraction; infringement; nonfulfillment; non-observance; rupture; schism; transgression; violation; **a.** dissentious; schismatic(al)
of etiquette: **n.** barbarism; *faux pas;* impropriety; solecism; **a.** indecorous; solecistic(al)
of trust: **n.** *trahison des clercs*

BREAD, *quality or state of being:* **n.** paneity

BREAK: (see "breach") **v.** bankrupt; fracture; fragment(al)ize; fragmentate; rupture; transgress; violate; **n.** abruption; abscission; armistice; c(a)esura; cessation; discontinuity; disruption; hiatus; interim; interruption; lacuna; recess; respite; schism; scission; **a.** hiatal
as in continued series: **n.** discontinuity; interregnum; lacuna
not possible to: see "unbreakable"
up: **v.** comminute; decompose; disjoin; divaricate; fractionalize; fractionate; liquidate; pulverize; schismatize; triturate; **n.** comminution; disintegration; dissolution; fragmentation; liquidation; trituration

BREAKABLE: **a.** fracturable; fragile; frangible; friable; **n.** fragility; frangibility; friability

BREAKING *down* (or BREAK-DOWN): **n.** catabolism; cataclasm; decomposition; disintegration; disruption; dissolution; prostration
process of (biological): **n.** catabolism
of faith: **n.** apostasy; perfidy; **a.** perfidious; traitorous
of status or situation, sudden: **n.** abscission
off: **n.** abruption; cessation; disruption
up: see under "break"

BREAST(S): **n.pl.** mammae; **a.** mammary; pectoral
excessive development: **n.** macromastia; **a.** bathycolpian; pneumatic
from the inmost: **adv.** *imo pectore*
having: **a.** mammiferous
having small: **n.** micromastia
having two: **a.** bimastic; **n.** bimasticism; bimasty
male, excessive development: **n.** gynecomastia
muscles: **n.pl.** pectorals
pin or ornament: **n.** pectoral

BREATH: **n.** anima(tion); emanation; exhalation; flatus; halitus; inhalation; inspiration; suggestion; utterance; vitality
of life: **n.** *élan vital;* pneuma; prana
shortness of: **n.** anhelation; brachypnea; dyspn(o)ea

BREATHING: **n.** inhalation; inspiration
difficult or painful: **n.** dyspn(o)ea; **a.** dyspneic
heavy: **a.** suspirious; **n.** suspiration
rapid: **n.** hyperpnea; hyperventilation; polypnea

BREECH: see "blunder" and "break"

BREED: (see "beget") **v.** multiply; pullulate
-half or mixed: **n.** hybrid; mestizo; *métis;* mongrel; mulatto
quickly or *abundantly:* **v.** pullulate; **n.** pullulation

BREVITY: (see "brief") **n.** conciseness; laconism; monosyllabicity; succinctness; terseness
in speech or expression: **n.** brachylogy; breviloquence; laconism; monosyllabicity;

a. breviloquent; cryptic(al); laconic(al); monosyllabic; succinct; **adv.** *paucis verbis*

BREW: **v.** concoct; contrive; decoct; **n.** concoction; decoction

BRIBE: **v.** suborn; **n.** douceur; gratuity; pourboire; sop to Cerberus; subornation
capable of taking: **a.** mercenary; venal
one taking fr. both sides: **n.** ambidexter
willingness to take: **n.** venality

BRIDEGROOM: **n.** *garçon d'honneur;* paranymph

BRIEF: (**see** "concise") **a.** compendiary; compendious; cryptic(al); ephemeral; epigrammatic; evanescent; fugacious; fugitive; laconic(al); monosyllabic; pithy; succinct; summary; telegramm(at)ic; terse; transient; transitory; vanishing; volatile; **n.** (**see** "brevity") abstract; compendium; epitome; inventory; summarization; summary; syllabus; **adv.** BRIEFLY: *en abrégé; paucis verbis*
in: **adv.** *paucis verbis*
in answering or talking: (**see** "brevity") **a.** monosyllabic; **n.** *monosyllabicity*
visit or stay: **n. or v.** sojourn

BRIGHT: **a.** auroral; aurorean; effulgent; illustrious; incandescent; irradiant; luminous; lustrous; nitid; opalescent; (re)fulgent; resplendent; scintillating; undimmed; **v.** BRIGHTEN: effulge; illuminate; refurbish; **n.** BRIGHTNESS: brilliance; effulgence; fulgor; fluorescence; incandescence; luminance; luminescence; luminosity; luster; nitidity; refulgence; refulgency; resplendence; resplendency; scintillation; vivacity
(*promising*): **a.** auspicious
witty and (bright), characterized by being: **a.** spirituel(le)

BRILLIANT: (**see** "bright") **a.** effulgent; glittering; illustrious; luminescent; luminous; meteoric; opalescent; scintillant; scintillating; splendent; splendrous; virtuosic; **n.** BRILLIANCE (**or** BRILLIANCY) *éclat;* effulgence; incandescence; luminance; luminescence; luminosity; luster; nitidity; refulgence; refulgency; resplendence; resplendency; scintillation; virtuosity; vivacity
and witty, to be: **a.** lambent; scintillating; scintillescent; spirituel(le); **n.** lambency; scintillation; **v.** scintillate
array or assemblage: **n.** galaxy
execution, as of mus.: **n.** bravura; *tour de force;* virtuosity; **a.** virtuosic
in color: **a.** iridescent; opalescent; **n.** iridescence; opalescence
momentarily: **a.** meteoric

BRING(ING) *forth, or about to:* **n.** parturition; **a.** aborning; parturient
together: (**see** "assemble") **v. or a.** correlate; **n.** correlation

BRINK: **n.** precipice

BRISK: **a.** alacritous; ebullient; effervescent; energetic; galvanic; spirited; stimulating; **a. or adv.** allegro; *con brio;* **n.** BRISKNESS: alacrity; ebullience; effervescence; spiritedness; vivacity; vividity

BRISTLES, *bearing:* **a.** chaetigerous; chaetophorous
having: (**see** "spiny") **a.** aristate; barbellate; exhinate; hispid; setaceous; setarious; setiferous; setigerose; setose

BRITTLE: **a.** evanescent; fragile; frangible; friable; perishable; tenuous; transitory; **n.** BRITTLENESS: fragility; frangibility; friability

BROKEN: **a.** bankrupt; contrite; disconnected; discrete; disunited; fractional; fractured; fragmental; fragmentary; humbled; interrupted; ruptured; spasmodic; subdued
-down: **a.** dilapidated; disreputable; tatterdemalion
that which cannot be: (**see** "unbreakable") **n.** irrefrangability; **a.** immarcescible; imperishable; indestructible; irrefrangable

BROTHEL: **n.** bagnio; bordel(lo); lupanar; seraglio
under police supervision: **n.** *maison de tolérance*

BROTHER *or sister:* **n. or a.** sibling

BROTHERHOOD: **n.** alliance; companionship; confraternity; confraternization; confrerie; fellowship; fraternity; sodality

BROTHERLY: **a.** affectionate; amicable; fraternal

BROWBEAT: **v.** bully; dictate; domineer; dragoon; hector; intimidate; overawe;

subdue; swashbuckle; **a.** dictatorial; domineering; swashbuckling; tyrannical; tyrannous

BROWN, *dark:* **a.** bruneous; brunescent; cordovan
beige: **a.** *café au lait;* fulvous

BRUISE: **v.** contuse; disable; traumatize; **n.** contusion; ecchymosis; laceration; lividity; petechia; trauma(tism)

BRUSQUE: **a.** see "abrupt"; **n.** BRUSQUENESS: abruptness; brusquerie

BRUTAL: **a.** barbarous; bestial; brutish; Caliban; feral; inhuman; Procrustean; troglodytic; vindictive

BRUTALITY: **n.** barbarity; brutishness; ferity; inhumanity
one practicing or advocating: **n.** brutalitarian; sadist

BUBBLING: **a.** ebullient; effervescent; effusive; exuberant; yeasty; **n.** ebulliency; effervescence; effusiveness; exuberance; yeastiness

BUD: **v.** burgeon; germinate; pullulate; **a.** BUDDING: burgeoning; emanating; emergent; pullulant; **n.** burgeoning; efflorescence; pullulation

BUFFOON: **n.** grobian; harlequin; merry-andrew; **n.** BUFFOONERY: harlequinade

BUGBEAR: **n.** *bête noire;* hobgoblin; *loup-garou*

BUILD: **v.** chisel; compose; contrive; fabricate; fashion; manufacture; **n.** composition; makeup; physique; stature
as to body type: **see under** "body"

BUILDING: **n.** edifice; fabrication; structure
pert. to: **a.** (archi)tectonic; architectural; constructional

BULGE: **v.** beetle; protrude; protuberate; **n.** convexity; gibbosity; protuberance; protrusion; **a.** (**see** "swollen") gibbous; obtrusive; protuberant; protrudent; protrusive

BULK: (**see** "largeness") **n.** aggregate; dimension; magnitude; majority; quantum; (**pl.** quanta); **a.** BULKY: corpulent; magnitudinous; massive; ponderous; unwield(l)y; voluminous; **n.** BULKINESS: corpulency; massivity; ponderosity; voluminosity

BULLY: (**see** "browbeat") **v.** bluster; hector; **n.** blusterer; hector

BUNGLING: **a.** amateurish; awkward; gauche; inept; inexpert; maladroit; unskillful; **n.** BUNGLER: *blanc-bec*

BURDEN: **v.** (en)cumber; freight; **n.** albatross; encumbrance; hindrance; impediment; imposition; incubus; infliction; millstone; obligation; onus; *onus probandi;* perplexity; responsibility; **a.** BURDENED: (en)cumbered; freighted; impedimental; impeditive; impregnated; obstructive; oppressed; **a.** BURDENSOME: cumbersome; cumbrous; formidable; grievous; onerous; oppressive; overpowering; ponderous; superincumbent
equal to the: **adv.** *par oneri*
of proof: **n.** onus; *onus probandi*

BUREAUCRAT: **n.** mandarin

BURIAL: **n.** deposition; inhumation; interment
ceremony: **n.** exequy; obsequy
clothes: **n.** cerecloth; cerement; shroud
pert. to: **a.** cemeterial; cinerary; funebrial; funereal; mortuary; sepulchral

BURLESKING *cynic:* **n.** pantagruelist; **a.** pantagruelian; **n.** pantagruelism

BURN: **v.** cauterize; deflagrate; incinerate; oxidize; scorify; torrify

BURNABLE: **a.** combustible; conflagrant; conflagratory; ignescent; (in)flammable; inflammatory

BURNING: **a.** ardent; conflagrant; consuming; urgent; vehement; **n.** cineration; conflagration; cremation; ustulation
to ashes: **n.** cineration
words: **n.pl.** *ardentia verba*

BURST *forth:* (**see** "blossom") **v.** burgeon; effloresce; **n.** efflorescence; proruption *or split open:* **v.** dehisce; **a.** dehiscent; dissilient; **n.** dehiscence; dissilience

BURSTING: **a.** burgeoning; dehiscent; efflorescent; **n.** dehiscence; efflorescence
open: **a.** dehiscent; dissilient; **n.** dehiscence; dissilience

BUSH, *beat about the:* **v.** *battre la campagne*

BUSINESS: **n.** clientele; commerce; commercialism; *commercium;* industrialism; industry; *jus commercii; métier;* mercantilism; patronage; pursuit

BUSINESSMAN: **n.** *homme d'affaires;* (**pl.** *gens d'affaires*)
uncultivated and conventional: **n.** Babbitt; **a.** Babbitical

BUSY: (**see** "diligent") **a.** assiduous; engaged; engrossed; industrious; occupied; operose; sedulous; **n.** assiduity; engagement; operosity; sedulity

BUSYBODY: **n.** gadfly; intermeddler; polypragmatist; pragmatic; quidnunc; zealot

BUTCHER, *rel. to:* **a.** carnificial

BUTTER, *resembling, yielding or containing:* **a.** butyraceous

BUTTERFLY, *pert. to or characteristic of:* **a.** lepidopterological; lepidopterous

BUTTOCKS: **n.** *derrière;* fundament; gluteus (maximus); (**pl.** glutei maximi); podex; posterior; **a.** pygal
enlarged or fatty: **n.** steatopygia; steatopygy; **a.** steatopygic; steatopygous
having beautiful or shapely: **a.** callipygian; callipygous

BUXOM: **a.** Junoesque

BUY *at own risk:* **n.** or **a.** *caveat emptor*
insane desire to: **n.** oniomania

BUYER: **n.** consumer; emptor; purchaser; vendee
beware, let the: **n.** or **a.** *caveat emptor*
of products or services of several sellers: **n.** monopsonist; monopsony; **a.** monopsonistic

BUYING *or selling of church office or preferment:* **n.** simony

BUZZ: **v.** bombinate; **n.** bombilation; bombination

BY *courage and faith:* **adv.** *animo et fide*
force of arms: **adv.** *vi et armis*
grace of God: **adv.** *Dei gratia*
hook or crook: **adv.** *à bis ou à blanc*
my fault: **adv.** *meâ culpâ*
the month: **adv.** *per mensem*
the way: **adv.** *en passant*
this sign thou wilt conquer: **adv.** *in hoc signo vinces*
virtue of being: **adv.** *qua*
way of example: **adv.** *exempli gratia* (*abb.* e.g.)
words of present tense: **adv.** *per verba de praesenti*

BYEGONE: **a.** extinct; outmoded; *passé;* quondam; **adv.** whilom; **n.** ancien regime; antiquity

BYPASS: (**see** "evade") **v.** circumnavigate; circumvent; detour; **n.** circumnavigation; circumvention; detour

BYWORD: **see** "proverb"

C

CABBAGE *warmed over* (*old story*): **n.** *crambe repetita*

CAESAR'S *river:* **n.** Rubicon

CALAMITY: **n.** cataclysm; catastrophe; holocaust; **a.** CALAMITOUS: cataclysmic; cataclysmal; catastrophic(al); holocaustic

CALCULATE: **see** "infer" **and** "predict"

CALCULATING, *art of:* **n.** algorism; **a.** algorismic

CALENDAR, *add to* (*as in leap year*): **v.** intercalate; **a.** intercalary; **n.** intercalation
present in use: **n.** Gregorian

CALF *of leg, muscle of:* **n.** gastrocnemius; (**pl.** gastrocnemii)
of leg, pert. to: **a.** gastrocnemial; sural
worship the golden: adorer le veau d'or

CALL: (**see** "name") **v.** denominate; entitle
forth: **v.** evocate; **a.** evocative; evocatory; **n.** evocation
together: **v.** convocate; muster; **a.** convocational; **n.** convocation; muster

CALLOUS: (**see** "cruel") **a.** adamant; anesthetic; dedolent; impertinent; impiteous; indifferent; indurative; inexorable; insensible; obdurate; unfeeling; **n.** CALLOUSNESS: impenitence; impenitency; induration
(*hardening of skin*): **n.** callosity

CALM: (**see** "appease") **v.** assuage; placate; temper; tranquilize; **a.** (**see** "peaceful") apathetic; assuasive; composed; dispassive; dispassionate; equanimous; grave; halcyon; hermetic(al); impartial; impassive; imperturable; imperturbed; impervious; insensate; judicial; lenitive; nepenthean; nonchalant; oasitic; pacific; philosophic(al); phlegmatic(al); phlegmatous; phlegmonic; placid; (re)quiescent; sedate; self-possessed; serene; sober; staid; stoic(al); stolid; tempean; temperate; tranquil; unagitated; unalarmed; unblinking; undisturbed; unexcited; unimpassioned; unperturbed; unruffled; untroubled; **n. see** "calmness"
act of making: **n.** sedation; tranquilization; **a.** sedative; tranquilizing
become: **v.** quiesce; tranquilize
medicine or agent for making: **n.** nepenthe; sedative; tranquilizer
(*sober*): **adv.** *mens aequa in arduis*
(*unconcerned*): **a.** indifferent; insouciant; lackadaisical; phlegmatic; pococurante; **n.** equanimity; insouciance; lackadaisy; phlegm

CALMING: **a.** anodynic; calmant; calmative; hesychastic; nepenthean; placative; placatory; sedative; tranquilizing; **adv.** *placidamente;* **n.** placation; propitiation

CALMNESS: **n.** apathy; assuagement; ataraxia; ataraxy; composure; *détente;* dispassion; equability; equanimity; forbearance; gravity; impassivity; imperturbability; imperturbation; indifference; lackadaisy; lassitude; nepenthe; nonchalance; passivity; phlegm; placidity; pococurantism; quietude; repose; (re)quiescence; *sang-froid;* sedation; serenity; sobriety; solemnity; tranquility; tranquilization; unexcitedness
of mind: **n.** *aequo animo;* equanimity

CAMP, *laying out or establishment of:* **n.** castrametation
rel. to: **a.** castrensian
temporary, or for the night: **n.** or **v.** bivouac; **n.** *pied-à-terre*

CANCEL: **v.** abolish; abrogate; countermand; delete; efface; expunge; invalidate; neutralize; nullify; obliterate; repudiate; rescind; revoke; vacate; **a.** CAN-

CELLABLE: abrogative; recissory; revocable; revocatory; revokable; **n.** CANCELLATION: abrogation; cessation; deletion; disaffirmance; disaffirmation; expunction; invalidation; nullification; recision
not capable of being (canceled): **(see** "unbreakable") **a.** inalienable; indefeasible

CANCER: **n.** carcinoma; malignancy; malignant neoplasm; sarcoma; **a.** CANCEROUS: cancroid; carcinomatous; malignant; sarcomatous
-producing: **a.** carcinogenic; **n.** carcinogen

CANDID: **a.** artless; disinterested; guileless; impartial; implicit; ingenuous; naive; straightforward; unfeigned; unflattering; unprejudiced; unreserved; unsophisticated; unsubtle; unvarnished; wholehearted

CANDIDATE *for admission:* **n.** postulance; postulancy; postulant

CANDLE, *burn both ends: brûler la chandelle par les deux bouts*

CANE *or reed, like or pert. to:* **a.** arundinaceous

CANNIBAL: **n.** anthropophaginian; anthropophagite; anthropophagus; (**pl.** anthropophagi); **n.** CANNIBALISM: anthropophagism; anthropophagy; cannibality; exophagy; **a.** CANNIBALISTIC: anthropophagous

CAPABLE: **(see** "able") **a.** accomplished; adequate; competent; consummate; qualified; sciential; virtuosic

CAPACITY: **n.** amplitude; attainment; capability; endowment; genius; intellect; intelligence; latitude; magnitude; potentiality; puissance; qualification; talent; virtuosity
increase: **v.** augment; enhance; potentiate; **n.** augmentation; enhancement; potentiation

CAPER: **(see** "frolic") **n.** capriccio; capriole; caracole; curvet; gambade; gambado; gambol; marlock; saltation

CAPITAL *letter(s)*: **n.** factotum; majuscule
letter(s), written in: **a.** majuscule

CAPITALIST: **n.** bourgeois; Philistine (**usu.** disparaging)
class: **n.** proprietariat; **a.** bourgeois; proprietarian

CAPRICE: **see** "whim"

CAPTIVATE: **(see** "allure" **and** "charm") **v.** enamor; enrapture; ensorcel(l); enthral(l); fascinate; transport; **n. see** "alluring"

CAPTURE, *open to:* **a.** expugnable; pregnable; vulnerable

CARAVAN: **n.** cavalcade; convoy; expedition; peregrination; safari

CARD(S), *by the:* **adv.** *à la carte*
fortune-telling by: **n.** cartomancy
lay one's on table: **n. or v.** *abattre son jeu*

CARE: **n.** attention; attentiveness; circumspection; consideration; custody; guardianship; management; paternalism; precaution; prudence; solicitude; supervision; tutelage; vigilance; **a.** custodial; supervisory; tutelary; tutorial
marked by great: **a.** solicitous; solicitudinous
take good: gardez bien
without: **(see** "carefree") **adv.** *sans souci; sine cura*

CAREFREE: **a.** debonair(e); *dégagé;* incautious; insouciant; irresponsible; jaunty; *sans souci;* undemanding; **n.** insouciance

CAREFUL: **(see** "cautious") **a.** analytical; attentive; calculating; circumspect(ive); conscientious; discreet; discriminating; discriminatory; heedful; judicious; meticulous; observant; provident; prudent(ial); punctilious; punctual; regardful; scrupulous; solicitous; vigilant; **n.** CAREFULNESS: **(see** "caution") circumspection; meticulosity; prudence; scrupulosity; solicitude
excessively: **a.** fastidious; finical; hypercritical; meticulous; particularistic; pedantic; punctilious; rabbinic(al); scrupulous; **n.** circumspection; fastidiousness; meticulosity; punctiliousness; scrupulosity; scrupulousness
of details: **a.** conscientious; meticulous; scrupulous; **n.** meticulosity; particularity; scrupulosity; scrupulousness

CARELESS: (see "indifferent") **a.** apathetic; casual; cursory; heedless; improvident; imprudent; inattentive; incautious; incurious; indiscreet; neglectful; negligent; oblivious; perfunctory; pococurante; promiscuous; random; slovenly; superficial; unconcerned; unfastidious; unmindful; unsolicitous

CARELESSNESS: **n.** improvidence; imprudence; inattention; incaution; incuriosity; indifference; indiscretion; neglect; negligence; nonchalance; perfunctoriness; pococurantism; promiscuity; remission; superficiality
through: **adv.** *per incuriam*
toward duty: **n.** laches

CARESS: **v.** embrace; fondle; **a.** CARESSIVE: affectionate; amative; endearing

CARETAKER: **n.** concierge; superintendent

CARNIVAL: **n.** *Mardi Gras*
like a: **a.** carnivalesque; festive

CAROUSE: **v.** roister; royster; **n.** CAROUSER: bacchanal; bacchant; (**fem.** bacchante); reveler; roysterer; **a.** CAROUSING: bacchanal(ian); bacchanalic; roystering; roysterous

CARP: **v.** cavil; censure; criticize; disparage; pettifog; **n.** cavil; pettifoggery; stricture; **a.** captious; hypercritical

CARRIAGE: (see "bearing") **n.** posture
porch for: **n.** *porte cochère*

CARRY-*all:* **n.** omnibus
away: **v.** ablate; disembogue; meander; **a.** ablative; deferent; efferent; **n.** ablation
out: see "accomplish" and "fulfill"

CARTHAGE *must be destroyed:* **n.** *delenda est Carthago*

CASE, *famous or celebrated:* **n.** *cause célèbre*
hard protective: **n.** carapace

CASH, *convert into:* **v.** liquidate; **n.** liquidation

CAST: **n.** matrix
off, as skin or shell: **v.** desquamate; exfoliate; exuviate; **a.** desquamative; desquamatory; exuvial; **n.** desquamation; exuviation

CASTE, *person of high:* **n.** Brahmin; kshatriya
person of low: **n.** pariah; sudra

CASTLE *in Spain (or in the air):* **n.** *château en Espagne*

CASTOR AND POLLUX, *of or like:* **a.** dioscuric

CASTRATE: **v.** asexualize; desexualize; emasculate; eunuchize; geld; spay; **n.** CASTRATION: asexualization; demasculinization; emasculation; eunuchism; gonadectomy; mutilation; orchidectomy

CASUAL: **a.** accidental; adventitious; dishabille; fortuitous; haphazard; impromptu; incidental; informal; precarious; random; uncertain; unexpected; unimportant; unstudied

CAT(S), *abnormal fear of:* **n.** aelurophobia; ailurophobia
characteristic of: **a.** feline; **n.** felinity
fondness for: **n.** ailurophilia; galeophilia
hater or hatred of: **n.** aelurophobe; ailurophobe; ailurophobia; galeophobia; gatophobia
having claws like: **a.** aeluropodous; ailuropodous; cheliferous
killing of: **n.** felicide
-lover: **n.** aelurophile; ailurophile
make sound like: **v.** or **n.** caterwaul
old (usu. fem.) **n.** grimalkin
resembling: **a.** feliform; feline; **n.** felinity

CATALOG(UE): **n.** *catalogue raisonné;* compendium; *repertorium;* repertory; **a.** catalogical

CATASTROPHE: **n.** Armageddon; holocaust
heightened action leading to: **n.** catastasis
violent and disordered: **n.** gotterdammerung

CATEGORY: (see "class") **n.** classification; concept; genre; lexicon; rubric

CATER *to passions and prejudices:* **v.** pander

CAUGHT *in the act:* **adv.** *in actu; (in) flagrante delicto;* **a.** redhanded

CAUSE: (**see** origin") **n.** determinant; etiology; genesis; provenance; **a.** etiological
and effect, rel. bet.: **n.** causality
final: **n.** *causa finalis*
final, containing or realizing: **n.** entelechy
final, study of: **n.** entelechy; teleology; **a.** teleological
for war: **n.** *casus belli*
nothing is w/o a (theory) : **n.** causality
of unknown: **a.** agnogenic; idiopathic; ignogenic
to effect: **n.** *a priori;* apriority; **a.** aprioristic

CAUSTIC: (**see** "biting" **and** "keen") **a.** acidulous; acrimonious; corrosive; incisive; malevolent; mordant; pyrotic; sarcastic; satirical; scathing; trenchant; virulent; vitriolic; **n.** CAUSTICITY: malevolence; mordacity; spinosity; virulence

CAUTION (**or** CAUTIOUSNESS): **n.** admonishment; (ad)monition; calculation; caveat; chariness; circumspection; cunctation; discretion; exhortation; heedfulness; meticulosity; prudence; vigilance; wariness; **v.** admonish; sermonize
from abundant: ex abundanti cautela

CAUTIOUS: (**see** "careful") **a.** admonitory; Argus-eyed; attentive; calculating; circumspect(ive); discreet; expectant; judicious; meticulous; monitorial; Nestorian; provident; prudent(ial); scrupulous
to be: (**see** "careful") **adv.** *festina lente* (make haste slowly)

CAVE-*dweller:* **n.** troglodyte; **a.** troglodytic(al)
explorer: **n.** speleologist; spelunker
science of exploring: **n.** speleology; **a.** speleological

CAVERN(S), *inhabiting:* **a.** cavernicolous

CAVIL: **v. see** "carp"; **n.** CAVILER: *advocatus diaboli* (devil's advocate)

CELEBRATE: **v.** commemorate; solemnize; **a.** commemoratory; **n.** CELEBRATION: commemoration; jubilation; jubilee; ovation; potlatch; solemnization

CELEBRATED *case:* **n.** *cause célèbre*

CELEBRITY: (**see** "big-wig") **n.** luminary
treat as: **v.** lionize

CELESTIAL: **see** "spiritual"
mysteries: **n. pl.** *arcana caelestia*

CELL *division, direct:* **n.** mitosis

CEMETERY: **n.** *campo santo;* Golgotha; necropolis

CENSOR *of morals or manners:* **n.** *censor morum*

CENSORIOUS: (**see** "faultfinding") **a.** calumnious; castigative; censorial; condemnatory; defamatory; excoriative; slanderous; stigmatic(al); vituperative

CENSORSHIP: **see** "censureship" **and** "exclusion"
of books, etc: **see under** "book(s)"
sign or mark of approval: **n.** imprimatur

CENSURE: (**see** "abuse") **v.** animadvert; berate; calumniate; castigate; chastise; excoriate; lambaste; opprobriate; reprobate; revile; scarify; stigmatize; vilify; vituperate; **n.** CENSURESHIP: animadversion; calumniation; excoriation; reprehension; reprobation; reproof; stricture; **a.** CENSURABLE: blameworthy; condemnatory; reprehensible

CENTER(S): **n.** axis; focus; ganglion; nidus; nucleus; omphalos; pivot; umbilicus; **v.** concentrate; converge; focus
as of development: **n.** nucleus
away from the: **a.** decentralizing; efferent; excentric
being in, or tending to stay at or near: **a.** centrality; centricity
force to the, or tending toward: **n.** centripetence
having common: **a.** concentric; **n.** concentricity
having many: **a.** decentralized; polycentric
having single: **a.** unicentric
moving from: **a.** centrifugal; efferent; **n.** centrifugalization; decentralization
moving to: **a.** afferent; centripetal; **n.** centripetalism
of attraction, interest or activity: **n.** cynosure; epicenter; Mecca; polestar

off, or w/o a: **a.** acentric; excentric(al)
originating in: **a.** centrogenic

CENTRAL: (**see** "basic") **a.** concentric; dominant; equidistant; essential; middlemost; pivotal; principal; umbilical; **a.** CENTRALIZING: amalgamative; centripetal; integrative; **n.** centrality

CENTURY: **n.** centenary; centennial; *siècle;* **a.** centenary; centennial
pert. to beg. of: **a.** centurial
pert. to close of: **a.** *fin-de-siècle*

CEREMONIAL: (**see** "formal") **a.** ceremonious; conventional; punctilious; ritualistic; solemn
attire: **n.** *grande toilette;* panoply
fuss: **n.** panjandrum

CEREMONIES, *master of:* **n.** ceremoniarius; compere; officiator

CEREMONY: (**see** "pomp") **n.** accolade; formality; ostentation; protocol; ritual(ity)
without: **adv.** *sans cérémonie; sans façon*

CERTAIN: **a.** absolute; apodictic(al); conclusive; explicit; incontestable; incontrovertible; indisputable; indubitable; ineluctable; inevitable; irrefrangible; irrefutable; undeniable; unequivocal; unerring; unmistakable; unquestionable; **adv.** CERTAINLY: *bien entendu;* ineluctably; inevitably; *sans doute;* unquestionably
absolutely: **a.** apodictic(al); indisputable; inevitable; irrefutable; unequivocal

CERTAINTY: **n.** accuracy; assurance; certitude; incontrovertibility; indisputability; indubitability; ineluctability; infallibility; positivism; reality; securement
believer in impossibility of: **n.** acataleptic; probabilism; probabilorism; probabilorist; **a.** acataleptic; probabilistic

CHAFE: **see** "annoy"

CHAIN: **v.** catenate; fetter; **n.** catena(tion); concatenation; vinculum

CHAIR, *from the:* **a.** or **n.** *ex cathedra*
protector for: **n.** antimacassar

CHAMBER(S): **n.** camera; concameration; cubiculum
divided into: **n.** cameration

CHANCE: **v.** hazard; venture; **n.** accidentality; *casus fortuitus;* contingency; fortuitiveness; fortuity; haphazardry; opportunity; peradventure; random; speculation; tychism; **a.** accidental; casual; contingent; fortuitous; haphazard; random
by: **a.** fortuitous; *par hasard; per accidens*
goodess of: **n.** Tyche
rule by: **n.** casualism; tychism

CHANGE(S): **v.** alchemize; alternate; commute; diversify; metamorphose; permutate; reciprocate; renegotiate; substitute; transfigure; transform; transmogrify; transmute; transplant; **n.** alternance; alternation; heterization; metamorphosis; materialization; modification; modulation; (per)mutation; reciprocation; (r)evolution; substitution; transfiguration; transformation; transition; transmogrification; transmutation; transplantation; variation
alternating: **n.** alternation; reciprocation; vicissitude
capable of: (**see** "correctable") **a.** alterable; labile; mutable; tractable
characterized by: **a.** chameleonic; inconstant; labile; variational; **n.** lability
completely, as in grotesque or strange manner: **v.** transmogrify; **n.** transmogrification
figure, form or outward appearance; **v.** transfigure; **n.** transfiguration
from one stage, cond., etc. to another: **n.** evolution; metastasis; transition; **a.** metastatic
hater or hatred of: **n.** misoneism; misoneist; **a.** misoneistic
in process of: **a.** transitional
in shape, form, substance, etc.: **v.** metamorphose; **n.** heterization; metamorphism; metamorphosis; **a.** metamorphic; metamorphous
liable to: (**see** "changeable") **a.** labile; mutable; **n.** lability; mutability
magic power to: **n.** alchemy; **a.** alchemic; alchemistic
necessary (changes) having been made: **adv.** *mutatis mutandis*
not capable of: **see** "unbreakable" **and** "unchangeable"
"of life": **n.** climacteric; climacterium; involution; menopause; **a.** climacteric; involutional; menopausal
of mind or heart (to better): **n.** penitence; reformation; repentance; resipiscence; **a.** penitent; penitential; repentent
of one thing into another, position, state

or form: **v.** metamorphose; metastasize; **a.** metamorphic; metamorphous; metastatic; **n.** heterization; metamorphosis; metastasis
one capable of indefinite: **n.** Proteus
one substance into another: **v.** transubstantiate; **n.** transubstantiation
subject to: (**see** "changeable") **a.** chameleonic; labile; mutable; protean
sudden: **n.** saltation
tendency against: **n.** inertia; **a.** immutable; inertial
tending to: **see** "liable to" **above**
times and customs: **adv.** *autre temps, autre moeurs*
wine and bread to blood and body of Christ (doctrine): **n.** transubstantiation

CHANGEABLE: **a.** adaptable; alterable; ambivalent; amenable; amphibolic; amphibolous; capricious; chameleonic; fickle; fluctuating; inconstant; iridescent; itinerant; labile; mercurial; mutable; nomadic; protean; Proteus-like; quicksilver; temperamental; unstable; vagrant; variational; versatile; whimsical; **n.** CHANGEABLENESS: adaptability; ambivalence; fickleness; iridescence; lability; mutability; versatility; volatility; volubility; whimsicality

CHANGING: **a.** evolutionary; transitional
constantly: **a.** kaleidoscopic
frequently or foolishly: **a.** capricious; chameleonic; protean; vertiginous
one form to another: **n.** heterization; metamorphosis; transmogrification; transubstantiation
patterns: **a.** kaleidoscopic

CHANNELED: (**see** "grooved") **a.** canalicular; canaliculate; cannel(l)ated; chamfered

CHAOS: **see** "confusion"

CHAPERON(E): **n.** *gouvernante;* governess; surveillant

CHAPTER, *as of an organization, member of:* **n.** capitulary
rel. to: **a.** capitulary

CHARACTER(S): **n.** constitution; disposition; reputation; temperament; texture
concealment of real: **n.** hypocrisy; hypocrite; **a.** hypocritical
in drama, etc.: **n.** persona; (**pl.** *corps dramatique; dramatis personae; personae*)
main, in story, drama, etc.: **n.** protagonist
pursuits influence: **n.** *abeunt studia in mores*
rel. to: **a.** characterological
standards, etc., of race or group: **n.** ethos; mores
study of development of: **n.** characterology; ethology; **a.** characterological; ethological

CHARACTERISTIC(S): **n.** accoutrement; attribute; haecceity; individuality; singularity; symptom; **a.** diacritical; distinguishing; individual; pathognomonic(al); peculiar; quintessential; symbolic(al); symptomatic(al); typical
odd or peculiar: (**see** "peculiarity") **n.** eccentricity; idiosyncrasy; oddity; singularity; vagary
quality: **n.** savor
study of acquired: **n.** ctetology; psychology
though untrue: **a.** *ben trovato*

CHARGE: **v.** enjoin; indict; **n.** accusation; ascription; behest; imposition; imputation; indictment; injunction; mandate; management; supervision
(*accusation*): **n.** gravamen

CHARGING: **a.** accusable; ascribable; attributive; imputable; imputative; mandatory
by, or as if by, oath: **n.** objuration

CHARITABLE: (**see** "generous") **a.** benefic(ent); benevolent; eleemosynary; gracious; humanitarian; lenient; philanthropic
person: **n.** charitarian; eleemosynar; humanitarian; philanthropist; Samaritan

CHARITY: (**see** "mercy") **n.** benefaction; beneficence; benevolence; generosity; largess(e); lenity; liberality; philanthropy

CHARLATAN: **see** "pretender"

CHARM: (**see** "entice") **v.** bewitch; captivate; enchant; enrapture; ensorcel(l); enthral(l); fascinate; transport; **n.** abracadabra; abraxis; amiability; amulet; enchantment; fetish; geegree; incantation; madstone; obeah; periapt; phylactery; seduction; talisman; witchery; **a.** CHARMING: (**see** "pleasing") arresting; bewitching; captivating; enchanting; fascinating; felicitous; irresistible; magnetic; mesmeric; personable; phylacteric; winsome

CHARTER: **n.** canon; constitution
of civil or political liberties: **n.** constitution; decalogue; *Magna C(h)arta*

CHARWOMAN: **n.** *femme de chambre; femme de ménage*

CHASE: **see** "hunting"
goddess of the: **n.** Artemis; Diana

CHASTITY: **n.** continence; pucelage; pudicity
vow of: **n.** *votum castitatis*

CHAT: **(see** "talk") **v.** confabulate; **n.** causerie; confabulation; conversation; **a.** CHATTY: discursive; garrulous; loquacious; **n.** CHATTER (*small talk*): bavardage

CHATTERBOX: **n.** *moulin à paroles*

CHEAP: **(see** "bargain") **a.** bedizened; Brummagem; chintzy; inexpensive; meretricious; picayune; picayunish; pinchbeck; tawdry; **n.** CHEAPNESS: bedizenment; flummery; trumpery
(*bargain*): **a.** *à bon marché*
(*flashy*): **a.** raffish; tawdry; trumpery

CHEAT: **v.** bamboozle; beguile; chicane; circumvent; cozen; defraud; delude; foist; victimize; **n.** CHEATER: **see** "pretender"; **n.** CHEATING: circumvention; cozenage; defraudation; imposture

CHECK: **v.** abort; checkmate; counteract; counterbalance; counterpoise; inhibit; obstruct; acclude; rebuff; repress; restrain; slacken; stymie; **a.** CHECKING: abortive; inhibitory; **n.** abortifacient; inhibition

CHEEK(S), *pert. to:* **a.** buccal

CHEER: **v.** inspirit; invigorate; solace; **n.** acclamation; applause; *éclat*

CHEERFUL: **a.** blithe; buoyant; ebullient; eudaemonic; euphoric; eupeptic; exhilarative; genial; jocular; jocund; optimistic; sanguinary; sanguine; sprightly; vivacious; volatile; **a. or adv.** allegro; *gemütlich;* **adv.** *de bonne grâce*
overly and irritatingly: **a.** Pollyannish; **n.** Pollyanna; Pollyannism

CHEERFULNESS: **(see** "merriment") **n.** ebullience; euphoria; exhilaration; geniality; jocularity; jocundity; joviality; sanguinity; sprightliness; vivacity
excessive: **n.** Pollyannism

CHEF: **n.** *chef de cuisine; cuisinier;* **(fem.** *cuisinière*); culinarian

CHERISH: **v.** embosom; enshrine; foster; idolize; spiritualize

CHEST: **n.** thorax; **a.** thoracic
pert. to (or lungs): **a.** pectoral; thoracic

CHEW: **v.** manducate; masticate; **a.** manducatory; masticatory; **n.** manducation; mastication; rumination

CHIEF: **a.** capital; cardinal; foremost; paramount; predominant; (pre)eminent; principal; sovereign; superior; supreme; **n.** **(see** "leader") director; hierarch; *imperator;* pendragon; sachem; sovereign; superior
item of a group: **n.** *pièce de résistance*
work: **n.** *chef d'oeuvre; magnum opus; meisterwerk*

CHILD: **(see** "children" **and** "offspring") **n.** changeling; infant; issue; juvenile; (s)cion; **a.** filial
attracted to parent of opp. sex:
daughter to father: **n.** Electra complex
son to mother: **n.** Oedipus complex
befitting a: **a.** dutiful; filial
gifted: **n.** prodigy; *wunderkind*
illegitimate; **n.** *filius nullius; filius populi;* mongrel; **a.** bar sinister
not befitting a: **a.** unduteous; undutiful; unfilial
of or rel. to study of: **a.** pedologic(al); **n.** pedologist; pedology
relationship or attitude of parent to: **n.** filiality
spoiled: **n.** *enfant gâté; enfant terrible*
state or period of development when becomes interested in opp. sex: **n.** altrigenderism
unmanageable; **n.** *enfant terrible*

CHILDBIRTH: **n.** accouchement; delivery; labor; parturition; travail; **a.** parturient

after: **a.** post-natal; post-partum
before: **a.** antenatal; antepartum; prenatal; prepartum
convalescent period following: **n.** puerperium
father takes bed during: **n.** couvade

CHILDHOOD: **n.** *jeune âge;* juniority
from: **adv.** *ab incunabilis*
lit. works designed for: **n.pl.** juvenilia
rel. to: **a.** juvenile; puerile
second: **n.** dotage
writings, drawings, etc. of: **n. pl.** juvenilia

CHILDISH: (**see** "petty") **a.** immature; infantile; infantine; infantive; juvenile; pantywaist; puerile; **n.** CHILDISHNESS: dotage; immaturity; infantility; juvenility; puerilism; puerility
behavior: **see under** "behavior"

CHILDREN: (**see** "offspring") **n.pl.** descendants; progeny; posterity; (s)cions
diseases of, study: **n.** pediatrics; **a.** pediatric; **n.** pediatrician
hatred or hater of: **n.** misopaedia; misopaedist
science or study of life and development of: **n.** pedology; pedologist
sexual inclination toward: **n.** pedophilia; pedophiliac

CHILL: **v.** infrigidate; **n.** frisson

CHIN: **n.** mental prominence (**or** protuberance)
pert. to: **a.** mental
point of: **n.** pogonion

CHINESE, *one fond of:* **n.** sinophil(e)

CHINK(S): **n.** aperture; cranny; interstice; lacuna
full of: **a.** rimose; rimous; rimulose

CHITCHAT: **n.** bavardage; small talk

CHIVALROUS *fighter:* **n.** *preux chevalier*

CHIVALRY, *having spirit or manners of:* **a.** chivalresque

CHOICE: (**see** "best") **n.** alternant; alternate; alternative; candidate; election; option; **a.** (**see** "choosing") discriminative; elegant; exquisite; fastidious; optimum; *recherché;* sumptuous; supernacular; supernal
power of: **n.** alternativity; option
where no real, or for want of better; **n.** *faute de mieux;* Hobson's choice

CHOIRMASTER: **n.** *choryphеus; maestro di cappella*

CHOOSE: **see** "determine"; **a.** CHOOSING: discretional; eclectic; optional; preferential; **a.** CHOOSY: **see** "careful"
or reject, ability to: **n.** alternativity; discretion; option

CHORUS *leader:* **see** "choirmaster"
of or pert. to: **a.** choreutic; choric

CHRONIC: (**see** "habitual") **a.** confirmed; deep-seated; ingrained; intractable; inveterate; irradicable; lingering; obstinate; persistent; prolonged; routine

CHRONOLOGICAL *error:* **n.** anachronism; prochronism; prolepsis; **a.** anachronistic; anachronous; proleptic

CHRIST, *doctrine that human being only:* **n.** psilanthropy; psilanthropism; psilanthopist
marks resembling wounds of: **n.pl.** stigmata

CHURCH *body:* **n.** diocese; episcopate; hierarchy
buying or selling of office or preferment: **n.** simony
excessive devotion to: **n.** ecclesiasticism; ecclesiolatry
leader: (**see** "priest") **n.** archimandrite; hegumen; hierophant; **a.** hierophantic
one estranged from: **n.** publican
pert. to: **a.** apostolic; ecclesiastic(al); ecclesiologic(al); ecumenical; encyclic(al); episcopal; hierarchial; sacerdotal; **n.** apostolicity
policy, also study of doctrines of: **n.** ecclesiology
sphere of authority: **n.** diocese; episcopate; hierarchy

CIRCLE: **see** "group"
reasoning in a: **n.** *circulus in probando*

CIRCUIT: **n.** ambit; circumference; circumnavigation; gyre; periplus; revolution; **a.** circumferential; peripheral
(*journey*): **n.** itineration

CIRCULAR: **a.** annular; cyclic(al); cycloid(al); cylindrical; elliptic(al); nummiform; nummular; orbicular; rotund; spherical; spheroid(al)
in definition: **n.** *circulus in definiendo*
movement: **n.** circumduction; circumgyration; **v.** circumduct; circumgyrate
state of being: **n.** circularity; rotundity; spheroidicity

CIRCUMFERENCE: **n.** ambit; perimeter; periphery; **a.** circumferential; peripheral

CIRCUMSTANCE(S): (**see** "condition") **n.** concomitant; contingency; episode; eventuality; inadvertency; incident; occurrence; particularity; posture; **a.** CIRCUMSTANTIAL: adventitious; contingent; inadvertent; incidental
bow to: **v.** temporize; **adv.** *tempori parendum* (one must yield to the times)
by force of: **adv.** perforce
dependent upon: (**see** "chance") **a.** precarious
suited to the: **a.** expedient; opportune; opportunistic; politic
taking advantage of: **a.** opportunistic; **n.** expediency; opportunism; opportunist

CITIZEN(S): **n.** burgher; citoyen; constituency; constituent; denizen; *habitué;* national; oppidan
leading: **n.pl.** *lumina civitatis*
of town: **n.** burgher; oppidan
of world: **n.** cosmopolitan; cosmopolite; **a.** cosmopolitan
of yesterday: **n.** *hesterni quirites*

CITIZENSHIP *of child determined by parent's:* **n.** *jus sanguinis*

CITY: **n.** metropolis; municipality; **a.** metropolitan; municipal; urban
very large: **n.** megalopolis
world-important, or of many nationalities: **n.** cosmopolis; **a.** cosmopolitan

CIVIL: (**see** "courteous") **a.** cultured; educated; genteel; nonclerical; parliamentary; secular; sophistical; **n.** laity
affairs, pert. to: **a.** communal; metropolitan; municipal; urban
liberties, advocate of: **n.** libertarian; **a.** libertarian
or civic pride, lack of: **n.** incivilism
order: **n.** polity
power or authority: **n.** temporality

CIVILITIES: **n.pl.** amenities; (the) proprieties; urbanities

CIVILIZED: (**see** "refined") **a.** debarbarized; **v.** debarbarize; **n.** debarbarization

CLAIM: **v.** maintain; postulate; **a.** CLAIMED: alleged; assertive
to possession: **n.** arrogation; **v.** appropriate; arrogate

CLAMOR: (**see** "uproar") **n.** alarum; alarums and excursions; brouhaha; hubbub; tumult; **a.** CLAMOROUS: blatant; boisterous; clangorous; demonstrative; importunate; pressing; strepitant; strepitous; vociferant; vociferous
of the forum: **n.** *forensis strepitus*

CLARIFICATION: **n.** *éclaircissement;* elucidation; enlightenment; exegesis; interpretation; **v.** CLARIFY: defecate; depurate; elucidate; elutriate; enlighten; explicate; illume; interpret; resolve; subtilize; unscramble; **a.** CLARIFYING: elucidative; elucidatory; exegetic(al); explanatory
further: **n.** epexegesis; **a.** epexegetic(al)

CLASH: **v.** encroach; impinge; **n.** **see** "conflict"

CLASS: (**see** "classification") **n.** category; clique; coterie; denomination; genre; (**pl.** genera); genus; phylum; (**pl.** phyla); rubric; **a.** categorical; generic; phyletic
by itself: **a.** *sui generis*
divided into many (classes): **a.** multipartite; polychotomous; polytomous; **n.** polychotomy
lesser nobility: **n.** *petite noblesse*
low: **n.** canaille; rabble; riffraff
lower middle (also members of): **n.** petite bourgeoisie
middle: **n.** Babbit(t)ry (**usu.** disparaging); bourgeois(ie); proletariat; **a.** Philistine (**usu.** disparaging); proletarian
of no definite: **a.** mongrel
propertied or capitalist (also members of): **n.** proprietariat; **a.** proprietarian
upper: (**see** "aristocrat") **n.** aristocracy; (**pl.** aristoi); gentry; nobility; patrician

CLASSICAL, *state or quality of being:* **n.** classicality

CLASSIFICATION: (**see** "class") **n.** categorization; category; compartmentaliza-

tion; departmentalization; departmentation; hierarchization; individualization; stratification; subordination; taxonomy; **a.** classificatory
science of: **n.** taxonomy; **a.** taxonomic(al)
something that escapes: **n.** *tertium quid*

CLASSIFY: **v.** alphabetize; categorize; collimate; compartmentalize; departmentalize; hierarchize; individualize; synthesize
difficult to: **a.** nondescript; **n.** *tertium quid*
not possible to: **a.** acategorical; amorphous; heterogeneous; unclassifiable

CLAWS, *bearing:* **a.** cheliferous
having (or nails): **a.** unguiferate

CLAY, *pert. to:* **a.** argillaceous

CLEAN: **v.** absterge; depurate; deterge; elutriate; expiate; expurgate; mundify; **a.** abstrusive; hygienic; immaculate; kosher; sportsmanlike; sterile; thoroughgoing; undefiled; unspoiled; unstained; unsullied; **n.** CLEANLINESS: immaculacy; sterility
slate: **n.** *tabula rasa*

CLEANSING: **a.** abstersive; cathartic; expiatory; purgatorial; **n.** ablution; abstersion; balneation; depuration; elutriation; expiation; lavage; lavation; lustration; purgation; purification
ceremonial: **n.** purgation
religious (washing): **n.** ablution; maundy

CLEAR: **v.** see "clarify"; **a.** (see "transparent") accessible; crystal(line); definitive; demonstrable; diaphanous; evident; exoteric; explicit; limpid; luculent; luminous; manifest; palpable; patent; pellucid; perspicacious; perspicuous; (trans)lucent; transpicuous; unambiguous; unencrypted; unequivocal; unhampered; unimpeded; unmistakable; unquestionable; unquestioned; **n.** CLEARNESS: clarity; diaphaneity; distinctness; explication; limpidity; luminosity; (pel)lucidity; perspicacity; perspicuity; sonority; translucence; translucency; transparency
and simple in style: **a.** limpid; unambiguous; unencrypted; unequivocal; **n.** limpidity
as a bell: **a.** orotund; resonant; sonorous; **n.** orotundity; sonority; sonorousness
as glass: **a.** crystal(line); hyaline
-cut: (see "decided") **a.** crystalline; inconfused
in lit. style: **a.** Addisonian
to make: (see "clarify") **v.** explicate; manifest; subtilize
to understanding: **a.** explicit; lucid; perspicacious; perspicuous; unequivocal; **n.** comprehensibility; lucidity; perspicuity

CLEARLY *presented or spoken:* **a.** articulate; explicatory; lucid

CLEFT *in two:* **a.** bipartient; bipartite; bisulcate; cloven; dichotomous; schismatic(al)

CLERGY(MAN): (see "church") **n.** cleric; ecclesiastic; hierophant; man of the cloth; prelate; pulpitarian; (pl. *gens d'église*)
function(s) of: **n.** clericature; (pl. spiritualities)
pert. to: **a.** clerical; ecclesiastical; ministerial; parsonic(al); prelatical; pulpitarian; sacerdotal; sacerdotical; **n.** clericality; ecclesiasticism
position of: **n.** clericature

CLERK, *pert. to:* **a.** clerical; **n.** clericality
position or function of: **n.** clericature

CLEVER **a.** adroit; astute; dexterous; discerning; habile; heady; ingenious; penetrating; perspicacious; resourceful; sagacious; sapient; **n.** CLEVERNESS: acumen; adroitness; astucity; dexterity; discernment; esprit; hability; ingeniosity; ingenuity; inventiveness; resourcefulness
feat: see "feat"
(skillful): **a.** adept; adroit; dexterous; habile; **n.** adroitness; dexterity; hability
turn of phrase (see "witticism") **n.** *jeu d'esprit*

CLEW (*or* CLUE): **n.** characteristic; criterion; (pl. criteria); indication; landmark; symptom

CLIMATE: (see "environment") **n.** clime; milieu
lit. or artistic, pert. to: **a.** *fin de siècle*

CLIMAX: (see "acme") **n.** climacterium; consummation; culmination; denouement;

flood tide; meridian; orgasm; pinnacle; summit; zenith

CLIMBER, *social:* **n.** arriviste; *nouveau riche;* opportunist; parvenu

CLINGING: **a.** adherent; adherescent; agglutinant; tenacious; viscous
by feet, as certain birds; **a.** adhamant

CLIPPINGS (*writings, etc.*): **n.pl.** excerpta; scrapiana

CLIQUE: **n.** cabal; camarilla; charmed circle; conclave; *corps d'élite;* coterie: junto; sodality
for dishonest or dishonorable ends: **n.** camorra

CLOAKED: **a.** cabalistic; clandestine; disguised; larvate(d); screened

CLOG: **v.** impede; obstruct; occlude; oppilate; **n.** impediment; occlusion; oppilation

CLOISTER, *confined in, or as if in:* **n.** claustration

CLOSE: (**see** "discontinue" **and** "near") **v.** obturate; occlude; **a.** CLOSED: imperforate; **a.** CLOSING. operculated; **n.** occlusion; obturation; **n.** CLOSENESS: (**see** "nearness") propinquity; proximity
at hand: **a.** adjacent; contiguous; imminent; **n.** adjacency; contiguity; imminence
together, to place: **v.** juxtapose; **a.** (**see** "adjacent") juxtapositional

CLOSURE *of passage or opening:* **n.** atresia; obturation; occlusion; stenosis
or limitation of debate: **n.** cloture

CLOT: **v.** coagulate; thrombose; **n.** coagulation; thrombosis

CLOTHE: **v.** accouter; array; caparison; habilitate; invest; portray; represent; swathe

CLOTHING (or CLOTHES): (**see** "dress") **n.pl.** accouterments; apparel; array(ment); attire; habiliments; regalia; toggery; vestments; vesture
act of: **n.** investiture
addicted to those of opp. sex: **a.** transvestic; **n.** transvestism; transvestite
pert. to (esp. men's): **a.** sartorial
splendid: **n. pl.** regalia

CLOUD(S): **v.** obfuscate; tarnish; **n.** nebula; nimbus; stigma; **a.** CLOUDY (or CLOUDED): fuliginous; murky; nebular; nebulated; nebulose; nebulous; nimbose; nubilous; obscure; overcast; roily; turbid; **n.** CLOUDINESS: fuliginosity; nebulosity; obnubilation; tenuosity; turbidity
in the: **adv.** *in nubibus*
rain: **n.** nimbus
scientific observation of: **n.** nepholognosy

CLOVEN: (**see** "cleft") **a.** bisulcate

CLOWN: **n.** buffoon; grobian; harlequin; jester; lubber; merry-andrew; Pierrot; **n.** CLOWNING: baboonery; buffoonery; clownery; clownishness; **a.** baboonish; buffoonish
boastful: **n.** scaramouche

CLUB: **n.** association; consortium; coterie; fraternity; sodality; sorority
lit. or scientific: **n.** athen(a)eum
of both sexes: **n.** fratority

CLUE: **see** "clew"

CLUMPS, *growing in:* (**see** "clustered") *a.* caespitose

CLUMSY: (**see** "awkward") **a.** cumbersome; cumbrous; elephantine; gauche; loutish; lumbering; maladroit; ponderous; ungainly; unwield(l)y; **n.** CLUMSINESS: cumbrousness; gaucherie; maladroitness; ponderosity; ungainliness

CLUSTER: **v.** agglomerate; aggregate; nucleate; **n.** agglomeration; aggregation; fascicle; nucleation; **a.** CLUSTERED: acervate; acervuline; aciniform; agglomerated; aggregatory; caespitose; fascicular

COARSE: **a.** artless; barbarous; brutish; earthy; Falstaffian; gauche; immature; incondite; indelicate; inelegant; inurbane; plebeian; ribald; scurrilous; squalid; tramontane; troglodytic; uncouth; unpolished; unrefined; vulgarian; **v.** COARSEN: vulgarize; **n.** COARSENESS: barbarism; barbarity; buffoonery; gaucherie; *grossiereté;* indelicacy; inurbanity; rascality; scurrility; vulgarity

and witty writings or books: **n. pl.** *facetiae*
person: **see under** "person"

COASTAL *region:* **n.** littoral

COATING, *hard:* **n.** carapace; incrustation
resulting fr. age or wear: **n.** patina

COAX: **v.** cajole; wheedle; **n.** cajolery; cajolement

COCKTAIL: **n.** apertif

CODE *message:* **n.** cryptogram
of conduct, accepted: **see under** "standards

COERCE: **v.** compel; discipline; dragoon; necessitate; **a.** COERCIVE: compelling; compulsatory; compulsory; obligatory; **n. see** "duress"
ability to: **n.** puissance

COEXIST(ING): **see** "living"
ability to: **a.** compossible; symbiotic; **n.** compossibility; symbiosis

COFFEE, *black:* **n.** *café noir*
small serving: **n.** *café noir;* demitasse
with cream: **n.** *café-crème*
with milk: **n.** *café au lait*

COFFIN: **n.** bier; catafalque; sarcophagus

COHERE: (**see** "stick") **v. or a.** conglutinate; **n.** conglutination

COIL: (**see** "spiral") **n.** convolution; entanglement; perplexity; whorl; **a.** COILED: convolute(d); gyrate; meandrine; tortile; volute

COIN *collector:* **n.** numismatist; **a.** numismatic(al)
of small value; **n.** picayune
-shaped: **a.** nummiform; nummular

COINCIDE: **v. see** "agree"; **a.** congruent; congruous

COLD: (**see** "unfeeling") **a.** arctic; boreal; frigid; glacial; hyperborean; marmoreal; **n.** frigidity; glaciation; gelidity
-blooded: (**see** "cruel") **a.** indurate; marblehearted; poikilothermal; poikilothermic; poikilothermous; premeditated; **n.** *sang-froid*
hands, warm heart: froides manis, chaudes amours
make: **v.** infrigidate
pert. to or producing: **a.** frigorific

COLLAPSE: (**see** "failure") **n.** dissolution; prostration; **v.** founder
catastrophic: **n.** cataclysm; *götterdämmerung;* holocaust

COLLECT: (**see** "accumulate") **v.** agglutinate; conflate; conglomerate; congregate; convoke; muster

COLLECTION: **n.** agglomeration; agglutination; aggregation; collectivity; colluvies; compendium; conflation; conglomeration; congregation; fascicle; ingathering; miscellaneity; nucleation; repertory; sylloge; (**pl.** congeries)
literary: **n.** anthology; crestomathy; (**pl.** adversaria; analecta; collectanea; *disjecta membra*)
of biographical sketches (or production of): **n.** prosopography
of stories by same author or on one subject: **n.** omnibus
of things in general: **n.** collectanea; heterogeneity; hodgepodge; miscellanea; miscellaneity; miscellany

COLLECTOR, *bird-egg:* **n.** oologist
coins: **n.** numismatist; **n.** numismatics
curios or objets d'art: **n.** curioso
postcards: **n.** deltiologist
shells: **n.** conchologist; conchology
stamps: **n.** philatelist; philately

COLLEGE, *life within walls of:* **a.** intramural; parietal; **n.** academe; academia
teaching or teachers: **n.** professordom; professoriat(e)

COLLISION: **n.** encroachment; impingement; infringement; renitency; retroaction; **a.** COLLIDING: encroaching; impingent

COLONIZER: **n.** oecist

COLONY: **n.** habituation; installation; protectorate; settlement

COLOR(S), *deprive of:* **v.** achromatize; decolorize; etiolate; **a. see** "colorless"
having many: **a.** heterochromous; multicolored; polychrom(at)ic; polychromatous; variegated

having one: **a.** homochromatic; monochrom(at)ic; unicolorous
having two: **a.** bichromatic; bichrome; bicolored; bicolorous; dichrom(at)ic
having various, or changeable in: **a.** allochromatic; chatoyant; iridescent; kaleidoscopic; varicolored; versicolor(ed)
neutral in: **a.** achromatic
of flesh: **a.** incarnadine
of same (uniform in): **a.** concolorate; concolorous
pert. to different, or having complex pattern of: **a.** heterochrom(at)ic; heterochromous; kaleidoscopic

COLORLESS: (**see** "dull") **a.** achlorophyllaceous; achlorophyllous; achromatic; achromatous; achromic; achromous; diatonic; **n.** achromatism

COLOSSAL: **see** "huge"

COLUMNIST: **n.** feuilletonist

COMA: **n.** carus; stupor; torpidity; torpor; **a.** comatose; stuporous; torpid; torporific

COMBAT: **v. see** "contend"; **n.** rencontre; **a.** COMBATIVE: (**see** "hostile") agonistic; armigerous; bellicose; belligerent; disputatious; martial; militant; oppugnant; pugnacious; taurine; unpacific
mock or futile: **n.** sciamachy

COMBINATION: (**see** "collection") **n.** agglutination; amalgamation; coalescence; coalition; conjoinment; conjugation; conjunction; conjuncture; consolidation; lamination; merger; (poly)synthesis; syncretism; synergism; **v.** COMBINE: (**see** "join") amalgamate; coalesce; conjoin; consolidate; laminate; syncretize; synthesize
of diff. ideas, persons or things: **n.** amalgam(ation); homogeneity
of many elements into one: **n.** polysynthesis(m)

COMBINED *action of drug or agent:* **n.** synergism; **v.** synergize; **a.** synergetic; synergic(al); synergistic(al)

COMBINING: **a.** amalgamative; coalescent; synergetic; synergic(al)
more than one use or quality: **a.** portmanteau
of various ideas, forces, etc. into workable result: **v.** synthesize; **n.** synthesis
two into one: **a.** biune; biunial

COME *between:* **v.** intermediate; interpose; intervene; **n.** intermediation; interposition; intervention
together: (**see** "meet") **v.** converge; rencounter; **n.** convergence; convergency

COMEDOWN: **n.** anticlimax; bathos; comeuppance; denigration; disappointment; setback; **a.** anticlimactic; bathetic; denigratory

COMEDY, *broad and low:* **n.** burlesk; burlesque; **a.** Aristophanic; Falstaffian; Rabelaisian
muse of: **n.** Thalia
plotless: **n.** harlequinade

COMFORT: **see** "ease"; **n.** COMFORTER: intercessor; paraclete; **a.** COMFORTING: consolatory; nepenthean; tranquilizing
drug or agent for: **n.** nepenthe; tranquilizer; **a.** nepenthean

COMIC: **n.** comedian; *farceur;* (**fem.** *farceuse*); harlequin; **a.** COMICAL: Aristophanic; burlesk; burlesque; farcical; harlequin; ludicrous; opera buffe; risible
talent: **n.** *vis comica*

COMMAND: (**see** "order" **and** "rule") **v.** imperate **n.** adjuration; caveat; fiat; imperative; mandament; mandate; mastery; precept
authoritative: **n.** caveat; fiat; mandate

COMMANDER: **n.** imperator

COMMANDING: **a.** august; authoritative; autocratic; exalted; grandiose; imperative; imperial; imperious; imposing; mandatory; peremptory; predominant
air: **n.** bravura

COMMEMORATE: **v.** celebrate; elegize; signalize; solemnize

COMMENCE: **see** "begin"

COMMENDABLE: **a.** admirable; approbatory; commendatory; complimentary; creditable; encomiastic(al); estimable; eulogistic; exemplary; honorific; laudable; laudative; laudatory; meritorious; panegyric(al); praiseworthy

COMMEND: **see** "extol"; **n.** COMMENDATION: (**see** "praise") approbation;

compliment; encomium; laudation; panegyric

COMMENTATOR: **n.** annotator; exegete; exegetist; expositor; glossator; scholiast

COMMERCIAL: **a.** mercantile; mercenary

COMMODIOUS: (**see** "roomy") **a.** baronial; capacious; cavernous; spacious

COMMON: **a.** communal; customary; demotic; epidemic; generic; habitual; hackneyed; heathenish; pagan; plebeian; prevalent; scurrile; scurrilous; undistinguished; universal; unrefined; vulgar; **n.** COMMONNESS: commonality; peasantry; prevalence; unrefinement; vulgarity
consent, by; **adv.** *communi consensu*
danger produces concord: **adv.** *commune periculum concordiam parit*
good: **n.** *commune bonum*
origin, having: **a.** monogen(et)ic; monogenistic
people: (**see under** "people") **n.** commonalty; proletariat(e); **a.** lumpen; plebeian; proletarian; proletariat(e)
sense: **n.** *bon sens;* prudence; sophrosyne
to both male and female: **a.** (am)bisexual; ambosexual; epicene; hermaphrodite; hermaphroditic(al)
to make: (**see** "debase" *and* "lower") **v.** heathenize; paganize; vulgarize

COMMONER: **n.** bourgeois; plebeian; roturier

COMMONPLACE: (**see** "dull") **a.** banal; bourgeois; *cliché;* hackneyed; pedestrian; platitudinal; platitudinous; plebeian; prosaic(al); stereotyped; stereotypical; trite; twice-told; uneventful; unglamorous; unglorified; **n.** COMMONPLACENESS: banality; bathos; peasantry; pedestrianism; platitudinism; triteness
expression or remark: **n.** bromide; *cliché;* platitude; shibboleth; stereotype; truism; **a.** bromidic; hackneyed; platitudinal; platitudinous; stereotyped; **v.** platitudinize
person addicted to use of the: **n.** platitudinarian

COMMOTION: **n.** agitation; Babelism; bouleversement; brouhaha; convulsion; flurriment; hurly-burly; perturbation; tempest in a teapot; tumult; turbulence; turmoil; **a.** perturbational; turbulent

COMMUNICATION: (**see** "speech") **n.** impartment; transmission
without means of: **a.** incommunicado

COMMUNITY: **n.** environment; environs; fellowship, microcosm; milieu; **a.** environmental; microcosmic(al)
affairs, active in: **a.** pragmatic
affairs, disinterested in: **n.** incivilism
of interest: **n.** affinity

COMPACT: **a.** compendious; consolidated; succinct; **n.** alliance; compendium; covenant

COMPANION: **n.** accessory; chaperone; cohort; compeer; consort; counterpart; escort
at table: **n.** commensal; **a.** commensal; **n.** commensality
boon: **n.** *alter ego; bon camarade*
close: **n** *alter ego*
gay and often irresponsible: **n.** Trojan
ghostly: **n.** doppelganger; doubleganger
he is known by his (companions): noscitur ex sociis
traveling: **n.** *compagnon de voyage*

COMPARABLE: (**see** "similar") **a.** commensurate; corresponding; equipollent; equiponderant; equivalent; homogeneous; homologous; proportionate; **n.** COMPARABILITY: commensurability; commensuration; equiponderance; equivalence; homogeneity

COMPARE: **v.** collate; contrast; equate; **a.** COMPARATIVE: analogical; analogous; approximate; metaphorical

COMPARISON: **n.** analogy; collation; metaphor; parable; simile; similitude
beyond: (**see** "superior") **a.** *ne plus supra; ne plus ultra; par excellence;* preeminent; supereminent
not capable of: **a.** incommensurable; incomparable; **n.** incommensurability

COMPASS: **see** "scope"

COMPASSION: (**see** "sympathy") **n.** commiseration
appeal(ing) to: **adv.** **or** **n.** *(argumentum) ad miserecordiam*

COMPASSIONATE: **see** "kind" **and** "sympathetic"
person: **n.** almoner; charitarian; elee-

mosynar; humanitarian; philanthropist; Samaritan

COMPATIBLE: (**see** "harmonious") **a.** congenial; congruent; consentaneous; consonant; homogenous; **n.** COMPATIBILITY: congeniality; congruity; consentaneousness; homogeneity

COMPEL: **v.** commandeer; discipline; dragoon; necessitate; **a.** COMPELLING: cogent; convincing; impelling; **n.** cogency

COMPENDIUM: (**see** "abstract") **n.** lexicon; sylloge

COMPENSATE: (**see** "offset") **v.** atone; counterbalance; counterpoise; countervail; recompense; remunerate; requite; **n.** COMPENSATION: honorarium; perquisite; recompense; remuneration; requital; restitution; solatium

COMPETENT: (**see** "able") **a.** adequate; capax; ingenious; panurgic; proficient; puissant; **n.** COMPETENCE: (**see** "ability") versatility
in many things: **a.** ambidextrous; ingenious; panurgic; versatile; **n.** ambidexterity; ingeniosity; panurgy; versatility
mentally: **n.** *compos mentis*

COMPETITION: **n.** concours; rivalry; **a.** COMPETITIVE: rivalrous
out of, or excluded from: **a. or adv.** *hors concours;* **adv.** *hors de combat*

COMPLAIN: (**see** "protest") **v.** bewail; expostulate; inveigh; lament; remonstrate; repine; **a.** COMPLAINING: clamorous; complaintive; querimonious; querulent; querulous
person who (complains): **n.** complainant; plaintiff; querulist

COMPLAINT: (**see** "objection") **n.** allegation; expostulation; jeremiad; lamentation; protest(ation); querulity; remonstration; remonstrance
essential part of: **n.** gravamen
sad: **n.** jeremiad; lamentation

COMPLETE: **v.** accomplish; complement; consummate; finalize; realize; **a.** accomplished; consummate; consummative; integral; plenary; replete; saturative; unabridged; unexpurgated; **a.** COMPLETED: (**see** "done") accomplished; concluded; consummated; established; finalized; realized; **adv.** COMPLETELY: *a capite ad calcem; à fond; cap-a-pie;* diametrically; *in toto;* utterly; **a.** COMPLETING: (**see** "ending") concluding; consummatory; **n.** COMPLETION: (**see** "accomplishment") actuality; actualization; complement; consummation; *coup de grâce; fait accompli;* finality; realization
it is (completed): **adv.** *consummatum est; fait accompli*

COMPLETENESS: **n.** consummation; finality; integrality; integrity; wholeness
in general: **n.** entelechy

COMPLEX: (**see** "abstract" **and** "intricate") **a.** complicated; daedal(ic); heterogeneous; labyrinthian; labyrinthine; sinuous; sophisticated; **n.** COMPLEXITY: complexus; complicacy; compositeness; entanglement; intricacy; involvement; labyrinth; maelstrom; sinuosity

COMPLIANCE: **n.** assiduity; concord; condescendence; conformance; facilitation; facility; harmony; obsequence; obsequency; obsequity; sequacity; **a.** COMPLIANT: accommodating; amenable; assentatious; assiduous; complaisant; docile; ductile; facile; malleable; obsequious; pliable; sequacious; servile; submissive; subservient; tractable; yielding

COMPLICATED: (**see** "complex") **a.** abstruse; Gordian; involuted; prolix; recondite; **n.** COMPLICATION: (**see** "complexity") complexus; complicacy; entanglement; intricacy; involution; involvement; sinuosity
aggregation or situation: **n.** complexus

COMPOSED: **see** "calm"; **n.** COMPOSURE: (**see** "serenity") countenance; equability; equanimity; phlegm; placidity; poise; posture; repose; *sang-froid;* self-possession; stability; temperament

COMPOUND: **see** "mixture"

COMPREHENSION: (**see** "knowledge") **n.** connotation; inclusion; intuition; understanding; **v.** COMPREHEND: **see** "understand"
beyond: (**see** "obscure") **a.** transcendent
by intellect alone: **n.** cognition; noesis; **a.** cognitive; noetic

COMPREHENSIVE: **(see** "universal") **a.** catholic; connotative; consolidated; ecumenical; encyclic; encyclopedic(al); intensive; synoptic; transcendental
all: **see under** "all"
view or range: **n.** panorama

COMPROMISE: **v.** adjust; arbitrate; embarrass; endanger; expose; humiliate; jeopardize; **n.** abatement; arbitration; concession; conciliation; embarrassment; humiliation; jeopardy; understanding
arrangement pending final settlement: **n.** *modus vivendi*

COMPULSORY: **see** "imperative"

COMPUNCTION: **n.** contrition; penitence: qualm; scruple; **a.** COMPUNCTIOUS: contrite; penitent(ial); qualmish; remorseful

COMRADE: **n.** associate; colleague; compeer; confrere; **n.** COMRADESHIP: *camaraderie; esprit de corps;* geniality
close or boon: **n.** *alter ego; bon camarade*

CONCEALMENT: **n.** clandestinity; delitescence; dissimulation; eclipse; obscuration; occultation; **v.** CONCEAL: camouflage; cache; dissemble; ensconce; obscure; secrete; sequester; **a.** CONCEALED: **(see** "hidden") abeyant; clandestine; covert; delitescent; dormant; larvate(d); latent; potential; quiescent; surreptitious; veiled
from law: **n.** abscondence
of crime: **n.** misprision
of facts: **(see** "fraud") **n.** subreption; *suppressio veri*

CONCEDE: **v.** acknowledge; acquiesce; capitulate; surrender

CONCEIT: **n.** *amour-propre;* caprice; egocentricity; egomania; ego(t)ism; flatulence; hauteur; *mauvaise honte; outrecuidance;* pomposity; presumption; self-esteem; **a.** CONCEITED: arrogant; bumptious; egomaniac(al); ego(t)istical; haughty; hubristic; opinionated; overweening; pragmatic; priggish; presumptuous
abnormal: **n.** egomania; hubris; **a.** egomaniac(al); hubristic
disagreeable: **n.** bumptiousness; presumptiousness
person with: **n.** cockalorum; egomaniac

CONCEIVE: **v.** apprehend; comprehend; concoct; contrive; fabricate; formulate; ideate; **a.** ideational; **n. (see** "concept") ideation

CONCENTRATE: **(see** "condense") **v.** agglutinate; assemble; centralize; conglomerate; consolidate; epitomize; nucleate; **a.** CONCENTRATED: inspissated; **n. see** "concentration"

CONCENTRATION: **n.** agglutination; concentrate; essence; inspissation; nucleation; polarization; quintessence
of power or authority: **n.** centralization
point: **n.** nidus; nucleus

CONCEPT(ION): **(see** "category") **n.** envisagement; hypothesis; ideation; postulate; presupposition; prochronism; prolepsis; rubric

CONCERN: **n.** altruism; anxiety; apprehension; concernment; solicitude; **a.** CONCERNED: apprehensive; distressed; disturbed; interested; solicitous; solicitudinous; versant; **adv.** CONCERNING: anent; *in re;* regarding; respecting
it's my own: **n.** *c'est mon affaire*

CONCESSION: **n.** acknowledgement; capitulation; condescendence; indulgence

CONCILIATE: **v.** appease; mollify; pacify; placate; propitiate; reconcile; tranquilize; **n.** CONCILIATION: appeasement; mollification; pacification; propitiation; tranquilization; **a.** CONCILIATORY: mollifying; pacific; placatory; propitiatory; propitious
offer or gesture of (conciliation): **n.** olive branch

CONCISE: **(see** "terse") **a.** aphoristic; compendious; comprehensive; cryptic(al); epigrammatic; laconic(al); pregnant; sententious; succinct; Tacitean; telegraphic; trenchant
in speech or expression: **(see under** "brevity") **n.** brachylogy; **a.** aphoristic

CONCLUSION: **n.** cessation; coda; consequence; consummation; (d)eduction; envoi; epilogue; finality; finalization; gradation; illation; inference; liquidation; settlement; termination *terminus ad quem;* **a. see** "ending"

exclamatory sentence or striking comment at (conclusion) of discourse: **n.** epiphonema
expressing a: **a.** desitive

CONCLUSIVE: (**see** "final") **a.** consummative; consummatory; decisive; definitive; determinative; illative; irrefutable; terminal; unanswerable; unequivocal

CONCORD: (**see** "agreement") **n.** congeniality; harmony; rapprochement; simultaneity; synchroneity; unanimity
in: **see** "harmonious"
restoring of: **n.** rapprochement

CONCRETE, *dealing with the:* **a.** idiographic; materialistic; pragmatic
entity: **n.** concretum; (pl. concreta)

CONCURRENCE: **n.** simultaneity; synchroneity; unanimity; **v.** CONCUR: **see** "agree"
not in: **a.** anachronous; asynchronistic; asynchronous; **n.** asynchronism

CONDEMN: **see** "censure"; **a.** CONDEMNING: condemnatory; damnatory
what is not understood: damnat quod non intelligunt

CONDENSE: **v.** abbreviate; abridge; compress; concentrate; consolidate; epitomize; inspissate
in rhetoric to emphasize: **n.** paraleipsis

CONDENSED *expression:* **n.** (**see** "maxim") aphorism; brachylogy

CONDESCENDING: (**see** "yielding") **a.** hoity-toity; patronizing
air or manner, with a: **a.** or **adv.** *de haut en bas*

CONDITION: **n.** circumstance; contingency; eventuality; facet; obstacle; plight; predicament; (pre)requisite; provision; proviso; reservation; status; stipulation
at any previous time: **n.** *status quo ante*
at any specified time: **n.** *status quo*
in same or existing: **n.** or **adv.** *in statu quo; status quo*
indispensable: **see** "indispensable"

CONDITIONAL: **a.** circumstantial; contingent; limitative; provisional; provisory; tentative; **n.** CONDITIONALITY: tentativeness

CONDOLE: **v.** commiserate; lament; **n.** CONDOLENCE: commiseration; compassion; **a.** CONDOLENT: compassionate

CONDUCT: (**see** "manage") **v.** escort; negotiate; **n.** (**see** "behavior") comport(ment); demeanor; deportment; management; mien; praxis
bad: **see** "misbehavior"
brutish or grotesque: **n.** baboonery; grossness; vulgarity
correctness of: **n.** correctitude; rectitude; scrupulosity
extravagant, shamelessly flamboyant or vainglorious: **n.pl.** heroics; theatrics
gracious acts of: **n.pl.** amenities; proprieties; urbanities
nice point of: **n.** meticulosity; punctilio
reasoning about, or false application of principles to: **n.** casuistry; **a.** casuistic
right or wrong, judge of: **n.** casuist; *censor morum;* moral sophist
study of human: **n.** praxeology; praxiology
usual or conventional: **n.** praxis

CONFEDERATE: **see** "associate"

CONFEDERATION: **see** "alliance"

CONFERENCE: **n.** caucus; colloquium; colloquy; confabulation; consultation; deliberation; dialogue; discussion; palaver; parley; seminar; symposium; **v.** CONFER: bestow; confabulate; consult; deliberate; endow
preliminary or informal: **n.** pourparler

CONFESSON(S), *receiver of:* **n.** confessarius
sacrament of: **n.** penance

CONFIDENCE: **n.** assurance; certainty; certitude; credence; positivism; presumption; **a.** CONFIDENT: assured; peremptory; presumptious; sanguine
bold show of: **n.** bravura; doughtiness; *tour de force*
lack of: **n.** diffidence; inferiority complex
over-: **n.** presumptiousness
tending to inspire: **a.** prepossessing

CONFIDENTIAL: (**see** "secret") **a.** classified; covert; esoteric; trustworthy; **adv.** CONFIDENTIALLY: covertly; *entre nous; inter nos; sub rosa*

CONFINE: **v.** circumscribe; demarcate; encompass; immure, impale; impound; imprison; incarcerate; **n.** CONFINEMENT: accouchement; circumscription; immurement; incarceration
place of: **n.** limbo

CONFIRM: (**see** "verify") **v.** authenticate; corroborate; establish; substantiate; validate; **n.** CONFIRMATION: affirmation; authentication; corroboration; investiture; substantiation; validation; **a.** CONFIRMATIVE: confirmatory; corroborative; corroboratory

CONFISCATE: **see** "take"

CONFLICT: (**see** "fight") **n.** antagonism; collision; encroachment; friction; impingement; **a.** CONFLICTING: antagonistic; antithetical; contending; contradictory; incompatible; incongruous; inconsistent; inharmonious; irreconcilable; **n.** CONFLICTION: antagonism; contrariety; disharmony; incompatibility; irreconcilability
vast, final, or conclusive: **n.** Armageddon

CONFORM: **see** "adapt"; **a.** CONFORMABLE: **see** "accepted"
one who (conforms): **n.** conventionalist; ritualist

CONFORMING *to standards:* (**see** "according to rule" **and** "standards") **a.** canonical; conventional; ethical; **adv.** *en règle;* **n.** canonicity; conventionality; propriety; rituality

CONFORMITY *at any cost, or by force:* **a.** procrustean
lack of: **n.** difformity; impropriety; recusancy; unconventionality

CONFUSE: (**see** "bewilder") **v.** bemuse; confound; disconcert; disorient; embrangle; obfuscate; perplex; perturb
by sounds, or by mingling of diff. language or cultures: **n.** Babelism; **v.** Babelize

CONFUSED (**or** CONFUSING): (**see** "baffling" **and** "bewildered") bemused; chaotic; disconcerted; *désorienté;* disordered; distraught; frantic; higgledy-piggledy (**or** higglety-pigglety); hugger-mugger; incoherent; indiscriminate; muddled; obfuscated; obfuscatory; perplexed
state of mind: **n.** disorientation; incoherence; obnubilation

CONFUSION: (**see** "disorder") **n.** anarchy; ataxia; Babelism; bewilderment; brouhaha; chaos; delirium; disarrangement; disarray; discomfiture; disorientation; embranglement; hugger-mugger; incoherence; katzenjammer; obfuscation; perplexity; turbidity; turmoil; welter; witches' brew
in: **adv.** *à l'abandon;* higgledy-piggledy; topsy-turvy
of sound or sense: **n.** Babelism
place or scene of: **n.** Bedlam

CONGRATULATE: **v.** commend; felicitate; macarize; **a.** CONGRATULATORY: gratulant; **n.** CONGRATULATION: commendation; felicitation

CONJECTURE: **n.** hypothesis; postulation; presumption; (pre)supposition; speculation; surmise; theorem; **a.** CONJECTURAL: hypothetical; stochastic; suppositional; supposi(ti)ous; theoretical

CONJUNCTION(S): (**see** "union") **n.** association
connecting by (words or sentences): **a.** syndetic
omission of in sentence: **n.** asyndeton; **a.** asyndetic
repetition of many in succession: **n.** polysyndeton; **a.** polysyndetic

CONJURER: **see** "magician"

CONNECTION: (**see** "association") **n.** affinity; alliance; colligation; conjunction; consanguinity; contiguity; continuity; liaison; ligature; nexus; relationship; symphysis; **a.** CONNECTED (**or** CONNECTING): affined; anastomotic; articulate(d); coadunate; coadunative; conjunctive; contiguous; osculant; syndetic
as by descent or derivation: **n.** apparentation; **v.** apparent
blood vessels or channels: **n.** anastomosis; **a.** anastomotic
necessary: **n.** causality
nerve(s): **n.** synapse; **a.** synaptic

CONQUER: **v.** overthrow; subdue; subjugate; surmount; vanquish; **n.** **see** "conquest"
or die: aut vincere aut mori

CONQUERABLE: **a.** domitable; expugnable; surmountable; vincible; vulnerable; **n.** CONQUERABILITY: domitability; expugnability; surmountability; vincibility
not: **see under** "conquered"

CONQUERED, *capable of being:* **see** "conquerable"
incapable of being: **a.** impregnable; inconquerable; inexpugnable; insurmountable; invulnerable; **n.** impregnability; inexpugnability; insurmountability; invincibility
woe to the: **adv.** *vae victis*

CONQUEROR: **n.** conquistador

CONQUEST: **n.** acquisition; debellation; reduction; subjection; subjugation; triumph

CONSCIOUS *of:* (**see** "aware") **a.** cognizable; cognizant; sensible; sentient; **n.** cognizance

CONSCIOUSNESS: (**see** "awareness") **n.** cognizance; percipience; percipiency; sentience; sentiency
below threshold or outside area of: **a.** subliminal; **n.** sublimination
twinge of: **n.** compunction; qualm; scruple; **a.** qualmish; scrupulous; **n.** scrupulosity

CONSECUTIVE: **a.** alphabetical; categorical; chronologic(al); sequel; sequent(ial); successional; successive

CONSENT: (**see** "accord" **and** "assent") **n.** approbation; concurrence; corroboration; permission; ratification; sufferance; unanimity
against, or against will: **adv.** *in invitum*
by common: **adv.** *communi consensu; d'un commun accord*
silence gives: chi tace assonsenti; qui tacet consentit
with general: **a.** consentaneous; consentient; consensual; unanimous; **n.** consension; consensus; unanimity

CONSEQUENCE(S): (**see** "weight") **n.** consecution; contrecoup; corollary; emanation; importance; ramification; residual; residue; residuum; sequela(e); **a.** CONSEQUENTIAL: corollary; residual; rational; self-important; sequent(ial)

CONSERVATION: **n.** economy; husbandry; perpetuation; planned management; preservation; sustentation; sustention; **a.** sustentative; **v.** CONSERVE: **see** "manage"

CONSERVATIVE: (**see** "old-fashioned") **a.** conventional; lethargic; reactionary; traditionalistic; unenterprising; **n.** mossback; Old-Guard(ist); pr(a)etorian; reactionary; standpatter; traditionalist; **n.** CONSERVATISM: conventionality; fundamentalism; traditionalism; traditionality
politically: **a.** Old-Guard; Metternichian

CONSIDERATION: **n.** advisement; attention; contemplation; deliberation; estimation; (ex)cogitation; honorarium; perpension; *quid pro quo;* reward; **v.** CONSIDER: (**see** "reflect") contemplate; deliberate; (ex)cogitate; perpend; ponder; take under advisement
for further: **adv.** *ad referendum*

CONSISTENT: (**see** "constant") **a.** commensurate; compatible; comportable; concordant; congenial; congruous; consentaneous; consonant; harmonious; invariable; isogenous; **n.** CONSISTENCY: compatibility; correspondence; harmony; homogeneity; isogeny; persistency
not: **see** "inconsistent"

CONSOLE: **see** "condole"

CONSOLIDATE: **see** "combine"

CONSPICUOUS: (**see** "outstanding") **a.** eminent; manifest; striking
by his absence: **adv.** *briller par son absence*
extremely: **a.** supereminent; **n.** supereminence

CONSPIRE: **v.** collude; connive; contrive; machinate; **a.** CONSPIRATIVE (or CONSPIRATORIAL) cabalistic; Catilinarian; collusive; collusory; conniving; **n.** CONSPIRACY: (**see** "plot") *association illégale;* cabal; collusion; confederacy; conjuration; connivance; intrigue; junto; machination

CONSTANT: (**see** "steady") **a.** continent; continual; continuous; immutable; incessant; invariable; perennial; persevering; resolute; steadfast; unceasing; undeviating; unfading; unfailing; uniform; unswerving

CONSTITUTION: **n.** character; decalogue; disposition; lustihood; Magna C(h)arta; ordinance; physique; stamina; temperament; virility
individual: **n.** crasis

CONSTRAINT: **see** "duress"

CONSTRICTION: (**see** "obstruction") **n.** coarctation; stenosis; strangulation

CONSTRUCT: (**see** "build") **v.** compose; confect; fabricate; improvisate; improvise; manufacture

CONSTRUCTION, *art of:* **n.pl.** (archi)-tectonics
pert. to: **a.** (archi)tectonic; constructional

CONSTRUCTIVE: **a.** affirmative; architectonic; definitive; inferred

CONSUMING: **a.** devouring; edacious; voracious; **n.** edacity; voracity

CONTACTING: **a.** contiguous; juxtapositional; tangential; **n.** (**see** "touching") apposition; contiguity; contingence; juxtaposition; tangency

CONTAGIOUS: **a.** communicable; epidemic; noxious; pestilential; **n.** contagium
state of being: **n.** contagiosity

CONTAMINATED: **a.** defiled; insanitary; polluted; septic; **v.** CONTAMINATE: **see** "defile"
morally: **a.** scrofulous; **n.** scrofulosis
not possible to (contaminate): **a.** incontaminable; incontaminate

CONTEMPLATION: **n.** anticipation; (ex)cogitation; expectation; meditation; **v.** CONTEMPLATE: anticipate; envisage; (ex)cogitate; meditate; ponder; postulate
mystical: **n.** orison

CONTEMPORARY: **a.** coetaneous; coeternal; coeval; coincident; concomitant; concurrent; contemporaneous; isochronous; simultaneous; synchronous; **n.** CONTEMPORARINESS: coetaneity; coeval(ity); contemporaneity; simultaneity; synchroneity

CONTEMPT: **n.** contumacy; contumely; denigration; depreciation; derision; despiciency; disdain; disparagement; hauteur; hubris; misprision; scurviness; **a.** CONTEMPTIBLE: contemptuous; contumelious; denigrating; derisible; derisive; despicable; despiteous; disdainful; haughty; hubristic; pitiable; scurrile; scurrilous; scurvy; toplofty
as a token of: **adv.** *par signe de mépris*
hold in: **v.** denigrate; deride; disdain; disparage; misprize
person regarded with: **n.** pilgarlic

CONTEND: **v.** antagonize; grapple; oppugn; **n.** CONTENTION: (**see** "controversy") altercation; competition; contestation; dissidence; donny-brook; litigiosity; rivalry; **a.** CONTENTIOUS: (**see** "hostile") belligerent; contradictious; disputable; disputatious; dissentious; factious; litigious; mutinous; seditious; tauraine; turbulent

CONTENT(ED): (**see** "calm") **a.** *sans souci;* unperturbed; **n.** CONTENTMENT: complacency; eudaemonia; eudaemony; euphoria; felicity; repose; satisfaction; tranquility

CONTEST: (**see** "oppose" **and** *"fight"*) **n.** agon; tournament; **n.** CONTESTING: agonistic(al); **n.** CONTESTANT: agonist
slight: **n.** skirmish; vellitation

CONTINGENCY: **n.** accidentality; casualty; eventuality; fortuitousness; fortuity; juncture

CONTINUE: **v.** perdure; perpetuate; perseverate; persevere; persist; **n.** CONTINUATION: (**see** "continuousness") perduration; perpetuation; perpetuality; perpetuity; perseveration; persistence; persistency; prolongation

CONTINUOUS (**or** CONTINUAL): **a.** consecutive; incessant; inveterate; perdurant; perennial; perpetual; persistent; progressive; recurrent; sempiternal; successive; unceasing; uninterrupted; **n.** CONTINUOUSNESS: (**see** "continuation") continuity; continuum; incessancy;

incessantness; inveterateness; perpetuality; perpetuity; perseveration; sempiternity
something which is: **n.** continuum

CONTOUR: (**see** "outline") **n.** configuration; conformation; silhouette

CONTRACT, *power to:* **n.** contractility

CONTRACTING: **a.** astrictive; binding; **n.** astriction; astrictive

CONTRADICTING *no one:* **adv.** *nemine contradicente* (**abb.** *nem con*); *nemine dissentiente*

CONTRADICTION: **n.** anomaly; antilogy; antinomy; antithesis; contrariety; incompatibility; paradox
in terms or ideas: **n.** antilogy; *contradictio in adjecto*

CONTRADICTORY: **a.** ambivalent; antonymous; contradictious; incompatible; inconsistent; paradoxical; repugnant; schizoid
attitude: **n.** ambivalence; paradoxicality

CONTRARY: (**see** "opposite" **and** "stubborn") **a.** absonant; adverse; ambivalent; antagonistic; antipodal; antithetic(al); cantankerous; contradictious; contrariant; contrarious; diametrical; discrepant; fractious; froward; incompatible; inverse; perverse; petulant; refractory
on the: **adv.** *per contra*
quite the: **adv.** *à rebours; tout au contraire; tout bien ou rien*
state of being: **n.** antithesis; contrariety; (**n.pl.** antipodes)
to the: **adv.** *a contrario; au contraire*

CONTRIBUTION, *small but all one can afford:* **n.** widow's mite

CONTRIBUTORY: (**see** "supplemental") **a.** accessorial; accessory; adjuvant; auxiliary; complemental; complementary; **n.** complementarity

CONTRIVE: **see** "invent"

CONTROL: (**see** "manage") **v.** dominate; govern; hierarchize; influence; manipulate; regulate; restrain; subdue; subjugate; superintend; **n.** (**see** "power") hierarchization; jurisdiction; manipulation; restraint; subjugation; **n.** CONTROLLER: comptroller; governor; manipulator; regulator; superintendent; supervisor
easy to: (**see** "pliant") **a.** controllable; educable; educatable; manipulatory; tractable; vulnerable; **n.** dirigibility; educa(ta)bility; tractability; vulnerability
impossible to: **a.** incoercible; incorrigible; irrepressible
of another, one who is under: **n.** *homo alieni juris*
self-: **see under** "self"

CONTROVERSY: **n.** argumentation; altercation; brannigan; contestation; disputation; dissention; polemics; **a.** CONTROVERSIAL: argumentative; contentious; dialectic; discursory; disputatious; eristic; polemic(al)
famous or celebrated: **n.** *cause célèbre*

CONVENIENCE: **n.** advantage; expedience; expediency; opportunity; **a.** CONVENIENT: advantageous; expedient; expeditional; opportune; seasonable

CONVENT, *occupant of:* **n.** cenobite; solitudinarian; **a.** cenobitic; solitudinarian

CONVENTION: **n.** academicism; decorum; (**pl.** decora); orthodoxy; proprieties; propriety
one who defies: **n.** beatnik; Bohemian; iconoclast; solecist; transgressor
outside: **a.** extracurricular

CONVENTIONAL: (**see** "accepted") **a.** academic; artificial; *au fait;* Babbit(t)ical; bourgeois; ceremonial; ceremonious; conventionalized; decorous; formal; nomic; orthodox(ical); pedantic; Philistine; stilted; traditional; tralatitious; **n.** CONVENTIONALITY: **n.** academicism; commonplaceness; conformity; conventionalism; formalism; (**pl. see** "proprieties")
person: **n.** academician; Babbitt; bourgeois; orthodoxian; Philistine; proprietarian
social usage, form or propriety: **n.** convenance; (the) amenities; (the) proprieties
to make: **v.** conventionalize; stylize

CONVERGENCE: **n.** concurrency; confluence; conflux; convergency; **a.** CONVERGENT: confluent

CONVERSANT: **see** "informed"

CONVERSATION: (**see** "discussion") **n.** causerie; colloquy; confabulation; conversazione; interlocution; parlance
clever or witty: **n.** repartee
of three: **n.** trialog(ue)
preliminary: **n.** pourparler
room set aside for: **n.** ex(h)edra; locutory

CONVERSATIONAL: **a.** colloquial; interlocutory; **n.** CONVERSATIONALIST: **n.** causeur; (**fem.** causeuse); raconteur
style, writing in: **n.** causerie; journalese

CONVERT: **v.** persuade; transform; transmute; **n.** disciple; neophyte; novice; proselyte
from another sect, belief, etc.: **v. or n.** proselyte

CONVINCING: (**see** "authoritative" **and** "evident") **a.** cogent; compelling; luculent; (per)suasive; plausible; telling

CONVULSION: **n.** grand mal; jactitation; orgasm; paroxysm; petit mal; seizure; **a.** CONVULSIVE: convulsionary; eclamptic; orgasmic; paroxysmal; spasmic; spasmodic(al)
state of: **n.** eclampsia

COOK, *chief:* **n.** *chef de cuisine; cuisinier;* (**fem.** *cuisinière*); culinarian
under- or assistant: **n.** *aide de cuisine*

COOKED *plainly:* **a.** *au naturel* (*also uncooked*)
well: **adv.** *bien cuit*

COOKING, *art of:* **n.** cuisine; epicurism; gastronomy; magirics
fine or high-class: **n.** *haute cuisine*
pert. to: **a.** culinary
plain: **n.** *cuisine bourgeoise*
prepared as at home: **a.** *bonne femme*
style of: **n.** cuisine; gastronomy

COOL: (**see** "calm" **and** "indifferent") **a.** composed; dispassionate; imperturbable; judicial; nonchalant; unperturbed; unruffled; **a.** COOLING: frigorific; **n.** COOLNESS: equanimity; indifference; nonchalance; phlegm; *sang-froid;* self-possession

COOPERATION: **n.** coadjuvancy; collaboration; commensalism; mutuality; reciprocality; reciprocity; symbiosis; synergism; synergy; **v.** COOPERATE: (**see** "unite") collaborate; **n.** COOPERATOR: collaborateur; collaborator; colleague; co-worker; phalansterian
bet. persons, animals or groups which may be otherwise incompatible: **n.** commensalism; mutualism; nutricism; parasitism; symbiosis; **a.** symbiotic(al)

COOPERATIVE: **a.** associative; collaborative; synergetic(al); synergic; synergistic
group living together; also building so used: **n.** phalansterianism; phalanstery

COORDINATION, *lack of:* **n.** astasia abasia; asynergia

COPPER, *bearing or containing:* **a.** cupriferous
pert. to, or to color of: **a.** cupr(e)ous

COPY: (**see** "imitate") **v.** duplicate; reproduce; transcribe; **n.** apograph; counterpart; duplicate; duplication; ectype; facsimile; replica; reproduction; transcription; **a.** apographal; ectypal
act or process of making: **n.** transumption

CORDIALITY: **see** "warmth"; **adv.** CORDIALLY: *à bras ouverts*

CORE: **see** "heart"

CORN (*on toe*): **n.** callosity; clavus; ecphyma

CORPSE, *like a:* **a.** cachectic; cadaverous

CORRECT: **v.** castigate; chasten; discipline; expiate; rectify; **a.** accurate; *au fait;* conventional; decorous; legitimate; orthodox; precise; rectitudinous; scrupulous
deviating from what is: **see** "deviating" **and** "deviation"
overly: **a.** meticulous; scrupulous; **n.** meticulosity; precisian; scrupulosity

CORRECTABLE: **a.** amenable; corrigible; perfectible; tractable; **n.** amenability; corrigibility; tractability

CORRECTION: (**see** "rebuke") **n.** amendment; chastening; chastenment; emendation; rectification; reformation

beyond: **a.** incorrigible; irreclaimable; irredeemable; irreformable; irremediable; irreparable
order for, of error: **n.** corrigendum; erratum; (**pl.** corrigenda; errata)

CORRECTIVE: **a.** amenable; amendatory; castigatory; correctional; emendatory; penal

CORRECTNESS: (**see** "accuracy") **n.** orthodoxy; scrupulosity
of judgment: **n.** rectitude

CORRESPONDING: **a.** accompanying; commensurable; commensurate; equivalent; homologous; isonomous; proportionate; **n.** CORRESPONDENCE: commensurability; commensuration; correlation; equiponderance; equivalence; homogeneity; reciprocation; **v.** CORRESPOND: (**see** "agree") coincide; correlate; equate; reciprocate
in value, structure, or position: **a.** homologous
person or thing: **n.** counterpart; homolog(ue)

CORROBORATIVE: **a.** adminicular; confirmatory; corroboratory; justificatory; vindicatory

CORRUPT: **v.** adulterate; debase; debauch; defile; demoralize; deprave; inquinate; pervert; pollute; putrefy; vitiate; **a.** CORRUPT (**or** CORRUPTIVE): Augean; cankerous; contaminated; contaminating; degenerate; demoralizing; immoral; infectious; mercenary; peccant; putrescent; putrid; tainted; venal
morally: **a.** degenerate; scrofulous; **n.** scrofulosis

CORRUPTION: **n.** contamination; debasement; debauchment; debauchery; degeneracy; defilement; demoralization; depravation; depravity; flagitiousness; putrefaction; putrescence; putridity; scrofulosis; squalor; venality
moral: **n.** degeneracy; scrofulosis; **a.** degenerate; scrofulous

COSMOS: **see** "universe"
worship of: **n.** cosmotheism

COST, *regardless of (or what it may)*: **adv.** *à tout prix; coûte que coûte*

COSTLY: **a.** dispendious; exorbitant; extortionate; extravagant; inestimable; invaluable; lavish; prodgial
victory: **n.** Cadmean victory; Pyrrhic victory

COSTUME: **see** "attire"

COUNCIL: **n.** assembly; quorum
of state (privy council) : **n.** *conseil d'état*

COUNSEL: **see** "advice" **and** "advocate"

COUNTENANCE: **n.** appearance; comportment; lineament; mien; physiognomy; sanction; visage; **v.** (**see** "support") encourage; sanction
is index of the soul: vultus est index animi

COUNTERACT: **v.** antagonize; contrapose; neutralize; nullify; **n.** **see** "opposition"

COUNTERATTACK: **n.** counteroffensive; repartee; ripost(e)

COUNTERCHARGE: **v.** recriminate; retaliate; **n.** recrimination; retaliation; **a.** recriminative; recriminatory; retaliative; retaliatory

COUNTERFEIT: (**see** "false") **v.** feign; imitate; pretend; simulate; **a.** (**see** "imitative") affected; apocryphal; artificial; Brummagem; colorable; delusive; ersatz; factitious; fraudulent; inauthentic; pretended; pseudo; simulated; spurious; supposititious; synthetic(al); uncanonical; **n.** **see** "imitation"

COUNTERFEITER: **n.** adulterator; imitant; impostor; imposture; mountebank; pretender

COUNTERMOVE: **n.** counteraction; *démarche*

COUNTLESS: **a.** incalculable; infinite; innumerable; legion; multitudinous; myriad; **n.** infinitude

COUNTRIFIED (**or** COUNTRYFIED): (**see** "rural") **a.** agrestic; bucolic; provincial; rustic; unsophisticated; **n.** peninsularity; provincialism; provinciality; rusticity

COUNTRY, *back (away fr. coast or cities)*: **n.** hinterland
born or living in the: **a.** rurigenous
girl or sweetheart: **n.** amaryllis
go to, live, or stay in: **v.** rusticate; **n.** rustication
holiday or retreat: **n.** villeggiatura
house or farm: **n.** villa; **a.** villatic
in the: **adv.** *en pays*
of or like: **a.** agrestic; countrified; idyllic; pastoral; provincial; rustic; Theocritean; unsophisticated
one's own: **n.** fatherland; **a.** patrial
person: **n.** agrestian; bucolic; provincial; rustic
person who came up in the world: **n.** *paysan parvenu*
pert. to a particular: **a.** autochthonous; enchorial; indigenous

COUNTRYMAN, *fellow:* **n.** compatriot

COUPLE: (**see** "unite") **v.** conjugate; **a.** COUPLED: coadunate; coadunative; conjugate
(*as hus. and wife*): **n.** dyad; **a.** dyadic

COUPLING: (**see** "union") **n.** accouplement; articulation; conjugation; copulation; junction; juncture; symphysis

COURAGE: **n.** audacity; dauntlessness; fortitude; gallantry; intrepidity; mettle; prowess; resolution; tenacity; **a.** COURAGEOUS: (**see** "bold") audacious; chivalrous; fortitudinous; Herculean; intrepid; resolute; Spartan
and faith, by: **adv.** *animo et fide*
incitement to: **n.** *sursum corda*
pretended: **n.** bravado; doughtiness
reckless: **n.** bravado; derring-do; doughtiness

COURSE: **v.** pulsate; surge; transverse; **n.** (**see** "journey" **and** "schedule") *démarche;* maneuver; procedure
of: **adv.** *bien entendu;* **int.** *parbleu!*

COURT(S), *authority or power of:* **n.** judicature; judiciary; jurisdiction
before, or under consideration by: **adv.** *sub judice*
capable or suitable for cons. by: **a.** justiciable
of law: **n.** judicature
pert. to: **a.** aulic; forensic; judicial; judiciary; juridical; juristic

COURTEOUS: (**see** "affable") **a.** attentive; chivalric; chivalrous; debonair(e); deferential; hospitable; ingratiating; parliamentary; suave; urbane
acts: **n. pl.** (the) amenities; (the) proprieties; urbanities
overly: **a.** deferential; obeisant; obsequious; servile; **n.** deferentiality; obeisance; obsequence; obsequiousness; obsequity; servility

COURTESY: **n.** address; *agréments;* amenity; civility; courtliness; deference; deferentiality; gentility; graciousness; gratuity; homage; indulgence; obeisance; politeness; politesse; protocol; suavity; urbanity; (**pl.** COURTESIES: *agréments;* amenities; proprieties; urbanities)
act of: **n.** devoir
given as a: **a.** complimentary; gratis

COURTLY: (**see** "courteous" **and** "polite") **a.** aulic; obsequious; stately; suave; unctuous

COVER: **v.** superimpose
under: **adv.** *à couvert*

COVERING: **n.** canopy; envelope; integument; marquee; operculum; superimposition

COVETOUS: **a.** acquisitive; *alieni appetens;* avaracious; extortionate; miserly; parsimonious; penurious; prehensile; rapacious; **n.** COVETOUSNESS: avarice; cupidity; pleonexia; venality

COW: **v.** browbeat; bulldoze; dishearten; intimidate; overawe; **n.** bovine; (**pl.** bovidae); ruminant

COWARD: **n.** caitiff; craven; dastard; poltroon; recreant; **a.** COWARDLY: caitiff; craven; dastardly; irresolute; lily-livered; poltroon(ish); pusillanimous; recreant; timorous; tremulous; **n.** COWARDICE: cowardliness; dastardliness; poltroonery; pusillanimity; recreancy; timidity

COWLED: **a.** cucullate(d)

COXCOMB: **n.** jackanapes; macaroni; popinjay

COY: **a:** coquettish; **n.** COYNESS: coquetry; dalliance; minauderie

COZY: **a**: gemultlich; intimate
place: **n.** snuggery

CRABBY: (**see** "cranky") **a.** *acariâtre;* acerb(ic); acidulent; acidulous; choleric; churlish; rebarbative; splenetic; vinegary; **n.** CRABBINESS: acerbity; asperity
person: **n.** crotcheteer; curmudgeon

CRACKLING: **a.** crepitant; **n.** crepitation

CRACKS, *full of:* **a.** rimose; rimulose

CRADLE: **n.** *crèche;* incunabula; infancy; matrix
from the: **adv.** *ab incunabulis*
song: **n.** berceuse

CRAFTSMAN: **n.** artificer; artisan

CRAFTY: (**see** "cunning") **a.** artful; astucious; astute; ingenious; insidious; insinuating; Machiavellian; politic; sophisticated; subtle; vulpine; **n.** CRAFTINESS: astuteness; astucity; callidity; diablerie; ingeniosity
esp. political: **a.** Machiavellian; **n.** Machiavellianism

CRAMPED: **a.** incapacious; incommodious

CRANKY: (**see** "crabby" **and** "peevish") **a.** cantankerous; choleric; crochety; irascible; petulant; querulous; splenetic; vinegary; **n.** CRANKINESS: (**see** "peevishness") acerbity; angularity; asperity; crotchiness; distemper; irascibility; querulousness

CRAVING: **a.** appetant; appetitious; desiderative; **n.** appetence; appetency; appetition; desideration; desideratum; yearning

CRAWLING, *adapted to:* (**see** "creeping") **a.** subreptary

CRAZED: **a.** berserk; distraught; frantic; frenetic; harassed; maniac(al); **n.** CRAZE: **see** "fad"
for one thing: **a.** monomaniac(al); **n.** monomania; monomaniac

CRAZY: **see** "insane"

CREATING, *all:* **see under** "all"

CREATION: **n.** cosmos; genesis; masterpiece; poiesis; universe; **v.** CREATE: (**see** "build") fabricate; generate; invent; reproduce
before: **a.** antemundane; premundane

CREATIVE: (**see** "original") **a.** constructive; demiurgic; formative; genetic; imaginative; ingenious; poietic; Promethean; (re)productive; **n.** poiesis
person: **n.** Prometheus
principle: **n.** *élan vital*

CREATIVELY *striving:* **a.** Dionysian

CREDIT: **n.** acknowledg(e)ment; ascription; recognition
for authorship, etc.: **n.** attribution; **a.** attributive
giving: **n.** ascription
letter of: **n.** *lettre de créance*
worthy of: **a.** commendable; creditable; **n.** creditability

CREDULOUS: **a.** gullible; naïve (**also** "naive"); naïvety; **n.** CREDULITY: gullibility; *naïveté* (**also** "naiveté")
person: **n.** gobemouche

CREED: (**see** "belief") **n.** confession; denomination; doctrine; dogma; philosophy; tenet
abandon: **v.** apostatize; **n.** apostate; apostasy; **a.** apostate; apostatic
one with no particular: **n.** anythingarian; aporetic; latitudinarian; nullifidian

CREEPING: **a.** procumbent; prostrate; reptant; reptatorial; reptilian; serpentine; serpiginous; subreptary

CREMATION: **n.** cineration

CRESCENT-*shaped:* **a.** lunate; lunular; lunulate; meniscoid

CRESTED: **a.** cristate; **n.** CREST: **see** "crown"

CRIME: **n.** defalcation; delict; embezzlement; felony; infraction; iniquity; malefaction; malfeasance; misdemeanor; offense; transgression
against state or king: **n.** *lèse majesté;* treason
associate in: **n.** accessory; *particeps criminis; socius criminis;* sorcerer's apprentice
capable of committing: **a.** *capax doli*
charge w/: **v.** (in)criminate; indict; **a.**

criminatory; (in)criminative; **n.** (in)crimination
concealment of: **n.** misprision; subreption
concernment w/: **a.** criminous
fact(s) necessary to establish: **n.** *corpus delicti*
minor: **n.** misdemeanor; transgression
on acct. of conviction for: **adv.** *propter delictum*
tending to involve in: **v.** incriminate; **a.** criminogenic; incriminatory; **n.** incrimination

CRIMINAL: **a.** blameworthy; culpable; disgraceful; extortionate; felonious; flagitious; illicit; iniquitous; malefic; malevolent; malignant; nefarious; nocent; reprehensive; unlawful; **n.** convict; culprit; delinquent; felon; infractor; malefactor; malfeasant; miscreant
intent: **n.** *mens rea*

CRINKLED: **a.** convoluted; crispate

CRIPPLED: **see** "lame"

CRISIS: **n.** climacteric; climacterium; (con)juncture; criticality; cruciality; crux; dilemma; exigency; predicament; **a.** CRISIC: (**see** "critical") dilemmatic; predicamental

CRITERION: **see** "standard"

CRITIC: (**see** "faultfinder") **n.** aristarch; carper; caviler; exegete; feuilletonist; pundit
bitter and envious; **n.** Zoilus; **a.** Zoilean
carping: **n.** momus
learned and severe: **n.** Aristarch(us)
of art(s) and fashion(s): **n.** cognoscente; connoisseur

CRITICAL: (**see** "crucial" **and** "dangerous") **a.** captious; censorial; censorious; climacteric(al); climactic(al); condemnatory; cynical; definitive; derisive; dilemmatic; exigent; imminent; resolute; scrupulous; squeamish
(dangerous): **a.** parlous
essay, exam. or analysis: **n.** critique; exegesis
moment: **see** "crisis"

CRITICISM: (**see** "censure") **n.** animadversion; critique; derision; diatribe; evaluation; impugnation; scarification; stricture
above or beyond: **a.** impregnable; invulnerable; unassailable
insensitive to: **a.** pachydermatous

CRITICIZE: (**see** "censure") **v.** animadvert; castigate; evaluate; execrate; fustigate; impugn; reprehend; upbraid
sharply: **v.** scarify

CRITICIZING *another for what he criticizes in others:* **n.** *tu quoque*

CROOKED: **a.** circuitous; devious; fraudulent; insidious; perfidious; sinuous; stealthy; surreptitious; tortuous; unconscionable; unprincipled; unscrupulous; vermiculate; villainous; **n.** CROOKEDNESS: circuity; deviousness; indirection; insidiousness; perfidy; surreptition; tortuosity; unscrupulosity; villainy

CROP(S), *goddess of:* **n.** Annona; Ops
production, study of: **n.** agronomics; agronomy; agronomist

CROSS: **a.** acidulous; bilious; choleric; contentious; decussate; fractious; irascible; perverse
-breeding, animal or plant produced by: (**see** "half-breed") **n.** hybrid; mongrel
-fertilization; **n.** allogamy; xenogamy; **a.** allogamous; xenogamous
making sign of the: **n.** signation
pert. to: **a.** crucial; cruciate
shaped like: **a.** cruciate; cruciform
swastica type: **n.** flyfot; gammadion; hakenkreuz
type of: **n.** avellan; *botonée; clechée; fleuretée;* Maltese; moline; patonce; quadrate
worship of (or crucifix): **n.** staurolatory

CROSSNG: **n.** chiasma; decussation; intersection
like an "x": **n.** decussation; **v.** decussate

CROSS-ROADS: **n.** carrefour; quadrivium; **a.** quadrivial
goddess of: **n.** Hecate; Trivia

CROUCHING: **a.** crouchant; couchant

CROW, *like or pert. to:* **a.** corvine

CROWD(S): **see** "multitude"
abnormal fear of: **n.** ochlophobia
in. a: **adv.** *en foule*

to please the: **adv.** *ad captandum (vulgus)*

CROWN: **n.** coronet; culmination; diadem; scepter; sovereignty; tiara
-prince; **n.** atheling; dauphin; **(fem.** dauphine; dauphiness)
with laurel: **n.** or **v.** laureate

CRUCIAL: **(see** "critical") **a.** climacteric(al); climactic(al); decisive; searching; **n.** CRUCIALITY: **(see** "crisis") criticality
experiment: **n.** *experimentum crucis*

CRUCIFIX: *worship of (or cross)*: **n.** staurolatory

CRUDE: **(see** "undeveloped") **a.** artless; gauche; immature; inapt; incondite; inept; primitive; primordial; rustic; unpolished; unskil(l)ful
person: **n.** buffoon; grobian; rustic

CRUDENESS (*or* CRUDITY): **n.** gaucherie; grobianism; impoliteness; immaturity; ineptness; ineptitude; pleb(e)ianism; primitivity; rusticity
social or lit.: **n.** gaucherie

CRUEL: **(see** "wicked") **a.** barbarous; despiteful; diabolical; dispiteous; Draconian; ferocious; impiteous; inexorable; inhuman; malicious; marblehearted; merciless; Neronian; procrustean; remorseless; ruthless; sadistic; satanic; Tarquinian; truculent; tyrannical; tyrannous; **n.** CRUELTY: barbarism; barbarity; callousness; ferity; induration; inhumanity; sadism

CRUMBLY: **a.** frangible; friable; pulverous; pulverulent

CRUSADER: **n.** Messiah; messiahship; **a.** CRUSADING: evangelical; evangelistic; messianic; zealous

CRUSH: **see** "annihilate" **and** "pulverize"

CRUTCH: **n.** prosthesis

CRY(ING): **n.** deploration; lachrymation; lacrimation; lamentation; ululation; **a.** lachrymal; lacrimal; lachrymose; lachrymatory; lacrimatory; larmoyant

CULMINATION: **(see** "acme") **n.** apogee; climacteric; climacterium; climax; consummation; meridian; zenith; **a.** CULMINANT: climacteric

CULTURE(S), *assimilation of:* **n.** enculturation; socialization
human, study of: **n.** ethnology; **a.** ethnologic(al)
imparting of or conditioning to: **v.** acculturize; **n.** acculturation
lacking in: **(see** "uncouth") **a.** bourgeoise; Philistinic; Philistinish; **n.** Babbitt; grobian; Philistine
mingling or confusion of: **n.** Babelism; **v.** Babelize
trend of (gen. moral state, etc.): **n.** zeitgeist

CULTURED **a.** (a)esthetic; cultivated; literate; polished; refined; urbane
not: **see** "culture, lacking in"

CUNNING: **a.** artful; artistic; astucious; astute; callid; crafty; daedal(ian); daedalic; dexterous; diplomatic; duplicitous; expedient; ingenious; insidious; parlous; sagacious; unscrupulous; **n.** artifice; astucity; callidity; craftiness; dexterity; ingeniosity; ingenuity; insidiousness

CURABLE: **(see** "remedial") **a.** curative; medicable; remediable; sanable; sanative; sanatory; therapeutic(al); tractable; vulnerary; **a.** CURATIVE: **see** "healing"

CURE: **(see** "remedy") **n.** remediation
-all: **n.** catholicon; elixir; nostrum; panacea; theriac

CURIO: **n.** bibelot; bric-a-brac; curiosity; knickknack; virtu; **(pl.** objet d'art)

CURIOSITY: **n.** inquisitiveness; piquancy; prurience; pruriency; rarity; **(pl.** curiosa)
arousing: **a.** provocative; provocatory

CURIOUS: **a.** inquisitive; inquisitorial; piquant; provocative; prurient
person: **n.** Pandora; quidnunc

CURLY: **a.** convolute(d); crispate; oundy; **n.** convolution; crispation

CURRENT **(see** "modern") **a.** coetaneous; coeval; contemporaneous; contemporary; existing; extant; popular; prevailing; prevalent; topical; **n.** contemporaneity; modernity; prevalence; topicality

CURSED (or CURSING): (**see** "detestable) **a.** accursed; anathematic(al); comminatory; execrable; imprecatory; maledictory; odious; **v.** CURSE: anathematize; blaspheme; comminate; execrate; imprecate; maledict; objurgate; **n.** anathema(tization); blasphemy; contamination; denunciation; execration; imprecation; malediction; malison; scourge

person or thing which is (*cursed*): **n.** anathema

CURT: (**see** "terse") **a.** brusque; condensed; laconic(al); unceremonious

CURTAIL: **v.** abbreviate; abridge; truncate

CURVE: **v.** arcuate; circumflex; **n.** arcuation; circumflexion; convolution; flexure; parabola; sinuosity; **a.** CURVED (or CURVING): archiform; arcuate; circumflex; convolute(d); crescentic; curvaceous; falciform; flexuous; undulating

inward: **a.** involute(d); **n.** concavity; incurvation; involution

outward: **n.** convexity

CUSTODIAN: **n.** Cerberus; chaperone; claviger; concierge; guardian; shepherd; superintendent

CUSTOM(S): (**see** "habit") **n.** consuetude; habitude; habituation; mores; observance; patronage; praxis; precedent; prescription; protocol; rubric

according to: (**see** "customary") **adv.** *ad usum* (**abb.** *ad us.*) *ex more; comme il faut*

depicting local or regional in lit. or art: **n.** costumbrista

group: **n. pl.** conventionalities; ethos; mores

CUSTOMARY: **a.** censuetudinary; conventional; *de rigueur; de règle;* nomic; prescriptive; prevalent; traditional; **adv.** *ad amussim; ad us(um); ex more*

CUT *off:* **v.** abscind; abscise; amputate; **n.** ablation; (ab)scission; amputation

out: **v.** ablate; bowdlerize; emasculate; enucleate; excise; expurgate; extirpate; resect

short: **v.** abbreviate; decapitate; syncopate

CUTE: **see** "coy"

CUTTING: (**see** "keen") **a.** acrimonious; caustic; incisive; mordant; penetrating; piquant; poignant; sarcastic; trenchant; **n.** excision; extirpation; rescission; scission

down: **n.** retrenchment

in parts: **a.** disjunction; dismemberment; dissolution; disunion; excision; mutilation; sundering

CYCLE(S), *life, or of organism:* **n.** ontogeny; ontogenesis; **a.** ontogenetic

moving or arranged in: **a.** cyclic(al); periodical; rhythmic(al)

CYNIC: **n.** Antisthenes; Diogenes; misanthrope; skeptic; Timon; **a.** CYNICAL: derisive; ironical; misanthropic(al); pessimistic; sarcastic; sardonic; satirical; **n.** CYNICISM: Dadism; derision; irony; pessimism; sarcasm; sardonicism; satire

burlesquing: **a.** pangruelian; **n.** pangruelism; pangruelist

D

DABBLER: (**see** "collector") **n.** amateur; dilettante; novice; sciolist

DAILY: **a.** diurnal; quotidian
anything that occurs: **n.** quotidian
occurring twice: **a.** semidiurnal

DAINTY: (**see** "airy") **a.** decorous; etherial; exquisite; fastidious; gossamery; *recherché;* DAINTINESS: (**see** "delicacy") ethereality; *friandise*

DALLY: **v.** dawdle; loiter; philander; procrastinate; shilly-shally; vacillate

DALLYING, *relaxed:* **n.** desipience; desipiency; **a.** *dégagé;* desipient

DAMAGES, *payment for:* **n.** remuneration; reparation(s)

DAMAGING: (**see** "injurious") **a.** destructive; detrimental; hurtful; inimical; malignant; nocent; nocuous; noxious; prejudicial; venomous

DAMN: **see** "curse"

DAMNATION, *also place of:* **n.** perdition

DANCE, *belly:* **n.** *danse du ventre*
for two persons; **n.** *pas de deux*
of death: **n.** *danse macabre*
tea: **n.** *thé dansant*

DANCER(S), *ballet, esp. star:* **n.** *coryphée* **(fem.)**
responsive movement bet. two, or groups of: **n.** antiphony; **a.** antiphonal; antiphonic

DANCING: **n.** choreography; terpsichore
muse of: **n.** Terpsichore
pert. to: **a.** saltatorial; saltatory; terpsichorean

DANDRUFF, *covered w/:* **a.** furfuraceous; scurfy

DANDY: **n.** Beau Brummel; coxcomb; dandiprat; *incroyable;* jackanapes; macaroni; *petit-maître;* popinjay; **n.** DANDYISM: foppishness

DANGER: (**see** "peril") **n.** Charybdis; crisis; imperilment; insecurity; instability; jeopardy; **v. see** "endanger"
common, produces concord: commune periculum concordiam parit
hidden: **n.** *anguis in herba* (snake in the grass); Trojan horse
impending: **n.** powder keg; sword of Damocles; **a.** Damoclean
pushing to limit of: **n.** brinksmanship
serving as warning of: **a.** sematic; **n.** *memento mori;* skull and crossbones

DANGEROUS: (**see** "menacing") **a.** critical; formidible; hazardous; ignitable; imminent; jeopardous; parlous; periculous; perilous; precarious; venturesome; venturous; vulnerable; **n.** DANGEROUSNESS: criticality; ignitability; jeopardy; venturousness; vulnerability
situation: **n.** hazard; jeopardy; precipice
to morals or social welfare: **a.** pernicious; pestiferous; pestilent(ial)

DARE *to know:* **adv.** *aude sapere*

DARING: (**see** "bold" **and** "dangerous") **a.** (ad)venturous; audacious; courageous; fortitudinous; Icarian; intrepid; perilous; picaresque; unconventional
action: **n.** bravura; derring-do
or reckless experience: **n.** escapade
romantic story of: **n.** bravura; derring-do; *tour de force;* **a.** picaresque
show of: **n.** bravura; derring-do; *tour de force*

DARK: (**see** "gloomy") **a.** adiaphanous; adumbral; atramental; atramentous; caliginous; Cimmerian; fuliginous; ignorant; inexplicable; iniquitous (**see** "wicked"); murky; mysterious; opaque; sinister; somber; stygian; tenebrous *in color, complexion or cast:* **a.** nigrescent; swart(hy)

DARLING: **see** "favorite"

DARKEN: **v.** adumbrate; denigrate; obfuscate; obscure
as if by shadowing: **v.** obtenebrate

DARKNESS: (**see** "night") **n.** fuliginosity; nigrescence; nigritude; obscurity; tenebrosity
after, comes light: **adv.** *post tenebras lux*
causing: **a.** tenebrific
comparative: **n.** umbra(ge)
of complexion: **n.** nigrescence; **a.** nigrescent; swart(hy)
Prince of: **n.** Ahriman
surrounded by: **a.** benighted; unenlightened

DASH: (**see** "spirit") **n.** dollop
headlong: **n.** tantivy

DATA, *factual or speculative:* **n.** armentarium; (**pl.** armamentaria)

DATE, *out of:* **see under** "out"

DAUGHTER *or son, pert. to:* **a.** filial; sibling; **n.** sibling

DAWDLE: (**see** "dally" **and** "delay") **a. n. or v.** shilly-shally

DAWN: **n.** aurora; **a.** auroral; aurorean; eoan
before: **a.** antelucan
goddess of: **n.** Aurora; Eos

DAY, *live for or enjoy the:* **n.** *carpe diem; in diem vivere; in horam vivere*
lucky: **n.** *dies fa(u)stus*
occurring three times per: **a.** terdiurnal
of this: **a.** hodiernal
of wrath or judgment: **n.** *dies irae*
pert. to: (**see** "daily") **a.** diurnal
pert. to half a: **a.** semidiurnal
to day, from: **adv.** *de die in diem* (**abb.** d.d. in d.)
unlucky: **n.** *dies infa(u)stus;* (**pl.** *nefasti dies*)
w/o a (day) being set: **a.** *sine die*

DAYDREAM(ING): **n.** autism; introspection; introspectiveness; phantasm; phantasy; reverie; stargazing; woolgathering; **a.** autistic; introspective; phantasmal

DAYLIGHT, *in broad:* **adv.** *en plein jour*

DAZE: **see** "bewilder"

DAZZLING: **a.** foudroyant; fulgent; fulgurant; fulgurating; fulgurous; iridescent; meteoric; prismatic; pyrotechnic; radiant; resplendent; splendorous; **n.** DAZZLEMENT: radiance; resplendence; resplendency

DEAD: (**see** "death") **a.** *ad patres;* amort; barren; deceased; defunct; demised; deserted; exanimate; extinct; inanimate; inert; inorganic; insensible; insentient; irrevocable; lifeless; monotonous; moribund; unresponsive
abnormal attachment to (corpses, etc.): **n.** necrophilia(c); necrophilism
abnormal fear of: **n.** necrophobia
civilly (dead): **a.** *civiliter mortuus*
communication with (claimed): **n.** necromancy; **n.** necromancer; **a.** necromantic
fear of the: **n.** necrophobia
hymn to: **n.** requiem
place for: (**see** "cemetery") **n.** charnel house; ossuary
place for burial of honored: **n.** pantheon
prayer for: **n.** *requiescat; requiescat in pace* (**abb.** r.i.p.)
say nothing but good of: **adv.** *de mortuis nil nisi bonum*
world of the: **n.** netherworld
worship of or excessive reverence for: **n.** manism; necrolatry; **a.** manistic; necrolatrous

DEADEN: **v.** anesthesize; benumb; hebetate; obscure; obtund; paralyze; stupefy; **n.** anesthesia; hebetation; hebetude; stupefaction; **a.** anesthetic; obtund(ent); stupefacient

DEAD-END (or DEADLOCK): (**see** "impasse") **n.** cul-de-sac

DEADLY: **a.** baneful; cadaverous; devastating; fatal; feral; implacable; internecine; lethal; lethiferous; malignant; malicious; mortal; mortiferous; noxious; pernicious; pestilent(ial); stygian; terminal; venomous; viperish; **n.** DEADLINESS: fatality; lethality; mortality
less than: **a.** subcritical; sublethal

DEAF, *sign lang. of:* **n.** dactylology

DEAFNESS: **n.** surdity

DEAL: **see** "apportion"

DEAR: **see** "expensive"

DEATH: (**see** "dead") **n.** annihilation; consummation; *debitum naturae;* defunction; demise; evanishment; exitus; extinction; fatality; mortality; quietus; **a.** DEATHLESS: **see** "eternal"; **n.** DEATHLESS: eternality; imperishableness; perpetuity; **a.** DEATHLY: (*see* "deadly") cachectic; cadaverous; morbid; moribund; stygian; terminal
abnormal fear of: **n.** necrophobia; necrophobiac
abode after of unbaptised: **n.** limbo
after: **a.** *post-mortem; post obitum;* posthumous
appearance of face when near: **n.** Hippocratic facies; **a.** cadaverous
arising, continuing, born or published after: **a.** posthumous
be mindful of: memento mori
before: **a.** antemortem
characteristic of: (**see** "deadly") **a.** stygian
easy and painless: **n.** euthanasia
evidence of (*sometimes figurative*): **n.** rigor mortis
exam. after: **n.** autopsy; necropsy; post mortem; **a.** post-mortem
exempt from: **n.** immortability; immortality; **a.** immortal
fated or foredoomed to: **a.** fey; moribund
fear of: **n.** thanatophobia
-like: **see** "deathly"
likely to cause: **see** "deadly"
made by reason or in expectation of: **a.** *mortis causa*
made or done after: **a.** post-mortem; posthumous
mercy: **n.** euthanasia
notice of: **n.** obituary; necrology; **a.** obitual; obituary; **v.** obituarize
occurring after: **a.** post-mortem; posthumous
occurring before: **a.** premortal; premortem; preterminal
of a part (*local*): **n.** necrosis
pert. to: **a.** mortuary
poem, song or oration of mourning: **n.** elegy; monody; threnody; **a.** elegaic; monodic
rate: **n** mortality
resembling: **a.** thanatoid
stiffening of body after: **n.** rigor mortis
to the: **a.** *à outrance;* lethal; mortal; mortiferous
to the point of: **adv.** *à l'extrémité; in extremis*
warning or reminder of: **n.** *memento mori;* skull and crossbones

DEBASE: **v.** adulterate; bastardize; contaminate; corrupt; defame; deglamorize; degrade; demean; denigrate; deteriorate; discredit; dishonor; heathenize; humble; minimize; paganzie; pejorate; pervert; stigmatize; sully; vilify; vitiate; vulgarize; **n.** DEBASEMENT: adulteration; degeneracy; deglamorization; depravation; depravity; dishonor; humiliation; squalidity; squalor; **a.** **see** "degrading"

DEBATE: **v.** argue; deliberate; discuss; **n.** argumentation; controversy; dialectic; disputation; dissension; **a.** DEBATABLE: contentious; controversial; controvertible; dialectical; disputatious; dubious; dubitable; equivocal; forensic; polemical; questionable; quodlibetic(al)
pert. to or suitable for: **a.** forensic; quodlibetic(al)
practice of: **n.pl.** forensics; polemics

DEBILITY: (**see** "weakness") **n.** adynamia; asthenia; cachexia; cachexy; debilitation; decrepitude; enervation; impotence; impotency; languor; **a.** DEBILITATED: (**see** "weak") adynamic; asthenic; cachectic; impotent
general, or fatigue: **n.** adynamia; myasthenia; myasthenia gravis

DEBRIS: (**see** "rubbish") **n.pl.** detritus; fragments; oddments; orts; trivia

DEBTS, *able to pay:* **a.** solvent; **n.** solvency
unable to pay: **a.** insolvent; **n.** insolvency

DEBUTANTE: **n.** ingenue

DECADENT: (**see** "out-of-date") **a.** antediluvian; archaic; archaistic; *démodé; fin-de-siècle;* moribund; obsolescent; *passé;* **n.** DECADENCE: **see** "deterioration"

DECAMP: **see** "elope"

DECAY: (**see** "rot") **v.** disintegrate; putrefy; putresce; **n.** decadence; decadency; decomposition; decrepitude; *délabrement;*

deterioration; dilapidation; disintegration; dissolution; labefaction; necrosis; putrefaction; putrescence; putridity
from old age: **n.** consenescence; **a.** consenescent
not subject to: **a.** indefectible; **n.** indefectibility

DECAYING *matter, feeding on:* **a.** saprophagous; saprophytic
matter, thriving on: **a.** saprophytic; **n.** saprophyte

DECEIT: (**see** "deception") **n.** artifice; chicanery; circumvention; cozenage; defraudation; desipience; dissimulation; duplicity; fabrication; hypocrisy; imposture; indirection; inveiglement; legerdemain; mendacity; obliquity; perfidy; sinuosity; stratagem; tortuosity; **a.** DECEITFUL: (**see** "deceptive" **and** "tricky") dissimulative; duplicitous; gnathonic; mendacious; obliquitous; perfidious; **n.** DECEITFULNESS: (**see** "deception") disingenuity; dissimulation; duplicity; fraudulence; indirection; obliquity

DECEIVE: **v.** bamboozle; beguile; cajole; camouflage; circumvent; cozen; defraud; dissemble; dissimulate; double-cross; ensnare; inveigle; mislead; outwit; victimize; **n.** DECEIVER: charlatan; dissembler; dissimulator; imposter; mountebank; rogue

DECENT: **a.** adequate; appropriate; chaste; decorous; demure; **n.** DECENCY: decorum; modesty; propriety; pudency; (**pl.** conventionalities; conventions; decencies; decora; proprieties)

DECEPTION: (**see** "deceit" **and** "trickery") **n.** artifice; bamboozlement; camouflage; chicanery; cozenage; defraudation; dissimulation; duplicity; fourberie; gambit; hanky-panky; hocus-pocus; ignis fatuus; legerdemain; mirage; obliquity; phonus-bolonus; prestidigitation; simulation; sinuosity; speciosity; stratagem; subterfuge; will-of-the-wisp
act of: **n.** beguilement; defraudation; duplicity; ludification; speciosity; triplicity
of the eye, as by painting: **n.** *trompe l'oeil*

DECEPTIVE: (**see** "misleading") **a.** alluring; barmecidal; cabalistic; clandestine; deceptious; dissembling; duplicitous; fallacious; illusional; illusory; mendacious; sirenic(al); specious; surreptitious

DECIDE: **see** "determine"
inability to: (**see** "waver") **n.** indecision; irresolution; vacillation
power to: **n.** discretion; **a.** discretionary
question or case: **v.** adjudicate; **n.** adjudication; **a.** adjudicative

DECIDED: (**see** "decisive") **n.** *fait accompli; res judicata*
that which can be: **a.** justiciable; resoluble; **n.** justiciability; resolubility

DECIDING, *act of:* **n.** adjudication; arbitrament; determination; umpirage; volition

DECISION: **n.** adjudication; arbitrament; conclusion; definitude; determination; judgment; mandate; resolution; settlement
irrevocable: **n.** (crossing the) Rubicon; point of no return

DECISIVE: (**see** "conclusive" **and** "final") **a.** absolute; authoritative; categorical; clear-cut; conclusive; crucial; definitive; determinative; implacable; indomitable; inexorable; unalterable; unmistakable; unequivocal
blow or answer: **n.** sockdolager
or authoritative group or tribunal: **n.** Aerophagus; **a.** Aerophagitic; **n.** Aerophagite
period or stage: **see** "crisis"
ultimately: **a.** apocalyptic(al)

DECLAMATORY: **a.** bombastic; Ciceronian; elocutionary; grandiloquent; oratorical; rhetorical

DECLARE: **v.** annunciate; asseverate; nuncupate; predicate; proclaim; promulgate; **n.** DECLARATION: manifesto; white paper; **a.** DECLARATORY: affirmative; assertorial; assertive; enunciative; expository; proclamatory
positively: **v.** asseverate; **n.** asseveration; **a.** asseverative

DECLINE: (**see** "decrease") **v.** degenerate; renege; retrocede; retrogress; retrograde; **n.** DECLINATION: decadence; degeneration; degenerescence; degradation; *dégringolade;* demotion; retrocession; retrogression
gradual, as fever or disease: **n.** lysis
in function, as organ or body; **n.** involution

period of: **n.** decadence; decadency; involution; **a.** decadent; involutional
rapid: **n.** *dĕgringolade*

DECORATE: **v.** adorn; embellish; emblazon; enrich; furbish; ornament; **n.** DECORATION: adornment; atmosphere; caparison; citation; decor; embellishment; emblazonment; embroidery; garnish(ment); garniture; medallion; **a.** DECORATIVE: **see** "attractive"

DECORUM: **see** "propriety"

DECREASE: (**see** "lessen") **v.** abate; diminish; dwindle; **n.** abatement; attenuation; declination; decrement; decrescence; decrescendo; degregation; degression; depreciation; diminuendo; diminution; retrenchment; retrogression; **a.** DECREASING: declinatory; decrescendo; decrescent; degressive; diminishing; reductionistic; reductive
gradual: **a.** or **n.** decrescendo; diminuendo; **n.** lysis

DECREE: **n.** decretum; fiat; judgment; mandate; ordinance; proclamation; pronouncement; pronunciamento

DECRY: **see** "belittle"

DEDICATE: **v.** consecrate; enshrine; hallow; sanctify; **a.** DEDICATORY: consecratory; dedicatorial; **n.** DEDICATION: consecration; devotion; devotement; enthusiasm; faithfulness; sanctification

DEDUCE: **v.** conclude; estimate; hariolate; **a.** **see** "deductive"; **n.** DEDUCTION: abatement; corollary; deductibility; hariolation; inference; inferentiality

DEDUCTIVE: **a.** deducible; illative; inferential
logic or reasoning: **n.** *a priori;* apriority; syllogism; synthesis; **a.** *a priori;* aprioristic; syllogistic(al)

DEED(S): **n.** achievement; exploit; gest(e); performance; *res geste;* transaction; **n.pl.** acta
justified by result: exitus acta probat
not words: facta non verba
not words are needed: non verbis sed factis opus est

DEEP: (**see** "mysterious") **a.** abstruse; abysmal; cavernous; hermetic(al); penetrating; profound; recondite; subterranean; unfathomed; **n.** (**see** "depth") bottomless
-bosomed: **a.** bathycolpian; pneumatic
-seated: **a.** adamant; chronic; confirmed; habitual; ingrained; inveterate; irradicable; obstinate; subterranean

DEEPEST *distress, from:* **n.** *de profundis*

DEEPNESS: (**see** "depth") **n.** abstrusity; profundity

DEFACE: **see** "disfigure"

DEFAME: (**see** "libel") **v.** asperse; calumniate; denigrate; disparage; malign; revile; slander; sully; traduce; vilify; **n.** DEFAMATION: aspersion; denigration; **a.** DEFAMATORY: calumnious; denigratory; slanderous; libelous

DEFEAT: (**see** "baffle") **v.** checkmate; conquer; frustrate; nullify; overcome; overthrow; subjugate; surmount; **n.** bouleversement; debacle; defeasance; discomfiture; downfall; frustration; labefaction; overthrow; repulse; subjugation; Waterloo
fear of: **n.** defeatism; **a.** or **n.** defeatist

DEFECT: (**see** "blemish" **and** "weakness") **n.** deficiency; foible; handicap; impediment; lacuna; shortcoming
because of a: **adv.** *propter defectum*
free of: (**see** "flawless") **a.** immaculate

DEFECTIVE: (**see** "imperfect") **a.** deficient; impedimental; incomplete; infelicitous; insufficient; lacunal; lacunar; *manqué;* mediocre; unsound; **n.** DEFECTIVENESS: defectibility
biologically: **a.** dysgenic

DEFENSE: **n.** aegis; apologia; argument; bulwark; extenuation; justification; (**pl.** apologetics; apologiae); **a.** DEFENSELESS: exposed; impotent; vulnerable; **n.** DEFENSELESSNESS: impotence; impotency; vulnerability; **a.** DEFENSIBLE: **see** "reasonable"
incapable of: (**see** "defenseless") **a.** indefensible; inexcusable; unjustifiable; untenable
means of: **n.** armament; (**pl.** armamen-

taria); *matériel;* muniment; munitions; weaponry
position for: **n.** *en garde*
systematic, as of a doctrine or particular action(s) : **n.pl.** apologetics

DEFER: **v.** capitulate; continue; intermit; postpone; prorogue; surrender; temporize; **n.** continuance; prorogation

DEFERENCE: **n.** capitulation; deferentiality; devoir; fealty; homage; humility; obeisance; veneration; **a.** DEFERENTIAL: reverential; venerative

DEFIANT: (**see** "bold") **a.** antagonistic; audacious; challenging; insolent; recalcitrant; refractory; **n.** DEFIANCE: audacity; challenge; confrontation; effrontery; impudence; opposition; refractoriness; temerity

DEFICIENT: (**see** "defective") **a.** mediocre; **n.** DEFICIENCY: dearth; *faiblesse;* foible; handicap; impediment; imperfection; inadequacy; lacuna; *manqué;* ullage; weakness
biologically or racially: **a.** dysgenic

DEFILE: **v.** befoul; contaminate; pollute; ravish; tarnish; violate; vitiate; **a.** DEFILED: contaminated; maculate; polluted; vitiated; **n.** DEFILEMENT: contamination; corruption; pollution

DEFINE: **v.** circumscribe; delineate; diagnose; diagnosticate; distinguish; identify; interpret
what is to be (defined) : **n.** definiendum
what serves to: **n.** defimens

DEFINING *technical terms, science of:* **n.** orismology; **a.** orismological

DEFINITE: **a.** absolute; circumscribed; cogent; definitive; determinate; determinative; dogmatic(al); explicit; material; mathematical; objective; particular; positive; tangible; unqualified; **n.** DEFINITENESS: (de)finitude; finality; inevitability; precision; tangibility

DEFLATED: **a.** kaput

DEFRAUD: (**see** "cheat") **v.** cozen; victimize; **n.** DEFRAUDATION: cozenage; defraudment

DEFY: **see** "oppose"

DEGENERATE: (**see** "decay") **a.** corrupt(ed); devitalized; effete; retrograde; **n.** DEGENERACY: *abâtardissement;* declination; degeneration; profligacy; retrogression

DEGRADE: (**see** "debase") **v.** demean; demote; denigrate; humble; humiliate; imbrute; pejorate; relegate; **n.** DEGRADATION: debasement; declination; humiliation; pejoration; squalidity; squalor; **a.** DEGRADING: (**see** "dishonorable") humiliating; humiliative; ignoble; ignominious; menial; mortifying; sordid; squalid

DEGREE: **see** "measure"
bachelor's: **a.** or **n.** baccalaureate

DEHUMANIZE: **v.** automate; automatize; barbarize; brutalize; mechanize; robotize

DEIFY: (**see** "exalt") **v.** apotheosize; canonize; enshrine; hallow; sanctify; spiritualize; transcend; transfigure; **n.** DEIFICATION: apotheosis; canonization; sanctification; transfiguration

DEITY: **see** "god"
evil: **n.** (**see** "devil") Ahriman; caco-d(a)emon
good: **n.** agathod(a)emon; ormuzd
local: **n.** numen

DEJECT: **v.** discourage; dishearten; dispirit; **a.** DEJECTED: abased: *à la mort;* disconsolate; disheartened; dispirited; funereal; humbled; inconsolable; inconsolate; melancholic; melancholy; prostrate; **n.** DEJECTION: **see** "depression" **and** "gloominess"

DELAY: **v.** continue; defer; impede; postpone; procrastinate; protract; retard; temporize; **n.** armistice; continuance; cunctation; deferment; detention; impediment; moratorium; obstructionism; postponement; procrastination; protraction; respite; retardation; suspension; temporization; **a.** DELAYING: impedimental; obstructive; procrastinating; procrastinatory; protractive
inexcusable: **n.** laches
there's danger in: periculum in morâ
without: **adv.** instanter; *sine morâ*

DELEGATE: **v.** commission; commit; depute; **n.** commissioner; deputy; representative; surrogate; **a.** DELEGATED: deputed; substitutionary; vicarial; vicarious

DELIBERATE: **v.** excogitate; meditate; ponder; **a.** (**see** "intentional") calculated; considered; premeditated; studied; **n.** DELIBERATION: attention; deliberateness; excogitation; ponderation; premeditation; reflection

DELICACY: **n.** *bonne bouche;* confection; *délicatesse;* ethereality; fragility; *friandise;* kickshaw; tidbit
extreme: **n.** fastidiousness; meticulosity; overniceness; overnicety; preciosity; squeamishness

DELICATE: (**see** "dainty") **a.** epicene; ethereal; fastidious; fragile; overnice; precarious; refined; sensitive; squeamish; superfine; uncertain

DELICIOUS: (**see** "appetizing") **a.** ambrosiac; ambrosial; delectable; delightful; enchanting; esculent; nectarean; nectareous; palatable; savory

DELIGHT: (**see** "charm") **n.** delectation; ecstasy; exuberance; exultation; festivity; gratification; jubilation; merriment; oblectation; rapture; ravishment; transport; **a.** DELIGHTFUL: delectable; delicious; Edenic; entrancing; felicitous; gratifying; luscious; paradisiacal

DELIRIOUS: **a.** frantic; frenetic(al); maniac(al); phrenetic(al); rabid; **n.** DELIRIUM: **see** "frenzy"

DELIVERANCE: **n.** atonement; emancipation; exoneration; extrication; liberation; manumission; reclamation; redemption; salvation; **a.** emancipative; extricable; redemptive; redemptory; salvatory; salvific

DELUDE: (**see** "deceive") **v.** bamboozle; circumvent; cozen; mislead; victimize; **n.** DELUSION: (**see** "deception") artifice; chimera; circumvention; cozenage; hallucination; *ignis fatuus;* illusion; phantasm(agoria); phantasma; (**pl.** phantasmata); wile; will-of-the-wisp; **a.** DELUSIVE: beguiling; deceptive; delusional; delusory; fallacious; phantasmagoric(al); unrealistic

DEMAGOGUE: **n.** ochlocrat; rabble-rouser; **a.** DEMAGOGIC(AL) rabble-rousing; **n.** DEMAGOGISM: demagogery; demagogy

DEMAND: (**see** "pray") **v.** expostulate; importune; necessitate; **a.** DEMANDING: (**see** "persistent") arduous; clamorous; exacting; importunate; onerous; taxing; vociferous

DEMOCRATIC: **a.** egalitarian; equalitarian; **n.** democratization; egalitarianism; *égalité;* popularization

DEMON(S): **see** "devil"
abode of all: **n.** pandemonium; **a.** pandemoniac(al)
like or pert. to: **a.** demoniac(al); demonic(al); fiendish; frantic; frenzied
lore of: **n.** diablerie; diabology
worship of: **n.** demonolatry

DEMONSTRATION: **n.** apod(e)ixis; effusion; effusiveness; exhibition; manifestation; **v.** DEMONSTRATE: exhibit; manifest; promulgate; reflect; **a.** DEMONSTRATIVE: (**see** "theatrical") apod(e)ictic(al); deictic; effusive; epideictic; exhibitive; gushing; overflowing; probative; unreserved; unrestrained
capable of: **a.** apodictic(al)

DEMORALIZING: **see** "corrupt"

DEMOTE: (**see** "depreciate") **v.** denigrate; minify; minimize; pejorate; **n.** DEMOTION: denigration; pejoration; relegation

DENIAL: **n.** (ab)negation; denegation; disaffirmance; disaffirmation; disavowal; disclaimer; renunciation; repudiation; **a.** disclamatory; elenc(h)tic; renunciative; renunciatory
self-: **see under** "self"
that admits or involves affirmative implication: **n.** negative pregnant

DENOUNCE: (**see** "censure") **v.** abrade; comminate; delate; denunciate; excoriate; inveigh; lambaste; stigmatize

DENSE: **see** "stupid"

DENUNCIATION(S): (**see** "accusation") **n.** anathema; commination; diatribe; fulmination; invective; vituperation; **a.** DENUNCIATORY: anathematic(al); comminatory; denunciative; fulminous; vituperative
shout or thunder forth: **v.** fulminate; **a.** fulminous; **n.** fulmination

DENY: (**see** "denial") **v.** abjure; (ab)negate; disclaim; disown; gainsay; renege; repudiate
not possible to: **a.** incontrovertible; irrefrangable; irrefutable

DEPENDABLE: **a.** authentic; authoritative; calculable; inerrable; inerrant; inerratic; infallible; predictable; trustworthy; yeomanly; **n. see** "reliability"

DEPENDANCE: **n.** reliance; relativity; succorance

DEPENDENT: **a.** adjective; adjectival; auxiliary; circumstantial; collateral; contingent; derivative; subsidiary; succursal
mutually: **a.** complementary; symbiotic(al)
servile: **n.** minion

DEPLORABLE: (**see** "wretched") **a.** calamitous; contemptible; despicable; disreputable; execrable; grievous; lamentable; odious; shocking; unfortunate; **n.** DEPLORATION: bewailment; lamentation

DEPORTMENT: (**see** "bearing") **n.** address; behavior; comportment; demeanor; mien

DEPOSIT: (**see** "sediment") **n.** deposition

DEPRAVE: **v.** corrupt; demoralize; depreciate; malign; pervert; pollute; **a.** DEPRAVED: (**see** "lewd") degenerate; dissolute; Neronian; putrid; vitiated; **n.** DEPRAVITY: degeneracy; demoralization; iniquity; putridity; turpitude

DEPRECIATE: (**see** "demote") **v.** denigrate; deprecate; disparage; minify; minimize; pejorate; revile; traduce; undervalue; vilify; vilipend; **n.** DEPRECIATION: denigration; disparagement; pejoration

DEPRESS: **v.** degrade; deject; dishearten; dispirit; humble; **a.** DEPRESSED: (**see** "sad") *à la mort;* dejected; dispirited; downcast; melancholic; vaporish; **a.** DEPRESSING: dispiriting; melancholy; *triste*

DEPRESSION: **n.** dejection; dispiritedness; doldrums; downswing; humiliation; mortification; nadir; *taedium vitae; tristesse*
greatest depth of: **n.** nadir
of spirit(s) **n.** melancholia; melancholy; (**pl.** doldrums; megrims)

DEPRIVATION *of authority:* **n.** deposition; dispossession; divestation; divestiture

DEPRIVING, *or tending to:* **a.** divestive; privative

DEPTH(S): **n.** abstrusity; acumen; acuteness; penetration; perspicacity; profundity
great: (**see** "deep") **n.** profundity
out of the: **adv.** *de profundis*

DEPUTY: (**see** "delegate") **n.** surrogate; representative

DERANGED: (**see** "disordered") **a.** *détraqué;* maniac(al); psychopathic

DERISION: **n.** asteism; burlesk; burlesque; caricature; contumely; denigration; irrision; ridicule; **a.** DERISIVE: ironical; irrisory; sarcastic; sardonic; satiric(al); scurrilous

DERIVATION: (**see** "descent" **and** "lineage") **n.** epiphenomenon; etiology; etymology; genesis; lineage; pedigree; provenance; stemma; **a.** DERIVATIVE: derivational; epiphenomenal; etiological; secondary; supplemental

DESCARTE'S *philosophy:* **n.** *cogito ergo sum*

DESCENDANT(S): **n.** issue; progeny; posterity; (s)cion; (**pl.** *les arrière-neveux*)

DESCENT: (**see** "derivation") **n.** ancestry; declension; declination; declivity; degradation; extraction; lineage; origination; pedigree; phylum; stemma; **a.** declinatory; declivitous
connect by: **v.** apparent; **n.** apparentation; derivation
fr. promising to disappointing: **n.** anticlimax; bathos; **a.** anticlimactic(al); bathetic
line of: **n.** ancestry; lineage; pedigree; **a.** phyletic
sudden: **n.** anticlimax; **a.** anticlimactic(al); bathetic
thru father: **a.** patrilineal; patrilinear
thru mother: **a.** matrilineal; matrilinear

DESCRIPTION: **n.** delineation; depiction; portraiture; portrayal; portrayment; **v.** DESCRIBE: delineate; depict; portray
vivid picturesque: **n.** hypotyposis

DESCRIPTIVE: **a.** delineative; descriptory; illuminating; illuminative; picturesque
list: **n.** *catalogue raisonné*

DESECRATION: (**see** "debasement") **n.** defilement; profanation; violation; vulgarization; **a.** profanatory

DESERT: **v.** abandon; abdicate; abscond; absquatulate; decamp; elope; forsake; renege; **n.** DESERTER: apostate; renegade; turncoat; **n.** DESERTION: abandonment; abdication; abrogation; abscondence; absentation; absquatulation; apostasy; defection; renunciation; tergiversation
a cause, party, etc.: **v.** apostasize; tergiversate

DESERVED: **a.** condign; merited; warranted

DESIGN: (**see** "purpose") **n.** arrangement; decoration; delineation; intendment; motif; scheme; DESIGNING: **see** "crafty"
evidence of in nature: **n.** teleology; **a.** teleological

DESIGNATE: **v.** circumscribe; identify; nominate; signify; specify; stigmatize; stipulate; **n.** DESIGNATION: (**see** "name") assignment; circumscription; connotation; nomination; specification; stipulation

DESIRABLE: (**see** "attractive") **a.** advantageous; advisable; appetible; appetitious; desiderative; expedient; optative; optimal; orective
less than: **a.** suboptimal; **a. or n.** suboptimum

DESIRE: **v.** covet; crave; desiderate; **n.** appetency; appetibility; appetite; appetition; aspiration; desideration; (**pl.** desiderata); Eros; inclination; orexis; passion; proclivity; propensity
appealing to: **a.** appetible; appetitive; **n.** appetibility
ardent: **n.** aspiration; desiderium; **a.** aspirational; desiderative
expressing: **a.** optative
habitual or uncontrollable: **n.** cacoethes
having great: **a.** gluttonous; insatiable; omnivorous; voracious; **n. see** "gluttony"
innate: **n.** conatus
lack of: **n.** inappetence
pert. to: **a.** appetitive; desiderative; epithumetic; orectic
sexual: **n.** concupiscence; Eros; libido
strong: **n.** appetency; appetition; desiderium; (**pl.** desiderata; desideria); **a.** appetitious
unsatisfied: **n.** insatiability; insatiety; **a.** insatiable
very weak: **n.** velleity

DESIRED, *something to be:* **n.** desideratum; desiderium; (**pl.** desiderata; desideria); optative

DESOLATE: (**see** "barren") **a.** dejected; *désolé;* melancholy; *triste*

DESPAIR: **n.** (**see** "depression") desperation; futility; hopelessness
expression of: **n.** *de profundis*
fashionable: **n.** *fin-de-siècle*
in: **adv.** *au désespoir;* **n.pl.** doldrums; megrims
never: **adv.** *nil desperandum*

DESPERATELY: **adv.** *à corps perdu;* appallingly; compelling; impetuously; indispensably; intensely; **a.** DESPERATE: (**see** "helpless") crucial; despondent; outrageous; overmastering; overpowering; **n.** DESPERATION: (**see** "despair") cruciality

DESPISABLE: **a.** contemptible; contemptuous; contumelious; despicable; execrable; leprous

DESPITE: **prep.** *malgré;* notwithstanding

DESPONDENT: **a.** disconsolate; discouraged; disheartened; dispirited; forlorn; hypochondriacal; melancholy; **n.** DESPONDENCY: apathetic inertia; dejection; dispiritment; hypochondriasis; melancholia; melancholy; (**pl.** doldrums; megrims)

DESPOT: **n.** anarch; autarch; authoritarian; autocrat; disciplinarian; martinet; rigorist; satrap; totalitarian; tyrant; **n.** DESPOTISM: absolutism; autocracy; totalitarianism; tyranny

DESPOTIC: **a.** absolute; absolutistic; anarchistic; arbitrary; autarchic(al); authoritarian; autocratic; dictatorial; dogmatic; domineering; hierarchic(al); imperative; imperious; Neronian; peremptory; rigorist(ic); totalitarian; tyrannical
official: **n.** satrap; totalitarian; **n.** satrapy

DESTINATION: **(see** "goal") **n.** terminus; *terminus ad quem*

DESTINY: **(see** "fate") **n.** doom; fortune
Hindu: **n.** karma
individual: **n.** *moira;* (**pl.** moirae)
of man, study or science of: **n.** eschatology; **a.** eschatological

DESTITUTE: **(see** "poor") **a.** impecunious; impoverished; indigent; **n.** DESTITUTION: **(see** "poverty") impecuniosity; impecuniousness; indigence; insolvency; mendicancy; pauperism; penury; squalor

DESTROY: **v.** annihilate; decapitate; deracinate; devastate; eradicate; exterminate; extirpate; immolate; **a.** DESTROYED: decimated; devastated; eradicated; kaput; **n.** DESTROYER: predator
large number: **v.** decimate; **n.** decimation

DESTRUCTION: **n.** annihilation; cataclysm; corrosion; demolition; deracination; devastation; dissolution; extinction; extirpation; immolation; invalidation; perdition
capacity for: **n.** destructivity
great or widespread: **n.** catastrophe; cataclysm; *götterdämmerung;* holocaust
malicious, of materials, machinery, etc.: **v. or n.** sabotage
place of: **see** "hell"

DESTRUCTIVE: **(see** "deadly") **a.** annihilative; annihilatory; baneful; corrosive; deleterious; devastating; devastative; inimical; malignant; noxious; pernicious; ruinous; subversive
metabolism: **n.** catabolism
mutually: **a.** internecine
of life: **(see** "deadly") **a.** lethal; malignant; pernicious; pestilent; pestiferous

DETACHED: **(see** "separate") **a.** aloof; discrete; dissociated; disunited; enisled; fragmented; hermetic(al); insular; insulated; isolated; segregated; unaffiliated; unbiased; **n.** DETACHMENT: abruption; dissociation; disunion; fragmentation; indifference; insularity; isolation; segregaton; unworldliness

DETAIL(S): **n.** circumstance; circumstantiality; meticulosity; minutia(e); particular(ity); specificality; **v.** particularize
excessively careful about: **a.** chromatic; finical; meticulous; minutiose; minutious; picayune; rabbinic(al); scrupulous
small: **n.** minutia; (**pl.** inconsequentia; minutiae; particularities; trivia[lities])

DETECT: **v.** apprehend; ascertain; descry; discern; elicit; unmask; **n.** DETECTION: ascertainment; discernment; discovery; elicitation; revelation; **a.** DETECTIVE: discerning; revelative; revelatory

DETERIORATION: **(see** "declination") **n.** decadence; declension; degeneration; degenerescence; *dégringolade; délabrement;* labefaction; retrocession; retrogression; **a.** DETERIORATING: decadent; declensional; declinatory; degenerative; deteriorative; retrograde; retrogressive

DETERMINE: **v.** adjudicate; ascertain; dijudicate; foreordain; regulate; resolve; **n.** DETERMINATION: **(see** "decision") conclusion; impulsion; resoluteness; resolution
nature or cause: **v.** diagnosticate; **a.** diagnostic; pathognomonic(al)

DETERMINED (**or** DETERMINING): **a.** decisive; definitive; dominative; foreordained; immovable; indomitable; predestined; peremptory; resolute; resolved; tenacious; unalterable; unwavering
person: **n.** Trojan

DETEST: **(see** "hate" **and** "loathe"); **a.** DETESTABLE: **(see** "bad") abhorrent; abominable; anathematic(al); contemptible; despicable; execrable; grievous; imprecatory; loathsome; odious; **n.** DETESTATION: abhorrence; abomination; anathema; contempt; despicability; loathsomeness; odium
person or thing (*detested*): **n.** abomination; anathema

DETRACT: **(see** "debase") **v.** calumniate; defame; denigrate; derogate; disparage; minify; minimize; **a.** DETRACTING:

denigratory; derogative; derogatory; disparaging; **n.** DETRACTION: (**see** "censure") calumny; denigration; derogation; disparagement; subtraction

DETRIMENTAL: (**see** "adverse") **a.** baneful; deleterious; hurtful; inimical; injurious; malefic; malignant; nocuous; noisome; pernicious; prejudicial

DEVELOP: **v.** burgeon; differentiate; evolve; effloresce; expound; flourish; incubate; maturate; mature
fail to: **v.** abort

DEVELOPED: **a.** culminant; differentiated; matured
in course of being: **adv.** *in statu nascendi;* **a.** aborning; burgeoning; florescent; maturescent; nascent; parturient
prematurely: **a.** precocious; **n.** precocity

DEVELOPMENT: (**see** "advancement") **n.** consummation; differentiation; evolution; florescence; incubation; maturation; maturescence; maturity; morphosis; ontogeny
capable of: **a.** viable; **n.** viability
in course of: **see under** "developed"
mode of, as organism or part: **n.** morphosis; **a.** morphotic
path or line of: **n.** trajectory
period of in young: **n.** puberty; pubescence; **a.** maturescent; pubertal; pubescent

DEVIATING: (**see** "devious" **and** "straying") **a.** aberrant; circuitous; divaricative; divergent; excursional; excursionary; excursive; parenthetic(al); serpentine; tortuous; **n.** DEVIATION: aberrance; aberration; circuity; detour; divergence; divigation; eccentricity; intransigence; sinuosity; tangency; tortuosity
fr. previous course: **a.** aberrant; tangent; **n.** aberration; tangency
fr. principles or rules: **a.** (ab)errant; aberrative; heteroclite; obliquitous; **n.** deviate; deviationist; heteroclite

DEVICE: **n.** accouterment; artifice; contrivance; insigne; (**pl.** insignia); invention; machination; stratagem

DEVIL(S): **n.** Apollyon; Beelzebub; Belial; cacod(a)emon; Diabolus; incubus (**pl.** incubi); Lucifer; Mephistopheles; succubus (**pl.** succubi)
advocate: **n.** *advocatus diaboli*
crafty and malevolent: **n.** Mephistopheles; **a.** Mephistophelian
follower of: **n.** diabolonian
govt. by: **n.** diabolarchy; diabolocracy
one possessed of: **n.** energumen
study of: **n.** demonology; demonologist; diabology
to pay, the: **n.** *diable à quatre; faire le diable à quatre*
work of: **n.** diablerie
worshipper of: **n.** diabolist; **n.** demonolatry

DEVILISH: (**see** "fiendish") **a.** demoniac(al); demonic(al); diabolic(al); diabolonian; ghoulish; hellish; infernal; Luciferian; malicious; Mephistophelian; Satanic(al); saturnine; **n.** DEVILTRY (**or** DEVILRY) diablerie; diabolism

DEVIOUS: (**see** "roundabout") **a.** ambagious; anfractuous; circuitous; labyrinthian; labyrinthine; louche; oblique; perverse; serpentine; sinister; sinuate; sinuous; tortuous; unscrupulous; **n.** DEVIOUSNESS: (**see** "deviation") anfractuosity; circuity; circumbendibus; indirection; sinuosity; tortuosity

DEVISE: **v.** bequeath; contrive; fabricate; machinate; premeditate
with evil intent: **v.** machinate; **n.** machination

DEVITALIZE: **v.** debilitate; desiccate; disembowel; emasculate; enervate; eviscerate; exenterate; **n.** DEVITALIZATION: **see** "weakness"

DEVOTEE: (**see** "follower") **n.** adherent; aficionado; (**fem.** aficionada); amateur; apostle; enthusiast; fanatic; liege man; minion; votary; zealot
fanatical or hired: **n.** energumen; mercenary; minion

DEVOTION: (**see** "worship") **n.** allegiance; enthusiasm; fealty; fidelity; loyalty; piety; reverence
fervent: **n.** fanaticism; fetishism; zealotry; **a.** fetishistic; zealous
to church, excessive: **n.** ecclesiolatry; religiosity; **a.** religiose

DEVOURING: **a.** annihilatory; consuming; corrosive; edacious; gluttonous; voracious

DEVOUT: **a.** devotional; pietistic(al); religiose; sacrosanct; sanctimonious
hypocritically: **a.** pietistic(al); religiose; sanctimonious; **n.** piosity; religiosity

DEW, *generating:* **a.** roriferous
rel. to: **a.** roric

DEXTERITY: **see** "agility"

DIAGNOSE: **v.** diagnosticate; identify; **a.** DIAGNOSTIC: distinctive; pathognomonic(al); prodromal; symptomatic

DIAGRAM: **n.** schema; (**pl.** schemata); **a.** diagrammatic(al); schematic

DIALECT(S), *local or provincial:* **n.** cant; colloquialism; jargon; vernacular(ism); vernacularity
student or study of: **n.** dialectologist; dialoctology; **a.** dialectological

DIALOGUE: **n.** causerie; collocution; colloquy; confabulation; interlocution
art of discussion and reason by: **n.** dialectics; **a.** dialectic(al)
pert. to: **a.** dialectic(al); dialogic; dialogistic; interlocutory

DIAMETRICALLY *opposite:* **a.** antipodal; antipodic; antithetic(al); **n.** antipode; antithesis

DIAMOND(S), *like in luster:* **a.** adamantine
to set with: **v.** diamondize
yielding: **a.** diamondiferous

DIARY, *private:* **n.** *journal intime*

DICE, *lowest number in:* **n.** ambsace

DICTATOR: **n.** anarch; authoritarian; autocrat; caudillo; commissar; despot; man on horseback; oligarch; tyrant; **a.** DICTATORIAL: arbitrary; authoritarian; autocratic; cavalier; despotic; doctrinaire; dogmatic(al); domineering; hierarchic(al); imperative; imperious; magisterial; oracular; overbearing; peremptory; totalitarian; **n.** DICTATORSHIP: absolutism; autocracy; Caesarism; monopolization; totalitarianism

DICTION: **n.** enunciation; phraseology; verbiage; vocabulary
bad: **n.** cacology

DICTIONARY, *author or compiler of:* **n.** lexicographer; lexicography
of names and terms: **n.** nomenclature; onomasticon
pert. to: **a.** lexicographic(al); Websterian

DIE *has been cast: jacta alea est*
we who are about to, salute: morituri te salutamus

DIET: **see** "menu"

DIFFER: **see** "disagree"

DIFFERENCE(S): (**see** "controversy") **n.** cleavage; differentia; discrepancy; discrimination; disparity; dissention; dissimilarity; dissimilitude; dissonance; distinction; divergence; diversity; heterogeneity; heterology; nuance; incongruity; inequality; (**pl.** differentiae)
in nature or kind: **n.** allogeneity; heterogeneity; **a.** allogeneous; heterogeneous
process of perceiving or expressing: **n.** differentiation
slight degree of: **n.** nuance
w/ the respective differences having been considered: mutatis mutandis

DIFFERENT: **a.** antipodal; antithetic(al); disparate; dissimilar; divergent; diverse; heterogeneous; heterologous; incongruent; incongruous; sundry
in operation or effect: **a.** heteropathic
quality or state of being: **n.** alterity; antipodes; antithesis; heterogeneity; incongruity

DIFFERING: **a.** antagonistic; differential; discordant; discrepant; discriminative; dissenting; dissonant; diverse; heterogeneous; incongruous; inharmonious; unharmonious
fr. standard(s) or norm: (**see** "impropriety") **a.** heteromorphic; **n.** heteromorphism; heteromorphosis; mutation; sport

DIFFICULT: (**see** "hard") **a.** arduous; devastating; exacting; formidable; frenetic; hectic; Herculean; incorrigible; intractable; intricate; involved; laborious; murderous; onerous; operose; overwhelming; perplexing; perverse; scabrous; strenuous; toilsome; unaccommodating; unmanageable; unyielding; vicissitudinous

position: **n.** dilemma; quagmire; quandary
problem: **n.** dilemma; entanglement; Gordian knot
route, passage, or series of experiences: **n.** *via dolorosa*

DIFFICULTY: (**see** "problem") **n.** dilemma; embarrassment; embroilment; entanglement; Gordian knot; imbroglio; impediment; maelstrom; obstacle; predicament; riptide; quagmire; quandary; strenuosity; vicissitude; vortex
in great: **adv.** *in extremis*
without: **adv.** *sans peine*

DIFFUSE: (**see** "wordy") **a.** osmotic; prolix; verbose; **n.** DIFFUSION: dispersion; dissemination; osmosis; prolixity; promulgation

DIG *up:* **v.** disentomb; disinter; exhume; **n.** exhumation

DIGESTION: **n.** assimilation; metabolism; **v.** DIGEST: assimilate; codify; comprehend; metabolize; **n.** (**see** "summary") abridgement; breviary; compilation; conspectus; pandect; prospectus; summation
having good: **a.** eupeptic; **n.** eupepsia
pert. to: **a.** peptic

DIGIT, *having but one (toe, finger, claw)*: **a.** monodactylous
having six: **n.** hexadactylism

DIGNITY: **n.** courtliness; decorum; eminence; ennoblement; gentility; grandeur; lordliness; majesty; nobility; solemnity; stateliness; (**pl.** amenities; civilities; convenances; conventions; decora; [the] proprieties); **v.** DIGNIFY: (**see** "exalt") aggrandize; ennoble; nobilitate; pedestal; **a.** DIGNIFIED: (**see** "stately") august; eminent; grandiose; imperial; magisterial; togated
affront to: **n.** *lèse majesté*
beneath one's: **a.** *infra dignitatem* (**abb.** infra dig.)
extreme or exaggerated: **n.** imperialism; magistrality; pomposity; pompousness; pontificality; pontification
high: **n.** sublimity
to maintain: se faire valoir

DIGRESS: **v.** detour; deviate; divaricate, divagate; diverge; meander; parenthesize; **n.** DIGRESSION: aberration; apostrophe; detour; discursion; divagation; divarication; ecbole; excursus; excursion, irrelevancy; parenthesis; tangency; tangent; **a.** DIGRESSIVE: aberrant; apostrophic; circuitous; devious; discursive; divaricative; divergent; excursional; excursionary; excursive; parenthetic(al); sinuous; tangent(i)al; Thackerayan; tortuous; vagrant
in rhetoric: **n.** ecbole; excursus
in speech or writing(s): **n.** apostrophe; excursus; **a.** apostrophic; excursive

DILAPIDATED: **a.** beggarly; disreputable; retrogressive; tatterdemalian; **n.** DILAPIDATION: **see** "decay"

DILEMMA: (**see** "predicament") **n.** nonplus; quagmire; quandary; **a.** DILEMMATIC: nonplussed

DILIGENT: **a.** assiduous; indefatigable; industrious; operose; painstaking; persevering; sedulous; solicitous; steadfast; **n.** DILIGENCE: (**see** "attention") assiduity; operosity; perseverance; sedulity; steadfastness

DILUTED: **a.** attenuated; homeopathic

DIM: (**see** "obscure") **v.** becloud; befog; eclipse; obfuscate; obnubilate; obscurify; **a.** caliginous; crepuscular; fuliginous; lackluster; opaque; **n.** DIMNESS: crepuscle; *demi-jour;* fuliginosity; nebulosity; obscuration

DIMINISHMENT: **n.** attenuation; declination; depreciation; diminuendo; diminution; extenuation; regression; retrenchment; **v.** DIMINISH: abate; attenuate; depreciate; dwindle; extenuate; palliate; recede, regress; retrench; **a.** DIMINISHING: ablatitious; decrescendo; diminuendo; extenuatory; regressive
in volume or force: **n.** or **a.** diminuendo

DIN: **see** "uproar"

DINING *hall:* **n.** refectory; *salle à manger*
science or art of: **n.** aristology

DINNER, *after:* **a.** postcibal; postprandial
before: **a.** precibal; preprandial

DIPLOMATIC *corps:* **n.** *corps diplomatique*

DIRE: (**see** "deadly") **a.** awesome; calamitous; catastrophic(al); cheerless; deplorable; desolate; desperate; disastrous; dispiriting; extreme; grievous; horrendous; horrific; implacable; mortal; overpowering

DIRECT: **v.** administer; focus; superintend; superscribe; supervise; **a.** absolute; categorical; explicit; immediate; pertinent; positive; unconditional; undeviating; unequivocal; **n.** DIRECTNESS: immediacy

DIRECTION: (**see** "control") **n.** command; inclination; objective; presidence; superintendence; superscription; supervision
maintenance of: **n.** directionality
reverse or change: **v.** commutate; **n.** commutation
to find right: **v.** orientate; **n.** orientation

DIRECTLY *opposite:* (**see** "diametrically opposite") **a.** antipodal; diametrical

DIRECTOR: **n.** administrant; comptroller; conductor; regisseur; superintendent
as opera: **n.** impresario

DIRGE: **see** "funeral ode or hymn"

DIRTY: **a.** Augean; bawdy; despicable; dishonorable; disreputable; excrementitious; feculent; filthy; immund; insanitary; ordurous; putrid; saprogenic; sordid; squalid; stercoraceous; unsportsmanlike; **n.** DIRTINESS: (**see** "filthiness") immundity; putridity; sordidness; squalidity; squalor

DISABLE: (**see** "weaken") **v.** disqualify; handicap; incapacitate; **a.** DISABLED: incapacitated; kaput; **adv.** *hors de combat;* **n.** DISABILITY: disadvantage; handicap; incapacity; incapacitation; invalidity
become (disabled): **v.** founder

DISAGREE: (**see** "dispute") **v.** contradict; contravene; **a.** DISAGREEING (or DISAGREEABLE): (**see** "discordant") antagonistic; disputatious; dissentient; dissenting; dissentious; dissentive; dissident; dissonant; distasteful; incompatible; incongruous; inconsistent; inconsonant; inharmonious; unharmonious; unpalatable; unpleasant; unsavory; **n.** DISAGREEMENT: (**see** "breach") contravention; *désagrément;* disharmony; disparity; disputation; dissentience; dissidence; dissonance; embroilment; entanglement; imbroglio; incompatibility; incongruity; inconsonance

DISAPPEARANCE: **n.** abscondence; depletion; diminution; evanishment; evanition

DISAPPOINTMENT: (**see** "defeat") **n.** anticlimax; bathos; contretemps; frustration; **a.** DISAPPOINTING: anticlimactic(al); bathetic; suboptimal

DISAPPROVAL: **n.** admonition; censure; condemnation; deprecation; disapprobation; reprobation; **v.** DISAPPROVE: (**see** "reject") censure; condemn; deprecate; discommend; discountenance; disparage; reprobate; **a.** DISAPPROVING: admonitory; censorious; deprecatory; deprecative; disapprobative; disapprobatory; **adv.** *en mauvaise odeur*
expression of: **adv. or n.** *à bas*

DISARRAY: (**see** "confusion") **n.** derangement; disarrangement; discomfiture; hodge-podge; mish-mash

DISASTER: **n.** adversity; calamity; cataclysm; catastrophe; debacle; holocaust; misadventure; mischance; **a.** DISASTROUS: calamitous; cataclysmal; cataclysmic; catastrophal; catastrophic(al); unpropitious
heightened point of action leading to: **n.** catastasis; epitasis
impending: **n.** imminence; sword of Damocles
sudden great: **n.** catastrophe; debacle; holocaust (*esp. fire*)

DISAVOWAL: **n.** disclamation; renunciation; repudiation

DISBELIEVER: (**see** "skeptic") **n.** agnostic; aporetic; dissenter; dissident; doubting Thomas; giaour; heretic; infidel; nullifidian; pyrrhonist; recusant; skeptic; theophobist; **n.** DISBELIEF: (**see** "doubt") incredibility; incredulity; misbelief; miscreance; skepticism; **a.** DISBELIEVING: **see** "skeptical"
(*freethinker*): **n.** latitudinarian

DISCARD(ING): (**see** "abandon") **n.** abandonment; banishment; defenestration; repudiation

DISCERNMENT: **n.** acumen; astucity; clairvoyance; clear-sightedness; detection; discrimination; judgment; penetration; perception; perspicacity; profundity; sagacity; sapiency; telegnosis; **a.** DISCERNING: analytical; astucious; astute; clairvoyant; discriminatory; discriminating; judicious; knowledgeable; penetrating; penetrative; perspicacious; sagacious; trenchant
impaired: **n.** astigmatism; impalpability; myopia; **a.** astigmatic(al); myopic

DISCHARGE: (**see** "dismissal") **n.** acquittance; elimination; profluvium

DISCIPLE: (**see** "follower" **and** "learner") **n.** adherent; apostle; proselyte; satellite; sectary; sectator; votary; **a.** DISCIPULAR: apostolic(al)

DISCIPLINARIAN, *strict:* **n.** martinet; precisian; rigorist; sabbatarian; tyrant

DISCIPLINARY: **a.** ascetic; austere; castigatory; disciplinatory; penitentiary; punitive
course or conduct: **n.** ascesis; asceticism; self-mortification

DISCIPLINE: **v.** castigate; chasten; chastise; **n.** (**see** "punishment") approach; castigation; chastenment; chastisement; method; self-restraint
subject to rigid: **v.** hierarchize; regiment

DISCIPLINED, *hardy:* **a.** *aguerri;* Spartan(ic)
self-: **a.** ascetic; **n.** ascesis; ascetic(ism); self-mortification

DISCLOSURE: **n.** apocalypse; divulgation; divulgence; exposition; exposure; manifestation; publication; revelation; **a.** DISCLOSING: expository; revelative; revelatory; **v.** DISCLOSE: (**see** "demonstrate") unbosom
prophetic: **n.** apocalypse; revelation; **a.** apocalyptic(al); apostolic(al); revelatory

DISCOLORATION *from bruise:* **n.** ecchymosis; petechia(e)
on skin: **n.** ecchymosis; macula; petechia(e); **a.** ecchymotic; petechial

DISCOMFORT: **n.** annoyance; chagrin; discomfiture; discomposure; disquietude; dysphoria; embarrassment; inquietude; malaise

DISCONNECTED: **a.** desultory; discrete; dissociated; disunited; fractional; rambling; staccato; **n.** DISCONNECTION: **see** "separation"

DISCONTENT(MENT): **n.** discomfiture; dissatisfaction; dysphoria; frustration; insubordination; malaise; sedition; **a.** DISCONTENTED: dissatisfied; insubordinate; malcontent; seditious; unsatisfied
stirring up: **a.** insubordinate; rebellious; seditious; turbulent

DISCONTINUE: (**see** "pause") **v.** abandon; intermit; interrupt; sever; surcease; suspend; terminate; **n.** DISCONTINUANCE: (**see** "removal") cessation; desistance; intermission; interruption; surcease; termination
from use: **v.** obsolesce; **n.** desuetude; obsolescence; **a.** archaic; obsolescent; obsolete
or end a session: **v.** prorogue; **n.** prorogation; *sine die*

DISCORD: **n.** antagonism; *brouillerie;* cacophony; disharmony; disruption; dissension; dissonance; incongruitv; inharmony; scission; variance; **a** DISCORDANT: (**see** "stubborn") absonant; cacophonous; contradictory; disputatious; dissociable; dissonant; gladiatorial; heterogeneous; incongruous; inconsonant; irreconcilable; quarrelsome
goddess of: **n.** Eris
harmony of (discordant harmony): **n.** *concordia discors*

DISCOURAGE: **v.** daunt; dishearten; dismay; dispirit; dissuade; intimidate; obstruct; **n.** DISCOURAGEMENT: (**see** "despondency") dissuasion

DISCOURSE: (**see** "lecture") **n.** conversation; descant; disquisition; dissertation; expiation; narration; treatise
formal: **n.** disquisition

DISCOURTESY: **n.** brusqueness; *brusquerie;* contumely; disrespect; impoliteness; incivility; insuavity; inurbanity; profanation; **a.** DISCOURTEOUS: **see** "disrespectful"

DISCOVER: **v.** ascertain; descry; determine; disinter; exhume; unearth; **n.** DISCOVERER: Columbus; pathfinder; trailblazer
by careful exam.: **v.** expiscate; **n.** expiscation; **a.** expiscatory

DISCOVERY: **n.** ascertainment; detection; disclosure; revelation
accidental: **n.** serendipity; **a.** serendipitous
helping, guiding or serving to: **a.** heuristic

DISCRETION: **n.** circumspection; diplomacy; finesse; moderation; prudence; restraint; **a.** DISCREET: (**see** "cautious" **and** "prudent") circumspect(ive); judicious; politic; reticent; silentious; taciturn
age of: **n.** *âge de raison*
marked by notable: **a.** Solomonic

DISCUSSION(S): (**see** "conversation") **n.** argumentation; colloquium; colloquy; confabulation; disputation; disquisition; exposition; expostulation; seminar; symposium; (**pl.** symposia); **v.** DISCUSS: confabulate; deliberate; expostulate
formal: **n.** disquisition; (**pl.** dialectics; forensics)
incidental: **n.** excursus
informal: **n.** causerie
on subtle or debatable point: **n.** quodlibet
pert. to: **a.** dialectic; forensic; quodlibetic
preliminary: **n.** pourparler
Socratic type: **n.** dialectics; **a.** dialectic(al)

DISEASE(S): **n.** affection; affliction; ailment; distemper; indisposition; infirmity; malady; malignancy; morbus; pathology; pathosis; visitation; **a.** DISEASED: contaminated; malignant; morbid; morbific(al); morbose; leprous; pathological; peccant; unwholesome
after-effects of: **n.** residual(s) residuum; sequala(e); **a.** residual; sequential
bringing, carrying or infected w/: **a.** pestiferous; pestilent(ial)
carrier: **n.** vector
causing or capable of causing: **a.** morbific(al); pathogenetic; pathogenic; **n.** pathogenicity
characteristic of a particular: **a.** pathognomonic(al); symptomatic
classification of: **n.** nosography; nosology; pathology
description of: **n.** nosography; nosology; pathology
imaginary: **n.** *malade imaginaire*
increase in: **n.** anabasis; exacerbation; **a.** anabatic; **v.** exacerbate
infectious or contagious: **a.** zymogenic; zymogenous; zymotic
made up of various symptoms: **n.** syndrome
not capable of causing: **a.** apathogenic; nonpathogenic; physiological; sterile
origination and development of: **n.** pathogenesis; pathogenicity; pathogeny; **a.** pathogen(et)ic; pathological
place of origin or orig. location: **n.** nidus; situs
produced by physician or treatment: **a.** iatrogenic
shifting in body location: **n.** metastasis; **v.** metastasize; **a.** metastatic
sign(s) of: **n.** stigma; (**pl.** stigmata); symptomatology
simulation of: **n.** malingering; pathomimesis
stage when outcome doubtful: **n.** amphibolia
study of: **n.** pathology
study of symptoms of: **n.** diagnostics; semeiotics; symptomatology
symptoms of: **n.** symptomatology; syndrome; **a.** diagnostic; pathognomonic(al); semeiotic; symptomatic; symptomatologic(al); syndromic
w/o recognized cause: **a.** essential; idiopathic

DISFAVOR: **n.** detriment; disadvantage; disesteem; disrepute; odium; **a.** detrimental; disadvantageous; disreputable; odious

DISFIGURE: **v.** maim; mutilate; scarify; uglify; **n.** DISFIGUREMENT: defacement; disfiguration; mayhem; scarification; uglification

DISGRACE: **v.** stigmatize; **n.** (**see** "contempt") dishonor; disrepute; ignominy; infamy; obloquy; odium; opprobrium; stigma; turpitude; **a.** DISGRACEFUL: (**see** "disreputable") criminal; dishonorable; ignominious; indign; infamous; inglorious; notorious; obloquious; opprobrious; shameful; stigmatical; unbecoming
mark of: **n.** odium; opprobrium; stigma; (**pl.** stigmata)

DISGUISE: **v. or n.** camouflage; counterfeit; masquerade; **a.** DISGUISED: clandestine; covert; incognito; obscure; surreptitious; *travesti(e)*
woman in: **n.** incognita

DISGUST: **v.** abominate; nauseate; **n.** abhorrence; abomination; antipathy; nausea; odium; repugnance; **a.** DISGUSTING: abhorrent; fulsome; loathsome; nauseating; *nauséeux;* odious; offensive; repugnant; repulsive; sickening; unpalatable; **adv.** *ad nauseam*
to the point of: **adv.** *ad nauseam*

DISH, *main or principal:* **n.** *pièce de résistance; plat du jour*
next to main: **n.** *entrée*
side: **n.** entremet(s)

DISHARMONIOUS: **(see** "divisive") **a.** allometric; cacophonic; cacophonous; discordant; disharmonic(al); disputatious; dissident; dissociable; dissonant; incongruous; **n.** DISHARMONY: **(see** "disagreement") antagonism; cacophony; discord(ance); dissention; dissidence; dissonance; incongruity; variance

DISHONEST: **(see** "dishonorable" **and** "tricky") **a.** deceitful; disingenuous; duplicitous; fraudulent; ignominious; knavish; Machiavellian; mendacious; perfidious; roguish; sinister; sinuate; sinuous; surreptitious; treacherous; unscrupulous; **n.** DISHONESTY: dishonor; disingenuity; duplicity; improbity; indirection; indirectness; infamy; knavishness; perfidy; roguery; roguishness; sinuosity; unscrupulosity; villany

DISHONOR: **n.** disrepute; ignominy; improbity; infamy; obloquy; opprobrium; stigma; **a.** DISHONORABLE: **(see** "base" **and** "dishonest") despicable; disesteemed; disgraceful; disreputable; ignoble; ignominious; infamous; inglorious; obloquious

DISINCLINATION *to act:* **(see** "laziness") **n.** inertia; inertness; **a.** inertial

DISINTEGRATION: **n.** decentralization; decomposition; demoralization; dissolution; fragmentation; putrefaction; **a.** DISINTEGRATIVE: disintegrable; putrefactive

of society or personal standards: **n.** anomie

DISINTERESTED: **a.** candid; impassionate; impersonal; **n.** DISINTERESTEDNESS: inertia; objectivity; passivity
adviser: **n.** *amicus curiae* (friend of the court)

DISJOIN(T): **v.** disarticulate; disarrange; discerp; dismember; luxate; **a.** DISJOINTED: disconnected; disordered; dissociated; inarticulate; incoherent; **n.** DISJOINTING: **(see** "separation") disarticulation; discerption; disjointure; dissociation

DISLIKE: **(see** "hate") **n.** abhorrence; alienation; antipathy; aversion; detestation; disaffection; disapprobation; disfavor; disinclination; displeasure; estrangement; hostility; odium; repugnance; **a.** DISLIKABLE: abhorrent; antipathetical; averse; odious; repugnant

DISLOCATION: **n.** disarticulation; displacement; disruption; luxation; **a. see** "displaced"

DISLOYAL: **(see** "disobedient" **and** "treacherous") **a.** disaffected; faithless; mutinous; perfidious; recreant; seditious; traitorous; unfaithful; **n.** DISLOYALTY: infidelity; perfidy; recreancy; sedition; traitorship; treachery; villainy
person: **n.** apostate; conspirator; recreant; renegade; traitor; villain
to country or govt.: **n.** anarchy; incivilism; traitorousness; treachery

DISMAL: **(see** "gloomy") **a.** Acheronian; Acherontic; calamitous; dispirited; dispiriting; funebrial; funebrous; funerary; funereal; lachrymose; lugubrious; melancholic; melancholy; **n.** DISMALITY: lugubrosity; melancholia

DISMAY: **(see** "fear") **n.** consternation; disenchantment; disillusionment; perturbation

DISMISSAL: **n.** *congé;* manumission
from office: **n.** deprivation; divestation; divestiture

DISOBEDIENCE: **n.** insubjection; insubordination; intractableness; mutiny; perfidy; recusance; recusancy; refractoriness;

treachery; unruliness; **a.** DISOBEDIENT: (**see** "disloyal") insubmissive; insubordinate; intractable; mutinous; recalcitrant; recusant; refractory; unruly

DISORDER: (**see** "confusion") **n.** alarums and excursions; anarchism; anarchy; Babelism; Bedlam; bouleversement; brouhaha; chaos; disarrangement; discomposure; dishevelment; disorganization; distemper; embroilment; irregularity; pandemonium; turbulence; turmoil; **a.** DISORDERED: chaotic; dishevel(l)ed; disorganized; farraginous; immethodic(al); inchoate; inchoative; incoherent; pandemoniac(al); turbulent; unhinged; **a.** DISORDERLY: (**see** "riotous") inordinate

in: **adv.** *à l'abandon*

place of great: **n.** Bedlam; capharnaum; mare's nest; pandemonium

wild: **n.** mania; pandemonium; **a.** maniac(al); pandemoniac(al)

DISORGANIZED: (**see** "disordered") **a.** deranged; disarranged; fragmental; fragmentary; indecisive; inveterate; unhinged; **n.** DISORGANIZATION: **see** "disorder"

DISOWN: **v.** abjure; disclaim; repudiate

DISPARAGING: **a.** denigrating; depreciatory; derogative; minimizing; pejorative; **n.** DISPARAGEMENT: denigration; deprecation; disgrace, indignity; meiosis; minimization; pejoration

word or phrase: **n.** epithet; **a.** epithetical

DISPARATE: (**see** "different") **a.** unequal

DISPLACED: **a.** *dépaysé;* ectopic; luxated; **n. see** "dislocation"

DISPLACEMENT, *as a bone:* **n.** luxation

DISPLAY: **v.** disclose; manifest; ostentate; **n.** blazonry; *étalage;* exhibition; fanfare; manifestation; ostent(ation); pageant; panoply; pomp; spectacle

colorful, rich (or empty): **n.** pageantry; panoply; **a. see** "showy" **and** "theatrical"

DISPLEASURE: **n.** annoyance; disapproval; discomposure; indignation; pique; umbrage; **a.** DISPLEASING: **see** "annoying"

DISPOSE *of, by killing or otherwise:* **v.** liquidate; **n.** liquidation

DISPOSED: (**see** "favorable") **a.** amenable; congenial; inclinable; inclinatory; suasive; tractable

DISPOSITION: (**see** "mood") **n.** administration; arrangement; character; diathesis; idiosyncrasy; inclination; liquidation; management; predisposition; proclivity; propensity

DISPOSSESS: **v.** commandeer; confiscate; expropriate; oust; sequester; usurp; **n.** DISPOSSESSION: abstraction; deprivation; divestiture; divestment; expropriation; ouster; sequestration; usurpation; **a.** DISPOSSESSED: (**see** "displaced") lumpen; uprooted

DISPROOF: **n.** confutation; refutation; **a.** DISPROVING: refutative; refutatory; **v.** DISPROVE: confute; controvert; rebut; refute

DISPROVED, *not capable of being:* **a.** incontrovertible; irrecusable; irrefutable

DISPUTE: **v.** contend; contest; contravene; controvert; polemize; **n.** DISPUTE (or DISPUTATION): (**see** "controversy") altercation; argument(ation); contravention; controversy; debate; dissension; invective; polemic; velitation; **a.** DISPUTATIOUS: (**see** "argumentative") controversial

one who (disputes): **n.** controversalist; disputant; polemic

practice of (disputation): **n.** dialectic(s); polemic(s); **a.** dialectic(al); polemic(al)

subject to (dispute): **a.** contentious; controvertible; controversial; debatable; disputatious; polemic(al)

DISQUIET(UDE): **n.** agitation; anxiety; chemistry; dyspathy; dysphoria; excitement; ferment; restlessness; uneasiness; unrest; **a. see** "annoying"

DISREGARD: **see** "ignore"

DISREPUTABLE: (**see** "disgraceful") **a.** despicable; ignoble; ignominious; infamous; inglorious; notorious; opprobrious; squalid; unrespectable

DISRESPECTFUL: **a.** contemptuous; contumelious; derisive; despicable; discourteous; impertinent; impolite; infamous; opprobrious; scurrilous; uncivil; **n.** DISRESPECT: contumely; discourtesy; incivility; misesteem; profanation
to things held sacred: **a.** profanatory; profane; sacrilegious

DISRUPTION: **n.** cataclasm; intrigue; **a.** DISRUPTIVE: cataclasmic

DISSATISFACTION: **n.** disapprobation; discontent; displeasure; dissidence; **a.** DISSATISFIED: (**see** "discontented") dissentious; factious; mutinous

DISSENT: (**see** "disagree") **n.** cleavage; disagreement; dissidence; nonconcurrence; recusance; recusancy

DISSENTER: **n.** dissentient; dissident; recusant; **n.** DISSENSION: **see** "dissent"

DISSENTING: **a.** dissentient; dissentious; dissident; factious; heretical; nonconforming
with no one; **adv.** *nemine dissiente*

DISSIMILAR: **a.** anomalistic; anomalous; disparate; incongruous; heterogeneous; **n.** DISSIMILARITY: anomalism; anomaly; divergence; divergency; heterogeneity; unlikeness

DISSOLUTE: **see** "lewd"

DISSOLVE: **v.** abrogate; decompose; deliquesce; disintegrate; liquefy; **a.** DISSOLVING: deliquescent; liquefactive; **n.** (**see** "disintegration") deliquescence; liquefaction

DISTANCE, *seeing at, or knowledge of things at:* **n.** clairvoyance; telegnosis

DISTANT: (**see** "haughty" **and** "remote") **a.** forane; tramontane; ultramontane; **n.** light year; ultima Thule

DISTASTE: **n.** abhorrence; abomination; antipathy; disinclination; disrelish; repugnance; revulsion; **a.** DISTASTEFUL: (**see** "disagreeable") augean; fastuous; fulsome; impalatable; insufferable; loathsome; nauseating; nauseous; noisome; obnoxious; offensive; repellant; repugnant; repulsive; revulsive; unpalatable
mood of scornful: **n.** fastidium

DISTENDED: (**see** "swollen") **a.** dilated; dila(ta)tive; gravid; inflated; patulous; tumescent; tumid; tympanic; **n.** DISTENTION: dila(ta)tion; tumescence; tumidity; turgescence; tympanites; tympany

DISTINCT: (**see** "separate") **a.** articulate; cogent; definitive; determinate; discernible; discrete; manifest; palpable; patent

DISTINCTION(S): (**see** "eminence") **n.** cachet; differentiation; discrimination; disparity; dissimilarity; subtlety
given to subtle or ridiculously fine: **a.** quodlibetic; **n.** subtlety; tenuosity
great: **n.** flamboyance
marked by appearance of: **a.** *distingué*
person of, in his field; **n.** *cordon bleu;* laureate; paladin
trifling or subtle: **n.** distinguo; nuance; quiddity; subtlety; tenuosity; **a.** quodlibetic

DISTINCTIVE: **a.** characteristic; diacritic; diagnostic; discriminating; *distingué;* flamboyant; honorific; illustrious; majestic; peculiar; signal; transcendent
character or tone: **n.** cachet; timbre
feature or characteristic: **n.** lineament
mark: **n.** cachet
or subtle quality: **n.** bouquet; cachet
property (of a thing): **n.** savo(u)r

DISTINGUISHED: **a.** celebrated; conspicuous; *distingué;* eminent; honorific; illustrious; majestic; prominent; signal; transcendent; **v.** DISTINGUISH: differentiate; discriminate; perceive; signalize; typify
in profession or field: **n.** *cordon bleu;* laureate; paladin

DISTINGUISHING: **a.** definitive; diagnostic; differential; signal
mark(s) on property (brand, etc.): **n.** differentia; differentiation; stigma; (**pl.** differentiae; stigmata)

DISTORTED: **a.** circuitous; tortuous; **n.** tortuosity; tortuousness

DISTORTION, *exaggerated or ludicrous:* **n.** caricature; Munchausenism

DISTRACTED: **a.** absent-minded; aloof; bemused; detached; disconcerted; distraught; perplexed; preoccupied; **n.** DISTRACTION: (**see** "confusion") perplexity; perturbation

DISTRESS: **n.** adversity; affliction; *angoisse;* bereavement; calamity; consternation; cruciation; mortification; penance; tribulation; **a.** DISTRESSED: harrowed; lacerated; tortured; **a.** DISTRESSING: agonizing; atrocious; calamitous; deplorable; flagrant; grievous; harrowing; heinous; hurtful; macaber; macabre; necessitous; vexatious
mental: **n.** dysphoria; psychalgia

DISTRIBUTION *center:* **n.** *entrepôt*

DISTRUST: **v.** misdoubt; **n.** apprehension; misdoubt; misgiving; suspicion

DISTURB: **v.** agitate; discompose; disconcert; disquiet; perturb; **n.** DISTURBANCE: (**see** "disorder") commotion; discomposure; interruption; perturbation; rabblement; tumult(ation); **a.** DISTURBING: (**see** "distressing") vexatious; **a.** DISTURBED: **see** "agitated"

DISUNITE: (**see** "disjoint") **v.** alienate; dissociate; **n.** DISUNITY: (**see** "separation") alienation; dissension; dissociation

DISUSE: **n.** desuetude; obsolescence

DIVERGE: **v.** bifurcate; detour; digress; divagate; divaricate; parenthesize; **n.** DIVERGENCE: bifurcation; detour; deviation; digression; dissimilarity; divagation; divarication; obliquity; parenthesis; tangency; **a.** DIVERGENT: deviant; deviating; parenthetical; tangent(ial)

DIVERSE: (**see** "distinct") **a.** heterogeneous; manifold; motley; multifarious; multiform; multiplex; multiplicious; multivarious; protean; variegated; **n.** DIVERSITY: (**see** "variety") diversification; heterogeneity; rotation; variegation; **v.** DIVERSIFY: intersperse; rotate; variegate

DIVIDE: (**see** "separate") **v.** alienate; bifurcate; dis(as)sociate; disjoint; dismember; disunite; divaricate; diverge; fractionalize; fractionate; **n.** **see** "division"
and rule: **adv.** *divide et impera*
into equal parts: **n., v.** or **a.** aliquot
into three parts: **see under** "divided"
unable to: **a.** indivisible; inextricable; inseparable

DIVIDED (or DIVIDING): **a.** bisulcate; cleft; cloven; discrete; disunited; divaricate; divergent; partite
into many parts or branches: **a.** multipartite; polychotomous; polytomous
into three parts: **a.** trichotomous; tripartite; **n.** trichotomy; tripartition; **v.** trisect
into two parts: **a.** bisected; bipartient; bipartite; dichotomous; **n.** bifurcation; dichotomy; **v.** bifurcate; bisect; dichotomize; halve
wall: **n.** septum

DIVINATION: (**see** "fortune-telling") **n.** metagnomy
false: **n.** pseudomancy; **a.** pseudomantic
forms of: **n.** astragalomancy; astromancy; catoptromancy; cleromancy; haruspication; numerology; omoplastoscopy; oneiromancy; ornithomancy; rhabdomancy; scapulimancy; sortilege

DIVINE: (*see* "sacred") **a.** ambrosiac; ambrosial; celestial; deific; olympian; superhuman; supernal
and human combined or working jointly: **n.** theanthropism; theanthrophy; **a.** theandric; theanthrophic
guidance or care: **n.** Providence
influence or inspiration: **n.** afflation; afflatus; theopneusty; **a.** theopneust(ic)
law: **n.** *jus divinum; jus ecclesiasticum*
law, by: **adv.** *jure divino*
making (divine): **v.** apotheosize; canonize; celestialize; deify; etherealize; spiritualize; **n.** apotheosis; deification; spiritualization
power, alleged: **n.** charism(a); **a.** charismatic
wisdom: **n.** Sophia; **a.** Sophian

DIVINELY *inspired:* **a.** charismatic; theopneust(ic)

DIVINITY, *good:* **n.** agathod(a)emon
individual opn. on: **n.** theologoumenon

DIVISIBLE: **a.** discerptible

DIVISION(S): **n.** alienation; apportionment; category; cleavage; decentralization; detachment; disagreement; discerp-

tion; disjunction; dismemberment; dissolution; distribution; disunity; divarication; divergence; fission; partition; phylum; polychotomy; schism; scission; separation; sundering
comprising more than two: **a.** polychotomous
cut into small: **a.** sectile; **n.** sectility
having many lateral: **a.** ramose; ramous
into independent or semi-independent units: **n.** compartmentalization; compartmentation; deparmentalization; departmentation; **v.** compartmentalize; departmentalize
into two opposites, or bet. two enemies: **n.** polarization; **v.** polarize
pert. to: **a.** divisional; fractional; phyletic; schismatic(al)
plant and animal kingdoms: **n.** phylum; regnum; **(pl.** genera; regna); **a.** phyletic

DIVISIVE: **a.** centrifugal; disharmonious; disintegrative; disjunctive; dissentious; dissociable; dissociative; factional; fissiparous; schismatic(al); schizoid; separatist; **n.** **(see** "division") fissiparousness

DIZZY: **a.** vertiginous; **n.** DIZZINESS: vertigo

DO: **see** "complete"
what you are doing (concentrate on business at hand): age quod agis

DOCTOR(S), *medical, pert. to:* **a.** Aesculapian; iatric(al)
pert. to disease or disorder caused by: **a.** iatrogenic; medicamentous

DOCTRINE(S): **n.** creed; **(pl.** credenda); dogma; philosophy; precept; tenet; theory
body of: **n.** organon
pert. to: **a.** doctrinaire; dogmatic(al)
secret or occult: **n.** cabala; cabalism; occultism; **a.** cabalistic

DOER: **n.** executant; facient

DOG(S), *abnormal fear of:* **n.** cynophobia
beware the: **adv.** *cave canem*
expert in training and care of: **n.** cynologist
genus: **n.** canis
in manger: canis in praesepi
let sleeping lie: quieta non movere
love me, love my (dog): qui m'aime, aime mon chien
lover of: **n.** canophilist; cynolatrist
pert. to or resembling: **a.** canine; cynoid
resembling or like: **a.** cynoid
study of: **n.** cynology
the race, or qualities of: **n.** caninity; dogginess
trainer of: **n.** cynologist
worship of: **n.** cynolatry; **n.** cynolatrist

DOGMATIC: **a.** authoritative; dictatorial; doctrinaire; doctrinal; magisterial; opinionated; pronunciative; sophomoric; **n.** DOGMA: **see** "creed" **and** "doctrine"
assertion: **n.** dixit
statement(s): **n.** dictum; **(pl.** dicta); dogmatism; *ipse dixit;* ipsedixitism

DOLLAR, *love of:* **n.** *amor nummi;* plutolatry

DOMAIN (or DOMINION): **(see** "estate") **n.** arrondissement; demesne; jurisdiction; principality; sovereignty

DOMESTIC: **a.** enchorial; indigenous; internal; **n.** domesticity; domesticality
animals and plants, science of propagation: **n.** thremmatology
establishment: **n.** menage

DOMESTICATED: **(see** "tame") **a.** *domitae naturae*

DOMICILE: **see** "abode"

DOMINANT: **(see** "powerful") **a.** (pre)-eminent; prepotent; prevalent; transcendent; **n.** DOMINATION: **(see** "authority") ascendency; dominance; sovereignty; **a.** DOMINATING: **(see** "commanding") autocratic; dominative; hegemonic; **n.** DOMINANCE: ascendency; preeminence; superordination; transcendency

DOMINION: **n.** dominance; domination; jurisdiction; seign(i)ority; sovereignty; supremacy; suzerainty; transcendency

DONATION: **see** "gratuity"

DONE: **a.** consummate(d); **n.** consummation; *factum est; fait accompli;* kaput
it is: actum est
that which was to be: quod erat faciendum **(abb.** q.e.f.)

DOOM, *foreshadowed:* **(see** "fate") **n.** handwriting on the wall; sword of Damocles; **a.** apocalyptic(al); Damoclean *prophet of:* **n.** Jeremiah; (**fem.** Cassandra)

DOOMED: **a.** destined; fey

DOOR(S), *behind or w/ closed:* **adv.** *à huis clos; januis clausis*
-keeper: **n.** concierge; ostiary; tiler; tyler

DOPEY: **see** "sluggish"

DORMANT: **a.** abeyant; comatose; cryptic; hibernant; latent; lethargic; potential; quiescent; stationary; torpid; **n.** DORMANCY: hibernation; latency; latescence; quiescence

DOT: **n.** punctation; punctum; **a.** DOTTED: motley; piebald; punctate(d); punctiform; variegated

DOTARD: **see** "fool"

DOUBLE: **a.** bigeminal; binary; duplex; **n.** *alter ego;* counterpart; duplicate; image; semblance; similitude; substitute; understudy; **n.** DOUBLENESS: dichotomy; duality; **a.** dualistic
-dealing: **n.** ambidexterity; duplicity; **a.** ambidextrous; duplicitous; Janus-faced; Janus-like; Machiavellian
-dealing, extreme: **n.** triplicity
meaning: **n.** double entendre; double entente; equivoque; (*also* equivoke); **a.** equivocal
vision: **n.** diplopia; **a.** diplopic

DOUBT: (**see** "skepticism" **and** "uncertainty") **n.** ambiguity; ambivalence; distrust; dubiety; dubiosity; dubitation; incertitude; incredulity; indecision; irresolution; miscreance; skepsis; skepticism; suspicion; **a.** DOUBTING: aporetic; dubitant; dubitative; incredulous; irresolute; skeptical; **n.** DOUBTER: (**see** "disbeliever") aporetic; doubting Thomas; nullifidian; pyrrhonist; skeptic
covert expression of: **n.** addubitation
expression of as where truth lies: **n.** *non liquet*
in: **adv.** *in ambiguo; in dubio*
lack of: **n.** credulity; gullibility; **a.** credulous; gullible
not open to: **see under** "question"
philosophical: **n.** skepsis
problem presenting, or passgae in speech or writing presenting a: **n.** aporia; (**pl.** aporiae)
room for: **n.** *ambigendi locus;* **a.** dubious
when in, do nothing: **adv.** *dans le doute, abstiens-toi*
without: (**see** "incontrovertible") **adv.** *sans doute; sine dubio*

DOUBTFUL: (**see** "vague") **a.** ambivalent; dubious; dubitable; equivocal; fabular; factious; improbable; incredible; incredulous; legendary; perilous; problematic(al); questionable; unlikely; unpredictable; unpromising
group (morally or legally): **n.** demimonde
outlook: **n.** skepsis

DOUGHY: **a.** magmatic; **n.** magma

DOWDY: **see** "untidy"

DOWN: **n.** floccus; lanugo; pubescence; **a.** DOWNY: (**see** "woolly") floccose; flocculent; lanuginous; puberulent; pubescent; villous
with: **adv.** *à bas*

DOWNCAST: (**see** "sad") **a.** cheerless; dejected; disheartened; dispirited; melancholic; melancholy; **n.pl.** doldrums; lachrymals, megrims

DOWNFALL: (**see** "ruin") **n.** debasement; degradation; *dégringolade;* labefaction; Waterloo

DOWNRIGHT: (**see** "out-and-out") **a.** arrant; forthright; unmitigated; utter

DOWNWARD: **a.** netherward
moving or bending: **a.** declensional; declinatory; **n.** declension; declination

DRAB: (**see** "dull") **a.** insipid; somber; subfusc(ous)

DRAFT, *rough:* **n.** *brouillon; ébauche*

DRAMA, *culminating event of:* **n.** catastrophe; climax; dénouement
featuring gruesome or horrible: **n.** guignol
heightened action, or complication leading to climax: **n.** catastasis
juvenile lead in: **n.** *jeune premier*
pert. to: **a.** dramatic; histrionic; theatric(al); thespian
problem (drama or play): **n.** *pièce à thèse*

DRAMATIC: (**see** "showy") **a.** artificial; compelling; declamatory; elocutionary; histrionic; operatic; stagy; theatric(al); thespian; **n.** DRAMATIST: dramaturge; playwright; **a.** dramaturgic(al)

DRASTIC: **see** "rigorous"
as to methods: **a.** procrustean

DRAW *away:* **v.** abduct; abstract; **n.** abduction; abstraction; **a.** ablatitious
back (*or in*): **v.** adduct; retract; **n.** adduction; retraction; retrenchment; **a.** retractile
forth (*or out*): **v.** attenuate; elicit; extract; protract; **n.** attenuation; elicitation; evocation

DRAWBACK: (**see** "hindrance") **n.** stultification

DRAWING(S), *pert. to:* **a.** delineative; graphic
scratched on walls, etc.: **n.** graffito; (**pl.** graffiti)
young person's (*children*): **n.pl.** juvenilia

DREAD: **a.** doughty; formidable; perilous; portentious; redoubtable; **n.** (**see** "anxiety") angst; apprehension; trepidation; trepidity; **a.** DREADFUL: (**see** "dire") awesome; fearful; horrendous; horrific; revolting

DREAM(S): **n.** chimera; fantasia; fantasy; *insomnium;* phantasm; (**pl.** phantasmata); **v.** fantasize; **n.** DREAMER: (**see** "visionary") fantasist; fantast; ideologist; ideologue; phantast; romancer; romanticist; utopian; **a.** DREAMY: (**see** "impractical") chimerical; fantastic; fantasque; languid; langorous; utopian
art of interpretation, or foretelling by: **n.** oneiromancy
day-: **see** "daydream"
god of: **n.** Oneiros
pert. to: **a.** chimerical; fantastic: oneiric; utopian
sick man's: **n.** *aegri somnis*
sick man's empty: **n.** *aegri somnia vana*
unrealistic or unrealizable: **n.** *chateau en Espagne;* chimera; **a.** chimerical; fantastic; utopian

DREARY: **see** "dismal"
quality or state of being: **n.** dreariment

DREGS: (**see** "rubbish") **n.** debris; exuviate; feculence; orts, residue; residuum; sediment; sordor

DRENCH: **see** "imbrue"

DRESS: (**see** "attire") **v.** accouter; accoutre; **n.** accoutrement(s); apparel; array(ment); drapery; habiliments; (in)-vestments; regalia; toggery; toilette; trappings; vesture
ceremonial: **n.** *grande toilette;* panoply; regalia
in full: **adv.** *en grande tenue; en grande toilette; endimanché*
-maker: **n.** *couturier;* (**fem.** couturière)
pert. to (*esp. men's*): **a.** sartorial; **n.** haberdashery
richly: **v.** caparison
up: **v.** caparison; tit(t)ivate; **n.** caparison; panoply; ragalia; tit(t)ivation

DRESSED *carelessly or partly:* **n.** deshabille; dishabille; **adv.** *en déshabillé*

DRESSING *gown:* **n.** *robe de chambre*

DRIFTER(S): **n.** flotsam and jetsam; gaberlunzie; itinerant; vagrant

DRINK: **v.** imbibe; **n.** beverage; potable; potation; libation
alcoholic: **n.** libation
ceremonial or as sacrifice: **n.** libation
craving for (*as alcoholic*): **n.** dipsomania; oenomania; potomania; **a.** dipsomaniac(al)
fit to (*drinkable*); **a.** potable; **n.** potability
greedily: **v.** ingurgitate
not fit to: **a.** impotable; undrinkable
of the gods (*or any delicious*): **n.** nectar; **a.** nectarean; nectareous

DRINKING: (**see** "alcoholism") **n.** bibation; inbibition; ingurgitation; libation; potation
addicted to: **see** "drunken"
bold or courageous when: **a.** pot-valiant
bout, or together: (**see** "spree" **below**) **n.** carouse; compotation
companion: **n.** compotator
fond of: **a.** convivial; crapulous; intemperate
mania for: **n.** dipsomania; *mania a potu*
rel. to: **a.** bibacious; bibitory; bibulous
song or light lyric: **n.** *air à boire;* Anacreontic

sparing in: **a.** abstemious; abstentinent; abstentious; **n.** abstentation; moderation
spree: **n.** bacchanal(ia); bender; brannigan; carouse; compotation

DRIVE: **v.** coerce; flagellate; impel; **n.** (**see** "incentive") conation; conatus; dynamism; impetus; momentum; vector; **a.** DRIVING: conational; conative; dynamic
away: **v.** aroint; dispel

DROLLERY: **n.** *drôlerie;* raillery; whims(e)y; whimsicality; whimsicalness

DROOPING: **a.** enervated; flaccid; lackadaisical; languid; languorous; lethargic; nutant; **n.** flaccidity; lackadaisy; languor; lethargy

DROP *by drop:* **adv.** *goutte à goutte*
falling in (drops): **a.** stillatitious
to the last **adv.** supernaculum

DROSS: (**see** "remains" **and** "sediment") **n.** *caput mortuum;* (**pl.** *caput mortua*)

DROWNING, *execution by:* **n.** noyade; Republican marriage

DROWSY: **a.** comatose; hypnogenic; hypnogenous; hypnogogic; lethargic; oscitant; somnolent; torpid; **n.** DROWSINESS: oscitancy; oscitation; somnolence

DRUG(S), (**see** "medicine") *combined action of* **n.** synergism; **a.** synergic(al); synergistic(al)
habit: **n.** narcoticism; opiumism
science of **n.** materia medica; pharmaceutics; pharmacology; **a.** pharmaceutic(al); pharmacological

DRUMMER: **n.** tympanist

DRUNK: **see** "alcoholic" **and** "drunken
bold or courageous when: **a.** pot-valiant; **n.** Dutch courage; pot-valor
to make: **v.** inebriate; intoxicate
weepingly: **a.** maudlin

DRUNKARD: (**see** "alcoholic") **n.** bacchanal; bacchant; (**fem.** bacchante); debauchee; dipsomaniac; inebriate; libertine; oenophilist; winebibber; **n.** DRUNKENNESS: (**see** "alcoholism") dipsomania; ebrosity; inebriation; (in)ebriety; intoxication; potomania

DRUNKEN: **a.** bacchanal(ian); bacchantic; bibacious; bibulous; crapulent; crapulous; dipsomaniacal; inebriate(d); inebrious
feast or party: **n.** bacchanal(ia); bender; brannigan; carouse; compotation orgy

DRY: (**see** "dull") **a.** anhydrous; arenaceous; dehydrated; desiccated; desiccative; jejune; monotonous; uninteresting; xerotic; **n.** DRYNESS: aridity; dehydration; desiccation; xerosis

DUCT, *body:* **n.** meatus

DUAL: **see** "two-fold"

DUEL: **n.** *affaire d'honneur;* rencounter; rencontre

DUET: **n.** *pas de deux*

DULL: (**see** "bland" **and** "commonplace") **a.** adenoid(al); anserine; apathetic; asinine; bromidic; brutish; comatose; conventional(ized); gleamless; hebetate; hebetudinous; insipid; jejune; lackadaisical; lackluster; languid; languorous; lethargic; lumbering; monotonous; moronic; obtuse; opaque; oscitant; pedestrian; phlegmatic(al); pointless; ponderous; prosaic; routinized; stolid; stereotyped; stylized; triste; unadventurous; uninspired; unresponsive; unsensational; vapid
(*lifeless*): **a.** comatose; inanimate; lethargic
or blunt, to make: **v.** hebetate; obtund
passage (as of book, play or music): **n.** longueur
statement: **n.** platitude
(*uninteresting*): **a.** insipid; jejune; prosaic(al); **n.** insipidity; jejunity

DULLARD: (**see** "person, dull," **etc.**) **n.** Boeotian; bromide

DULLNESS: **n.** apathy; hebetude; inanity; infestivity; insensitivity; insipidity; jejunity; lethargy; mirthlessness; monotony; obtuseness; opacity; oscitancy; platitude; ponderosity; prosaism; stereotypy; stoginess; stolidity; stupidity; tepidity; tristesse *mental:* **n.** crassitude; hebetude; mental retardation; moronity; obtuseness; obtusity; stupidity

DUMMY: **n.** *homme de paille* (man of straw)

DUNG: (**see** "feces") **n.** ordure; (**pl.** rejectamenta)
containing or like: **a.** fecal; ordurous; stercoraceous
living in: **a.** fimicolous; merdivorous; stercoricolous

DUPE: **see** "deceive"

DUPLICATE: (**see** "double") **n.** counterfeit; counterpart; facsimile

DURATION: (**see** "endurance") **n.** longanimity; perseverance; protension
unlimited: **n.** infinitude; infinity; perpetuality; perpetuity; saeculum

DURESS: **n.** coercion; constraint; durance; imprisonment; incarceration; restraint

DUSKY: **a.** somber; obfusc(ous)

DUST, *abnormal fear of:* **n.** amathophobia
covered with: **a.** pulverulent

DUSTY: **a.** pulverous; pulverulent

DUTIFUL: **a.** deferent(ial); duteous; filial; **n.** deference; deferentiality

DUTY: **n.** devoir; dharma; liability; obligation; onus; responsibility
abandonment of: **n.** abdication; apostasy; defection
ethics of: **n.** deontology; **a.** deontological
misconduct or neglect of: **n.** irresponsibility; maladministration; misfeasance; misprision
of nobility or rich to less fortunate: **n.** *noblesse oblige*
outside regular: **a.** extracurricular; supererogative; supererogatory
rel. to: **a.** deontic; duteous; obligatory
required by: **a.** *de règle; de rigueur;* imperative; obligatory; preemptory
to do my: faire mon devoir

DWARF: **n.** diminutive; homunculus; (**pl.** homunculi); lilliputian; Rumpelstiltskin; sesquipedal; **a.** DWARFISH: diminutive; homuncular; lilliputian; microscopic; nanitic; nanous; sesquipedalian; **n.** DWARFISHNESS: dwarfism; nanism

DWELLING: **n.** domicile; habitation; **a.** domiciliated; imminent; inherent; residentiary

DYE: **v.** imbue; tinge

DYING: **a.** agonal; expiring; fey; moribund; **adv.** *in articulo mortis; in extremis*
person: **n.** moribund

DYNAMIC: (**see** "powerful") **a.** kinetic

E

EACH *his own, to: suum cuique*

EAGER: (see "ardent") **a.** agog; desirous; ecstatic; enthusiastic; fanatical; fervent; impetuous; importunate; insatiable; intent; rapturous; ravenous; solicitous; voracious; zealous; **n.** EAGERNESS: (see "enthusiasm") ardor; demonstrativeness; empressement; lust; solicitude
for gratification: **a.** gluttonous; rapacious; ravenous; voracious
for praise: **a.** esurient; **n.** captation; esurience

EAGLE *does not catch flies: aquilla non capit muscas*
of or like an: **a.** aquiline

EARLIEST: **a.** primeval; primitive; primordial
in time: **a.** primordial; ultimate
part or stage: **n.** primordium; (pl. primordia)

EARLY: **a.** embryonic; incipient; matinal; matutinal; nascent; precipitate; premundane; primeval; primitive; primordial; punctual; seasonable; timely
development: **n.** precocity; **a.** precocious
stage, in: **a.** embryonic; incipient; incunabulum; infancy; nascent; rudimentary
work of art, book, record, etc.: **n.** incunabulum; (pl. incunabula)

EARNEST: (see "eager") **a.** fervent

EARS, *excessive largeness of:* **n.** macrotia; **a.** macrotous
having: **a.** auriculate
pricked up: **n.** *arrectis aribus*

EARTH: (see "universe") **n.** *terra firma*
and heavens, rel. to or affecting both: **a.** cosmotellurian
as a center: **n.** geocentricism; **a.** geocentric(al)
deep within the: **a.** chthonian; chthonic; plutonic; subterranean
goddess of: **n.** Ceres; Tellus Mater
inhabited portion: **n.** ecumene
inhabitant of: (see "man") **n.** earthling; tellurian; **a.** terrigenous
lying beneath: **a.** nether; subterranean
lying, dwelling or active on or above: **a.** superterranean; superterraneous; **n.** superterranean; superterrene
of or arising from: **a.** telluric; terrestrial
of this: see "worldly"
power of people of: **n.** cosmocracy
rel. to: **a.** planetary; telluric; terranean; terraneous; terrestrial
theory of origin, etc.: **n.** cosmogony

EARTHBORN: **a.** human; terrigenous

EARTHEN: **a.** terraceous

EARTHLY: (see "earthly") **a.** cosmopolitan; factual; global; mundane; planetary; realistic; sublunary; telluric; temporal; terrene; terrestrial

EARTHQUAKES, *pert. to:* **a.** seismic(al)
study of: **n.** seismology

EARTHY: (see "vulgar") **a.** carnal; chthonian; chthonic; Falstaffian; heathenish; Hogarthian; mortal; mundane; pagan; Rabelaisian; *risqué;* terrestrial; worldly

EASE: **v.** alleviate; assuage; compromise; extenuate; mitigate; moderate; placate; relax; tranquilize; **n.** alleviation; assuagement; detachment; disengagement; leisure; naturalness; palliation; quietude; relaxation; repose; tranquility; **a.** see "easy"
at: **adv.** *à l'aise*
difficult to, or incapable of (easing): **a.** implacable; inexorable; intractable; unappeasable
something which (eases): **n.** alleviant; lenitive; nepenthe; palliative; tranquilizer
tending to: **a.** alleviative; alleviatory; conciliatory; extenuating; extenuative;

lenitive; mitigating; nepenthean; palliative; placative; placatory; tranquilizing
with dignity: **n.** *otium cum dignitate*
without dignity: **n.** *otium sine dignitate*

EASILY: **adv.** *sans gêne*
managed, taught or controlled: **a.** docile; educable; educatable; governable; malleable; maniable; manipulable; manipulative; manipulatory; pliable; tractable; **n.** docility; malleability; tractability

EASING: **a.** alleviative; alleviatory; anesthetic; consolatory; lenitive; nepenthean; mitigative; palliative; palliatory; **n.** alleviation; *détente;* mitigation; palliation; tranquilization

EAST: **n.** Levant; Orient; **a.** **see** "oriental"
face or turn to: **v.** orientate

EASTER *or Lent, pert. to:* **a.** lenten; paschal; quadragesimal

EASTERN: **a.** oriental; ortative
hemisphere, rel. to: **a.** gerontogeous

EASY: **a.** accessible; complaisant; effortless; facile; indulgent; lenient; tractable
and casual in manner: **a.** cavalier; *dégagé;* jaunty; unconcerned; unconstrained; **adv.** *sans gêne;* **n.** *un air aisé*
come (easy) go (easy): **n.** *cito parit; quod cito acquiritur*
going: **a.** apathetic; *dégagé;* indifferent; jaunty; unconstrained
job: **n.** sinecure

EAT: **v.** consume; corrode; devour; ingest; ingurgitate; manducate

EATABLE: (**see** "food") **n.** comestible; edible; **a.** alimentary; cibarious; comestible; edible; esculent
not: **a.** inedible; inesculent
state of being: **n.** edibility

EATER: **n.** gastronome(r)
gluttonous: **n.** bon-vivant; cormorant; glutton; gourmand; **a.** crapulent; edacious; omnivorous
heavy: **n.** cormorant; gourmand; trencherman

EATING: **n.** ingestion; ingurgitation; manducation; **a.** consuming; corrosive; devouring; edacious; ingestible; ingestive; voracious
after: **a.** post-cibal; post-prandial
any sort of food: **a.** omnivorous; pantophagous
before: **a.** ante cibum
both animal and vegetable food: **a.** amphivorous
earth, dirt, clay, etc.: **n.** geophagy; pica
fast: **n.** tachyphagia
fond of: **a.** convivial; gluttonous; gourmand; **n.** *bon-vivant;* epicure; gastronome(r); gourmand; gourmet; sybarite; trencherman; **a.** epicurean
huge capacity for: **n.** edacity; gluttony; voracity
injurious, unusual or nonedible things: **n.** allotriophagy; geophagy; paroexia; pica
science of good: **n.** cuisine; epicureanism; gastronomy
sparing: **a.** abstemious
together: **a.** commensal; **n.** commensal(ity)

ECCENTRIC: (**see** "peculiar") **a.** aberrant; anomalous; atypical; bizarre; cantankerous; capricious; crotchety; fantastic; idiosyncratic; off-center; **n.** aberrant; Bohemian; deviant; **n.** ECCENTRICITY: (**see** "peculiarity") aberrance; aberrancy; aberration; *bizarrerie;* idiosyncrasy; quiddity; quirk

ECHO: **n.** polyphony; repercussion; reverberation; **a.** echoic; polyphonic; polyphonous; reverborative; reverboratory

ECONOMICS: **n.** plutology; plutonomy; **a.** ECONOMIC(AL): frugal; profitable; prudent
(economic) satisfaction: **n.** ophelimity

ECONOMY: **n.** frugality; husbandry; prudence; retrenchment; **v.** ECONOMIZE: curtail; husband; retrench
extreme: **n.** austerity
unreasonable: **n.** parsimony; **a.** cheeseparing; parsimonious

EDDY: **n.** Charybdis; vortex; whirlpool; **a.** vortiginous

EDIBLE: **see** "eatable"

EDICT: **n.** fiat; mandate; mandatum; manifesto; ordinance; proclamation; pronouncement; pronunciamento; ukase; **a.** edictal

EDIT: **v.** compile; emend; redact; **n.** redaction; **n.** EDITOR: diaskeuast; *redacteur;* redactor

EDITION, *first:* **n.** *editio princeps;* princeps

EDUCATED: **a.** enlightened; erudite; learned; lettered; literate; philomathic(al); scholarly; tutored; **v.** EDUCATE: **see** "teach"
or enlightened class: **n.pl.** cognoscenti; illuminati; intelligensia; literati; **n.** cognoscente; clerisy; litterateur; literatus; savant
self-: **a.** autodidactic; **n.** autodidact

EDUCATION: **(see** "background" **and** "learning") **n.** breeding; curriculum; discipline; erudition; instruction; learning; pedagogics; pedagogy; refinement; scholarship; scholasticism; tuition; **a.** EDUCATIONAL: academic; didactic; doctrinal; educative; instructive; pedagogic(al); propaedeutic(al); scholastic(al); tutorial
general (education) and breeding: **n.** curriculum

EDUCATOR(S): **(see** "teacher(s)") **n.** pedagog(ue)
pretentious speech or writing(s) of: **n.** pedag(u)ese; pedantry

EERIE: **a.** fantastic; grotesque; mysterious; phantasmal; phantasmic; uncanny; weird; **n.** grotesquerie

EFFECT: **v.** accomplish; execute; **n.** **(see** "outcome" **and** "result") appearance; causatum; consequence; encroachment; impingement; infringement; manifestation; residuum; sequel; sequela; **(pl.** sequelae)
done for: **see** "stagy"
to cause: **n.** *a posteriori;* **a.** aposterioristic

EFFECTIVE (or EFFECTUAL): **a.** consequential; efficacious; efficient; executive; substantious; telling; **n.** EFFECTIVENESS: effectivity; efficacity; efficacy
make more: **v.** augment; enhance; potentiate; **n.** augmentation; enhancement; potentiation

EFFEMINATE: **a.** gynecoid; muliebral; womanlike; **n.** EFFEMINACY: androgyny; femineity; femininity; muliebrity
boy or man: **n.** androgyne; androgynus; milksop

EFFICIENCY: **n.** accomplishment; competency; consummation; effectiveness; effectuality; efficacity; efficacy; expedition; ingenuity; **a.** EFFICIENT: accomplished; adept; competent; consummate; dexterous; effective; efficacious; expeditious; ingenious; professional; proficient; virtuosic

EFFIGY, *to form or represent as:* **(see** "model") **v.** effigiate; **n.** effigiation; **a.** effigial
used in primitive magic: **n.** *envoûtement*

EFFORT: **n.** application; conatus; endeavor; exertion; nisus
act of making: **n.** conation; **a.** conative
close or continuous: **(see** "diligence") **n.** assiduousness; assiduity; **a.** assiduous
requiring constant and often ineffective: **a.** Sisyphean; Sisyphian

EFFUSIVE: **a.** demonstrative; ebullient; exuberant; gushing; scaturient; unreserved; unrestrained; **n.** EFFUSIVENESS: ebullience; ebulliency; ebullition; exuberance; unreserve; unrestraint

EGG(S), *collector or student of bird:* **n.** oologist; oology; **a.** oologic(al)
having young by: **a.** oviparous; ovoviviparous; **n.** oviparity; ovoviviparity
living or feeding on: **a.** oophagous
membrane: **n.** oolemma; vitilline (membrane)
-shaped or like: **a.** ooid(al); ovate; ovicular; oviform; ovoid(al)

EGGHEAD: **see** "intellectual"

EGOTISM: **see** "selfishness" **and** "self-importance"

EGYPTIAN *writing, ancient:* **n.** cuneiform; hieroglyphic(s)

EIGHT, *pert. to or group or series of:* **a.** octadic; **n.** octad
-sided or angled figure: **n.** octagon; **a.** octagonal
years, happening every or lasting for: **a.** octennial

EIGHTY *to 90 years, person of, or rel. to this period:* **a.** or **no.** octogenarian

EINSTEIN'S *theory:* $e = mc^2$

EITHER *to conquer or to die: aut vincere aut mori*

EJECT: (**see** "banish") **v.** disbar; dispossess; oust; regurgitate

ELABORATE: **v.** (**see** "develop") expaciate: **a.** (**see** "large") complicated; diligent; intricate; painstaking; stupendous; **n.** ELABORATION: exegesis; expaciation

in ornamentation: **a.** garish; rococo

production: **n.** extravaganza; spectacular

ELATED: **a.** buoyant; ecstatic; enraptured; eudamonic(al); euphoric; exhilarated; exultant; heady; intoxicated; rapturous; **n.** ELATION: (**see** "rapture") ecstasy; euphoria; exultation; rapture; transport

ELDER: **n.** patriarch; **a.** ELDERLY: (**see** "aged") anile; antiquated; *d'un certain âge;* senile; venerated; **n.** anility; antiquity; senescence; senility

ELECTIONS, *scientific study of:* **n.** psephology; **a.** psephological; **n.** psephologist

ELEGANCE: **n.** comeliness; concinnity; courtliness; gentility; luxe; refinement; *savoir faire;* sumptuosity; urbanity; **a.** ELEGANT: concinnous; exquisite; luxurious; polished; *recherché;* sumptuous; supernacular; supernal

of simple: **adv.** *simplex munditiis*

ELEGANTLY *dressed or maintained:* **a.** *soigné;* (**fem.** *soignée*); modish; well-groomed

ELEGY: **see** "funeral ode or hymn"

ELEMENT: **n.** component; constituent; factor; ingredient; integral; integrant; **a.** ELEMENTAL: (**see** "fundamental") hypostatic(al); integral; introductory; ultimate

out of one's: **a.** *dépaysé*

ELEMENTARY: (**see** "fundamental") **a.** abecedarian; abecedary; inchoate; incomplex; initiatory; primitive; primordial; rudimental; rudimentary

instruction: **n.** propaedeutics; **a.** propaedeutic(al)

ELEPHANT(S): **n.** pachyderm

do not catch mice: elephantus non capit murem

ELEVATE: (**see** "raise") **v.** edify; enhance; enlighten; ennoble; escalate; exhilarate; pedestal; refine; spiritualize; sublimate; transcend; **n.** ELEVATION: edification; enhancement; enlightenment; **a.** edificatory

character of: **v.** ennoble; spiritualize; sublimate; **n.** ennoblement; spiritualization; sublimation

ELIMINATE: (**see** "abolish") **v.** decimate; dele(te); exclude; expunge; exscind; extirpate; oust; resect; **n.** ELIMINATION: decimation; deletion; deracination; divestation; extirpation; ouster

not capable of (elimination): **a.** ineliminable; ineradicable; inexterminable; inextinguishable; inextirpable; irradicable; irrepressible; unquenchable

ELITE: (**see** "aristocrat" **and** "superior") **n.** aristocracy; (**pl.** aristoi); *bas bleu;* bluestocking; *crème de la crème;* magnifico; *ne plus supra; ne plus ultra;* supernaculum; (**pl.** *gens de condition*)

principles and practices of the: **n.** aristocratism

ELOPE: **v.** abscond; absquatulate; **n.** ELOPEMENT: abscondence; absquatulation

ELOQUENCE: (**see** "speech") **n.** facundity; **a.** ELOQUENT: Ciceronian; Demosthenic; Demosthenian; facund; impassioned; oratorial; oratoric(al)

ELUSIVE: (**see** "baffling") **a.** impalpable; insidious; intangible; lubric(i)ous; saponaceous; subtle; **n.** ELUSIVENESS: insidiousness; intangibility; lubricity; subtility

EMACIATED: **a.** attenuated; cadaverous; enfeebled; macilent; marasmic; tabescent; **n.** EMACIATION: atrophy; attenuation; macies; marasmus; tabefaction; tabescence

EMANATION: (**see** "outcome") **n.** aura; cachet; effluence; effluvium; efflux

EMBARRASSMENT: **n.** abashment; chagrin; discomfiture; discomposure; disconcertion; discountenance; encumbrance; frustration; humiliation; impediment; mortification; perturbation; **v.** EMBARRASS: daunt; discomfit; discompose; disconcert; humble; humiliate; mortify
without: **adv.** *sans gêne*

EMBEDDED: **a.** encapsulated; impacted; nidulant

EMBELLISH: **see** "adorn"

EMBEZZLE: **v.** appropriate; defalcate; misappropriate; peculate; purloin; **n.** EMBEZZLER: defalcator; peculator

EMBEZZLEMENT: **n.** abstraction; defalcation; malversation; (mis)appropriation; peculation; substraction

EMBITTER: **(see** "anger") **v.** exacerbate; **n.** exacerbation; exacerbescence; rancor; **a.** EMBITTERED: rancorous

EMBLEM(S): **n.** insigne; **(pl.** insignia); symbol; **a.** EMBLEMATIC: representative; symbolic(al)
for a book: **n.** colophon

EMBODIMENT: **(see** "personify") **n.** avatar; epiphany; incarnation; incorporation; (im)personification; quintessence

EMBRACE: **v.** adopt; circumscribe; comprehend; comprise; embosom; encompass; enfold; incorporate; undertake; **n.** EMBRACEMENT: accolade; comprehension; incorporation; **a.** EMBRACING: circumscriptive; comprehensive; encircling; enclosing; inclusive; incorporated; osculant

EMERGE: **v.** burgeon; debouch; disembogue; effloresce; egress; emanate; evolve; materialize; **n.** EMERGENCE: burgeoning; debouchment; debut; efflorescence; egression; emanation; evolution
as a river: **v.** disembogue
as from outlet: **v.** debouch

EMERGENCY: **n.** crisis; dilemma; exigency; **a. see** "critical"

EMIGRATION: **(see** "flight") **n.** egression; exodus; hegira

EMINENCE: **n.** conspicuity; conspicuousness; esteem; magnificence; majesty; paramouncy; prestige; prominence; resplendency; salience; saliency; superiority; transcendence; transcendency
great: **n.** preeminence; principality

EMINENT: **(see** "famous" **and** "illustrious") **a.** august; celebrated; conspicuous; *distingué;* distinguished; estimable; honorific; immortal; inimitable; leonine; magnific(al); magnificent; majestic; paramount; prestigious; prominent; (re)splendent; sovereign; superlative; transcendent
in rank or authority: **n.** *cordon bleu*
person: **(see** "person of high rank, etc.") **n.** eminentissimo

EMOTION(S): **(see** "feeling") **n.** affectivity; ecstasy; emotionality; emotivism; emotivity; rapture; rhapsody; vehemence
appeal(ing) to: **adv.** *ad captandum (vulgus)*
display of: **n.pl.** histrionics; hysterics; melodramatics
frenzy of: **n.** nympholepsy; orgasm; Saturnalia
lacking or incapable of: **see under** "feeling"
relieved by talking, etc.: **n.** abreaction; catharsis; **a.** abreactive; cathartic

EMOTIONAL: **a.** affective; ecstatic; effusive; emotive; histrionic; hysteric(al); (melo)dramatic; passionate; rhapsodic; theatric(al); vehement; **n.** emotionality
interest or involvement: **n.** ecstasy; empressement; fervor
wildly: **a.** dithyrambic; rapturous; rhapsodic(al)

EMPHASIZE: **v.** accelerate; accent(uate); enhance; exacerbate

EMPHATIC: **a.** coercive; cogent; compelling; dogmatic; forceful; imperative; pronounced; vehement; vigorous
in speaking: **a.** lexical
statement: **n.** adjuration; asseveration

EMPIRE *within an empire:* **n.** *imperium in imperio*

EMPTY: **a.** barren; frivolous; fustian; inane; meaningless; pretentious; uninhabited; unoccupied; vacuous; **n.** EMPTINESS: barrenness; inanition; inanity;

nihility; nullibicity; nullibiety; senselessness; shallowness; vacuity; vacuum
as by pouring, or as a river: **v.** disembogue
(*pretentious*): **n.** flummery; pageantry
space: **n.** vacuity; vacuum
spaces, aversion to: **n.** *horror vacui*

ENABLING: (**see** "permissive") **a.** empowering; facultative

ENCAMPMENT: **n.** castrametation; etape

ENCHANT: (**see** "allure") **v.** bewitch; captivate; ensorcel(l); enthral(l); mesmerize; **a.** ENCHANTING: captivating; Circean; fascinating; sirenic(al); **n.** ENCHANTMENT: bewitchment; captivation; conjuration; ensorcel(l)ment; fascination; gramary(e); incantation; necromancy; sorcery; sortilege

ENCHANTRESS: **n.** *charmeuse;* Circe; *femme fatale;* lamia; vampire

ENCIRCLE: (**see** "surround") **v.** circumnavigate; circumscribe; circumvallate; embosom; embrace; encompass; impale; immure; **a.** ENCIRCLING: circumambient; circumferential; encompassing; peripheral

ENCLOSE: (**see** "encircle") **v.** circumscribe; embosom; environ; incarcerate; invaginate; sheathe; **n.** ENCLOSURE: empalement

ENCLOSED *tract, territory, etc.:* **n.** enclave

ENCOMPASSING: (**see** "encircling") **a.** ambient; circumferential; enveloping

ENCOURAGE: **v.** animate; embolden; expostulate; exhort; foment; hearten; inspire; inspirit; instigate; promote; sanction; stimulate; **n.** ENCOURAGEMENT: approbation; excitation; exhortation; expostulation; fomentation; incentive; instigation; patronage; protreptic; sanction; sponsorship; **a.** ENCOURAGING: auspicious; (ex)hortative; (ex)hortatory; inspirational; inspiriting; persuasive; propitious; protreptic(al); psychagogic; sanctionative

ENCUMBRANCE: **n.** embarrassment; impediment; incubus; perplexity; **a.** impedimental

END: (**see** "conclusion," "discontinue," "ending" **and** "objective") **v.** abolish; abrogate; consummate; culminate; dis(as)sociate; terminate; **n.** abrogation; accomplishment; achievement; annihilation; coda; consequence; consummation; culmination; denouement; destination; dis(as)sociation; dissolution; eventuality; exitus; expiration; finality; finis; goal; omega; *sine die;* termination; terminus; **a.** ENDED: **see** "completed"
act or stroke that (ends): **n.** *coup de grâce*
beginning of the: **n.** *commencement de la fin*
coming to an: **a.** moribund
crowns the work: finis coronat opus
directed or tending toward an: **a.** teleological; telic
impossible to: **a.** inconclusible
in itself, having: **a.** autotelic
in or at the: **adv.** *in fine*
look to the: respicere finem
near the: **a.** subterminal
to the bitter: **adv.** *à outrance*
to the, or at the: **adv.** *ad fin(em)*
weigh well the: **adv.** *avise la fin*

ENDANGER: **v.** imperil; jeopardize

ENDEARMENT, *short term of (pet name)*: **n.** hypocorism; hypocoristic; **a.** hypocoristic

ENDEAVOR: **v.** essay; strive; **n.** conatus; essay; experiment; nisus; speculation; undertaking; venture; **a.** conative; experimental; speculative; venturous

ENDING: (**see** "conclusion" **and** "end") **n.** desinence; disintegration; dissolution; epilogue; finis; liquidation; **a.** consummative; desinent(ial); desitive; finitive; terminal; terminative; terminatory; **a.** ENDED: **see** "finished"

ENDLESS (**see** "enduring" **and** "everlasting") **a.** boundless; illimitable; incessant; infinite; interminable; interminate; measureless; perpetual; protracted; sempiternal; unceasing; **adv.** *ad infinitum*
in time: (**see** "eternity") **n.** infinity; perpetuity

ENDOWMENT: **n.** accomplishment; ap(p)anage; largess(e); perquisite; talent

ENDURANCE: **n.** continuance; continuity; diuturnity; fortitude; longanimity; longev-

ity; monumentality; perdurability; perdurance; permanence; perseverance; perseveration; propensity; sempiternity; stamina; sufferance; tolerance; toleration; **v.** ENDURE: abide; brook; countenance; perdure; survive; tolerate; undergo; withstand; **a.** ENDURING: (**see** "chronic") abiding; classic; diuturnal; established; immarcescible; long-suffering; monotonous; monumental; patient; (per)durable; permanent; perseverant; persistent; protensive; sempiternal
contest: **n.** marathon

ENDURES, *he conquers who: vincit qui patitur*

ENEMY: **n.** adversary; antagonist; competitor; opponent

ENERGY: **n.** dynamism; gusto; impetus; motivity; potency; puissance; verve; vivacity; **a.** ENERGETIC: (**see** "brisk") dynamic(al); forceful; resolute; strenuous; vigorous; **adv.** *con brio*
generating: **a.** calorigenic
intense: **n.** athleticism; strenuosity
lacking in: (**see** "weak") **a.** lymphatic(al)
science of: **n.** dynamics; energetics

ENFORCED: **a.** coercive; compulsory; disciplinary; mandatory; obligatory; peremptory; tyrannical; **n.** ENFORCEMENT: coercion; compulsoriness; duress; oppression

ENFORCER *of discipline:* (**see** "disciplinarian") **n.** martinet; rigorist; tyrant

ENGAGE: **v.** betroth; participate; plight; **n.** ENGAGEMENT: assignation; betrothal; betrothment; espousal; involvement; plight; prepossession; rendezvous; tryst

ENGLAND (**or** ENGLISH), *hate(r) of:* **n.** anglophobe; anglophobia; **a.** anglophobic
love(r) of: **n.** anglomania; anglomaniac; anglophile; anglophilia; **a.** anglomaniacal; anglophilic
study of lang. or lit. of: **n.** anglistics

ENGLISHMAN: **n.** Sassenach

ENJOY *the present:* **n.** *carpe diem; in diem vivere; in horam vivere*

ENJOYMENT: (**see** "pleasure") **n.** delectation; ecstasy; exultation; gusto; zest; **a.** ENJOYABLE: (**see** "pleasurable") delectable; entertaining; zestful
devoted to: **a.** apolaustic; hedonic; hedonistic; sensuous; sybaritic; voluptuous
of foolish trifles: **n.** desipience; desipiency

ENLARGE: **v.** aggrandize; amplify; dilate; elaborate; enhance; exacerbate; expatiate; hypertrophy; intumesce; magnify; omnify; protuberate; tumefy; **a.** ENLARGED: augmented; enhanced; hypertrophic; (in)tumescent; tumefactive; turgescent; turgid; **n.** ENLARGEMENT: accession; aggrandizement; augmentation; expansion; expaciation; (in)tumescence; majoration; tumefaction; tumidity; turgescence

ENLARGING *upon:* **a.** amplificatory; augmentative; **n.** augmentation; enhancement; expatiation

ENLIGHTENMENT: (**see** "revelation") **n.** *éclaircissement;* edification; illumination; **v.** ENLIGHTEN: (**see** "teach") edify; educate; elucidate; illuminate; irradiate; **a.** ENLIGHTENING: edificatory; illuminant; illuminating; illuminative
person of high: **n.** illuminato; (**pl.** cognoscenti; illuminati; intelligensia)

ENLIVEN: **v.** animate; exhilarate; inspirit; invigorate; quicken; vivify

ENMITY: (**see** "hate") **n.** animosity; animus; antagonism; antipathy; malevolence; pique; rancor; **a.** antagonistic(al); antipathetic(al); malevolent; provocative; rancorous

ENORMOUS: (**see** "huge") **a.** colossal; cyclopean; cyclopic; gargantuan; inordinate; magnitudinous; titanic; **n.** ENORMITY: amplitude; colossality; magnitude

ENOUGH: (**see** "ample") **a.** adequate; copious; **adv.** *quantum sufficit* (**abb.** q.s.)
and more: satis superque
is as good as a feast: satis quod sufficit (what suffices satisfies)

ENRICH: (**see** "adorn") **v.** diamondize; fertilize; garnish; lard

ENROLL: **v.** impanel; matriculate; **n.** matriculation

ENSNARE: (**see** "deceive" **and** "entice") **v.** circumvent; entrap; **n.** circumvention; entrapment

ENSUING: **see** "following"

ENTANGLE: **v.** confuse; embrangle; embroil; ensnare; entrap; **n.** ENTANGLEMENT: complexity; complication; embranglement; embroilment; imbroglio; intricacy; involution; labyrinth; maelstrom; morass

ENTER: **v.** infiltrate; ingress; penetrate; permeate; **n.** ENTERING (**or** ENTRY): incursion; ingression; invasion; penetration
freedom or right to: **n.** access; *entrée;* ingress
not permitting to: **a.** impenetrable; imperforate; impermeable; imperviable; impervious

ENTERTAINMENT: (**see** "amusement") **n.** diversion; divertissement; recreation; **a.** ENTERTAINING: (**see** "amusing") divertive; festive; recreative
of strangers: **n.** xenodochy

ENTHUSIASM: **n.** ardor; dash; ebullience; ebulliency; ecstasy; *élan;* euphoria; exhilaration; exuberance; fanaticism; fervency; impetuosity; transport; vehemence; vigor; zest; **a.** ENTHUSIASTIC: ardent; dithyrambic; ebullient; ecstatic; euphoric; exuberant; fervent; flamboyant; glowing; impassioned; intense; lyrical; (per) fervid; profuse; rapturous; rhapsodic(al); unrestrained; vehement; zealous; zestful; **n.** ENTHUSIAST: buff; devotee; energumen; *exalté;* fanatic; zealot
unrestrained: **n.** lyricism; **a.** dithyrambic; lyrical; rhapsodic(al)

ENTICE: (**see** "charm") **v.** allure; attract; cajole; captivate; entrap; inveigle; **a.** ENTICING: alluring; beguiling; bewitching; captivating; Circean; engaging; exotic; glamorous; orphic; picturesque; prepossessing; seducible; seductive; sirenic(al); **n.** ENTICEMENT: allure(ment); entrapment; inveiglement; seducement; seduction; temptation

ENTIRE: **a.** comprehensive; integral; *pur et simple;* undiminished; undivided; unexpurgated; unimpaired; **adv.** ENTIRELY: (**see** "completely") *in toto; tout à fait;* **n.** ENTIRETY: aggregate; integrality; integrity; totality
something which is: **n.** integral; totality

ENTITY: **n.** existent; monad
abstract: **see under** "abstract"

ENTRAILS, *pert. to:* **a.** enteral; enteric; intestinal; splanchnic; visceral
remove: **v.** disembowel; eviscerate; exenterate
soothsayer who examined: **n.** haruspex; **a.** haruspical

ENTRANCE: **n.** access; adit(us); atrium; *entrée;* ingress(ion); introitus; os
rel. to: **a.** liminal

ENTRANCING: (**see** "enticing") **a.** delightful; rapturous
as of music: **a.** orphic(al)

ENTREAT: (**see** "beseech" **and** "pray") **v.** adjure; implore; supplicate; **a.** ENTREATING: adjuratory; precative; precatory; supplicative; supplicatory; **n.** ENTREATY: (**see** "prayer") adjuration; imprecation; obsecration; petition; solicitation; supplication

ENTRY: **see** "entering"
violent or forceful: **n.** intrusion; irruption

ENVELOP(E): (**see** "surround") **n.** container; integument; wrapper; **a.** ENVELOPING: ambient; circumferential; encompassing; pervading; pervasive

ENVIRONMENT: (**see** "background") **n.** ambiance; ambience; ambiente; entourage; environs; habitat; milieu; *mise en scène;* surroundings; vicinage; vicinity
adaptation to: **n.** acclimatization; bionomics; ecology; habitation; inurement; orientation
in artificial: **a.** or **adv.** *in vitro*
local: **n.** habitat; milieu; vicinage; vicinity; (**pl.** environs)
molded by: **a.** alloplastic; **n.** alloplasticity
native or natural: **n.** habitat(ion)
pert. to: **a.** ecological; environmental; vicinal

responsive to and in harmony w/: **a.** syntonic; syntonous; **n.** syntony
serving to bring in rel. w/: **a.** projicient; **n.** projicience
study of w/ rel. to living organisms: **n.** behavioristics; bionomics; ecology; **a.** behavioristic; bionomic; ecological

ENVY: **n.** jaundice; prejudice; resentment
is blind: invidia est caeca
without: **adv.** *sine invidia*

EQUAL: **(see** "equalize") **v.** equate; **a.** adequative; commensurable; commensurate; coordinate; corresponding; equable; equipollent; equiponderant; equivalent; isometric; proportionate; tantamount; uniform; **n.** (see "equality") coeval; compeer; equivalent; peer
age or period: **n.** coetaneity; contemporaneity; **a.** coetaneous; coeval; contemporaneous; contemporary
first among (equals): **n.** *primus inter pares*
in (equal) fault: **adv.** *in pari delicto*
in force, weight or rank: **a.** equipollent; equiponderant; equivalent; isonomic
in status or rank: a. coeval; coordinate; isonomous; **n.** coeval; compeer; contemporary; isonomy
make: **v.** adequate; equate; **a.** adequative; **n.** adequation
obligations w/ mutual rights and duties: **a.** reciprocal; syna(l)lagamatic
other things being: **adv.** *c(a)etera desunt; ceteris paribus*
pace or proportion: **a.** or **adv.** *pari passu*
to each person: **a.** or **adv.** *per capita*
to the burden: **adv.** *par oneri*
without: **adv.** *hors concours; sans pareil*

EQUALITY: **n.** adequation; commensurability; equiponderance; equivalence; isonomy; parity; uniformity
before law: **a.** isonomous; **n.** isonomy
conducive to: **a.** democratic; egalitarian
favoring: **a.** democratic; equalitarian; Rouseauesque; Rouseauistic
one who advocates: **n.** egalitarian; equalitarian; libertarian; Rouseauist

EQUALIZATION: **n.** adequation; balance; equilibrium; equipoise; equiponderance; equiponderation; isonomy; osmosis; proportionality; stabilization; **v.** EQUALIZE: equate; equiponderate; librate; neutralize; stabilize; unify; **a.** EQUALIZING: egalitarian; isonomous; osmotic; unifying

EQUILIBRIUM, *internal:* **n.** homeostasis; **a.** homeostatic

EQUIP: **v.** accouter; accoutre; capacitate; caparison; habilitate; **n.** EQUIPMENT: accouterment(s); accoutrement(s); apparatus; appointments; appurtenance(s); armamentaria; caparison; equipage; habiliment(s); impedimenta; instrumentaria; *matériel;* panoply; paraphernalia; trappings

EQUIVALENT: **(see** "equal") **a.** adequative; commensurate; congruent; counterpart; equipollent; equiponderant; homogeneous; isonomous; synonymous; tantamount
an: **(see under** "equal") **n.** *quid pro quo*
in meaning or result: **a.** equipollent; equiponderant; synonymous; **n.** equiponderance; **v.** equiponderate
treat or regard as: **v.** equate
word or phrase: **n.** equivoque **(also** equivoke)

EQUIVOCAL: **(see** "evasive") **a.** ambiguous; ambivalent; amphibologic(al); cryptic; dubious; enigmatic; indeterminate; multivocal; problematic(al); questionable

ERA, *pert. to end of:* **a.** *fin de siècle*

ERADICATE: **v.** annihilate; decimate; deracinate; exterminate

ERASE: **(see** "eliminate") **v.** dele(te); expunge; obliterate; **n.** ERASURE: deletion; excision; expunction; extirpation; obliteration
incapable of being (erased): **a.** immarcescible; imperishable; indelible; ineradicable; inexpungeable; inexpungible; inextirpable; irradicable; **n.** indelibility; ineradicableness; inextirpableness; inexpungibility

ERECT: **(see** "vertical") **v.** construct
posture, pert. to: **a.** orthograde; orthostatic
state or quality of being: **n.** perpendicularity; verticality
walking: **a.** orthograde; orthostatic

EROSION: **n.** ablation; cavitation; corrasion; corrosion; denudation; depletion; deterioration; detrition; ulceration
carry away by: **v.** ablate; **a.** ablative
formed by: **a.** terrigenous
products of: **n.pl.** detritus

EROTIC: **see** "lewd"
books, pictures, etc.: **n.pl.** erotica; esoterica; facetiae; pornography

ERR (*to*), *is human: errare humanum est; humanum est errare*

ERRATIC (**or** ERRING): **a.** (ab)errant; capricious; circuitous; desultory; devious; eccentric; fallible; fluctuating; nomadic; tangent(ial); unpredictable; vagarious; vagrant; **n.** aberrancy; caprice; deviation; eccentricity; erraticism; fallibility; vagary

ERRONEOUS: (**see** "incorrect") **a.** apocryphal; fallacious; inaccurate
doctrine or belief: **n.** pseudodox(y); **a.** pseudodox

ERROR: (**see** "blunder") **n.** corrigendum; deviation; discrepancy; erratum; fallacy; *faux pas;* inaccuracy; indiscretion; *lapsus linguae;* miscalculation; misconception; misinformation; transgression
acknowledgment w/ apology: **n.** *amende honorable;* apologia
capable of: **v.** fallible; **n.** fallibility
correction of, order for: **n.** corrigendum; erratum; (**pl.** corrigenda; errata)
fond of finding in others: **a.** captious
grammatical: **n.** catachresis; parapraxia; solecism; **a.** catachrestic(al); solecistic(al)
incapable of: **a.** inerrable; inerrant; infallible; **n.** inerrability; inerrancy; infallibility
social, or in etiquette: **n.** barbarism; *faux pas; gaffe; grivoiserie;* impropriety; *lapsus linguae;* solecism
word pointing out: **adv.** sic

ESCAPADE: (**see** "adventure") **n.** gambit; gest(e); harlequinade; peccadillo; ploy

ESCAPE: **see** "elope"
to have a narrow: **v.** *échapper belle*

ESCORT: **v. or n.** chaperone; shepherd; **n.** cicerone; entourage; retinue; *vis-à-vis*

ESSAY: **v. or n.** endeavor; **n.** (*see* "treatise") discourse; disquisition; dissertation; exegesis; **n.** ESSAYIST: feuilletonist; polemist; polemicist

ESSENCE: (**see** "embodiment") **n.** attribute; aura; cachet; concoction; decoction; epitome; principle; virtuality
having (essence) or substance: **a.** coessential; consubstantial; **n.** consubstantiality
in: **adv.** basically; essentially; fundamentally
of the: **a.** essential; indispensable
purest or ultimate: **n.** quintessence; **a.** quintessential

ESSENTIAL: (**see** "basic") **a.** cardinal; characteristic; componental; constitutional; fundamental; hypostatic(al); idiopathic; indispensable; inherent; integral; intrinsic; quintessential; substantial; substantive; vital; **adv.** ESSENTIALLY: *au fond;* basically; fundamentally; inherently; **n.** (**see** "requirement") component; constituent; essentiality; indispensability; prerequisite; *sine qua non;* **n.** desideratum; desiderium; integrality; (**pl.** desiderate; desideria)
cond. or qualification: **n.** prerequisite; *sine qua non*
in form or nature: **adv.** *sub specie aeternitatis;* **n.** quiddity; quintessence
nature or meaning: (**see** "embodiment") **n.** epiphany
not quite: **a.** subessential; suboptimal
part: **n.** component; constituent; quintessence
part(s), deprive of: **v.** devitalize; disembowel; emasculate; eviscerate; exenterate
quality, fact or thing: **n.** essentiality; fundamentality; indispensability; quiddity; quintessence

ESTABLISHED: **a.** conclusive; determinate; determinative; documented; ensconced; enshrined; ingrained; institutive; inveterate; ordained; substantiated; **v.** ESTABLISH: endow, ensconce; inaugurate; institute; ordain
long and firmly: **a.** chronic; inveterate
something conclusively: **n.** probatum; (**pl.** probata)

ESTABLISHMENT: **n.** installation; institution
doctrine of opposition to: **n.** antiestab-

lishmentarianism; disestablishmentarianism

opposing disestablishmentarianism: **n.** antidisestablishmentarianism

ESTATE: **n.** ap(p)anage; demesne; freehold; hereditament(s); patrimony; principality; tenure

ESTEEM: (**see** "honor") **v.** appreciate; venerate; **n.** deference; distinction; eminence; estimableness; estimation; illustriousness; majesty; popularity; prestige; prominence; reverence; veneration; **a.** ESTEEMED: (**see** "eminent") celebrated; commendatory; estimable; illustrious; majestic; meritorious; praiseworthy; prestigious; venerated

place of highest: **n.** hall of fame; pantheon

state of being in high: **n.** perihelion

worthy of: **see** "esteemed" **above**

ETERNAL: (**see** "everlasting") **a.** ceaseless; diuturnal; immarcescible; immortal; immutable; indefectible; infinite; perpetual; sempiternal; supertemporal

make: **v.** eternalize; perpetuate

state of being: **n.** diuturnity; eternality; perpetuity

truths or realities: **n.pl.** (the) eternities

ETERNITY: **n.** diuturnity; eon; eternality; eviternity; Ewigkeit; immortability; immortality; infinitude; infinity; perpetuality; perpetuity; sempiternity

from: **adv.** *ab aeterno*

to: **adv.** *in aeternum*

ETHEREAL: **a.** celestial; diaphanous; empyreal; empyrean; exquisite; heavenly; insubstantial; tenuous; **n.** ETHEREALITY: diaphaneity; insubstantiality; tenuity

ETHICAL: **see** "accepted" **and** "moral"

quality or character: **n.** ethicality

ETIQUETTE: **n.** ceremony; conventiality; decorum; formality; protocol

breach of: **n.** barbarism; *faux pas; gaffe;* impropriety; solecism

EULOGY: (**see** "praise") **n.** commendation; encomium; eulogium; laudation; panegyric; **a.** EULOGISTIC(AL): (**see** "praiseworthy") commendatory; elegaic; encomiastic; laudatory; panegyrical

EVASION: **n.** artifice; circumvention; equivocation; stratagem; subterfuge; tergiversation; **v.** EVADE: circumvent; equivocate; finesse; maneuver; tergiversate; **a.** EVASIVE: disingenuous; duplicitous; equivocal; evanescent; nebulous; oblique

in speech: **n.** circumbendibus; circumlocution; periphrasis; sophistry; **a.** circumlocutious; circumlocutory; periphrastic

EVEN: (**see** "equal") **a.** equable; impartial; serene; uniform; unruffled

mind in circumstances of difficulty: mens aequa in arduis

EVENING, *of the, occurring or appearing at:* **a.** crepuscular; vespertinal; vespertine

party or gathering: **n.** *soirée*

EVENT(S): **n.** circumstance; circumstantiality; contingency; episode; experience; occurrence; phenomenon

important: **n.** breakthrough; landmark

in all: **adv.** *en tout cas*

prepared for either: **adv.** *in utrumque paratus*

series of: **n.** chain reaction; continuity; continuum

EVENTUAL: **see** "final" **and** "inescapable"

EVER: **see** "everlasting"

for: **adv.** *in aeternum;* in perpetuity; *in perpetuum*

for (ever) and (ever): **adv.** *in saecula saeculorum*

EVERGREEN: **a.** perennial; perpetual; sempervirent; unceasing

EVERLASTING: (**see** "forever") **a.** (a)eonian; amaranthine; diuturnal; continual; eternal; immarcescible; imperishable; incessant; indefectible; indelible; indestructible; *in saecula saeculorum;* interminable; perpetual; sempiternal; unceasing; unfadable; unfading; **n.** EVERLASTINGNESS: (**see** eternity") diuturnity; eviternity; immortability; immortality; perpetuity; sempiternity

EVERYONE: **pron.** *tout le monde*

EVERYWHERE: **a.** boundless; infinite; omnipresent; peregrine; prevalent; ubiquitous; universal; **n.** omnipresence; ubiquity; universality

EVIDENCE: **n.** criterion; (**pl.** criteria); demonstration; indication; manifestation; symptom; testimony; token; **a.** EVIDENT: (**see** "apparent") cognizable; conspicuous; demonstrable; discernible; luculent; manifest; palpable; patent; perceivable; perceptible; ponderable; rampant; recognizable; sensible; symptomatic; tangible

EVIL: (**see** "wicked") **a.** baleful; depraved; demoniacal; diabolic(al); guileful; iniquitous; malefic(ent); malevolent; malicious; malign(ant); miscreant; noxious; pernicious; pestiferous; pestilent; serpentine; sinister; sinistrous; vicious; **n.** (**see** "wickedness") abomination; calamity; depravity; diabolism; disaster; malefaction; maleficence; malum; misfortune; sinisterity

and good, theory that world divided into: **n.** Manichaeism; **a.** Manichaeistic

because prohibited by law: **adv.** *malum prohibitum*

designed to avert or turn aside: **a.** apotropaic

-doer: **n.** criminal; culprit; delinquent; felon; malefactor; miscreant

in itself, or inherently: **adv.** *malum in se*

intent: **n.** malice aforethought; *malus animus;* **adv.** maliciously; *malo animo*

magic ritual, etc. to avert or overcome: **n.** apotropaism; **a.** apotropaic

mark of: **n.** mark of the beast; stigma; (**pl.** stigmata)

spirit(s): **n.** cacod(a)emon

person possessed by: **n.** demonaic; energumen

to him who (evil) thinks: honi soit qui mal y pense

to invoke: **v.** anathematize; imprecate; **a.** anathematic(al); imprecatory; **n.** anathema; imprecation

world is (doctrine): **n.** malism

EVOLUTION: (**see** "advancement" **and** "change") **n.** development; metamorphosis; ontogeny; phylogeny; transformation; unfoldment; **n.** EVOLUTIONIST: developmentarian

regressive: **n.** categenesis; **a.** catagenetic

EX (*former*): **a.** or **n.** ci-devant; emeritus

EXACT: (**see** "precise") **v.** extort; **a.** ceremonious; conscientious; definitive; determinate; literal; literatim; mathematical; meticulous; punctilious; scrupulous; slavish; undeviating; verbatim; word-for-word; **n.** EXACTNESS: (**see** "accuracy") definitude; determinacy; exactitude; fidelity; meticulosity; precision; scrupulosity

information: **n.** chapter and verse

minutely: **adv.** *à la lettre; ad literam;* meticulous; punctilious; scrupulous

not: (**see** "inexact") **a.** imponderable

EXACTING: (**see** "demanding") **a.** arduous; exigent; fastidious; meticulous; onerous; precise; scrupulous

EXACTLY: (**see** "exact" **and** "literally") **adv.** accurately; *ad amussim*

as written: (**see** "word-for-word") **adv.** *ad lit(t)eram;* verbatim

EXAGGERATE: **v.** amplify; enhance; magnify

tendency to: **n.** meglomania; mythomania; **a.** megalomaniac(al); Munchausen

EXAGGERATED (**or** EXAGGERATIVE): **a.** amplificatory; bizarre; eccentric; extravagant; fustian; hyperbolic(al); mythomaniac(al); *outré;* overweening

EXAGGERATION: **n.** megalomania; Munchausenism; mythomania; phantasm(ata)

extravagant or for effect: **n.** hyperbole; **a.** hyperbolic(al)

EXALTATION: **n.** aggrandizement; apotheosis; canonization; deification; enhancement; ennoblement; enshrinement; nobilitation; spiritualization; stellification; transcendence; transfiguration; **v.** EXALT: aggrandize; apotheosize; canonize; deify; enhance; ennoble; enshrine; nobilitate; pedestal; spiritualize; stellify; subtilize; transcend; transfigure; **a.** EXALTED: aggrandized; apotheosized; canonized; deified; enhanced; ennobled; enshrined; magnific(al); nobilated; pedestalized; stellified; transfigured

of mood or spirits: **n.** euphoria; *sursum corda;* **a.** euphoric

EXAMINATION: (**see** "analysis") **n.** anatomy; critique; exploration; inquest; inquiry; inquisition; investigation; perlustration; perscrutation; probe; **a.** analytic(al); exploratory; inquisitive; inquisitorial

critical: **n.** critique

EXAMINE: **v.** analyze; anatomize; collate; explore; interrogate; investigate; perlustrate; scrutinize
minutely: **v.** analyze; anatomize

EXAMPLE: **n.** archetype; exemplar; exemplification; exemplum; paradigm; paragon; precedent; prototype; specimen; typification; **a. see** "exemplary"
chief: **n.** *ne plus supra*
for, or by way of: **n.** or **adv.** *exempli gratia* (**abb.** e.g.)
most typical: **n.** quintessence; **a.** quintessential
to others, an: **n.** *instar omnium*
to serve as: **v.** exemplify; typify; **n.** exemplification; typification

EXCEED: **v.** excel; surpass; transcend; **a.** EXCEEDING: inordinate; transcendent; **adv.** parlous; **n.** transcendency

EXCELLENCE: **n.** arete; preeminence; superiority; transcendence; **a.** EXCELLENT: (**see** "best" **and** "finest") admirable; *euge;* marvelous; meritorious; mirific; *ne plus ultra; nulli secundus;* paramount; preeminent; prominent; signal; significant; supernal; superordinary; surpassing; stellar; transcendent; unparalleled; unprecedented; valiant; **adv.** *à la bonne heure; catexochen; par excellence*
model of: (**see** "example") **n.** paragon; phoenix

EXCELLING: **a.** preeminent; supereminent; transcending; **v.** EXCEL: **see** "exceed"

EXEMPTION, *not subject to:* **a.** irrecusable
taking: **a.** excipient
to a rule: **n.** non obstante

EXCEPTIONAL: (**see** "choice") **a.** extraordinary; inexplicable; nonpareil; novel; preternatural; supernal; supernatural; superordinary; unexampled; unprecedented

EXCERPTS, *literary:* **n.pl.** analecta; analects; collectanea; chrestomathy; *disjecta membra;* miscellanea; *morceaux choisis;* scrapiana

EXCESS: **n.** copiosity; exorbitance; exorbitancy; extravagance; inordinateness; intemperance; luxus; nimiety; plethora; prodigality; redundancy; satiety; *satis superque;* superabundance; superabundancy; supererogation; superfluity; superflux; surfeit; surplusage; **a.** EXCESSIVE: (**see** "extravagant") copious; exorbitant; extreme; immoderate; inconsolable; inordinant; intemperant; lavish; nimious; pleonastic; plethoric; profuse; redundant; replete; superabundant; superfluous; superlative; unconscionable
avoid: **adv.** *ne quid nimis*
in number: **a.** superfluous; supernumerary; **n.** superfluity; superflux; supernumerary
of words: **n.** prolixity; redundancy; verbiage; verbosity

EXCHANGE: **v.** barter; commute; reciprocate; substitute; **n.** commutation; *quid pro quo;* reciprocity; **a.** commutable
science of, esp. international: **n.** cambistry

EXCITED: (**see** "delirious") **a.** agitato; febrile; frenetic; hectic; **v.** EXCITE: (**see** "stir") fillip; inflame; stimulate; suscitate; **a.** EXCITATORY: excitable; hysteric(al); ignitable; incitatory; incitative; provocative; riotous; stimulatory
capable of being: (**see** "excitatory" **above**) **n.** ignitability
extremely: **a.** or **adv.** berserk; rapturous(ly)

EXCITEMENT: **n.** agitation; fomentation; furore; incitation; incitement; instigation; rapture; transport
great: **n.** alarum; alarums and excursions; orgasm; **a.** orgasmic; orgiastic
intense emotional: **n.** ecstasy; raptus; **a.** ecstatic; **v.** ecstasiate; ecstasize
state of: **n.** agitation; fanteeg; fantigue; raptus

EXCLAMATION: **n.** ecphonesis; ejaculation; expletive; vociferation; **a.** EXCLAMATORY: ejaculatory; expletive; expletory; vociferant; vociferous

EXCLUDE: **v.** debar; disbar; eliminate; excommunicate; ghettoize; ostrasize; preclude; prohibit; reject; segregate; **n.** EXCLUSION: (**see** "separation") censorship; debarring; excommunication; ostracism; rejection; segregation; sequestration

EXCLUSIVE: **a.** exclusivistic; fashionable; stylish; undivided; **n.** exclusivism; exclusivity
group: (**see** "clique") **n.** cabal; charmed circle; *corps d'elite;* coterie

EXCOMMUNICATE: **v.** anathematize; interdict; ostracize; **n.** EXCOMMUNICATION: anathema(tism); anathematization; ostracism; **a.** anathematic(al)

EXCREMENT(S): **n.** defecation; elimination; feculence; ordure; (**pl.** dejecta; egesta; excreta; feces); **v.** EXCRETE: defecate; egest; eliminate; **a.** EXCRETORY: depurant; egestive; excretious
abnormal interest in: **n.** coprophilia; **a.** coprophilous
rel. to or to study of: **a.** excremental; scatologic(al)
study of or interest in: **n.** coprology; scatology; skatology

EXCUSE: **v.** absolve; conciliate; condone; extenuate; intellectualize; overlook; palliate; pardon; rationalize; **n.** absolution; amnesty; condonation; dispensation; extenuation; indulgence; intellectualization; justification; palliation; pardon; provocation; rationalization; remission; **a.** EXCUSABLE: apologetic; conciliatory; condonable; *ein mal, kein mal;* excusatory; justificatory; pardonable; placable; venial; vindicatory
he who (excuses) himself, accuses himself: qui s'excuse, s'accuse

EXECUTION, *means of:* **n.** decapitation; electrocution; garrote; guillotine; lapidation; noyade; Republican marriage; strangulation

EXECUTIONER, *rel. to:* **a.** carnificial

EXEMPLARY: (**see** "commendable") **a.** exemplificative; exemplificatory; monitory; paradigmatic(al); prototypal; prototypic(al)

EXEMPTION: (**see** "freedom") **n.** dispensation; immunity; impunity

EXHALATION: **n.** effluvium; emanation; expiration; flatus; **a.** effluvial

EXHAUST: **v.** deplete; discharge; evacuate; **n.** effluvium; (**pl.** effluvia); **a.** EXHAUSTED: depleted; effete; impoverished; **n.** EXHAUSTION: depletion; inanition
riches or supplies: **v.** depauperate; improverish; pauperize

EXHIBITION, *boastful:* **n.** ostentation; **a.** ostentatious

EXHILARATED: (**see** "cheerful") **a.** ebullient; euphoric; exhilarative; heady; intoxicated; rapturous; zestful

EXILE: **v.** banish; expatriate; ostracize; relegate; **n.** banishment; Diaspora; expatriation; fugitivity; ostracism; relegation

EXISTENCE: (**see** "being") **n.** actuality; entity; reality
as a person or individual: **n.** individuation
beginning to have: **a.** aborning; nascent; parturient; **adv.** *in fieri*
capacity to compete for: **n.** vagility
cause or ground of: **n.** *ratio essendi*
physical: **n.** corporality; corporeity; materiality; substantiality; substantivity; **a.** corporeal; substantive
rel. to: **a.** noumenal; ontic; ontological
science or study of: **n.** ontology; **a.** ontological
something w/o: **n.** ethereality; nonentity; nullity

EXISTING: **a.** existential; extant; **adv.** *in esse*
at same time: **see** "contemporary"
something which is: **n.** actuality; corporality; corporeity; entity; existent; materiality; reality; substantiality

EXIT: **n.** egress(ion); exeunt

EXONERATE: **v.** absolve; exculpate; vindicate; **n.** EXONERATION: exculpation; **a.** EXONERATED: exculpable; exculpatory

EXORBITANT: (**see** "excessive") **adv.** *hors de prix*

EXPAND: **v.** amplify; augment; delate; dilate; enhance; inflate; intumesce; tumefy; **a.** EXPANDING: proliferous; tumefactive; tumescent; **n.** EXPANSION: amplification; development; exacerbation; proliferation; tumescence; tympany

EXPANDED *or spread out:* (**see** "expanding") **a.** patulous

EXPECTED: **a.** anticipated; contemplated; contingent; inchoate; inchoative; incipient; potential; prospective; **n.** EXPECTATION: anticipation; assumption; contemplation; expectancy; prospect; supposition
act or conduct: **n.** devoir
doing more than: **a.** supererogative; supererogatory; **n.** supererogation; **v.** supererogate

EXPECTING: **a.** anticipant; anticipatory; **n.** anticipant

EXPEDIENT: (**see** "fit") **a.** advisable; astucious; astute; expediential; opportune; opportunistic; politic; **n.** EXPEDIENCY (or EXPEDIENCE): makeshift; temporization
last: **n.** *à outrance; dernier ressort; pis aller*

EXPEDITION: (**see** "quest") **n.** acceleration; entrada; promptness; reconnaissance; safari

EXPEL (**or** EXPULSION): **see** "exile"

EXPENDITURE: **n.** disbursement; dispensation

EXPENSE(S), *at great:* **adv.** *à grands frais*
regulating: **a.** sumptuary

EXPENSIVE: (**see** "costly") **a.** confiscatory; dispenditious; extravagant; lavish; sumptuous
very: **a.** exorbitant; **adv.** *hors de prix*

EXPERIENCE: (**see** "background" **and** "knowledge") **n.** versatility; **a.** EXPERIENCED: adept; capable; competent; consummate; knowledgeable; practiced; seasoned; versant; versatile
based on: **a.** empirical; existential; experiential; materialistic; pragmatic; utilitarian
beyond or outside of: **a.** intuitive; metempirical; **n.** fourth dimension
brief but unpleasant: **n.** *mauvais quart d'heure*
is mistress of fools: experientia stultorum magistra
reliance on rather than science: **a.** empiric(al); **n.** empiric(ism)
teaches: **n.** *experientia docet*
thru imaginary participation: **n.** identification; vicariousness; **a.** vicarious

EXPERIMENT, *crucial:* **n.** *experimentum crucis*

EXPERIMENTAL: **a.** contingent; empirical; tentative

EXPERT: (**see** "skillful") **a.** adept; (ambi)dexterous; *au fait;* proficient; versatile; virtuosic; **n.** adept; ambidexterity; artiste; connoisseur; expertise; past master (or mistress); virtuoso
in realms of fine arts or fashion: **n.** artiste; cognoscente; connoisseur; doyen; (**fem.** doyenne); esthete; illuminato; **a.** esthetic
opinion: **n.** expertise

EXPERTNESS: (**see** "skill") **n.** (ambi)-dexterity; deftness; expertise; hability; virtuosity
degree of: **n.** habilitation; technique; virtuosity

EXPLAIN: **v.** elucidate; expatiate; explicate; exposit; expound; interpret; justify; rationalize; resolve; translate; **n.** EXPLAINER: elucidator; exegete; exegetist; explanator; exponent; interpreter; translator
not able to: (**see** "mysterious") **a.** inexplicable; insoluble

EXPLANATION: (**see** "justification") **n.** clarification; *éclaircissement;* elucidation; exegesis; expatiation; explication; exposition; interpretation; rationale; rationality; translation
additional: **n.** excursus; epexegesis
art of: **n.** exegetics; hermeneutics
avoid by giving reasonable, but not too plausible (explanation): **v.** intellectualize; rationalize; **n.** intellectualization; rationalization
making more obscure by: obscurum per obscurius

EXPLANATORY: **a.** analytical; discursive; epexegetic(al); essayistic; exegetic(al); explicative; explicatory; expository; expositive; hermeneutic; interpretative; paraphrastic(al); resolutive; resolutory *article:* **n.** disquisition; exegesis; interpretation

EXPLODE: **v.** detonate; fulminate; **a.** EXPLOSIVE: detonative; fulminous; •pyrotechnic(al); **n.** EXPLOSION: detonation; fiasco; fulmination

EXPLOIT: **v.** cultivate; manipulate; utilize; **n.** (**see** "deed") achievement; gest(e); **a.** EXPLOITING: predaceous; predacious; predatory; **n.** EXPLOITATION; predacity; utilization

EXPLORE: **v.** examine; investigate; probe; reconnoiter; **n.** EXPLORATION: (**see** "survey") examination; inquest; investigation; probe; prospection; reconnaissance; reconnoiter; safari

EXPOSE: **v.** denudate; denude; unmask; **n.** denudation; *exposé;* **a.** EXPOSING: denudative; **a.** EXPOSED: **see** "attack, open to"

EXPOUND: **see** "explain"; **n.** EXPOUNDER: advocate; exegete; exponent

EXPRESSION: (**see** "remark") **n.** diction; locution; manifestation; mien; phraseology; physiognomy; utterance
concise or condensed: **n.** aphorism; brachylogy
extravagant or high-flown: **n.** vaporing; **a.** vaporing; vaporizing; **v.** vaporize
facial, denoting disorder, etc.: **n.** facies
lacking in: **a.** inexpressible; impassive; **n.** impassivity
nice facility of: **n.** *curiosa felicitas*
pedantic or academic: **n.** scholasm
polite: **n.** euphemism; **a.** euphemistic
studied facility of: **n.** curiosa felicitas

EXPRESSIVE: **a.** articulate; eloquent; emphatic; indicative; meaningful; sententious; significant; **n.** EXPRESSIVENESS: eloquence; expressivity; plangency

EXPURGATE: **v.** bowdlerize; emasculate; expunge; purge

EXTEMPORARY: (**see** "off-hand") **a.** autoschediastic; extemporaneous; extempore; impromptu; improvised; improviso; spontaneous; unpremeditated; **n.** EXTEMPORIZATION: autoschediasm; extemporaneity; improvisation; improviso; spontaneity; **v.** EXTEMPORIZE: *ad lib;* improvise

EXTENT: (**see** "scope") **n.** ambit; amplitude; caliber; compass; comprehensiveness; latitude; **a.** EXTENSIVE: comprehensive; (en)cyclopedic(al); far-reaching; illimitable; latitudinal; latitudinous; magnitudinous; measureless; panoramic
to a certain: **adv.** *pro tanto*
to indicate the: **v.** quantify

EXTENUATE: **see** "ease"

EXTERMINATE: (**see** "destroy") **v.** abolish; annihilate; decimate; demolish; deracinate; eradicate; execute; extirpate; **n.** EXTERMINATION: abolishment; annihilation; decimation; eradication; extirpation

EXTERNAL (**or** EXTERIOR): **a.** adventitious; ectal; exogenous; exoteric; extraneous; extrinsic(al); foreign; peripheral; superficial; ulterior; **n.** EXTERNALITY: exteriority; extraneity; periphery
appearance: **see under** "aspect"
control, subject to: **a.** heteronomous

EXTOL: (**see** "exalt") **v.** applaud; approbate; commend; deify; glorify; enhance; enshrine; eulogize; laud; panegyrize; spiritualize; **a.** EXTOLLING: (**see** "commendable") eulogistic; panegyric(al)

EXTRA: **a.** accessory; additional; adjunctive; *de trop;* redundant; superfluous; superior; supernumerary; **n.** redundance; redundancy; superabundance; supererogation; superfluity; supernumerary
work: **n.** supererogation; **a.** supererogant; supererogatory

EXTRACT: (**see** "abstract") **n.** concentrate; decoction; decoctum; elicitation; extraction; genealogy; (quint)essence

EXTRANEOUS: (**see** "foreign") **a.** accidental; extrinsic; irrelevant; ulterior; unrelated; **n.** accidentality; extraneity

EXTRAORDINARY: (**see** "rare") **a.** bizarre; *extraordinaire;* inordinate; melodramatic; phenomenal; prodigious; sensational *person or thing:* **n.** anomaly; extravaganza; mutation; phenomenality; phenomenon; prodigality; prodigy; *rara avis;* spectacular; sport

EXTRASENSORY *perception:* **n.** telesthesia

EXTRAVAGANCE: **n.** enthusiasm; exorbitance; extravagancy; extravaganza; luxuriance; nimiety; opulence; prodigality; profligacy; profusion; rampancy; redundance; superabundance; superfluity; superflux; wantonness; **a.** EXTRAVAGANT: (**see** "superfluous") dispendious; exorbitant; gothic; immoderate; inordinate; intemperate; lavish; luxuriant; luxurious; nimious; prodigal; profligate; rampant; redundant; unrestrained; wanton
controlling or regulating: **a.** sumptuary

EXTREME(S): (**see** "odd") **a.** arrant; bizarre; consummate; eccentric; egregious; extravagant; fanatical; fantastic(al); immoderate; inordinate; maximum; notorious; *outré;* overweening; ultimate; uncompromising; **adv.** unco
act(s): **n.** ultraism
at the: **adv.** *ad extremum*
circumstances, in: **adv.** *in articulo mortis; in extremis*
course bet. two: **a.** or **n.** *via media*
limit: (**see** "extremity") **n.** outrance

EXTREMIST(S): (**see** "radical") **n.** *avant-garde;* ultraist
opinions, principles, etc. of: **n.** ultraism
pert. to: **a.** *avant-garde;* fanatical; ultraistic(al)

EXTREMITY, *last or utmost:* **n.** *à outrance; dernier ressort;* outrance; *pis aller*

EXTRICATE: **see** "free"

EXUBERANT: **see** "rank" **and** "unbridled"

EXUDE: **v.** emanate; osmose; percolate; transude; **n.** EXUDATION: extravasation; osmosis; transudate; transudation; **a.** EXUDATIVE: osmotic; transudative

EYE(S), *almond-shaped:* **n.** *yeux en amande*
bulging: **a.** exophthalmic; **n.** exophthalmos (**also** exophthalmus)
cross: **n.** exotropia; exotropism
glance of the: **n.** oeillade
having or involving one: **a.** monocular; monophthalmic
having or pert. to two: **a.** binocular
inequality in size of pupils: **n.** anisocoria
quick movement of, fr. one point to another: **n.** saccadic (movement)
study or student of: **n.** ophthalmology; ophthalmologist
twinkling of: **n.** *clin d'oeil*
watering of: **n.** epiphora
with naked: **adv.** nudis oculis; **a.** macroscopic

EYEBROW(S): **n.** supercilium; (**pl.** supercilia)
loss of: **n.** anaphalantiasis

EYELASH: **n.** cilium; (**pl.** cilia); **a.** ciliary

EYELID(S): **n.** blepharon; palpebrum; (**pl.** palpebra); **a.** palpebral

F

FABLE: **n.** allegory; apologue; fabrication; fabulosity; legend; myth; untruth; **a.** FABULAR (or FABULOUS): allegorical; apocryphal; fictitious; mythical; parabolical; Scheheradazian; **n.** FABLER: allegorist; fabulist; improvisatore; (**fem.** improvisatrice); improvisor; mythmaker; mythologist; parabolist

express in: **v.** allegorize; fabulize; mythasize; mythologize; parabolize

pert. to: **a.** Aesopian; Aesopic; allegoric(al); fabular; mythologic(al); parabolical

FABRICATE: (**see** "construct") **v.** fabulize; improvisate; improvise; **a.** improvisatorial; improvisatory

FACE: **v.** beard; brave; challenge; **n.** assurance; audacity; countenance; effrontery; facade; facet; impudence; obverse; physiognomy; visage

having large: **a.** megaprosopous

makeup: **n.** maquillage

rel. to: **a.** prosopic

-to-face: **adv.** *affronté; front à front; tête-à-tête; vis-à-vis;* **n.** confrontation

trust not the: fronti nulla fides; ne fronti crede

FACIAL *feature or expression:* (**see** "countenance") **n.** lineament; mien; physiognomy; (**pl.** facies); **a.** physiognom(on)ic(al)

feature(s) where sign of disease: **n.pl.** facies (**or** Hippocratic facies)

makeup (cosmetic, as paint, etc.) **n.** maquillage

FACING: **see** "face-to-face"

FACT(S): **n.** actuality; circumstance; datum; (**pl.** data); *fait accompli;* occurrence; **a.** FACTUAL: (**see** "earthly") empirical; **n.** FACTUALITY: facticity

after the: **a.** *ex post facto; post-factum;* retrospective

by the: **a.** **or** **n.** *ipso facto;* **a.** *de facto*

consider (something unreal) as (fact): **v.** materialize; pragmatize; rationalize

fraudulent concealment of: **n.** subreption

ignorance of the (excuses): ignoranti facti (excusat); **pl.** *ignoranti factorum (excusat)*

inescapable and unalterable: **n.** facticity

speak for themselves: res ipso loquitur

state of being a: **n.** facticity; factuality

surrounding a crime, etc.: **n.pl.** *res geste*

w/o ref. to pertinent (facts) or materials: **adv.** *in vacuo*

FACTIONAL: **see** "divisive"

FAD: (**see** "fancy") **n.** caprice; foible; megrim; monomania; vagary; whim

latest: **n.** *dernier cri*

FADE: **v.** etiolate; evanesce; languish; **a.** FADELESS: amaranthine; immarcescible; indelible

FAIL, *as in health:* **v.** decline; flag; languish; retrogress

to develop: **v.** abort; **a.** **or** **adv.** abortive

FAILURE: **n.** abstention; bankruptcy; *brutum fulmen;* catastrophe; *culbute;* defalcation; defection; delinquency; dereliction; deterioration; fiasco; insolvency; miscarriage; neglect; omission; pretermission

to act: **n.** inexecution; laches; misfeasance; nonfeasance; nonperformance

to appear: **n.** absentation; abstention

utter: **n.** catastrophe; **a.** catastrophic(al)

FAINT: **n.** swoon; syncope; **a.** (**see** "dim") caliginous; indistinct; obscure

-hearted: **a.** irresolute; pusillanimous; **n.** pusillaniminity

FAIR: (**see** "honest") **a.** comely; dispassionate; equitable; honorable; impartial;

impersonal; judicial; moderate; unbiased; unprejudiced; **n.** FAIRNESS: detachment; disinterestedness; equity; impartiality; judiciality

FAITH: (**see** "belief" **and** "religion") **n.** assurance; confidence; conviction; doctrine
abandon: **v.** apostasize; **n.** apostate; apostasy
acceptance of dogmatic statements on: **n.** fideism
alone assures salvation: **n.** solifidianism
articles of: **n.** credenda
bad, with or in: **adv.** or **a.** *mala fide(s)*
branch of theology dealing w/: **n.** pistology
defender of the: **n.** *fidei defensor*
good: **n.** *uberrima fides*
implicit: **n.** *uberrima fides*
pert. to or explaining: **a.** pistic
reliance on alone: **n.** fideism

FAITHFUL: **a.** accurate; incorruptible; reliable; resolute; staunch; steadfast; unswerving; unwavering; **n.** FAITHFULNESS: allegiance; devotion; fealty; fidelity; loyalty; obedience; steadfastness

FAITHLESS: **see** "false" **and** "treacherous"

FAKE: **see** "counterfeit"

FALL, *sudden:* **n.** anticlimax; **a.** anticlimactic(al)

FALLACY: (**see** "deception") **n.** casuistry; idolum; illogicality; illusion; paradox(icality); phantasy; pseudology; pseudoxy; sophism; sophistry; **a.** FALLACIOUS: (**see** "deceptive" **and** "false") apocryphal; illogical; paralogistic; pseudological; pseudox; sophistical
formal: **n.** paralogism; **a.** paralogistic
in thinking: **see under** "thinking"
logical: **n.** *petitio principii*

FALLING *of organ or part:* **n.** prolapse; prolapsus; ptosis
steeply: **a.** precipitant; precipitate; precipitous

FALSE: (**see** "artificial" **and** "hypocritical") **a.** apocryphal; arrant; apostate; apostatic; barmecidal; counterfeit (**q.v.**); dishonorable; duplicitous; faithless; fictitious; fictive; ignominious; illusional; illusive; illusory; inauthentic; infamous; Machiavellian; mendacious; meretricious; mythical; paradoxical; perfidious; pseudological; pseudo(x); renegade; specious; spectral; spurious; traitorous; treacherous; treasonable; unauthentic; untrustworthy; **n.** FALSENESS: (**see** "hypocrisy") duplicity; inaccuracy; inveracity; mendacity; misrepresentation; paradoxicality; perfidy; speciosity; treachery; unfaithfulness
and scandalous story, esp. in politics: **n.** canard; roorback
belief or conception: **n.** delusion; hallucination; misconception; pseudodox: **a.** delusional; delusionary; delusive; pseudodox
fantastically or romantically: **a.** Munchausen; pseudological; **n.** Munchausenism
front: **n.** Potemkin village; Trojan horse
modesty or shame: **n.** *malus pudor;* **a.** puritanical
notably or splendidly: **adv.** *splendide mendax*
opinion or doctrine: **n.** or **a.** pseudodox; **n.** pseudodoxy
pathos: **n.** bathos; maudlinism; sentimentalism
pretense: (**see** "sham") **n.** dissemblance; dissimulation; Trojan horse
reasoning: (**see** "illogical") **v.** paralogize
suggestion: **n.** *suggestio falsi*
swearing: **n.** perjury; **a.** perjur(i)ous
thinking, form of: (**see under** "thinking") **n.** idolum
writing(s) **see** "falsely or wrongly attributed writing(s)"

FALSEHOOD: (**see** "lie") **n.** canard; cretinism; fabrication; fabulation; falsity; invention; inveracity; mendacity; misrepresentation; pretense; pseudology; roorback; unveracity
hint of: **n.** *suggestio falsi*
minor: **n.** fib; tarradiddle
suggestion of: **n.** *suggestio falsi*

FALSELY *or wrongly attributed writing(s)*: **n.** apocryph; pseudepigraph; pseudograph; (**pl.** anagignoskomena; apocrypha; pseudepigraphia); **a.** apocryphal; pseudepigraphic(al); pseudepigraphous

FALSIFIED, *fantastically:* **a.** Munchausen; pseudological; **n.** Munchausenism

FAME: (see "eminence") **n.** distinction; *éclat;* notability; notoriety; prestige; renown; reputation; repute

FAMILIARITY: **n.** confidentiality; informality; intimacy; **a.** FAMILIAR: *au fait;* confidential; conversant; customary; intimate; intrusive; proverbial; unceremonious; versed; **v.** FAMILIARIZE: (see "accustom") acclimatize; acquaint; habituate; orientate; popularize
acting with: **a.** avuncular
too much breeds contempt: nimia familiaritas parit contemptum

FAMILY, *centered around husband's:* **a.** patrilocal
centered around mother's: **a.** matrilocal
head of (fem.): **n.** materfamilias; matriarch; **a.** matriarchal
head of (m.): **n.** paterfamilias; patriarch; *père de famille;* **a.** patriarchal
life: **n.** domesticity; ménage
relating or peculiar to a: **a.** gentilitial; gentilitious
pert. to: **a.** familial; familistic
tree: **n.** ancestry; genealogy; lineage; paternity; pedigree

FAMINE: **n.** dearth; exigency; starvation

FAMOUS: (see "eminent") **a.** celebrious; celebrated; classic; *distingué;* distinguished; illustratory; illustrious; leonine; notable; notorious; renowned; reputable; venerable
incident or case: **n.** *cause célèbre*

FAN: (see "follower") **n.** *aficionado;* (**fem.** *aficionada*); apostle; buff; devotee; enthusiast; votary
shaped like: **a.** rhipidate

FANATIC: (see "radical") **n.** bigot; energumen; enthusiast

FANCY: (see "fad" and "daydream") **n.** capriccio; caprice; chimera; *fata morgana;* megrim; phantasm(ata); phantasy; vaporosity; **a.** extravagant; premium; whimsical; **a.** FANCIFUL: (see "fantastic") capricious; chimerical; ethereal; grotesque; imaginary; quixotic; romantic; vaporous; whimsical; **n.** ethereality; fantasticality; grotesquerie; whimsicality
food or dish: **n.** kickshaw; tidbit
impossible or foolish: **n.** chimera; fantasy; **a.** chimerical; fantastic; utopian

FANFARE: **n.** blazonry; fanfaron; fanfaronade; flourish; tantara; tantatara

FANTASTIC(AL): (see "fanciful" and "odd") **a.** baroque; bizarre; capricious; eccentric; extravagant; fantasque; gothic; grotesque; irrational; preposterous, preternatural; supernatural; unearthly; unrealistic; **n.** FANTASTICALITY: ethereality; grotesquerie; whimsicality
render (fantastic): **v.** fantasticate; **n.** fantastication; fantasticism

FANTASY: **n.** apparition; autism; ethereality; fantasticality; hallucination; phantasm(ata); reverie; vagary
lit. or mus.: **n.** extravaganza; fantasia

FAR: (see "remote") **a.** forane; tramontane; ultramontane; ultramundane
away place: **n.** ultima Thule

FARCE: **n.** buffoonery; burlesque; extravaganza; forcemeat; harlequinade; opera bouffe; ridiculosity

FARCICAL *character:* **n.** harlequin; opera bouffe

FAREWELL: (see "goodbye") **n.** adieu; *chant du cygne* (swan song); *congé;* envoi; valediction
a last: **n.** *ultimum vale*
bidding or saying, or farewell utterance: **n.** valediction; **a.** apopemptic; valedictory
hymn or ode: **n.** or **a.** apopemptic

FAR-FETCHED: (see "ridiculous") **a.** catachrestic(al); laborious; preposterous; *recherché*

FARMING: **n.** agrarianism; agriculture; agronomics; agronomy; geoponics; husbandry; **n.** FARMER: agriculturist; agronomist; granger; husbandman; ruralist
pert. to: **a.** agrarian; agricultural; agronomical; geoponic

FAR-OFF *or unknown region:* **n.** ultima Thule; **a.** tramontane; ultramontane; ultramundane

FARSIGHTED: (see "prophetic[al]") **a.** hyperopic; presbyopic; presbytic; **n.** presbyopia

FARTHEST: **a.** farthermost; remotest; ultimate
possible point or limit: **n.** ultima Thule

FASCINATING: **a.** captivating; Circean; enchanting; enthralling; irresistible; mesmeric; sirenic(al); **v.** FASCINATE: (**see** "allure") bewitch; captivate; enamor; enchant; ensorcel(l); enthral(l); mesmerize
woman: **n.** Circe; *femme fatale;* intrig(u)ante

FASHION: (**see** "make" **and** "fad") **n.** *dernier cri*
after a: ad instar
high: **n.** *beau monde; haute couture; haut ton*
in a cavilier: **adv.** *à la hussarde*
latest: **n.** *dernier cri*
man of: **n.** *homme du monde*
people of: **n.pl.** *gens du monde*
woman of: **n.** *femme du monde;* mondaine; sophisticate

FASHIONABLE: **a.** *à la mode;* jaunty; *le bon ton;* modish; mondain(e); *recherché; soigné(e)*; sophisticated; ton(n)ish
despair: **a.** *fin-de-siècle*
society: **n.** *beau monde;* (**pl.** *beaux mondes*); *grand monde; haut monde*
world: **n.** *le beau monde; le monde*

FAST: (**see** "prompt") **a.** accelerated; *à corps perdu;* celeritous; expeditious; expeditive; Gaderine; intemperate; meteoric; precipitate; precipitous; velocious; **adv.** **or a.** allegro
day: **n.** *jour maigre*

FAT: (**see** "stout") **a.** adipose; corpulent; pinguid; **n.** (**see** "fattiness" **and** "obesity") adiposity; corpulence; pinguidity
excess on hips or buttocks: **n.** steatopygia; steatopygy; **a.** steatopygic; steatopygous
formation of: **n.** adipogenesis; **a.** adipogenous; adipogenetic
inclined to be: **a.** liparous
pert. to: **a.** adipose; corpulent; pinguid
producing or causing: **see** "fattening"

FATAL: (**see** "deadly") **a.** calamitous; disastrous; feral; lethal; lethiferous; malicious; malignant; mortal; mortiferous; pernicious; pestilent(ial)

FATALISM: **n.** determinism; necessarianism; predestination; predetermination

FATE(S): (**see** "doom") **n.** destiny; disaster; Moira; (**pl.** Moirai); portion; predestination; predetermination; Providence; will of the gods
Hindu: **n.** karma
omen of (esp. one's own): **n.** handwriting on the wall
oppose: **n.** *Fata obstant*
The Three: (**or** "Destinies"): Greece (Moerae **or** Moirai); Clotho (spins thread of life); Lachesis (assigns each to his destiny); **and** Atropos (cuts thread at death); Roman counterparts (Parcae): Nona; Decuma; Morta

FATHER: **n.** ancestor; author; genitor; patriarch; precursor; predecessor; procreator; prototype
centered upon: **a.** patricentric
derived fr. name of: **a.** patronymic(al)
descended thru: **a.** patrilineal; patronymic(al); **n.** patrilineage
inherited from: **a.** patriclinous; patroclinous; **n.** patrimony
killing of, also killer: **n.** patricide
like a: **a.** paternal(istic); **n.** paternalism
like (father), like son: tel père, tel fils
marked by authority of: **a.** patripotestal
of the family: **n.** paterfamilias; patriarch; *père de famille;* **a.** patriarchal
pert. to duty to: **a.** filial
power of: **n.** *patria potestas;* **a.** patripotestal
relationship thru: **n.** agnate; agnation; patrilineage; **a.** agnatic; patrilineal; patronymic(al)
side of family: **a.** paternal

FATHERHOOD: **n.** paternality; paternity; **a.** paternal

FATHERLY *care or conduct:* **n.** **or a.** paternality; **n.** paternalism; **a.** paternalistic

FATIGUE: **n.** dyspn(o)ea; enervation; exhaustion; hypokinesia; hypokinesis; impuissance; lackadaisy; languor; lassitude; lethargy; listlessness; weariness; **a.** FATIGUED: adynamic; dyspn(o)eic; enervated; languescent; languorous; lassitudinous; lethargic
becoming (fatigued): **a.** languescent

FATTENING: **a.** lipogenous; pinguescent; steatogenous; **a.** FATTY: adipose; oleaginous; unctious; unctuous; **n.** FATTINESS: (**see** "obesity") adiposis; lipomatosis

FAULT(S): **n.** culpa(bility); delinquency; dereliction; foible; imperfection; misdemeanor; neglect; negligence; peccadillo
by my: **a.** *mea culpa*
every man has his: nemo sine vitiis nascitur
in equal: **adv.** *(in) pari delicto*
slight: **n.** foible; peccadillo; veniality

FAULTFINDING: (**see** "critical") **a.** captious; carping; censorial; censorious; condemnatory; cynical; hypercritical; querulous; scrupulous; **n.** FAULTFINDER: carper; caviler; censor; critic; cynic; *frondeur;* malcontent; momus
given to: **n.** captiousness; cynicism; scrupulosity

FAULTLESS: (**see** "innocent") **a.** immaculate; impeccable; impeccant; indefectible; infallible; irreproachable; undeviating; unerring; **n.** FAULTLESSNESS: immaculacy; impeccability; indefectibility

FAULTY: (**see** "imperfect") **a.** amiss; dilapidated; suboptimal; substandard; unsound
in reasoning or logic: **a.** paralogistic; **n.** paralogism
or mixed use of metaphors: **n.** catachresis; **a.** catachrestic(al)

FAVOR: **v.** abet; countenance; encourage; **n.** approbation; condescension; indulgence; patronage; sponsorship
as a: **adv. or a.** ex gratia; **a.** complimentary; gratis; gratuitous
popular: **n.** *aura popularis*
to find, or bring into good: **v.** ingratiate; **a.** ingratiating; ingratiatory

FAVORABLE: (**see** "advantageous") **a.** approbative; approbatory; auspicious; beneficial; benign(ant); commendatory; condescending; disposed; gracious; inclinable; ingratiating; preferential; propitious; salutary; strategetic; strategic(al); tendentious; wholesome
most: **a. or n.** optimal; optimum
omen: **n.** *omen faustum*

FAVORED, *person highly:* **n.** *persona grata;* (**pl.** *personae gratissimae*)

FAVORITE: **n.** cosset; *mignon;* partisan; *persona grata*
servile: **n.** minion; toady

FAVORITISM: **n.** bias; cordiality; encouragement; partiality; patronage; predilection; sanction
in placing in desirable jobs: **n.** nepotism; **a.** nepotal; nepotic; **n.** nepotist

FAWN: **v. or n.** grovel; kow-tow; **a.** FAWNING: deferential; gnathonic; obsequious; oleaginous; parasitical; servile; sycophantic; toadying; unctuous; **n.** deference; obsequiousness; obsequity; servility; sycophancy; toadying; unctuosity; unctuousness

FEAR: **n.** apprehension; consternation; disquietude; misgiving; timidity; trepidation; **v.** apprehend; cower; eschew; suspect
abnormal, of animals: **n.** zoophobia
of being alone: **n.** autophobia; monophobia
of being buried alive: **n.** taphephobia
of being chastized: **n.** rhabdophobia
of being touched: **n.** aichmophobia
of cat(s): **n.** aileurophobia; ailurophobia; galeophobia; gatophobia
of close(d) places or being shut in: **n.** claustrophobia
of crowds: **n.** ochlophobia
of darkness: **n.** nyctophobia
of death or dead: **n.** necrophobia; thantophobia
of disease: **n.** hypochondria; pathophobia
of dog(s): **n.** cynophobia
of drafts or wind: **n.** aerophobia; anemophobia
of dust: **n.** amathophobia
of fire: **n.** pyrophobia
of foreigners or what is foreign: **n.** xenophobia
of God's wrath: **n.** theophobia
of heights or high places: **n.** acrophobia
of human society: **n.** apanthropophobia; apanthropia; apanthropy
of ideas: **n.** ideophobia
of insanity or going insane: **n.** lyssophobia
of lightning or storms: **n.** astraphobia
of male sex: **n.** androphobia; apandria
of meeting people: **see** "of human society" **above**
of night or darkness: **n.** nyctophobia
of number 13: **n.** triskaidekaphobia
of open or public places: **n.** agoraphobia
of pain: **n.** algophobia

of particular place(s): **n.** topophobia
of poisoning: **n.** toxiphobia
of pollution by contact w/ objects, or of being unclean: **n.** mysophobia
of punishment: **n.** rhabdophobia
of Satan: **n.** Satanophobia
of sharp-pointed objects: **n.** aichmophobia
of sleep: **n.** hypnophobia
of society: **see** "of human society" **above**
of solitude: **n.** autophobia; monophobia
of sound(s): **n.** phonophobia
of storms or lightning: **n.** astraphobia
of thunder: **n.** astrophobia; brontophobia; tontitrophobia; tonitruphobia
of uncleanliness: **n.** mysophobia
of winds or drafts: **n.** aerophobia; anemophobia
of woman or women: **n.** gynephobia
of work: **n.** ergasiophobia; ergophobia
of wrath of God: **n.** theophobia

FEARFUL: **a.** appalling; apprehensive; horrendous; horrific; pavid; timorous; **a.** FEARLESS: (**see** "brave") audacious; chivalrous; courageous; dauntless; impavid; indomitable; intrepid; *sans peur;* temerarious; undauntable; undaunted; **n.** FEARLESSNESS: audacity; chivalry; fortitude; intrepidity; **a.** FEARSOME: awe-inspiring; doughty; formidable; horrendous; redoubtable

FEASIBLE: **see** "possible"

FEAST: **n.** convivium; **n.** FEASTING: conviviality; epulation; **a.** convivial; epulary; festive

FEAT *of arms:* **n.** *action d'éclat*
of strength, skill or ingenuity: **n.** gymnastic(s); gyration; *passe-passe; tour de force*

FEATHER(S), *birds of a:* **n.pl.** *gens de même famille*
loss of: **n.** deplumation; molting; **a.** callow; deplumate

FEATURE(S): **n.** characteristic; facies; landmark; lineament; peculiarity; physiognomy
facial or distinguishing: **n.** countenance; facies; habitus; lineament; physiognomy; physique; visage; **a.** lineamental; physiognomic(al); physiognomonic(al)
odd, peculiar or remarkable: **n.** eccentricity; oddity; peculiarity; singularity
outward: **n.** physiognomy
surface or natural: **n.** topography

FEBRUARY *29th:* **n.** bissextile (day); intercalary (day)

FECES: (**see** "dung") **n.** excrement; feculence; ordure; (**pl.** (d)ejecta; egesta; excreta; (r)ejectamenta); **a.** FECAL: excremental; excrementi(ti)ous; scatologic(al); steracoraceous; stercoral
abnormal interest in: **n.** coprophilia

FEE: (**see** "wage") **n.** emolument; honorarium
one taking fr. both sides: **n.** ambidexter

FEEBLE: **a.** adynamic; asthenic; debilitated; decrepit; flaccid; impotent; impuissant; insipid; insubstantial; languid; languorous; pointless; unsubstantial; **n.** FEEBLENESS: (**see** "fatigue" **and** "weakness") adynamia; decrepitude; impotence; impotency; impuissance; tenuity
-mindedness: **n.** amentia; cretinism; idiocy; imbecility; moronity; oligophrenia

FEEL: (**see** "felt") **v.** palpate; **n.** experience; palpation; sensation
ability to: **n.** esthesia; sentience; sentiency
one's way: **v.** *aller à tâtons*

FEELING: (**see** "enthusiasm") **n.** affectation; affection; atmosphere; consciousness; conviction; emotion; fondness; impression; opinion; perception; responsiveness; sensation; sensibility; sentience; sentiency; senitment
arouse: **v.** impassion; **a.** (**see** "ardent") impassionate; impassioned
capable of: **a.** conscious; esthetic; sensible; sentient
drug or agent to destroy: **n.** analgesic; anesthesia; anesthetic; anodyne
examine by: **v.** palpate; **n.** palpation
for others: **n.** altropathy; altruism; **a.** altruistic
for those in same situation as oneself: **n.** alter-egoism; identification
incapable of: (**see** "unfeeling") **a.** impassible; impassive; impiteous; **n.** impassibility
lacking in: **a.** anesthetic; apathetic; expressionless; impassive; impiteous; inanimate; incompassionate; indurate; indura-

tive; insensate; insensitive; insentient; phlegmatic; stoical; unimpressionable; unfeeling; **n.** analgesia; anesthesia; anesthetic; impassivity; insensitivity; insentiency
loss of: **n.** analgesia; anesthesia; **a.** analgesic; anesthetic; anodynic
loss of power to recognize by: **n.** asterognosis
of having been at place before: **n.** *déjà vu(e)*; parmnesia
power to recognize by: **n.** stereognosis
sudden or violent change in: **n.** revulsion
tender or sorrowful: **n.** pathos; **a.** pathetic
with: **adv.** *con expressione;* **n.** pathos; **a.** pathetic
without: **see** "unfeeling"

FEET, *hanging by, as certain birds:* **a.** adhamant
having: **a.** pedigerous
having four: **a.** quadrupedal; tetrapod; tetrapodous; **n.** quadruped; tetrapod
having large: **a.** or **n.** macropod; **n.** macropodia; **a.** sciapodopous
having many: **a.** or **n.** multiped; polyped
having small: **a.** micropodal; micropodous; **n.** micropod
having two: **a.** biped(al); **n.** biped
pert. to or accomplished by the: **a.** pedal; podal(ic)

FEIGN: (**see** "pretend") **v.** allege; fabricate; **a.** FEIGNED: (**see** "artificial") fictitious
illness: **v.** malinger; **n.** malingerer; malingering; pathomimesis

FELLOW, *good:* **n.** bon ami; bon enfant
member or worker: (**see** "associate") **n.** coadjutor; coeval; confrere; cohort; colleague

FELLOWSHIP: **n.** alliance; association; brotherhood; camaraderie; comity; communion; foundation; fraternity; sociality; sodality
good: **a.** *bon camaraderie;* bonhom(m)ie; conviviality; *esprit de corps;* geniality
united in: **a.** consociate; consociative

FELT, *capable of being:* **a.** palpable; tactual; tangible; **n.** tactility; tangibility
incapable of being: **a.** impalpable; insentient; intangible

FEMALE: (**see** "woman") **a.** (**see** "feminine") distaff; effeminate; womanish; womanlike
centering or centered on: **a.** gynecocentric
diseases of (incl. study): **n.** gynecology; **a.** gynecological
external genitals of: **n.pl.** muliebria; pudenda; **n.** vulva
govt. by: **n.** gynecocracy
having form or structure like: **a.** gynecomorphic; gynecomorphous
homosexual: **n.** lesbian; sapphist; tribadist; uranist; urning; **a.** homoerotic; lesbian
leader, leading figure, etc.: **n.** doyenne
seductive: **see** "enchantress"
small: **n.** microgyne; *petite dame*

FEMININE: **a.** distaff; effeminate; feminal; gynecian; gynecic; maidenly; muliebral; womanish; womanly; **n.** FEMININITY: effeminacy; feminality; femineity; muliebriety
domination by or emphasizing interests of: **n.** gynecocentrism; **a.** gynecocentric
loss of qualities: **n.** defeminization; masculinization
the eternal: **n.** Ewig-Weibliche

FENCE: **v.** circumscribe; equivocate; impale; **n.** bulwark; circumscription; impalement; palisade; septum; stockade

FENCER: **n.** foilsman; sabreur; swordsman

FERMENTATION, *rel. to or caused by:* **a.** fermentative; zymotic
science dealing with: **n.** zymology

FEROCITY: **n.** acharnement; barbarity; ferity; impetuosity; savagery; truculency; **a.** FEROCIOUS: (**see** "barbaric") feral; sanguinary; tartarly; vandalic

FERTILE: (**see** "fruitful") **a.** abounding; abundant; exuberant; fecund; fructuous; productive; profuse; prolific; proligerous; uberous; **n.** FERTILITY: (**see** "fruitfulness") fecundity; prolificity; **v.** FERTILIZE: enrich; fecundate; fecundify; fructify; generate; impregnate; pollinate; prolificate; spermatize; **n.** FERTILIZATION: enrichment; fecundation; impregnation; pollination; prolification

FERVOR: **see** "zeal"

FESTER: **v.** corrupt; maturate; putrefy; suppurate; **a.** putrefactive; suppurative; **n.** maturation; putrefaction; suppuration

FESTIVE: **a.** carnivalesque; celebrious; convivial; festivous; *Mardi Gras;* sportive; **n.** FESTIVAL: conviviality; epulation; jamboree; *Mardi Gras;* symposium; **n.** FESTIVITY: (**see** "gaiety") jollification; jollity; merrymaking

FEUD: *as bet. families:* **n.** vendetta

FEVER: **n.** agitation; calenture; delirium; febricity; (hyper)pyrexia; impetuosity; **a.** FEVERISH: (**see** "fiery") febrile; inflammatory; pyretic; pyrexial; pyrexic; **n.** FEVERISHNESS: febrility
abnormally high: **n.** hyperpyrexia; **a.** hyperpyrectic
something to reduce: **n.** antipyretic; febrifuge; **a.** antipyretic
subsidence of: **n.** defervescence; lysis; **a.** defervescent; lytic

FEW: **n.** minority; sparcity; sparsity
govt. by or state so governed: **n.** oligarchy; **a.** oligarchic(al)
words, in a: (**see** "brevity") **adv.** *paucis verbis*

FEWNESS: (**see** "scarcity") **n.** dearth; exigency; exiguity; paucity; scantiness; sparcity; sparsity

FIB, *minor:* **n.** prevarication; taradiddle; white lie

FICKLE: **a.** capricious; chameleonic; crotchety; erratic; flighty; inconstant; mercurial; quicksilver; unpredictable; whimsical; **n.** FICKLENESS: *légèreté;* mercurality; quicksilver

FICTIONAL: **see** "imaginary"

FICTITIOUS: **see** "illusory"

FIDDLE, *resembling in outline:* **a.** pandurate; panduriform

FIDGETY: (**see** "nervous") **a.** restive; restless

FIELD(S): **see** "domain"
growing in or pert. to: **a.** agrarian; agrest(i)al; agrestic; campestral
of interest or authority: **n.** baliwick; domain; jurisdiction; *métier;* milieu; province; sphere

FIEND: **n.** demon; energumen; fanatic; **a.** FIENDISH: avernal; demoniac(al); demonic(al); diabolical; frantic; frenzied; infernal; malevolent; Mephistophel(i)an; sardonic; satanic; saturnine
crafty and malevolent: **n.** Mephistopheles

FIERCE: (**see** "cruel") **a.** feral; ferine; ferocious; inhuman; leonine; lupine; merciless; pugnacious; taurine; truculent; **n. see** "ferocity"

FIERY: (**see** "rash") **a.** animated; ardent; blazing; choleric; combustible; evangelistic; fervent; fervid; feverish; flammable; igneous; impassioned; impetuous; inflamed; irascible; mettlesome; passionate; spirited; vehement; vivacious

FIFTEEN *year existence or celebration:* **n. or a.** quindecennial

FIFTEENTH *century:* **n. or a.** quattrocento

FIFTH *day, occurring every:* **a.** quintan

FIGHT: **v.** impugn; **n.** belligerency; contention; contest; controversy; engagement
against: **v.** contest; militate

FIGHTER: (**see** "boxer") **n.** pugilist
chivalrous: **n.** *preux chevalier*

FIGHTING, *given to:* **a.** agonostic; antagonistic; bellicose; belligerent; disputations; militant; oppugnant; pugnacious; taurine; truculent; **n.** bellicosity; pugnacity

FIGMENT *of the mind:* (**see** "ghost") **n.** apparition; phantasm(agoria); phantom; specter

FIGURATIVE: **a.** allegorical; anagogical; metaphoric(al); parabolic(al); synecdochic(al); tralatitious; tropological
language: **n.** tropology

FIGURE: **v.** calculate; compute; **n.** digit; numeral
fine: **n.** *belle tournure*
having shapely or well-developed: **a.** curvaceous; pneumatic
of speech: **n.** litotes; metaphor; simile;

synecdoche; tralatition; trope; **a.** metaphoric(al); synecdochic(al); tralatitious; **v.** metaphorize
use of: **n.** tropology; **a.** tropological

FILE: **n.** dossier

FILLED: (**see** "full") **a.** gravid; replete

FILMY: **a.** diaphanous; ethereal; insubstantial; membranous; pellucid; pellicular; pelliculate; tenuous

FILTH (**or** FILTHINESS): **n.** contamination; corruption; defilement; excrement; excreta; fecula; feculence; immundity; offal; ordure; pollution; putrefaction; putrescence; putridity; recrement; sordidness; squalidity; squalor; **a.** FILTHY: (**see** "obscene") augean; excremental; excrementitious; feculent; immund; impetiginous; noxious; ordurous; putrid; scatologic(al); sordid; squalid; stercoraceous; verminous
abnormal attraction to: **n.** coprophilia; mysophilia; scatology
covered with or abounding in: **a.** feculent; **n.** feculence
interest in: **n.** scatology; **a.** scatological
produced by, or originating fr. decomposition of: **a.** pythogenic
worship of: **n.** *aischrolatreia*

FINAL: (**see** "conclusive" **and** "decisive") **a.** consummative; consummatory; (de)-finitive; dernier; last-ditch; telic; terminal; terminative; ultimate; **adv.** FINALLY: *ad extremum; en fin;* eventually; ultimately; **n.** FINALITY: (de)finitude; inevitability; perfection; teleology; ultimateness
act or appearance: **n.** *chant du cygne* (swan song)
argument: **n.** *ultimo ratio*
cause: **n.** *causa finalis*
destiny or purpose of man. study of: **n.** eschatology
part: **n.** epilogue
proposition or condition: **n.** ultimatum

FINANCES: **n.** exchequer
rel. to: (**see** "money, pert. to") **a.** financial; fiscal; sumptuary
rel. to public: **a.** cameralistic
science of public: **n.** cameralistics

FINANCIALLY *responsible:* **a.** solvent; **n.** solvency

FIND: (**see** "discover") **n.** *découverte*
impossible to: **a.** introuvable
lucky: **n.** *ben trovato;* serendipity; **a.** serendipitous
rich: **n.** bonanza; El Dorado
when looking for something else: **n.** serendipity; **a.** serendipitous; **n.** serendipitist

FINE: **a.** attenuated; comminuted; excellent; exquisite; homeopathic; tenuous; **n.** FINEST: *crème de la crème; élite; ne plus supra; ne plus ultra;* nonpareil; nonesuch; *rara avis*
arts: **n.pl.** *beaux-arts*
extremely: **a.** homeopathic; impalpable
or penalty: **n.** amercement; **v.** amerce
writing(s): **n.pl.** *belles-lettres;* **a.** belletristic

FINERY: **n.** adornment; caparison; frippery; ornamentation; regalia

FINGER(S) (**or** toe): **n.** dactyl(u)s; digit
abnormal size: **n.** dactylomegaly
having five: **a.** pentadactyl(ate); **n.** pentadactylism
having six: **n.** hexadactylism
holding up two: **n.** bidigitation; **v.** bidigitate
interlock as in folded hands: **v.** interdigitate
little: **n.** minimus; pinkie; pinky
middle: **n.** medius
resembling or shaped like: **a.** dactyloid; digitate; digitiform
ring: **n.** annulary
thumb: **n.** pollux
use in sign language: **n.** dactylology

FINGERPRINT(S): **n.** dactylogram
study of: **n.** dactylography; **n.** dactylographer

FINICAL: **see** "overnice"

FINISH: **see** "complete"; **a.** FINISHED: accomplished; *au fait;* consummated; culminated; kaput; perfected; proficient; *soigné;* (**fem.** *soignée*); terminated

FINISHING: (**see** "ending") **a.** consummatory
stroke or blow: **n.** *coup de grâce*

FIRE(S): **n.** combustion; conflagration; holocaust; **a.** conflagratory; igneous
add oil to: *oleum addere camino*

bet. two: **adv.** *entre deux feux*
catch: **v.** conflagrate; ignite; **a.** ignescent
divination by use of: **n.** pyromancy
fear of: **n.** pyrophobia
formed by: **a.** igneous; pyrogenic
great destructive, or great destruction by: **n.** holocaust
hypothetical principle of: **n.** phlogiston
one w/ compulsion to start or watch: **n.** firebug; pyromaniac
wilfully causing: (**see** "firebug") **n.** arson; **n.** or **a.** incendiary
-yielding: **a.** pyrophoric

FIREBUG: **n.** arsonist; incendiary; pyromaniac; pyrophile

FIREWORKS (*incl. verbal*): **n.** girandole; petard; pyrotechnic(s); (**pl.** *feux d'artifice*); **a.** pyrotechnic(al)

FIRM: (**see** "steady") **a.** adamantine; determined; established; impregnable; indissoluble; ineradicable; inexpugnable; inflexible; preemptory; resolute; sustained; unassailable; unconquerable; unfaltering; unflinching; unshaken; unwavering; unyielding; **n.** FIRMNESS: adhesiveness; determination; indissolubility; persistency; resolution; solidarity; solidity; tenacity; vertebration
of purpose: **adv.** *tenax propositi*

FIRST: **a.** (ab)original; elementary; embryonic; inaugural; inceptive; inchoate; indigenous; initial; initiatory; introductory; maiden; nascent; preeminent; primeval; primitive; primo(rdial); primogenital; pristine; rudimental; rudimentary; **adv.** *ab ovo;* **n.** aboriginal; aborigine; alpha; preeminence; princeps
among equals: **n.** *primus inter pares*
at: **adv.** *d'abord; au premier abord;* **a.** *prima facie*
attempt: **n.** *coup d'essai*
born, rights of: **n.** primogeniture
edition: **n.** *editio princeps; princeps*
in rank, etc.: **n.** precedence; preeminence; primacy; priority; supremacy
in time: **a.** primordial
one, or that which is: **n.** premier; princeps
or among the: **adv.** imprimis
place, in the: **adv.** imprimis
principles, science of: **n.** archelogy
prize or award: **n.** *cordon bleu; grand prix*
-rate: **a.** *soigné;* (**fem.** *soignée*); stellar
step: **n.** *premier pas*
to last, from: **adv.** *ad primo ad ultimum*

FISH *chowder:* **n.** bouillabaisse
-eating: **a.** ichthyophagous; piscivorous; **n.** ichthyophagist
expert on science of: **n.** ichthyologist
feeding on: **see** "eating" *above*
of a region: **n.** piscifauna
pert. to or resembling: **a.** ichthyic; ichthyoid; ichthyological; piscatorial; piscatory; piscine
shaped like, or having some features of: **a.** ichthyomorphic
state of being: **n.** piscinity
study of or treatise on: **n.** halieutics; ichthyology; piscatology

FISHERMAN: **n.** angler; piscator; Waltonian

FISHING: **n.** piscation
art of or treatise on: **n.** halieutics; ichthyology; piscatology
pert. to: **a.** halieutic(al); ichthyological; piscatorial; piscatory

FISSURE: **n.** sulcus; **a.** sulcate

FIT(S): (**see** "fitting") **a.** condign; expedient; felicitous; ideal; idoneous; kosher; legitimate; pertinent; prudent; **n.** paroxysm; seizure; tantrum; **n.** FITNESS: (**see** "suitability") adaptability; adaptitude; appropriateness; aptitude; competency; decorum; (**pl.** decora); eligibility; expediency; idoneity; propriety; seemliness; soundness; suitability
and starts, by: **adv.** *par accès*
out: **see** "equip"

FITTING: (**see** "appropriate") **a.** apropros; *comme il faut;* congruent; congruous; consonant; decorous; idoneous; legitimate; pertinent; relevant; seemly; **n.** accessory; adjunct; apropository; attachment; idoneity
to be: **v.** behoove
together, as ends of bone: **n.** coaptation

FIVE: **n.** cinque; pentad
arranged in sets of, or divided into 5 parts: **a.** pentamerous; quinary; quinate
articles or points, rel. to: **a.** quinquarticular
athletic events: **n.** penthalon

consisting of, or 5th in rank: **a.** quinary; quinate

consisting of or including, or 5 times as great: **a.** or **v.** qunituple; **n.** quintuplet

figure w/ 5 sides and angles: **n.** pentagon; **a.** pentagonal

objects in square, one each corner and one in middle: **n.** quincunx; **a.** quincuncial

-sided: **a.** pentagonal

the number, group of, or period of 5 years: **n.** pentad

-year event or celebration: **n.** quniquennial; quinquennium

years, period of: **n.** lustrum; pentad; quinquennium

years, taking place every or lasting: **a.** quinquennial

FIX: **v.** arrange; attach; concentrate; determine; implant; install; radicate; stabilize; **n.** cruciality; dilemma; implantation; plight; predicament; **a.** dilemmatical; predicamental

FIXED: **(see** "firm" **and** "stubborn") **a.** immobile; immovable; immotile; immutable; inadaptable; inalterable; incommutable; inerratic; inflexible; irrevocable; irreversible; sedentary; sessile; stab(i)le; stabilized; unswerving; unyielding; **n. see** "inflexibility"

idea: **n.** delusion; *idée fixe;* obsession

FLABBY: **a.** ductile; flaccid; languid; plastic; supple

FLAG: **n.** colors, ensign; pennant; pennon; standard; vexillum

for boat: **n.** bougee; burgee

of devotion or courage: **n.** oriflamme

-waver: **n.** chauvinist; jingoist; patrioteer; **(pl.** patriotics)

FLAGRANT: **(see** "wicked") **a.** egregious; execrable; flagitious; glaring; heinous; malicious; nefarious; rampant; vicious

FLAKE: **v.** desquamate; exfoliate; **n.** desquamation; exfoliation; lamina; **a.** FLAKING: desquamative; desquamatory; exfoliative; lamellar; lamelliform; laminar

FLAME: **n.** luminescence

bursting into: **a.** fulgurating; ignescent; inflammatory; volatile

producing, or bright with: **a.** flammiferous; ignescent

FLARING: **(see** "showy") **a.** bouffant(e); dazzling

FLASH, *as lightning or spiritual:* **n.** fulguration

FLASHING: **a.** fulgurating; meteoric; pyrotechnic(al)

as colors: **a.** iridescent; **n.** iridescence

as pain: **a.** fulgurant; fulgurating; fulgurous; lancinating

FLASHY: **(see** "gaudy") **a.** garish; meretricious; ostentatious; tawdry

FLAT: **(see** "bland") **a.** horizontal; immature; insipid; jejune; juvenile; monotonous; planar; palnate; prostrate; uninteresting; **n.** horizontality; insipidity; jejunity; monotony; prostration

FLATTER: **v.** beguile; blandish; cajole; ingratiate; panegyrize; sycophantize; wheedle; **n.** FLATTERY: adulation; allurement; banishment(s); cajolement; cajolery; obsequiousness; sycophancy; unction; unctuosity; **n.** FLATTERER: adulateur; **(fem.** adulatrice); eulogist; proneur; sycophant

FLATTERING: **a.** adulatory; ingratiating· ingratiatory; panegyric(al); sycophantic(al); unctuous

falsely: **a.** gnathonic; sycophantic(al); toadying

FLAVOR, *high:* **(see** "taste") **n.** *haut goût*

FLAWLESS: **(see** "perfect") **a.** immaculate; impeccable; impeccant; indefectible; irreproachable; **n.** FLAWLESSNESS: **(see** "perfection") immaculacy; impeccability; indefectibility

FLEE: **v.** absquatulate; elope; evade; fugitate; **n. see** "flight"

FLEECY: **(see** "woolly") **a.** lanate; laniferous

FLEETING: **(see** "vanishing") **a.** deciduous; diaphanous; ephemeral; ephemerous; ethereal; evanescent; fugacious; gossamer; impermanent; instantaneous; momentary; perishable; preterient; semelfactive; shadowy; temporal; transient; transitory; unenduring; vaporous; volatile; unsubstantial; **n.** caudicity; diaphaneity; ephemerality; ethereality; fugacity; impermanence; volatility

FLESH-*colored:* **a.** incarnadine
-eating: **a.** carnivorous; creophagous; sarcophagic; sarcophagous; sarcophilous; **n.** carnivority; creophagy; sarcophagy
embody in: **v.** humanize; incarnate; **a.** incarnate
of or composed of: **a.** sarcous
used as food: **n.** carnivosity; creophagy; sarcophagy

FLESHINESS: (see "obesity") **n.** corpulence

FLEXIBLE: **a.** compliant; lissom(e); lithe(some); manageable; pliable; resilient; supple; tractable; willowy; **n.** FLEXIBILITY: amenability; elasticity; lissomeness; maneuverability; mobility; plasticity; tractability

FLICKERING: **a.** fulgurating; lancinating; 'ambent; meteoric; uncertain

FLIGHT: **n.** elopement; fugitation; hegira; migration; volitation
capable of: **a.** volitant
engaged in headlong: **a.** Gaderine

FLIGHTY: **a.** anile; capricious; helter-skelter; hoity-toity; frivolous; imaginative; mercurial; pompous; quicksilver; quixotic; scatterbrained; utopian; volatile

FLIMSY: **a.** diaphanous; enfeebled; ethereal; ineffective; insubstantial; superficial; tenuous; trifling; unsubstantial; **n.** FLIMSINESS: diaphaneity; ethereality; tenuity; tenuousness; unsubstantiality

FLIPPANCY *in writing or speech:* **n.** persiflage; **v.** persiflate; **n.** persifleur

FLIRT: **v.** philander; **n.** coquet(te); philanderer; **a.** FLIRTATIOUS: amorous; vampirish; **n.** FLIRTATION: coquetry; dalliance; passade; philander; toying
amorous (flirtation): **n.** *oeillade*
female (flirt): **n.** amourette; amoureuse; coquette; intrigante; nymph(et)
male (flirt): **n.** coquet; philander(er)

FLOAT(ING) *in air:* **n.** levitation; **v.** levitate
on surface: **a.** supernatant

FLOCKS, *living in:* **a.** gregarious

FLOG: **v.** chastise; flagellate; lambaste

FLOOD: **v.** deluge; inundate; overflow; **n.** cataclysm; cataract; deluge; freshet; inundation; spate; **a.** FLOODED (or FLOODING): cataclysmic(al): deluginous; diluvial; inundatory
after the (Biblical): **a.** postdiluvian
before the: **a.** antediluvian
fresh, or sudden heavy rain: **n.** freshet; spate
violent: **n.** avalanche; cataclysm; debacle; deluge

FLORID: (see "ornate" and "showy") **a.** erubescent; melismatic; rubescent; rubicund; rufous; **n.** FLORIDITY: erubescence; rubescence; rubicundity

FLOUR *or meal, of or like or made from:* **a.** farinaceous

FLOURISH: **v.** blossom; brandish; burgeon; effloresce; flaunt; prosper; **a.** FLOURISHING: affluent; efflorescent; palmy; prosperous; rampant; **n.** affluence; efflorescence; fanfare; tan(a)tara
rhetorical: **n.** circumgyration

FLOWERING *again:* **a.** reefflorescent; remontant

FLOWERLESS: **a.** agamous; cryptogamous

FLOWERS, *bearing:* **a.** anthophorous; floriferous
description of: **n.** anthography
feeding on: **a.** anthophagous; anthophilous
living among: **a.** anthophilous

FLOWERY: (see "showy") **a.** bombastic; (ef)florescent; embellished; euphuistic; floriferous; florulent; grandiloquent; inflated; rhapsodic; rubescent

FLOWING: **a.** canorous: cantable; (con)fluent; cursive; derivative; deriving; effluent; emanant; mellifluent; mellifluous; mellisonant; perfluent; **n.** liquidity
back: **a.** refluent; reflux; regurgitate; **n.** refluence

musically: **a.** canorous; cantable; sonorous
out or forth: **a.** effluent; profluent; **n.** effluence; emanation; profluvium
sweetly or smoothly: **a.** mellifluent; mellifluous; mellisonant; profluent; sonorous
together: **a.** confluent; coursing; cursive

FLUCTUATE: (**see** "waver") **v.** oscillate; undulate; vacillate; **n.** FLUCTUATION: ambivalence; oscillation; vacillation; **a.** ambivalent; mercurial

FLUENCY *of speech:* **n.** *copia verborum;* eloquence; facundity; grandiloquence; liquidity; loquaciousness; loquacity; mellifluence; verbosity; **a.** FLUENT: euphonious; facile; liquid; loquacious; mellifluous; unembarrassed; verbose

FLUFFY: (**see** "woolly") **a.** flocculent

FLUORESCENCE: **n.** luminescence; phosphorescence

FLUSHED, *to become* (*or red*): **v.** empurple; **n.** rubescent

FLUTED: **a.** cannel(l)ated; channeled

FLUTTER: **v.** fluctuate; palpitate; quiver; vibrate; volitate; **a.** FLUTTERING: (**see** "confusion") palpitant; volitant; **n.** palpitation; vibration; volitation

FLY, *able to* (*or flying*): **a.** volitant; volitorial
as hither and thither: **v.** volitate

FOCAL *point* (*focus*): **n.** centrum; cynosure; epicenter; nidus; nucleus; omphalos; umbilicus

FOE: **n.** adversary; antagonist; combatant; competitor; opponent

FOG: **n.** bewilderment; brume; perplexity; uncertainty; vapor; **a.** FOGGY: brumous; caliginous; confused; nubilous; tenuous; vague; vaporous

FOIL, *person serving as:* **n.** deuteragonist

FOLD: **v.** embosom; envelop(e); intertwine; plicate; **n.** congregation; (con)-volution
or bend back: **v.** replicate

FOLIAGE, *shade-giving;* **n.** boscage; umbrage; **a.** foliaceous; umbrageous

FOLKWAYS: **n.pl.** mores
study of: **n.** ethnology; **a.** ethnological

FOLLOW(S), *disposition to:* **n.** sequacity; tractability
it does not: **n.** *non sequitur* (**abb.** non seq.)
that (*or those*) *which:* **n.** *et sequens* (**abb.** et seq.); (**pl.** *et sequentes; et sequentia;* (**abb.** et seq., et seqq. or et sqq.))
that which does not: **n.** *lucus a non lucendo; non sequitur* (**abb.** non seq.)
that which logically: **n.** *sequitur*

FOLLOWER(S): **n.** abettor; acolyte; adherent; aficionado; (**fem.** aficionada); apostle; attendant; audience; claque; clique; cohort; devotee; disciple; enthusiast; entourage; escort; fanatic; henchman; liege man; partisan; retainer; retinue; sectary; sectator; votary; zealot; **a.** FOLLOWING: consecutive; (con)sequential; ensuant; ensuing; sequent
loyal or hired: (**see** "mercenary") **n.** Hessian; janissary; janizary; liege man; minion
small group of: **n.** claque; corporal's guard
zealous: **n.** militant; minion; sectary

FOLLY: **n.** absurdity; *bêtise;* desipience; fatuity; imprudence; inanity; indiscretion; indulgence; infatuation; lunacy
utter: **n.** idio(t)cy

FOND: (**see** "loving") **a.** affectionate; amatory; amorous; ardent; devoted; enamored; **n.** FONDNESS: (**see** "appetite") affection; attachment; diathesis; partiality; penchant; predilection; propensity

FOOD(S): (**see** "cooking") **n.** aliment; comestible(s); cuisine; edible(s); grist; ingesta; nourishment; nutrient; nutriment; nutrition; nutritive; pabulum; provender; subsistence; sustenance; sustentation
American Indian: **n.** pem(m)ican
and drink: **n.** refection
art of preparation: **n.** cuisine; gastronomy
assimilation of: **n.** anabolism; **a.** anabolic
conversion into energy: **n.** metabolism; **a.** metabolic

craving for unnatural articles of: **n.** allotriophagy; geophagy; parorexia; pica
dry, for livestock: **n.** provender
eating any sort of: **a.** omnivorous; pantophagic; pantophagous; polyphagous
eating both animal and veg.: **a.** amphivorous
eating living organisms: **a.** biophagous
eating only a few kinds of: **a.** oligophagous
eating single kind of: **a.** monophagous
high class: **n.** *haute cuisine*
judge or lover of fine: **n.** *bon-vivant;* epicure; gastronome(r); gourmet; sybarite; trencherman
living on many or various kinds of: **a.** pantophagous; polyphagous; **n.** polyphagia
lover of good: **see** "judge or lover of fine" **above**
manner of preparing: **n.** cuisine; gastronomy
pert. to: **a.** alimental; alimentary; alimentative; cibarian; cibarous; culinary; gastronomic(al); nutrimental; nutritious; nutritive; trophic; **n.** gastronomy
reheated (left over): **n.** or **a.** *réchauffé*
science of: **n.** cuisine; dietetics; gastronomy; nutrition; sitology; trophology
uncooked: **adv.** *au naturel*
warmed over: **n.** or **a.** *réchauffé*

FOOL(S): (**see** "fop") **n.** Abderite; idiot; imbecile; nincompoop; *radoteur;* simpleton
fortune favors: fortuna favet fatuis
learned: **n.** morosoph
not such a: pas si bête

FOOLED, *people wish to be: populus vult decipi*
world wishes to be: mundus vult decipi

FOOLHARDY: (**see** "reckless") **a.** adventurous; Icarian; incautious; temerarious

FOOLISH: (**see** "silly") **a.** fatuous; inane; inept; infatuated; preposterous; puerile; **n.** FOOLISHNESS: (**see** "irrationality") fatuity; ineptitude; insipidity; *niaiserie*
act or remark: (**see** "absurdity") **n.** *bêtise; gaffe;* ridiculosity; solecism
cause to appear: **v.** infatuate; stultify
laughing: **a.** Abderian

FOOT: (**see** "feet") **n.** pedal extremity
done or going on: **a.** *à pied;* pedestrian
having but one: **n.** or **a.** monopod

FOOTPRINT: **n.** spoor; vestige; (**pl.** vestigia)

FOP: (**see** "dandy") **n.** Beau Brummel; coxcomb; incroyable; jack-a-dandy; jackanapes; *petit maître;* popinjay; **a.** FOPPISH: dandiacal; dandified

FOR *and against:* **adv.** *pro et contra*
ever and ever: (**see** "everlasting") **adv.** *in saecula saeculorum*
now: **adv.** *pro tunc*
public good: **adv.** *pro bono publico*
so much: **adv.** *pro tanto*
the present: **adv.** *pro nunc*
this occasion only: **adv.** *pro hoc vice*
this purpose: **adv.** *ad hoc*
virgins and for boys: virginibus puerlesque
want of better: **adv.** *faute de mieux*
whose benefit (or what purpose)?: **adv.** *cui bono?*

FORBEARANCE: (**see** "mercy") **n.** clemency; compassion; fortitude; leniency; lenity; longanimity; long-suffering; patience; resignation; toleration; **a.** FORBEARING: (**see** "patient") compassionate; indulgent; lenient; longanimous; tolerant

FORBIDDEN: **a.** inhibitory; prohibited; taboo; tabu; verboten; **v.** FORBID: (**see** "ban") enjoin; inhibit; interdict; prohibit; **a.** FORBIDDING: (**see** "dangerous") disagreeable; formidable; hazardous; inhibitory; menacing; repellant
list of books, etc.: **n.** *index expurgatorious; index liborum prohibitorum*

FORCE: **v.** coerce; constrain; dragoon; oblige; **n.** coercion; cogency; compulsion; constraint; duress; dynamism; impetus; import; impulsion; potency; restraint; validity; vis
acting from behind: **n.** *vis a tergo*
appealing to: **a.** or **adv.** *a baculo*
by main: **adv.** *manu forti*
by its own: **adv.** *proprio vigore*
creative or decisive (as institution, idea or person): **n.** demiurge
dynamic or creative: **n.** numen
equal, having: **a.** equiponderant; equivalent; tantamount
equal, use against: **v.** countervail
from behind: **n.** *vis a tergo*
from the front: **n.** *vis a fronte*
life: **see** *"vital"* **below**

marked by great: **a.** dynamic; Herculean; Samsonian; titanic; titanian
moving or impelling: **n.** animus; impetus
of or by own: **adv.** (*ex*) *proprio vigore; proprio motu*
overwhelming, as of nature: **n.** *force majeure; vis major*
powerful or angry, effect or expression of: **n.** terribilita
rel. to: **a.** dynamic(al); **n.** dynamism
terrible or irresistible: **n.** juggernaut
vital: **n.** *anima mundi; élan vital;* mana
w/ the whole: viribus totis

FORCED: **see** "coercive"; **a.** FORCEFUL: (**see** "emphatic" **and** "vigorous") dynamic; impactful; intrusive; resounding
acceptance: **n.** Hobson's choice

FOREARM: **n.** antebrachium

FOREBODING: (**see** "foretelling") **a.** apprehensive; portentous; premonitory; **n.** apprehension; augury; portent; premonition; presage; presentiment; prognostication
disaster or doom: **a.** apocalyptic(al); handwriting on the wall

FORECAST: (**see** "foretell") **v.** prognosticate; prophesy; **n.** prognosis; prognostication; **a.** divinatory; oracular; orphic; prognostic; prophetic

FOREFATHER(S): **n.** ancestor; antecedent; ascendant; forebear; forerunner; precursor; primogenitor; procreator; progenitor; (**fem.** progenitress; progenetrix); prototype
pert. to: **a.** ancestorial; ancestral; primogenitorial; primogenitive

FOREFRONT: **n.** *avant-garde;* van(guard)

FOREGO: (**see** "renounce") **v.** precede; **a.** FOREGOING: antecedent; preceding

FOREGROUND: **n.** proscenium

FOREHEAD: **n.** frons; metopion; sinciput; **a.** metopic; sinciputal

FOREIGN: **a.** adventitious; exotic; extraneous; extrinsic; forane; irrelevant; heterochthnous; heterogeneous; peregrinate; tramontane; **n.** FOREIGNNESS: extraneity; heterogeneity
(*far-off*): **a.** ultramontane; untramundane; **n.** ultima Thule
one attracted to (foreign) things, people or places: **n.** xenophile; **a.** xenophilous
to: **prep.** dehors
to the subject: **adv.** *à propos de bottes; à propos de rien;* irrelevant

FOREIGNER: **n.** alien; auslander; exoteric; outlander; peregrine; Philistine; tramontane
abnormal fear of, or what is foreign: **n.** xenophobia; **a.** xenophobic; **n.** xenophobe

FOREKNOWLEDGE: (**see** "intuition") **n.** precognition; precognitum; prescience; **a.** precognitive; prescient

FORERUNNER: **n.** ancestor; antecedent; antecessor; *avant coureur; avant-garde;* forebear; harbinger; herald; pioneer; precursor; predecessor; premonitor; trailblazer; vanguard

FORESEE: (**see** "foretell") **v.** adumbrate; anticipate; divine; envisage

FORESHADOW: **see** "foretell"

FORESIGHT: (**see** "institution") **n.** foreknowledge; precognition; prescience; *prospiciénce;* prospection; prudence; **a.** precognitive; prescient
deficiency of: **n.** amblyopia; astigmatism; myopia; **a.** astigmatic; myopic
having, or characterized by: **a.** precognitive; prescient

FOREST(S), *pert. to or inhabiting:* **a.** nemoral; sylvan; sylvatic; sylvestrian

FORETASTE: **n.** prelibation

FORETELLING: (**see** "foreboding") **a.** adumbrated; apocalyptic(al); Delphian; Delphic; divinatory; fatidic; oracular; presageful; prophetic(al); pythonic; **n.** adumbration; divination; foreshadowing; prognostication; **v.** FORETELL: adumbrate; augur; auspicate; forecast; predict; prefigure; presage; presignify; prognosticate; prophesy; portend; vaticinate
imminent disaster or doom: **a.** apocalyptic(al); **n.** apocalypse

FOREVER: (**see** "everlasting") **adv.** *ab aeterno; ad infinitum; in adfinitum; in aeternum;* incessantly; in perpetuity; *in perpetuum; in saecula saeculorum*

FOREWARNED *is forearmed: praemonitus praemunitus*

FOREWORD: **see** "preface"

FORFEIT, *take over on:* **v.** amerce; confiscate; **a.** confiscatory; **n.** FORFEITURE: amercement; confiscation

FORGED: **a.** counterfeit; spurious; supposititious; **n.** FORGERY: counterfeit; fabrication; invention; pseudograph; supposition

FORGET: **v.** obliviate; **a.** FORGETFUL: (**see** "careless") abstracted; oblivious; unmindful
do not: **adv.** *ne obliviscaris*

FORGETFULNESS: **n.** lethe; oblivescence; oblivion; obliviscence
rel. to or causing: **a.** Lethean
something causing (as drug, potion, etc.): **n.** nepenthe; **a.** nepenthean

FORGIVABLE: **see** "excusable"; **n.** FORGIVENESS: absolution; amnesty; conciliation; condonation; indulgence; remission; **a.** FORGIVING: absolutory; clement; compassionate; conciliatory; indulgent; placable; magnanimous; merciful

FORGOTTEN, *cond. or fact of being:* **n.** oblivescence; oblivion; obliviscence

FORK: **v.** bifurcate; dichotomize; divaricate; **n.** FORK (**or** FORKING): bifurcation; dichotomization; dichotomy; divarication; **a.** FORKED: bidigitate(d); bifid; bifurcate(d); dichotomous; forcipate; forficulate; furcate; furciform

FORM(S): (**see** "outline") **n.** ceremony; configuration; conformation; contour; conventionality; liturgy; perspective; ritual; silhouette; **v. see** "make"
according to: (**see** "rule") **a.** conventional; *de règle; de rigueur;* formal; ritualistic
as a matter of (form) only: **a.** perfunctory; *pro forma (tantum)*
assuming various: **a.** polymorphic; polymorphous; **n.** polymorphism; polymorphy; **n.** polymorph
beautiful: **n.** *belle tournure*
beginning to: **a.** aborning; nascent; parturient; **adv.** *in fieri*
combining human and animal: **a.** therianthropic; **n.** therianthropism
existing in different: **a.** allotrophic; **n.** allotrophy
for sake of: **see** "as matter of" **above**
give individual (form) to: **v.** individualize; individuate; **n.** individualization; individuation
having a single: **a.** monomorphic; monomorphous
having more than one: **a.** pleomorphic; pleomorphous; polymorphic; polymorphous
having, occurring or passing through several or various: **a.** polymorphic; polymorphous; **n.** polymorphism
having identical or similar: **a.** isomorphic; **n.** isomorphism
in its essential: **adv.** *sub specie aeternitatis*
varied in: **a.** allotropic; **n.** allotropy
word (form) or formation, study of: **n.** morphology

FORMAL: **a.** academic; ceremonial; ceremonious; conventional; dogmatic; formalistic; liturgical; mechanical; pedantic; pharisaic(al); punctilious; ritualistic; scholastic(al); stylized; syntactical

FORMALITIES, *observance of trivial or petty:* **n.** punctilio; **a.** punctilious

FORMALITY: **n.** academicism; ceremonial(ism); ceremony; conventionality; liturgy; pedantry; regularity; ritual(ism); rituality; solemnity

FORMATION, *in course of:* **a.** aborning; in production; *in statu nascendi;* nascent; parturient; **n.** nascency
in layers: **n.** hierarchization; stratification; **a.** stratified; stratose
in line or series: **n.** echelon; linearity

FORMATIVE: (**see** "creative") **a.** constructive; demiurgic; developmental; fictile; impressionable; nascent; plastic

FORMER: **n.** antecedent; cidevant; emeritus; (**pl.** emeriti); **a.** ancient; antecedent; anterior; bygone; cidevant; elapsed; onetime; quondam; **adv.** erewhile; whilom
life, supposed remembering of: **n.** anamnesis; **a.** anamnestic
system, govt., etc.: **n.** *ancien régime*

FORMLESS: **a.** amorphous; chaotic; heterogeneous; immaterial; inchoate; incorporeal; nebulous; spiritual; **n.** FORMLESSNESS: heterogeneity; immateriality; incorporeality; incorporeity; nebulosity

FORMULA: **n.** doctrine; philosophy; prescription; recipe; **a.** doctrinaire; doctrinal; formulaic
magic: alkahest
secret: **n.** nostrum

FORMULATE: **v.** confect; concretize; fabricate; forge; materialize; synthesize

FORTIFY: **v.** lace; munify; **a.** castellated

FORTUNATE: **a.** auspicious; beneficial; benign(ant); dexter; opportune; propitious; prosperous; reasonable; timely
man: **n.** *homme de fortune*

FORTUNE: (**see** "fate") **n.** destiny; fortuity; prosperity; success
accident of: **n.** serendipity; vicissitude; **a.** serendipitous; vicissitudinous
favors bold: audaces fortuna juvat
favors brave: fortes fortuna adjuvat
favors daring: audentes fortuna juvat
favors fools: fortuna favet fatuis
goddess of: **n.** Tyche
helps those who help themselves: faber est quisque fortunae suae
if (fortune) favors: si fortuna fuvat

FORTUNE-TELLER: **n.** necromancer; Nostradamus; prognosticator; physiognomist; soothsayer

FORTUNE-TELLING: (**see** "propheti-c(al)") **n.** prognostication
by cards: **n.** cartomancy
by crystal-gazing or mirrors: **n.** catoptromancy
by dreams: **n.** oneiromancy

FORTY, *lasting 40 days or consisting of:* **a.** quadragesimal
persons 40 to 50 years of age: **n.** or **a.** quadragenarian; **a.** quadragenarious

FORUM, *clamor of the:* **n.** *forensis strepitus*

FORWARD: **a.** *en avant*

FOUL: **a.** carious; disagreeable; entangled; feculent; fetid; leprous; loathsome; mephitic; noisome; noxious; pestilent(ial); polluted; putrescent; putrid; treacherous
-smelling: see "stink" **and** "stinking"

FOULNESS: **n.** feculence; fetidness; loathsomeness; mephitis; noisomeness; pestilence; pollution; putrefaction; putrescence; putrescency; putridity; stench
accumulation of: **n.** colluvies

FOUNDATION: (**see** "base") **n.** endowment; fundament; *point d'appui;* principum; substratum
from the: de fond en comble

FOUR, *consisting of, including or multiplied by:* **n.** or **a.** quadruple; **a.** quaternary
directions, leading in or meeting at a point: **a.** quadrivial; **n.** quadrivium
-fold: **a.** or **n.** quadrigeminal; tetrad; **a.** quadruple; quadruplicate
group or set of, or composed of 4 parts: **n.** or **a.** quaternary; quaternity; tetrad; **a.** quarternate
member of such group: **n.** quaternary
in sets or groups of: **a.** or **n.** quaternary; **a.** quaternate
-letter word: **n.** tetragram
liberal arts: **n.** quadrivium; **a.** quadrivial
lines, stanza or poem of: **n.** quatrain
parts, divide into: **v.** quadrisect; **n.** quadripartition; **a.** quadripartite
persons, group of: **n.** *partie carée;* quadrumvirate; quartet; quaternary; tetrad
series of, as books, operas, etc.: **n.** tetralogy
-sided or angled figure: **n.** quadrangle; **n.** or **a.** quadrilateral
threatening forces: **n.** Four Horsemen (of the Apocalypse)
union of: **n.** quaternity
years, lasting or occurring every: **n.** or **a.** quadrennial
years, period of: **n.** Olympiad; quadrennium

FOURTH *anniversary:* **n.** quadrennium; **a.** quadrennial
in order: **a.** quaternary

FOWLS, *domestic, science of:* **n.** alectryonology

FOX-*like:* **a.** alopecoid; vulpine

FRACTION: **n.** fragment; modicum; moiety; quantum; (pl. quanta); segment; **a.** FRACTIONAL: aliquot; fragmental;

fragmentary; inconsiderable; insignificant; segmental

FRAGILE: (see "fleeting") a. diaphanous; ephemeral; ethereal; evanescent; frangible; nebulous; tenuous; unsubstantial; n. FRAGILITY: diaphaneity; ephemerality; ethereality; evanescence; nebulosity; tenuity

FRAGMENT(S): (see "fraction") n. detritus; morceau; morsel; residue; segment; a. see "fractional"
assembled to make picture, etc.: n. collage; montage
of erosion, etc.: n. detritus
scattered or lit.: n.pl. analecta; collectanea; disjecta membra; scrapiana; n. chrestomathy

FRAGRANT: (see "savory") a. ambrosiac; ambrosial; aromatic; balmy; redolent; refreshing; n. FRAGRANCE: aroma(ticity); bouquet; effluvium; emanation; redolence
to make: v. aromatize

FRAILTY: n. infirmity; insubstantiality; susceptibility; tenuousness; tenuity; a. FRAIL: (see "brittle" and "sickly") fragile; frangible; infirm; valetudinarian
in character: n. foible

FRAMEWORK: n. anatomy; cadre; parenchyma; skeleton

FRANCE: see "French"

FRANK: (see "candid") a. artless; demonstrative; guileless; *ingénu;* (*fem. ingénue*); ingenuous; manifest; straightforward; unreserved; unvarnished

FRANTIC: a. berserk; delirious; demoniac(al); demonic(al); frenzied; maniac(al); phrenetic; rabid; n. see "frenzy"

FRAUD: n. adventurer; artifice; charlatan; circumvention; conjurer; deception; delusion; dissimulation; duplicity; empiric; fraudulence; humbug; hypocrite; imposition; imposter; imposture; mountebank; prestidigitator; pretender; stratagem; subreption; trickster; a. FRAUDULENT: (see "counterfeit") duplicitous; perfidious; sinister
marked or done by: a. clandestine; duplicitous; fraudulent; surreptitious
pious: n. *fraus pia*

FREAK: n. capriccio; caprice; crochet; lusus; monstrosity; mutation; sport; vagary; whimsey; whimsicality; a. FREAKISH: bizarre; capricious; crochety; eccentric; fanciful; notional; uncertain; vagarious; whimsical
of nature: n. *lusus naturae;* monstrosity; mutation; sport

FRECKLE(S): n. ephelis; (pl. ephelides); lentigo; a. lentiginous

FREE: v. absolve; detach; disburden; disencumber; disentangle; emancipate; enfranchise; manumit; unfetter; unshackle; unyoke; a. (see "unrestrained") autonomic; autonomous; complimentary; emancipated; exempt; frank; generous; gratis; gratuitous; independent; ingenuous; prodigal; self-determining; sovereign; spontaneous; unburdened; unbuttoned; unconfined; unencumbered; unenslaved; unenthralled; unfettered; unhampered; unlimited; unobstructed; unrestricted; untrammeled; voluntary; adv. FREELY: *avec abandon*
and easy: a. apathetic; cavalier; *dégagé;* indifferent; jaunty; lenient; unconcerned; unconstrained; adv. capriccioso; *sans gêne; sans souci*
choice or will: n. *liberum arbitrium*
-for-all: n. donny-brook
from blame: v. absolve; exculpate; exonerate; vindicate; n. exculpation; vindication; a. exculpable; exculpatory
gift: n. gratuity; lagniappe; largess(e); a. complimentary; gratis
not: see "restrained"
set (free): v. disencumber; disentangle; emancipate; extricate
to move about: a. vagile
will or choice: n. *liberum arbitrium*

FREEDOM: n. authority; autonomy; *carte blanche;* dispensation; emancipation; immunity; impunity; independence; liberation; license; manumission; self-determination; unrestraint; unrestrictedness
from obligation: n. disengagement; disentanglement; immunity; impunity
having: a. latitudinal; latitudinous
of conduct or action: n. impunity; latitude
prevent: v. immobilize

FREETHINKER: n. agnostic; aporetic; *esprit fort;* latitudinarian; nullifidian; n. FREETHINKING: agnosticism; latitudinarianism; nescience

FREEZING *to solid or semi-solid:* **n.** congealation; **a.** congealative

FRENCH, *hater of anything:* **n.** Francophobe; gallophobe; **n.** Francophobia; gallophobia
lover of anything: **n.** Francophile; gallophile
prejudice in favor of: **n.** gallomania; gallophobia

FRENZY: **n.** deliration; delirium; fanaticism; mania; orgasm; rabidity; raptus; **a.** FRENZIED: (**see** "frantic") berserk; corybantic; furibund; hectic; orgasmic; orgiastic
of emotion: **n.** nympholepsy; **a.** nympholeptic

FREQUENCY: **n.** commonality; perpetuality; prevalence

FREQUENTER: **n.** *habitué*

FRESH: (**see** "sassy") **a.** additional; blooming; inexperienced; invigorating; neoteric; original; succulent; unspoiled; untainted; unwilted; vernal; youthful; **v.** FRESHEN: refurbish; renovate; modernize; vernalize; **n.** FRESHENING (**or** FRESHNESS): crispness; innovation; invigoration; refurbishment; renovation; spontaneity; succulency; vernalization; vividity; youthfulness

FRETFUL: (**see** "irritable") **a.** fractious; ill-humored; impatient; irascible; peevish; pettish; petulant; querulous; restive; restless; waspish; **n. see** "irritability"

FRICTION, *wearing by:* **n.** attrition; erosion

FRIEND(S): (**see** "follower") **n.** adherent; benefactor; colleague; compeer; companion; confrere; confidant; Damon and Pythias; devotee; partisan; patron; *protégé*
are proved by adversity: amici probantur rebus adversis
close or bosom: **n.** *alter ego; ami de coeur*
close and trusted (intimate): **n.** *alter ego;* catercousin; confidant; (**fem.** confidante); *fidus Achates*
dear: **n.** *bon ami; cher ami;* (**fem.** *chère amie*); *mon vieux*
next (one who acts for incompetent, as minor or person non compos): **n.** *prochein ami*
of the court: **n.** *amicus curiae*
of the human race: **n.** *amicus humani generis*
old: **n.** *mon vieux*
true and faithful: **n.** confidant(e); *fidus Achates;* partisan; sectary

FRIENDLESS: **adv.** *sans amis*

FRIENDLY: **a.** accessible; affable; affectionate; ami(c)able; amical; bonhomous; companionable; compatible; (con)genial; convivial; courteous; favorable; fraternal; gregarious; neighborly; propitious; sociable; sympathetic; **n.** FRIENDLINESS: affinity; amicability; bonhom(m)ie; camaraderie; (con)geniality; conviviality; cordiality; *esprit de corps;* geniality; graciosity; graciousness; gregariousness; hospitality; intimacy; joviality; sociability
warmly: **a.** bonhomous

FRIENDSHIP: (**see** "friendliness") **a.** affinity; amicability; intimacy
act of gaining or contracting: **n.** contesseration
making or restoration of: **n.** *rapprochement*

FRIGHTEN: **v.** intimidate; petrify; terrorize; **a.** FRIGHTFUL (**or** FRIGHTENING): (**see** "ghastly") appalling; formidable; grotesque; hideous; horrendous; horrific; perilous; portentous; prodigious; redoubtable

FRIGID: (**see** "cold") **a.** gelid; glacial; hyperborean; passionless; **n.** frigidity; gelidity

FRILL: **n.** affectation; bauble; extravagance; flummadiddle; superfluity

FRINGED: **a.** circumferential; lacinate; laciniose

FRIVOLOUS: (**see** "gay" **and** "playful") **a.** frolicsome; hoity-toity; inconsequential; irrelevant; light-minded; superficial; yeasty; **n.** FRIVOLITY: absurdity; irrationality; *légèreté;* levity; nugacity; superficiality; yeastiness
person: **n. or a.** futilitarian
young woman: **n.** soubrette

FROGS *and mice, parody on (Homer?):* **n.** Batrachomyomachy

feeding on: **a.** batrachophagous
of, like, or pert. to: **a.** batrachian; batrachoid

FROLIC: **(see** "caper") **n.** boutade; caprice; carousal; *espièglerie;* festivity; *fredaine;* gambol; marlock; vagary; **a.** FROLICSOME: **(see** "playful") antic; *espiègle; folâtre;* larkish; mirthful; prankish; **n.** FROLICSOMENESS: *gaminerie;* roguery

FROM *a part one may infer the whole:* **n.** *ex pede Herculem; ex ungue leonem*
a single instance one may infer the whole: ab uno disce omnes
day to day: **adv.** *de die in diem*
deepest distress: **n.** *de profundis*
elsewhere, or other source: **a.** or **adv.** *aliunde*
olden time: **adv.** *ab antiquo*
one, learn all: ab uno disce omnes
the beginning: **see** "beginning"
the chair: **a.** or **adv.** *ex cathedra*
the greatest to the least: a maximus ad minima
the part may recognize the whole: **n.** *ex pede Herculem; ex ungue leonem*
within: **adv.** *ab intra;* **a.** endogenous
without: **(see** "foreign") **a.** exogenous

FRONT: **n.** anterior; anticus; *avant coureur; avant-garde;* countenance; façade; obverse; physiognomy; vanguard
as of coin or medal: **n.** obverse
being in: **a.** anterior; *avant-garde;* **n.** anteriority

FRONTIER: **see** "border"

FROSTY: **a.** boreal; gelid; pruinose; pruinous; unfriendly; **n.** FROSTNESS: gelidity

FROTH: **n.** despumation; effervescence; spume; **a.** FROTHY: effervescent; spumescent

FROWZY (or FROWSY): **a.** scabrous; slatternly; squalid; unkempt

FROZEN: **(see** "cold") **a.** gelid; hyperborean; immobile; petrified; refrigerated; solidified; **n.** gelidity

FRUGALITY: **(see** "thrift") **n.** exiguity; parcity; parsimony; paucity

FRUIT, *bear:* **v.** fructify; **a.** fructiferous; fructuous; **n.** fruition
bearing none: **a.** acarpous; barren; infertile; infructuous; sterile
business of growing, marketing, etc.: **n.** pomology; **n.** pomologist
-eating: **a.** carpophagous; frugivorous
residuum after expressing juice: **n.** magma

FRUITFUL: **(see** "fertile") **a.** abounding; exuberant; fecund; feracious; fructiferous; fructificative; fructuous; fruitive; gravid; procreant; prolific; proligerous; uberous; **n.** FRUITFULNESS: fecundity; frutescence; gravidity; productiveness; prolificacy
to make: **v.** fructify

FRUITLESS: **see** "futile"

FRUSTRATE: **(see** "baffle") **v.** circumvent; impede; outwit; stultify; **n.** FRUSTRATION: circumvention; disappointment; impediment; stultification; **a.** FRUSTRATING: self-defeating; stultifying

FULFILL: **v.** accomplish; consummate; execute; fructify; implement; **n.** FULFILLMENT: **(see** "end") accomplishment; consummation; execution; fruition; implementation; **a.** consummative; implementary

FULL: **a.** abounding; abundant; comprehensive; copious; orotund; plenary; plentitudinous; plethoric; replete; sated; surfeited; torrential; unexpurgated; **n.** FUL(L)NESS: abundance; amplitude; copiosity; copiousness; plen(t)itude; plethora; repletion; satiation; satiety; surfeit
in: **adv.** *in extenso; in pleno*
-toned: **a.** resonant; rotund; sonorous

FUNCTION(S): **see** "purpose" **and** "occupation"
having various: **a.** polymorphic; polymorphous; **n.** polymorphism; polymorphy
impaired or abnormal: **n.** dysfunction; malfunction; **a.** afunctional; malfunctional
lack of, not due to apparent injury or disease: **n.** abiotrophy; hysteria; **a.** abiotrophic; hysterical
of office, etc.: **n.** attribute; attribution; perquisite; **a.** attributive

FUNCTIONAL: **a.** occupational; psychogen(et)ic; psychological; psychosomatic;

physiological; utilitarian; **n.** psychogenesis; psychosomatics

FUNCTIONING, *normal, of organism, pert. to:* **a.** functional; operational; psysiological

FUNDAMENTAL: (**see** "basic") **a.** constitutional; essential; indispensable; inherent; primal; primary; primitive; substratal; substrate; substrative; underlying; ultimate; **adv.** *au fond;* **n.** FUNDAMENTALITY: essentiality; intrinsicality; primality; primitivity; quintessence; ultimacy; (**pl.** ultimacies)

FUNERAL: **n.** exequy; (**or pl.** exequies); inhumation; interment; obsequy; (**pl.** obsequies); sepulcher; sepulchre; sepulture; solemnities
ode, hymn or commendation: **n.** coronach; dirge; elegy; epicede; epicedium; epitaph; monody; obituary; requiem; threnody; **a.** elegaic; epicedial; epicedian; monodic; threnodial; threnodic
oration: **n.** eloge; elogy; encomium
service(s): **n.pl.** exequies; obsequies; solemnities
song: **see** "ode, hymn, etc." **above**
suitable for or pert. to: **a.** exequial; funebrial; funebrous; funereal; funerary; mortuary; sepulchral

FUN-*loving:* **a.** gelogenic; jocular; roguish

FUNNY: (**see** "laughable") **a.** facetious; farcical; gelastic; harlequin; humorous; jocose; ludicrous; risible
action or remark: **n.** facetiosity; farcicality; ridiculosity
yet serious: **a.** ludicropathetic; ludicroserious

FURIOUSLY: **see** "mercilessly"

FURNITURE, *household, of or rel. to:* **a.** mobiliary

FUROR(E): **see** "hubbub"

FURROW: **n.** chamfer; sulcus; **a.** sulcate

FURTHER: **a.** additional; ulterior

FURY: (**see** "anger" **and** "madness") **n.** acharnement; agitation; frenzy; impetuosity; rabidity; truculence; truculency; vehemence; **a.** FURIOUS: energetic; frenzied; furibund; impetuous; maniac(al); turbulent

FUSE: **v.** amalgamate; ankylose; anneal; coalesce; conflate; connate; syncretize; synchronize; **n.** amalgamation; ankylosis; conflation; connation; syncretism; synchronism

FUSS: **see** "hubbub;" **a.** FUSSY: (**see** "overnice") grandmotherly

FUTILE: **a.** abortive; frivolous; fruitless; futilitarian; inadequate; ineffective; ineffectual; otiose; sterile; unrewarding; **n.** FUTILITY: frivolity; fruitlessness; inadequacy; ineffectuality; otiosity; uselessness
one engaged in (futile) pursuits, or believing in futility of human striving: **n. or a.** futilitarian

FUTURE: **a.** prospective; subsequent; **n.** futurity
in the: **adv.** *in futuro*

G

GAIETY: **n.** animation; buoyancy; ebullience; euphrosyne; exhilaration; exuberance; festivity; *gaieté de coeur;* geniality; jocularity; jocundity; jollification; jollity; joviality; jubilation; lightheartedness; merrymaking; nepenthe; nonchalance; revelry; sprightliness; vivacity; yeastiness; **a. see** "gay"

GAIN: **n.** acquirement; acquisition; aggrandizement; augmentation; compensation; enhancement; emolument; increment; **a.** GAINFUL: (**see** "profitable") compensatory; remunerative; remuneratory

for sake of: **adv.** *lucri causâ*

interested in or undertaken for: **a.** commercial; mercenary; mercantile; quaestuary; venal

spirit of: **n.** fiscality

GALL: (**see** "anger") **n.** acerbity; assurance; audacity; effrontery; impudence; presumption; rancor; temerity; **a. see** "annoying"; **v. see** "annoy"

GALLANT: (**see** "brave") **a.** cavalier; chivalresque; chivalric; chivalrous; magnanimous; stately; urbane; **n.** (**see** "lover") cavalier; *cavalier servente;* chevalier; cicisbeo; **n.** GALLANTRY: **see** "bravery"

and dashing man, as in liberating victims of tyranny: **n.** pimpernel

GALLOP, *rapid, or at a:* **n.** or **a.** tantivy

GAMBLING, *pert to:* **a.** aleatory

GANG: (**see** "mob") **n.** camorra; canaille; carbonari

member of: **n.** camorrista

GAP: **n.** aperture; caesura; chasm; discontinuity; hiatus; interim; intermission; interregnum; interruption; interspace; interstice; interval; lacuna; parenthesis; vacuity; **a.** hiatal; lacunal; lacunar; parenthetical

GAPE: **v.** dehisce; oscitate; **n.** dehiscence; oscitance; oscitation; **a.** GAPING: cavernous; oscitant; patulous

GARBAGE: (**see** "waste") **n.** offal; recrement; refuse; sordes

GARDEN *party:* **n.** *fête champêtre*

pert. to or suitable for: **a.** hortensial

vegetables, herbs, etc.: **n.** potagerie(s)

GARMENT: **n.** habiliment; vestment

ecclesiastical: **n.** cassock; chasuble; soutane

worn as sign of mourning, penitence or project: **n.** sackcloth

GARNISH: **v.** adorn; diamondize; embellish; furbish; lard; **n.** GARNISH (or GARNISHMENT): adornment; embellishment; ostentation; panoply

GARTER, *Order of, motto: honi soit qui mal y pense*

GAS, *intestinal:* **n.** borborygmus; crepitation; crepitus; flatulence; flatus

GATHER: **v.** agglutinate; assemble; coagulate; collate; concentrate; conclude; conglomerate; infer; marshal(l); muster; **n.** GATHERING: (**see** "collection") agglutination; assemblage; assembly; colluvies; concourse; congregation; coterie; parliament

GAUDY: (**see** "ornate" **and** "showy") **a.** baronial; baroque; bedizened; blatant; brummagem; chintzy; extravagant; flamboyant; garish; grotesque; meretricious; ornate; rococco; **n.** GAUDINESS: bedizenment; blatancy; flamboyance; ostentation; panoply; showiness

GAUZY: see "filmy"

GAY: a. Anacreontic; affable; amiable; blithe(ful); buoyant; carnivalesque; cavalier; convivial; debonair(e); ebullient; ecstatic; effervescent; euphoric; exuberant; frivolous; frolicsome; genial; hoity-toity; jaunty; jocular; jocund; jovial; joyous; jubilant; nonchalant; phrenetic; Pythian; revelrous; rhapsodic(al); riant; roguish; *sans-souci;* spirited; vivacious; volatile; yeasty; n. see "gaiety"

GEAR: (see "equipment") n.pl. accoutrements; apparatus; appointments; paraphernalia; toggery; trappings

GEM, *surface of:* n. bezel; facet
uncut but somewhat polished: n. cabochon

GENERAL: a. cosmic; cosmopolitan; customary; ecumenical; encyclic(al); encyclopedic(al); generic; pandemic; prevalent; universal; unrestricted; n. GENERALITY: catholicity; ecumenicity; universality
effect: n. *tout ensemble*
in: adv. *en masse*

GENERATION: n. development; procreation; production
spontaneous: n. abiogenesis; autogenesis

GENERATIVE *principle in nature, worship of:* n. phallicism

GENEROUS: (see "charitable") a. altruistic; beneficent; benevolent; bountiful; charitable; chivalrous; copious; indulgent; lavish; munificent; philanthropic(al); profuse; n. GENEROSITY: beneficence; benevolence; largess(e); liberality; magnanimity; munificence; openhandedness; philanthropy; prodigality
extremely: a. lavish; prodigal; n. prodigality
person: (see "person, charitable") n. philanthropist; Samaritan

GENIAL: (see "friendly") a. affable; amiable; benignant; bonhomous; debonair(e) genteel; nonchalant; n. GENIALITY: (bon)camaraderie; bonhom(m)ie; conviviality; *esprit de corps;* gentility; joviality

GENITALS, *external, either sex:* n.pl. genitalia; pudenda
female: n.pl. genitalia; muliebria; pudenda; vulva

GENIUS. n. aptitude; disposition; intellect; propensity; talent
local, or of a place: n. *genius loci*

GENTLE: a. chivalresque; chivalric; chivalrous; conciliatory; considerate; courteous; courtly; docile; favonian; genteel; lenient; pacific; placid; tractable; tranquil; n. GENTLENESS: chivalry; docility; gentility; leniency; lenity; mansuetude; refinement

GENTLEMAN: n. galantuomo; gentilhomme; mynheer; seignior; seigneur; a. GENTLEMANLY: seigneurial; seign(i)orial
young: n. yo(u)nker

GENUINE: (see "sincere") a. apostolic(al); authentic; authoritative; *bona fide;* canonical; documented; ingenuous; kosher; legitimate; official; orthodox; simon-pure; straightforward; unadulterated; unaffected; unalloyed; unfeigned; n. GENUINENESS: apostolicity; canonicity; ingenuousness; legitimacy; sincerity
not: see "counterfeit"

GESTURE(S): v. gesticulate; n. deportment; gesticulation; a. gesticulatory
fine, graceful or pleasing, but sometimes meaningless and overcourteous: n. *beau geste*
study of, as means of communication: n. pasimology

GET: v. acquire; comprehend; obtain; secure; n. acquisition; acquirement; comprehension; obtainment; obtention; procurement; securement

GHASTLY: (see "frightful") a. awesome; cadaverous; corpselike; grisly; gruesome; hideous; livid; macabre; morbid; repellent; repulsive; spectral; terrifying; n. GHASTLINESS: grisliness; lividity; morbidity; repulsiveness

GHOST: n. animus; apparition; chimera; *deceptio visus;* delusion; eidolon; manes; phantasm(ata); phantom; poltergeist; revenant; shadow; specter; wraith; a. GHOSTLY: chthonian; delusive; illusory; shadowy; spectral; spiritual; supermundane; supernatural

(*ghostly*) *counterpart or companion:* **n.** alter ego; doppelganger
noisy: **n.** poltergeist

GIANT: **n.** behemoth; brobdingnagian; colossus; Gargantua; goliath; Paul Bunyan; Polypheme; **a.** GIGANTIC: (**see** "huge") behemothian; brobdingnagian; Bunyanesque; cyclopean; cyclopic; elephantine; Gargantuan; giantesque; Herculean; polyphemian; polyphemic; polyphemous; prodigious; **n.** GIANTISM: gigantism; macrosomia
with a (*giant*) *stride:* **adv.** *à pas de géant*

GIDDY: **a.** capricious; flighty; frivolous; gyratory; heady; vertiginous; volatile; **n.** vertigo

GIFT: (**see** "gratuity") **n.** aptitude; benefaction; benefice; beneficence; bequest; devise; faculty; largesse(e)
free: **n.** gratuity; lagniappe; largess(e); **a.** complimentary; gratis
giver adds to the: autcor pretiosa facit
of kindness: **n.** benefaction; benefice; beneficence; benevolence; **a.** beneficent; benevolent

GIFTED *person or thing:* **n.** *bel esprit;* prodigality; prodigy

GILDED: **a.** aureate; festooned; luxurious; meretricious; ornate; prosperous; tassellated; tawdry; **v.** GILD: **see** "adorn"
"youth": **n.** *jeunesse doré;* (**fem.** *dorée*)

GIN: **n.** *spiritus juniperi*

GIRL: **n.** belle; colleen; damsel; demoiselle; mademoiselle; maid(en); minx; nymph
adolescent or immature: **n.** backfisch(e)
country: **n.** amaryllis
mischievous, bold or boisterous: **n.** gamine; hoyden; minx; tomboy; **a.** gamine; hoydenish
promiscuous but technically virgin: **n.** *demi-vierge*
slender: **n.** sylph; **a.** sylphic; sylphlike
young: **n.** ingénue; *jeune fille;* junior miss; soubrette

GIST: **n.** essence; quintessence; sum and substance

GIVE-*and-take:* **v.** reciprocate; **n.** compromise; *quid pro quo;* reciprocation; reciprocity; **a.** reciprocative
in: **see** "yielding"
out: **v.** administer; dispense; distribute; **n.** administration; disbursement; dispensation; distribution
up: **v.** abjure; capitulate; disclaim; divest; relinquish; submit; surrender; **n.** abjuration; capitulation; relinquishment; resignation; submission
with expectation of receiving: **n.** or **v.** potlatch

GIVER: **n.** benefactor; donor; eleemosyner; grantor; philanthropist; testator
adds value to gift: auctor pretiosa facit

GLANCE: (**see** "glimpse" **and** "rebound") **v.** effleurer; ricochet
amorous: **n.** *oeillade*
brief: **n.** *aperçu; clin d'oeil*
rapid, or covering wide field: **n.** *coup d'oeil*

GLARING: (**see** "gaudy") **a.** audacious; flagrant; garish; glowering; impudent

GLASS, *of or like:* **a.** crystal(line); hyaline; sanidinic; vitreous; vitric

GLEAM: **v.** coruscate; fulgurate; phosphoresce; radiate; rutilate; scintillate; **n.** coruscation; fluorescence; fulguration; phosphorescence; **a.** GLEAMING: clinquant; corsucant; coruscating; fulgent; fulgurant; lambent; luminous; lustrous; phosphorescent; rutilant; **n.** clinquant; coruscation; fulguration; lambency; luminosity; phosphorescence

GLIMPSE: (**see** "glance") **n.** adumbration; *aperçu; clin d'oeil; coup d'oeil;* inkling

GLOOM (**or** GLOOMINESS): **n.** dejection; depression; despondency; disconsolation; hypochondria(sis); melancholia; melancholy; morbidity; morosity; murkishness; pessimism; sableness; saturninity unsociability; (**pl.** doldrums; lachrymals; megrims)
causing: **a.** luctiferous; tenebrific

GLOOMY: (**see** "peevish") **a.** Acheronian; Acheronic(al); Cimmerian; dejected; disconsolate; disheartened; disheartening; dolorous; dyspeptic; funebrial; funebr(i)ous; funereal; hypochondriacal; inconsolable; melancholic; melancholy; morose; pessimistic; plutonian; plutonic; satur-

nine; sepulchral; splenetic; stygian; tenebrific; tenebrous; unsociable
person: **n.** atrabilarian; hypochondriac; melancholiac; pessimist

GLORY: **n.** effulgence; eminence; grandiloquence; grandiosity; illustriousness; luminosity; luster; magnificence; repute; resplendence; resplendency; splendor; sublimity; **v.** GLORIFY: (**see** "exalt") apotheosize; deify; glamorize; idealize; romanticize; stellify; **n.** GLORIFICATION: apotheosis; canonization; deification; exaltation; glamorization; sanctification; stellification
born to: **adv.** *natus ad gloriam*
cloud of: **n.** nimbus
to the Father (God): **n.** ascription; Gloria in Excelsis; Gloria Patri

GLOSS: **see** "veneer"; **a.** GLOSSY: lustrous; nitid; **n.** GLOSSINESS: (**see** "sheen") luster; nitidity

GLOW, *sunrise or sunset:* **n.** alpenglow

GLOWING: **a.** ardent; candent; enthusiastic; fervent; impassioned; (in)candescent; intense; (per)fervid; phosphorescent; refulgent; **n.** (in)candescence; phosphorescence; refulgence; refulgency

GLUEY: **a.** glutinous; tenacious; viscous; **n.** glutinosity; tenacity; viscosity

GLUM: **see** "gloomy"

GLUTTON: **n.** apician; cormorant; epicure; gormand(izer); gourmand; gourmet; **v.** gormandize; **a.** GLUTTONOUS: bulimic; cormorant; crapulent; crapulous; edacious; epicurean; polyphagous; rapacious; ventripotent; voracious; **n.** GLUTTONY: (**see** "appetite, excessive") bulimia; crapulence; edacity; gulosity; insatiability; rapacity; voracity

GO: (**see** going") **v.** depart; diminish; elapse; proceed; wane
before: (**see** "going before" **and** "preliminary") **v.** precede; transcend; **n.** precedent
-between: **n.** diplomat(ist); emissary; *entrepreneur;* (**fem.** *entrepreneuse*); intercessor; intermediary; internuncio; mediator; moderator; propitiator
in peace: **adv.** *vade in pace*
permission to: **n.** *congé*

GOAL: (**see** "aim" **and** "intent") **n.** ambition; destination; ideal; intention; Mecca; terminus; *terminus ad quem*
distant: **n.** Thule; *ultima Thule*
extreme or highest: **n.** consummation

GOAT, *of or like:* **a.** capric; caprid; caprine; hircine

GOD(S): **n.** Almighty; divinity; Jehovah; Pantocrator; Providence
appearance or revelatory manifestation of: **n.** epiphany; **a.** epiphanic
as center, central interest or ultimate concern: **n.** theocentrism; **a.** theocentric
bad: **n.** Ahriman; cacod(a)emon; (**see** "devil")
being willing, or w/ sanction of: **adv.** *Deo volente*
belief in or worship of several or many: **n.** polytheism; **a.** polytheistic(al)
blood of the (gods): **n.** ichor
by grace of: **adv.** *Dei gratia*
doctrine that but one: **n.** monotheism; **a.** monotheistic(al)
drink of the (gods): **n.** nectar
favored our undertakings: annuit coeptus
fear of wrath of: **n.** theophobia
festival honoring the (gods): **n.** panegyris
fit for, or food for (gods): **n.** ambrosia; **a.** ambrosial
forbid: **adv.** *absit omen*
formed an image of: **a.** theomorphic; **n.** theomorphism
from machine; deux ex machinâ
glory to: **see** "praise to" **below**
good or beneficial: **n.** agathod(a)emon
government or rule by: **n.** theocracy; theonomy; **a.** theocratic; theonomous
hatred or hater of: **n.** theophobia; theophobist
having ruled otherwise: diis (or dis) aliter visum
having appearance or nature of a: **a.** Adonic; deiform
helps those who help themselves: otiosis nullus adsistit Deus
humbles the proud: Dieu abaisse les superbes
hymn to: **n.** doxology; *te deum;* theody
incarnation of: **n.** epiphany
inferior or subordinate: **n.** demiurge; subdeity
narrative of miraculous deeds of (god) or hero: **n.** aretalogy
of the people (popular or state-recognized): **n.** pantheon

praise be to: **adv.** *laus Deo*
praise to: **n.** ascription; doxology; *Gloria in Excelsis; Gloria Patria; laus Deo;* **a.** doxological; **v.** doxologize
revelation or manifestation of: **n.** epiphany
thanks to: **n.** *Deo gratias*
will of the: **n.** moira
will provide: Deus providebit; Dominus providebit
wills it: Deus vult
with us: **adv.** *Dieu avec nous*
worship of a: **n.** theolatry
worship of all: **n.** pantheism; **a.** pantheistic(al); **n.** omnist; pantheist
worship of foreign or unsanctioned: **n.** allotheism
worship of many: **n.** polytheism; **a.** polytheistic(al)
worship of one: **n.** henotheism; monolatry; monotheism; **a.** monolatrous; monotheistic

GODLINESS: **n.** *pietas*

GOD-MAN: **n.** theanthropos

GODSEND: **n.** *trouvaille*

GOING *before:* (**see** "preliminary") **a.** antecedent; anticipating; anticipatory; expectant; introductory; precedent; preceding; precursory; prefatorial; premonitory; prevenient; **n.** precedent
out: **v.** egress; **n.** egression

GOLD, *accursed greed of: auri sacra fames*
bearing or containing: **a.** auric; auriferous; aurous
cloth of: **n.** *drap d'or*
distinctive properties of: **n.** aureity
pert. to or like: **a.** auric; aurous
supposed element to produce: **n.** elixir; philosopher's stone

GOLDEN: **a.** aureate; aurelian; aureous; auric; auriferous; aurulent; halcyon
age: **n.** millennium; (**pl.** millennia); *siècle d'or*
calf, worship of: **n.** *adorer le veau d'or*
mean: **n.** *ariston metron; aurea mediocritas; le juste milieu*

GOOD: **a.** adequate; admirable; advantageous; beatific; blissful; cardinal; decorous; delicious; nutritious; prime; propitious; profitable; saintly; salubrious; salutary; seraphic; superlative; worthy
all things tend to ultimate (theory): **n.** agathism; agathist
and evil, composed of both: **a.** agathocacological; agathokakological; Jekyll-and-Hyde
and evil, theory that world divided into: **n.** Manichaeism; **a.** Manichaeistic
appearing to be: **a.** hypocritical; religiose; sanctimonious; **n.** hypocrisy; odor of sanctity; religiosity; sanctimoniousness; sanctimony
auspices: **n.** *bonis avibus*
breeding or manners: **n.** *bon ton;* gentility; *savoir faire;* suavity; urbanity
common: **n.** *commune bonum*
deed or act: **n.** benefaction; benefice; beneficence; benevolence; mitzvah; **a.** benefic(ent); benevolent
doctrine of: **n.** agathology
-evening: **n.** *bonsoir*
faith: **n.** *aberrima fides; bona fide(s); bonne foi*
-fellowship: **n.** *(bon) camaraderie; bonhom(m)ie;* conviviality; *esprit de corps;* geniality; joviality; **a.** bonhomous; convivial; genial; jovial
-for-nothing: **a.** fustian
for whose?: **n.** *cui bono?*
genius: **n.** agathod(a)emon
great: **n.** *magnum bonum*
help: **n.** *bon secours*
highest or greatest: **n.** *summum bonum*
-humored: **see** "gay"
incapable of either harm or good: **a.** adiaphoristic; adiaphorous
-looking: **a.** comely; personable; pulchritudinous
-morning: **n.** *bonjour; buenas dias*
-natured: **a.** affable; amiable; benign; (con)genial; gracious
-night: **n.** *buenas noches*
order or management: **n.** eutaxy; husbandry
position for observation or action: **n.** coign (of vantage)
pretending to be: **see** "appearing to be" **above**
science or doctrine of: **n.** agathology
supreme or highest: **n.** *summum bonum*
taste: **n.** *decorum;* **a.** *decorous*
to the (good) all things are (good): omnia bona bonis
-will: **n.** benevolence; *bienveillance; bonne volonté; bonté*

GOODBYE: **n.** *à bientôt;* adeus; adieu; *à tout à l'heure; au revoir; auf wiedersehen; bene vale; bon voyage; congé; riverderchi* *biding or pert. to:* **a.** apopemtic; valedictory

GOODNESS, *appearance or reputation of:* **n.** hypocrisy; odor of sanctity; religiosity; sanctimoniousness

GOOSE, *like a:* **a.** anserine
-pimples: **n.** *arrectores pilorum; cutis anserina;* horripilation

GORGE: **v.** gormandize; satiate; surfeit; **n.** gluttony; satiation; satiety

GORGEOUS: (**see** "grand") **a.** dazzling; flamboyant; magnificent; resplendent; splendaceous; splendacious

GOSSIP: **n.** blatherskite; *caqueterie;* magpie; quidnunc; rumormonger; scuttlebutt
piece of: **n.** *on-dit*
unsavory: **n.** *chronique scandaleuse*

GOURMET: (**see** "glutton") **n.** *bon-vivant;* epicure; gastronome(r); gourmand; trencherman

GOVERN: **see** "command"

GOVERNMENT(S): **n.** administration; bureaucracy; dominion; polity; regime(n); sovereignty
by all the people: **n.** pantarchy; pantisocracy; **a.** pantocratic
by best men: **n.** aristarchy
by fools: **n.** foolocracy
by devil(s): **n.** diabolarchy; diabolocracy
by few, also state so governed: **n.** oligarchy: **a.** oligarchic(al)
by harlots: **n.** pornocracy
by many persons: **n.** polyarchy; **a.** polyarchic
by middle class: **n.** mesocracy
by old men: **n.** gerontocracy
by one person: **n.** autocracy; dictatorship; monarchy; monocracy
by rich: **n.** plutocracy
by small ruling class: **n.** aristocracy
by two persons: **n.** diarchy; duumvirate; dyarchy
by woman or women: **n.** gynarchy; gynecocracy; matriarchy
by worst men: **n.** kakistocracy
ceremonial forms of dealing bet.: **n.** protocol
former or old: **n.** *ancien regime*
founded on system or code of laws: **n.** nomocracy
military: **n.** stratocracy
rel. to: **a.** governmental; gubernatorial; statal; **n.** statecraft
subject to that of another (govt.) **n.** heteronomy; **a.** heteronomous
suspension of, or interval bet. leaders: **n.** interregnum
within a govt.: **n.** *imperium in imperio*
without a head: **a.** acephalous

GRAB: **v.** appropriate; arrogate; capture; confiscate; sequester; **n.** appropriation; arrogation; capture; confiscation; sequestration

GRACE: **n.** attractiveness; benefaction; clemency; considerateness; dispensation; elegance; felicity; lenity; polish; thoughtfulness
characterized by exquisite (grace) and refinement: **a.** spirituel(le)
(prayer): **n.** benediction; invocation; **a.** benedictory; invocatory
with good: **adv.** *de bonne grâce*

GRACEFUL: **a.** gracile; lissome; lithe(some); nymphean; nymphlike; soigné(e); svelt(e); sylphic; sylphlike; symmetrical; **n.** GRACEFULNESS: **see** "slenderness"

GRACIOUS: (**see** "courteous") **a.** affable; auspicious; benign(ant); merciful; **adv.** GRACIOUSLY: *de bonne grâce;* **n.** GRACIOUSNESS: (**see** "grace") benignity; condescension; graciosity; lenity; mercifulness

GRADE: (**see** "rank") **n.** echelon; gradation; standing; station

GRADUAL: **a.** fractional; fragmentary; imperceptible; incremental; piecemeal; progressive; subtle; **adv.** GRADUALLY: *di grado in grado;* inchmeal; *poco a poco*
state or quality of being: **n.** graduality; imperceptibility

GRAIN, *against the:* **adv.** *à contre coeur; à rebours*
of or like: **a.** farinaceous; frumentaceous

GRAMMATICAL *arrangement:* **n.** syntax
inflection: **n.** conjugation

GRAND: (**see** "great") **a.** august; baronial; cosmic; exalted; flamboyant; grandiloquent; grandiose; Homeric; illustrious; imposing; impressive; magnificent; magniloquent; majestic; ostentatious; preeminent; princely; prominent; rococo; stately; sublime; sumptuous; transcendent
state of being or feeling: **see** "grandeur"

GRANDEUR: **n.** flamboyancy; grandiloquence; grandiosity; grandity; impressiveness; magnificence; majesty; regality; sublimity; sumptuousness
delusions of: **n.** megalomania; **a.** megalomaniacal; **n.** megalomaniac

GRANDIOSE: (**see** "grand") **a.** apocalyptic(al); bombastic; cosmic; Homeric; imposing; majestic; turgid
in speech or expression: (**see** "flowery") **a.** grandiloquent; magniloquent; rubescent

GRANT: **v.** award; concede; vouchsafe; **n.** **see** "gratuity

GRANTED, *taken for:* (**see** "self-evident") **adv.** sub silento

GRANTING, *act of:* **n.** accordance; concession

GRAPES, *clustered or shaped like:* **a.** aciniform; botryoid(al); botryose; racemose

GRASPING: (**see** "greedy") **a.** acquisitive; *alieni appetens;* avaricious; covetous; miserly; prehensile; prehensive; tenacious
adapted for: **n.** prehensile; prehensive; **n.** prehension; prehensility
person: **n.** curmudgeon

GRASS(ES), *feeding on:* **a.** graminivorous
rel. to or resembling: **a.** gramineal; gramineous; graminoid
study of: **n.** agrostology; **n.** agrostologist

GRATIFICATION: **n.** delectation; satiation; satiety
showing: **a.** congratulatory; gratulant

GRATIFY: (**see** "please") **v.** delectate; indulge; satiate
that which (gratifies): **n.** emollient; placebo; tranquilizer; unction

GRATING: **a.** strident; stridulous; **n.** crepitus; stridor; stridulation

GRATUITY: **n.** benefaction; benefice; beneficence; benevolence; douceur; honorarium; lagniappe; largess(e); perquisite; pourboire
given w/ a purchase: **n.** lagniappe

GRAVE: (**see** "important") **a.** authoritative; funereal; melancholy; mortuary; saturnine; sepulchral; sombrous; tumular(y); **n.** columbarium; mausoleum; ossuary; repository; sepulcher; terminus
cloth: **see under** "burial"

GRAVESTONE *inscription:* **n.** epitaph; *hic jacet*

GREASY: **a.** adipose; butyraceous; oleaginous; lardaceous; pinguid; saponaceous; sebaceous; unctuous; **n.** GREASINESS: lubricity; pinguidity; unctuosity; unctuousness

GREAT: (**see** "grand") **a.** distinguished; estimable; incalculable; incomputable; magnanimous; monumental; predominant; (pre)eminent; prominent; renowned
events or deeds: **n.** magnalia; magnality
in amount: **n.** abundance; magnitude; plethora; preponderance
in magnitude and extent: **a.** cosmic; encyclopedic(al); magnitudinous; panoramic
very: **a.** incalculable; inestimable; supereminent; transcendent
work: **n.** *chef-d'oeuvre; magnum opus; meisterwerk; piece de résistance*
year: **n.** *annus magnus*

GREATER, *in amount, weight, power, etc.:* **a.** preponderant; **n.** plurality; preponderance

GREATEST: **a.** maximal; maximum; *ne plus supra; ne plus ultra;* paramount; preeminent; sovereign; utmost
degree: **n.** optimum
from the (greatest) to the least: a maximus ad minima

GREATNESS: **n.** grandeur; grandiosity; magnanimity; magnitude; monumentality; nobleness; predominance; (pre)eminence; prominence; renown; sublimity; transcendence
delusions of: **see under** "grandeur"
personal: **n.** grandeur

GREECE, *worship or veneration of:* **n.** Hellenism; philhellenism; **a.** philhellene; philhellenic; **n.** philhellene; philhellenist

GREEDY: (**see** "grasping") **a.** acquisitive; avaricious; bourgeois; covetous; extortionate; gluttonous; insatiable; mercenary; parasitic(al); prehensile; prehensive; rapacious; ravenous; venal; voracious; **n.** GREED(INESS): (**see** "avarice") covetousness; cupidity; eagerness; miserliness; rapacity; voracity
person: (**see** "glutton") **n. or a.** cormorant

GREEN: (**see** "immature") **a.** ultramarine; verdant; verdurous; virescent; virid; **n.** GREENNESS: verdancy; verdure; virescence; viridity; **a.** GREENISH: aeruginous; verdigrisy; virescent; viridescent

GREENHORN: (**see** "amateur") **n.** *blancbec*

GREENSICKNESS: **n.** chlorosis

GREET: **v.** accost; address; salute; welcome

GREETING, *act of:* **n.** devoir; salaam; salutation; salute; **a.** salutatory
or opening, as in a letter: **n.** salutation; **a.** salutational; salutatory

GRIEF: **n.** affliction; desolation; dolor; heartache; lamentation; melancholy; misadventure; misfortune; mortification; tribulation; tristesse; **a.** GRIEVED: disconsolate; inconsolable; lamented
banishing or mitigating: **a.** nepenthean; **n.** dolorfuge; nepenthe
causing: **a.** dolorific
characterized by: **a.** dolorous; funereal; grievous; lamentable; melancholy
come to: **v.** founder
road or course of: **n.** *via doloroso*
scene or occasion of great: **n.** Gethsemane

GRIEVANCE: **n.** annoyance; displeasure; gravamen; lament(ation); oppression

GRIM: (**see** "ghastly") **a.** ferocious; forbidding; gruesome; grisly; inexorable; macabre; morbid; moribund; obdurate; plutonian; plutonic; relentless; ruthless; uncompromising

GRIMACE: **n.** moue; *simagrée*

GRIMY: (**see** "dirty") **a.** scabrous; squalid; sullied; **n.** squalidity; squalor

GRIND: **v.** abrade; comminute; harass; masticate; pulverize; triturate

GRITTY: **a.** arenaceous; plucky; resolute; sabulous

GROOVED: **a.** caniculate; cannellated; chamfered; channeled; scorbiculate; sulcate; **n.** GROOVE: **n.** chamfer; sulcus
two-: **a.** bisulcate

GROPE: **v.** *aller à tâtons;* **n.** GROPING: *tatonnement*

GROSSNESS: **n.** barbarity; crassitude; crassness; indecency; scurrility; vulgarity

GROTESQUE: **see** "odd"
manifestation(s): **n.** bizarrerie; fantasia; *fata morgana;* grotesquerie; grotesquery; *ignis fatuus;* phantasmagoria; will-of-the-wisp

GROUCHY: **see** "irritable"

GROUND(S): (**see** "justification") **n.** foundation; rationale; terrain
contour of: **n.** terrain; topography
growing in the: **a.** terrestrial
growing on the: **a.** terricolous
living under: **a. or n.** subterranean; subterrestrial; **n.** subterrene
solid: **n.** *terra firma*
under the: **a.** submundane; subterranean; subterrestrial

GROUNDLESS: **a.** baseless; unfounded

GROUP(S): (**see** "classify") **v.** agglutinate; assemble; categorize; coagulate; colligate; conglomerate; congregate; muster; **n.** (**see** "class" **and** "collection") assemblage; battery
authoritative: **n.** Areophagus; **a.** Areophagitic; **n.** Areophagite
centered in one's social: **a.** egocentric; ethnocentric; sociocentric; **n.** sociocentrism
comprising more than two: **a.** polychotomous
controlling: **n.** hierarchy; **a.** hierarchic(al)

degraded or contemptible: **n.** lumpen proletarial; **a.** lumpen
elder and often reactionary member of: **n.** mandarin
entire membership of: **n.** plenum; **a.** plenary
exclusive: **n.** cabal; charmed circle; claque; clique; *corps d'élite;* coterie
gathering in a: (see "sociable") **a.** gregarious; **n.** gregariousness
general, as a corporation: **n.** commonal(i)ty
habits, manners and customs of: **n.** mores
in a: **adv.** *en masse*
large: **n.** hecatomb; legion; multitude
list of members of: **n.** matricula; roster; rota
literary, philosophical or artistic: **n.** athen(a)eum; cenacle
living together cooperatively: **n.** phalanstery; **a.** or **n.** phalansterian
member of: **n.** congregant
miscellaneous: **n.** *omnium-gatherum*
of best in any category; **n.** *corps d'élite; crème de la crème*
of many tribes, kingdoms, etc: **n.** polyarchy; **n.** polyarchic
of miscellaneous persons: **n.** menagerie
of three: **n.** *ménage à trois;* ternion; triad; trio; triumvirate
one who secedes and forms new: **n.** Adullamite
opinions, doctrines, etc. of a: **n.** ideology
powerful, effective, well-organized, etc.: **n.** powerhouse
scientific or literary: **n.** athen(a)eum; cenacle
secret: **n.** cabel; junta; **a.** cabalistic
select: **n.** charmed circle; *corps d'élite;* quorum

GROUPING: **a.** agglutinative; aggregatory; cumulative; **n.** alignment; pattern

GROVE: **n.** boscage
rel. to or inhabiting: **a.** nemoral

GROVELING: (see "servile") **a.** reptilian

GROW: **v.** augment; enhance; maturate; mature; **n.** see "growth"
together: **v.** ankylose; coalesce; **n.** accretion; ankylosis; coadunation; coalescence; concrescence; concretion; conglomeration; **a.** ankylosed; coadunate; coadunative

GROWING *at high elevations:* **a.** alpestrine
luxuriantly: **a.** rampant; **n.** rampancy
on living tissues: **a.** biogenous
wild, in fields, etc.: **a.** agrest(i)al

GROWTH: **n.** accretion; augmentation; concrescence; development; differentiation; enhancement; evolution; excrescence; maturation; maturescence; neoplasm; proliferation; ramification
gradual: **n.** accrescence; accretion; evolution
or enlargement: **n.** excrescence; neoplasm
original (of anything, as new industry, etc.) : **n.** naissance
over-: **n.** hypertrophy; **a.** hypertrophic
source of natural: **n.** physis
under-: **n.** atrophy; degeneration; hypotrophy

GRUDGE: (see "hatred") **n.** animosity; animus; malice; pique; resentment

GRUESOME: (see "ghastly") **a.** cadaverous; grisly; macabre; morbid; morbific; morbose; sinister

GUARANTOR: **n.** adpromissor; protector; warrantor

GUARDIAN *of manners or morals:* **n.** *custos morum*
spirit: **n.** *alter ego*
watchful: **n.** Argus; Cerberus; chaperone

GUARDIANSHIP: (see "care") **n.** paternalism

GUARDS, *who guards the?: quis custodiet ipsos custodes?*

GUESS: **v.** anticipate; conjecture; deduce; divine; estimate; hariolate; hypothesize; infer; postulate; presage; prognosticate; surmise; **n.** augury; conjecture; deduction; divination; estimation; hariolation; hypothesis; postulation; prognosis; prognostication; prophesy; supposition; surmise; **a.** GUESSING: academic; conjectural; divinatory; hypothetical; postulatory; presumptive; prophetic(al); suppositional; supposititious; suppositive; theoretical

GUESSWORK: **n.** conjecture; hariolation; haruspication; postulation; supposition

GUEST: **n.** invitee

GUIDE: (**see** "measure") **n.** cicerone; cynosure; dragoman; mentor; polestar; precedent; supervisor; **n.** GUIDANCE: (**see** "supervision") chaperonage; ciceronage; guardianship; paternalism
serving to: **a.** didactic; heuristic; normative; prescriptive
sightseeing: **n.** cicerone

GUIDEBOOK: (**see** "handbook") **n.** Baedeker; itinerary; *vade mecum*

GUIDING, *as by hand:* **n.** manuducation; **a.** manuducative; manuducatory

GUILE: **n.** artifice; deceit; dissimulation; duplicity; rascality; stratagem; subtlety; treachery; **a.** GUILELESS: artless; credulous; gullible; ingenuous; naive; **n.** GUILELESSNESS: artlessness; credulity; cullibility; gullibility; ingenuousness; *naïveté*

GUILT: **n.** criminality; culpa(bility); delinquency; dereliction; reprehensibility; reprehension
acknowledgment of personal: **n.** *mea culpa*
confession of: **n.** peccavi
feeling of: **n.** compunction; contrition; penitence; remorse; repentance
freeing or forgiveness from: **n.** absolution; amnesty; atonement; expiation; purgation; redemption; **a.** absolutory; expiatory; redemptive
impute: **v.** incriminate; inculpate
sense of: **n.** compunction; contrition; penitence; remorse; **a.** compunctious; contrite; intropunitive; penitent; remorseful; self-accusatory

GUILTY: **a.** blameworthy; contrite; culpable; demeritorious; indictable; nocent; penitent; reprehensible; reprehensive
person: **n.** criminal; culprit; felon; misdemeanant; misfeasor

GULLIBLE: **a.** credulous; naïve; **n.** GULLIBILITY: credulity; cullibility; *naïveté*

GUMMY: **a.** glutinous; viscous

GUSH: **v.** regurgitate; **n.** regurgitation; **a.** GUSHING: **see** "demonstrative"
forth: (**see** "effusive") **a.** scaturient

GYPSIES, *of or rel. to:* **a.** tzigane

H

HABIT(S): **n.** addiction; assuetude; constitution; consuetude; demeanor; disposition; habitude; pattern; physique; praxis; rota; rote; routine
bad or uncontrollable: **n.** cacoethes
become accustomed to: **v.** habituate; **n.** habituation
great is the power of: magna est vis consuetudinis
group: **n.pl.** mores
law(s) regulating on religious or moral grounds: **n.** sumptuary (law)
person addicted to: **n.** *habitué;* routineer
state of being controlled by: **n.** habituality; habituation

HABITUAL: (**see** "chronic") **a.** adamant; confirmed; consuetudinal; customary; inveterate; persistent; routine; HABITUATE: **see** "accustom"
pursuits pass over into character: abeunt studia in mores

HAIR: **n.** capillus; chevelure; pilus; thatch
covered w/ fine or wool: **a.** lanate; lanuginose; lanuginous; laniferous; pubescent; velutinous; villoid
crew-cut: **n.** (*cheveux*) *en brosse*
erection due to cold, fear, etc.: **n.** *cutis anserina;* horripilation; piloerection
falling out of: **n.** depilation; psilosis; **a.** psilotic
false: **n.** postiche; toupee
golden: **a.** aurocephalous
grayness or whiteness of: **n.** canities
having dark or black: **a.** melanocomous; melanous
having red: **a.** hirsutorufous; rufous; xanthous; **n.** phrrhotism
having straight smooth: **a.** leiotrichous; lissotrichous
having wooly or curly: **a.** ulotrichous; **n.** ulotrichy
having yellowish, red, auburn or brown: **a.** xanthous
kinky or crinkled, pert. to: **a.** encomic
like a: **a.** capilliform
loss of coloring in: **n.** canites; poliosis
of the head: **n.** chevelure
pubic: **n.** byssus; escutcheon
site of: **n.** *mons veneris* (**fem.**) pubic triangle
rel. or pert. to: **see** "hairy"
remove: **v.** depilate; **n.** depilant; depilatory; depilation
study of: **n.** trichology
wavy, having: **a.** cymotrichous

HAIR-RAISING: **a.** horripilant; **a.** HAIR-SPLITTING: casuistic; sophistical; specious; **n.** casuistry; dialectics; pilpul; sophistry; speciosity

HAIRY: **a.** ciliate; comose; comous; crinate; criniferous; crinitory; hirsutal; hirsute; piliferous; pilose; pilous; polytrichous; villous; **n.** HAIRNESS: crinosity; hirsutism; pilosis; pilosism; pilosity; trichosis; **a.** HAIRLESS: atrichic; atrichous; depilous; glabrate; glabrescent; glabrous
covering, as animal's: **n.** pelage
growth, covered w/: **a.** crinate; criniferous; **n.** crinosity; pelage
or threadlike: **a.** capillaceous; **n.** capilliform

HALF: (**see** "halved") **a.** imperfect; partial; **n.** mediety; moiety
-"baked:" **a.** immature; malentendu
-breed: (**see under** "breed") **n.** hybrid; mestizo; *métis;* mongrel

HALL, *of or pert. to:* **a.** aularian

HALLOWED *place:* **n.** bethel; bethesda; halidom(e); sanctuary; *sanctum sanctorum*

HALLUCINATION(S), *that which produces:* **n.** hallucinogen

HALO: **n.** aura; aureola; aurora; anthelion; corona; nimbus

HALT: **see** "discontinue"

HALTING *place:* (**see** "hostelry") **n.** anchorage; haven; étape; terminus

HALVED: **a.** bifid; bipartite; bisected; cloven; dichotomous; dimidiate; **n.** bifurcation; dichotomy; dimidiation

HAND(S), *enlargement of:* **n.** chiromegaly
having four: **a.** quadrumanous
having no: **a.** amanous
having or pert. to two: **a.** ambidextrous; bimanous; bimanual
largeness of: **n.** chiromegaly
leading by the: **n.** manuducation; **a.** manuductive; manuductory
left: **n.** *mano sinistra;* **a.** sinistral
on the other: **adv.** *per contra*
opened so as to show palm; **a.** *ap(p)aumé*
pert. to, made or worked by: **a.** manual
right: **n.** dextrality; *mano destra;* **a.** dextral; **a. or adv.** *main droite*
seizure by: **n.** manucaption; **n. or v.** manucapture
sign lang. by use of: **n.** dactylology
use of in talking: **v.** gesticulate; **n.** gesticulation; **a.** gesticulatory
use of both equally: **n.** ambidexterity; **a.** ambidextrous; bimanual
use of one: **a.** unidextral
with a strong: **adv.** *manu forti*

HANDBOOK: **n.** Baedeker; enchiridion; manual; promptuary; *vade mecum*

HANDED *down:* (**see** "traditional") **a.** tralatitious

HANDICAP: (**see** "disability") **n.** encumbrance; impediment; incubus

HANDSOME: **a.** adonic; comely; *fait à peindre;* personable
young man: **n.** Adonis; *un beau garçon*

HANDWRITING: **n.** chirography; (manu)script(ion); **a.** chirographic
bad or careless: **n.** cacography; griffonage; scrawl
fine or beautiful: **n.** calligraphy; **a.** calligraphic; **n.** calligrapher
illegible: **n.** hieroglyphic(s)
large: **n.** macrography; **a.** macrographic
of author, written in: **a.** holographic(al); onomastic; **n.** holograph
on the wall: mene, mene; tekel, upharsin
one's own: **n.** autograph; autography; **a.** autographic(al)
pert. to: **a.** scriptorial; scriptory
study of: **n.** bibliotics; graphology
written in one's own: **a.** autographic(al); holographic; onomastic

HANDY: (**see** "convenient") **a.** adroit; dext(e)rous; facile; habile; ingenious; resourceful; **n.** HANDINESS: adeptness; dexterity; expertise; virtuosity
-man: **n.** factotum; *genius loci*

HANG: **v.** (im)pend; pendulate; suspend; **a.** HANGING: (**see** "impending") abeyant; appendicular; pendent; pendulant; pendular; pendulous; pensile; suspended; **n.** pendency; pendulation; pendulosity; pendulousness

HAPHAZARD: **see** "random"

HAPPENING: **see** "contingency" **and** "incident"; **v.** HAPPEN: befall; betide; supervene; transpire
at same time: **see under** "time"

HAPPINESS: **n.** beatitude; bliss; ecstasy; eud(a)emonia; euda(e)monism; felicity; seventh heaven; transport
bringing, or designed to promote: **a.** beatific; felicific; **v.** beatify
incapacity for: **n.** anhedonia; **a.** anhedonic
place of blissful: **n.** Eden; Elysium; paradise
"science of:" **n.** eudaemonics
transcendent: **n.** beatitude; ecstasy; **a.** beatific; ecstatic

HAPPY: (**see** "blissful") **a.** appropriate; auspicious; blithesome; buoyant; ecstatic; edenic; elysian; eud(e)emonic(al); felicific; felicitous; gelastic; gelogenic; halcyon; harmonious; opportune; rapturous; revelrous; *sans-souci*
always: **adv.** *semper felix*
extremely: **a.** dithyrambic; ecstatic; euda(e)monic(al); rapturous; rhapsodic(al)
make extremely: **v.** enrapture; imparadise; transport

HARASS: **v.** bedevil; dragoon; exhaust; importune

HARD: (**see** "difficult" **and** "stern") **a.** adamant(ine); arduous; exacting; grievous; impenetrable; incorrigible; inflexible; intractable; laborious; ruthless; strenuous; unrelenting; unsparing; **v.** HARDEN: concretize; fortify; habituate; indurate; inure; ossify; petrify; **a.** HARDENED: adamantine; concretive; confirmed; congelative; impenitent; indurated; insensate; insusceptible; inured; inveterate; marmoreal; obdurate; ossified; petrous; unrepentant; **n.** HARDNESS: impenitence: induration; petrification; sclerosis; strenuosity

-hearted: **(see** "unfeeling") **a.** impenitent; impervious; obdurate; unemotional

like marble: **a.** adamantine; marmoreal; petrous

HARDENING: **n.** concretization; congealment; congelation; induration; ossification; petrification

of the arteries: **n.** arteriosclerosis; **a.** arteriosclerotic

HARE: **n.** coney; lagomorph; **a.** leporid

-brained: **a.** *écervelé*

-lip: **n.** cheilognathus; cheiloschisis

HARM: **(see** "injury") molestation

immune to: **a.** impassible; invulnerable; **n.** impassibility; invulnerability

incapable of (harm) or good: **a.** adiaphoristic; adiaphorous

HARMFUL: **(see** "bad") **a.** baleful; baneful; deleterious; detrimental; inimical; malefic; malevolent; malicious; malign(ant); nocent; nocuous; noxious; prejudicial; scatheful; sinister; unbenevolent; venomous; virulent; **n.** HARMFULNESS: maleficence; malevolence; malignancy; sinisterity; toxicity

to health or morals: **a.** malign(ant); noxious; pernicious; venomous; virulent

HARMLESS: **(see** "innocent") **a.** beneficent; benign(ant); impotent; inoffensive; innocuous; innoxious; insipid; salutary

something which is: **n.** innocuity

HARMONIOUS: **a.** affable; Apollonian; Apollonic; Apollonistic; assonant; canorous; companionable; compatible; concinnous; concordant; congruent; congruous; consonant; *en rapport;* euphonic(al); euphonious; eurhythmic; mellifluent; mellifluous; mellisonant; melodic; melodious; reconciliatory; rhythmic(al); sociable; sonorous; symphonic; symphonious; synchronic(al); synchronous; syncretic; syncretistic; unisonant

not: **(see** "harsh") **a.** cacophonous; discordant; dissident; dissonant; incompatible; incongruous; inharmonious; **n.** atonality; cacophony; discordance; dissonance

HARMONIZE: **(see** "agree") **v.** coordinate; correlate; mediate; orchestrate; reconcile symphonize; synchronize; syncretize; tranquilize

having power or tendency to: **a.** conciliatory, henotic; irenic; pacific(atory); tranquilizing

HARMONY: **n.** affability; amity; assonance; compatibility; concinnity; concordance; congruence; congruency; congruity; consonance; coordination; cosmos; euphony; mutuality; orchestration; rapport; reconciliation; reconcilement; symmetry; symphony; synchroneity; syncretism; tranquility; unanimity

discordant; **n.** *concordia discors*

in: **(see** "harmonious) **a.** *en rapport*

in art, etc.: **n.** synaesthesis

HARSH: **(see** "rigorous" **and** "severe") **a.** acerb(ic); acidulous; antagonistic; asperous; astringent; cacophonous; discordant; disharmonious; dissonant; Draconian; ferocious; inclement; relentless; ruthless; strident; truculent; uncharitable; unharmonious; **n.** HARSHNESS: acerbity; asperity; discordance; discordancy; inclemency; mordacity; rigor

in temperament: **a.** acidulent; acidulous; vinegary

sound(s): **n.** cacophony; **a.** cacophonic; cacophonous; discordant; dissonant; immelodious; ineuphonious; strident; unharmonious

HAS-BEEN: **n.** or **a.** ci-devant; emeritus; **a.** quondam

HASH: **n.** gallimaufry; goulash; haricot; heterogeneity; hodgepodge; medley; olla podrida; potpourri; ragout; *réchauffé;* salmagundi; slumgullion

HASTE: **(see** "abruptness") **n.** acceleration; alacrity; celerity; dispatch; *empressement;* expediency; expedition; facility; impetuosity; impulsivity; precipitateness; precipitancy; precipitation; rapidity; su-

perficiality; **n.** HASTINESS: alacrity; celerity; festination; rapidity; superficiality; **a.** HASTY: (**see** "rash") accelerated; celeritous; cursory; desultory; festinate; impatient; impulsive; incautious; indiscreet; precipitant; precipitate; precipitous; subitaneous; superficial
make (haste) slowly: **adv.** *eile mit weile; festina lente; speude bradeos*

HASTENER: **n.** accelerant; catalyst; gadfly; precipitator; stimulator

HATE: (**see** "hatred" **and** "loathe") **v.** abhor; abominate; anathematize; **a.** HATEFUL: abhorrent; abominable; anathematic(al); defamatory; despicable; detestable; excreable; fastuous; heinous; invidious; loathsome; nauseous; objectionable; obnoxious; odious; opprobrious; outrageous; repellent; repugnant; repulsive; **n.** HATER: antipathist
object of: **n.** *bête noir(e)*

HATRED: (**see** "aversion") **n.** abhorrence; abomination; anathema; animosity; animus; antagonism; antipathy; detestation; enmity; malevolence; malice; malignity; odium; rancor; repugnance; repugnancy
arousing: **a.** antipathetic(al); antipathic
without: **adv.** *sine odio*

HAUGHTY: (**see** "proud") **a.** arrogant; cavalier; contemptuous; contumelious; despiteful; disdainful; egotistical; fastuous; grandiose; hoity-toity; hubristic; patronizing; petulant; pompous; pontifical; portentous; peremptory; prideful; supercilious; toploftical; toplofty; **n.** HAUGHTINESS: arrogance; contempt; contumacy; despicableness; despicability; disdain; fastuosity; hauteur; hubris; lordliness; morgue; vainglory

HAUNT: **n.** environ(s); habitat; milieu; purlieu; rendezvous

HAWK, *resembling:* **a.** accipitral; accipitrine

HAZARD: **see** "danger"

HAZY: **a.** ethereal; indefinite; indistinct; nebular; nebulose; nebulous; obscure; tenuous; vague; **n.** HAZINESS: (**see** "cloudiness") ethereality; nebulosity; tenuosity; vaporosity

HEAD(S): **n.** caput; (pl. capita); cranium
affecting both sides of: **a.** amphicranial; bicranial
affecting one side of: **a.** hemicranial
back of: **n.** occiput; **a.** occipital
bald: **n.** pilgarlic
black-: **n.** comedo
golden-colored: **a.** aurecephalous
having a: **a.** cephalous
having abnormally small: **a.** microcephalic; microcephalous; **n.** microcephaly
having large: **a.** megacephalic; megacephalous; **n.** megacephaly
having many: **a.** hydra-headed
of the house, fem.: **n.** *mater familias;* matriarch
of the house, male: **n.** *chef de famille; pater familias;* patriarch
out of the (fr. memory): **adv.** *ex capite*
pain in: (**see** "headache") **n.** *cephalalgia*
pert. to: **a.** capital; cephalic; cranial
pointed: **a.** acrocephalic; **n.** acrocephaly
tax: **n.** capitation; **a.** capitation; per capita
thickness of (or skull): **n.** pachycephalia; pachycephaly
to foot, from: **adv.** *cap-à-pie*
to heel, from (completely): **adv.** *capite ad calcem*
to remove: **v.** decapitate; guillotine; obtruncate; **n.** decapitation
toward the: **adv.** cephalad
two better than one: due teste valgano piú d'una sola; nemo solus satis sapit
without a: **a.** acephalic; acephalous; **n.** acephalia

HEADACHE: **n.** cephalalgia; cephalodynia; *mal de tête;* megrim; migraine
both sides: **n.** amphicrania; bicrania; **a.** amphicranial; bicranial
one side: **n.** hemicrania; **a.** hemicranial

HEADLONG: (**see** "rash") **a.** Gaderine; impetuous; precipitant; precipitate; precipitous; **adv.** *à corps perdu; tête baissée*

HEADSTRONG: **see** "stubborn"

HEALING: **a.** assuasive; balsamic; curative; lenitive; medicamental; medicamentous; medicative; medicinable; medicinal; remedial; resoluble; restorative; sanative; therapeutic(al); vulnerary
agent (as medicine or plant): **n.** therapeutant
by first intention: **a.** *per primam*

power of nature: **n.** *vis medicatrix naturae*
promoting of: (**see** "healthful") **a.** curative; lenitive; remedial; restorative; sanative; therapeutic(al); vulnerary
science of: **n.** iatrics; iatrology; therapeusis; therapeutics
slow in: **a.** indolent

HEALTH: **n.** prosperity; robusticity; tonicity; vigor; vitality
abnormal anxiety over: **n.** hypochondria(sis); **a.** hypochondriacal; valetudinarian; **n.** hypochondriac; valetudinarian
conducive to: **see** "healthful" **and** "healing"
goddess of: **n.** Hygeia; Salus
in normal or good: **n.** eucrasia; eudaemonia; euphoria; normality
in poor: **n.** dyscrasia; **a.** valetudinarian
recovery or restoration of: **v.** convalesce; recuperate; **n.** convalescence; recuperation; **a.** convalescent; recuperative; recuperatory

HEALTHFUL: **a.** curative; hygienic; invigorating; restorative; salubrious; salutary; salutiferous; wholesome; **n.** HEALTHFULNESS: salubrity; salutariness; wholesomeness
not: **see** "unhealthy"

HEAP: **n.** accumulation; acervation; agglomeration; aggregation; congeries; **a.** acervuline; cumulative; pyramidal

HEAR *the other side:* **adv.** *audi alteram partem*
willing to: **a.** acousmatic

HEARSAY: **n.** *on dit; oui-dire;* scuttlebutt

HEART: (**see** "gist") **n.** affection; cardia; cor(e); disposition; interior
coming fr. the (as subjective or emotional): **a.** pectoral; **adv.** *imo pectore*
fast beating of: **n.** tachycardia
fear of disease of: **n.** cardiophobia
from bottom of one's: **adv.** *imo pectore;* **a.** pectoral
from the: **see** "sincere"
of the matter, in: **adv.** *in medias res*
pert. to, or to disease of: **a.** cardiac; cardiological
shaped like: **a.** cordate; cordiform
slow beating of: **n.** bradycardia
study of disease of: **n.** cardiology; **n.** cardiologist

HEARTH, *goddess of:* **n.** Hestia; Vestia

HEAT: (**see** "hot") **n.** calefaction; calescence; candescence; temperature
formed by, as rock: **a.** igneous
generating: **a.** calorigenic; igneous
great: **n.** candescence
pert. to: **a.** calefacient; calefactory; calescent; calorific; ignescent; igneous; pyrogenic; pyrogenous; thermal; thermic
producing or produced by: **a.** calefacient; igneous; pyrogenic; pyrogenous; thermal; thermic
treatment by use of: **n.** thermotherapy
unusual sensitiveness to: **n.** hyperthermalgesia

HEATHEN: **n.** idolater; pagan; **n.** HEATHENISM: heathendom; heathenry; idolatry; paganism; **a.** HEATHENISH: foreign; irreligious; pagan; uncircumcised; unenlightened; unfamiliar

HEAVEN(S): (**see** "sky") **n.** celestial sphere; Eden; Elysium; empyrean; firmament; paradise; Utopia; Valhalla; **a.** HEAVENLY: (arch)angelic; beatific; blissful; (super)celestial; edenic; elysian; empyreal; ethereal; firmamental; Olympian; paradisiac(al); paradisial; paradisian; rapturous; sublime; supernal
above the: **a.** supercelestial
and earth, rel. to or affecting both: **a.** cosmotellurian
of or from the: **a.** ethereal; supernal
study of: **n.** astronomy; uranology
there is rest in: in coelo quies
up to the (ref. to theory that land ownership includes air above): **adv.** *usque ad coelum*

HEAVY: **a.** burdensome; consequential; elephantine; grievous; massive; oppressive; ponderous; saturnine; substantious; weighty

HEDGE: **n.** septum; **v.** encircle; equivocate; obstruct

HEED: (**see** "attention") **n.** apprehension; attentiveness; circumspection; cognizance; perception; **a.** HEEDFUL: advertent; calculating; cautious; circumspect; mindful; vigilant; wary; **a.** HEEDLESS: (**see** "reckless") inattentive; incautious; incogitable; incogitant; neglectful; oblivious; precipitate; remiss; unobservant; unmindful; **n.** HEEDLESSNESS: *étourderie;* inattention; inobservance

HEIGHT(S): (**see** "acme") **n.** altitude; elevation; eminence; pinnacle
fear of: **n.** acrophobia; **a.** acrophobic
natural: **n.** stature
pert. to: **a.** altitudinous; culminant

HEIGHTEN: **v.** accent; aggravate; augment; enhance; exacerbate; exaggerate; exalt; intensify

HEIR *apparent:* **n.** atheling; crown prince; dauphin; **n.** primogeniture(ship)

HELL: **n.** Abaddon, Acheron; Avernus; barathrum; gehenna; Hades; inferno; limbo; Pandemonium; perdition; Sheol; Tartarus; **a.** HELLISH: Acheronian; Acherontic(al); chthonian; chthonic; demoniac(al); devilish; infernal; pandemoniac(al); sheolic; sulfurous; sulphurous; stygian
descent to is easy: facilis descensus Averno

HELP: **v.** abet; alleviate; collaborate; facilitate; participate; succor; **n.** (**see** "assistance") adminicle; administeration; (co)adjuvancy; cooperation; encouragement; **int.** *au secours!;* **a.** HELPFUL: (**see** "beneficial") accessory; advantageous; alleviatory; auspicious; constructive; convenient; cooperative; obliging; opportune; propitious; remedial; salutary; subsidiary; therapeutic (**see** "curative"); **a.** HELPING: adminicular; auxiliary; cooperative; corroborative; participative; **a.** HELPLESS: (**see** "defenseless") bewildered; *brutum fulmen;* feckless; impotent; impuissant; incapacitated; incompetent; ineffective; inefficient; nugatory; powerless; **n.** HELPLESSNESS: impotency; impuissance; inability; incapacity; incapability
designed to: **a.** alleviatory; cooperative; remedial
good: **n.** *bon secours*
with God's: **adv.** *Dieu aidant*
yourself and heaven will help you: aide-toi, le ceil t'aidera

HELPER: (**see** "aide") **n.** accessory; adjutant; adjuvant; adminicle; aide-de-camp; ancillary; auxiliary; benefactor; coadjutor; (**fem.** coadjutress; coadjutrix); collaborator; collaborateur; colleague; confederate; confrere; participant; participator

HENCHMAN: **n.** mercenary; minion; *particeps criminis;* participant; satrap; *socius criminis*

HERALD: (**see** "forerunner") **n.** *avant-courrier; avant-garde;* harbinger; precursor

HERBS, *living on:* **a.** herbivorous
study of: **n.** phytology; **n.** botanist; phytologist

HERD(S), *leader of:* **n.** patriarch
living in: **a.** gregarious

HERE *and everywhere:* **adv.** *hic et ubique*
and there: **adv.** *par ci par là; passim*
lies: **adv.** *hic jacet*
there, and everywhere: **adv.** *hic et ubique*
today, gone tomorrow: **adv.** *aujourd'hui roi, demain rien*

HEREDITARY: (**see** "inborn") **a.** ancestral; congenital; familial; hereditable; innate; lineal; linear; paternal; patriarchal; patrimonial
disposition (to disease, etc.): **n.** diathesis

HERETIC: (**see** "unbeliever") **n.** apostate; heresiarch; nonconformist; schismatic; **a.** HERETICAL: **see** "unorthodox"
labeling as a: **n.** mark of the beast

HERETOFORE: **a.** Ci-devant; hitherto; quondam; **n.** ci-devant; has-been; *status quo ante*

HERITABLE *property:* **n.** hereditament(s); patrimony

HERITAGE: **n.** hereditament; inheritance; legacy; patrimony; **a.** patrimonial

HERMIT: **n.** anchorite; cenobite; eremite; isolate; recluse; solitudinarian; troglodyte
like a, or pert. to: **a.** anchoritic; cenobitic; eremitic(al); hermitic; troglodytic

HERO: **n.** Argonaut; demigod(dess)
in a play: **n.** protagonist

HEROIC: **a.** chivalrous; courageous; dauntless; extreme; Homerian; Homeric; il-

lustrious; intrepid; powerful; radical; resolute; Samsonian; undaunted
mockingly or satirical: **a.** Hudibrastic

HESITATE: **v.** demur; fluctuate; linger; shilly-shally; vacillate; **a.** HESITANT: (**see** "indisposed") dubitant; dubitative; shilly-shally; vacillatory; **n.** HESITATION: demur; dubitation; indisposition; pausation; vacillation

HICCUP (or HICCOUGH): **n.** singultus

HICK: **see** "boor"

HIDDEN: (**see** "secret") **a.** abeyant; abstruse; arcane; cabalistic; clandestine; covert; cryptic(al); cryptogenic; delitescent; dormant; enigmatic(al); esoteric; inapparent; inherent; larvate(d); latent; occult; potential; quiescent; recondite; surreptitious; ulterior; undercurrent; undisclosed; unexplained; veiled
danger: **see under** "danger"
significance, having a: **a.** cryptogrammic
state of being, or something that is: **n.** abstrusity; arcanum; clandestinity; obscuration; occultation; sequestration

HIDE: **v.** abscond; cache; camouflage; conceal; ensconce; obscure; secrete; sequester; **n.** (**see** "skin") abscondence; obscuration; sequestration
away: **v.** abscond; cache; **n.** HIDEAWAY: hermitage; nidus; redoubt; refuge; retreat
from law: **v.** abscond; fugitate; **n.** abscondence; fugitation
one's self: **v.** abscond; ensconce

HIGH: (**see** "lofty") **a.** altitudinous; eminent; extravagant; sublime; supernal; top-echelon; towering
extremely: **a.** stratospheric(al); supernal
fashion or social standing: **n.** *bon ton; haut ton;* **a.** *à la hussarde*
-flown: **see** "pretentious"
in class or field: **a.** aristocrat; Brahmin; *cordon bleu;* eminentissimo; luminary; magnifico; mahatma; minion; nonesuch; paladin; panjandrum; paradigm; paragon; patrician; **a.** (super)eminent; supernal
point: **see** "apex"
society: **n.** *grand monde; haut monde*
-sounding: **a.** grandiloquent; magnific(al)
spirits: **n.** ebullience; ebulliency; ebullition; ecstasy; euphoria; exuberance; **a.** (**see** "spirited") ebullient; ecstatic; euphoric; exuberant
status or prestige: **n.** cachet

HIGHEST: **a.** classic; meridional; paramount; preeminent; supereminent; supernal; supreme
distinction: **n.** *cordon bleu; grand prix*
in the: **adv.** *in excelsis*
point: **see** "apex"
region(s): **n.** *1.* stratosphere; *2.* inosphere; *3.* mesosphere; *4.* exosphere
type: **n.** *ne plus supra; ne plus ultra*

HIGHWAY, *main:* **n.** *camino real*

HILL, *small or low:* **n.** hillock; hummock; namelon; monticule; monticulus; **a.** HILLY: tumular; tumulose; tumulous

HINDER: (**see** "block") **v.** impede; **n.** HINDRANCE: barnacle(s); barrier; encumbrance; impediment; obstruction; perplexity; stultification; **a.** impedimental; obstructive

HINT: **v.** allude; imply; insinuate; suggest; **n.** forewarning; illusion; innuendo; insinuation; insinuendo; suggestion; **a.** insinuative; insinuatory
that something is worse than said: **n.** parale(i)psis; paralipsis

HIRED: **a.** commercial; mercenary; mercantile; venal; **n.** HIRELING: (**see** "mercenary") myrmidon; pensionary

HISS: **v.** (as)sibilate; **n.** sibilance; sibilant; sibilation; **a.** sibilant

HISTORIAN: **n.** analyst; annalist; chronicler; Herodotus; historiographer

HISTORIC, *state of being:* **n.** historicity
to render or make: **v.** historify; historicize

HISTORICAL *records:* **n.pl.** annals; **a.** annalistic

HISTORY: (**see** "ancestry") **n.** annals; biography; chronicle; historiography
as of word or custom: **n.** phylogenesis,

phylogeny; **a.** phylogenic; **n.** phylogenist
give appearance of (historical) verity or significance: **v.** historicize
goddess of: **n.** Saga
muse of: **n.** Clio
of immaterial thing, as word or custom: **n.** phylogenics; phylogeny; **a.** phylogenic
period just before recorded: **n.** protohistory; **a.** protohistoric(al)
personal: **see** "autobiography"
record in, or as: **v.** historicize; historify
study or knowledge of: **n.** historiology
writing of: (**see** "historian") **n.** historiography; **a.** historiographic(al); **v.** historicize; historify

HIT *or miss:* **adv.** *à tort et à travers;* (at) random; **a.** aimless; desultory; haphazard; random

HITCH: **n.** contretemps; misadventure; mishap

HOARSE: **a.** raucous; strident; stridulent; stridulous; **n.** HOARSENESS: phonasthenia; raucity; stridency; stridor; stridulation; strid(ul)ence

HOAX: (**see** "fraud") **n.** imposture; mare's nest

HOCUS-POCUS: (**see** "nonsense") **n.** abracadabra; legerdemain; prestidigitation; thaumaturgy

HODGE-PODGE: (**see** "hash" **and** "mixture") **n.** colluvies; gallimaufry; *macédoine; omnium-gatherum;* pasticcio; pastiche; potpourri; ragout; smorgasbord

HOG(S), *like or rel. to:* **a.** porcine; suoid; swinish

HOLE: **n.** aperture; (con)cavity; excavation; lacuna; orifice; perforation; punctulum; puncture
in body: **n.** aperture; fistula; foramen; (**pl.** foramina); meatus; orifice; os

HOLLOW: **n.** concavity; sinus; **a.** concave; insincere; lacunal; lacunar; treacherous
-sounding: **a.** tympanic; tympanitic

HOLY: (**see** "sacred") **a.** hallowed; immaculate; sacrosanct; saintly; sanctified; **a.** HOLIER-THAN-THOU: Pecksniffian; religiose; sacrosanct; sanctimonious; **n.** Pecksniffianism; religiosity; sanctimoniousness; sanctity; **n.** HOLINESS: godliness; sacramentality; sacredness; saintliness; sanctification; sanctitude; sanctity
of holies: **n.** adytum; sanctum; *sanctum sanctorum*
place: **n.** bethesda; halidom(e); sanctuary
pretending to be: **see** "holier-than-thou" **above**
Roman Empire: **n.** *Sacrum Romanum Imperium* (**abb.** S.R.I.)
thing considered: **n.** halidom(e)

HOMAGE: **a.** adoration; allegiance; deference; deferentiality; fealty; fidelity; obeisance; reverence; sacredness; veneration
supreme: **n.** latria

HOME: **n.** abode; domicile; habitation; headquarters; hearthstone; ingleside; *lares et penates*
love of: **n.** inhabitiveness
sweet: **n.** *dulce domum*

HOMELAND, *extreme or exaggerated love of:* **n.** chauvinism
pert. to: **a.** compatristic; patrial

HOMELESS: **adv.** *sans abri*

HOMESICKNESS: **n.** *mal du pays;* nostalgia; **a.** nostalgic

HONEST: **a.** *bona fide;* candid; conscientious; equitable; honorable; impartial; incorrupted; incorruptible; ingenuous; judicial; legitimate; meticulous; rectitudinous; reputable; scrupulous; uncorrupt(ed); upright ; **n.** HONESTY: *bona fide(s); bonne foi;* candor; fidelity; integrity; judiciality; probity; propriety; rectitude; scrupulosity; sincerity; truthfulness; uprightness; veracity

HONEY-*colored:* **a.** melichrous; nectarous
containing or resembling: **a.** melleous; nectarous
producing: **a.** melliferous; nectariferous

HONEYCOMB, *like a:* **a.** alveolate; faveolate; faviform

HONEYED, *as words or speech:* **a.** melodic; melleous; melliferous; mellifluent; mellifluous; mellisonant
words: **n.** *paroles mielleuses*

HONOR(S): (see "esteem") **v.** canonize; commemorate; deify; dignify; elevate; enhalo; ennoble; laureate; revere; worship; **n.** approbation; deference; deferentiality; eminence; ennoblement; homage; integrity; izzat; obeisance; prestige; reverence; veneration
as a token of: **a. or adv.** *causa honoris; honoris causa*
conferring, conveying or implying: **a.** commendatory; eulogistic; honorific; laudatory
with: **adv. or a.** *cum laude*
with high: **adv. or a.** *magna cum laude*
with highest: **adv. or a.** *summa cum laude*
word of: **n.** *parole d'honneur*
worthy of: (see "praiseworthy") **a.** laureate

HONORABLE (or HONORED): **a.** belaurel(l)ed; chivalric; chivalrous; estimable; illustrious; laureated; laurel(l)ed; prestigious; reputable; respectable; revered; venerable; venerated; **n.** HONORABLENESS: honorificabilitudinitatibus; honorificabilitudininity; prestige; prestigiousness; reputability; respectability

HOODED (or HOODSHAPED): **a.** cowled; cucullate

HOOFS, *animal having:* **n.** ungulate
shaped like or having: **a.** ungular; ungulate

HOOK *or by crook:* **adv.** *à bis ou à blanc*
shaped like: **a.** aduncous; ancistroid; ankyroid; aquilline; falciform; **n.** aduncity

HOOT, *as an owl:* **v.** ululate; **n.** ululation; **a.** ululant

HOPE: **n.** anticipation; confidence; enthusiasm; expectancy; optimism; reliance; **a.** HOPEFUL: auspicious; confident; enthusiastic; euphoric; expectant; optimistic; promising; sanguine; utopian; **n.** HOPEFULNESS: buoyancy; confidence; enthusiasm; euphoria; expectancy; sanguinity; optimism; **a.** HOPELESS: immitigable; incorrigible; irreclaimable; irredeemable; irretrievable
anchor of: **n.** *ancora spei*
faint: **n.** velleity
good: **n.** *spes bona*
while I breathe I (hope): *spero dum spiro*

HORIZONTAL: **a.** decumbent; prone; prostrate; recumbent; supine; **n.** HORIZONTALITY: decumbency; reclination; recumbency

HORN(S), *having:* **a.** corniculate
having two: **a.** bicorn(ed); bicornous; bicornuate
of plenty: **n.** *corne d'abondance;* cornucopia; **a.** cornucopian
without: **a.** aceratophorous; polled

HORNY (or HORNLIKE) **a.** corneous

HORRIBLE: (see "ghastly") **a.** abhorrent; abominable; appalling; excruciating; execrable; formidable; grisly; gruesome; horrendous; horrific; macabre
to relate: **adv.** *horribile dictu*

HORROR, *something that provokes:* **n.** *danse macabre*

HORSE(S), *art of riding or training:* **n.** equitation; manège
broken-down: **n.** rosinante
caper or circle: **n. or v.** caracole
-drawn vehicle: **n.** hippomobile
family or species: **n.** equidae; **a.** equine
flesh, eating of: **n.** hippophagous; hippophagism; **n.** hippophagist
-loving: **a.** philhippic
pert. to: **a.** equestrian; equinal; equine; hippoid
rearing on hind legs: **n.** pesade
study or student of: **n.** hippologist; hippology
turn on one spot: **n.** caracole; passade
violent check by pull on reins: **n.** saccade

HORSEBACK: **adv.** *à cheval*

HORSEMAN: **n.** cavalier; chevalier; dragoon; equestrian; (**fem.** equestrienne); **n.** HORSEMANSHIP: equestrianism; equitation; *haute école;* manège

HORSESHOE-*shaped:* **a.** hippocrepiform

HOSPITAL: **n.** *maison-dieu; maison de santé*
for contagious diseases: **n.** lazaretto

HOSPITALITY: **n.** amicability; bonhom(m)ie; camaraderie; (con)geniality; convivality; cordiality; graciosity; graciousness; xenodochy; **a.** HOSPITABLE: amicable; bonhomous; companionable; (con)genial; convivial; cordial; gracious; gregarious; neighborly; receptive; sociable
to strangers: **n.** xenodochy

HOST *at dinner:* **n.** amphitryon

HOSTEL(RY): (**see** "hotel") caravansary; xenodochium

HOSTILE: (**see** "aggressive") **a.** a(d)verse; antagonistic; antipathetic; bellicose; belligerent; contentious; discordant; disaffected; feral; gladiatorial; inimicable; inimical; irreconcilable; malevolent; martial; mutinous; provocative; pugilistic; pugnacious; rancorous; rebellious; repugnant; truculent; umbrageous; unassuageable; unfavorable; unfriendly; vehement; warlike; **n.** HOSTILITY: animosity; animus; antagonism, antipathy; bellicosity; cleavage; combativeness; combativity; disaffection; discordance; ferity; friction; inimicalness; irreconcilability; pugnacity; rancor; truculence; umbrage; vehemence
bitterly: **a.** venomous; virulent
in (hostile) or unfavorable surroundings: **adv.** *in partibus (infidelium)*
meeting: **n.** rencontre

HOT: **a.** ardent; candent; choleric; fervent; impetuous; incalescent; incandescent; pungent; thermal; thermic; vehement
and moist: **a.** sulfurous; sulphurous; sultry; sweltering; torrid; **n.** torridity

HOTEL(S): **n.** caravansary; hostel(ry); imaret; xenodocheum
and inns, lore of: **n.** xenodocheinology

HOUR, *live for the:* **adv.** *carpe diem; in horam vivere*

HOUSE: **v.** contain; shelter; **n.** (**see** "abode") chateau; domicile; habitation; mansion; tenement
head of: **see under** "head"
mistress of: **n.** chatelaine; materfamilias

HOUSEHOLD, *also persons who share:* **n.** menage
deities or tutelaries: **n.pl.** lares; penates
effects, most valued: **n.pl.** lares and penates
mistress of: **n.** chatelaine; materfamilias; matron
of misc. persons: **n.** menagerie
of three, one the lover of one of spouses: **n.** *ménage à trois*

HOUSEKEEPING: **n.** ménage

HOVER: **v.** cower; librate; linger

HOW: **adv.** *quo modo?*

HOWLING *joyously:* **a.** roborant; **v.** HOWL: ululate; **n.** ululation

HUBBUB: (**see** "ado") **n.** agitation; Babelism; brouhaha; coil; hullabaloo; turmoil

HUE: **n.** aspect; complexion; tincture

HUG: **v.** embosom

HUGE: (**see** "giant") **a.** amplitudinous; astronomical; behemoth(ian); brobdi(n)gnagian; Bunyanesque; colossal; cyclopean; dinosauric; elephantine; gargantuan; gigantesque; gigantic; Herculean; heroic; Homeric; immeasurable; imposing; leviathan; macroscopic; magnitudinous; mammoth; mastadonic; monstrous; monumental; oceanic; Olympian; polyphemian; polyphemic; polyphemous; prodigious; pyramidal; pythonic; stratospheric(al); titanic; tremendous; **n.** HUGENESS: (**see** "immensity") amplitude; colossality; enormity; indefinitude; magnitude; prodigality
grotesquely: **a.** gigantesque
something that is: **n.** behemoth; colossus; leviathan; titan

HULLABALOO: **see** "hubbub" **and** "ado"

HUM: **v.** bombinate; murmur; susurrate; **n.** bombination; murmur; susurration

HUMAN(S): (**see** "man" **and** "mankind") **n.** Adamite; anthropoid; earthling; hominid(ae); *homo sapiens;* individual; mortal; **a.** anthropoid(al); anthropomorphic; anthropopathic; compassionate; earthborn; finite; humane; mortal; sympathetic
action, produced or induced by: **a.** (arti)factitious; **n.** artifact; (**pl.** *fructus industriales*)
affairs, pert. to: **a.** mundane

and animal forms combined (as centaur): **n.** therianthropism; **a.** therianthropic

below: **a.** infrahuman; subhuman

characteristics, ascription to animal(s): **n.** anthropomorphism; anthropopathism; **a.** anthropomorphic; anthropopathic

characteristics, ascription to god(s): **n.** anthropopathy; anthropophuism; embodiment; incarnation; **n.** anthropopathite

characteristics, ascription to inanimate objects: **n.** humanization; pathetic fallacy; personification

feelings, ascribed to something not human: **a.** anthropopathic; **n.** anthropopathism

figure, as architectural support: **n.** antic; caryatid (fem.); telamon (male)

figure, representation of: **n.** anthropomorph; humunculus; manikin

figure, use in primitive magic: **n.** *envoûtement*

flesh, eating of: see "cannibalism"

form, changing into: **n.** anthropomorphosis; (pl. anthropomorphoses); **a.** anthropomorphic; anthropomorphous

form, in: **a.** incarnate; personified; **n.** embodiment; incarnation

form or shape, having: **a.** anthropomorphic; anthropomorphous

law, by: **adv.** *jure humano*

less than: **a.** infrahuman; subhuman

pert. to: **a.** anthropoid; anthropogenic; anthropic(al); mortal

qualities, attributed to nature or objects: **n.** embodiment; humanization; incarnation; pathetic fallacy

qualities, deprive of: **v.** barbarize; brutalize; dehumanize; robotize

resembling: **a.** anthropomorphic; anthropomorphous; anthropoid(al); humanoid

study of in rel. to environment and to other organisms: **n.** anthropomony; ecology

study of origin and development: **n.** anthropogenesis; **a.** anthropogenetic

study or student of: **n.** anthropologist; anthropology; **a.** anthropological

unsuitable for: **a.** subhuman

wisdom about: **n.** anthroposophy

HUMANE: **see** "human"

HUMANITARIAN: **see** "person, charitable"

HUMANITY: (**see** "man" **and** "mankind") **n.** anthropopathy

HUMANIZE: **v.** civilize; incarnate; personify; refine; **n.** HUMANIZATION: civilization; embodiment; incarnation; personification; refinement

animals or things: **v.** anthropomorphize; personify; **n.** anthropomorphism; embodiment; incarnation; pathetic fallacy; personification; **a.** anthropomorphic; anthropomorphous

HUMBLE: **v.** debase; degrade; demean; denigrate; humiliate; minify: **a.** (**see** "meek") genuflectory; modest; self-effacing; submissive; unpretentious; **n.** HUMBLENESS: **see** "humility"

people: **n.pl.** *gens de peu*

HUMBUG: **n.** blague; flummery; hypocrisy; hypocrite; imposter; pretension

HUMILIATING: **a.** degrading; humiliative; ignominious; mortifying; **n.** HUMILIATION: abasement; abashment; chagrin; chastenment; debasement; mortification; **n.** HUMILITY: (**see** "self-denial") abjection; abnegation; humbleness; self-effacement

place of (humiliation): **n.** Canossa

HUMOR: **n.** badinage; caprice; comicality; disposition; farcicality; inclination; jocosity; jocularity; joviality; temperament; **n.** HUMORIST: *farceur;* (**fem.** *farceuse*)

bad: (**see** "ill-humored") **n.** distemper; dudgeon

coarse: **a.** Falstaffian; Rabelaisian

cynical: **n.** Pantagruelism; **a.** Pantagruelic; Pantagruelian; **n.** Pantagruelist

sense of: **n.pl.** risibles

HUMORLESS: **a.** serious; unmirthful

HUMOROUS: (**see** "laughable") **a.** facetious; farcical; jocose; jocular; jovial; ludicrous; Rabelaisian; risible; waggish; whimsical; **n.** HUMOROUSNESS: *espièglerie;* ludicrousness; waggishness; whimsicality

action or remark: **n.** farcicality; jocosity

grotesquely: **a.** baboonish; **n.** baboonery

HUMPBACK: **n.** gibbosity; kyphosis; **a.** gibbous; kyphotic

HUNDRED *fold:* **a.** or **v.** centuplicate; **a.** HUNDREDTH: centisimal
years: **see** "one hundred"

HUNGER: (**see** "appetite") **n.** edacity; gulosity; voracity; **a.** HUNGRY: gluttonous; insatiable; rapacious; ravenous; voracious
abnormal or continuous: **n.** bulimia; hyperorexia; **a.** bulimic; hyperorectic
acknowledges no law: la fame non vuol leggi
for praise, honor, etc.: **n.** captation; esurience; **a.** esurient

HUNTING: **n.** (the) chase; venation; **n.** HUNTER: chasseur; huntsman; ja(e)ger; Nimrod
as art or sport: **n.** cynegetics; shikar; venery
expedition: **n.** safari
goddess of: **n.** Artemis; Diana
of, used for, fond of or living by: **a.** venatic
rel. to: **a.** cynegetic; venatic

HURRAH!: **int.** *evviva!;* ole!

HURRIEDLY: **adv.** *à corps perdu; à la volée;* impetuously

HURTFUL: (**see** "injurious") **a.** atrocious; baneful; deleterious; flagrant; grievous; heinous; inimical; malignant; nocent; nocuous; noxious; pernicious; traumatic; venomous

HUSBAND(S): **n.** consort; spouse
and wife: **n.** *vir et uxor*
dear: **n.** *caro sposo*
having one at a time: **n.** monandry; monogamy; **n.** monandrist; monogamist; **a.** monandrous; monogamic; monogamous
having two or more at a time: **n.** bigamy; polyandry; polygamy; **n.** bigamist; polyandrist; polygamist; **a.** bigamous; polyandrous; polygamous
located or centered around family of: **a.** patrilocal
or wives, having more than one at a time: **n.** bigamy; polygyny; **n.** bigamist; polygamist; polygynist; **a.** bigamous; polygamous; polygynous
right of the: **n.** *jus mariti*

HUZZY: **n.** doxy; slattern; trollop; wench

HYMN *of praise or thinksgiving:* (**see** under "praise") **n.** doxology; magnificat; *te deum;* theody

HYPOCRISY: (**see** "pretense") **n.** (dis)simulation; duplicity; Pharisaism; piosity; religiosity; sanctimoniousness; self-righteousness; speciosity; Tartuffery; **n.** HYPOCRITE: (**see** "pretender") dissembler; dissimulator; Pecksniffian; Tartuf(f)e; **a.** HYPOCRITICAL: dissimulative; Pecksniffian; pretentious; religiose; sanctimonious; specious; Tartuffian; **adv.** *à la Tartuffe*

HYPOTHETICAL: **see** "theoretical"
principle of fire: **n.** phlogiston

I

I, *excessive use of letter:* **n.** iotacism
think, therefore I am: cogito ergo sum

IDEA(S): **(see** "notion") **n.** abstraction; concept(ion); conceptus; **(pl.** concepti); impression; percept(ion); supposition
advanced in: **a.** *avant-garde; fin-de-siècle;* **n.** *avant-garde; avant-gardist(e)*; visionary
contradiction in: **n.** antilogy
express variously by means of synonyms: **v.** synonymize
fear or distrust of: **n.** ideophobia
fixed: **n.** *idée fixe*
formulate: **v.** conceptualize; ideate; **n.** conceptualization; ideation; **a.** conceptualistic; ideational; ideative
full of or pregnant w/: **a.** tumefacient
happy: **n.** *curiosa felicitas*
one accepting new: **n.** neoteric
one hating new: **n.** misoneist
originating: **a.** ideogenetic
suggestive of, rel. to or concerned w/: **a.** ideologic(al)
with no exact word for: **n.** anonym(e)

IDEAL(ISTIC): **a.** aerial; altitudinarian; chimerical; doctrinaire; messianic; paradisaic(al); paradisical; paradisial; paradisic; platonic; platonistic; poetic(al); romantic; sentimental; quixotic(al); utopian; visionary; **n.** IDEALIST: altitudinarian; *avant-gardist(e)*; Don Quixote; utopian; visionary; **n.** IDEALIZATION: apotheosis; canonization; deification; spiritualization; stellification; **v.** IDEALIZE: apotheosize; canonize; deify; spiritualize; stellify

IDEALOGY: **see** "ideology"

IDENTICAL: **(see** "equal") **a.** congruent; equivalent; indistinguishable; isonomous; synonymous; tantamount; **n.** IDENTICALITY: equivalence; selfsameness; synonymity

IDENTIFICATION, *sympathetic:* **n.** empathy; **a.** empath(et)ic; heteropathic; **v.** IDENTIFY: diagnosticate; recognize; **n.** IDENTIFIABILITY: identification; **a.** identificatory

IDENTITY, *individual:* **n.** individuality; ipseity
in essence or substance: **n.** homoousia
of nature, meaning or significance: **n.** synonymity
self w/ another: **n.** empathy; identification; **a.** empath(et)ic; heteropathic

IDEOLOGY: **n.** philosophy; speculation; *weltanschauung*

IDIOM: **n.** colloquialism; parlance; patois; vernacular

IDIOTIC: **see** "stupid"

IDLE: **a.** *désoeuvré;* faineant; groundless; indolent; lackadaisical; *le bras croisés;* otiose; slothful; superfluous; trivial; vacuous
remark: **n.** vaporing
talk: **n.** caquet
the (unemployed persons): **n.pl.** flotsam and jetsam; *les sans-travail*

IDLENESS **(or** IDLING): **(see** "inaction") **n.** aimlessness; disoccupation; *flânerie; idlesse;* inactivity; indolence; leisure; otiosity; sedentation; triviality
pleasant: **n.** *dolce far niente*

IDLER: **n.** badaud; dawdler; *fainéant; flaneur;* **(fem.** *flaneuse*); loiterer; sluggard; vagrant

IDOL: **(see** "image") **n.** effigy; demigod(dess)
worship: **n.** am harrez (Jewish); iconolatry; idolatry

IGNORANCE: **n.** agnosticism; benightedness; *bêtise;* crassitude; ignoration; illiteracy; inscience; nescience; rusticity; sciolism
appealing to: **adv.** *ad ignorantum*
of the fact(s) excuses: ignoranti facti excusat; (pl.) *ignoranti factorum excusat*
of the law excuses no one: ignorantia legis nemnem excusat
gross: **n.** *ignorance crasse*
state of: ignoration; incognoscibility

IGNORANT: **a.** agnostic; analphabetic; artless; benighted; illiterate; incognoscible; inerudite; inscient; nescient; unbookish; uncultured; unenlightened; uninstructed; unlearned; unlettered; unschooled; unsophisticated; untaught; untutored
person: **n.** am haarez; analphabet; ignoramus; illiterate; Philistine; sciolist

IGNORE: (**see** "neglect") **v.** disregard; elide; **n.** IGNORATION: disregard; elision

ILL: (**see** "sick") **a.** *à la mort;* aeger; hurtful; inauspicious; indisposed; infirm; maladive; morbid; morbific; morbose; pernicious; unpropitious; untoward; valetudinarian
-advised: **adv.** *mal avisé*
breeding: **n.** *mauvais ton*
health: **n.** cachexia; malaise; **a.** cachectic
-humored: **a.** cantankerous; captious; churlish; contentious; disputatious; irascible; pettish; petulant; pugnacious; querulous; waspish; **n.** distemper; dudgeon
-mannered or ill-bred: **a.** *mal elevé(e)*
-matched: **a.** disparate; dissociable; heterogen(e)ous; incompatible; incongruous
-natured or tempered: (**see under** "bad") **a.** bilious; cantankerous; irascible; perverse; surly
-will: (**see** "hostility") **n.** animosity; animus; antagonism; enmity; malevolence; malice; malignity; rancor
-will, full of or moved by: **a.** antagonistic; contemptuous; despiteful; despiteous; malevolent; malicious; rancorous
will, let there be no: **adv.** *absit invidia*

ILLEGAL: (**see** "unlawful") **a.** adulterine; contraband; criminal; illegitimate; illicit; misbegotten; nugatory; unauthorized; unsound
performance of legal act: **n.** malfeasance; misfeasance

ILLEGITIMATE: **a.** counterfeit; debased; erratic; illogical; irregular; misbegotten; spurious; supposititious; unwarranted
birth: **n.** *bar sinister*
child: **n.** *filius nullius; filius populi;* mongrel

ILLICIT *love affair:* **n.** amour; intrigue; liaison; rendezvous

ILLITERATE: (**see** "ignorant") **a.** analphabetic; **n.** analphabet(ic)

ILLNESS, *recovery period:* **n.** convalescent; recuperation; **a.** convalescent; recuperative

ILLOGICAL: (**see** "unreasonable") **a.** acategorical; equivocal; fallacious; incoherent; incongruous; inconsequent; inconsistent; parabolical; paralogical; paralogistic; rambling; **n.** ILLOGICALITY: incoherence; incoherency; paralogism; unreasonableness; unsoundness
explanation: **n.** *lucus a non lucendo; non sequitur* (**abb.** non sec.)

ILLUMINATING: **a.** enlightening; fluorescent; incandescent; luminescent; luminiferous

ILLUSION: **n.** anamorphosis; apparition; chimera; *fata morgana;* hallucination; hallucinosis; *ignis fatuuis;* mirage; misapprehension; misconception; phantasm(ata); revenant; spectrum
of being somewhere before: **n.** *déjà vu(e)* (phenomenon); paramnesia

ILLUSIVE: (**see** "ghostly") **a.** barmecidal; chimerical; deceptive; fatuitous; fictitious; illusionistic; illusory; imaginary; phantasmagoric(al); phantasmal; phantasmic; phantom, prestidigitatorial; prestidigitatory; spectral

ILLUSTRATIVE (**or** ILLUSTRATIONAL): **a.** delineative; demonstrative; descriptive; descriptory; pictorial; picturesque; representative; **n.** ILLUSTRATION: **see** "picture"

ILLUSTRIOUS: (**see** "eminent") **a.** august; celebrated; distinguished; formidable; honorific; immortal; luscent; magnific(al); magnificent; majestic; prestigious; redoubtable; regal; (re)splendent; signal; transcendent

IMAGE(S): (**see** "likeness") **n.** *alter ego;* conception; counterpart; effigy; portrait; replica; (re)semblance; sculpture; similitude; simulacrum
breaker of: **n.** iconoclast; a. iconoclastic
pert. to: **a.** conceptual; concipient
use in primitive magic: **n.** *envoûtement*
veneration of: **n.** fetishism; iconoduly
worship of: **n.** fetishism; iconolatry; idolatry

IMAGINARY: (**see** "illusive") **a.** apocryphal; apparitional; chimerical; fanciful; fictitious; fictive; idealistic; ideational; imaginational; *in nubibus;* insubstantial; legendary; mythical; quixotic; simulated; supposititious; unreal(istic); utopian; veritable; visionary; **v.** IMAGINE: conceive; fabricate; fictionalize; ideate; meditate; mythologize; surmise
animal or thing: **n.** centaur; chimera; cyclops; *ens rationis;* griffon; gyascutus; kraken; mermaid; minotaur; phoenix; sphinx
creature, regarded as embodiment of absolute absurdity: **n.** coquecigrue
disease: **n.** *malade imaginaire*
invalid: **n.** hypochondriac; valetudinarian
perception, auditory or visual: **n.** delusion; hallucination; hallucinosis; **a.** hallucinatory
place: **n.** never-never country; *weissnichtwo*
place of high romance: **n.** Graustark; **a.** Graustarkian

IMAGINATION: **n.** genius; phantasy; resourcefulness; unreality
capacity for: **n.** ideaphoria
fantastic: **n.** *fata morgana*
lacking in: **a.** frigid; insipid; monotonous; pedantic; pedestrian; pointless; prosaic; unimaginative; unleavened

IMBECILE: **n.** *impos animi*

IMITATION: **n.** burlesque; caricature; counterfeit; emulation; imitant; mimesis; mimicry; mockery; parody; postiche; pretense; sequacity; simulacrum; simulation; **v.** IMITATE: counterfeit; emulate; feign; pretend; reproduce; simulate; **a.** IMITATIVE: (**see** "counterfeit") derivative; echoic; emulatory; emulous; epigonic; epigonous; mimetic; onomatopoe(t)ic; sequacoius; slavish; **n.** IMITATIVENESS: imitancy; **n.** IMITATOR: (**see** "impostor") epigone
as of speech or behavior: **n.** mimesis; mimicry; **a.** mimetic; mimical
lit. or mus. work: **n.** epigonism; postiche
satirical or grotesque: **n.** or **v.** burlesque; caricature

IMMATERIAL: **a.** apparitional; asomatous; diaphanous; ethereal; gossamery; illusionary; incorporeal; insubstantial; irrelevant; spiritual; transcendent; unimportant; **n.** IMMATERIALITY: diaphaneity; ethereality; incorporeality; incorporeity; insubstantiality; irrelevancy

IMMATURE: **a.** fledgling; impubic; infantile; infantilistic; juvenile; nouveau; puerile; unfinished; unripe; **n.** IMMATURITY: incunabulum; infancy; infantility; juniority; juvenility; nonage; puerilism; puerility; verdancy

IMMEASURABLE: (**see** "vast") **a.** imponderable; incommensurable; infinite; unfathomable

IMMEASURABLY *great or low:* **a.** abysmal

IMMEDIATE: (**see** "direct") **a.** presto; proximate; **adv.** IMMEDIATELY: forthwith; instanter; straightway; *tout de suite;* **n.** IMMEDIACY: directness; instantaneity

IMMENSE: **see** "huge"; **n.** IMMENSITY: colossality; immeasurability; indefinitude; magnitude; vastitude; vastity

IMMODERATE: **a.** bizarre; eccentric; exaggerated; exorbitant; extravagant; inordinate; intemperate: *outré;* overweening; unreasonable; **n.** IMMODERATION: extravagance; gulosity; inordinancy; insobriety; intemperance

IMMODEST: **a.** brazen; *grivois;* indecorous; indelicate; uninhibited; unrestrained; unseemly; **n.** IMMODESTY: boldness; forwardness; impropriety; impudicity; indecency; indecorum; indelicacy

IMMORAL: (**see** "lewd") **a.** dissolute; licentious; pornographic; profligate; unedi-

fying; unprincipled; unsavory; wanton; **n.** IMMORALITY: (**see** "lewdness") obliquity
excess of (immorality) : **n.** orgy; Saturnalia; **a.** orgiastic; Saturnalian

IMMORTAL: **see** "eternal"

IMMOVABLE: (**see** "fixed") **a.** implanted; obdurate; sessile

IMPARTIAL: **a.** candid; dispassionate; equitable; impersonal; judicial; judicious; unbiased; unprejudiced; **n.** IMPARTIALITY: detachment; disinterestedness; fairness

IMPASSABLE: (**see** "unconquerable") **a.** impenetrable; imperforate; impermeable; impervious; insurmountable; **n.** impenetrability; impermeability

IMPASSE: **n.** cul-de-sac; deadlock; (horns of a) dilemma; obstruction; predicament; stalemate

IMPASSIONED: **a.** delirious; dithyrambic; evangelistic; fanatical; hysterical; impetuous; maniac(al); (per)fervid; vehement; zealous

IMPASSIVE: (**see** "calm") **a.** apathetic; comatose; expressionless; hermetic(al); imperturbable; inanimate; insensate; invertebrate; motionless; nonchalant; phlegmatic; spineless; stolid; torpid; torporific; unimpressible; unperturbed

IMPATIENT: **a.** anxious; apprehensive; choleric; fidgety; impetuous; intolerant; pettish; petulant; precipitate; premature; previous; restive; waspish

IMPEDIMENT: (**see** "hindrance") **n.** cul-de-sac; embarrassment; encumbrance; obstruction

IMPENDING: (**see** "pressing") **a.** approaching; emergent; imminent; incumbent; inevitable; threatening
disaster or doom: **n.** handwriting on the wall; sword of Damocles; **a.** apocalyptic(al); Damoclean

IMPERATIVE: (**see** "required") **a.** compulsory; *de rigueur; de règle;* obligatory; peremptory; prerequisite; **n.** command; injunction; mandate; mandatum; prerequisite

IMPERCEPTIBLE: **a.** gradual; subliminal; subtle; **n.** IMPERCEPTIBILITY: graduality
to touch or mind: **a.** impalpable; subliminal

IMPERFECT: (**see** "defective") **a.** atelic; contingent; dilapidated; imperfective; inadequate; inchoate; inchoative; incipient; potential; rudimentary; suboptimal; substandard; **n.** IMPERFECTION: **see** "blemish"

IMPERIOUS: **see** "lordly"

IMPERISHABLE: (**see** "eternal") **a.** immarcescible; immarcessible; immortal; indestructable; perpetual; **n.** IMPERISHABLENESS: eternality; perpetuality; perpetuity; subtility

IMPERSONAL: (**see** "impartial") **a.** infrahuman; inhuman; mechanical; **n.** personality
to make: **v.** dehumanize; depersonalize; robotize; **n.** dehumanization; depersonalization

IMPERSONATION: **see** "personation"

IMPETUOUS: (**see** "abrupt" **and** "hasty") **a.** *à corps perdu;* impassioned; impulsive; intractable; (per)fervid; precipitate; restive; vehement; **n.** impetuosity; impulsivity

IMPISH: (**see** "whimsical") **a.** puckish; **n.** IMPISHNESS: puckishness; whimsicality

IMPLEMENT(S): **see** "equipment"

IMPLICATION: **n.** connotation; deduction; entanglement; inference; insinuation; insinuendo; significance; signification; **a.** IMPLIED: connotative; implicit; inferred; insinuated; tacit; **v.** IMPLY: allude; connote; infer; insinuate; intimate; purport
affirmative: **n.** negative pregnant

IMPLYING *something beyond what is obvious:* **a.** subintelligential

IMPOLITE: (**see** "rude") **a.** dedecorous; discourteous; indecorous; inurbane; uncivil; uncourtly; uncouth; unmannerly; unpolished; unrefined; **n.** IMPOLITENESS: (**see** "discourteousy") incivility; inurbanity

IMPORTANCE: **n.** concernment; consequence; cruciality; eminence; moment; prestige; signality; significance
of great: **a.** basilic(al); crucial; monumental
person of little: **n.** nonentity
thing of: **n.** *pièce de résistance*
thing of little: (**see** "trifle") **n.** bagatelle; bauble; geegaw; gewgaw; gimcrack; inconsequence; inconsequentiality; infinitesimality; minutia; nihility; nullity; (**pl.** inconsequentia; minutiae; trivia)

IMPORTANT: **a.** acute; basic; basilic(al); consequential; crucial; determinative; fundamental; impactful; impactive; influential; momentous; monumental; paramount; pivotal; prominent; signal; significant; strategic; stratagetic
feeling or acting: **a.** consequential; pompous; **n.** flatulence; pomposity; pontificality; pursiness
matters or events: **n.** memorabilia
person or thing: **n.** bashaw; colossus; mogul; panjandrum; potentate; sachem; sagamore; tycoon

IMPOSING: (**see** "commanding") **a.** august; exalted; grandiose; imperial; magnific(al); magnificent; majestic; regal; **n.** grandiosity; majesty; regality
in style: (**see** "pretentious") **a.** grandiloquent; sonorous
upon: **n.** imposture

IMPOSSIBLE: **a.** chimerical; fantastic; impracticable; insuperable; insurmountable; invincible; unacceptable; unrealistic; unsurpassable; **n.** IMPOSSIBILITY: impracticability; insuperability; invincibility
advocacy of something that is: **n.** impossibilism; **n. or a.** impossibilist

IMPOSTOR (or IMPOSTER): **n.** Cagliostro; charlatan; epigone; humbug; mountebank; Pharisee; pretender; quacksalver; **n.** IMPOSTURE: charlatanry; hocus-pocus; mountebankery

IMPOTENCE: **n.** fecklessness; feebleness; helplessness; sterility; weakness
sexual: **n.** anaphrodisia; impotency

IMPRACTICABLE: **a.** imprudent; infeasible; insuperable; unrealistic

IMPRACTICAL: (**see** "visionary") **a.** academic; doctrinaire; dogmatic(al); escapist; feckless; idealistic; implausible; inexcutable; irresponsible; ivory-tower(ed); pedantic; poetic(al); quixotic(al); romantic; speculative; theoretic(al); unfeasible; visionary

IMPREGNATION: **n.** fecundation; fertilization; indoctrination; spermatization
by external contact only: **n.** adosculation

IMPRESSION: **n.** impact; imprint; indentation; influence
brief: **n.** *aperçu*
total or over-all: **n.** *tout ensemble*

IMPRESSIVE: (**see** "grand" **and** "imposing") **a.** impactful; penetrative; **n.** IMPRESSIVENESS: grandeur; grandiloquence; grandiosity; magnificence; opulency; penetrativity

IMPRISON: **v.** confine; immure; incarcerate; restrain; **n.** IMPRISONMENT: confinement; durance (vile); immuration; immurement; incarceration; limbo; restraint

IMPROBABLE: **see** "uncertain"

IMPROMPTU: (**see** "off-hand") **a.** *ad lib(itum)*; autoschediastic; extemporaneous; extemporary; extempore; improvisatorial; improvisatory; improviso; impulsive; spontaneous; unpremeditated; unstudied; **v. see** "improvise"; **n.** ad lib; autoschediasm; improvisation

IMPROPER: (**see** "unwise") **a.** *à propos de rien;* errant; illicit; immodest; impertinent; inaccurate; inappropriate; incongruous; indecent; indecorous; indelicate; inexpedient; insubordinate; insurgent; irrelevant; rebellious; scabrous; solecistic; unacceptable; unbecoming; uncomely; unethical; unseasonable; unseemly; untoward; **n.** IMPROPRIETY: barbarism; *faux pas; gaffe; grivoiserie;* solecism
action or behavior: (**see** "impropriety") **n.** insubordination; insurgence; insurgency; insurrection
highly: **a.** malodorous

IMPROVE: **v.** (a)meliorate; augment; enhance; rectify; refine; **a.** ameliorative; **n.** IMPROVEMENT: (a)melioration; enhancement; perfectionment; refinement; reformation

capable of (improvement): (see "correctable") **a.** perfectible
designed to (improve): **see** "remedial"
not subject to (improvement): **see under** "correction" **and** "incurable"

IMPROVISE: **v.** *ad lib;* extemporize; improvisate; **n.** IMPROVISATION: *ad lib(itum)*; autoschediasm; **a.** IMPROVISED: **see** "impromptu"

IMPRUDENT: (**see** "rash" **and** "unwise") **a.** audacious; impolitic; impracticable; improvident; injudicious; procacious

IMPUDENT: (**see** "sassy") **a.** audacious; contemptuous; contumelious; disrespectful; forward; insolent; malapert; shameless; supercilious; toplofty; unmannerly; **n.** IMPUDENCE: (**see** "sassiness") cheekiness; impudency; incivility; procacity

IMPULSE: (**see** "incentive") **n.** impetus; incitement; instigation; nisus; spontaneity; **a.** IMPULSIVE: (**see** "rash" ballistic; capricious; impetuous; spontaneous; unpremeditated; **n.** IMPULSIVENESS: impetuosity; impetuousness; impulsivity; spontaneity

IMPURE: (**see** "lewd") **a.** adulterated; defiled; macular; unchaste; unrectified; unwholesome; **n.** IMPURITY: adulteration; contamination; corruption; defilement; pollution; putrescence
make: **v.** adulterate; debauch; defile; impurify

IN *a few words:* **adv.** *paucis verbis*
all events: **adv.** *en tout cas*
all seriousness: **adv.** *au grand sérieux*
bad faith: **adv.** *mala fide(s)*
being: **a.** or **adv.** *in esse;* **n.** existent
equal fault: **adv.** *(in) pari delicto*
few words: **adv.** *paucis verbis*
one way or another: **adv.** *à bis ou à blanc*
passing: **adv.** *en passant*
short, or in a word: **adv.** *ad summam*
so many words: **adv.** *totidem verbis*
spite of: **prep.** mauger; maugre; notwithstanding; *quand même*
spite of oneself: **adv.** *malgré lui*
the first place: **adv.** *imprimis*
the first place cited: **adv.** *loco primo citato* (**abb.** *loc. primo cit.*)
the function, capacity or character of: **adv.** qua
the place cited or quoted: **adv.** *loco citato* (**abb.** *loc. cit.*)
the same place: **adv.** *ibidem* (**abb.** *ibid.*)
the work cited or quoted: **adv.** *opere citato* (**abb.** *op. cit.*)
this place: **adv.** *hoc loco*
what manner or way?: **adv.** *quo modo?*

INABILITY: **see** "helplessness" **and** "weakness"
statement expressing: **n.** *non possumus*

INACCURATE: (**see** "incorrect") **a.** apocryphal; discrepant; erroneous; fallacious; inexact; **n.** INACCURACY: discrepancy; erratum; fallacy; imprecision; inexactitude; inexactness; misconception

INACTION: (**see** "sloth") **n.** acedia; deliquescence; dormancy; ennui; fecklessness; idleness; indolence; inertia; inertness; lassitude; lethargy; otiosity; passivity; quiescence; quietude; slothfulness; supinity; torpidity; torpor; **a.** INACTIVE: anergic; comatose; deliquescent; dormant; faineant; feckless; inanimate; indolent; inoperative; latent; lethargic; otiose; quiescent; sedentary; slothful; supine; torpid; withdrawn; **n.** INACTIVITY: (**see** "idleness") faineance; faineancy; *fainéantise;* idleness; inertia; otiosity; paralysis; passivity; quiescence; sedentation; stasis; *status quo*
pleasant: **n.** *dolce far niente*

INADEQUATE: (**see** "ineffective") **a.** deficient; disabled; disproportionate; futile; impotent; inefficacious; insufficient; perfunctory; **n.** INADEQUACY: (**see** "deficiency") dearth; incapacitation; inefficacy; insufficiency

INADVISABLE: **a.** contraindicative; disadvantageous; impolitic; impracticable; inappropriate; inexpedient; inopportune; **n.** INADVISABILITY: contraindication

INANE: (**see** "empty") **a.** fatu(it)ous; feckless; insubstantial; jejune; pointless; puerile; shallow; stratospheric(al); vacant; vacuous; **n.** INANITY: (**see** "emptiness") hollowness; inanition; lethargy; marasmus; shallowness; vacuity

INAPPROPRIATE: (**see** "unsuitable") **a.** impertinent; inapposite; inapt; incongruous; inexpedient; infelicitous; inopportune; malapropos; unbecoming

INATTENTIVE: **a.** absent-minded; abstracted; astigmatic; bemused; distant; distraught; harum-scarum; heedless; incogitable; incogitant; incurious; negligent; oscitant; preoccupied; remiss; **n.** INATTENTION: **(see** "neglect") abstraction; heedlessness; ignoration; inadvertency; incogitancy; incuriosity; misfeasance; oscitancy; oscitation; preoccupation; remission

INAUGURATE: **v.** auspicate; induct; initiate; install; institute; introduce; invest; **n.** INAUGURATION: accession; induction; installation; institution; investiture; **a.** INAUGURATIVE: auspicatory; initiatory; introductory

INBORN: **(see** "innate") **a.** ancestral; cognate; congenital; connate; constitutional; endogamous; endogenous; familial; hereditary; idiopathic; inbred; indigenous; ingrained; inherent; inherited; intrinsic; institutional; intuitive
tendency: **n.** diathesis; predisposition

INCAPABLE: **a.** feckless; helpless; impotent; powerless; sterile, **n. see** "helplessness"
of being weighed or measured: **a.** immeasurable; imponderable

INCENTIVE: **(see** "incitement") **n.** catalyst; fillip; incitation; inducement; instigation; motivation; provocation; stimulant; stimulation; stimulus

INCEPTION: **(see** "beginning" **and** "origin") **n.** inauguration; initiation; principium

INCIDENTAL: **a.** accessory; adventitious; casual; collateral; concomitant; concurrent; circumstantial; digressive; episodic(al); extraneous; fortuitous; intervenient; parenthetic(al); subordinate; tangential; **adv.** INCIDENTALLY: apropos; casually; en passant; obiter; parenthetically; secondarily; **n.** INCIDENT: **(see** "event") circumstance; circumstantiality; concomitant; contingency; episode; phenomenon
remark or comment: **(see under** "parenthetical") **n.** digression; interlocution; *obiter (dictum)*; **a.** interlocutory; parenthetical

INCITE: **(see** "stimulate") **v.** actuate; animate; flagellate; foment; instigate; suscitate; **n.** INCITEMENT: concitation; fomentation; incitation; instigation; provocation; **a.** INCITING: animative; catalytic; hortative; hortatory; incitory; provocative; stimulatory
to courage or fervor: **n.** *sursum corda*

INCLINATION(S): **n.** acclivity; affectation; diathesis; gradient; partiality; penchant; predilection; (pre)disposition; prejudice; proclivity; propensity; tendency; versant; **a.** INCLINABLE: (pre)-disposed; suasible; tendentious; **a.** INCLINING: accliv(it)ous; inclinatory
natural born: **n.** diathesis; predisposition; tropism
slight: **n.** velleity
to act in response to stimulus: **n.** tropism
worldly: **n.pl.** mundanities

INCLUSIVE: **a.** capacious; comprehensive; cyclopedic(al); encompassing; **n.** INCLUSIVENESS: comprehensibility; **v.** INCLUDE: **see** "embrace"
all-: **see under** "all"

INCOMPATIBLE: **(see** "disagreeing") **a.** discordant; immiscible; incongruous; inconsistent; irreconcilable; repugnant; uncongenial

INCOMPETENT: **a.** impertinent; inapt; incapacitated; inept; unqualified; **n.** INCOMPETENCE: inaptitude; incapacitation; incapacity
as evidence: **a.** impertinent; inadmissible
mentally: **a.** *non compos (mentis)*
totally: **a. or n.** *asinus ad lyram* (ass at the lyre)

INCOMPLETE: **(see** "partial" **and** "rudimentary") **a.** contingent; defective; deficient; elementary; fractional; fractionary; fragmental; fragmentary; imperfect(ed); inchoate; inchoative; incipient; potential; truncated; unperfected

INCOMPREHENSIBLE: **a.** ambiguous; enigmatic(al); impenetrable; indefinite; nebulous; numinous; undecipherable; unintelligible; **n.** INCOMPREHENSIBILITY; ambiguity; enigma; indefinitude; nebulosity

INCONSISTENT: **a.** antagonistic; contradictuous; discordant; discrepant; immiscible; incompatible; incongruous; inharmonious; irreconcilable; paradoxical; repugnant; **n.** INCONSISTENCY: contrariety; incompatibility; incongruity; misalliance; *non sequitur* (**abb.** *non seq*); paradox(icality); (**pl.** contrarieties)

INCONSTANT: (**see** "fickle") **a.** alternating; ambivalent; capricious; chameleonic; fluctuating; mercurial; mutable; quicksilver; spasmodic; unstable; vacillating; vagrant; variable; vertiginous

INCONTROVERTIBLE: (**see** "certain") **a.** immutable; incontestable; indisputable; irrecusable; irrefrangible; irrefutable; **adv.** *sans doute; sine dubio*

INCONVENIENT: **a.** disadvantageous; discommodious; embarrassing; inappropriate; incommodious; inexpedient; inopportune; unseasonable; **n.** INCONVENIENCE: disadvantage; handicap; impediment; **v.** (**see** "annoy") discommode; embarrass; incommode

INCORPORATION: **n.** amalgamation; embodiment; incarnation; inclusion

INCORRECT: (**see** "erroneous" **and** "unseemly") **a.** fallacious; imprecise; improper; inaccurate; solecistic; unbecoming; **n.** fallacy; imprecision; impropriety; inaccuracy

spelling, writing or printing of words: **n.** cacography; pseudography

INCREASE: (**see** "multiply") **v.** aggrandize; augment; enhance; exacerbate; propagate; **n.** accruement; accumulation; additament; advancement; agglutination; aggrandizement; augmentation; concrescence; enhancement; exacerbation; increment; intensification; majoration; multiplication; progress(ion)

gradual: **n.** accrescence; accretion; agglutination; **a.** incremental

in severity, as disease: **v.** exacerbate; **n.** exacerbation; exacerbescence

in size, as organ or part: **v.** hypertrophy; tumesce; **n.** hypertrophy; tumescence

rel. to: **a.** accessorial

size, power, riches, etc.: **v.** aggrandize; augment; **n.** aggrandizement; augmentation

to utmost: **v.** maximalize

INCREASING: **a.** (ac)cumulative; augmentative; escalating; exacerbative; multiplicative; pyramiding

capable of: **a.** accumulable

INCURABLE: **a.** immedicable; incorrigible; insanable; intractable; irremediable; irreparable

wound: **n.** *immedicable vulnus*

INDECENCY: (**see** "immodesty" **and** "obscenity") **n.** grossness; impudicity; indelicacy; ribaldry; scurrility; **a.** INDECENT: (**see** "improper" **and** "lewd") *grivois;* immodest; ribald; scurrilous; unseemly

concerned with or replete with: **a.** cloacal; coprophilous; scatologic(al)

INDECISION: (**see** "doubt") **n.** ambivalence; fluctuation; incertitude; indecisiveness; irresolution; **a.** INDECISIVE: (**see** "vague") ambivalent; capricious; inconclusive; indefinite; indistinct; invertebrate; irresolute; vacillating; wavering

INDECISIVENESS, *pathological:* **n.** *folie du doute*

INDEFINITE: (**see** "ambiguous," "uncertain" **and** "vague") **a.** aoristic; equivocal; heterogeneous; imprecise; inconclusive; indeterminable; indeterminate; indefinitive; *sine die;* unformalized; unmathematical; **n.** INDEFINITENESS: (**see** "uncertainty") ambiguity; indefinitude; nebulosity

in form: **a.** amorphous; ethereal; nebular; nebulous; vaporous

period, for an: **a. or adv.** *sine die*

INDELICATE: (**see** "coarse" **and** "lewd") **a.** immodest; salacious; scabrous; tactless; unrefined; **n.** INDELICACY: immodesty; salaciousness; salacity; scabrousness

INDEPENDENT: (**see** "free") **a.** autonomic; autonomous; individualistic; objective; self-governing; sovereign; unconstrained; undoctrinaire; unregimented; **n.** INDEPENDENCE: autarchy; autonomy; emancipation; objectification; sovereignty; unconstraint

INDESCRIBABLE: (**see** "awful") **a.** ineffable; inenarrable

INDESTRUCTIBLE: (**see** "everlasting") **a.** adamantine; immarcescible; irrefragable; inviolable; **n.** see "everlastingness"

INDETERMINATE: (**see** "indefinite") **a.** aoristic; capricious; dubious; indefinitive; irresolute

INDEX: (**see** "indication") **n.** concordance; repertory; token; (**n.pl.** indexes; indices)
of forbidden books: **n.** *index expurgatorius; index liborum prohibitorum*
of topics: **n.** *index rerum*
of words or terms: **n.** *index verborum*

INDIA, *of or rel. to:* **a.** Bharati; Indic
study of, or its people: **n.** Indology; **a.** Indological

INDIAN *food:* **n.** pem(m)ican

INDICATION: (**see** "clew") **n.** criterion; gesticulation; hallmark; insigne; (**pl.** insignia); symbol; symptom; **a.** INDICATIVE: emblematic(al); pathognomonic(al); prodromal; significant; significative; significatory; suggestive; symbolic(al); symptomatic

INDICATOR: **see** "measure"

INDIFFERENCE: (**see** "apathy") **n.** acedia; detachment; inappetency; inertia; insouciance; lackadaisicalness; lackadaisy; languor; listlessness; minauderie; nonchalance; phlegm; pococurantism; *sangfroid;* stoicism; stolidity; supineness; supinity
religious or moral: **n.** adiaphoria; adiaphorism; agnosticism; **a.** adiaphorous; agnostic; laodicean

INDIFFERENT: (**see** "aloof" **and** "careless") **a.** anapodictic; apathetic; cursory; detached; disinterested; imperturbable; incurious; insipid; insouciant; insusceptible; invertebrate; lackadaisical; languid; languorous; laodicean; lethargic; mechanical; nonchalant; phlegmatic; pococurante; stolid; unconcerned; unenthusiastic
person: **n.** adiaphorist; laodicean; pococurante

INDIGNATION: **see** "anger"; **n.** INDIGNITY: affront; infamy; *lèse majesté;* unpleasantry

INDIRECT: **a.** ambagious; circumlocutious; circumlocutory; circuitous; circumstantial; collateral; consequential; deceitful; devious; mediate; oblique; roundabout; serpentine; **n.** INDIRECTION: ambiguity; circuity; circumbendibus; circumlocution; circumstantiality; deceitfulness; deviousness; duplicity; sinuosity; tortuosity
in expression: **a.** circumlocutious; circumlocutory
in speaking or writing: **a.** circumlocutory; **n.** circumbendibus; circumlocution; *oratio obliqua*
ways or proceedings: **n.** ambage(s)

INDISCREET: (**see** "rash") **a.** heedless; imprudent; incautious; inconsiderate; injudicious; untactful; **n.** INDISCRETION: heedlessness; imprudence; incaution; injudiciousness; untactfulness

INDISCRIMINATE: **a.** desultory; haphazard; heterogeneous; hit-or-miss; indistinguishable; promiscuous; random; **n.** INDISCRIMINATION: heterogeneity; promiscuity

INDISPENSABLE: **a.** *de rigueur;* essential; fundamental; obligatory; (pre)requisite; *sine qua non*
condition or thing: **n.** condition precedent; *conditio sine qua non;* essentiality; indispensability; (pre)requisite

INDISPOSED: **a.** aeger; a(d)verse; disinclined; hesitant; loath; reluctant; unfriendly; unwilling

INDISPUTABLE: (**see** "incontrovertible") **a.** apodictic(al); incontestable; indubitable; irrefrangible; undeniable; unquestionable

INDISTINCT: (**see** "hazy" **and** "vague") **a.** amorphous; ethereal; nebulous; nebular; vaporous
area: **n.** penumbra; twilight zone

INDIVIDUAL: **a.** idiomatic(al); ontogenetic; personal; **n. see** "person"
characteristic: **n.** haecceity; individuality
entity or being, as dist. from a group: **n.** individuum
identity: **n.** individuality; ipseity
mark or signature: **n.** idiograph

INDOLENCE: **see** "inactivity"

INDUCTIVE *reasoning:* **n.** empiricism; epagoge; **a.** *a posteriori;* aposterioristic; empirical; inductive

INDUSTRIAL *workers:* **n.** proletariat; **n.** or **a.** proletarian

INDUSTRIOUS: (**see** "busy") **a.** assiduous; attentive; diligent; indefatigable; operose; persevering; zealous

INDUSTRY: (**see** "diligence") **n.** assiduity; diligence; industriousness; laboriousness; operosity; perseverance; sedulity; steadfastness
leisurely: **n.** *otiosa sedulitas*

INEFFECTIVE: **a.** abortive; feckless; flaccid; impotent; incapable; ineffectual; inefficacious; **n.** INEFFECTIVENESS: flaccidity; impotency; ineffectuality

INEFFICIENT: **a.** inept; **n.** INEFFICIENCY: maladministration; **v.** maladminister

INEQUALITY: **n.** anomalism; anomaly; disparity; disproportion; dissimilarity; divergence; diversity; imparity; inequity; injustice; **a. see** "unequal"
of rank, quality, form, etc.: **n.** imparity

INERTIA: **n.** indisposition; inertness; *vis inertiae*

INESCAPABLE: (**see** "certain") **a.** *che sarà sarà;* ineluctable; ineludible; inevitable; unavoidable; unescapable; **n.** INESCAPABILITY: ineluctability; inevitability; inevitableness

INEXACT: (**see** "incorrect") **a.** desultory; equivocal; erroneous; imponderable; imprecise; **n.** INEXACTITUDE: equivocality; imponderability; imprecision; inevitability
things which are: **n.pl.** *imponderabilia*

INEXCUSABLE: **a.** inexpiable; irremissible; unforgivable; unjustifiable; unpardonable; unprovoked

INEXISTENCE: **n.** nonentity; nonexistence; nullibicity; nullity

INEXPERIENCED: (**see** "immature") **a.** amateurish; callow; fledgling; incompetent; inconversant; inexpert; maladroit; unfledged; uninitiated; unseasoned; unskilled; untrained; verdant
person or thing: **n.** fledgling

INEXPLICABLE: **a.** preternatural; supermundane; supernatural

INFALLIBILITY: **see** "perfection"

INFAMOUS: **a.** abhorrent; arrant; atrocious; dedecorous; despicable; execrable; heinous; ignominious; inglorious; nefarious; obloquial; opprobrious; **n.** INFAMY: abasement; ignominy; obloquy; odium; opprobrium

INFANCY: **n.** *bas âge;* incunabulum; (**pl.** incunabula); minority; nonage
in: **adv.** *in statu pupillari*

INFATUATION: (**see** "passion") **n.** *béguin*

INFECTION: **n.** contagion; corruption; pathology; septicity; **a.** INFECTIOUS (or INFECTIVE): communicable; contagious; contaminating; corruptive; demoralizing; pathological; septic; **n.** INFECTIVENESS: contagiosity; infectivity
source or center of: **n.** nidus

INFER: **v.** conclude; (d)educe; surmise; **n.** INFERENCE: conclusion; corollary; (d)eduction; illation; **a.** INFERENTIAL: denotative; illative; putative
from a trend: **v.** extrapolate; **n.** extrapolation

INFERIOR: **a.** *déclassé;* mediocre; nether; subaltern(ate); subnormal; suboptimal; subordinate; substandard; **n.** INFERIORITY: mediocrity; subnormality; subordination
as a judge: **n.** puisne
in status or quality: **a.** subaltern(ate); suboptimal; **n.** subaltern(ant); subalternation

INFERNAL: (**see** "hellish") **a.** avernal; chthonian; chthonic; diabolical; fiendish; flagitous; horrific; malevolent; Mephistophelian; (pan)demoniac(al); stygian; tartarean

INFERTILE: (**see** "barren") **a.** infecund; sterile; unfruitful; unproductive; **n.** INFERTILITY: barrenness; infecundity; sterility

INFINITE: (**see** "eternal") **a.** boundless; cosmic; illimitable; immeasurable; inex-

haustible; limitless; unlimited; **n. see** "eternity"
amount: **n.** inconsequentiality; infinitesimality; iota; negligibility; scintilla; **a.** infinitesimal

INFIRM: **see** "weak"

INFLAMMATION: **n.** congestion; phlegmasia; phlogosis; suppuration; **a.** INFLAMMATORY: ignescent; incendiary; phlogenic; phlogenetic; phlogistic; provocative; seditious; suppurative
allaying: **n. or a.** antiphlogistic; calmative
producing: **a.** phlogenetic.

INFLATED: (**see** "swollen") **a.** bombastic; exaggerated; flatulent; incrassate; magniloquent; pompous; portentous; tumescent; turgescent; turgid; tympanic; tympanitic; **n.** INFLATION: distention; flatulence; (in)tumescence; pomposity; tumidity; turgidity; turgidness; tympany

INFLEXIBLE: (**see** "stubborn") **a.** immutable; implacable; implastic; impliable; indocile; inductile; indurate; indurative; inexorable; intransigeant; intransigent; irreconcilable; obstinant; refractory; relentless; retractable; unalterable; uncompromising; unmodifiable; unrelenting; unyielding; **n.** INFLEXIBILITY: immutability; immutableness; implacability; implacableness; implasticity; indocility; induration; inexorability; intransigence; intransigentism; obstinacy; refractoriness; relentlessness; rigidification; rigidity; unalterability; unmodifiability; unyieldingness

INFLICT: **v.** impose; perpetrate

INFLUENCE: **v.** actuate; affect; impel; impregnate; infuse; modify; predominate; **n.** (**see** "authority") impulsion; patronage; predomination; prestige; puissance; **a.** INFLUENTIAL: (**see** "powerful") effective; hierarchic(al); potent; prominent
divine: (**see** "halo") **n.** afflation; afflatus; charism(a)
impervious to: (**see** "impassive") **a.** hermetic(al); unperturbed
pervasive or noxious: **n.** miasma; **a.** miasmal; miasm(at)ic

INFORM: **v.** acquaint; delate; enlighten; instruct; **a.** INFORMED: (**see** "up-to-date") *au courant; au fait;* cognizant; conversant

INFORMAL: **a.** colloquial; *en famille;* irregular; unceremonious; unconventional; unofficial; unorthodox; **adv.** *en famille; sans façon;* unceremoniously

INFORMER: **n.** delator; quidnunc

INFRINGE: **v.** contravene; encroach; intrude; transgress; trespass; violate; **n.** INFRINGEMENT: breach; contravention; encroachment; infraction; intrusion; nonfulfillment; piracy; plagiarism; transgression; trespass

INFURIATED: **see** "mad"

INGREDIENT: (**see** "part") **n.** component; constituent; element; **a.** componental

INHERENT: (**see** "inborn") **a.** connatal; connate; essential; immanent; inalienable; indwelling; inseparable; intrinsic; latent; native; potential; subjective; **n.** essentiality; intrinsicality
not: (**see** "foreign") **a.** adventitious; extraneous; peripheral

INHERITABLE: **a.** descendible; hereditable; hereditary; transmissible
characteristic: **n.** mutation
tendency **n.** diathesis; tropism; **a.** diathetic

INHERITANCE: **n.** benefaction; heritage; hereditament(s); legacy; patrimony
esp. from father: **n.** patrimony

INHERITED: (**see** "inborn") **a.** congenital; hereditary; innate
fr. father or paternal line: **a.** patroclinical; patroclinic; **n.** patrimony
fr. mother or maternal line: **a.** matroclinical; matroclinic; matroclinous

INHUMAN: (**see** "cruel") **a.** barbarous; diabolical; dispiteous; Draconian; impersonal; infrahuman; inhumane; mechanical (q.v.); Neronian; ruthless; satanic; subhuman; superhuman; truculent; **n. see** "cruelty"
to make: **v.** dehumanize; mechanize; robotize

INITIAL: (**see** "beginning") **a.** incipient; inchoative; initiatory; rudimental; **adv.** INITIALLY: *ab initio;* aborigine; *ab ovo*

INITIATED, *known only to the:* **a.** epoptic; esoteric
one who has been: **n.** epopt; initiate

INITIATIVE, *by one's own:* **adv.** *proprio motu*

INITIATOR: **n.** actuator; bellwether; catalyst; inceptor; originator

INJURIOUS: (**see** "harmful") **a.** deleterious; inimical; invidious; malignant; pernicious
to health: **a.** contagious; inimical; malignant; nocuous; nocent; noisome; noxious; pernicious; venomous

INJURY: **n.** detriment; impairment; lesion; mayhem; mutilation; trauma(tism)
by violence or force: **a.** traumatic; **v.** traumatize; **n.** mayhem; trauma(tism)
following, or result of: **a.** post-traumatic; residual
patient endurance of: **n.** forbearance; longanimity; long-suffering; **a.** longanimous
residual(s) or result(s) of: **n.** disablement; disability; handicap; impairment; incapacitation; residuum; sequala; (**pl.** sequalae)
unmerited: **n.** crown of thorns; martyrdom

INKY: **a.** atramental; atramentous

INN (**or** LODGE): **n.** auberge; caravansary; hospice; hostel(ry); poseda; xenodochium

INNATE: (**see** "inborn") **a.** congenital; hereditary; idiopathic; inherited; intrinsic
desire: **n.** conatus
intelligence: **n.** *élan vital;* entelechy
quality: **n.** largesse

INNER *nature or character:* **n.** interiority

INNERMOST *part(s)*: **n.** penetrale; (**pl.** penetralia); sanctuary; *sanctum sanctorum*

INNOCENT: **a.** Arcadian; artless; blameless; candid; cherubic; faultless; guileless; immaculate; impeccable; impeccant; inculpable; ingenuous; innocuous; inoffensive; irreproachable; lily-white; *naïve* (also naive); pastoral; seraphic; unaware; undefiled; undisguised; undissembled; unsullied; unsuspecting; untainted; virtuous; **n.** INNOCENCE: artlessness; blamelessness; immaculacy; impeccability; inculpability; ingenuousness; innocuousness; *naïveté;* simplicity; verdancy
something which is: **n.** innocuity

INNUENDO: (**see** "hint") **n.** aspersion; connotation; insinuation

INOFFENSIVE: (**see** "peaceful") inobnoxious

INOPPORTUNE: (**see** "untimely") **a.** impracticable; inappropriate; inconvenient; inexpedient; intempestive; malapropos; unseasonable; unsuitable

INQUIRY: (**see** "investigation") **n.** disquisition; inquest; inquisition; **a.** INQUISITIVE: disquisitive; inquisitorial

INSANE: **a.** chaotic; compulsive; delirious; frantic; frenzied; incompetent; irrational; lunatic; maniacal; *non compos (mentis)*; psychotic; *tête exaltée;* (tête exaltée)
fear of becoming: **n.** lyssophobia
wildly: **a.** berserk; dithyrambic; maniac(al)

INSANITY: **n.** aberration; alienation; *amentia folie;* dementia; incompetency; lunacy; psychosis
of two (hus. and wife): **n.** *folie à deux*
religious: **n.** theomania

INSCRIPTION(S), *on plaque, monument, etc.:* (**see** "gravestone") **n.** epigraph
scratched on walls, etc.: **n.** graffito; (**pl.** graffiti)

INSECURITY: **n.** apprehensiveness; apprehension; incertitude; instability; jeopardy; peril

INSENSITIVE: **a.** analgesic; anesthetic; apathetic; inanimate; insensate; insentient; lethargic; obtuse; pachydermatous; philistine; philistinic; unimpressionable; **n.** INSENSIBILITY (**or** INSENSITIV-

ITY): analgesia; apathy; carus; coma; insentience; lethargy; obtuseness; obtusity; stupor; torpor; trance
person: **n.** pachyderm; **a.** pachydermatous

INSERT: **v.** intercalate; interlard; interpolate; interpose; intromit; **n.** entredeux; intercalation; interpolation; **a.** INSERTING (**or** INSERTED): intercalary; interlarded; interpolated
at intervals: **v.** intersperse
bet. two: **n.** entredeux

INSIGHT: **n.** acumen; clairvoyance; discernment; discrimination; empathy; intuition; penetration; perception; perspicacity; perspicuity; understanding
gifted w/ mental or moral: **a.** prehensile; prescient; spirituel(le)
intuitive: **n.** aperçu; intuition; prescience
natural: **n.** *lumen naturale*

INSIGNIFICANT: (**see** "small") **a.** commonplace; contemptible; immaterial; infinitesimal; irrelevant; minuscule; trivial; **n.** INSIGNIFICANCE: infinitesimality; minitude; triviality
thing(s): **see** "importance, things of little or slight"

INSINCERE: **a.** artificial; counterfeit; deceitful; disingenuous; duplicitous; fulsome; hypocritical; meretricious; specious; theatrical; **a. or adv.** tongue in cheek; **n.** INSINCERITY: artificiality; bathos; dissimulation; duplicity; hypocrisy; sentimentalism; sentimentality; theatricality
person: **n.** charlatan; mountebank; *poseur;* (**fem.** *poseuse*); pretender

INSIPID: (**see** "bland") **a.** cloying; commonplace; jejune; mawkish; savorless; trite; uninteresting; unsavory; vapid; **n.** INSIPIDITY: jejunity; vapidity

INSISTENT: (**see** "urgent") **a.** conspicuous; exigent; importunate; persevering; persistent; pressing; prominent

INSOLENT: (**see** "sassy") **a.** arrogant; audacious; contemptuous; contumelious; hubristic; impudent; overbearing; **adv.** INSOLENTLY: *avec audace;* **n.** INSOLENCE: arrogance; audacity; cheekiness; contempt(uousness); contumacy; contumely; effrontery; flippery; haughtiness; hubris; impertinence; impudence; protervity; sauciness
person: **n.** jackanapes

INSPECTION: (**see** "examination") **n.** probe; reconnaissance; scrutiny; surveillance; **a.** inspectorial
person(s) making: **n.** inspectorate; surveillant

INSPIRATION: **n.** afflation; afflatus; enthusiasm; inhalation; stimulant; stimulation; **v.** INSPIRE: animate; encourage; exhilarate; imbue; infuse; inhale; motivate; prompt; **a.** INSPIRING: (**see** "stimulating") afflated; infusive

INSTABILITY: (**see** "unbalance") **n.** apprehensiveness; incertitude; inconstancy; insecurity

INSTALLMENT(S), *printed in:* **n.** feuilleton

INSTANCE: **n.** circumstance; exception; illustration; suggestion
for: **adv.** *exempli gratia* (**abb.** e.g.)

INSTANT: **n.** *clin d'oeil;* instantaneity; **a.** INSTANTANEOUS: momentary; semelfactive; simultaneous; **n.** simultaneity

INSTIL(L): **v.** implant; indoctrinate; infiltrate; innoculate; insinuate; introduce

INSTINCT: **n.** appetency; intuition; propensity

INSTRUCTION: (**see** "teaching") **n.** discipline; education; indoctrination; information; precept; **v.** INSTRUCT: discipline; edify; educate; indoctrinate; **a.** INSTRUCTIVE: didactic(al); edificatory; educational; expository; moralistic; preceptive
elementary or preparatory: **n.** propaedeutics; **a.** propaedeutic(al)
oral: **n.** catechesis; **a.** catechetic(al); catechistic; **v.** catechize
theory of art of: **n.** didactics; propaedeutics; pedagogy

INSTRUMENT(S): (**see** "equipment") **n.pl.** armamentaria; instrumentaria

INSUFFICIENCY: **n.** dearth; deficiency; inability; inadequacy; incompetency; paucity

INSULT: **see** "indignity"

INTACT: **see** "whole"

INTANGIBLE: **a.** aeriform; amorphous; diaphanous; ephemeral; impalpable; imperceptible; incorporeal; insubstantial; nebular; nebulous; vague; vaporous; **n.** INTANGIBILITY: aeriality; ephemerality; (**pl.** ephemera; ephemeralities) incorporeality; insubstantiality; nebulosity
process or function: **n.** chemistry; mystique

INTEGRATIVE: (**see** "unifying") **a.** centralizing; centripetal; integrable

INTEGRITY: **n.** candor; completeness; entireness; sincerity; soundness

INTELLECT: **see** "reason"
comprehension by: **n.** cognition; noesis; **a.** cognitive; noetic

INTELLECTUAL(S): **n.** academe; *bel esprit;* cognoscente; illuminato; literato; literatus; luminary; pedant; savant; sophist; (**pl.** cognoscenti; illuminati; intelligentsia; literati); **a.** cerebral; cognitive; dianoetic; epistemic; epistemological; gnostic; sagacious; sophic(al)
depth: **n.** intellectuality; profundity; rationality
food (figurative): **n.** pabulum
hostility toward: **n.** anti-intellectualism
state of being, or intellectual power: **n.** intellectuality; luminosity; sagacity
treat or analyze (intellectually): **v.** intellectualize; rationalize; **n.** intellectualization; rationalization
wandering or quest: **n.** odyssey; **a.** odyssean

INTELLIGENCE: **n.** acquaintance; acumen; comprehension; information; intellectuality; luminosity; mentality; perspicacity; perspicuity; sagacity; sapience; **a.** INTELLIGENT: **see** "intellectual" **and** "rational"
innate: **n.** *élan vital;* entelechy
lack of: **n.** amentia; insipience; moronity; nescience
pert. to or having: **a.** intelligential

INTEMPERATE: **a.** immoderate; inclement; incontinent; inordinate; **n.** INTEMPERANCE: acrasia; acrasy; immoderation; inclemency; incontinence; insobriety
in eating or drinking: (**see** "alcoholic" **and** "glutton") **a.** crapulent; crapulous; **n.** crapulence; gulosity

INTENSE (**or** INTENSIVE): (**see** "burning") **a.** comprehensive; consuming; consummatory; inspissate(d); vehement; zealous; **n.** INTENSIFICATION (**or** INTENSITY): concentration; enhancement; enthusiasm; exacerbation; potency; profundity; saturation; strenuosity; temperature; vehemency; **v.** INTENSIFY: accentuate; augment; deepen; emphasize; enhance; exacerbate; exaggerate; sharpen; strengthen

INTENT (**or** INTENTION): (**see** "design" **and** "motive") **n.** ambition; animus; contemplation; determination; import; intendment; purport; resolve; significance
criminal: **n.** malice aforethought; malice prepense; *mens rea;* premeditation
with evil: (**see under** "evil") **adv.** maliciously; *malo animo*
without: (**see** "accidental") **a.** unpremeditated; unmotivated

INTENTIONAL: **a.** calculated; deliberate; designed; permissive; premeditated; purposeful; voluntary
quality or state of being: **n.** designedness; intentionality

INTENTIONALLY *so written:* **adv.** *sic*

INTERCHANGE: **v.** alternate; reciprocate; **n.** alternation; mutuality; *quid pro quo;* reciprocation; reciprocity; **a.** INTERCHANGEABLE: alternating; commutable; mutual; reciprocal; reciprocative

INTERCONNECTING: **a.** anastomotic; syndetic

INTEREST(S): (**see** "concern") **n.** attraction; consciousness; curiosity; inquisitiveness
center of: **n.** cynosure; Mecca; polestar
community of: **n.** affinity
in others: **a.** allocentric
in self: **a.** egocentric; **n.** egocentricity
lack of: **n.** acedia; ennui; lackadaisy;

melancholia; otiosity; slothfulness; tepidity; torpor; unconcern
level of: **n.** intensity; temperature
of local or current: **a.** topical; **n.** topicality
one having great diversity of: **n.** Proteus
rate higher than legal: **n.** usury; **a.** usurious

INTERESTING: **a.** absorbing; attractive; divertive; engrossing; intriguing; piquant; provocative; succulent; **a.** INTERESTED: (**see** "concerned") versant

INTERFERE: **v.** intercede; interlope; intermeddle; interpose; interrupt; intervene; intrude; obtrude; supervene; **n.** INTERFERENCE: ingerence; intercession; interposition; intervention; intrusion; **a.** INTERFERING: adventitious; supervenient
do not: **adv.** *noli me tangere*

INTERIOR: (**see** "internal") **a.** domestic; **n.** INTERIORITY: domesticality; internality; internalization
country: **n.** hinterland; **a. or n.** up-country

INTERLOCK: **v.** interdigitate; interlace; **n.** interdigitation

INTERLUDE: **n.** armistice; hiatus; intermezzio; intermission; interregnum; interruption; parenthesis; respite; stasimon

INTERMEDIATE: **a.** equidistant; medial; mesothetic

INTERMISSION: (**see** "pause") **n.** armistice; *entr'acte;* interlude; interruption

INTERNAL: **a.** domestic; endogenous; inherent; internecine; intestinal; intramural; intraneous; intrinsic; municipal
state of being: **n.** domesticality; interiority; internality; internalization
to make: **v.** interiorize; internalize; **n.** interiorization; internalization

INTERNATIONAL *law:* **n.** *jus gentium; jus inter gentes*
state or cond. of being: **n.** internationality

INTERPOSE: (**see** "interfere") **v.** arbitrate; interpolate; intervene; mediate; mediatize; **n.** INTERPOSITION: arbitration; interpolation; mediation

INTERPRETATION: **n.** elucidation; exegesis; explanation; explication; exposition; **a.** INTERPRE(TA)TIVE: divinatory; exegetic(al); explanatory; expository; hermeneutic; prophetic(al); revelatory; significative; **v.** INTERPRET: (**see** "clarify") construe; decipher; elucidate; explicate; illustrate; translate
additional: **n.** epexegesis
by reading into it one's own: **n.** eisegesis; **a.** eisegetical
science of: **n.** exegetics; hermeneutics

INTERPRETER: **n.** annotator; dragoman; exegete; exponent; expounder; expositor; hierophant; scholiast
of dreams: **n.** oneirocritic

INTERRUPT: (**see** "interfere") **v.** arrest; intercept: intermit; pretermit; **n.** INTERRUPTION: (**see** "pause") armistice; arrest; disruption; hiatus; interlocution; intermission; interpolation; pretermission; suspension

INTERRUPTIVE *utterance:* **n.** interlocution

INTERSECT: **v.** anastomose; bisect; collide; decussate; transect; **n.** INTERSECTION: anastomosis; chiasma; collision; decussation

INTERVAL: (**see** "gap," "interlude"; **and** "pause") **n.** armistice; c(a)esura; hiatus; intermission; interstice; parenthesis; rupture
bet. two reigns: **n.** interregnum

INTERVENE: (**see** "interfere") **v.** arbitrate; interject; interpose; mediate; **a.** INTERVENING: interjacent; interjaculatory; interjectional; interpolated; intervenient; mediatorial; mediatory; parenthetical
one who does: **n.** intercessor; intermediary; intervenient; mediator

INTERVENTION: **n.** arbitration; intercession; interposition; intervenience; (inter)mediation
supernatural, into human affairs: **n.** theurgy

INTESTINES: **n.pl.** viscera
pert to: **a.** alvine; splanchnic; visceral
rumbling sound(s) in: borborygmus; crepitation; flatus; **a.** borborygmic

INTIMATE: (see "familiar") **a. or adv.** *à deux;* **a.** contubernal; *tête-à-tête*

INTIMIDATE: **v.** browbeat; bulldoze; bully; cow; daunt; dishearten; dragoon; hector; terrorize

INTOXICATED: (**see** "drunken") **a.** heady; inebriated
person: **see** "alcoholic"
that which (intoxicates): **n.** inebriant; intoxicant

INTRICATE: **a.** abstruse; convoluted; daedalian; daedal(ic); entangled; Gordian; inexplicable; inextricable; involuted; labyrinthian; labyrinthine; **n.** INTRICACY: abstrusity; complexity; labyrinth

INTRIGUE: (**see** "plot") **n.** artifice; cabal; chicanery; collusion; coup; machination; subtlety; **a.** INTRIGUING: **see** "attractive"

INTRIGUER, *female:* **n.** Circe; *femme fatale;* intrig(u)ante; siren

INTRINSIC: **see** "inborn" **and** 'inherent"

INTRODUCTION: (**see** "preface") **n.** debut; exordium; innovation; manduction; preamble; prelude; prelusion; preparation; proem; prolegomenon; prologue; prolusion; propaedeutic; unveiling; **v.** INTRODUCE: **see** "open"
brief: **n.** proem
literary: **n.** isagoge

INTRODUCTORY: **a.** antecedent; elementary; inductive; initiatory; innovatory; isagogic(al); liminary; manductive; manductory; precursory; prefatorial; prefatory; preliminary; preludial; preludious; prelusive; premonitory; presaging; prolegomenous; prolusory; propaedeutic(al); rudimentary
study, as of Bible history, etc.: **n.pl.** isagogics
work (lit.) **n.** prodromus

INTROSPECTIVE: **a.** autistic; **n.** INTROSPECTION: autism; introspectiveness; introspectivity; reverie; self-examination

INTRUDE: **see** "interfere"

INTUITION: **n.** anschauung; apprehension; clairvoyance; conception; eidos; foreknowledge; percipience; precognition; prescience; **a.** INTUITIVE: (**see** "inborn") clairvoyant; percipient; prescient
learn by: **v.** intuit
reasoning by: **n.** *a priori;* apriority; **a.** aprioristic

INVADER: **n.** incursionist

INVALID: **a.** nugatory; null and void; unlawful; unsound; **n. or a.** valetudinarian

INVALIDATE: (**see** "weaken") **v.** nullify; repeal; stultify; vitiate

INVALUABLE: **a.** incalculable; inestimable; priceless

INVASION: **n.** aggression; assault; encroachment; incursion; inroad; transgression; **a.** incursionary; invasive

INVENT: **v.** contrive; create; devise; excogitate; fabricate; machinate; originate; **a.** INVENTIVE: creative; ingenious; innovational; **n.** INVENTIVENESS: creativity; ingeniosity; ingenuity

INVENTORY: **n.** catalog(ue); compendium; schedule; summary; survey; syllabus; tariff

INVESTIGATION: **n.** catechesis; catechism; disquisition; inquest; inquisition; interrogation; perscrutation; reconnaissance; scrutiny; survey; **a.** INVESTIGATIVE: disquisitive; exploratory; investigational; probative; zetetic; **v.** INVESTIGATE: inquisit; probe; **n.** INVESTIGATOR: **see** "searcher"

INVIGORATING: **a.** animating; bracing; exhilarative; roborant; stimulating; tonic

INVINCIBLE: (**see** "unconquerable") **a.** Achillean; unswerving

INVITATION, *pert. to or containing:* **a.** invitatory

INVOCATION: (**see** "prayer") **n.** *absit omen;* bismillah; enforcement; incantation; supplication

INVOLUNTARY: **a.** accidental; automatic; autonomic; inexorable; instinctive; irreparable; mechanical; uncontrollable; unmotivated; unwilling; **n.** automaticity; mechanicality

INVOLVE: **v.** complicate; embarrass; embroil; entangle; implicate; interpenetrate; permeate; **a.** INVOLVED: abstruse; complicated; confused; inextricable; intricate; involute(d); labyrinthian; labyrinthine; **n.** INVOLVEMENT: (**see** "confusion") complexity; embroilment; entanglement; involution

INWARD: **a.** centripetal; domestic; endogenous; immanent; intrinsic; **n.** INWARDNESS: immanence; intrinsicality; intrinsicalness

IRE: **see** "anger"

IRIDESCENT: **a.** kaleidoscopic; lustrous; margaritaceous; nacereous; opalescent; pavonine

IRK: **see** "annoy"; **n.** IRKSOMENESS: (**see** "depression") *taedium vitae*

IRON, *containing or bearing:* **a.** ferric; ferriferous; ferruginous
pert. to: **a.** ferric; ferruginous

IRONIC(AL): (**see** "biting") **a.** Hudibrastic; sarcastic; satirical; **a. or adv.** tongue in cheek; **n.** IRONY: asteism; contempt; disapprobation; dissimultation; satire; sarcasm
buffoonery: **n.** Pantagruelism; **a.** Pantagruelian; **n.** Pantagruelist

IRRATIONAL: (**see** "absurd") **a.** addlepated (or brained); alogical; asinine; Dionysian; fatuous; grotesque; imbecilic; illogical; psychotic; rattle-brained; unbounded; **n.** IRRATIONALITY: absurdity; fatuity; foolishness; imbecility; psychosis; unreasonableness
action or speech: **n.** deliration; delirium
statement or reasoning: **n.** alogism

IRREGULAR: (**see** "abnormal") **a.** anomalous; arrhythmic; atypical; baroque; clandestine; distorted; diverse; eccentric; heteroclite; heteromorphic; inordinate; intermittent; promiscuous; sporadic; tumultuary; **n.** IRREGULARITY: aberration; anomaly; arrythmia; asymmetry; caprice; delinquency; deviation; eccentricity; promiscuity; sporadicity; unevenness

IRRELEVANT: (**see** "unrelated") **a.** *à propos de bottes; à propos de rien;* extraneous; extrinsic; heterogeneous; impertinent; inapplicable; inapposite; inconsequential; *nihil ad rem;* tangential; **n.** IRRELEVANCE: extraneity; impertinence; inappositeness; inconsequentiality; irrelevancy

IRREPARABLE: **a.** intractable; irremediable; irretrievable; irreversible
injury: **n.** *immedicable vulnus*

IRRESISTIBLE: (**see** "alluring" **and** "charming") **a.** mesmeric

IRRESOLUTE: **see** "undecided"

IRRESPONSIBLE: (**see** "irrational") **a.** arbitrary; feckless; harum-scarum; impractical; scatterbrained; visionary

IRREVERENCE: **n.** blasphemy; impiety; irreligiosity; *lèse majesté;* profanation; sacrilege; undutifulness; ungodliness; **a.** IRREVERENT: atheistic; blasphemous; impious; irreligious; irreverential; sacrilegious; undutiful; worldly

IRRITABILITY: **n.** animosity; fretfulness; iracundity; irascibility; petulance; querulousness; waspishness; **a.** IRRITABLE: (**see** "peevish") acrimonious; bilious; cankered; cantankerous; caustic; choleric; churlish; crochety; fretful; fractious; iracund; irascible; perverse; pettish; petulent; splenetic(al); testy; touchy; waspish
being in state of: **n.** fantod(s)

IRRITATE: (**see** "aggravate") **v.** abrade; annoy; chafe; exacerbate; exasperate; gall; incense; intensify; nettle; provoke; stimulate; **a.** IRRITATING: **see** "annoying"; **n. or a.** IRRITANT: abradant; provocative; **n.** provocation

ISLAND(S), *group or cluster of:* **n.** archipelago
inhabiting an: **a.** enisled; insular; nesiote
pert. to: **a.** insular; **n.** insularity

ISOLATE: **v.** detach; enisle; ghettoize; immure; maroon; quarantine; seclude; segregate; **a.** ISOLATED: discrete; ivory-towered; quarantined; segmental; segmentary; segregated; sporadic; **n.** ISOLATION: ascesis; decentralization; immurement; incarceration; insularity; insulation; quarantine; segregation; sequestration

ISSUE: **v.** circulate; debouch; disembogue; egress; emanate; evacuate; extravasate; **n.** (**see** "child") debouchment; eggress(ion); emanation; emergence; extravasation; issuance; outflow
without: **adv.** *sine prole*

IT *is done:* **n.** *factum est; fait accompli;* **a.** consummated
is said: **n.** *on-dit*

ITEM, *lavishly decorated or utilitarian:* **n.** botique

ITCH: **n.** agitation; ferment; prurience; pruritus; restlessness
to do something: **n.** cacoethes

ITSELF, *by or in:* **adv.** inherently; intrinsically; *per se;* simpliciter; **n.** perseity

J

JACK-*of-all-trades:* **n.** factotem; *homme à tout faire;* pantologist; Proteus

JAGGED: (**see** "uneven") **a.** lancinate; lancinose; serrate(d)

JARGON: (**see** "slang") **n.** abracadabra; argot; balderdash; baragouin; cant; Chinook; Choctaw; dialect; gibberish; lingo; patois

JAUNTY: **a.** affable; affected; debonair(e); fashionable; genial; nonchalant; raffish; rakish; *soigné(e)*; sprightly; stylish; **n.** geniality; nonchalance; sprightliness

JAW(S), *having large:* **a.** pachygnathous
having long: **a.** longirostrine
having projecting: **a.** prognathous
having receding lower: **a.** opistognathous
pert. to: **a.** gnathic
pert. to lower: **a.** genial; mandibular; mental

JEALOUSY, *professional:* **n.** *jalousie de métier;* **a.** JEALOUS: invidious

JERKY: **a.** saccadic

JEST: **n.** banter; *drôlerie;* drollery; *mot pour rire; plaisanterie;* **n.** JESTER: (**see** "fool") *farceur;* (**fem.** *farceuse*); merry-andrew; railleur
in: **adv.** *pour rire*

JEW(S), *of or rel. to:* **a.** Hebraic; Judaic(al); **n.** Hebraism; Judaism
things or lit. pert. to: **n.** Hebraica; Judaica

JEWEL(S): **n.** bijou(terie)
imitation: **n.** or **a.** Brummagem

JEWISH *boy at age 13, also rite;* **n.** *bar mitzvah* (*also* bar mitzvot(h))
girl at age 13, also rite: **n.** bath (or bas or bat) mitzvah

JOB, *soft or easy:* **see** "snap"

JOINED: (**see** "coupled") **a.** affined; associated; concatenate; contiguous; intercatenated; **a.** JOINING: convergent; **n.** colligation; communication; concatenation; conjugation; copulation; juncture; **v.** JOIN: agglutinate; amalgamate; articulate; associate; coagment; coalesce; colligate; communicate; concatenate; conjugate; consolidate; copulate; harness; interconnect; interlock; matriculate

JOINT: **n.** articulation; commisure; juncture; synchondrosis; **a.** JOINTED (or JOINED): (**see** "connected") articulate

JOKE: (**see** "jest") **n.** facetiosity; farcicality; jocosity; jocularity; jocundity; **a.** JOKING: (**see** "jolly") facetious; jocose; jocular; jocund; jovial
for sake of the: **adv.** *joci causâ*

JOKER: **n.** *farceur;* (**fem.** *farceuse*); humorist; railleur

JOLLY: **a.** convivial; genial; jocular; jocund; jovial; sportive; **n.** **see** "joviality"

JOURNEY: **v.** itinerate; peregrinate; safari; **n.** entrada; expedition; itinerary; itineration; odyssey; peregrination; pilgrimage; safari
extended: **n.** odyssey
for safety (flight): **n.** hegira
have a pleasant: **adv.** *bon voyage*
pert. to: **a.** itinerant; Odyssean; peripatetic; viatic(al)

JOVIALITY: **n.** conviviality; jocosity; jocundity; jocularity

JOY: (**see** "delight") **n.** allégresse; beatitude; ecstasy; exuberance; exaltation; felicity; festivity; gaiety; gratification; jubilation; merriment; transport; **a.** JOY-

FUL (or JOYOUS): (**see** "gay") blithe; buoyant; carnivalesque; ecstatic; elated; exuberant; exultant; gratulant; jovial; jubilant; jubilean; rapturous; triumphant; zestful; **n.** JOYFULNESS: exuberance; exultation; joviality; jubilance; jubilation; jubilee
foretaste of: **n.** *joie anticipée*
of living: **n.** *joie de vivre;* zest
shout for: **v.** jubilate; **n.** jubilation; **n.** jubilarian

JUDGE(S): **v.** adjudicate; analyze; arbitrate; discriminate; **n.** (ad)judicator; arbitrator; arbiter; connoisseur; critic; judicature; judiciary
junior: **n.** puisne
of arts or fashion: **n.** cognoscente; connoisseur
rigorous: **n.** Rhadamanthus; **a.** rhadamanthine
wise: **n.** Solomon

JUDGED, *capable of or liable to be:* **a.** judicable; justiciable

JUDGING: **a.** analytical; discretionary; discriminatory; judicative; judicial; judicious

JUDGMENT: **n.** acumen; circumspection; criticism; discernment; discretion; discrimination; insight; intuition; judicality; judicium; penetration; perception; prudence; rationality; sagacity; wisdom; **a.** judgmental
lacking: **a.** immature; malentendu
sound or soundness of: **n.** sagacity; **a.** **see** "judicious"

JUDICIOUS: (**see** "wise") **a.** circumspect; discerning; judgmatic(al); rational; sagacious

JUGGLING, *skillful feat of:* **n.** legerdemain; *passe-passe;* prestidigitation; *tour de force*

JUICY: **a.** piquant; racy; succulent; **n.** piquancy; succulence; succulency

JUMBLE: (**see** "confusion") **n.** colluvies; disarrangement; farrago; *fatras;* gallimaufry; heterogeneity; hodge-podge; medley; olla podrida; potpourri; salmagundi; **a.** JUMBLED: disarranged; farraginous; hugger-mugger; indiscriminate; macaronic
confused: **n.** capharnaum; mare's nest

JUNCTION: **see** "union"

JUMP: **v.** saltate; **n.** saltation; **a.** capering; salient; saltant

JUNIOR: **a. or n.** puisne; subaltern(ate); subordinate; **a.** juvenile; youthful
state of being: **n.** juniority

JURISDICTION: **n.** authority; bailiwick; cognizance; control; domain; province; sovereignty; territory
being within: **n.** *intra vires;* **a.** justiciable
having full: **a.** plentary; plenipotent(ial); plenipotentiary; **n.** plenipotentiary
state of exceeding: **n.** *ultra vires*

JURY, *act of influencing illegally:* **n.** embracery

JUST: **a.** accurate; conscientious; deserved; equitable; impartial; incorruptible; merited; rectitudinous; righteous; unbiased
cause: **n.** *justa causa*
inflexibly: **a.** Rhadamanthine
once, nothing counts: ein mal, kein mal

JUSTICE: **n.** dharma; equity; impartiality; integrity; rectitude; righteousness; rightfulness
pert. to: **a.** forensic; judicatory; juridical; juristic; justiciary
rel. to administration of: **a.** justiciary
with. **adv.** *à bon droit*

JUSTIFIABLE: (**see** "legal") **a.** legitimate; justificatory; vindicatory; warrantable

JUSTIFICATION: **n.** apologia, exoneration; extenuation; rationale; vindication

JUSTIFIED, *something that is to be:* **n.** justificandum

JUSTIFY, *something that serves to:* **n.** justificans; justification; **a.** justificative; justificatory

JUSTIFYING: **a.** extenuative; justificative; justificatory; vindicatory

JUTTING: **a.** bulbous; protuberant; salient; **n.** protuberance; protuberancy; salience; saliency

JUVENILE: (**see** "young" **and** "youthful") **a.** ephebic; immature; puerile; **n.** juniority; juvenility
lead in a play: **n.** *jeune premier*

K

KEEN: (see "caustic") **a.** acrimonious; appercipient; astucious; astute; discerning; incisive; moradacious; mordant; penetrating; perspicacious; piquant; poignant; pungent; sagacious; trenchant; **n.** KEENNESS: acumen; asperity; astucity; perspicacity; piquancy; poignancy; pungency; sagacity
mindedness: **n.** acumen; astucity; astuteness; perspicacity; **a.** acuminous; analytical; appercipient; astute; perspicacious

KEEP *silent and be counted a philosopher:* **n.** *sile, et philosophus esto*

KEEPSAKE. **n.** bibelot; knickknack; memento; *objet d'art;* virtu

KERNEL: **n.** chromosome; nidus; nucleus; quintessence

KEY, *pass or master:* **n.** *passe partout*
to riddle or puzzle: **n.** *le mot de l'eigme*

KICK: **n.** *coup de pied*

KILL: (see "annihilate") **v.** assassinate; decapitate; dispatch; execute; immolate; suppress
by cutting throat: **v.** jugulate
by stoning: **v.** lapidate; **n.** lapidation

KILLING *of brother, also the killer:* **n.** fratricide; **a.** fratricidal
same for father: **n.** patricide; **a.** patricidal
same for husband by wife: **n.** matricide; **a.** matricidal
same for inafnt: **n.** infanticide; **a.** infanticidal
same for king: **n.** regicide; **a.** regicidal
same for mother: **n.** matricide; **a.** matricidal
same for parent: **n.** parenticide; parricide; **a.** parricidal; parricidious
same for sister: **n.** sorocide; **a.** sorocidal
same for wife by hus.: **n.** matricide; uxoricide; **a.** uxoricidal
same for woman or women: **n.** femicide; **a.** femicidal

KIND(S): **a.** amiable; auspicious; beneficent; benevolent; benign(ant); charitable; clement; compassionate; cordial; gracious; grandfatherly; humane; indulgent; philanthropic; propitious; Samaritan; sympathetic; **n.** see "class"
all, pert. to or producing: **a.** omnifarious
having same (kind) or nature: **a.** consubstantial; **n.** consubstantiality
of another: alieni generis
of its own: **a.** *sui generis*
only one of his or its: **a.** *sui generis;* unique; **n.** uniquity

KINDNESS: **n.** amiability; benevolence; benignancy; benignity; clemency; complaisance; congeniality; cordiality; lenity; philanthropy; *prévenance*

KINDRED: **a.** cognate; congeneric; congenerous; congenital; consanguineous; sympathetic; **n.** see "kinship"

KING(S): **n.** dynast; emperor; imperator; monarch; regulus; rex; sovereign
last of the: **n.** *ultimus regnum*
petty or vassal: **n.** (sub)regulus
right and privileges of: **n.** regalia; regality
today, tomorrow nothing; aujourd'hui roi, demain rien
who has lost power (do-nothing king): **n.** *roi fainéant*

KINGDOM: **n.** demesne; domain; dominion; dukedom; jurisdiction; principality; realm; sultonate; vizierate

KINGLY: **a.** august; basilic(al); imperial; leonine; majestic; monarchial; palatine; regal; royal; sovereign

KINSHIP: **n.** affinity; agnation; consanguinity; congener; propinquity; relationship

KISS: **v.** caress; osculate; **n.** osculation
parting: **n.** baiser d'adieu

KISSING: **a.** osculant; oscular; osculatory; **n.** osculation
"science of:" **n.** philematology

KITCHEN: **n.** cuisine
pert. to: **a.** culinary
utensils: **n.** *batterie de cuisine*

KNAVISH: (**see** "dishonest") **a.** deceitful; fraudulent; frolicsome; unscrupulous; **n.** KNAVISHNESS: (**see** "dishonesty") unscrupulosity; **n.** KNAVE: (**see** *"scamp"*) *scapin*

KNEE-*cap:* **n.** patella; **a.** patellar
-like: **a.** geniculate
space behind: **n.** popliteal (space)
to bend, as in reverence: **v.** or **a.** geniculate; kow-tow; **v.** genuflex; **n.** genuflection; genuflexion

KNEEL(ING): **n.** genuflection; genuflexion; **adv.** *à genoux;* **a.** genuflectory
in respect: **see under** "knee"

KNIGHT: **n.** chevalier; Galahad; paladin; protagonist; templar
gallant: **n.** *preux chevalier*
like a: **a.** chivalresque; chivalric; chivalrous; equestrian

KNOCKDOWN *blow:* **n.** recumbentibus

KNOLL: **n.** hillock; hummock; tumulus

KNOT: **n.** excrescence; exostosis; gibbosity; knurl; protuberance; **a.** KNOTTY: **see** "difficult"

KNOW, *dare to:* **adv.** *aude sapere*
-how: **n.** expertise; *savoir-faire;* technique; virtuosity
in the: **adv.** (be) *à la page*
thyself: **adv.** *gnothi seauton; nosce te ipsum; te nosce*

KNOWABLE: **a.** cognoscible; cognoscitative; cognizable; knowledg(e)able; perceivable; percipient; ratiocinative

KNOWING: **a.** apprehensive; astute; cognitative; cognitional; cognitive; cognoscible; cognoscitive; discerning; epistemonic(al); gnostic; intelligenced; knowledg(e)able; penetrating; perceptive; percipient; sagacious; scient(ial); sophisticated
all things: **a.** omniscient; pansophic(al); **n.** omniscience; pansophism
before hand: **a.** precognitive; **n.** precognition; **v.** precognize
having power of: **a.** cognoscitive

KNOWLEDGE: (**see** "learning") **n.** acquaintance; apperception; cognition; cognizance; comprehension; episteme; erudition; information; perception; sagacity; scholarship; science; scientia; sophistication
denial of any basis for: **n.** nihilism; **a.** nihilistic; **n.** nihilist
depreciation of or opposition to: **n.** anti-intellectualism; obscurantism; **a.** obscurant(ic)
ground of: **n.** *ratio cognoscendi*
having great or infinite: **a.** bibliognostic; encyclopedic(al); omniscent; pansophic(al); **n.** encyclopedism; omniscence; pansophism; **n.** bibliognost; pansophist; virtuoso
great or penetrating: **n.** profundity; **a.** encyclopedic(al)
half-: **n.** *demi-savoir*
imparting: (**see** "teaching") **a.** informative; instructive; tutorial
impossibility of arriving at certain: **n.** acatelepsy; **a.** acateleptic
instinctive: (**see** "intuition") **n.** Anschauung; cognition; *savoir-faire;* **a.** cognitive; intuitive
intellectually certain: **n.** episteme; **a.** epistemic; epistemological
investigation or study of nature of: **n.** epistemology; gnoseology
lack of: **n.** ignoration; inscience; nescience
love of: **n.** epistemophilia; philomathy
method, means or agency of communicating: **n.** organon
one interested in pursuit of: **n.** co(g)noscente; illuminato; savant; virtuoso
possessing great or extensive: **a.** (en)cyclopedic(al); omniscent; pansophic(al)
preliminary: **n.** foreknowledge; praecognitum; precognition
private or secret bet. two persons: **n.** privity; **a.** *à deux*

process of: **n.** cognition; **a.** cognitional; cognitive

rel. or pert. to: **a.** cognitional; cognitive; epistemonic(al); gnostic; sciental

sacred, body of: **n.** hierology; **a.** hierologic(al); **n.** hierologist

secret or mysterious: **n.** arcanum; **(pl.** arcana); **a.** arcane

show of: **n.** didacticism; pedantry; sciolism; **a.** pedantic; sciolistic; sciolous

study or theory of: **n.** epistemology; gnoseology; **a.** epistemonic(al)

superficial: **n.** sciolism; **a.** sciolistic; sciolous; **n.** sciolist

theory of: **n.** epistemology; gnosology; **a.** epistemonic(al)

universal, or system embracing all: **n.** pansophism; pansophy; **a.** pansophic(al)

useful, pert. to: **a.** chrestomathic(al)

L

L, *excessive use of letter, as in stuttering:* **n.** lallation; lambdacism

LABOR, *characterized by great:* **(see** "laborious") **a.** Herculean; yeoman
conquers all: labor omnia vincit
convict, system of: **n.** peonage
the palm is not gained w/o (labor): palma non sine pulvere

LABORIOUS: **a.** arduous; Herculean; industrious; onerous; operose; slavish; toilsome; yeoman; **n.** LABORIOUSNESS: operosity
very (unending toil): **a.** Sisyphean

LABORIOUSLY *study, etc.:* **v.** lucubrate; **n.** lucubration

LACKING: **a.** desiderative; deficient; devoid; exigous; insufficient; **n.** LACK: **(see** "deficiency") dearth; deficiency; desideratum; desiderium; **(pl.** desideria); exigency; exiguity; famine; inadequacy; insufficiency; requirement
in factual or historical basis; **a.** fictional; mythologic(al)

LADY: **n.** domina; donna
beautiful: **n.** *belle dame*
beautiful w/o mercy: **n.** *la belle dame sans merci*
great or aristocratic: **n.** *grande dame*
young: **n.** damsel; demoiselle; ingenue; *jeune fille*

LAKES, *pert. to or found in:* **a.** lacustral; lacustrine
situated bet.: **a.** interlacustrine

LAMB, *as gentle as a:* **n.** *doux comme un agneau*
of God: **n.** *agnus Dei*

LAME: **a.** claudicant; halting; maimed; spavined; **n.** claudication

LAMENT: **(see** "bewail") **v.** deplore; elegize; **n.** elegy; epicede; epicedium; threnody; **a.** LAMENTABLE: deplorable; despicable; doleful; grievous; lachrymose; mournful; plaintive; plangorous; sorrowful; **n.** LAMENTATION: **(see** "complaint") epicedium; lachrymation; languishment

LAND: **(see** "earth") **n.** domain; dominion; terrain
and water, consisting of both: **a.** amphibian; terraqueous; **n.** amphibian
area: **n.** terrain; terrene; topography
doctrine of equitable distribution: **n.** agrarianism
living or growing on or in: **a.** terrestrial; terricolous
native, pert. to: **a.** compatriotic; patrial
of one's birth: **n.** *natale solum*
promised: **n.** (land of) Canaan
rel. to: **a.** agrarian; terrene
take for public use: **v.** expropriate; sequester; **n.** eminent domain; expropriation; sequestration

LANDHOLDING, *vast or extensive:* **n.** barony

LANDMARK: **n.** cairn

LANDSCAPE: **n.** panorama; paysage; scenery; terrain; topography

LANGUAGE(S): **n.** idiom; parlance; tongue; vernacular
abusive: **n.** billingsgate; invective; scurrility; vituperation; **a.** scurrilous; vituperative
affectation in: **n.** preciosity
ambiguity in: **n.** amphibology; circumlocution; **a.** amphibological; amphibolous; circumlocutious
artificial, affected, or excessive elegance of: **n.** ephuism; preciosity; **a.** euphuistic(al); phraseological

careful in lit. style: **a.** Addisonian; stylistic
characteristic of a particular: **a.** idiomatic; provincial
characterized by mixture of: **a.** macaronic; **n.** Babelism
clear and polished: **a.** Addisonian
clear in: **a.** explicit; limpid; unambiguous; uncryptic; unequivocal
common, or functioning as (signs, etc.): **n.** *lingua franca*
common, ordinary, local or native: **n.** patois; vernacular(ism); vernacularity; vulgate
confused: (**see** "jargon") **n.** Babelization; Babelism
confusion of: **n.** Babelism; polyglot
containing several: **a.** polyglot; polylingual
deceptive: **n.** flummery
expert in: **see** "linguist"
familiar w/ or using but one: **a.** monoglot; monolingual
familiar w/ or using two or more: **a.** bilingual (*two*); polyglot; polylingual
figurative: **n.** tropology
foolish: **n.** balderdash; flatulence; flummery; gasconade; gibberish; jabberwock(y); kompology; lallation; **a.** jargonistic; **v.** jargonize
having same: **a.** colingual
high-sounding and usu. unimportant: **a.** bombastic; euphuistic; grandiloquent; rhapsodic; rubescent; **n.** bombast; grandiloquent; rubescence
in plain: **adv.** or **a.** *en clair;* **adv.** *nudis verbis*
incorrect use of: **n.** abusage
informal or conversational: **n.** colloquialism; vernacular; **a.** colloquial; vernacular
knowledge of: **n.** linguistry; philology
international: **see** "universal" **below**
living: **n.** vernacular
native: (**see** "regional or local" **below**) **a.** or **n.** vernacular; **n.** patois
nonsense: **see** "foolish" **above**
obscene, uncontrollable or excessive use of: **n.** coprolalia
of criminals: **n.** argot
preciseness or over-preciseness of: **n.** preciosity; purism; **n.** precieuse; purist
regional or local: **a.** or **n.** vernacular; **n.** colloquialism; dialect; dialectalism; koine; patois; villagism; **a.** dialectal
rel. to: **a.** glottological; lingual; linguistic; phonetic
rel. to origin of: **a.** dialectic; glottogonic; lingual(istic); vernacular
science of: **n.** glottology; linguistics; philology
sign: **n.** dactylology; *lingua franca*
smallest unit of: **n.** glosseme
speaking in unknown or imaginary: **n.** glossolalia
speaking one: **a.** monoglot; monolingual
speaking or pert. to two: **a.** bilingual; **n.** bilingualism; bilinguality
speaking or pert. to several: **a.** multilingual; polyglot; polylingual
specialist in: **see** "linguist"
specialist in English: **n.** anglicist
study of: **n.** glottology; linguistics; linguistry
study of English: **n.pl.** anglistics
universal: **n.** esperanto; pasigraphy
use of substandard: **n.** barbarism; vernacularism; vernacularity; vulgarism

LAPEL *flower(s)*: **n.** boutonniere

LAPSE: (**see** "pause") **n.** apostasy; backslide; caudicity; declination; decline
as of memory: **n.** parapraxia; parapraxis

LARD, *of or like:* **a.** amyloid; lardaceous; oleaginous

LARGE: (**see** "huge") **a.** abundant; capacious; comprehensive; copious; formidable; generous; grandiose; immeasurable; lavish; magnitudinous; monstrous; portentous; prodigal; spacious; **n.** LARGENESS: colossality; comprehensiveness; grandiosity; immensity; magnitude; massivity; monumentality; vastity; voluminosity
and ornate: **a.** baronial; magnificent; palatial
fantastically: **a.** Bunyanesque
in body: **a.** macrosomatic; macrosomatous; **n.** macrosomatic
number: **n.** hecatomb; legion; multitude; spate

LASSITUDE: (**see** "laziness") **n.** adynamia; enervation; ennui; hypokinesia; lackadaisy; languor; lethargy; listlessness; weariness; **a.** LASSITUDINOUS: adynamic; comatose; hypokinesic; lackadaisic(al); languorous; lethargic

LAST: (**see** "final" **and** "endure") **v.** abide; perdure; **a.** conclusive; concluding; definitive; dernier; eventual; extreme; terminal; ultimate

at: **adv.** *ad extremum*
but one (next to last): **n.** penult; **a.** penultimate
but two: **n.** antepenult; **a.** antepenultimate
degree: **adv.** *ad extremum*
resort: **n.** *dernier ressort; pis aller; ultima ratio*
word (*most modern*): **n.** *dernier cri;* ultimate

LASTING: (**see** "eternal") **a.** abiding; boundless; diuturnal; indelible; indissoluble; inefaceable; interminable; perseverant; pertinacious; protracted; unceasing; **n.** diuturnity; indissolubility; perpetuality; perpetuity; pertinacity
indefinitely: **a.** aeonian; in perpetuity

LASTLY: **adv.** *en fin*

LATE: (**see** "recent") **a.** advanced; dilatory; procrastinative; procrastinatory; neoteric; **n.** LATENESS: eleventh hour; **a.** LATER: (**see** "after") posterior; subsequent; succedent

LATENT: **a.** abeyant; delitescent; dormant; inactive; potential; quiescent; sessile; **n.** LATENCY: (**see** "possibility") deliquescence; dormancy; incubation; potentiality; quiescence; quietude

LATEST *fashion, or most authoritative thing:* **n.** *dernier cri*

LATIN, *of or pert. to:* **a.** Latinian; Latinic; **n.** Latinism; Latinity; latinization

LAUD: **v.** acclaim; applaud; approbate; commend; deify; extol; felicitate; macarize; panegyrize; **a.** LAUDABLE (or LAUDATORY): commendatory; encomiastic; eulogistic; panegyrical; praiseworthy; **n.** LAUDATION: approbation; commendation; deification; encomium; eulogy; extolment; panegyric

LAUGH: **v.** cachinnate; ridicule; **n.** cachinnation
able to or inclined to: **a.** risible; **n.** risibility

LAUGHABLE: (**see** "funny") **a.** cachinnatory; farcical; ludicrous; mirthful; *pour rire;* riant; ridiculous; risible
yet serious: **a.** ludicropathetic; ludicroserious

LAUGHTER: **n.** cachinnation; risibility
causing or pert. to: **a.** gelastic; gelogenic; risible; **n.** risibility
given to: **a.** Abderian
inextinguishable: **n.** *asbestos gelos*
loud or unrestrained: **n.** cachinnation; **a.** cachinnatory
sarcastic: **n.** irrision
to excite: **v.** *pour faire rire*

LAVISH: **v.** squander; **a.** affluent; Babylonian; Babylonic; exorbitant; extravagant; exuberant; improvident; inordinate; Lucullan; luxurious; magnificent; opulent; prodigal; profuse; (super)abundant; sumptuous; unstinted; **n.** LAVISHNESS: (**see** "abundance") affluence; affluency; extravagance; exuberance; magnificence; opulence; opulency; prodigality; sumptuosity

LAW(S): **n.** canon; code; command(ment); covenant; enactment; formula; jurisprudence; legislation; mandate; ordinance; precept; procedure; regulation; statute
according to: **adv.** *secundum legem;* **a.** nomological
based on: **a.** *de jure;* nomothetic
basic: **n.** constitution; decalogue; *Magna C(h)arta*
by reason or by operation of: **a.** *ipso jure*
by right of: **a.** *de jure*
civil order under good: **n.** eunomy
common: **see** "unwritten" **below**
conformity to: **n.** dharma; legitimation
digest of: **n.** *corpus juris;* pandect
divine: **n.** *jus divinum; jus ecclesiasticum*
divine, by: **adv.** *jure divino*
exact: **n.** *strictum jus; summum jus*
-giver: **n.** Solon; thesmothete
govt. founded on system of: **n.** nomocracy
having no standing in (w/o legal effect or validity): **a.** invalid; *nullius juris*
human, by: **adv.** *jure humano*
international: **n.** *jus gentium; jus inter gentes*
letter of (strict): **n.** *strictum jus* (or *ius*); **adv.** *stricti(ssimi) juris*
-maker: **see** "-giver" **above**
moral: **n.** *dharma*
natural: **n.** *jus naturae; jus naturale*
of marriage: **n.** *jus con(n)ubii*
of nations: **see** "international" **above**
of organic life: **n.** organonomy
of place or locality: **n.** *lex loci*

of retaliation: **n.** *lex talions*
of the land: **n.** *lex terrae*
pert. to or in accordance w/: **a.** judicatory; juridical; juristic; nomological
public: **n.** *jus publicum*
regulating habits (moral or religious grounds): **n.** sumptuary (law); **a.** sumptuary
science or system of: **n.** jurisprudence
spirit of the: **n.** *mens legis*
strict: **see under** "letter of" **above**
under color of: **adv.** *sub colore juris*
unwritten or common: **n.** *jus commune; lex non scripta*
written or statute: **n.** *jus scriptum*

LAWFUL: (**see** "legal") **a.** authorized; canonical; constitutional; legitimate; permitted; rightful; **adv.** *de jure;* **n.** LAWFULNESS: **see** "legality"

LAWLESS: (**see** "unrestrained") **a.** anarchic; anomalous; contumacious; Dionysian; disobedient; insubordinate; insurgent; mutinous; piratical; recalcitrant; recusant; refractory; riotous; seditious; transgressive; unbounded; ungoverned; unlicensed

LAWMAKING *or drafting:* **n.** nomography; nomology

LAWSUIT(S), *given to carrying on:* **a.** litigious
in action or pending: **adv.** *pendente lite*

LAWYER: (**see** "advocate") **n.** attorney; barrister; counselor
pert. to: **a.** advocatory; barristerial
woman: **n.** Portia

LAX: (**see** "remiss") **a.** immoral; undutiful; unobservant; unprincipled

LAYER: **n.** hierarchization; lamina; stratification; stratum; **a.** LAYERED: laminal; laminar; laminated; stratal; stratified; superimposed

LAYMAN: **n.** esoteric; (**pl.** laity)

LAZY: **a.** comatose; dilatory; faineant; hebetudinous; hypnotic; indolent; inertial; lackadaisical; languid; lethargic; oscitant; otiose; remiss; slothful; sluggish; somniferous; spiritless; torpescent; torpid; unenterprising; **n.** LAZINESS: (**see** "sloth") faineancy; *fainéantise;* inanition; inertia; indolence; lackadaisy; lassitude; lethargy; oscitancy; otiosity; remission; sluggishness; supinity; torpidity
or idle person: **n.** faineant

LEACH: **v.** lixiviate; **n.** lixiviation; **a.** lixivious

LEAD, *containing or producing:* **a.** plumbiferous
having color of: **a.** plumbeous

LEADER(S): (**see** "guide") **n.** archimandrite; bellwether; chairman; conductor; executive; governor; hierophant; maestro; pacemaker; premier; president; primate; protagonist; speaker; spokesman; wheelhorse; **n.** LEADERSHIP: aegis; authority; chieftainry; command
masterful and potent: **n.** mogul; tycoon
military, or w/ mil. following: **n.** caudillo
of a chorus: **n.** choragus; choregus; coryphaeus
of a school, as painting, music, writing, etc.: **n.** *chef d'école*
of a group or body: **n.** dean; doyen; (**fem.** doyenne)
of thought, taste, or opn.: **n.** *avant-garde;* connoisseur; vanguard
politics: **n.** sachem
sect: **n.** coryph(a)eus; hierarch; **a.** hierarchic(al)
tending to follow any: **a.** sequacious; **n.** sequacity
without a: **a.** acephalic; acephalous

LEADING: (**see** "chief") **a.** enlightened; foremost; principal; salient; signal; stellar
act of: **n.** manuduction; **a.** manuductive; manuductory
"-light": **n.** luminary
position in a movement, etc., also those leading: **n.** *avant-garde;* vanguard

LEAGUE: (**see** "association") **n.** alliance; amalgamation; coalition; confederation; entente

LEAN: **a.** angular; attenuated; deficient; emaciated; infertile; macilent; tabescent; unproductive; unremunerative; **n.** LEANNESS: angularity; emaciation; macilency; tabescence

LEANING: (**see** "tendency") **n.** conatus; flair; partiality; penchant; predilection; (pre)disposition; prejudice; propensity; susceptibility; **a.** inclinatory; tendentious

LEAP(S): **n.** catapault; gambade; gambado; gambol; saltation
proceeding by: **a.** saltatory
-year: **n.** bisextile (year)

LEAPING: **a.** capering; saltant; saltatorial; saltatorian; saltatory; subsultory; subsultive
adapted for or rel. to: **a.** saltatorial

LEARN: **v.** acquire; ascertain; memorize
all from one: **adv.** *ab uno disce omnes*
by intuition: **v.** *intuit*

LEARNED: (**see** "educated") **a.** academic; Aristotelian; enlightened; erudite; lettered; literate; omniscient; pansophic; philomatic(al); polymathic(al); profound; scholarly
affectedly: **a.** bookish; pedantic; pansophist
exhaustedly: **a.** omniscient; pansophic(al); **n.** omniscience; pansophism; pansophy
person: **see under** "person"
world, the: **n.** *le monde savant*

LEARNER: (**see** "beginner") **n.** abecedarian; alphabetarian; apprentice; catechumen; inceptor; novice; novitiate; probationer; trainee; understudy
who begins late in life: **n.** *opsimath*

LEARNING: (**see** "knowledge") **n.** culture; enlightenment; erudition; omniscience; philology; sapience; scholarship; schoolcraft
encyclopedic: **n.** polymath(y): **a.** polyhistoric; polymathic(al); **n.** polyhistor(ian)
given to excess: **a.** intellectualistic; **n.** intellectualism; intellectualist; rationalism
helping, serving or guiding in: **a.** heuristic
hostility to: **n.** anti-intellectualism; anti-intellectualist
lover or love of: **n.** intellectualist; intellectualism; philologist; philomath(y); **a.** philomathic(al)
man of great: **see** "person, learned"
one of encyclopedic: **n.** polyhistor(ian); polymath
one who parades: **n.** pedant; sciolist; **a.** pedantic; sciolistic; sciolous; **n.** pedanticism; pedantry; sciolism
period of: **n.** apprenticeship; catecumnenate; novitiate
person of great: **see** "person, learned"
pert. to: **a.** erudite; palladian
pretender to: **n.** pedant; sciolist; **a.** pedantic; sciolistic; sciolous
show of: **n.** didacticism: intellectuality; pedanticism; pedantry; sciolism
useful, pert. to: **a.** chrestomathic(al)

LEATHER, *pert. to* (*leathery*): **a.** coriaceous

LEAVE, *by your:* **adv.** *pace tua*
for travel, education, etc.: **n.** sabbatical; shemittah; **a.** sabbatical
-taking: (**see** "goodbye") **n.** adieu; *congé;* devoir; valediction; **a.** valedictory

LEAVES, *feeding on:* **a.** phyllophagic; phyllophagous
shedding: **a.** deciduous
to strip off: **v.** defoliate; **n.** defoliation

LECHEROUS: **see** "lustful"

LECTURE: (**see** "discussion") **n.** castigation; colloquium; colloquy; discourse; disquisition; dissertation; dressing-down; excursus; homily; reprimand; reproof; riot-act; symposium; treatise; **v.** castigate; reprimand; reprove; sermonize; **n.** LECTURER: (**see** "speaker") *conférencier*
pert. to: **a.** admonitory; castigatory; disquisitional; dissertative; homiletic

LEFT: **a.** larboard; port; sinistral
hand: **n.** *mano sinistra;* minor hand
handed but trained to use right hand in writing: **a.** dextrosinistral
-handedness: **n.** maneinism; sinistrality; **a.** sinistral; sinistromanual
toward or on the: **a.** gauche; sinister; sinistrad; sinistral
turning to: **a.** levogyrate; levogyre; levorota(to)ry; **n.** levogyration; levorotation

LEG(S), *front of the:* **n.** antecnemion
having long: **a.** or **n.** macropod; **a.** macropodal
having short: **a.** brachyskelic; brachyskelous
lower portion of: **n.** cnemis; tibia
rel. to: **a.** crural; femoral
upper portion of: **n.** femur

LEGAL: **a.** authorized; constitutional; *de-jure;* juridical; juristic; justifiable; lawful; legitimate; licit; official; permissive;

permitted; statutory; warrantable; **n.** LEGALITY: legitimacy, lawfulness
capacity, power or jurisdiction: **n.** competence
effect, w/o: **a.** nugatory; null and void; **n.** *nullius juris*
ineligibility or incompetency: **n.** incapacity; incompetency; *non compos (mentis)* **a.** *doli incapax;* incompetent; *non compos (mentis)*
it is: **n.** licit
person: **n.** *homo legalis*

LEGALLY *competent:* **a.** *capax negotii; compos mentis; doli capax; sui juris*
incompetent: **see under** "legal"

LEGENDARY: **a.** aprocryphal; fabulous; fictitious; mythical; mythological; traditional; tralatitious; unwritten

LEGIBLE: **a.** comprehensible; decipherable; scrutable; understandable

LEGITIMATE: **see** "legal"

LEISURE, *at:* **a.** otiose; **adv.** *en retraite;* **n.** otiosity
breeds vice: otia dant vitia

LENGTH, *at:* **a. or adv.** *in extenso*
pert. to: **a.** longitudinal
speak or write at: **v.** expatiate; **n.** expatiation

LENGTHEN: **v.** elongate; expand; extend; prolong; protract; **a.** LENGTHENING: protractive; **n.** protraction; **a.** LENGTHWISE: longitudinal

LEOPARD, *pert. to or resembling:* **a.** pardine

LESS: *so much the: quoad minus*
than required: **a.** submarginal; subminimal; subnormal; suboptional; substandard

LESSEN: (**see** "decrease") **v.** abbreviate; adulterate; alleviate; attenuate; demote; depreciate; disparage; extenuate; minify; mitigate; mollify; palliate; temper
repute or esteem of: **v.** decry; degrade; denigrate; derogate; disparage; minify; pejorate; **n.** degradation; denigration; derogation; disparagement; pejoration; **a.** degradative; denigratory; derogative; derogatory
seriousness of: **v.** dulcify; extenuate; minify; mitigate; mollify; palliate

LESSENING: (**see** "reduction") **n.** abatement; attenuation; decrescendo; demotion; diminution; diminuendo; extenuation; mitigation; mollification; palliation; **a.** ablatitious; alleviatory; decrescent; extenuative; palliative; palliatory; subtractive
of virulence: **n.** attenuation

LETHARGY: (**see** "lassitude" **and** "laziness") **n.** apathy; lassitude; **a.** LETHARGIC: **see** "slow"

LETTER(S), *devotion to or worship of:* **n.** grammatolatry
-for-letter: **a.** literally; literatim; verbatim; **n.** literality
-for-letter and word-for-word: **adv.** *literatim et verbatim*
men of: **n.pl.** *gens de lettres; hommes de lettres*
observing the, rather than spirit: **a.** formal; hypocritical; pharisaic(al); ritualistic
of credit: **n.** *lettre de créance*
opening of: **n.** salutation; superscription
person of: **n.** *homme de lettres; littérateur; litterato; litteratus;* (**pl.** *gens de lettres; hommes de lettres; intelligentsia; literati*)
pert. to: **a.** epistolary
representing diff. sounds in diff. words: **n.** heterography
transposition of, as in reading or writing: **n.** metathesis; strephosymbolia
-writer: **n.** epistolarian; **a.** epistolary
-writing, practice or art of: **n.** epistolography; **a.** epistolary

LEVEL: **n.** echelon; plateau; **a.** balanced; equipotential; horizontal; planate; unexcited; uniform; **n.** horizontality

LEWD: **a.** Anacreontic; aphrodisiac; carnal; concupiscent; concupiscible; cyprian; debauched; depraved; dissolute; ithyphallic; lascivious; lecherous; libidinous; licentious; lubricious; lustful; obliquitous; obscene; pornographic; profligate; prurient; salacious; satyric; scrofulous; sensual; venereal; venereous; wanton; **n.** LEWDNESS: amorosity; carnality; concupiscence; debauchery; depravity; impudicity; lasciviency; lasciviousness; lechery; libidinousness; lubricity; obliquity; obscenity; profligacy; pruriency; salacity; sensuality; wantonness
person: **see** "libertine"

LIABILITY: **n.** drawback; likelihood; obligation; obnoxiety; responsibility

LIAR: **n.** Ananias; fabricator; fabulist; prevaricator; pseudologist; pseudologue
consummate: **n.** *menteur à triple étage*
pathological: **n.** pseudologue
should have good memory: mendacem memorem esse oportet

LIBEL (**see** "defame") **n.** aspersion; calumny; defamation; lampoon; satire; slander; **a.** LIBELOUS: calumnious; defamatory; slanderous

LIBERAL: **a.** abundant; bounteous; bountiful; copious; generous; hospitable; knowledg(e)able; latitudinarian; lavish; magnanimous; munificent; philanthropic; prodigal; **n.** latitudinarian; philanthropist; Young Turk; **n.** LIBERALITY: copiosity; generosity; hospitality; munificence; openhandedness; philanthropy

LIBERATE: **see** "free"; **n.** LIBERATOR: emancipator; manumitter; Messiah; redeemer; redemptor; (**fem.** redemptrix); **a.** messianic

LIBERTINE: **n.** cyprian; debauchee; lecher; paillard; profligate; sensualist; satyr; thelemite; voluptuary
state of being: **n.** debauchery; lechery; libertinage; profligacy; sensuality

LIBERTY, *destruction or destroyer of:* **a.** or **n.** liberticide

LIBRARY: **n.** athenaeum; atheneum; bibliotheca; *bibliothèque;* **n.** LIBRARIAN: *bibliothécaire; bibliothecarian*

LICE, *pert. to or infected w/:* **a.** pedicular; pediculous; verminous; **n.** pediculosis

LICENSE: (**see** "unrestraint") **n.** franchise; privilege; licentiousness
poetic: **n.** *licientia vatum*
to publish or print (*under censorship*): **n.** imprimatur

LIE: (**see** "falsehood") **v.** equivocate; fabricate; fabulate; prevaricate; tergiversate; **n.** (**see** "liar") canard; equivocation; exaggeration; fabrication; fabulation; hyperbole; inveracity; mendacity; prevarication; pseudology; roorback; tergiversation; **a.** prevaricative; tergiversatory
abnormal tendency to: **n.** mythomania; pseudology
pathological or exaggerated: **n.** Munchausenism; pseudology

LIEN: **n.** encumbrance; hypothecation; mortgage

LIFE: (**see** "biography") **n.** animation; spirit; vitality; vivaciousness; vivacity
absence of: (**see** "death") **n.** abiosis; defunction; **a.** abiotic
centering in or on: **a.** bio-centric; **n.** bio-centrist
cycle, single organism: **n.** ontogeny; **a.** ontological
development fr. preexisting: **n.** biogenesis; biogeny; **a.** biogenic; biogenous
during: **adv.** *durante vita; intra vitam*
force: **n.** *anima mundi; élan vital;* mana
full of: **see** "lively"
generating of: **n.** (bio)genesis; **a.** biogenetic(al); biogenous
history: **see** "biography"
long or great span of: **n.** longevity; macrobiosis; **a.** macrobian; macrobiotic
necessity of: (**see** "food") **n.** aliment; **a.** alimental; alimentary
organic, law of: **n.** organonomy
philosophy of: **n.** ideology; weltanschauung
prime of: **n.** *fleur de l'âge*
prolonging, art of: **n.** macrobiotics
process: **n.** anabolism; **a.** anabolic
producing: **n.** (bio)genesis; **a.** biogenetic(al); biogenous
return to: **n.** anabiosis; resurrection; resuscitation; reviviscence
science and development: **n.** biology; **a.** biologic(al)
scientific investigation of: **n.** biognosis; (**pl.** biognoses)
such is: c'est la vie; sic eunt fata hominum
vigor of: **n.** *élan vital; vis vitae*
way of: **n.** *modus vivendi*
weariness of: **n.** *taedium vitae*

LIFELESS: (**see** "spiritless") **a.** adenoid(al); amort; apathetic; colorless; comatose; defunct; exanimate; inanimate; inert; insensible; insentient; insipid; lethargic; quiescent; torpid; unconscious; unresponsive; vapid; **n.** LIFELESSNESS: defunction; immobility; insentience; insipidity; quiescence; quietude; torpidity; vapidity

LIGHT: (see "easy") **a.** diaphanous; ethereal; imponderous; inconsiderable; luminary; luminiferous; luminous; weightless; **n.** fluorescence; illumination; incandescence; luminary; luminescence; luminosity; phosphorescence; scintillation
abnormal fear of or sensitivity to: **n.** photophobia; **a.** photophobic
(airy), as in mus. dir.: **a.** sfogato
and brilliant: **a.** lambent; scintillating; scintillescent; **n.** lambency; scintillescence; **v.** scintillate
and shade (as in painting), interplay of: **n.** chiaroscuro
avoiding: **a.** lucifugal; lucifugous; photophobic
impervious to: **a.** opaque; **n.** opacity
let there be: **adv.** *fiat lux*
movement in response to: **n.** photokinesis; tropism; **a.** photokinetic
of the world: **n.** *lux mundi*
producing or giving off: **n.** illuminant; incandescence; luminosity; **a.** incandescent; lucific; luminescent; luminiferous; luminous; phosphorescent; photogenic
reflected, pert. to: **a.** catoptric(al)
requiring abundant: **a.** photophilic; photophilous
science of: **n.** actinology; catoptrics; optics; photics
sensitivity to: **n.** photophobia; **a.** photophobic
spirit of: **n.** Ormuzd
thriving in or loving: **a.** photophilic; photophilous
treatment by use of: **n.** actinotherapy; heliotherapy

LIGHTHEARTEDNESS: **n.** blitheness; buoyancy; ebullience; euphoria; jauntiness; nonchalance; sprightliness

LIGHTNING, *abnormal fear of:* **n.** astraphobia
of or like: **a.** fulgurant; fulgurous; fulmin(e)ous
strikes highest peaks: feriuntque summos fulgura montes

LIKABLE: **a.** appealing; attractive; comely; contential; personable; simpatico; sympathetic; **n.** LIKABLENESS: likability

LIKE: (see "akin" and "similar") **v.** esteem; relish
delights in like: similis simili gaudet

LIKELY: (see "possible") **a.** apparent; conjectural; credible; ostensible; plausible; presumable; presumptive; probable; *prima facie;* promising; specious; verisimilar; *vraisemblable;* **n.** LIKELIHOOD: liability; probability; speciosity; verisimilitude; verisimility; *vraisemblance*

LIKENESS: (see "image") **n.** analogy; counterpart; equivalence; facsimile; parity; (re)semblance; similarity; similitude
bad or ludicrous: **n.** caricature
or affinity of nature: **n.** assonance
rough: **n.** assonance, caricature

LIKING: **n.** diathesis; gusto; inclination; penchant; predilection; preference; propensity; relish
preconceived: **n.** inclination; predilection; predisposition; prejudice; propensity
strong: **n.** penchant

LIMBER: (see "pliant") **a.** flaccid; gracile; lissom(e); lithe(some); **n.** flaccidity; lissomeness; lithesomeness

LIMBS, *having those adapted to grasping:* **a.** prehensile
having those adapted to running: **a.** cursorial

LIMIT(S): (see "confine") **v.** circumscribe; demarcate; discriminate; regulate; **n.** boundary; circumscription; demarcation; restriction; solstice; terminus; (**pl.** confines; purlieus); **a.** LIMITED (or LIMITING): adjectival; adjective; circumscribed; cloistral; confined; confining; demarcative; denominational; finite; parochial; prescribed; provincial; qualificatory; restrictive; sectarian
established: **n.pl.** metes and bounds
without: **adv.** *ad infinitum;* **a.** inexhaustible; infinite; limitless; **n.** infinitude; infinity

LIMITATION: (see "limit") **n.** circumscription; delimitation; finitude; restriction
of debate: **n.** clôture

LIMITLESS: (see "unrestrained") **a.** boundless; uncircumscribed; unmeasured

LIMP: **a.** flaccid, spiritless; **n.** claudication; flaccidity; **a.** LIMPING: claudicant; **n.** claudication

LINE(S), *formation in, or series:* **n.** collineation; echelon; regimentation
in straight: **a.** (col)linear; **n.** collineation; linearity
marked with: **a.** linear(istic); lineate; **n.** lineation
of action: **n.** demarche; maneuver
of or rel. to a: **a.** lineal; linear
situated bet.: **a.** interlineal; interlinear; **v.** interlineate; **n.** interlineation

LINEAGE: **(see** "derivation" **and** "descent") **n.** ancestry; background; genealogy; heredity; pedigree; stemma

LINGUIST: **n.** glottologist; linguistician; philologist; **a.** glottological; linguistic(al); philologic(al)

LINIMENT: **n.** embrocation; linimentum

LINK: **(see** "join") **v.** (con)catenate; interlock; **n.** catena; concatenation; juncture; liaison; nexus; suture; vinculum; **a.** LINKED: **(see** "joined") concatenate; intercatenated

LION, *characteristic of or resembling:* **a.** leonine
fr. the claw one may recognize the: ex ungue leonem

LIP(S): **n.** labium; **(pl.** labia); **a.** labial
biting of: **n.** cheilophagia
having large: **a.** macrocheilous; **n.** macrocheilia
moving as in speech or singing but w/o sound: **n.** mussitation
produce sound by: **v.** labialize; phonate

LIQUID, *becoming:* **a.** liquescent
reduce to: **v.** liquefy; **n.** liquefaction

LIST(S): **n.** agendum; **(pl.** agenda); catalog(ue); enumeration; inventory; repertory; tariff; **a.** catalogical
of banned books, etc.: **see under** "books"

LISTENING: **a.** acousmatic; audient

LISTLESS: **(see** "lazy") **a.** comatose; dilatory; dispirited; enervated; inattentive; lackadaisical; lackluster; languid; languorous; lethargic; spiritless; supine; vacuous; **n.** LISTLESSNESS: abiotrophy; apathy; lackadaisy; languor; lassitude; lethargy; otiosity

LITANY: **n.** rogation; supplication

LITERAL: **(see** "word-for-word") **a.** categorical; exact; obvious; prosaic; textual; unimaginative; **adv.** LITERALLY: *à la lettre; au pied de la lettre;* explicitly; virtually; **n.** LITERALITY: exactitude; grammatolatry; prosaism

LITERARY: **(see** "bookish") **a.** erudite; scholarly
adaptation: **n.** rifacimento
attack: **n.** *coup de plume*
collection: **n.** anthology; chrestomathy; collectanea; *disjecta membra;* **(pl.** adversaria; analecta; collectanea; miscellanea); **a.** anthologized; **v.** anthologize
composition, short and reminiscent: **n.** feuilleton
crudity: **n.** gaucherie
excerpts or fragments: **see** "excerpts" **and** "collection" **above**
group or coterie: **n.** *cénacle*
ornamentation: **n.** asiaticism; floridity; grandiloquence; mandarinism; rubescence; **a.** mandarin
patron(age): **n.** Maecenas; Maecenasship; Maecenatism
person: **n.** belletrist; bellelettrist; *homme de lettres; litterateur; literato(r); literatus;* **(pl.** *gens de lettres; hommes de lettres; intelligentsia; literati*)
scraps, misc.: **(see** "collection" **above)** **n.pl.** ana; scrapiana
selected passages: **n.pl.** analecta; analects; collectanea; *morceaux choisis*
sketch: **n.** feuilleton
style, clear and polished: **a.** Addisonian
lofty: **n.** *la morgue littéraire*
ornate and complex: **see** "ornamentation" **above**
ornate, exaggerated or artificial: **n.** gongorism; lyricism; rubescence
popular: **n.** journalese
sublimity of: **a.** Miltonic
theft: **n.** piracy; plagiarism; **a.** piratical; plagiaristic; **v.** plagiarize
work, catering to popular taste: **n.** feuilleton; **n. or a.** journalese
chief: **see under** "chief"
closely imitating previous work: **n.** pastiche
containing two parts contrasting or matching each other: **n.** diptych
developing character fr. child to adulthood: **n.** entwicklungsroman
early development or spiritual education of main character: **n.** Bildungsroman

ornamental embellishment or accessory to: **n.** paregon; (pl. parega)
prelim, or introductory: **n.** prodromus; prologue
w/ notes by diff. persons, or w/ variant readings of the text: **n.** or **a.** variorum
w/ real persons, events, etc. disguised: **n.** *roman à clef*

LITERATURE, *high-class:* **n.** *belles-lettres;* **a.** belletristic; **n.** belletrist; bellelettrist
lover of: **n.** belletrist; bellelettrist; literarian; philologist
morbid or scandalous creation in: **n.** *chronique scandaleuse; fleur du mal*
specialist in: **see** "literary person"
specialist in English: **n.** anglicist
study of: **n.** philology
substandard or sensational: **n.** kitsch
undue interest in: **n.** belletrism; belleslettrism

LITHE: **see** "graceful"

LITIGATION, *rel. to:* **a.** litigious; *n.* litigiosity

LITTLE: (**see** "petty" **and** "small") **a.** contemptible; diminutive; exiguous; inconsiderable; lilliputian; microscopic; miniature; paltry; trifling; trivial
bit: **see** "in quantity" **below**
-by-little: **adv.** inchmeal; piecemeal; *petit à petit; peu à peu; poco a poco*
ever so (*little*): **adv.** *tant soit peu*
in quantity: (**see** "touch") **n.** modicum; moiety; *soupçon;* triviality; *un peu*
man: **n.** homunculus
minds are caught w/ trifles: parva leves capiunt animas
things befit little man: parvum parva decent

LIVE: **v.** dwell; reside; subsist; **a. see** "lively"; **n.** (**see** "life") viability
ability to (*live*) *elegantly:* **n.** *savoir vivre*
beings, bringing forth: **a.** parturient; proligerous; viviparous; **n.** parturition; viviparity
for the day: **n.** *carpe diem; in diem vivre; in horam vivere*
while we (*live*), *let us* (*live*): *dum vivimus, vivamus*

LIVELY: (**see** "sprightly") **a.** alacritous; animated; blithe; ebullient; effervescent; exhilarative; exuberant; fervent; fervid; frolicksome; impassioned; intense; lighthearted; piquant; spirited; spiritous; vehement; vigorous; vital; vivacious; volatile; **n.** LIVELINESS: (**see** "animation") ebullience; effervescence; exhilaration; intoxication; invigoration; sprightliness; vivacity
in music: **a.** *animo; capricio; con brio*

LIVING *again:* **a.** redivivus; reincarnated; resurgent; resurrected; **n.** resurgence; resurrection
high and well, one who does: **n.** *bon-vivant;* boulevardier; epicurean; flâneur; gastronome(r); gourmet; **a.** epicurean; sybaritic
manner of: **n.** *modus vivendi*
pledge: **n.** *vivum vadium*
things, produced from or inhabiting: **a.** biogenous
together: **a.** cohabiting; contubernal; **n.** cohabitation
dissimilar organisms where advantageous to both: **n.** symbionticism; symbiosis; **a.** symbiotic(al)

LOAD: (**see** "burden") **n.** encumbrance; impediment; incubus; ponderosity

LOAFER: **n.** chairwarmer; flaneur; loiterer; vagrant; (**pl.** flotsam and jetsam)

LOATH: **see** "indisposed"

LOATHE: **v.** abhor; abominate; anathematize; detest; execrate; **a.** LOATHING (**or** LOATHSOME): (**see** "hateful") abhorrent; abominable; anathematic(al); cloying; detestable; disgusting; odious; offensive; repugnant; unprincipled; **n.** abhorrence; abomination; antipathy; aversion; detestation; execration; *nausée;* odium; qualmishness; repugnance; repugnancy

LOCAL: (**see** "native") **a.** autochthonous; edaphic; parochial; peninsular; provincial; regional; sectional; topical; vicinal
as to country: **a.** enchorial
in viewpoint, customs, etc.: **n.** parochialism; peninsularity; provincialism

LOCALITY: **n.** locus; (**pl.** loci); milieu; purlieu; vicinage; vicinity

LODGING, *esp. temporary:* **n.** *pied-à-terre*

LOFTY: (**see** "high") **a.** altitudinous; celestial; divine; eminent; ethereal; gran-

diloquent; heavenly; magniloquent; Olympian; stately; supreme; supernal; towering
thoughts, ideas, etc., or given to: **a. or n.** altitudinarian; **a.** spirituel(le)

LOGIC: **n.** *ars artium;* syntactics
bad: **n.** sophism; sophistry; **a.** alogical; sophistical
beyond scope of: **a.** metaphysical
contrary to: (**see** "illogical") **n.** affirmation (or assertion) of the consequent; alogism; denial of the antecedent; dereism; formal fallacy; *ignoratio elenchi;* illicit process; paralogism; *petitio principii;* material fallacy; verbal fallacy; **a.** alogical; dereistic; paralogistic; sophistical
specialist in: **n.** dialectician; logician

LOGICAL: (**see** "rational" **and** "reasonable") **a.** Aristotelian; Cartesian; cogent; coherent; consistent; dialectical; dianoetic
argumentation: **n.** dialectic(s); **a.** dialectical
result: **n.** consequence; logicality; **a.** consequential

LOITERER: (**see** "loafer") **n.** flaneur; vagrant

LONG: **v.** desiderate; hanker; languish; pine; yearn; **a.** (**see** "eternal") diuturnal; elongated; sempiternal; seven-league; **n.** diuturnity; sempiternity
life: **n.** longanimity; longevity; macrobiosis; **a.** longanimous
lived, also one who has lived long: **n. or a.** centenarian; macrobian; **a.** longevous
story or account: **n.** iliad
-winded: **a.** garrulous; loquacious; prolix; repetitious; verbose; **n.** garrulity; loquaciousness; loquacity; verbosity
word(s): **see under** "word"

LONGING: (**see** "craving") **a.** appetent; appetitious; desiderative; **n.** appetency; appetite; appetition; desiderata; desideration
ardent: **n.** desiderium; (**pl.** desideria)

LOOK(S): **n.** appearance; aspect; countenance; expression; mien; physiognomy; semblance; visage
acquired fr. long custom or settled use: **n.** patina
good: **n.** *beaux yeux*

LOOP, *shaped like:* **a.** ansiform

LOOSE: **a.** desultory; detached; disengaged; dissolute; licentious; rampant; unconnected; wanton

LOOSENING, *gradual, as in disease:* **n.** lysis
of restraint: **n.** (re)laxation

LOPSIDED: (**see** "uneven") **a.** asymmetric(al); unsymmetric(al)

LORD: **n.** kyrios; (**also** kurios)
be with you: Dominus vobiscum
direct us: Domine dirige nos

LORDLY: (**see** "overbearing") **a.** archidiaconal; arrogant; dignified; honorable; honored; imperial; imperious; majestic; stately
personage: **n.** magnifico
style, in: **a.** baronial; *en grand seigneur*

LORDSHIP: **n.** domain; dominion; seigneury; seign(i)ory; sovereignty

LORE: **see** "learning"

LOSS: **n.** casualty; depreciation; (de)privation; destruction; detriment; diminution; disintegration; divestation; elimination; eradication; forfeiture; misfortune; perdition
complete or irreparable: **n.** perdition; **a.** irretrievable

LOST, *likelihood or capability of being:* **n.** amissibility; **a.** amissible
not capable of being: **a.** inamissible; **n.** inamissibility

LOT: **see** "fate"

LOTION: **n.** embrocation; emollient; liniment

LOTS, *act of casting:* **n.** sortition
divination or prophecy by: **n.** cleromancy; sortilege

LOUD: **a.** blatant; clamorous; clangorous; forte; multivocal; ostentatious; stentorian; stentorious; tumultous; vociferous
and abusive: **a.** scurrilous; thersitical
and piercing: **a.** calliopean; stentorian; stentorious; stertorous
moderately: **adv.** *mezzo-forte*

very: **a.** stentorian; stentorious; stentorophonic; (**mus.** forte; fortissimo)

LOUDNESS: **n.** amplitude; blatancy; magnitude; volume
increasing in: **a.** or **n.** crescendo

LOUSY: **a.** pedicular; pediculous; verminous; **n.** pediculosis

LOUT: **n.** grobian; oaf; yokel

LOVE: **n.** affection; amorosity; amorousness; amour; benevolence; devotion; *la belle passion; la grande passion;* passion; tenderness
affair: **n.** *affaire d'amour; affaire de coeur*
esp. if secret or illicit: **n.** amour; intrigue; liaison; rendezvous; tryst
passing: **n.** amourette; passade
trifling or ephemeral, also woman involved: **n.** amourette
conquers all: amor vincit omnia
devotee of: **n.** amo(u)rist; gallant
goddess of: **n.** Aphrodite; Venus
great (also object of great): **n.** *grand(e) passion*
illicit: **n.** amour; intrigue; liaison; rendezvous; **a.** Paphian; wanton
in: **a.** amorous; enamored; infatuated
-letter or note: **n.** *billet d'amour; billet doux*
-making: **n.** amour(s); courtship
natural: **n.** affection; storge
non-sensual: **a.** Platonic; **a.** Platonism
of country: **n.** *amor patriae*
of friends or one's fellows: **n.** philia
of offspring: **see under** "offspring"
of possession: **n.** *amor habendi*
of the dollar (money): **n.** *amor nummi;* plutolatry
overcomes all things: omnia vincit amor; amor vincit omnia
overwhelming (love) at first sight: **n.** *coup de foudre*
passionately, to: **v.** *aimer éperdument*
pledge of: **n.** *gage d'amour*
renewal of: **n.** *redintegratio amoris*
self-: **n.** *amour de soi; amour-propre;* autophilia; autotheism; egocentricity; ego(t)ism; iotacism; narcissism; **a.** autotheistic(al); egocentric; narcissan; narcissistic; narcistic; **n.** autophiliac; egocentrist; narcissist
to distraction, to: aimer éperdument
writings about: **n.** amoristics

LOVER(S): **n.** amour; amo(u)rist; Casanova; cavalier; devotee; gallant; inamorato; Lothario; paramour; Romeo; servente; (**fem.** inamorata; paramour)
are fools: amantes amentes
daring or romantic: **n.** cavalier; Lochinvar
of married man or woman: **n.** paramour
of married woman: **n.** cicisbeo
promiscuous and unscrupulous: **n.** Casanova

LOVING: (**see** "amative") **a.** affectionate; amatory; amorous; enamored; painstaking
state of: **n.** amorosity; amorousness

LOW: (**see** "despondent" **and** "vulgar") **a.** contemptible; despicable; dishonorable; groveling; Hogarthian; ignoble; ignominious; leprous; plebeian; reptilian; vulgarian
fellow: **n.** *polisson;* vulgarian
state of being: **n.** contemptibility; despicability; ignobility; ignominy; vulgarity

LOWER: (**see** "debase") **a.** inferior; nether
in status, esteem, character, quality, etc.: **v.** animalize; bastardize; deglamorize; degrade; dehumanize; demean; denigrate; derogate; devalorize; devaluate; disparage; humble; minify; minimize; pejorate; traduce; **n.** debasement; declension; deglamorization; degradation; demotion; denigration; minimization; pejoration; plebification; traduction
morale of: **v.** debauch; demoralize; **n.** debauchment; demoralization
to middle or intermediate position: **v.** mediatize
world, of or rel. to: **a.** chthonian; plutonian; plutonic; subterranean

LOWERING *in social status or class:* (**see under** "lower") **a.** *déclassé;* declensional; declinatory

LOWEST: **a.** bathetic; nethermost
point: **n.** bathos; nadir; perigee

LOWING (*as do cows*): **n.** or **a.** mugient

LOWLY: **see** "humble"

LOYAL: **a.** abiding; adhering; allegiant; faithful; obedient; tenacious; unswerving; yeomanly

follower: **n.** aficionado; devotee; janissary; mercenary; minion
in everything: loyal en tout

LOYALTY: **n.** allegiance; constancy; devotion; faithfulness; fealty; fidelity
among friends: **n.** *bonhom(m)ie; camaraderie; esprit de corps;* philia
in name or form only: **n.** lip service

LUCK, *bad:* **n.** ambsace; misfortune; **a. see** "unlucky"
good, charm for: **see** "charm"
pert. to: **a.** aleatory

LUCKY: (**see** "fortunate") **a.** auspicious; favorable; miraculous; providential; **adv.** *benigno numine*
day: **n.** *dies fa(u)stus*
find: **n.** *ben trovato;* serendipity; **a.** serendipitous

LUKEWARM, *esp. in religion:* **n.** or **a.** Laodicean
quality or state of being: **n.** tepidity

LULLABY: **n.** berceuse

LUMP: **n.** protuberance
in one: **a.** *en masse; en toto;* holus-bolus
in throat: **n.** *globus hystericus*

LUNCH(EON): **n.** *déjeûner;* tiffin

LUNGE (*incl. verbal*): **n.** repartee; ripost(e)

LUNGS, *or chest, pert. to:* **a.** pectoral; pneumonic; pulmonic; respiratory; thoracic

LURE: (**see** "entice") **v.** inveigle; **n.** inveiglement

LUSH: **see** "luxuriant"

LUST: (**see** "lewdness") **n.** carnality; concupiscence; eagerness; enthusiasm; **a.** LUSTFUL: (**see** "lewd") lecherous; paphian; randy

LUXURIANT: (**see** "fertile") **a.** affluent; exuberant; florid; flourishing; inventive; opulent; plenteous; prodigal; profuse; proliferous; sumptuous; superabundant; uberous

LUXURIOUS: (**see** "lavish") **a.** Babylonian; baronial; Lucull(i)an; opulent; palatial; sumptuous; sybaritic; *voluptuaire;* voluptuous; voluptuary

LUXURY: **n.** affluence; extravagance; luxe; luxuriousness; princeliness; sensuality; *volupté;* voluptuosity; voluptuousness
one fond of: **see under** "pleasure"
take delight in: **v.** luxuriate; revel; voluptuate

LYING: **a.** equivocative; mendacious; prevaricative; tergiversatory
down: **a.** couchant; decubital; decumbent; incumbent; recumbent; supine; **n.** accumbency; deambulation; decubation; decubitus; decumbency; reclination; recumbency
down with head up: **a.** couchant
face down: **a.** procumbent; prone; prostrate
on back: **a.** decubital; supine; **n.** decubation; dorsal decubitus; reclination; recumbency; supinity

LYNX, *like or pert. to:* **a.** lyncean

M

MACHINE: **n.** apparatus; appliance; automaton; engine
God from a: **n.** *deus ex machinâ*
like a: **a.** automatous; mechanical; mechanomorphic; **n.** mechanicality
to make like: **v.** automate; automatize; dehumanize; mechanize; robotize

MAD: (**see** "angry") **a.** bedlamite; berserk; demented; distracted; furious; impetuous; lunatic; maniac(al); senseless; **n.** MADNESS: aberration; acharnement; deliration; delirium; derangement; ecstasy; fanaticism; hallucination; insanity; lunacy; mania; rashness
(*out of one's mind*): **a.** *acharné; aliéné;* berserk; demented; fey; maniac(al); psychotic
whom Jupiter wishes to destroy he first makes (mad): quem Juppiter vult perdere, dementat prius

MADMAN: **n.** bedlamite; maniac; noncompos; psychopath

MAGAZINE *or newspaper style of writing:* **n. or a.** journalese

MAGIC: abracadabra; alchemy; conjuration; conjury; diablerie; enchantment; gramary(e); incantation; legerdemain; necromancy; prestidigitation; sorcery; thaumaturgy; theurgy; witchcraft; witchery; wizardy; **a.** MAGICAL: alchemic(al); alchemistic(al); cabalistic; hermetic(al); incantatory; mystic; necromantic; numinous; phylacteric; recondite; sorcerous; talismanic(al)
black: **n.** necromancy
formula: **n.** alkahest
power (magical): **n.** alchemy
primitive, using image or likeness: **n.** *envoûtement*
spell or sorcery: **n.** alchemy; conjuration; incantation
symbol of: (**see** "charm") **n.** pentacle; pentagram; talisman
word: **n.** abracadabra; abraxis; presto

MAGICIAN: **n.** conjurer; enchanter; magus; (**pl.** magi); necromancer; prestidigitator; shaman; sorcerer; soothsayer; thaumaturge; thaumaturgist; theurgist; wizard; warlock
great: **n.** archimage

MAGNANIMITY: **n.** chivalry; generosity; philanthropy; **a.** MAGNANIMOUS: (**see** "liberal") chivalric; chivalrous; philanthropic

MAGNATE: **n.** nobleman; peer; tycoon
local (big-bug): **n.** panjandrum

MAGNIFICENT: (**see** "grand") **a.** imperial; leonine; majestic; palatial; regal; spectacular; sumptuous; **n. see** "grandeur"

MAID, *lady's:* **n.** Abigail; soubrette
of honor: **n.** *dame d'honneur; fille d'honneur*

MAIDENLY: **a.** daphnean; maidenish; modest; virginal

MAIMED: **a.** mangled; mutilated; truncated; **n.** mayhem

MAIN *item or event, or main dish at meal:* **n.** *pièce de résistance*

MAINTENANCE: **n.** alimentation; sustenance; sustentation; **a.** sustentative

MAJESTIC: (**see** "kingly") **a.** grandiose; imperial; regal; statuesque; **n. see** "grandeur"

MAJORITY: **n.** adulthood; maturity; predominance; predominancy
rule of the: **n.** arithmocracy

MAKE: **v.** concoct; confect; contrive; fabricate; fashion; invent; manufacture; synthesize
haste slowly: **adv.** *festina lente; speude bradeos*
up: **v.** compose; fabricate; improvisate; improvise; recoup; **n.** improvisation; morphology; recoupment; **a.** improvisatorial; improvisatory
facial (paint, cosmetics, etc.): **n.** maquillage
up for: **v.** requite; **n.** requital

MAKER: **n.** artificier; author; craftsman; fabricator; manufacturer; producer

MAKESHIFT: **n.** expediency; expedient; improvisation; *pis aller;* **a.** emergency; extemporaneous; (ex)temporary; improvisatorial; impromptu

MAKEUP: **n.** aggregate; arrangement; chemistry; composition; disposition; morphology
of face: **n.** maquillage

MALE(S), *abnormal fear of or aversion to:* **n.** androphobia; apandria
and female, common to both: **a.** ambisexual; ambosexual; bisexual; epicene
attracted to the (human) **a.** androphilic; anthropophilic; anthropophilous
centering or centered on: **a.** androcentric
diseases of (study): **n.** andrology
dominated by: **a.** androcentric; androcratic; **n.** androcracy
generative organ: **n.** membrum virile; penis; phallus; priapium; **a.** phallic; priapic
homosexual: **n.** uranist; urning; **n.** uranism
political and social supremacy of: **n.** androcracy
producing or tending to produce: **a.** androgenous
shape and appearance of: **a.** andromorphous; masculine; **n.** masculinity
worship of generative organ (as principle of nature): **n.** phallicism

MALIGN: **(see** "censure") **v.** calumniate; **a.** baneful; malevolent; malignant; pernicious; sinister

MALIGNANT: **(see** "poisonous") **a.** baleful; baneful; cancerous; injurious; lethal

MALNUTRITION: **n.** cachexia; cacotrophy; malnourishment; tabescence

MAN: **(see** "mankind" **and** "person") **n.** anthropoid; earthling; hominian; hominid; hominoid; *homo (sapiens)*; mortal; terrene; (**pl.** *hominidae*)
-about-town: **n.** *bon vivant;* boulevardier; flâneur; (**fem.** flâneuse)
attracted to: **a.** androphilic; anthropophilic; anthropophilous
centering on, or as center of all things: **a.** anthropocentric; **n.** anthropocentrism
chivalrous: **n.** cavalier; chevalier; **a.** cavalier
differs fr. everything else (theory): **n.** anthropocentrism; anthropopism
distribution of, study: **n.** anthropogeography; ethnogeography
effeminate: **n.** androgyn(e); hermaphrodite; **a.** androgynous; hermaphroditic(al)
state of being (effeminate): **n.** androgyneity; androgynism; androgyny; hermaphroditism
fall of, before the: **a.** prelapsarian
family of: **n.pl.** *anthropoidea; hominidae; homo sapiens*
fit: **n.** *idoneus homo*
hatred of: **n.** misandry; misanthropy; timonism
knowledge of nature of: **n.** anthroposophism; anthroposophy; **a.** anthroposophic(al)
learned: **see** "scholar"
little (dwarf): **n.** homunculus; (**pl.** homunculi)
mean or wicked: **n.** caitiff; Procrustean; Sadist
mechanical: **n.** android; automaton; golem; robot
melancholy or pensive: **n.** *il pensieroso*
newly-married: **n.** benedict
-of-all-work: **see** "jack-of-all-trades"
of dignity and aristocratic mien: **n.** *grand seigneur*
of fashion (or of the world): **n.** *homme du monde*
of intellect or wit: **n.** *homme d'esprit*
of iron: **n.** *un homme d'airain*
of letters: **see under** "person"
of straw: **n.** *homme de paille*
of the world: **see under** "world"
of worth: **n.** *homme de bien;* (**pl.** *gens de condition*)
pert. to: **a.** android; anthropic; anthropogenic; anthropoidal; anthropomorphic; masculine
prominent in his field: **n.** Brahmin; doyen; mogul; nabob; tycoon
resembling: **a.** anthropoid(al)
rich: **n.** *homme de fortune*

sociological study of: **n.** anthroposociology
study of distribution of: **n.** anthropogeography; ethnogeography
of origin and development of: **n.** anthropogenesis; anthropogeny; **a.** anthropogenetic
talented or gifted: **n.** man of parts
wise; **n.** Nestor; Solomon
worship or deification of: **n.** anthropolatry
wretched or unfortunate: **n.** caitiff
young: **n.** ephebe; yo(u)nker; **a.** ephebic

MANAGE: (**see** "control") **v.** administer; cultivate; direct; govern; husband; manipulate; negotiate; superintend; supervise; **n.** MANAGEABILITY: docility; manipulability; tractability; **a.** MANAGEABLE: (**see** "plastic" **and** "pliant") governable; tractable
easy to: **see** "easily managed"
hard to: (**see** "stubborn") **a.** intractable; obstinate; recalcitrant; refractory

MANAGEMENT: **n.** administration; cultivation; direction; dispensation; disposition; economy; government; husbandry; manipulation; negotiation; superintendence; supervision
good or thrifty: **n.** eutaxy; husbandry
prudent in: **a.** politic
skillful in: (**see** "expert") **a.** executive; tactical

MANAGER: **n.** administrant; administrator; comptroller; director; executive; gerent; impresario; manipulator; superintendent; supervisor; **a.** MANAGERIAL: administrative; supervisory
clever and skillful: **n.** tactician
of apartment or rooming house: **n.** concierge
pert. to duties of: **a.** administrative; managerial; supervisory

MANDATORY: **a.** coercive; compelling; compulsory; enforced; exigent; impelling; obligatory; prerequisite; **n.** coertion; compulsoriness; exigency

MANHOOD: **n.** adulthood; *âge viril;* majority; masculinity; maturity; potency
garment (toga) to symbolize: **n.** *toga virilis*
Jewish, attaining age 13, also rite: **n.** bar mitzvah

MANIA: (**see** "fear") **n.** cacoethes; delirium; frenzy; hysteria; **a.** delirious; hysterical; maniac(al)

MANIFESTATION(S): **see** "embodiment"
grotesque or bizarre: **see** "grotesque"

MANIFOLD: (**see** "many") **a.** abundant; complex; multifarious; multitudinous; numerous; replicate

MANIPULATED, *that which is to be:* **n.** manipulandum

MANIPULATION, *skillful feat of:* **n.** *passe-passe; prestidigitation; tour de force*

MANKIND: (**see** "man") **n.** *homo sapiens;* mortality; (**pl.** *anthropoidae; hominidae*)
hate or distrust of: **n.** misandry; misanthropism; misanthropy; timonism
hater of: **n.** misanthrope; misanthropist
study of, or pert. to: **a.** anthropology; **a.** anthropological

MANLY: (**see** "brave") **a.** masculine; puissant; virile; **n.** MANLINESS: arete; chivalry; gallantry; masculinity; potency; puissance
deeds, womanly words (motto of Md.): fatti maschii, parole femine

MANNER: **n.** bearing; demeanor; deportment; mien; ostent; posture; procedure; *quo modo*
easy: (**see** "easy") **n.** *un air aisé*
in a bad: **adv.** *malo modo;* **a.** maladroit
obliging: **n.** *prévenance*
of living: **n.** *modus vivendi*
of operating or working: **n.** *modus operandi*

MANNERISM: **n.** affectation; artificiality; eccentricity; foible; idiosyncrasy; preciosity; singularity; whimsicality

MANNERS: (**see** "courtesy") **n.** breeding; decorum; demeanor; etiquette; savoir-faire; suavity; urbanity; **n.pl.** mores
artificial or affected: **n.pl.** artificialities; histrionics; theatrics
censor of: **n.** *censor morum*
contrary to or against good: **adv.** *contra bonos mores;* **a.** *mal élevé(e)*
fine: **n. or a.** *bon ton; savoir-faire*
good: **n.** *savoir vivre*
group: **n.pl.** mores

guardian of: **n.** *censor morum; custos morum*
nice point of: **n.** punctilio; punctilious

MANUAL: (**see** "handbook") **n.** ench(e)iridion; *vade mecum*
of customs or usages: **n.** consuetudinary

MANURE: (**see** "dung") **n.** excrement; feculence; ordure; (**pl.** (d)ejecta; excreta; excrementa; feces)

MANY: (**see** "manifold" **and** "numerous") **a.** divers(e); multifarious; multifold; multiple(x); multiplicious; multitudinous; myriad; sundry; **n.** multeity; multifariousness; multiplicity; multitude; plurality
-colored: **a.** kaleidoscopic; multi-colored; prismatic
-sided: **a.** multifaceted; multilateral; multiphasic; multivarious; versatile; **n.** versatility
things, having power to do: **a.** multipotent
values, having: **a.** multivalent; multivalued; polyvalent

MAR: **see** "disfigure"

MARBLE, *of, like or pert. to:* **a.** marmoraceous; marmoreal

MARGINAL: **a.** circumferential; limitrophe; peripheral
note(s): **n.** annotation; apostil(le); postil; scholium; (**pl.** adersaria; marginalia; scholia)
to make: **v.** postil

MARK(S): **n.** characteristic; defacement; disfiguration; indication; scarification; stigma; (**pl.** differentia; stigmata); **v.** characterize; deface; disfigure; scarify; signalize; stigmatize; typify
bearing a: **a.** stigmatiferous
distinguishing: **n.** aura; cachet; earmark; hallmark; imprimatur; stigma; (**pl.** stigmata)
off: **v.** circumscribe; delimit; subtend
of shame or discredit: **n.** mark of the beast; stigma; (**pl.** stigmata)
time: **v.** temporize; **n.** temporization

MARRIAGE: **n.** conjugality; connubiality; espousal; matrimony; nuptials; wedlock
absence, nonregulation or nonrecognition of: **n.** agamy
after: **a.** post-nuptial
before: **a.** antenuptial; premarital
bet. persons unsuited: **n.** *mésalliance;* misalliance
bet. royal and commoner, wife and children not royal: **a.** or **n.** morganatic
hater or hatred of: **n.** misogamist; misogamy; **a.** misogamic
outside tribe, clan, etc.: **n.** exogamy; **a.** exogamous
pert. to: **a.** conjugial; connubial; epithalmic(al); hymeneal; marital; matrimonial; **n.** conjugality; connubality; matrimony
plural: **n.** bigamy; polyandry; polygamy; polygyny; **a.** bigamous; polandrous; polygamous; polygynous
rate: **n.** nuptiality
related by: **n.** affine
rules and conventions (laws) governing: **n.** *jus con(n)ubii*
second: **n.** deuterogamy; digamy; **a.** digamous
song or poem: **n.** epithalamion; epithalamium; hymenal
state: **n.** connubiality; matrimony
tie: **n.** *vinculum matrimonii*
to one hus. at a time: **n.** monandry; **a.** monandrous
to one person at a time: **n.** monogamy; **a.** monogamous
to one wife at a time: **n.** monogyny; **a.** monogynous
w/ one of lower status: **n.** *mésalliance;* misalliance
w/ one of other race: **n.** miscegenation
within tribe or group: **n.** endogamy; inmarriage; **a.** endogamic; endogamous
w/o tribe or group: **n.** exogamy; **a.** exogamic; exogamous

MARRIAGEABLE: **a.** nubile; **n.** nubility

MARRIED *man, esp. recently:* **n.** benedict
person, one newly: **n.** neogamist

MARSH(ES), *living or thriving in:* **a.** palustrine; uliginose
pert. to: **a.** fenny; paludal; paludous; palustral; uliginose

MARVEL: **n.** miracle; phenomenon; prodigy; (**pl.** mirabilia; phenomena); **a.** MARVELOUS: meritorious; mirific; transcendent; **adv.** *à merveille; magnifique*

MARY, *worship or veneration of:* **n.** hyperdulia; Mariolatry

MASCULINE: (see "male") **a.** android
characteristics, having (as in fem.): **a.** amazonian; android; gynandrous
having shape or appearance: **a.** andromorphous
interests, dominating or emphasizing: **a.** androcentric

MASCULINITY: see "manliness"
female: **n.** amazonism; defeminization
lacking vigorous: **a.** effeminate; epicene; feminine

MASKED: (see "disguised") **a.** cabalistic; cryptic; incognito; larvate(d); latent

MASS: **v.** agglomerate; agglutinate; aggregate; assemble; concentrate; conglomerate; muster; **n.** aggregate; agglutination; conglomeration; magnitude; ponderosity; spissitude
solidified: **n.** concretion; **a.** concretionary; **v.** concretize

MASSIVE: (see "huge") **a.** elephantine; monumental; substantial

MASTER: **v.** conquer; dominate; overawe; overcome; overpower; subdue; subjugate; vanquish; **n.** MASTERY: ascendency; command; dominion; subjugation; superiority
of ceremonies: **n.** ceremoniarius; compere; officiator
of one's own art or profession, also title for such: **n.** *cher maître;* virtuoso
of self: **n.** *compos sui*
one who is his own: **n.** *paterfamilias; (homo) sui juris;* **a.** *sui juris*
stroke: **n.** *coup de maître*

MASTERFUL: (see "arrogant" and "skillful") **a.** commanding; domineering; imperative; imperious; preemptory; sovereign

MASTERPIECE, *as art or lit.*: **n.** *chef d'oeuvre; magnus opus;* meisterwerk; *pièce de résistance*

MASTURBATION: **n.** autoeroti(ci)sm; onanism

MAT, *picture:* **n.** *passe partout*

MATCH: **v.** correspond; harmonize; **n.** counterpart

MATCHLESS: **a.** consummate; incommensurable; incomparable; inimitable; *ne plus supra; ne plus ultra;* peerless; (super)eminent; superlative; transcendent; unparalleled; **n.** incommensurability; incomparability; inimitability

MATE: see "companion"; **n.** MATED: see "coupled"

MATERIAL(S): **a.** corporeal; essential; important; mechanical; palpable; pertinent; physical; ponderable; relevant; sensible; substantial; tangible; **n.** corporeality; corporeity; materiality; physicality; substantiality; tangibility
array or store of: **n.** armamentarium; (pl. armamentaria; instrumentaria)
not: (see "immaterial") **a.** asomatous; impalpable; incorporeal; intangible; transcendent
thing: **n.** corporeality; materiality; *matériel;* (pl. corporeals; *res corporales; matériel*)

MATERIALISM: **n.** barbarism; Darwinism; evolution(ism); heterodoxy; Philistinism; physicism; pragmatism; utilitarianism; **n.** MATERIALIST: corporealist; Darwinist; evolutionist; heterodox; physicist; pragmatist; Sadducee; utilitarian

MATERIALISTIC: **a.** banausic; bourgeois; democritean; faustian; moneymaking; philistine; philistinic; physicalistic; pragmatic; utilitarian
doctrine or theory: **n.** physicism
world of the: **n.** Philistia

MATERIALIZE: **v.** hypostatize; reify; **n.** MATERIALIZATION; hypostatization; reification

MATHEMATICS, *love(r) of:* **n.** philomath; philomathy; **a.** philomathic(al)

MATRIMONY: see "marriage"
bonds of: **n.** *vinculum matrimonii*

MATTED: **a.** cespitose

MATTER: (see "material") **n.** corporality; materiality; substance; substantiality
in heart or substance of the: **adv.** *in medias res*
it's no: **n.** *n'importe*
-of-fact: (see "prosaic") **a.** literal; *terre à terre;* utilitarian; **n.** literality;

practicality; prosaism; pragmatism; utilitarianism
small: **n.** *peu de chose*

MATURE: (**see** "adult" **and** "develop") **v.** maturate; **n.** MATURITY: adultness; maturation

MAXIM: (**see** "witticism") **n.** adage; aphorism; apothegm; axiom; dictum; epigram; gnome; logion; sententia; **a.** aphoristic; apothegmatic(al); gnomic(al); sentential

MAXIMUM: **see** "greatest"

MAZE: **n.** conglomeration; convolution; intricacy; labyrinth; maelstrom; perplexity; sinuosity
like: **a.** daedalian; daedal(ic); labyrinthine

MEAGER: **a.** exigous; infinitesimal; **n.** MEAGERNESS: dearth; exiguity; famine; parcity; paucity; squalor; stringency

MEAL: **n.** collation; repast; tiffin
after: **a.** postcibal; postprandial
before: **a.** precibal; preprandial
complete w/ fixed price: **a.** or **n.** *table d'hôte*
each item at separate price: **a.** or **n.** *à la carte*
light: **n.** collation; tiffin
main dish of: **n.** *entree; pièce de résistance; plat de résistance*
rel. to: **a.** cibarian; prandial
side dish(es) of: **n.** entremet(s)
-time: **n.** *heure du repas*

MEAN: **v.** connote; denote; import; signify; **a.** (**see** "wicked") contemptible; despicable; intermediary; intermediate; reptilian; **n.** average; intermediary
golden: **n.** *ariston metron; aurea mediocritas; juste-milieu*
person: **n.** Beelzebub; caitiff; procrustean; sadist

MEANING(S): **n.** acceptation; connotation; denotation; drift; gist; import; interpretation; purport; significance; signification; tenor; understanding
expressing complete substantive: **a.** categorematic
not: **a.** syncategorematic
having but one: **a.** or **n.** univocal
having many: **a.** polysemous; **n.** polysemy
generally accepted, as of word: **n.** acceptation
identity of: **n.** synonymity; **a.** synonymous
implied but not expressed: **n.** subaudition; subintelligitur; **a.** tacit
looseness of: **n.** ambiguity; **a.** ambiguous
of double or doubtful: **a.** ambiguous; amphibolic(al); amphibolous; equivocal; **n.** ambiguity; amphibologism; amphibology; equivoque
of similar or same; **n.** synonym; **a.** synonymic; synonymous
symbolic, or underlying theme: **n.** mythos; (**pl.** mythoi)

MEANINGFUL: **a.** definitive; expressive; knowledg(e)able; pregnant; sententious; significant

MEANINGLESS: (**see** "purposeless") **a.** aimless
talk: **n.** balderdash; Choctaw; flummery; galimatias; gibberish

MEANNESS: (**see** "wickedness") **n.** despicability; duplicity; knavery; parvanimity; rascality; **a.** despicable; duplicitous; parvanimitous

MEANS: **n.** channel; instrument(ality); instrumentation; intermediary; medium; *modus operandi; quo modo;* resources; vehicle; wherewithal

MEANTIME (or MEANWHILE): **n.** interim; interval
for or in the: **adv.** *ad hoc; ad interim*

MEASURE: **n.** amplitude; barometer; capacity; coefficient; criterion; (**pl.** criteria); indication; magnitude; thermometer; touchstone; yardstick
beyond: **adv.** *abundantly; à outrance;* excessively
in things, there is: est modus in rebus

MEASURED: **a.** calculated; deliberate; limited; rhythmical
capable of being: **a.** commensurable; finite; measurable; mensural; mensurative; ponderable; quantitative
not capable of being: **a.** imponderable; incommensurable; unfathomable; **n.** incommensurability

MEASURELESS: **see** "boundless"

MEASURING, *act of or pert. to:* **n.** mensuration; **a.** mensurable; mensural; mensurative

MECHANICAL: **a.** automatic; automatous; autonomic; inhuman; involuntary; perfunctorious; perfunctory; stereotyped; **n.** automaticity; mechanicality; **n.** MECHANIC; artisan; mechanician
man, or one who acts or thinks as: **n.** android; automaton; golem; robot
to make: **v.** automatize; dehumanize; mechanize; robotize; **n.** automation; automatism; dehumanization; mechanization; robotization

MEDDLE: **(see** "interfere") **v.** interlope; interpose; intervene; intrude; obtrude; tamper; **n.** MEDDLER: **(see** "busybody") interloper; intervenient; Meddlesome Mattie; quidnunc; **a.** MEDDLESOME (or MEDDLING): impertinent; intrusive; officious; (poly)pragmatic(al); **n.** MEDDLESOMENESS: impertinence; impudicity; intrusiveness; polypragmatism

MEDIATE: **see** "interpose"; **n.** MEDIATOR: arbitrator; conciliator; intercessor; intermediary; intervenient; placator

MEDICAL: **a.** Aesculapian; iatric(al)
instruments, equipment, etc.: **n.pl.** armamentaria; instrumentaria
practitioner: **n.** Aescalapius; physician; therapist
treatment: **n.** iatrics; medicament; medicant; medication; therapeusis; therapeutant; therapeutics; therapy

MEDICINE(S): **n.** medicament; medicant; medication; pharmaceutical; simple; specific; therapeusis; therapeutant; therapeutic; (**pl.** *materia medica*)
disease caused by, or by med. treatment: **a.** iatrogenic; medicamentous
false, or to please patient: **n.** placebo
favorite or quack: **n.** nostrum; panacea
pert. to: **a.** Aesculapian; iatric(al); medicative; medicinal; pharmaceutic(al); therapeutic(al); theriac(al)
science or art of: **n.** iatrics; iatrology; pharmaceutics; therapeutics

MEDICINAL: **a.** medicative; medicinable; pharmaceutic(al); salutary; sanative; salutiferous; therapeutic(al); theriac(al)

MEDIOCRE: **see** "ordinary"

MEDITATE: **v.** consider; contemplate; deliberate; (ex)cogitate; lucubrate; ponder; reflect; **n.** MEDITATION: cerebration; cogitation; contemplation; lucubration; reflection; rumination; **a.** MEDITATIVE: **(see** "reflective") apollonian; apollonic; apollonistic; cogitable; cogitabund; cogitative; contemplative; deliberative; nomothetic; pensive; purposeful

MEDLEY: **n.** brouhaha; charivari; farrago; fatras; heterogeneity; hodgepodge; *macédoine; mélange;* miscellany; olla podrida; olio; omnium-gatherum; pastiche; potpourri; salmagundi; *tripotage*
of confused sounds: **n.** Babelism; brouhaha; gallimaufry; pasticcio; pastiche
of familiar tunes: **n.** fantasia

MEEK: **a.** forbearing; humble; invertebrate; phlegmatic; placid; submissive; unpretentious; **n.** MEEKNESS: abnegation; forbearance; humbleness; humility; mansuetude; submission; submissiveness

MEET: **v.** assemble; confront; congregate; decussate; encounter; intersect; fulfill; satisfy
casually: **v.** rencounter

MEETING: **n.** amalgamation; assemblage; assembly; collocation; concourse; concursion; confluence; conflux; confrontation; congregation; congress; convention; convergence; conversazione; convocation; decussation; encounter; intersection; junction; juncture; rendezvous; tryst
for exchange of ideas; **n.** symposium
hostile: **n.** rencounter; rencontre
minimum to conduct: **n.** quorum
place; or secret: **n.** concourse; *point de réunion;* rendezvous; tryst
private or secret: **see under** "secret"

MELANCHOLY: (see "sad") **a.** atrabilarious; atrabiliar; atrabilious; dispirited; hypochondriacal; **n.** MELANCHOLY (or MELANCHOLIA) apanthropia; apanthropy; doldrums; hypochonaria(sis); lachrymals; megrims
person: **n.** atrabilarian; hypochondriac; melancholiac; valetudinarian
to make, depict as or indulge in: **v.** melancholize

MELLOW(ED): **a.** classic; matured; orotund; resonant; sonorous; **n.** orotundity; sonority

MELODIOUS: **a.** ariose; canorous; cantabile; dulcet; euphonious; lyric(al); mellifluous; melodic; orphic; sirenic(al); sonorous; symphonous; symphonizing; unisonant
"nonsense": **n.** *nugae canorae*

MELODY: **n.** descant; diapason; euphony; harmonization; harmony; lyric; orchestration; sonority; symphony; syncopation
art of inventing: **n.** melopoeia; **a.** melopoe(t)ic
consisting of or rel. to two or more: **a.** contrapuntal; polyphonic; polyphonous; polyrhythmic
having a single: **a.** monophonic; monophonous
single dominant or prevailing: **n.** leitmotif; leitmotiv

MELT: (**see** "dissolve") **v.** ablate; deliquesce; disintegrate; dissipate; liquefy; **a.** MELTING: deliquescent; liquescent; **n.** deliquescence; liquefaction

MEMBERS, *attended by all:* **n.** plenum; quorum; **a.** plenary

MEMBRANE, *pass thru:* **v.** osmose; transude; **n.** osmosis; transudate; transudation

MEMORANDUM: (**see** "reminder") **n.** *aide-memoire;* (**pl.** *aides-memoire*); memento; memoir
preliminary: **n.** protocol

MEMORIAL: **n.** cenotaph; commemoration; memento; monument; plaque; trophy

MEMORY: **n.** recollection; reminiscence; retrospection; **a.** reminiscent(ial)
aid to: (**see** "memorandum"): **n.** *aide-memoire;* (**pl.** *aides-memoire*); *memoria technica;* **a.** mnemonic; **n.** mnemonics
from: **adv.** *ex capite*
gap in: **n.** amnesia; **a.** amnesic
goddess of: **n.** Mnemosyne
helping: **a.** mnemonic
increased or exceptionally keen: **n.** hypermnesia
lack or loss of: **n.** amnesia; **a.** amnesic
lapse or slip of: **n.** *lapsus memoriae;* parapraxia; parapraxis
of blessed: **adv.** *beatae memoriae*
pert. to, helping or meant to help: **a.** mnemonic
science of, or art of improving: **n.** mnemonics
weak: **n.** *mémoire débile*

MEN: **see** "man"
business: **n.pl.** *gens d'affaires; hommes d'affaires*
group of best: **n.** *corps d'elite*
hatred of: **n.** misandry; misanthropy; timonism
military: **n.pl.** *gens de guerre*
of lesser merit: **n.pl.** *di minores*
of letters: **n.pl.** *gens de lettres; hommes de lettres; literati*
of outstanding merit (eminent): **n.pl.** *di majores*

MENACE: **v.** jeopardize; **n.** anathema; commination; charybdis; jeopardy; minacity; sword of Damocles; **a.** MENACING: (**see** "dangerous") imminent; minacious; minatorial; ominous

MENSTRUATION: **n.** catamenia; menorrhea; menses
absence of, or abnormal stoppage: **n.** amenorrhea
end of ("change of life") **n.** menopause; **a.** menopausal
onset or beg. of (at puberty): **n.** menarche; **a.** menarcheal; menarchial
painful: **n.** dysmenorrhea
previous to onset: **n.** premenarche; **a.** premenarcheal; premenstrual
profuse: **n.** menorrhagia

MENTAL: **a.** appercipient; cerebral; ideological; intellectual; metaphysical; noological; phrenic; psychic(al); psychologic(al); subjective
aberration: **n.** deliration; delirium; delusion; hallucination; hallucinosis; illusion; mania; psychosis
activity: **see** "thought"
modified by: **a.** ideoplastic
confusion or impairment: (**see** "aberration" **above**) **n.** dementia; obnubilation; psychosis
deficiency: **n.** amentia; aphronia; cretinism; feeblemindedness; idiocy; imbecility; moronity; oligophrenia; **a.** cretinous; moronic; oligophrenic
derangement: (**see** "aberration" **above**) **n.** *alienation mentale;* (**or.** *d'esprit*)
deterioration: **n.** dementia
disorder: **n.** aberration; alienation; dementia; psychosis; **a.** psychotic

impression: **n.** conception; **a.** conceptual; concipient

pain or distress: **n.** dysphoria; psychalgia

perception: **n.** apperception; prehension; **a.** apperceptionistic

distorted: **n.** astigmatism; myopia; **a.** astigmatic(al); myopic

phenomena, of or rel. to: **a.** mentalistic; psychological

study of: **n.** noology; psychology; (**pl.** psychostatics); **a.** noological; psychological

study of abnormal: **n.** psychiatry; **a.** psychiatric

reservation: **n.** *arrière pensée*

MENTALITY, *lack of:* (**see** "mental deficiency") **n.** amentia; cretinism; dementia; moronity

loss of: **n.** dementia; psychosis

MENTALLY *competent:* (**see** "legally competent" **and** "sane") **a.** capax; *compos mentis*

defective but brilliant or apt in some special field: **n.** *idiot savant*

incompetent or deficient: **a.** amental; cretinous; demented; *doli incapax;* incapacious; *non compos (mentis)*; psychotic

slow: **see** "slow-witted"

MENTOR: (**see** "guide") **n.** cicerone; counsellor; preceptor; tutor

MENU: **n.** *carte du jour;* dietary; regimen

MERCENARY: **n.** condottiere; Hessian; hireling; janissary; Myrmidon; pensionary; **a.** avaricious; commercial; mercantile; venal

MERCY: (**see** "charity") **n.** benignity; clemency; commiseration; compassion; lenity; toleration; **a.** MERCIFUL: (**see** "tender") clement; compassionate; forbearing; indulgent; lenient; sympathetic; tolerant; warm-hearted; **a.** MERCILESS: austere; barbarous; disputatious; imperative; implacable; inclement; inexorable; inquisitorial; intolerant; Neronian; obdurate; pitiless; relentless; remorseless; unfeeling; unsympathetic; **adv.** *avec archarnement; sans merci*

killing: **n.** euthanasia

MERGER: (**see** "union") **n.** absorption; alliance; amalgamation; coadunation; coalescence; coalition; concursion; confluence; fusion; osmosis; **a.** MERGING: amalgamative; coalescent; confluent; osmotic

MERIT: **n.** commendableness; eminence; estimableness; exemplarity; prestige

having: (**see** "meritorious") **a.** eminent; estimable; prestigious

having no (merit) or demerit: **a.** adiaphorous; **n.** adiaphoron

of lesser, persons of: **n.** *di minores*

of outstanding, persons of: **n.** *di majores*

MERITED: **a.** condign; warranted; **a.** MERITORIOUS: commendable; commendatory; creditable; eminent; estimable; exemplary; praiseworthy; prestigious

MERRY: **a.** blithe(some); carnivalesque; debonair; exuberant; exultant; festive; frolicsome; genial; hilarious; jaunty; jocund; jovial; joyous; mirthful; sportive; **n.** MERRIMENT: exuberance; exultation; festivity; geniality; hilarity; jocularity; jocundity; joviality; jubilation; sportiveness

MERRYMAKING, *wild and riotous:* **n.** carousal; orgy; **a.** carnivalesque; orgiastic

MESS: (**see** "mixture") **n.** conglomeration; heterogeneity; hodgepodge

MESSAGE(S), *code:* **n.** cryptogram

serving as conveyor of: **a.** internuncial; internunciary

MESSENGER: (**see** "forerunner") **n.** apostle; harbinger; herald; internuncio

MESSMATE: **a.** or **n.** commensal; **n.** commensality

METAPHOR(S): **n.** allegory; anagoge; metonymy; synecdoche; trope; **v.** allegorize; metaphorize

faulty or mixed use of: **n.** catachresis; **a.** catachrestic(al)

METAPHYSICAL: (**see** "supernatural") **a.** extraphysical; preternatural; stratospheric(al)

METHOD(S): (**see** "procedure") **n.** approach; discipline; *métier; modus operandi;* technique

lacking in: **(see** "disordered") **a.** immethodical
of doing things: **n.** expertise; methodology; *modus operandi;* technique; virtuosity
temporary: **n.** *modus vivendi*

METHODICAL: **see** "orderly"

METRICAL *accent:* **n.** cadence; ictus

MIDDAY *meal:* **n.** tiffin
rel. to: **a.** meridian

MIDDLE: **see** "center"
aged: **adv.** *entre deux âges;* **a.** *d'âge moyen*
ages: **n. or a.** medieval; *moyen-age*
class: **n.** bourgeois(ie)
course: **see** "way" **below**
ground: **(see** "way" **below) n.** limbo
-man: **n.** entrepreneur; **(fem.** entrepreneuse); (inter)mediary; intervenient
of action; or in midst of things: **adv.** *in media(s) res*
-of-the-road, person of: **n.** centrist; moderant; moderate
position: **(see** "intermediate") **a.** mesothetic
put in the: **v.** mediatize
way: **n.** *ariston metron; aurea mediocritas;* golden mean; *juste milieu; mezzo termine; tertium quid; via media*

MIDDLING: **see** "so-so"

MID-MORNING: **a. or n.** antemeridian

"MIDNIGHT OIL," *burn the:* **v.** lucubrate; **n.** lucubration

MIDST: **see** "middle"

MIGHT: **(see** "power") **n.** capacity; potency; puissance; resources
w/ all one's: **adv.** *à tout force; manibus pedibusque; totis viribus*

MIGHTY: **(see** "powerful") **a.** efficacious; efficient; extraordinary; Herculean; invincible; momentous; (omni)potent; puissant; Samsonian
in battle or arms: **a.** armipotent

MIGRATION: **n.** diaspora; hegira; **a.** MIGRATORY: nomadic

MILD: **(see** "peaceful") **a.** amiable; assuasive; clement; compassionate; complaisant; considerate; favonian; lenient; lenitive; temperate; tepid; tolerant; tranquil; **n.** MILDNESS: benignity; clemency; compassion; consideration; lenity; tranquility
make or become: **v.** mitigate; mollify; palliate; placate; tranquilize; **a.** mitigatory; palliative; palliatory; placative; placatory

MILITARY *expert:* **n.** Clauzewitz; **a.** Clauzewitzian
government: **n.** stratocracy
pert. to the: **a.** martial
supplies or equipment: **n.pl.** armentaria; armaments; impedimenta; *matériel;* **n.** armamentarium

MILK, *excessive secretion of:* **n.** polygalactia
feeding on: **a.** galactophagous; lactivorous
secretion of: **n.** lactation; **n.** lactescent
yielding or conveying: **a.** galactophorous; lactiferous

MILKY: **a.** lacteous; lactescent; opalescent; **n.** MILKINESS: lactescence; opalescence

MIMICRY: **n.** caricature; imitation; impersonation; mimesis; mimetism; **a.** echoic; mimetic; mimical; onomatopoe(t)ic

MIND(S): **n.** cerebrum; consciousness; faculty; intellect; intelligence; mentality; nous; psyche; rationality; reason; sensorium; sentiment; understanding
absence of: **(see** "absent-mindedness") **n.** *absence d'esprit;* amentia
action of: **(see** "thought") **n.** cerebration; lucubration; mentation
confused or impaired state of: **n.** dementia; obnubilation; psychosis
diversion fr. reality: **n.** escapism; identification
existing in the: **a.** endopsychic; psychogen(et)ic; psychosomatic; **n.** *ens rationalis;* psychogenesis
impress on the: **v.** inculcate; indoctrinate
keenness of : **n.** acumen; discernment; discrimination; perspicacity; perspicuity; shrewdness
little, are caught w/ trifles: parva leves capiunt animas
of or rel. to one's own: **a.** autopsychic
peace of: **see** "contentment"
pert. or rel. to: **(see** "mental") **a.** cere-

bral; intellectual; noological; psychologic(al)
pleasing or acceptable to: **a.** palatable
-reading: **n.** clairvoyance; telepathy; **a.** clairvoyant; telepathic
smallness of: **n.** parvanimity; **a.** lilliputian; parvanimitous
sound: **n.** competent; *compos (mentis)*; **n.** competency
sound in sound body: mens sana in corpore sano
study of: **n.** noology; psychiatry; psychology
unsound: **n.** *non compos (mentis)*
weak of: **n. or adv.** *impos animi*
with an equal: **adv.** *aequo animo*
with calmness of: **adv.** *aequo animo;* **n.** equanimity; sophrosyne
with one: **(see** "unanimous") **adv.** *uno animo*

MINE, *rich:* **n.** bonanza; El Dorado

MINERALS, *study of:* **n.** mineralogy; oryctology; **n.** mineralogist; oryctologist

MINGLE: **v.** amalgamate; concoct; confuse; conglomerate; infiltrate; integrate; interlard; interpolate; intertwine

MINIATURE: **a. or n.** diminutive; lilliputian; **n.** epitome
in: **adv.** *en petit; in parvo; in petto*
universe or any large unit: **n.** microcosm; **a.** microcosmic

MINOR: **see** "age, under legal" **and** "secondary"

MINUTE: **see** "small"
(be) up to the: **adv.** (be) *à la page*

MIRACLE(S): **n.** anomy; **(pl.** mirabilia); **a.** miraculous
narrative of those of god or hero: **n.** aretalogy
performance of: **n.** thaumaturgy
performer of: **n.** thaumaturgus; **(n.pl.** thaumaturgi)
pert. to: **a.** thaumaturgic(al)
study or lore of: **n.** thaumatology
worker: **n.** thaumaturge; thaumaturgus; **a.** thaumaturgic(al)

MIRAGE: **(see** "deception") **n.** corposant; *deceptio visus; fata morgana;* St. Elmo's fire

MIRROR(S), *pert. to:* **a.** catoptric(al); specular
study or science of: **n.** catoptrics

MIRTH: **see** "joy"

MISAPPLY: **v.** defalcate; embezzle; misappropriate; **n.** MISAPPLICATION: defalcation; embezzlement; malfeasance; misfeasance; subtraction

MISBEHAVIOR: **(see** "misconduct") **n.** delinquency; malbehavior; malconduct

MISBELIEF: **n.** miscreance

MISCELLANEOUS: **a.** assorted; heterogeneous; hodge-podge; indiscriminate; promiscuous; **n.** MISCELLANY: **(see** "medley") bric-a-brac; heterogeneity; hodge-podge; olla podrida; *omnium gatherum;* **(pl.** miscellanea; varia)
collection, as notes, etc.: **n.pl.** adversaria; collectanea; *disjecta membra;* miscellanea
quality or state of being: **n.** miscellaneity

MISCHANCE: **n.** calamity; catastrophe; contretemps; misadventure; misfortune; mishap

MISCHIEF: **n.** diablerie; hanky-panky; hocus-pocus; impishness; mischievousness
source of great: **n.** Pandora's box

MISCHIEVOUS: **a.** impish; injurious; malevolent; roguish; venomous
antic(s): **n.** escapade; harlequinade; ploy
conduct or manner: **n.** diablerie; impishness

MISCONCEPTION: **n.** delusion; hallucination; illusion; misapprehension; misinterpretation

MISCONDUCT: **n.** beastliness; bestiality; delinquency; malbehavior; malconduct; misbehavior; sociopathy
in office: **n.** defalcation; malfeasance; misfeasance; **a.** malfeasant
one guilty of: **n.** delinquent; malfeasor; misdemeanant; misfeasor

MISDEED: **(see** "offense") **n.** defaction; defalcation; delinquency; felony; malfeasance; misdemeanor; misfeasance

MISERABLE: **a.** contemptible; discreditable; shameful; worthless; wretched
act of making or state of becoming: **n.** immiserization

MISERLY: (**see** "stingy") **a.** acquisitive; avaricious; churlish; covetous; extortionate; frugal; penny-pinching; penurious
person: **n.** curmudgeon; Scrooge

MISERY: **see** "agony"
acute: **n.** purgatory
causing: **a.** afflictive
expression of: **n.** *de profundis*
place of great: **n.** Gethsemane; purgatory

MISFORTUNE: **n.** adversity; bereavement; calamity; catastrophe; holocaust; misadventure; mishap; tribulation; visitation; **a. see** "unfortunate"
great or sudden: **n.** *angoisse;* calamity; catastrophe; holocaust; **a.** calamitous; catastrophic(al)
never comes alone: nullium infortunium solum
prophetess of: **n.** Cassandra; **a.** Cassandr(i)an

MISHAP: (**see** "accident") **n.** contretemps

MISLEADING: (**see** "deceptive") **a.** ambiguous; ambivalent; delusional; delusionary; delusive; equivocal; factitious; illusive; **v.** MISLEAD: (**see** "deceive") bamboozle; defraud; delude; equivocate; victimize
ideal: **n.** *ignis fatuus;* will-of-the-wisp

MISREPRESENTATION: **see** "falsehood" **and** "falseness"

MIST: **n.** brume; nebula; obscurity; **a.** MISTY: brumous; caliginous; crepuscular; nubilous; vaporific; vaporish; vaporous; volatile

MISTAKE: (**see** "fault" **and** "error") **n.** erratum; fallacy; inadvertence; inadvertency; misapprehension; misconception; misperception; misprision; misunderstanding; oversight; **a.** MISTAKEN: **see** "erroneous"
grammatical or social: **see under** "error"

MISTRESS: **n.** amour; inamorata; paramour
of house: **n.** chatelaine; materfamilas; matriarch; matron

MISUNDERSTANDING: **n.** *brouillerie;* disagreement; dissention; imbroglio; malentendu; misapprehension; misinterpretation; misperception; misprision; **v.** MISUNDERSTAND: misapprehend; misinterpret; **a.** MISUNDERSTOOD: malentendu; misapprehended; misinterpreted

MISUSE: **v.** defalcate; embezzle; misappropriate; misapply; **n.** defalcation; embezzlement; misapplication; misappropriation

MIXED: **a.** amalgamated; amalgamative; farraginous; hyphenated; macaronic; **v.** MIX: amalgmate; coalesce; commingle; conglomerate; interfuse; interlard; intermingle; levigate; triturate
capable of being: **a.** miscible; **n.** miscibility
not: **a.** immiscible; incommiscible
origin, race, varieties, etc.: **n.** heterogeneity; hybrid(ization); **a.** heterogeneous; hybrid; **v.** hybridize
use of metaphors: **n.** catachresis; **a.** catachrestic(al)

MIXTURE: **n.** amalgam(ation); commingling; concoction; confection; conglomeration; farrago; gallimaufry; heterogeneity; hodgepodge; hyphenation; medley; miscellanea; miscellaneity; miscellany; pastiche; potpourri; salmagundi; smorgasbord; tagraggery
confused: **n.** farrago
of elements, ideas, peoples, etc.: **n.** amalgam(ation); heterogeneity; tagraggery
of race(s): **n.** miscegenation
produced by or constructed from: **n.** or **a.** hybrid; mongrel

MOANING: **a.** plangorous

MOB: (**see** "gang") **n.** canaille; claque; clique; riffraff; varletry
govt. or rule by: **n.** mobocracy; ochlocracy; **a.** mobocratic; ochlocratic

MOCKERY: **n.** asteism; badinage; burlesque; caricature; counterfeit; derision; futility; imitation; mimesis; mimicry; parody; persiflage; raillery; ridicule; sarcasm; satire
a deplorable: **n.** *flebile ludibrium*

MODE: **see** "method"

MODEL: **n.** archetype; *beau idéal;* ectype; exemplar; exemplum; mannequin; man(n)ikin; matrix; microcosm; paradigm; paragon; prototype; replica; **a.** (**see** "exemplary") archetyp(ic)al
of human, as for anatomy class: **n.** anthropomorph; homunculus; man(n)ikin
pert. to: **a.** archetypal; ectypal; exemplar; paradigmatic; prototypal
quality or state of being: **n.** exemplarity
use in primitive magic: **n.** *evoûtement*

MODERATE(S): (**see** "ease") **v.** mitigate; mollify; restrain; temper; tranquilize; **a.** (**see** "calm") mitigatory; modest; prudent; reasonable; **adv.** *allegretto; non troppo*
in eating, drinking, etc.: **a.** abstemious; abstentious; continent; temperate
one who is: **n.** centrist; moderant; moderate
something that (moderates): **n.** moderant; tranquilizer

MODERATION: (**see** "prudence") **n.** abstention; abstinence; continence; discretion; golden mean; moderateness; restraint; temperance
is best: ariston metron
wise: **n.** prudence; sophrosyne

MODERN: **a.** *au courant;* contemporary; *dernier cri; fin-de-siècle; moderne;* modernistic; neoteric; progressive; topical; **n.** MODERNITY: modernness; topicality
person or writer: **n.** *moderne;* neoteric
state of being: **n.** modernity
tastelessly or pretentiously: **a.** *moderne*

MODESTY: **n.** demurity; diffidence; maidenliness; pudency; pudibundity; pudicity; verecundity; **a.** MODEST: chaste; decorous; demure; diffident; humble; moderate; unassuming; unboastful; unobtrusive; unostentatious; unpresuming; unpretentious; verecund; virginal; virtuous
appeal(ing) to: **adv.** *ad verecundiam*
exaggerated or excessive: **n.** decorousness; priggishness; prudery; pudency; pudibundity; pudicity; **a.** priggish; prudish; pudibund
false: **n.** *malus pudor*

MODIFY: **see** "alter"

MODULATED, *capable of being:* **a.** modificatory; modulatory; **n.** modulability

MOISTURE (or MOISTNESS) **n.** aquosity; humectation; humidity; **a.** MOIST: aqueous; hydrogenous
capable of taking up: **a.** bibitory
induced by or absorbed fr. air: **a.** hygroscopic

MOLD: (**see** "model") **n.** matrix

MOLDED, *capable of being:* **see** "pliant"

MOLT (or MOULT): **v.** deplumate; exfoliate; exuviate; **n.** deplumation; ecdysis; **a.** deciduous; deplumate; exfoliative

MOLTEN *rock:* **n.** magma

MOMENT: **n.** consequence; consideration; instant; weight
at the: **adv.** *in articulo*
at the opportune: (**see** "timely") **adv.** *dextro tempore*

MOMENTARY: (**see** "fleeting") **a.** ephemeral; evanescent; instantaneous; semelfactive; transient; transitory; **n.** MOMENTARINESS: ephemerality; instantaneity

MOMENTOUS: **a.** consequential; crucial; epochal; memorable; paramount; prominent; signal; weighty

MONASTERY, *occupant of:* **n.** cenobite; **a.** cenobitic; **n.** cenobitism

MONETARY: **a.** financial; numismatic(al); nummary; pecuniary; quaestuary; sumptuary

MONEY, *appeal(ing) to:* **n.** or **adv.** *(argumentum) ad crumenam*
as evil, or personified: **n.** mammon
devoted to getting: **a.** mammonish; **n.** mammonism; mammonist; mammonite
devotion to or worship of: **n.** *amor nummi;* mammonism; plutolatry; plutomania
excessive regard for: **n.** fiscality
having none: (**see** "poor") **a.** impecunious; indigent; **n.** impecuniosity; indigence
large sum of: **n.** king's ransom
love of: **n.** *amor nummi;* mammonism; plutolatry; plutomania
motivated only by: **a.** commercial(istic); mercantile; mercenary; quaestuary; venal; **n.** commerciality; venality

pert. to control of: **a.** financial; fiscal; sumptuary
pert. to or involving: **a.** financial; fiscal; monetary; numismatic(al); nummary; nummulary; pecuniary; quaestuary; sumptuary; **n.** commerciality
ready: **n.** *argent comptant*
worship of: **n.** plutolatry; plutomania

MONK: **n.** cenobite; monastic; **a.** cenobitic; solitudinarian

MONKEY (**or** APE): **n.** anthropoid; primate; simian; **a.** anthropoidal; simian; simious; **n.** simianity

MONOTONOUS: (**see** "dull") **a.** banal; stereotyped; stereotypical; **n.** MONOTONY: (**see** "dullness") prosaism

MONSTER: **n.** behemoth; fiend; Frankenstein; leviathan; monstrosity
fabulous: **n.** chimera; dragon; gorgon; ogre; phoenix; sphinx

MONSTROUS: (**see** "huge") **a.** atrocious; Caliban; grotesque; heinous; hideous; prodigious

MONTH(S), *by the:* **adv.** *per mensam*
lasting two: **a.** bimestral
pert. to: **a.** mensual
six: **n.** semester; **a.** semestral

MOOD: **n.** disposition; inclination; proclivity; temper(ament)
in bad: **see** "irritable"
of scornful distaste: **n.** fastidium; squeamishness; **a.** fastigial

MOODINESS: (**see** "sullenness") **n.** hypochondriasis; melancholia; melancholy; (**pl.** doldrums; megrims); **a.** MOODY: ambivalent; hypochondriacal; melancholic; temperamental

MOON, *full or at time of full:* **a.** plenilune
goddess of: **n.** Artemis; Astarte; Diana; Luna
study of: **n.** selenology
supposed inhabitant of: **n.** lunarian

MORAL(S): **n.** allegory; apologue; ethics; mores; (the) moralities; **a.** allegorical; didactic; righteous; tropological; virtuous
against good: **adv.** *contra bonos mores*
censor of: **n.** *censor morum*
false application of reasoning about: **n.** casuistry; **a.** casuistic
guardian of: **n.** *custos morum*
having no (moral) merit or demerit: **a.** adiaphoristic; adiaphorous; **n.** adiaphorism; adiaphoron; **n.** adiaphorist
law: **n.** dharma
obligation or command: **n.** categorical imperative
obligation, study of: **n.** deontology
outside bounds of: **a.** amoral; immoral; **n.** amorality; immorality
persons who profess strict: **n.** (the) *unco guid*
strictness of: **n.** piosity; precisian; rigorism; sabbatarian; **a.** puritanic(al); sabbatarian
to lower: **v.** debauch; **n.** debauchment; **n.** debaucher
trend or spirit of the time: **n.** zeitgeist
w/o (moral) sensibility, as infants: **n.** or **a.** amoral

MORALISTIC: **a.** admonishing; didactic(al); sabbatarian; sermonic; **v.** MORALIZE: admonish; lecture; sermonize

MORALLY *contaminating:* **a.** scrofulous; **n.** scrofulosis
corrupt or unrestrained: (**see** "lewd") **a.** dissolute; lecherous; libertine; licentious; profligate; scrofulous
degrading, that which is: **n.** ordure
strict: **a.** puritanical; rectitudinous; sabbatarian; **n.** piosity; probity; propriety; rectitude; scrupulosity
those who profess to be: **n.** (the) *unco guid*
weak or unwholesome: **a.** maladive; scrofulous; **n.** scrofulosis

MORBID: (**see** "diseased") **a.** cachectic; cadaverous; grisly; gruesome; maladive; morbose; scrofulous; **n.** MORBIDITY: cachexia

MORNING: **n.** *ante meridiem;* matin
pert. to: **a.** antemeridian; matinal; matutinal

MOROSE: **see** "gloomy"

MORSEL: **see** "delicacy"

MORTAL: **see** "man" **and** "perishable"

MORTGAGE: **n.** hypothecation; **v.** hypothecate; impignorate

MOSAIC: **see** "variegated" **and** "variegation"

MOTHER: **n.** ancestress; genetrix; (**pl.** genetrices); mater; **a.** maternal(istic); **n.** MOTHERHOOD: maternity
centering on: **a.** matricentric
derived or inherited fr. side of: **a.** matroclinal; matroclinic; matroclinous
killing of, also killer: **n.** matricide; **a.** matricidal
lineage based on or thru: **n.** matrilineage; **a.** matrilineal; matrilinear
marked by authority of: **a.** matripotestal
of the family: **n.** materfamilias; matriarch; **a.** matriarchal
rel. to or to side of family: **a.** maternal(istic); matrilateral; matrilinean; matrilinear; **n.** maternity; matrilineage
ruler of family or clan: **n.** materfamilias; matriarch(ate); matriarchy; **a.** matriarchal; matriarchic

MOTION, *by one's own:* **adv.** *motu proprio; proprio motu; proprio vigore*
constantly in: **a.** volitant; **n.** volitation
loss of voluntary: **n.** catalepsy; paralysis; **a.** cataleptic; paralytic
perpetual: **n.** *moto perpetuo; perpetuum mobile*
pert. to or resulting from: **a.** kinetic
science of: **n.** dynamics; kinetics

MOTIONLESS: (**see** "still") **a.** impassive; quiescent

MOTIVE: **n.** consideration; design; determinant; fillip; impetus; impulse; incentive; inducement; intendment; intention; motif; motivation; provocation; stimulus
concealment of false: **n.** hypocrisy; **a.** hypocritical; **n.** hypocrite
ulterior: **n.** *arrière-pensée*
without: **a.** unmotivated; unpremeditated

MOTOR *control, loss or weakness of:* **n.** akinesia; akinesis; catalepsy; paralysis; **a.** akinetic; cataleptic; paralytic

MOTTO: (**see** "maxim") **n.** epigraph; epigram
beginning of book or chapter: **n.** epigram
reverse of U.S. seal: annuit coeptus
U.S.A.: e pluribus unum

MOULT: **see** "molt"

MOUND: **n.** hummock; tumulus

MOUNTAIN(S): *are in labor: parturiunt montes*
beyond the: **a.** tramontane; transmontane; ultramontane
climbing: **n.** alpinism; alpinist
process of formation: **n.** orogeny; **a.** orogenetic; orogenic
situated at foot or near base of: **a.** subalpine; submontane
situated between: **a.** intermontane
situated beyond: **a.** ultramontane
situated on farthest side of: **a.** transalpine; transmontane
situated on nearest side of: **a.** cismontane
study of: **n.** orography; orology
within the: **a.** intramontane

MOUNTAINEERS *are always freemen:* **n.** *montani semper liberi* (motto of W. Va.)

MOUNTAINOUS: **a.** alpestrine

MOURNFUL: (**see** "sad") **a.** deplorable; doleful; lamentable; luctiferous; threnodic; **n.** MOURNFULNESS: (**see** "sadness") lugubrosity

MOURNING *garment:* **n.** sackcloth

MOUTH, *away from:* **adv.** aborad; aboral
by way of (as medicine): **adv.** *per os;* peroral
having large: **a.** macrostomus; patulous; **n.** macrostomia
having small: **a.** microstomatus; microstomus; **n.** microstomia
pert. to: **a.** buccal; labial; oral; oscular
surrounding the: **a.** circumoral
w/ closed: **adv.** *à bouche fermée* **a.** or **adv.** bouche fermée

MOVE: **v.** actuate; advance; affect; (e)migrate; impel; influence; proceed; **n.** (**see** "movement") *démarche;* (e)migration; maneuver; transplantation; **a.** MOVING: impressive; pathetic; persuading; poignant; touching
with suddenness: **v.** or **n.** catapult

MOVEABILITY: **n.** flexibility; maneuverability; mobility; motility; **a.** MOVABLE: inconstant; maneuverable; mobile; motile

MOVEMENT: **n.** activity; advancement; automation; *démarche;* dynamism; (e)migration; impetus; locomotion; maneuver; momentum; proceeding; procession; progression; transition; trend; velocity

MUCH *in little:* **n.** *multum in parvo*

MUDDY: **a.** roiled; roily; turbid; **n.** turbidity

MULTIPLY: (**see** "increase") **v.** augment; burgeon; poliferate; propagate; pullulate; reproduce; **a.** MULTIPLYING: burgeoning; proliferous; reproductive

MULTITUDE: **n.** aggregation; concourse; host; legion; manifold; multiety; multiplicity; myriad; ruck

MURDER: **see** "killing"
mania for: **n.** phonomania

MURKY: **a.** fuliginous; obscure; turbid; **n.** MURKINESS: fuliginosity; obscurity; turbidity

MURMUR: **v.** susurate; **n.** susuration; susurus; **a.** mormorando; purling; susurant; susurus
act of (murmuring): **n.** murmuration

MUSCLE(S): **n.** sinew(s); thews
sense: **n.** kinesthesia; proprioception; **a.** kinesthetic; proprioceptive

MUSCULAR *uncoordination:* **n.** astasia-abasia; astasis; ataxia; **a.** ataxic
power: **n.** thews

MUSES, *the nine:* **n.** Calliope; Clio; Erato; Euterpe; Melpomene; Polymnia; Terpsichore; Thalia; Urania

MUSIC: **n.** harmonization; harmony; melody; syncopation
art or science of writing: **n.** composition; melopoeia; musicography; **a.** melopoe(t)ic
closing piece: **n.** coda; epilogue; postlude; postludium
excessive or abnormal liking for: **n.** melomania; melomaniac
god of: **n.** Apollo
muse of: **n.** Euterpe
opening piece: **n.** overture; pr(a)eludium; prelude
pert. to: **a.** Euterpean; harmonious; melodious; melophonic
study of: **n.** musicology; **a.** musicological; **n.** musicologist

MUSICAL: (**see** "harmonious") **a.** aeolian; canorous; dulcet; euphonic; euphonious; melic; melodious; orotund; sonorous; symphonic; symphonious; **n.** phantasia; revue
composition of varied themes: **n.** medley; montage; pastiche
embellishment: **n.** arabesque
humorous or whimsical melody: **n.** fantasia; quolibet
tones, entire compass of: **n.** diapason; **a.** diapasonal

MUTENESS: **n.** inarticulateness; obmutescence

MUTINOUS: **see** "lawless"

MUTUAL: **a.** alternate; alternating; coincident; common; complementary; correlative; homogeneous; interdependent; reciprocal; respective; synal(l)gamatic; synchronous
quality or state of being: **n.** interdependence; mutuality; reciprocality; synchroneity

MUTUALLY *antagonistic things or qualities:* **n.pl.** incompatibilities
dependent: **a.** complementary; interdependent; reciprocal; symbiotic(al)
destructive: **a.** internecine
not (mutually) possible: **a.** incompossible; **n.** incompossibility

MY *goodness!:* **adv.** *ma foi!*

MYSTERIOUS: (**see** "hidden") **a.** arcane; cabalistic; clandestine; cryptic(al); enigmatic(al); esoteric; exotic; extraphysical; glamorous; hermetic(al); incomprehensible; inexplicable; inscrutable; obscure; occult; oracular; orphic; picturesque; preternatural; recondite; sibylline; supernatural; surreptitious; tenebrific; tenebrious; uncanny; unfathomed; **n.** MYSTERIOUSNESS: incomprehensibility; inscrutability; mysticality
beliefs or attitudes surrounding person or thing: **n.** mystique
invested w/ (mysterious) significance: **a.** fetishistic; **n.** mystique
manner, in a: **a.** or **adv.** mysterioso
person: **n.** enigma; paradox; sphinx
process or function: **n.** arcanum; (**pl.** arcana); chemistry; mystique

MYSTERY: **n.** arcanum; conundrum; enigma; incomprehensibility; oracularity; paradoxicality; perplexity
celestial: **n.pl.** *arcana caelestia*
interpreter of: **n.** mystagogue
of mysteries: **n.** *arcanum arcanorum*

MYSTIC(AL): (**see** "mysterious") **a.** anagogical; cabalistic; cryptic; enigmatic(al); epoptic; esoteric; mysterial; occult; oracular; orphic(al); paradoxic(al); stratospheric(al); symbolic(al); telestic
beliefs, attitudes, etc. surrounding person or thing: **n.** aura; cachet; halo; mystique; nimbus
doctrine(s): cabala; cabalism; mystagogy; **a.** cabalistic; mystagogic
quality: **n.** mysticality; mystique
teacher or interpreter of the: **n.** mystagogue; **a.** mystagogic

MYSTIFY: **see** "bewilder"

MYTH(S): **n.** anecdote; fabulosity; legend; saga
engaged in making: **a.** mythopoe(t)ic(al); **n.** mythopoesis
to build or construct: **v.** mythologize

MYTHICAL: **a.** allegorical; apocryphal; arcane; fabricated; fabular; fabulous; fantastic; fictitious; legendary; parabolical; visionary
divest of the: **v.** deglamorize; demythologize; **n.** deglamorization; demytholization

N

NAIL(S): **n.** ungual; unguis
animal(s) having: **n.** unguiculate; (**pl.** unguiculata)
-biting: **n.** onychophagia; onychophagy; phaneromania
having: **a.** unguiferate; unguiculate

NAÏVE: **a.** artless; candid; credulous; gullible; ingenuous; innocent; unfeigned; unphilosophic; unsophisticated; **n.** NAÏVETE: artlessness; credulity; gullibility; ingenuosity; ingenuousness; simplicity

NAKED: **a.** *au naturel;* denudate; denuded; destitute; dishabille; divested; exposed; *in puris naturalibus;* obvious; *sans vêtements; tout nu;* unattired; unclothed; undraped; **n.** NAKEDNESS: starkness
eye, exam. or study by: **n.** macrography; macroscopy; *nudis oculus;* **a.** macroscopic; megascopic
partly: **n.** dishabille
practice of going: **n.** Adamitism; gymnosophy; nudism; **n.** gymnosophist
truth: **n.** *nuda veritas*

NAME(S): **v.** denominate; designate; entitle; identify; nominate; specify; stipulate; style; **n.** agnomen; appellation; appellative; cognomen(ation); (de)nomination; designation; epithet; eponym; matronym(ic); nomenclature; patronym(ic); rubric; sobriquet
act of calling or addressing by: **n.** compellation
additional, as honor (as Eric the Red): **n.** agnomen
application of wrong: **n.** misnomer
assumed, or nickname (**see** "nickname"): **n.** agnomen; alias; hypocoristic; *nom d'emprunt;* sobriquet
author, assumed by: **see** "fictitious" **below**
author's own, in: **adv.** *proprio nomine;* **a.** onomastic; onomatous; onymous
bad or objectionable: **n.** caconym; epithet; **n.pl.** *gros mots*
bearing no: **a.** anonymous; innominate
Christian: **see** "first" **below**
courtesy title (as Hon.): **n.** honorific
derived fr. father or male line: **n.** patronym; **a.** patronymic
derived fr. mother or fem. line: **n.** matronym(ic); metronym(ic)
descriptive, disparaging or abusive: **n.** epithet; **a.** epithetical
different for same thing, use of: **n.** heteronomy; **a.** heteronymous
different, having: **a.** heteronymous
existing in (name) only: **a.** nominal; titular; **n.** titular(it)y
false or unknown: **n.** anonym(e); anonymity; pseudonym; pseudonymity; **a.** anonymous; pseudonymous
family, or thru father: **n.** patronym; **a.** patronymic
family or surname: **n.** cognomen; *nom de famille;* patronym; **a.** patronymic; surnominal
feminine but used as pseudonym by man: **n.** pseudogyny; **a.** pseudogynous
fictitious: **n.** alias; allonym; *nom de guerre; nom de plume;* pseudonym; pseudonymity; **a.** pseudonymous
first or personal: **n.** Christian (name); forename; *nom de baptême; petit nom;* praenomen
for divine being: **n.** theologumenon
formed fr. a person's: **n.** antonomasia; eponym; **a.** antonomastic; eponymous
full or complete: **n.** *nom et prénom*
god or divine being, for: **n.** theologumenon
good, or well suited: **n.** euonym; **a.** euonymous
having no: **a.** anonymous; innominate
idea, use of person's for: **see** "formed fr. a person's" **above**
in author's own: **adv.** proprio nomine; **a.** onomatous; onymous
in (name) only: **a.** nominal; titular; **n.** titular(it)y

inapplication or wrong: **n.** misnomer
known by various: **a.** polyonymous; **n.** polyonymy
last: **see** "family" **above**
maiden: **n.** *nom de jeune fille*
male, but used by fem. as pseudonym: **n.** pseudandry
many for one person or thing: **n.** polyonymy; **a.** polyonymous
married woman using maiden: **n.** Lucy Stoner
mother, derived fr.: **see** "derived" **above**
no (name), having or bearing: **a.** anonymous; innominate
objectionable or bad: **n.** caconym; epithet; **a.** epithetic(al)
of one thing for that of another associated w/ or suggested by it: **n.** antonomasia; metonymy; synecdoche; **a.** antonomastic; metonymic(al); synecdochical
only, in: **a.** nominal; *pro forma;* titular; **n.** titular(it)y
pen: **see** "fictitious" **above**
pet, or of endearment: **n.** hypocorism; hypocoristic; *petit nom*
place, or indicative of origin, natural locale, etc.: **n.** toponym; **a.** toponymic(al)
plurality of: **n.** polyonymy; **a.** polyonymous
same, having: **a.** homonymic; homonymous
science of: **n.** nomenclature; onomatology; semantics; terminology
secret: **n.** cryptonym; pseudonym; **a.** cryptonymous; pseudonymous
stage: **n.** *nom de théâtre*
study of personal: **n.** anthropoponymy; onomastics
surname: **see** "family" **above**
system or catalog(ue) of: **n.** nomenclature; onomasticon
title or word in place of: **n.** antonomasia; **a.** antonomastic
two, combined use of: **a.** binomial
two or more, having: **a.** homonymic; homonymous
two persons of same, either of: **n.** homonym; **a.** homonymous
under assumed: **a.** incognito; (**fem.** incognita); pseudonymous
under the (name) of: **adv.** *sub nomine*
unmarried: **see** "maiden" **above**
use of diff. for same thing: **n.** heteronymy; **a.** heteronymous
use of person's for an idea: **see** "formed fr. a person's" **above**
use of title or word in place of: **see** "title, etc." **above**
various, having or known by: **a.** polyonymous; **n.** polyonymy
writer, bearing that of: **see** "author's own" **above**
wrong: **n.** misnomer

NAMED *suitably:* **a.** eunonymous

NAMELESS: **a.** anonymous; incognito; indescribable; inexpressible; innominate; unacknowledged; **n.** NAMELESSNESS: anonymity

NAMELY: **adv.** *c'est-à-dire;* scilicet (**abb.** scil.); videlicet (**abb.** viz.)

NAMESAKE: **n.** homonym

NARCOTIC: **n.** anesthetic; anodyne; nepenthe; opiate; somniferent; soporific; stupefacient; **a.** anesthetic; somniferous; soporiferous; stupefactive

NARRATIVE: **n.** iliad; narration; odyssey; saga

NARROW: (**see** "petty") **a.** bigoted; circumscribed; illiberal; incapacious; incommodious; insular; parochial; prejudiced; provincial; restricted; sectarian; stenotic
attachment to sect, party, etc.: **n.** sectarianism; **a.** parochial; sectarian
limits, having: **a.** municipal; parochial; provincial
-minded: **a.** bigoted; *borné;* denominational; illiberal; insular; insulated; isolated; parochial; pedantic; peninsular; prejudiced; provincial; sectarian; **n.** NARROW-MINDEDNESS: bigotism; bigotry; exiguity; Grundyism; illiberality; insularism; insularity; parochiality; parvanimity; (pen)insularity; provincialism; sectarianism
-minded person: **see under** *"person"*

NASTY: **see** "dirty"

NATIONS, *comity of:* **n.** *comitas gentium; comitas inter gentes*
law of: **see** "law, international"
understanding bet.: **n.** *entente (cordiale)*

NATIVE: **n.** aboriginal; aborigine; authchthon; domestic; indigen(e); inhabitant; (**pl.** *les aborigènes*); **n.** aboriginality; endemicity; endemism; **a.** aboriginal; autochthonal; autochthonic; autochthonous; demotic; domestic; edaphic; enchorial;

endemial; endemic(al); indigenous; inherent; innate; original; natal; primitive
animal, people or plant: **n.** aboriginal; aborigine; autochthon; indigin(e); **a.** aboriginal; autochthonous
environment: **n.** habitat(ion); milieu
land, pert. to: **a.** compatriotic; natal; patrial
not: (see "foreign") **a.** heterochthonous
soil: **n.** *natale solum*

NATURAL: (**see** "physical" **and** "sincere") **a.** artless; candid; congenital; endogenous; essential; hereditary; inborn; ingrained; inherent; innate; instinctive; spontaneous; unaffected; unpremeditated; unsophisticated; unstudied; **n.** naturality
differing fr. or beyond the: (**see** "supernatural") **a.** paraphysical; parapsychological; preternatural; supermundane
endowment or adjunct: **n.** ap(p)anage
feeling or behavior: **n.** naturality; **a.** naturalesque
forces, purposeful use of: **n.** telesia; telesis
insight: **n.** *lumen naturale*
law: **n.** *jus naturae; jus naturale*
not: (see "foreign") **a.** artefactitious; artificial; illusive; **n.** artefact; artificiality; Brummagem; counterfeit
products: **n.pl.** *fructus naturales*
state: **n.** *al fresco; au naturel*
state of being: **n.** naturality; **a.** naturalesque
tendency: (**see** "inclination") **n.** appetence; appetency; conatus; diathesis; idiosyncrasy

NATURALIZED: **a.** acclimated; adapted; heterochthonous

NATURE(S): (**see** "character") **n.** constitution; inclination; proclivity; propensity; (quint)essence; texture
according to, or second-: **adv.** *secundum naturam*
as one w/ God (doctrine): **n.** pantheism; **a.** pantheistic(al)
ascription of soul to things: **n.** anthropopsychism; **a.** anthropopsychic
being of a diff.: **a.** heterogeneous; hetero(o)usian
close to: **n.** primitivism; **a.** primitivistic
conforming closely to or imitating: **a.** naturalesque
essential: **n.** quiddity; quintessence; virtuality; **a.** quidditive; quintessential; **adv.** *sub specie aeternitatis*
evidence of design in: **n.** teleology; **a.** teleological
freak of: **n.** *lasus naturae;* monstrosity; sport
having same (nature) or kind: **a.** consubstantial; **n.** consubstantiality
having two or mixed: **a.** amphibious; **n.** amphibian
healing power of: **n.** *vis medicatrix naturae*
law of: **see under** "natural"
of beings, description of: **n.** ontography; **a.** ontographic
of things, in the: **adv.** *de rerum naturâ; in rerum naturâ*
pert. to or derived fr. laws of: **a.** or **n.** cosmonomic
unbiased or undistorted: **a.** or **adv.** naturâle; **a.** naturalesque
wisdom about: **n.** physiosophy
worship of, or of natural forces: **n.** cosmotheism; pantheism; physiolatory; priaprism; **a.** pantheistic(al); physiolatrous; **n.** pantheist; physiolater; physiolatrist

NAUSEA, *to point of: usque ad nauseam*

NAUSEOUS (or NAUSEATING): (**see** "revolting") **a.** abominable; bilious; disgusting; fulsome; loathsome; *nauséeux;* offensive; qualmish; repugnant; sickening; squeamish

NAVEL: **n.** omphalos; omphalus; umbilicus
meditation while gazing at: **n.** omphaloskepsis; **n.** hesychast; omphalopsychite; **a.** hesychastic
pert. to: **a.** omphalic; umbilical
resembling, or depressed like: **a.** umbilicate(d)

NAVIGATION, *pert. to:* **a.** marine; maritime; nautical; naval; oceanic

NEAR (or NEARBY): **a.** adjacent; approaching; contiguous; imminent; impending; neighboring; propinquant; propinquous; proximate; **adv.** NEARLY: *à peu près;* quasi
East: **n.** Levant; **a.** Byzantine; Levantine
-sighted: **a.** myopic; purblind; **n.** myopia

NEAREST *in time, relation or degree:* **a.** propinquitous; **n.** prochein; propinquity
to point of attachment or origin: **a.** proximal; proximate; **adv.** proximad

NEARNESS: **n.** adjacency; (appro)propinquity; contiguity; proximity
in time, place, relationship, etc.: **n.** propinquity; proximity

NEAT: **a.** concinnate; concinnous; fastidious; immaculate; modish; natty; proportional; shipshape; *soigné;* (**fem.** *soignée*); spruce; uncluttered; **a.** NEATNESS: concinnity; fastidiousness

NECESSARY: **a.** essential; imperative; incumbent; inevitable; indispensable; indispensible; inexorable; mandatory; needful; obligatory; (pre)requisite; unavoidable; unpreventable
changes having been made: mutatis mutandis

NECESSITY: (**see** "need") **n.** desideratum; essential(ity); exigency; indispensability; obligation; (pre)requisite; requirement; *sine qua non*
by force of: **adv.** perforce
has no law: necessitas non habet legem
mother of invention (*or of arts*): *mater artium necessitas*
of life: **n.** aliment; **a.** alimental

NECK: **n.** cervix; collum; **a.** cervical
having a long: **a.** longicollous; macrauchen

NECKLINE, *low:* **n.** décolletage; **a.** décollete

NEED(S): (**see** "necessity" **and** "poverty") **n.** deficiency; desideratum; desiderium; essential(ity); exigency; indispensability; *manque;* obligation; (pre)-requisite; requirement; (**pl.** desiderata; desideria)

NEEDLE, *shaped like:* **a.** acerate; acerose; acerous; acicular; aciculate(d); belonoid

NEEDLESS: **a.** gratuitous; unessential; unnecessary

NEEDY: (**see** "poor") **a.** desiderative; destitute; insolvent; necessitous; pressing

NEGATION: **n.** annihilation; contraindication; denial; disclaimer; nonentity; nullification; obliteration; **a.** NEGATIVE: negatory; neutral; privative; **n.** negativity
expressing: **n.** negatory; **n.** negativism; negativity
but implying affirmation: **n.** negative pregnant

NEGLECT: **v.** disregard; ignore; misprize; pigeonhole; pretermit; **n.** (**see** "failure") delinquency; dereliction; disregard; ignoration; inattention; indifference; indolence; nonobservance; omission; pretermission; procrastination
of duty: **n.** abandonment; delinquency; dereliction; laches; malfeasance; misfeasance
place or condition of: **n.** limbo

NEGLIGENCE: **n.** delinquency; ignoration; inadvertence; inattention; indifference; laches; malfeasance; misfeasance; nonobservance; omission; remission; **a.** NEGLIGENT: delinquent; improvident; inadvertent; inattentive; indifferent; neglectful; remiss; unmindful
gross: **n.** *crassa negligentia; culpa lata*

NEGROES, *dislike or fear of:* **n.** negrophobia; negrophobe
one friendly to: **n.** negrophile

NEIGHBORHOOD: **n.** habitat; milieu; propinquity; proximity; purlieu(s); suburb(s); vicinage; vicinity; (**pl.** alentours; confines; environs); **a.** NEIGHBORING: (**see** "adjacent") attingent; contiguous; limitrophe; propinquant; tangent(i)al; vicinal; **a.** NEIGHBORLY: (**see** "friendly") amicable; gregarious

NEPHEW, *pert. to:* **a.** nepotal; nepotic

NERVE: (**see** "gall") **n.** audacity; effrontery; fortitude; intrepidity; sinew; temerity
center: **n.** plexus
junction: **n.** synapse; **a.** synaptic

NERVOUS: **a.** agitated; apprehensive; excitable; fidgety; hysterical; irritable; neurotic; restless; restive; timorous; volatile; **n.** NERVOUSNESS: agitation; excitation; irritability; nervosity; neurosis; neuroticism; psychoneurosis; psychosis; (**pl.** fantods)
and excited: **a.** agitato

NEST: **n.** abode; aerie; nidus; retreat
build a: **v.** nidify; nidificate; **n.** nidification; nidulation; **a.** nidificant
leaving shortly after hatching: **a.** nidifugous
living in, or sharing w/ another: **a.** nidicolous

NETWORK: **n.** complex; labyrinth; plexus; *reseau;* (**pl.** *reseaux*); reticulation; reticulum

NEUTRAL: (**see** "indifferent") **a.** adiaphorous; disinterested; dispassionate; impersonal; nonpartisan; unbiased; **n.** NEUTRALITY: adiaphoria; detachment; indifference

NEVER *despair: nil desperandum*

NEVERTHELESS: **adv.** *tout de même*

NEW: **a.** immature; inexperienced; modern(istic); nascent; neoteric; novel; nouveau; pristine; renovated; unaccustomed; unexampled; unfamiliar; unprecedented; **n.** NEWNESS: **see** "freshness"
doctrine: **n.** neology
hater or hatred of something (new) or strange: **n.** misoneism; misoneist; xenophobia; xenophobe; **a.** misoneistic; xenophobic
introducing something (new): **a.** innovative; innovatory; **n.** debut; inauguration; innovation
something which is: **n.** innovation; neoteric
word or new use for old: **n.** neologism; neoterism

NEWCOMER: (**see** "upstart") **n.** Johnny-come-lately; *nouveau riche; parvenu*

NEWLY *arrived or developed:* **a.** nascent; neoteric; nouveau; **n.** innovation; neoteric

NEWSPAPER *or magazine style of writing:* **n.** journalese

NEXT: (**see** "adjacent") **a.** contiguous; prochein; proximal; sequacious
to the last: **a.** penultimate

NICE: (**see** "agreeable") **a.** decorous; demure; discriminating
overly: **a.** fastidious; squeamish; **n.** fastidiousness; preciosity; scrupulosity

NICETY, *to a:* **adv.** *ad unguem*

NICKNAME: **n.** agname; agnomen; cognomen; epithet; hypocorism; hypocoristic; moni(c)ker; *petit nom;* sobriquet

NIGHT: **see** "darkness"
at: **adv.** *à la belle étoile;* **a.** nocturnal; **n.** nocturnality
attack by: **n.** camisado
-blindness: **n.** hemeralopia; nyctalopia
club: **n.** *boîte de nuit;* truncheon
functioning at: **a.** nocturnal; **n.** nocturnality
going about at: **n.** noctambulation; noctivigation; **a.** noctivigant; noctivagous
-gown: **n.** *robe de nuit*
happening, active or functioning at: **a.** nocturnal; **n.** nocturnality
pert. to: **a.** nocturnal; **n.** nocturnality
stay up or out all: **v.** pernoctate; **n.** pernoctation
-stick: **n.** truncheon

NIGHTMARE: **n.** apprehension; *cauchemar;* incubus; oneirodynia; *pavor nocturnus;* vexation
something like: **n.** Walpurgis Night; *Walpurgisnacht*

NIMBLE: (**see** "agile") **a.** dexterous; lissom(e); supple; **n.** NIMBLENESS: agility; dexterity; elasticity; flexibility; legerity; lissomeness; suppleness

NINE, *group or set of:* **n.** ennead; **a.** enneadic
pert. to or based on: **a.** novenary
-sided: **n.** or **a.** nonagon

NINETIETH: **a.** nonagesimal

NINETY, *person over but less than 100:* **n.** nonagenarian
pert. to such person or period: **a.** nonagenarian

NO *one is sufficiently wise by himself: nemo solus satis sapit*
sooner said than done: aussitôt dit, aussitôt fait; dictum ac factum

NOBILITY: **n.** aristocracy; eminence; gentility; gentry; grandeur; magnanimity; noblesse; patriciate; peerage; sublimity; (**n.pl.** aristoi); **a.** aristocratic; nobiliary
duty of: **n.** *noblesse oblige*
lesser: **n.** *petite noblesse*
pert. to: **a.** aristocratic; nobiliary; patrician

NOBLE: **a.** aristocratic; eminent; exalted; illustrious; lofty; magnanimous; magnificent; majestic; patrician; princely; sub-

lime; **n.** NOBLEMAN: aristocrat; grandee; magnificio; patrician; peer; **(pl.** aristoi)
birth or status: **n.** aristocracy; noblesse; patriciate; peerage
in mind: **a.** magnanimous; spirituel(le)

NOBODY: **n.** *homme de rien; pessorbius orti*

NODDING, *act of, esp involuntary:* **n.** nutation; **a.** nutant; nutational

NOISE: **(see** "uproar") **n.** acoustics; Bedlam; blatancy; brouhaha; cacophony; charivari; clamor; detonation; pandemonium; phonics; tintamar(re); tintinnabulation; tumult; **a.** NOISELESS: **see** "silent"
great and confused: **n.** charivari; pandemonium; tintamar(re); **a.** pandemoniac(al); tintinnabulary; tintinnabulous
loud: **n.** detonation
place of: **n.** Bedlam; pandemonium

NOISY: **a.** agitated: Bedlam; blatant; boisterous; cacophonous; clamorous; clangorous; demonstrative; effusive; obstreperous; pandemoniac(al); raucous; riotous; roisterous; sonorous; strepitant; strepitus; stridulous; termagant; thunderous; tumultuary; tumultuous; turbulent; undisciplined
ominously: **a.** thunderous
rumor: **n.** *fama clamosa*

NONCHALANCE: **see** "indifference"

NONCONFORMISM: **n.** *avant-gardism,* dissidence; heresy; recusance; recusancy; **n.** NONCONFORMIST: **(see** "disbeliever") *avant-garde;* beatnik; Bohemian; dissenter; dissident; heresiarch; heretic; mossback; recusant; renegade; schismatic; schismatist; standpatter; ultraconservative; **n.** NONCONFORMITY: **see under** "conformity"

NONESSENTIAL: **a.** dispensable; gratuitous; supererogant; supererogative; supererogatory; unessential
items: **n.pl.** marginalia

NONINTERFERENCE, *doctrine of:* **n.** or **a.** *laissez-faire;* **(also** laisser-faire); **n.** *caveat emptor*

NONPROFESSIONAL, *as in art:* **n.** amateur; dilettante; **a.** dilettantish; **n.** dilettantism

NONSENSE: **n.** abracadabra; absurdity; amphigory; balderdash; blatherskite; fandangle; fiddle-faddle; flamdoodle; flummadiddle; folderol; hocus-pocus; imbecility; malarkey; *niaiserie;* nugacity; *nugae canorae;* stultiloquence; stultiloquy; tarradiddle; tomfoolery; trumpery; **(pl.** trivia); **a.** NONSENSICAL: absurd; amphigoric; capricious; fanciful; imbecilic; ludicrous; macaronic; notional; preposterous; whimsical
as talk: **n.** Choctaw; galimatias; gibberish; jabberwock(y)
melodious: **n.** *nugae canorae*
pretentious: **n.** amphigory; **a.** amphigoric
verse or prose: **n.** amphigory; **a.** amphigoric

NOON, *before:* **n.** *ante merediem;* **a.** antemeridian
rel. to: **a.** meridian

NORM(AL), *as to physical function:* **a.** physiological
conformity to: **(see** "according to rule") **n.** normality
sub-: **a.** subaverage; suboptimal; substandard

NORTH *star:* **n.** cynosure; lodestar; polestar

NORTHERN: **a.** arctic; boreal; hyperborean; septentrional
region(s), pert. to: **a.** arctic; hyperborean
region(s), resident of: **n.** hyperborean

NOSE: **n.** nasus; olfactus; organon; proboscis
-bleed: **n.** epistaxis; rhinorrhagia
hair in: **n.** vibrissa; **(pl.** vibrissae): **a.** vibrissal
having, esp. if large: **a.** nasute
hooked type: **a.** aduncous; aquiline
turned up: **n.** *nez retroussé;* **a.** retrousse
well-developed: **a.** nasute

NOT *too much:* **a. or adv.** *non troppo*

NOTABLE (or NOTED): **a.** celebrated; distinguished; eminent; illustrious; important; impressive; majestic; memorable; memorious; noteworthy; observable; prominent; remarkable; renowned; salient; signal; significant; striking; supereminent

NOTCH: **v.** denticulate; serrate; **n.** denticulation; serration; **a.** NOTCHED: dentate; denticulate(d); dentiform; serrate(d); serrulate

NOTE(S), *collection of:* **n.** adversaria; scrapiana
marginal: **see under** "marginal"
personal: **n.pl.** anecdotes; personalia
things worthy of: **n.pl.** notabilia
varied: **a.** miscellanea; scrapiana
well: **adv.** *nota bene* (**abb.** *n.b.*)
worthy of: **adv.** *notatu dignum*

NOTEBOOK, *looseleaf:* **n.** cahier
student's: **n.** *index rerum*

NOTED: **see** "notable"

NOTHING: *from or out of:* **a.** or **adv.** *ex nihilo*
out of comes (nothing): **adv.** *de nihilo nihil; ex nihilo nihil fit*
thing amounting to: **n.** bagatelle; nihility; nonentity; nullity; triviality; (**pl.** trivia)
to come to: **v.** *n'aboutir à rien*

NOTHINGNESS: (**see** "trifle") **n.** annihilation; bagatelle; cipher; naught; nihility; nonentity; nullity; oblivion; triviality; (**pl.** trivia); vacuity; vacuum

NOTICE: (**see** "heed") **v.** recognize; **n.** advertence; announcement; apprehension; attention; awareness; cognizance; conspicuity; conspicuousness; knowledge; observation; prominence
take particular: **adv.** *nota bene* (**abb.** n.b.)

NOTICEABLE: **a.** arresting; conspicuous; manifest; observable; obvious; palpable; perceptible; prominent; salient; signal

NOTION: (**see** "idea") **n.** apprehension; bibelot; conception; inclination; inkling; knickknack; understanding; vagary; whimsicality; **a.** NOTIONAL: crotchety; imaginary; theoretical; unreal; visionary; whimsical

NOTORIOUS: (**see** "notable") **a.** arrant; celebrated; discreditable; disreputable; ignominious; inglorious; unmitigated; villainous

NOTWITHSTANDING: **prep.** *malgré;* mauger; maugre; *quand même;* **adv.** howbeit; nevertheless; *nonobstante*

NOUN, *made fr. common name:* **n.** antonomasia; **a.** antonomastic
verbal: **n.** gerund

NOURISHING: **a.** alible; alimental; alimentative; invigorating; nutural; nutritious; nutritory; nutritive; strengthening
not: **a.** inalimental; innutrious

NOURISHMENT: (**see** "food") **n.** aliment(ation); collation; forage; nutriment; pabulum; sustenance
derived parasitically fr. others: **a.** paratrophic
healthy or good: **n.** eutrophy; **a.** eutrophic
lacking in: **a.** atrophic; distrophic; inalimental; innutrious; oligotrophic; **n.** atrophy; dystrophia; dystrophy

NOVEL: **see** "new"; **n.** NOVELTY: innovation; neoteric; newness
developing character fr. child to adulthood: **n.** entwicklungsroman
about early development or spiritual education of main character: **n.** Bildungsroman
leading character in: **n.** agonist
philosophical type: **n.** *roman à thèse*
w/ real persons, events, etc. disguised: **n.** *roman à clef*

NOVICE: (**see** "beginner" **and** "learner") **n.** neophyte; neoteric; tyro

NOW: **adv.** *in praesenti*
and always: ora e sempre
for then: **adv.** *nunc pro tunc;* **a.** *ex post facto*
or never: **adv.** *nunc aut nunquam*

NOWHERE, *state or quality of being:* **n.** nullibicity; nullibiety

NUDE: **see** "naked"; **n.** NUDISM: Adamitism; gymnosophy; naturalism; **n.** NUDIST: Adamite; gymnosophist

NULL: **a.** invalid; nonexistent; nugatory; *nullius juris;* void; **n.** NULLITY: nihility; **v.** NULLIFY: abolish; abrogate; invalidate; negate; rescind; stultify; **n.** NULLIFICATION: invalidation; stultification; vitiation

NUMB: **see** "blunt"

NUMBER: **n.** aggregate; legion; magnitude; multitude; myriad; quantity
indefinitely large: **n.** legion; myriad
large: **n.** hecatomb; manifold; multeity; multifariousness; multiplicity; **a.** manifold; multifarious; myriad

NUMBERLESS: (**see** "unlimited") **a.** innumerable; innumerous; **n.** innumerability

NUMEROUS: (**see** "many") **a.** manifold; multifarious; multiplex; multitudinous; myriad; plentious; plentiful; populous; **n.**

NUMEROUSNESS: manifold; multeity; multiplicity; numerosity; plurality

NUN: **n.** cenobite; recluse; religious; sanctimonial; **a.** cenobitic; **n.** cenobitism

NUTRITION: (**see** "food" **and** "nourishment") **n.** diatetics; **a.** NUTRITIOUS: **see** "nourishing"
fundamental, involving metabolic change in tissues: **n.** metabolism; trophism
healthy or good: **n.** eutrophy
science of: **n.** dietetics; trophology

NUTS, *bearing:* **a.** nuciferous
living on: **a.** nucivorous

NUTSHELL, *in a:* **adv.** *in nuce*

O

OATH: (**see** "curse") **n.** adjuration; affirmation; attestation; blasphemy; execration; expletive; imprecation; malediction
being bound by: **a.** objurgative; **n.** objurgation
breaking of: **n.** perjury; **a.** perjur(i)ous
pert. to: **a.** juratory
united by common: **n.** adjuration; conjuration

OBEDIENT: **a.** acquiescent; amenable; biddable; compliant; deferential; docile; malleable; obeisant; obsequious; submissive; tractable; **n.** OBEDIENCE: compliance; conformity; deference; docility; submission
to be servilely or humbly: **v.** genuflect; kow-tow

OBESE: (**see** "stout") **a.** corpulent; orbicular; portly; pyknic; rotund; **n.** OBESITY: adiposis; adiposity; avoirdupois; corpulence; embonpoint; pinguidity; plumpness; portliness; pursiness; steatosis; stoutness

OBJECT: (**see** "protest") **v.** cavil; demur; expostulate; remonstrate; **n.** (**see** "aim") intention; materiality; objective
mental rather than real: **n.** numenon
of human effort or workmanship: **n.** artefact; artifact; (**n.pl.** *fructus industriales*); **a.** artefactitious; artifactitious

OBJECTION: **n.** exception; protest(ation); remonstrance; remonstration; scruple; **a.** OBJECTIONABLE: (**see** "offensive") disagreeable; distasteful; inappropriate; inexpedient; loathsome; nauseous; noisome; obnoxious; rebarbative; reprehensible; repugnant; repulsive; revolting, unpleasing

OBJECTIVE: (**see** "intent") **n.** aspiration; *quaesitum;* **a.** material; postival

OBLIGATION: **n.** encumbrance; liability; onus; responsibility; **a.** OBLIGATED: behooving; imperative; incumbent; pledged; **a.** OBLIGATORY: *de rigueur;* imperative; incumbent; mandatory; prerequisite
ethics or science of moral: **n.** deontology; **a.** deontological
imposing mutual: **a.** synal(l)agmatic
rel. to: **a.** deontic; obligatory

OBLIGED, *much:* **adv.** *bien obligé*

OBLIGING: **a.** amiable; cooperative; obligatory
manner: **n.** *prevénance*
not: **a.** *désobligeant*

OBLIQUE: (**see** "devious") **a.** duplicitous; evasive; indirect; louche; perverse; sinister

OBLIVION: **n.** forgetfulnes; lethe; limbo; obliviscence; nirvana; **a.** OBLIVIOUS: (**see** "unaware") lethean; oblivial; nirvanic

OBNOXIOUS: **see** "objectionable"

OBSCENE: (**see** "lewd") **a.** ithyphallic; lascivious; pornographic
books, pictures, etc.: **n.** erotica; esoterica; facetiae; pornography
cult of the: **n.** aischrolatreia
language, excessive or uncontrollable use of: **n.** coprolalia

OBSCENITY: **n.** coprolalia; coprology; pornography; scatology; vulgarism; vulgarity
fondness for or preoccupation w/: **n.** coprophilia; scatology; **a.** cloacal; coprophilous; scatologic(al)
study of: **n.** coprology; pornography
worship of: **n.** aischrolatreia

OBSCURE: (**see** "vague") **v.** adumbrate; becloud; bedim; obfuscate; obnebulate;

obnubilate; **a.** abstruse; ambiguous; ambivalent; cabalistic; caliginous; crepuscular; cryptic(al); Delphian; Delphic; enigmatic(al); equivocal; fuliginous; incomprehensible; inscrutable; obfuscatory; recondite; transcendent; unfathomable; **n.** OBSCURITY: (**see** "confusion") abstrusity; ambiguity; ambivalence; fuliginosity; inconspicuousness; obfuscation; oblivion; obscuration; opacity; profundity; seclusion; turbidity
area: **n.** limbo; penumbra; twilight zone
literary style: **n.** obscuranti(ci)sm

OBSERVABLE: (**see** "noticeable") **a.** detectable; discernible; **a.** OBSERVANT: alert; attentive; heedful; mindful; (on the) *qui vive;* perceptive; percipient; regardful
fact or event: **n.** phenomenon; (**pl.** phenomena); **a.** phenomenal

OBSERVATION: **n.** descant; observance; reflection; utterance
based on one's: **a.** autoptic
if under suspicion: **n.** surveillance; **a.** surveillant
keenness of: **n.** acumen; percipience; percipiency; perspicacity; perspicuity; **a.** acuminous; percipient; perspicacious

OBSERVE: (**see** "commemorate" **and** "see") **v.** celebrate; solemnize; witness
unable or unwilling to: **a.** astigmatic(al); purblind; myopic; **n.** astigmatism; myopia

OBSESSION: **n.** compulsion; *idée fixe;* impulse; preoccupation; mania

OBSOLETE: **a.** antediluvian; antiquated; archaic; outmoded; *passé;* rudimentary; timeworn; vestigial
become by lapse of time: **v.** obsolesce; superannuate; **n.** depletion; obsolescence; superannuation
becoming: **a.** obsolescent; **n.** depletion; obsolescence; **v.** obsolesce

OBSTINATE: (**see** "stubborn") **a.** *entêté;* pertinacious; pervicacious; tenacious; unpliable; unrepentant; unyielding; **n.** OBSTINACY: (**see** "stubbornness") adamancy; asininity; contumely; inveteracy; persistence; pertinacity; pervicaciousness; pervicacity; tenacity

OBSTRUCT: **v.** barricade; encumber; impede; incommode; occlude; oppilate; retard; **n.** OBSTRUCTION: (**see** "impasse") barrier; embolus; impediment; (**pl.** impedimenta); obstacle; oppilation; stenosis; strangulation; **a.** OBSTRUCTIVE: impedimental; impedimentive; impeditive; obstruent; occlusive; oppilative; stenotic

OBTAIN: **see** "get"

OBVIOUS: **a.** conspicuous; evident; literal; manifest; palpable; patent; prominent; unambiguous; unequivocal; **n.** OBVIOUSNESS: conspicuity; conspicuousness; manifestness; patency
beyond or below what is: **a.** subintelligential; subliminal

OCCASIONAL: **a.** episodic(al); incidental; infrequent; sporadic
state of being: **n.** infrequency; occasionality; sporadicity

OCCUPANCY: **n.** incumbency; (in)habitation; occupation; residency; tenancy; tenure; **n.** OCCUPANT: incumbent; inhabitant; tenant; **a.** OCCUPATIONAL: employmental; habitudinal; industrial; professional; vocational

OCCUPIED *mentally:* **a.** abstracted; versant

OCCURRENCE: **n.** circumstance; episode; incident
unexpected or embarrassing: (**see** "accident") **n.** contretemps

OCCURRING *at same time:* **a.** coetaneous; coeval; coincident(al); coinstantaneous; coinciding; concomitant; concurrent; contemporaneous; contemporary; coordinant; harmonious; synchronic(al); synchronous; synchronistic(al); unanimous; **n.** coetaneity; concurrency; contemporaneity; simultaneity; synchronicity; synchrony; unanimity
later: **a.** subsequent(ial); supervenient; **n.** supervenience; supervention; **v.** supervene

OCEAN(S): (**see** "sea") **n.** brine; deep
beyond the: **see under** "sea"
inhabiting depths of: **a.** bathyal(ic); bathybic; bathypelagic; bathysmal; benthic; benthopelagic; suboceanic
pert. to: **a.** marine; maritime; oceanic; pelagic; thalassic

to deep part of: **a.** bathyal(ic); bathybic; bathypelagic; bathysmal
study of: **n.** oceanography; thalassography

ODD: (**see** "unrealistic") **a.** anomalous; atypical; azygous; bizarre; capricious; eccentric; fantastic(al); grotesque; haphazard; idiosyncratic; inexplicable; nondescript; occasional; *outré;* singular; vagarious; whimsical; **n.** ODDITY: (**see** "peculiarity") bizarrerie; caprice; curiosity; eccentricity; fantasticality; grotesquerie; h(a)ecceity; idiosyncrasy; particularity; quiddity; singularity; vagary; whim(sicality)
at (odds): **see** "unharmonious"
character: **n.** *drôle de corps*

ODOR: **n.** aroma(ticity); cachet; effluvium; emanation; estimation; fragrance; redolence; repute
disagreeable or noxious: **n.** aromaticity; effluvium; (**pl.** effluvia); mephitis; nidor; **a.** (**see** "stinking") effluvial; fetid; malodorous; mephitic; nidorous; noisome; odiferous
giving off: **a.** aromatic; odoriferous; odorous; olent; redolent

ODORLESS: **a.** inodorous; scentless

OF *course:* **adv.** *bien entendu*
this day: **a.** hodiernal

OFF-COLOR: **a.** dubious; *risqué*

OFFENSE: **n.** affront; delict(um); delinquency; dudgeon; felony; malfeasance; malum; misdemeanor; misfeasance; pique; resentment; transgression; trespass; **v.** OFFEND: affront; pique; transgress; trespass; **a.** OFFENSIVE: (**see** "attack" **and** "objectionable") blatant; defamatory; displeasing; distasteful; execrable; fetid; invidious; loathsome; noisome; (ob)noxious; obtrusive; odious; reprehensible; repugnant; repulsive; ribald(rous); ridiculous; unsavory; verminous; **n.** OFFENSIVENESS: blatancy; objectionability; repugnance; repugnancy; unsavoriness
caught in act of committing: **adv.** (in) *flagrante delicto;* red-handed
minor: **n.** culpa; delinquency; misdemeanor; peccadillo; veniality; **n.** delinquent; misdemeanant
none intended: **adv.** *absit invidia*
opening position for: **n.** *en garde*
slight: **see** *"minor"* **above**

OFFENDED *easily:* **a.** squeamish; umbrageous; **n.** squeamishness

OFFER: **v.** proffer; tender

OFFERING *of thanksgiving, sacrifice, etc.:* **n.** oblation

OFFHAND: (**see** "impromptu") **a.** *ad lib(itum)*; autoschediastic; *brevi manu;* casual; extemporaneous; extemporary; extempore; improvisatorial; improvisatory; improviso; impulsive; informal; spontaneous; unceremonious; unconventional; unpremeditated; unstudied; **adv.** *currente calamo*
something done (offhand): **n.** autoschediasm; improvisation

OFFICE *attire or vestments:* **n.** pontificalibus
by virtue of: **n.** or **a.** *ex cathedra;* **a.** *ex officio;* functional; perquisite; *virtute officii*
functions of: **n.** officialdom; **a.** (ad)-ministerial; administrative
-holder(s): **n.** functionaire; functionary; incumbency; incumbent; officialdom; officiality
investing into: **n.** inauguration; installation; investiture
no longer in, or power ended: **a.** emeritus; *functus officio;* superannuated
of honor or profit: **n.** preferment
power or function going with: **n.** attribution; perquisite

OFFICIAL(S): **a.** accredited; authoritative; authorized; cathedral; sanctioned; **n.** functionaire; functionary; incumbency; incumbent; officialdom; officiary
language of: **n.** federalese; officialese
pedantic: **n.** bureaucrat; mandarin; pedantocrat
state of being: **a.** authoritative; **n.** officialism; officiality

OFFICIOUS: **see** "meddlesome"

OFFSET: **v.** checkmate; compensate; counteract; counterbalance; counterpoise; countervail; reimburse

OFFSHOOT: **n.** digression; outgrowth; ramification; ramus; tangent; **a.** tangent(i)al

OFFSPRING: **n.** descendant(s); issue; posterity; progeniture; progeny; (s)cion
having two at birth: **a.** biparous
incapacity for producing: **a.** barrenness; sterility
love of: **n.** philoprogeneity; philoprogenitiveness; storge; **a.** philoprogenitive
producing female: **a.** thelygenic; thelytokous
producing male: **a.** androgenous
production of: **a.** philoprogenitive

OGLE, *amorous:* **n.** oeillade

OIL, *bearing or producing:* **a.** oleaginous; oleiferous

OILY: (**see** "elusive") **a.** deceitful; lardaceous; lubric(i)ous; oleaginous; pinguid; saponaceous; servile; suave; unctuous; **n.** OILINESS: lubricity; plasticity; saponaceousness; unctuosity

OINTMENT: **see** "salve"

OLD: (**see** "ancient") **a.** aboriginal; antebellum; antediluvial; antediluvian; antemundane; antiquated; antique; archaic; archaistic; decrepit; grandfatherly; immemorial; ogygian; paleolithic; paleozoic; *passé;* patriarchal; preadamite; prehistoric; prelapsarian; primeval; primitive; protohistoric; troglodytic; venerable; **adv.** *ab antiquo*
-age: **n.** anecdotage; autumn of life; caducity; decrepitude; dotage; evening of life; senectitude; senility
decay from: **n.** consenescence
growing or onset of: **n.** senescence; **a.** senescent; **v.** senesce
pert. to: **a.** caducous; gerontal; gerontic; senile
study of: **n.** geriatrics; gerontology; nostology
-fashioned: **a.** antebellum; antediluvian; antiquated; archaic; archaistic; conservative; dated; decadent; *démodé;* demoded; fuddy-duddy; Neanderthal; obsolescent; obsolete; old hat; outmoded; *passé;* reactionary; troglodytic; *vieux jeu;* **n.** ancientry; antiquation; decadence; obsolescence
ideas: **n.** fogyism
person or thing: **n.** antediluvian; antequarian; fogram; fogrum; fuddy-duddy; mossback; stick-in-the-mud; ultraconservative
love of what is (old): **n.** archaeolatry; archai(ci)sm
men children twice: ***bis pueri senes***
order: **n.** *ancien regime*
person: **n.** antediluvian; antequarian; cidevant; dotard; fogram; fogrum; graybeard; Methuselah; patriarch; preadamite; veteran
esp. over 100: **n.** centenarian; macrobian
preference for what is (old): **n.** archaeolatry; archai(ci)sm
story: **n.** *crambe repetita*
-womanish: **a.** anile; **n.** anility
world, rel. to: **a.** gerontogeous
worship of what is: **n.** archaism; archaeolatry

OLDEST *example of some category:* **n.** dean; doyen (**fem.** doyenne)
person of class or group: **n.** dean; doyen; (**fem.** doyenne); patriarch

OMEN: **n.** augury; auspice; divination; foretoken; handwriting on the wall; harbinger; portent; precursor; presage; presentiment; **a.** OMINOUS: augural; augurous; fateful; gravid; imminent; inauspicious; menacing; portentous; premonitory; sinister; unpropitious
favorable: **n.** *omen faustum*
may there be no evil (omen): **n.** *absit omen*
of good: **a.** auspicious; *de bon augure*

OMISSION: (**see** "failure") **n.** delinquency; exclusion; misfeasance; neglect; preterition; pretermission
in rhetoric or grammar: **n.** ellipsis; paral(e)ipsis (**or** paralepsis)

OMIT: **v.** exclude; forbear; ignore; neglect; overlook
as letter or vowel: **v.** elide; **n.** elision

OMITTED *parts of work, printed as supplement:* **n.pl.** paralipomena

ONCE: **a.** bygone; elapsed; quondam; **adv.** erewhile; whilom
at: (**see** "prompt") **a.** instantaneous; momentaneous; *tout de suite*
for all: **adv.** *semel pro semper*

ONE-AND-ONE-HALF *as great, or ratio of:* **a.** sesquialteral

ONE-HUNDRED-AND-FIFTY, *pert. to, or 150th anniversary:* **a.** or **n.** sesquicentennial

ONE-HUNDRED *fold:* **v.** or **a.** centuplicate; **a.** centuple
years, period of: **n.** centenary; centennial; **a.** centenary
years, person of: **n.** or **a.** centenarian; **n.** macrobian

ONENESS: **n.** omneity; unanimity; unicity; uniquity; unity

ONESELF, *in spite of:* **adv.** *malgré soi*

ONE-SIDED: **a.** excentric(al); *ex parte;* factionary; partisan; self-serving; unilateral

ONE-THOUSAND, *group of, or period of 1000 yrs.:* **n.** chiliad; millennium

ONE *year old:* **a.** annotinous

OOZE: **v.** extravasate; osmose; transudate; transude; **n.** extravasation; transudation; **a.** osmotic; transudative

OPAQUE: **a.** adiaphorous; fuliginous; impervious; nubiferous; obscure; unintelligible

OPEN: **v.** extend; inaugurate; introduce; unfold; unveil; **a.** (**see** "free") accessible; dehiscent; exoteric; frank; gaping; liable; manifest; notorious; patent; patulous; undisguised; undissembling; unfeigned; unobstructed; unrestricted; **adv.** OPENLY: *ex professo;* unconcealed; unreservedly; **n.** OPENNESS: artlessness; *naïveté;* patency; unobstructedness
air: **a.** or **adv.** *à la belle étiole; al fresco;* hypaethral; *sub Jove;* upaithric
to attack or assault: **a.** vulnerable; **n.** vulnerability
-worked: **a.** *à jour; ajouré; ajourisé*

OPENING: (**see** "outlet") aperture; breach; *débouché;* fenestration; foramen; gambit; hiatus; inauguration; opportunity; orifice; os; **a.** inauguratory; initiatory; orificial
absence or closing of an: **n.** atresia; imperforation; stenosis; **a.** imperforate
as of career: **n.** debut; debutant(e); inauguration; investiture
of body: **n.** aperture; fistula; foramen; meatus; orifice; os; sinus
of speech or treatise: **n.** exordium; prologue
of symphony or mus. composition: **see under** "music"

OPERATE, *as by hand:* **v.** manipulate; **n.** manipulation; **a.** manipulable; manipulatable; manipulatory

OPERATING: **a.** functional; operational; physiologic(al); **n.** OPERATION: functioning; processus
not: **a.** afunctional; defunct; quiescent

OPINION(S): (**see** "belief") **n.** conclusion; consensus; conviction; diagnosis; impression; judgment; persuasion; sentiment
collection of, on a subject: **n.** symposium
difference of: (**see** "controversy") **n.** brannigan
express an: **v.** editorialize; opine; pontificate
fond of one's own: **a.** philodoxical; **n.** philodox
formal statement of: **n.** dictum; judgment
general: **n.** consensus; unanimity; **a.** consentaneous; consentient; unanimous
in defiance of general: **adv.** or **a.** *contra mundum*
in my: **adv.** *à mon avis; me judice*
so many men, so many (opinions): quot homines, tot sententiae
unity of: **n.** consentience; solidarity; unanimity

OPINIONATED: (**see** "stubborn") **a.** autotheistic; bigoted; conceited; doctrinaire; doctrinal; dogmatic; officious; *opiniâtre;* philodoxical; pontifical; pragmatic(al); prejudiced; sophomoric; vainglorious
person: **n.** dogmatist; philodox; **a.** dogmatic; philodoxical

OPPONENT: **n.** adversary; antagonist; assailant; competitor; defendant; disputant
attacking rather than issue: **adv.** *ad hominem;* **n.** *(argumentum) ad hominem*

OPPORTUNITY: (**see** "chance") **n.** conjuncture; occasion; **a.** OPPORTUNE: (**see** "pertinent") advantageous; *à propos;* auspicious; expedient; miraculous; propitious; providential; seasonable; tempestive; timely
grasp the: **n.** *carpe diem*
makes the thief: occasio facit furem

OPPOSE: **v.** antagonize; confront; contravene; counteract; countervail; militate; thwart; withstand
by argument: **v.** impugn; oppugn; **n.** impugnation; oppugnation
directly: **v.** contrapose; polarize; **n.** contraposition; polarity; polarization
inclined to: **a.** argumentative; militant; oppositious; oppositive; pugnacious
w/ equal weight: **v.** counteract; counterbalance; counterpoise; countervail; **a.** oppositious; oppositive

OPPOSED (**or** OPPOSING): (**see** "contrary") **a.** adversative; adverse; antagonistic; antipathetic(al); antonymous; argumentative; contralateral; contrariant; militant; oppositional; oppositious; oppositive; pugnacious
determinedly: **a.** oppositious

OPPOSITE: **a.** antagonistic; antipathetic(al); antipodal; antipodean; antipodic; antithetic(al); antonymic; antonymous; contradictory; converse; diametrical; incompatible; **prep.** vis-à-vis; **n.** antipod; (**pl.** antipodes); antithesis; antonym; complement; counterpart
directly: **a.** antipodal; antipodean; antithetic(al); diametrical; inverse
gather or concentrate at (opp.) extremes or poles: **v.** polarize; **n.** polarity; polarization
looking or acting in (opp.) ways: **a.** double-dealing; duplicitous; Janus-faced; Janus-like
position directly: **n.** antithesis; contraposition; polarity; polarization; **v.** contrapose; polarize; **a.** antithetic(al)
state of being: **n.** antipodes; antithesis; contrariety; contrawise; **a.** antipodean; diametrical
tendency: **n.** ambitendency; ambivalence
to: **adv.** *ex adverso; ex adversum*

OPPOSITION: **n.** antagonism; antipathy; confrontation; contraposition; contrariety; contravention; disaffinity; hostility; oppugnation; recalcitration; refractoriness; repugnance; **a.** oppositious; oppositive; **adv.** *au contraire*
having natural: **a.** antipathetic(al)
one engaged in: **n.** antipathist; opponent
to traditions, etc.: **n.** disestablishmentarianism; **a.** oppositious; oppositive

OPPRESS: **v.** dragoon; overburden; persecute; tyrannize; **a.** OPPRESSIVE: exacting; grievous; onerous; Tarquinian; tyrannic(al); tyrannous; **n.** OPPRESSION: tyranny

OPTICAL *effect or illusion:* **n.** *deceptio visus; fata morgana; ignis fatuus;* mirage; phantasmagoria; phantasmagory; **a.** illusional; phantasmagoric(al); kaleidoscopic(al)

OPTIMISTIC: **a.** confident; eupeptic; euphoric; expectant; heartening; hopeful; Micawberish; Pollyann(a)ish; promising; roseate; sanguine; sanguinic; **n.** OPTIMISM: (**see** "hopefulness") euphoria; Micawberism; Pollyann(a)ism; sanguinity

OPTIONAL: **a.** alternative; discretional; discriminative; elective; facultative; preferential; voluntary

ORAL: **a.** buccal; nuncupative; parol(e); phonetic; tacit; *viva voce;* vocal; **adv.** *ore tenus*
instruction: **n.** catechism; catachresis; **a.** catechetic(al); catechistic; **v.** catechize

ORATION: **n.** declamation; **n.** ORATOR: Demosthenes; rhetor(ician); spellbinder; (**fem.** oratrix); **a.** ORATORICAL: Ciceronian; Demosthenean; Demosthenic; declamatory; rhetorical

ORBIT, *point farthest out:* **n.** apogee
point nearest in: **n.** perigee

ORDEAL, *trial by:* **n.** *dei judicium*

ORDER: (**see** "arrangement") **n.** adjuration; caveat; command; concinnity; cosmos; curriculum; direction; discipline; disposition; eutaxy; fiat; formation; harmonization; harmony; husbandry; injunction; mandate; mandatum; ordinance; precedence; precept; protocol; regime; requisition; symmetry; uniformity; **v. see** "arrange"
according to time: **n.** chronology; **a.** calendric(al); chronologic(al)
arranged in: **a.** alphabetical; categorical; chronological; consecutive; *en règle; en suit;* methodical; ordinal; pragmatic; regimental; sequacious; sequential; seriatim; successional; systematic; **adv.** *par ordre alphabetique;* **n.** consecution; regimentation; sequence; sequent; seriality
authoritative: **n.** decretal; fiat; injunc-

tion; mandate; mandatum; ordinance; **a.** mandatory
good: **n.** concinnity; economy; eutaxy; husbandry
in: **see** "arranged in" **above**
lack of: **see** "confusion"
not in: **a.** inconsecutive; inconsequent; inordinate
of rank, bring into: **v.** coordinate; **n.** coordination

ORDERLY: (**see** "peaceful" **and** "rule, according to") **a.** alphabetical; compatible; congruent; congruous; consonant; harmonious; methodic(al); methodological; parliamentary; programmatic; rational; shipshape; systematic
arrangement: **n.** concinnity; eutaxy; syntax; **a.** Apollonian; concinnate; concinnous
system: **n.** cosmos

ORDINARY: (**see** "commonplace") **a.** administrative; average; conventional; indifferent; inferior; habitual; mediocre; middling; nomic; nominal; second-rate; uncosmic; uneventful; **n.** mediocrity

ORE, *rich vein of:* **n.** bonanza; El Dorado

ORGANIC: **a.** constitutional; functional; fundamental; inherent; physiological; structural; systemic
life, laws of: **n.** organonomy

ORGANISM: **n.** organization; system
very small: **n.** animalcule; animalculum; (**pl.** animalcula(e))

ORGANIZATION: **n.** administration; arrangement; constitution; cosmos; establishment; hierarchization; regimentation; stratification; structure; system(ization); **v.** ORGANIZE: (**see** "arrange") mobilize; orchestrate; **n.** ORGANIZER: impresario

ORGANS, *internal body:* **n.pl.** viscera; **a.** splanchnic; visceral

ORGY: **n.** bacchanal(ia); carousal; saturnalia; **a.** ORGIASTIC: bacchanal(ian); bacchantic; Dionysiac(al); Dionysian; saturnalian

ORIENTAL: **a.** Byzantine; Levantine; ortative
materials, as lit., artistic or archaeologic: **n.** Orientalia

ORIGIN(S): (**see** "beginning" **and** "source") **n.** ancestry; causation; derivation; etiology; genesis; inauguration; inchoation; nascency; incipience; parentage; primordium; (**pl.** primordia); provenance; provenience
beginning to form: **a.** aborning; embryonic; nascent; parturient; **n.** nascency
doctrine of: **n.** archology
fr. the: **adv.** *ab incunabulis; ab initio;* **a.** primordial
having common: **a.** monogen(et)ic; monogenistic
having more than one source of: **a.** polygenetic
identity of: **n.** isogeny; **a.** isogenous
of known: **a.** phenerogen(et)ic
of unknown: **a.** cryptogenic; idiopathic
pert. to: **a.** embryonic; genetic; inaugural; inceptive; inchoate; inchoative; nascent; rudimental; rudimentary
place of: **n.** *natale solum;* provenance
source and (origin): **n.** *fons et origo*
spontaneous: **n.** idiogenesis; **a.** idiogen(et)ic
study of: **n.** etiology; **a.** etiological

ORIGINAL: **a.** aboriginal; authentic; causative; fontal; generative; genetic; germinal; germinative; inceptive; inventive; naissant; neoteric; primitive; primogenial; primogenital; primordial; pristine; protogenic; prototypal; seminal; spermatic(al); underivative; **n.** (**see** "native") ectype; neoteric
daringly: **a.** Promethean
growth or tissue: **n.** naissance
not: (**see** "counterfeit") **a.** derivative; unoriginal

ORIGINALITY: **n.** ingenuity; ingenuosity; inventiveness

ORIGINATING *at various places or times:* **a.** polygenetic
spontaneously: **see under** "origin"

ORNAMENT: **v.** (**see** "adorn") embellish; **n.** adornment; embellishment; exornation; garniture; ornamentation; **a.** ORNAMENTAL: (**see** "ornate") festooned; spangled; tasellated

ORNATE: (**see** "showy") **a.** arabesque; aureate; aurelent; aurelian; clinquant; baronial; baroque; bombastic; flamboyant; florid; grandiloquent; magniloquent; orotund; ostentatious; resplendent; rococo; sumptuous

ORNERY: see "contrary"

OSTENTATIOUS: see "ornate"

OSTRICH(ES), *pert. to:* **a.** struthian; struthious
resembling: **a.** struthi(oni)form

OTHER *persons, centering interest or attention on:* **a.** allocentric
things being equal: cetera desunt; ceteris paribus
with many (others): **adv.** *cum multis aliis*

OTHERNESS: **n.** alterity; diversity

OUT-and-out: (see "absolute") **a.** arrant; complete; confirmed; consummate; downright; notorious; shameless; sheer; thoroughgoing; unmitigated; unqualified; utter
of action: (see "retired") **adv.** *hors de combat*
-of-date: (see "old-fashioned") **a.** antediluvian; archaic; archaistic; decadent; *démodé;* demoded; effete; *fin-de-siècle;* moribund; Neanderthal; neolithic; obsolete; outmoded; *passé;* troglodytic; *vieux jeu*
of many, one: e pluribus unum
of the mouths of babes: ex ore infantum
of this world: **a.** untramundane

OUTBURST: (see "outpouring") **n.** ebullition; eruption; fantod; fusillade; paroxysm; spate; **a.** ebullient; paroxysmal

OUTCAST: **n.** abject; castaway; expatriate; Ishmael; leper; offscouring; pariah; reprobate; **a.** abject; expatriate; Ishmaelitish; reprobative
status of being: **n.** pariahdom; pariahism

OUTCOME: **n.** conclusion; consequence; consummation; dénouement; emanation; exitus; progeny; residual; residuum; **a.** consequential; consummative; residual
possible: **n.** eventuality; possibility; probability

OUTCRY: (see "uproar") **n.** bruit; clamor; conclamation; vociferation
making loud: **a.** blatant; boisterous; clamorous; vociferous
of multitude or many: **n.** conclamation; **a.** conclamant

OUTDOOR(S): **a.** *al fresco;* extraforaneous; hypoethial; hypaethral; upaithric; **adv.** *al fresco*

OUTFIT: **v.** accouter; accoutre; caparison; **n.** armamentarium; equipage; equipment; (**pl.** accoutrements; caparisons; paraphernalia; regalia; trappings)

OUTGROWTH: (see "consequence") **n.** ramification

OUTLET: (see "opening") **n.** aperture; egress; orifice; os; **a.** orificial
as for goods or trade: **n.** *débouché*
as of river or stream: **n.** debouchment

OUTLINE: (see "summary") **v.** adumbrate; delineate; diagram; **n.** abridgement; adumbration; *aperçu;* circumference; compendium; configuration; conformation; conspectus; contour; delineation; diagram; portrayal; prospectus; schema; silhouette; synopsis
faint: **n.** adumbration
form, in: **a.** diagrammatic(al); schematic

OUTLOOK: (see "view") **n.** configuration; expectation; mentality; panorama; perspective; perspectivity; prognosis; prognostication; prospect
limited in: **a.** cloistral; egocentric; parochial; provincial; sectarian

OUTMODED: (see "out-of-date") **a.** obsolete; troglodytic; **n.** obsoleteness; obsoletism
or discarded status: **n.** desuètude

OUT-OF-DATE: see **under** "out"

OUTPOURING: (see "outburst") **n.** debouchment; *épanchement*
unusually large, as of words: **n.** spate

OUTRAGE: **n.** affront; dishonor; indecency; indignity; infamy; *lèse majesty;* **a.** OUTRAGEOUS: abhorrent; arrant; atrocious; extravagant; fantastic; flagrant; heinous; infamous; monstrous; notorious; unconscionable

OUTSET, *from:* (see "beginning") **adv.** *ab initio; ab initium; ab ovo;* **a.** aboriginal; primordial; **n.** primordium

OUTSIDE, *coming fr. the:* **a.** adventitious; exogenous; extraneous; extrinsic; **n.** extraneity; invection
growing or developing from: **a.** exogenous
regular duties or work: **a.** extracurricular; supererogatory; **n.** extracurriculum
surface: **n.** externality; perimeter; periphery; **a.** peripheral

OUTSIDER: **n.** auslander; exoteric; Ishmael; layman; tramontane

OUTSTANDING: **(see** "excelling" **and** "noted") **a.** conspicuous; noticeable; paramount; pending; prominent; salient; signal; significant; significative; stellar; (super)eminent; supreme; unresolved; **n.** conspicuity; predominance; predominancy; saliency; signality
item of a group: **n.** *pièce de résistance*

OUTWARD *form or appearance:* **n.** configuration; physicality; physiognomy; semblance; silhouette

OUTWEIGH: **v.** preponderate; surpass; **a.** precedental; preponderant; **n.** preponderance

OUTWIT: **v.** circumvent; frustrate; victimize; **n.** circumvention

OVAL: **a.** curvilinear; elliptic(al); nummiform; nummular; ovate; ovoid; spherical; spheroidal

OVER: **see** "finished" **and** "excessive"

OVERACTING (or OVERACTED): **n.** histrionics; theatrics; **a.** histrionic; theatrical

OVERBEARING: **(see** "haughty") **a.** arbitrary; arrogant; autocratic; cavalier; compelling; despotic; dictatorial; dogmatic; domineering; imperative; imperious; insupportable; lordly; masterful; preponderating; supercilious

OVERCOME: **v.** conquer; demolish; domineer; overpower; overwhelm; subdue; surmount; vanquish
incapable of being: **a.** insubvertible; insuperable; insurmountable; invincible; inviolable; invulnerable; sacrosanct; unconquerable; **n.** insuperability; invulnerability

OVERCONFIDENT: **a.** overweening; presumptuous; **n.** OVERCONFIDENCE: **see** "presumption"

OVERDECORATED: (or OVERDRESSED): **a.** bedizened; **n.** bedizenment; **v.** bedizen
man who is (overdressed): **n.** Beau Brummel

OVERDO: **v.** cloy; satiate; supererogate

OVEREAT: **v.** gormandize; **n. see** "gluttony"

OVERFLOWING: **a.** abundant; copious; cornucopian; inundatory; redounding; redundant; scaturient; superabundant; torrential; **n.** cornucopia; deluge; inundation; profusion; redundance; redundancy; spate; superabundance

OVERINDULGENCE (*any activity*): **n.** orgy; satiation; satiety; **a.** orgiastic

OVERLAPPING: **a.** jugate

OVERLOOK: **v.** condone; disregard; ignore; pretermit; superintend; **n.** condonation; pretermission; surveillance

OVERNICE: **a.** euphemistic; fastidious; fastigial; meticulous; nice Nelly; per(s)-nickety; prudish; scrupulous; squeamish; **n.** OVERNICETY: correctitude; fastidiousness; fastidium; finicality; meticulosity; per(s)nicketiness; scrupulosity

OVERPOWERING: **(see** "overwhelming") **a.** copious; torrential

OVERSHADOW: **v.** adumbrate; eclipse; **n.** adumbration; eclipse; **a.** adumbral

OVERSTATEMENT: **n.** embellishment; exaggeration; hyperbole; ornamentation; **a.** hyperbolic(al)

OVERTHROW: **v.** demolish; dethrone; dislodge; exterminate; overturn; unhorse; vanquish; **n.** bouleversement; *coup d'état;* débacle; deféasance; labefaction
incapable of: **see under** "overcome"

OVERTURNING: **a.** anatreptic; refuting

OVERWHELM: **(see** "defeat") **v.** confound; deluge; demolish; inundate; submerge; vanquish; **a.** OVERWHELMING: deluginous; devastating; ineffable; inundatory; murderous; **n.** flood tide; ineffability; inundation

OWL(S), *rel. to or like:* **a.** strigine

OWN: **v.** acknowledge; concede

OWNERSHIP: **n.** proprietary; proprietorship; **a.** proprietary
pride in or consciousness of: **a.** proprietorial; proprietous

OXYGEN *deficiency:* **n.** anoxemia; cyanosis; **a.** anoxemic; cyanotic

P

PACE, *at equal:* **a.** or **adv.** *pari passu*

PACIFY: (**see** "appease") **v.** ameliorate; assuage; conciliate; mitigate; mollify; placate; propitiate; reconcile; tranquilize; **n.** PACIFICATION: amelioration; conciliation; mitigation; tranquilization; **a.** PACIFICATORY: (**see** "peaceful") conciliatory; irenic(al); pacifistic; placative; propitiative

PAGE (*of book*), *rel. to:* **a.** paginal
to number: **v.** paginate; **n.** pagination

PAIN: **n.** affliction; agony; anguish; distress; dolor; lancination; martyrdom; paroxysm; penance; punishment; throe; torment; travail
agent to destroy or deaden: **n.** analgesic; anesthetic; anodyne; hypnotic; opiate; **a.** analgesic; anodynic; hypnotic
capacity to endure: **n.** forbearance; longanimity; sufferance; tolerance
causing: **a.** afflictive; dolorific
fear of: **n.** algophobia
flashing: **a.** fulgurant; fulgurating; fulgurous; lancinating
high sensitivity to: **n.** hyperalgesia; hyperalgia; **a.** hyperalgesic
incapable of: **a.** impassible; insentient; **n.** impassibility; insentience
intense: **n.** agony; travail; **v.** travail
lessened sensitivity to: **n.** analgesia; anesthesia; hypalgesia; **a.** analgesic; hypalgesic
lessening: **a.** assuasive; lenitive; mitigatory; obtundent; palliative; palliatory; **n.** lenity
loss of: **n.** anesthesia; **a.** anesthetic
mental, or of mental origin: **n.** dysphoria; psychalgesia; **a.** dysphoric
of labor (*childbirth*): **n.** or **v.** travail
piercing: **see** "flashing" **above**
pleasure in inflicting: **n.** algophilia; sadism; **a.** algophilic; sadistic; **n.** algophilist; sadist
in inflicting or receiving: **n.** algophilia; **a.** algophilic
in receiving: **n.** algophilia; masochism; **a.** algophilic; masochistic; **n.** algophilist; masochist
rectal: **n.** proctalgia
rel. to or causing: **a.** algedonic; algetic; algogenic
relieving: (**see** "lessening" **above**) **a.** alleviatory; narcotic; opiate; opiatic; palliative; palliatory; remedial
sensitivity to: **n.** (hyper)algesia

PAINFUL: **a.** afflictive; agonal; dolorific; distressing; excruciating; irksome; torminous; tortuous; troublesome; vexatious
route or series of experiences: **n.** *via dolorosa*
to touch: **a.** hyperalgesic; hyperesthetic; hypersensitive

PAINTING *of genre or still-life, or of mean or sordid subjects:* **n.** rhyparography; **a.** rhyparographic

PAIR(S): **v.** conjugate; **n.** conjugation; counterpart(s); duality; dyad; partnership; **a.** PAIRED: bigeminal; binary; duplex; dyadic; jumelle
growing in: **a.** didymous

PALE: **a.** achromic; anemic; ashen; cadaverous; etiolated; ghastly; ischemic; livid; pallid; **n.** etiolation; ghastliness; ischemia; lividity; pallidity

PALLIATE: **see** "lessen"

PALMIST: **n.** chirognomist; chiromancer; **n.** PALMISTRY: chirognomy; chiromancy

PAMPER: (**see** "caress") **v.** mollycoddle

PAMPHLET: (**see** "manual") **n.** brochure; monograph; treatise

PANTING: **n.** anhelation; dyspnea; hyperpnea; palpitation

PAPER: **see** "essay"
resembling: **a.** papyraceous

PAR: (**see** "equality") **n.** normality; parity
under: (**see** "inferior") **a.** suboptimal; substandard

PARABLE *in form, or expressed by:* **a.** parabolic(al); **v.** parabolize

PARADISE: **n.** Abraham's bosom; Eden; elysium; Nirvana; oblivion; utopia; **a.** PARADISIAC(AL): Edenic; elysian; nirvanic; utopian

PARAGON *of excellence or beauty:* **n.** phoenix

PARALLEL: **a.** analogous; companion; concurrent; correlative; correspondent; equidistant; paradromic; **n.** *alter ego;* analog(ue); correlative; counterpart
to make: **v.** collimate; parallelize; **n.** collimation; parallelization

PARAPHRASE: **n.** *oratio obliqua;* recapitulation; restatement

PARASITE: **n.** saphrophyte; sponger; sycophant; today; **a.** PARASITIC(AL): saphrophytic; sycophantic(al); **v.** sycophantize

PARDON: **v.** absolve; acquit; condone; excuse; remit; **n.** absolution; acquittal; amnesty; condonation; indulgence; remission; **a.** PARDONABLE: **see** "excusable"
me: **n.** *pardonnez-moi*

PARENT(S): **n.** ancestor; author; genitor; (**fem.** genetrix; **pl.** genetrices); originator; producer; progenitor
acting as, or being in place of: **adv.** *in loco parentis*
murder of, also murderer: **n.** parenticide; parricide; **a.** parricidal; parricidious
rel. bet. child and: **a.** filial; parental
transmitting characteristics of both: **a.** amphigonic; amphigonous

PARENTAL *love or affection:* **n.** philoprogenitiveness; storge
power, subject to: **a.** unemancipated

PARENTHETIC(AL): **a.** ejaculatory; episodic(al); incidental; interjaculatory; interjectional; interjectural; interlocutory; tangential; *adv. par parenthèse*
remark(s): **n.** dictum; digression; *gratis dictum; obiter dictum;* scholium; tangent; (**pl.** *obiter dicta; scholia*)
speech: **n.** interlocution; **a.** interlocutory

PARISH, *pert. to:* **a.** parochial

PARK, *wooded:* **n.** arboretum

PARODY: **n.** burlesque; caricature; lampoon; satire; travesty
in nature of: **a.** parodistic; satirical

PART(S): **n.** component; constituent; element; fragment; integral; ingredient; integrant; moiety; particularity; quantum; (**pl.** quanta); sector; segment; **a.** componental; constituent; integral; **v.** **see** "divide"
complex aggregation of: **n.** complexus
divided into many: **a.** multipartite; polychotomous; polytomous
into three: **a.** trichotomous; tripartite; **n.** trichotomy; tripartition; triplex
into two: **a.** bifid; bifurcated; bipartite; dichotomous; **n.** dichotomy
from the (part) one may recognize the whole: ex pede Herculem; ex ungue leonem
necessary: **n.** component; constituent; essentiality

PARTED: **a.** bifid; bifurcated; cloven; dichotomous; estranged; partite

PARTIAL: (**see** "incomplete") **a.** biased; fractionary; fragmental; fragmentary; predisposed; prejudiced; segmented

PARTIALITY: (**see** "bias") **n.** partisanship; predilection
on acct. of: **adv.** *propter affectum*
undue or invidious: **n.** chauvinism

PARTICIPANT: **n.** antagonist; combatant; (**pl.** *dramatis personae*)

PARTICULAR: (**see** "careful") **a.** captious; fastidious; finical; scrupulous; **n.** characteristic; particularity
state or fact of being: **n.** particularity; scrupulosity

PARTING: (**see** "separation") **n.** cleavage; disjunction; dismemberment; disso-

lution; disunion; estrangement; sundering
word: (**see** "farewell") **n.** envoi

PARTISAN: (**see** "follower") **n.** advocate; aficionado; factionary; sectarian; sympathizer; **a.** denominational; factionary; sectarian

PARTNER: **a.** associate; coadjutor; colleague; confederate; confrere; consort; partaker; participant; **n.** PARTNERSHIP: accomplicity; alliance; association; participation
in crime: **n.** accomplice; ***particeps criminis; socius criminis***

PARTY: (**see** "celebration") **n.** potlatch

PASS: **v.** admit; authorize; exceed; intromit; terminate; **n.** (**see** "permit") crisis; intromission; predicament
(*palm off as genuine*): **v.** foist
permission to: **n.** ***passe partout;*** passport; visa

PASSAGE, *in or during:* **adv.** ***in transitu***

PASSION: (**see** "zeal") **n.** ardor; ***béguin;*** enthusiasm; evangelism; fervor; infatuation; martyrdom; suffering; torridity; transport
abnormal sexual: **n.** erogeneity; eroticism; erotomania

PASSIONATE: **a.** ardent; bacchanalian; bacchic; Dionysian; ebullient; evangelistic; faustian; fervent; impassioned; impetuous; intense; orgiastic; precipitate; sultry; torrid; vehement
protest or cry: **n.** ***cri de*** (*or* ***du***) ***coeur***
violently: **a.** sulfurous; sulphurous; voluptuous

PASSIVE: (**see** "patient") **a.** inactive; inert; inexcitable; invertebrate; negative; obedient; quiescent; receptive; stoical; submissive; supine; unresisting; unresponsive; **n.** PASSIVENESS: inactivity; passivity; stoicism; submissiveness

PASSOVER, *pert. to:* **a.** paschal

PASSWORD: **n.** countersign; ***mot de passe; mot d'ordre; mot du guet; passe parole;*** sesame; shibboleth; watchword

PAST, *influence of, as controlling or restricting the present:* **n.** mortmain
longing for: **n.** nostalgia; **a.** nostalgic
person or thing of: **n.** antediluvian; antequarian; cidevant; mossback; patriarch
surveying the: **n.** memoir(s); reflection; reminiscence; retrospection

PASTE, *make into:* **v.** levigate

PASTIME: **n.** passetemps

PASTORAL: (**see** "rural") **a.** Arcadian; bucolic; geoponic; georgic; idyllic; innocent; picturesque; rustic; Theocritean

PATH, *the beaten is the safe:* ***via trita, via tuta***

PATIENCE: **n.** composure; endurance; equanimity; forbearance; fortitude; imperturbability; indulgence; leniency; lenity; longanimity; long-suffering; perseverance; resignation; submission; sufferance; toleration; **a.** PATIENT: (**see** "forbearing") bovine; composed; charitable; dispassionate; enduring; imperturbable; longanimous; philosophic(al); resigned; sedate; stoical; temperate; tolerant; unimpassioned
something which exhausts: **n.** abradant; irritant; provocation

PATRIOT, *fanatical:* **n.** chauvinist; flagwaver; jingoist; patrioteer; superpatriot; superzealot

PATRIOTISM: **n.** ***amor patriae***
display of, or writings and speeches on: **n.pl.** patriotics
extreme or fanatical: **n.** chauvinism; ethnocentrism; jingoism; spread-eagleism; super-patriotism

PATRONIZING *manner or behavior:* **n.** condescendence; condescension

PATTERN: (**see** "model") **n.** archetype; *beau idéal;* characteristic; configuration; conformation; exemplar; exemplum; modality; orthodoxy; paradigm; paragon; precedent; prototype; stereotype; syndrome; yardstick
having but one structural: **a.** monomorphic; monomorphous

PAUNCH: **see** "abdomen"

PAUSE: **v.** intermit; **n.** armistice; c(a)esura; cessation; *entr'acte;* hiatus; inter-

mission; interregnum; moratorium; respite; **a.** cessative
as in speech: **n.** hiatus; **a.** hiatal

PAWN: **v.** hypothecate; (im)pignorate; pledge; **n.** hypothecation; impignoration

PAY: **v.** compensate; indemnify; liquidate; recompense; reimburse; remunerate; satisfy; **n. see** "payment" **and** "salary"

PAYMENT: (**see** "compensation") **n.** defrayal; honorarium; liquidation; remittance; remuneration; retribution
where no set fee: **n.** honorarium

PEA, *resembling in size or shape:* **a.** pisiform

PEACE: (**see** "calmness") **n.** nirvana; pacification; quiescence; (re)conciliation; repose; serenity; tranquility
(be) with you: **n.** *pax vobiscum; sholom aleichim*
go in: **adv.** *vade in pace*
goddess of: **n.** Irene; Minerva; Pax
offer or gesture of: **n.** olive branch
promoting: (**see** "peaceful") **a.** irenic; pacific; peaceable; **n.** peaceability
rest in: **adv.** *requiescat in pace* (**abb.** R.I.P.)

PEACEFUL: (**see** "calm") **a.** affable; amiable; appeasing; conciliatory; (con)genial; halcyon; harmonious; henotic; irenic(al); neighborly; nirvanic; oasitic; pacific(atory); pacifistic; pastoral; quiescent; serene; tempean; tranquil; unaggressive; unagitated; undisturbed; **n.** PEACEFULNESS: amiability; pacification; placability; serenity; tranquility; tranquilization

PEACE-MAKER: **n.** conciliator; intercessor; mediator; placater
blessed are the (peacemakers): *beati pacifici*

PEACOCK, *of or resembling:* **a.** pavonian; pavonine

PEAK: (**see** "acme") **n.** apogee; climax; culmination; flood tide; maximum; meridian; pinnacle; summit; ultimate; zenith; **a.** apogeal; apogean; apogeic; maximum; supernal; zenithal

PEARL-*bearing:* **a.** margaritiferous

PEARLY: **a.** iridescent; lustrous; margaritaceous; nacreous; opalescent

PECULIAR: (**see** "odd") **a.** aberrant; anomalous; atypical; bizarre; characteristic; eccentric; grotesque; heterogeneous; idiocratic; idiosyncratic; *outré;* unconventional; whimsical; **n.** PECULIARITY: (**see** "oddity" **and** "whim") bizarrerie; caprice; characteristic; eccentricity; haecceity; idiasm; idiocrasy; idiosyncrasy; individuality; particularity; quiddity; quirk; singularity; uniquity; vagary; whimsicality
to a particular group or person: **a.** idiomatic(al)
to the individual: **a.** idiopathic; innate

PEDESTAL, *place upon a:* **see** "deify" **and** "exalt"

PEEL: **v.** decorticate; desquamate; excoriate; exfoliate; exuviate; **a.** PEELING: deciduous; desquamative; desquamatory; exfoliative; exuviative; **n.** decortication; desquamation; ecdysis; excoriation; exfoliation; exuviation

PEEPER: **n.** peeping Tom; scopophiliac; *voyeur;* **a.** PEEPING: scopophilic; voyeuristic; **n.** scopophilia; voyeurism

PEERLESS: **a.** immutable; incomparable; incommensurable; majestic; matchless; *ne plus ultra;* optimum; paramount; preeminent; sovereign; (super)eminent; superlative; superexcellent; unequaled; unsurpassable
person or thing: **n.** nonpareil; nonesuch; paragon; phoenix

PEERS, *before one's:* **a. or adv.** *coram paribus*
by one's own: **adv.** *per pares*

PEEVISH: (**see** "gloomy") **a.** atrabilarious; atrabiliar; atrabilious; caustic; choleric; fretful; irascible; irritable; petulant; querulous; restive; splenetic; testy; waspish; **n.** PEEVISHNESS: (**see** "crankiness") distemper; irascibility; petulance; pique; protervity; querulousness
person: **n.** atrabilarian; curmudgeon

PEN *name:* **see under** "name"
slip of the: **n.** *lapsus calami*
with running: **adv.** *currente calamo*

PENAL: **a.** castigatory; corrective; disciplinary; expiatory; penitentiary; punitive; reformative; reformatory; retributive; retributory; **v.** PENALIZE: **(see** "punish") amerce

PENALTY: **(see** "punishment") **n.** amercement; chastisement; expiation; penance; retribution
appeal to: **n. or adv.** (*argumentum*) *ad baculum*
deserved: **n.** comeuppance; condignity; deserts; **a.** condign
pay the: **v.** atone; expiate
required or done under: **a.** penal; punitive; subpoenal

PENDING: **a.** abeyant; imminent; impending; *in fieri;* pendent (**or** pendant); pendular; pendulous; provisional; undecided; undetermined; **n.** PENDENCY: abeyance; abeyancy; imminence; imminency; pendulation; pendulosity; suspension

PENETRATE: **v.** impenetrate; permeate

PENETRATED, *capable of being:* **a.** penetrable; permeable; pervious
incapable of being: **a.** impenetrable; impermeable; imperforate; imperviable; impervious
thoroughly: **a.** permeated

PENETRATING: **(see** "keen") **a.** astute; discerning; incisive; osmotic; penetrative; perforating; permeable; piquant; poignant; sagacious; trenchant

PENITENCE: **(see** "regret") **n.** attrition; compunction; contrition; remorse; repentance; **a.** PENITENT: contrite; remorseful; repentant

PENITENTIAL *suffering:* **n.** satispassion

PENMAN: **n.** calligrapher; chirographer; **n.** PENMANSHIP: calligraphy; chirography; **a.** calligraphic; chirographic

PENNILESS: **(see** "poor") **a.** bankrupt; impecunious; indigent; *sans le sou;* **n.** PENNILESSNESS: bankruptcy; impecuniosity; insolvency; mendicancy

PENSIVE: **a.** cogitable; cogitabund; cogitative; contemplative; meditative; reflective

PEOPLE(S): **(see** "person") **n.** commonalty; *homo sapiens;* mankind; multitude; nation; populace; race; throng
common: **n.pl.** commonalty; demos; *hoi polloi; le bas peuple;* lumpen proletariat; multitude; pleb(e)ian; populace; population; *profanum vulgus;* proletariat; *vulgus ignobile;* **a.** lumpen; plebeian; proletarian; proletariat(e)
considered boobs: **n.pl.** booboisie
dregs of the: **n.pl.** *faex populi*
formed of or inhabited by many: **a.** polyethnic
group of varied: **n.** menagerie
high class: **see** "nobility"
humble: **(see** "common" **above) n.pl.** *gens de peu*
in general: **n.** commonalty; *hoi polloi;* masses; multitude
lower class: **see** "rabble"
middle class: **n.** bourgeois(ie)
of fashion: **n.pl.** *gens du monde*
of rank: **n.pl.** *gens de condition*
pert. to: **a.** demotic; ethnic; popular
pert. to all: **a.** cosmopolitan; pandemic; universal; **n.** pandemia
primitive, study of: **n.** agriology; anthropology
relating to or peculiar to a: **a.** gentilitial; gentilitious
to please the: **adv.** (*argumentum*) *ad captandum* (*vulgus*)
upper class: **see** "nobility"
voice of the: **n.** *vox populi* (**abb.** vox pop.)
wish to be fooled: populus vult decipe

PERCEIVABLE (**or** PERCEPTIBLE): **a.** cognizable; cognoscible; cognoscitative; comprehensible; discernible; intelligible; observable; palpable; recognizable; tangible
barely: **a.** liminal
not: **a.** subliminal
readily: **a.** translucent
to senses: **a.** corporeal; discernible; palpable; patent; sensible; tangible; **n.** corporeality; corporeity; sensibility; tangibility

PERCEIVE, *having power or capacity to:* **a.** (ap)percipient; perspicacious; **n.** cognizance; percipience; percipiency; perspicacity
instrument or apparatus for (perceiving): **n.** sensorium
unable or unwilling to: **a.** astigmatic(al); insentient; myopic; strabismic; **n.**

astigmatism; insentience; myopia; strabismus

PERCEPTION: (**see** "knowledge") **n.** apprehension; cognizance; comprehension; consciousness; discernment; insight; observation; percipience; (re)cognition; sensibility
below: **a.** subliminal; **n.** sublimination
gifted w/: **a.** (ap)percipient; clairvoyant; prehensile; telepathic
imaginary or unreal: **n.** delusion; *fata morgana;* hallucination; hallucinosis; *ignis fatuus;* illusion; phantasmagoria; will-of-the-wisp; **a.** delusive; hallucinatory; illusive; phantasmagoric(al)
keen: **n.** acumen; clairvoyance; cryptesthesia; hyperesthesia; percipience; perspicacity; sagacity; **a.** clairvoyant; hyperesthetic; percipient; sagacious
lacking in: **a.** astigmatic(al); insentient; myopic; strabismic
of distant objects, events, etc.: **n.** clairvoyance; extra sensory perception; telegnosis; telepathy; telesthesia
of what not normally perceptible: **n.** clairsentience; clairvoyance; extra sensory perception; telegnosis; **a.** clairsentient; clairvoyant

PERCEPTIVE: **a.** cognitive; cognitional; knowing; observant; penetrating; percipient; perspicacious; sensible; sensitive; sentient; trenchant
not: (**see** "stupid") **a.** imperceptive; impercipient; **n.** impercipience

PERFECT: (**see** "flawless") **a.** accurate; consummate; exemplary; expert; immaculate; inerrable; inerrant; inerratic; infallible; integral; inviolate; plenary; proficient; saintly
incapable of being made: **a.** imperfectible; **n.** imperfectibility
more than: **a.** pluperfect; superlative
to make: **v.** perfectivize; **n.** perfectivization

PERFECTION: **n.** accomplishment; *beau idéal;* completion; consummation; excellence; exemplarity; expertise; finality; immaculacy; impeccability; indefectibility; inerrancy; infallibility; integrality; maturity; perfectibilism; perfectibility; proficiency; saintliness; virtuosity; wholeness; **n.** PERFECTIONIST: perfectibilist; perfectibili(tari)an; *précieuse;* precisian; precisionist; purist
highest: **n.** *cordon bleu; ne plus supra; ne plus ultra;* supermundane; supernaculum
symbol of: **n.** *cordon bleu;* exemplarity; *grand prix*
tendency to fall short of: **n.** defectibility

PERFORMER: **see** "actor" **and** "doer"

PERFUMED: **see** "scented"

PERHAPS: **a. or adv.** peradventure

PERIL: (**see** "danger") **n.** Charybdis; hazard; insecurity; instability; jeopardy; **a.** PERILOUS: destructive; explosive; icarian; jeopardous; malignant; parlous
at his own: **adv.** *suo periculo*

PERIOD(S): **n.** cycle; eon; epoch; era; *siècle*
for indefinite: **a.** *sine die;* **adv.** *ad infinitum;* **n.** infinity
division into: **n.** periodization
latent or incubation: **n.** deliquescence; dormancy; latency; quiescence
of great happiness or prosperity: **n.** golden age; millennium
of long duration: **n.** millennium; saeculum
of success or achievement: **n.** fluorescence
recurring at indefinite: **a.** cyclic(al)

PERIODIC(AL): **a.** cyclic(al); etesian; intermittent; recurrent; rhythmical

PERIPHERAL: (**see** "external") **a.** circumferential; distal; marginal; peripheric

PERISHABLE: (**see** "fleeting") **a.** caducous; deciduous; ephemeral; evanescent; fugacious; mortal; transitory; volatile; **n.** PERISHABLENESS: caducity; evanescence; fugacity; perishability; transience; volatility

PERMANENT: (**see** "eternal" **and** "lasting") **a.** immarcescible; immutable; imperishable; indefaceable; indelible; indestructable; indissoluble; ineffaceable; ineradicable; inextirpable; invariable; irreversible; irrevocable; (per)durable; perdurant; unalterable; **n.** PERMANENCE (**or** PERMANENCY) durability; indissolubility; ineffaceability; perdurance; persistence

PERMISSION: **n.** authorization; sanction; sufferance; tolerance; toleration; **a.** PERMISSIVE: authorized; elective; empowering; enabling; facultative; indulgent; lawful; legitimate; licit; official; optional; sanctioned; sanctionative; tolerant; undemanding
involving or implying: **a.** authoritative; sanctionative; tolerant
to depart: **n.** *congé*
with: **adv.** *avec permission*

PERMIT: **v.** acquiesce; authorize; concede; countenance; empower; franchise; sanction; tolerate; **n.** franchise, *laissez-passer;* license; permittance
graciously: **v.** vouchsafe

PERMITTED: **(see** "permissive") **a.** allowed; licit; permissible
beyond what is: **adv.** *ultra licitum; ultra vires*
not: **a.** impermissible; **n.** impermissibility
within what is: **adv.** *intra vires*

PERPENDICULAR, *state of being:* **n.** perpendicularity

PERPETUAL: **(see** "permanent") **a.** immortal; incessant; persistent; sempiternal; unceasing; undying; **v.** PERPETUATE: **(see** "endure") eternalize; immortalize; preserve; **n.** PERPETUATION: eternalization; immortalization; perpetuality; perpetuity
motion: **n.** *moto perpetuo; perpetum mobile*
state of being: **n.** perpetuality; perpetualness; perpetuation; perpetuity

PERPLEX: **(see** "bewilder") **v.** complicate; confuse; disconcert; embrangle; entangle; interweave; **a.** PERPLEXED: anxious; bewildered; disconcerted; distracted; distraught; nonplus(s)ed; **n.** PERPLEXITY: conglomeration; cruciality; *cul-de-sac;* dilemma; embarassment; embranglement; embroilment; entanglement; exigency; imbroglio; impasse; labyrinth; morass; plight; predicament; puzzlement; quandary

PERPLEXING: **(see** "puzzling") **a.** bewildering; disconcerting; enigmatic(al); inexplicable
situation or position: **see** "perplexity"

PERSECUTE: **v.** afflict; dragoon; oppress; torment; tyrannize; **n.** PERSECUTOR: sadist; Torquemada; tyrant; **n.** PERSECUTION: oppression; torment; tyranny

PERSIST: **v.** perpetuate; persevere; sustain; **a.** PERSISTENT: **(see** "stubborn") demanding; determined; enduring; importunate; indefatigable; indomitable; lingering; obstinate; perpetual; pressing; solicitous; tenacious; **n. see** "stubbornness"

PERSON(S): **(see** "man" **and** "people") **n.** existent; personality; propositus; specimen; subject; **(pl.** *dramatis personae)*
affected and snobbish: **n.pl.** *gens à chichis;* **n.** *poseur;* **(fem.** *poseuse)*
aggressive: **n.** arrivist(e); pusher
among other: **adv.** *inter alios*
bad: **(see** "base" **below) n.** *enfant terrible*
bald-headed: **n.** pilgarlic
base and despicable: **n.** barbarian; Beelzebub; brutalitarian; caitiff; malefactor; Mephistopheles; miscreant; renegade; reprobate; ribald; rogue; sadist; scapegrace
bigoted: **see** "narrow-minded" **below**
bold and saucy: **n.** malapert; picaroon
bragging or blustering: **n.** braggart; rodomontade; swashbuckler
careless: **n.** pococurante; superficialist
charitable: **n.** almoner; *amicus humani generis;* charitarian; eleemosynar; humanitarian; philanthropist; Samaritan
clever and cultivated: **n.** *bel esprit*
clumsy: **n.** stumblebum
coarse: **see** "vulgar" **below**
common: **(see** "rabble") **n.** bourgeois(ie); commonality; *hoi polloi;* plebeian; *roturier*
compassionate: **see** "charitable" **above**
contrary or inconsistent: **n.** paradox
conventional: **see under** "conventional"
cowardly: **n.** dastard; poltroon; recreant
crabby: **n.** crotcheteer; curmudgeon
creative: **n.** Prometheus; **a.** Promethean
crude: **n.** buffoon; grobian; rustic
cultivated: **n.** *bel esprit;* literatus
degraded and contemptible: **n.** lumpenproletariat
determined: **n.** *esprit fort;* Trojan
distinguished in his field: **n.** Brahmin; *cordon bleu;* laureate; paladin; pantheon
domineering: **n.** autocrat; Napoleon; tyrant
dull, stupid or clownish: **n.** Abderite;

Babbitt; Boeotian; bromide; buffoon; dullard; flibbertigibbet; goose; grobian; harlequin; Juke; Merry Andrew; nincompoop; pachyderm; scaramouche

eccentric: **n.** beatnik: Bohemian; zealot

esteemed: (**see** "of high rank" **below**) **n.** pantheon

frivolous: **n. or a.** flibbertigibbet; futilitarian

functioning as a (as corpn., state, etc.): **n.** *universitas personarum*

generous: **see** "charitable" **above**

gigantic: **see** "giant"

gloomy: **n.** cynic; dismal Jimmie; gloomy Gus; pessimist

good-natured: **n.** *bon diable; bon naturel*

greedy: (**see** "self-centered" **below**) **n.** glutton; mercenary

hater of new things or ideas: **n.** misoneist; **a.** misoneistic

of wisdom or knowledge: **n.** anti-intellectualist; misopher; misophist

high in class or field: (**see** "of high rank" **below**) **n.** pantheon

ignorant: **n.** am haarez; analphabet; ignoramus; Philistine; sciolist

ill-disciplined, turbulent: **n.** bashibazouk; *enfant terrible*

important: **n.** bashaw; celebrity; colossus; cynosure; grandee; luminary; magnate; mogul; notability; notoriety; panjandrum; poo(h)bah; potentate; sachem; sagamore; tycoon

in (person): **adv.** *in propria persona*

inconsistent or contrary: **n.** paradox

indecisive: **n.** invertebrate; milksop; milquetoast

insensitive: **n.** pachyderm

insignificant: **n.** pipsqueak

insincere: **n.** charlatan; mountebank; *poseur;* (**fem.** *poseuse*); pretender

insolent: **n.** jackanapes; malapert

intellectual: (**see** "intellectual(s)") **n.** *bel esprit*

irresponsible: **n.** apostate; charlatan; *enfant terrible;* maverick; mountebank; pretender

irritable: **n.** atrabilarian; crotcheteer; curmudgeon; Tartar

large: **see** "giant"

lazy or idle: **n.** faineant

leading: (**see** "important" **above**) **n.** luminary

learned: (**see** "intellectual[s]") **n.** academe; academician; *bel esprit;* Brahmin; erudite; *homo multarum literarum;* illuminato; philologist; polyhistor; polymath; pundit; rhetorician; savant; scholar; sophist; (**pl.** illuminata; intelligentsia; literati)

legal: **n.** corporation; *homo legalis*

lewd: **see** "libertine"

liberal: **n.** charitarian; eleemosynar; humanitarian; latitudinarian; libertarian; philanthropist

literary: **see under** "literary"

living high and well: **n.** *bon vivant; bon viveur; sybarite*

low: **n.** groundling(s); *polisson;* vulgarian

materialistic: **n.** Babbitt; Gradgrind; Philistine

mean: **see** "base and despicable" **above**

mentally defective but brilliant in some field: **n.** idiot savant

miserly: **n.** curmudgeon; Scrooge

modern: **n.** moderne; neoteric

mysterious: **n.** enigma; paradox; sphinx

narrow-minded: **n.** bigot; lilliputian; pedant; Philistine; quidnunc; sectarian

of great size or power: **n.** colossus; gargantua; titan

of high rank, respect or importance: **n.** aristocrat; bashaw; Brahmin; eminentissimo; luminary; magnifico; mahatma; minion; *ne plus ultra;* nonesuch; paladin; panjandrum; paradigm; paragon; patrician; (**pl.** aristoi)

of humble origin: **n.** *filius terrae*

of letters: **n.** *homme de lettres; literateur; literato; literatus;* (**pl.** *gens de lettres; literati*)

of little importance: **n.** mediocrity; nihility; nonentity; reprobate

of low rank or repute: (**see** "rabble") **n.** *polisson;* vulgarian

of oustanding quality, or firm in course or object: **n.** paladin; paradigm; protagonist

offensive or pernicious: **n.** cocatrice

old: (**see under** "old") **n.** macrobian

opinionated: **n.** dogmatist; philodox; sectarian

overly precise in lang.: **n.** *précieuse; précieux;* purist

peerless: **n.** nonesuch; nonpareil; paragon; phoenix

pernicious: **n.** cocatrice

plucky: **n.** Trojan

pompous: **n.** Aldibrontiphoscophornio; panjandrum

powerful or wealthy: **n.** Croesus; leviathan; mogul; plutocrat; potentate; powerhouse; titan; tycoon

practical: **n.** practician; pragmatist; materialist; utilitarian

precise or punctilious: **n.** perfectibilist; perfectibilitarian; *précieuse; précieux;* precisian; precisionist
presumptuous: **n.** coxcomb; fantastico; jackanapes
prominent: (**see** "important" **above**) **n.** celebrity; luminary; notability; notoriety
quarrelsome: **n.** rantipole; termagant
ragged: **n.** ragamuffin; tatterdemalion
rascally: **see** "base and despicable" **above**
rash: **n.** hotspur
rowdy: **n.** yahoo
saintly and righteous: **n.** zaddik
saucy and bold: **n.** malapert; picaroon
self-centered: **n.** autotheist; egocentric; egocentrist; ego(t)ist; *flâneur;* (**fem.** *flâneuse*); hedonist; iotacist; misanthropist; narcissist; solipsist; sycophant; sybarite
self-important: **n.** megalomaniac; **a.** autotheistic
sensuous: **see under** "sensuous"
shiftless: **n.** prodigal; vagabond; (**pl.** flotsam and jetsam)
silly: (**see** "dull, stupid or clownish" **above**) **n.** *gobe-mouche*
simple: **n.** Abderite; *bon enfant;* nincompoop
skillful: **see** "expert"
small: **see** "dwarf"
small-minded: **see** *"narrow-minded"* **above**
snobbish and affected: **n.** poseur; (**fem.** *poseuse*); (**pl.** *gens à chichis*)
something carried about the (person): **n.** *vade mecum*
strict: **n.** disciplinarian; martinet; Pharisee; precisian; rigorist; ritualist; sabbatarian
strong-minded: **n.** *esprit fort;* Trojan
stubborn: **n.** intransige(a)nt; recalcitrant
stupid: **see** "dull, stupid or clownish" **above**
swaggering: **n.** braggadocio; rodomontade
talkative: **n.** blatherskite; popinjay
timid: **n.** invertebrate; milksop; milquetoast; nervous Nellie
turbulent, ill-disciplined: **n.** bashibazouk; *enfant terrible*
unconventional: **n.** beatnik; Bohemian; heretic; heterodox; solecist
uncouth: **see** "vulgar" **below**
unique: **n.** nonpareil; nonesuch; paragon; phoenix; uniquity
unusual: **n.** *rara avis*
unwelcome: **n.** *persona non grata*
vagrant: **n.** itinerant; peregrine; peripatetic; vagabond: (**pl.** flotsam and jetsam)
vain: **n.** coxcomb; dandiprat; jackanapes; macaroni; popinjay
visionary. **n.** altitudinarian; doctrinaire; dogmatist; idealist; ideologist; ideologue; theorist; utopian
vulgar or coarse: **n.** Babbitt; Falstaff; grobian; libertine; plebeian; plugugly; reprobate; vulgarian; yahoo
wasteful: **n.** prodigal; profligate; spendthrift; wastrel
weak: (**see** "indecisive" **above**) **n.** invertebrate; valetudinarian
wealthy: **n.** Croesus; leviathan; Midas; mogul; plutocrat; tycoon
welcome or acceptable: **n.** *persona grata; persona gratissimo;* (**pl.** *personae gratissimae*)
wicked: **see** "base and despicable" **above**
wise: **n.** mahatma; Nestor; patriarch; sage; Solomon
with fine mind: **n.** *bel esprit*
with undefined status: **n.** hybrid; maverick; mongrel
witty: **n.** Aristophanes; *bel esprit; homme d'esprit*
working-class: **n.** bourgeois(ie); proletarian; proletariat
worthless: **see** "rogue"
worthy: (**see** "of high rank" **above**) **n.** mahatma; paradigm

PERSONAL *anecdotes, notes, belongings, etc.:* **n.pl.** personalia
effects, most valued: **n.pl.** lares and penates
feelings or attitudes, based on: **a.** attitudinal
history: **see** "autobiography"
property: **n.** personalty; (**pl.** personalia)
remove (personal) from: **v.** depersonalize; impersonalize; **n.** depersonalization; impersonalization

PERSONALITY: **n.** disposition; egoity; individuality; personeity; temperament
split: **n.** schizophrenia; schizophreniac; schizophrenic

PERSONALLY: **adv.** *in propria persona*

PERSONATION: **n.** anthropomorphism; anthropomorphization; embodiment; impersonation; incarnation; personification; prosopopeia; **a.** anthropomorphic; anthropomorphous; personificative

of animals, as in art or lit.: **v.** anthropomorphize; zoomorphize; **n.** anthropomorphism; zoomorphism
speech or lit. for rhetorical purposes: **n.** apostrophe; prosopopeia; **a.** apostrophic

PERSONIFY: **v.** anthropomorphize; apostrophize; embody; incarnate; zoomorphize

PERSPIRATION: **n.** diaphoresis; excreta; exudation; sudation; sudor; transpiration; (**pl.** egesta); **v.** PERSPIRE: egest; excrete; transpire
absence of: **n.** anhidrosis; anhydrosis
agent or drug checking: **n.** an(h)idrotic; anhydrotic; antiperspirant
agent or drug, etc., producing: **n.** diaphoretic; sudorific
excessive: **n.** hidrosis; hyperhidrosis; polyhidrosis
foul-smelling: **n.** bromidrosis; kakidrosis
lack of or deficiency in: **n.** adiaphoresis; anhidrosis; anhydrosis
pert. to: **a.** diaphoretic; egestive; excrementious; sudoriferous; sudorific

PERSUADE: (**see** "allure") **v.** exhortate; expostulate; **a.** PERSUASIVE: (**see** "encouraging") exhortative; expostulatory

PERTINENT: **a.** *ad rem;* applicable; apposite; appropriate; apropos; categorical; commensurate; congruent; felicitous; germane; material; opportune; proportional; proportionate; relevant; **n.** PERTINENCE: aproposity; pertinency; relevance; relevancy
not: **a.** *à propos de rien;* inapposite; inappropriate; irrelevant
to present matter: **adv.** *ad rem*

PERVERSE: **see** "contrary"

PESSIMISM: **n.** melancholia; miserabilism; weltschmerz; **n.** PESSIMIST: cynic; dismal Jimmie

PET: **see** "caress" **and** "favorite"
name: **n.** hypocorism; hypocoristic; *petit nom*

PETITION: (**see** "prayer") **n.** complaint; entreaty; obsecration; solicitation; supplication; **a.** PETITIONARY: beseeching; supplicative; supplicatory; **n.** PETITIONER: applicant; candidate; orator; (**fem.** oratrix); postulant; supplicant

PETTY: (**see** "childish" **and** "trifling") **a.** contemptible; frivolous; ignoble; insignificant; lilliputian; meager; paltry; parochial; pettifogging; picayune; picayunish; scurvey; shabby; subordinate; trivial; unimportant; **n.** PETTINESS: parochialism; parochiality; parvanimity; triviality

PETULANT: **see** "irritable"

PHANTASY: **see** "fantasy"

PHASE(S): (**see** "aspect") **n.** facet; transition
having many: **a.** multiphasic; polyphasic

PHENOMENA, *science dealing w/:* **n.** phenomenology
secondary: **n.pl.** epiphenomena; **n.** epiphenomenon; **a.** epiphenomenal
state of being (phenomenal): **n.** phenomenality; **a.** phenomenological

PHILANTHROPIST: **see** "person, charitable"

PHILOSOPHER, *keep silent and be counted a: sile, et philosophus esto*
natural: **n.** physiologizer; physiologue

PHILOSOPHY: (**see** "doctrine") **n.** credo; *scientia scientiarum*
pretender or dabbler in: **n.** philosophaster
spurious or pretended: **n.** philosophastry; sciosophy; **a.** philosophastering

PHOTOGRAPHIC: **a.** photogenic

PHRASE(S): (**see** "word") **n.** diction
in formal and not always sincere: **a.** phraseological; **n.** lexiphanicism

PHRASEOLOGY: **n.** diction; parlance; syntax
pretentious: **n.** lexiphanicism

PHYSICAL: (**see** "natural") **a.** corpor(e)al; material(istic); palpable; physiological; ponderable; somatic; tangible; **n.** corporeality; corporeity; materiality; physicality; substantiality
beyond the: **see** "supernatural"
form or construction: **n.** constitution; habitus; physique
predominance of the: **n.** physicality
skill or energy, pert. to or requiring:

a. manual; muscular; physical
treatment: **n.** physiatrics; physical medicine (or therapy); physiotherapy
specialist in: **n.** physiatrist; physiotherapist

PHYSICIAN, *disease or disorder produced by or by treatment:* **a.** iatrogenic; medicamentous
pert. to: **a.** Aesculapian; iatric(al)
stock in trade of: **n.** armamentarium; *materia medica;* (**pl.** armamentaria; instrumentaria)

PHYSIQUE: **n.** constitution; habitus; physicality

PIANO, *display of expertness in playing:* **n.** expertise; virtuosity; (**pl.** pianistics)
female player: **n.** pianiste
pert. to: **a.** pianistic

PICTURE: **v.** delineate; depict(ure); illustrate; photograph; portray; represent; **n.** configuration; delineation; iconography; illustration; portraiture; similitude
composite: **n.** collage; (photo)montage
writing(s): **n.pl.** curiologics; hieroglyphics; **a.** curiologic(al); hieroglyphic(al)

PIECEMEAL: **a.** aliquot; fractional; fractionary; fragmentary; *par pièces*

PIERCE: **v.** impale; lancinate; penetrate; perforate; puncture; transfix

PIGEON(S), *of or rel. to:* **a.** peristeronic

PILE: **n.** accumulation; agglomeration; aggregation; congeries
up: **v.** (ac)cumulate; agglomerate; pyramid; **a.** cumulative

PILLAGE: **v.** despoil; devastate; plunder; **n.** brigandage; depredation; (de)spoliation; rapine

PIMPLY: **a.** papuliferous; papulose; **n.** papule

PINCH: **v.** compress; constrict; impinge, vellicate; **n.** exigency; impingement; juncture; predicament; vellication; vicissitude

PIOUS: **a.** consecrated; devotional; devout; religious; reverent; sanctified
excessively or falsely: **a.** hypocritical; religiose; sanctimonious; **n.** odor of sanctity; piosity; religiosity; sanctimoniousness
fraud: **n.** *fraus pia*
not: (**see** "disbeliever") **a.** adiaphorous; aporetic; blasphemous; impious; irreligious; sacreligious

PIRATE: **n.** buccaneer; corsair; freebooter; picaroon; privateer; **a.** piratical
flag: **n.** Jolly Roger

PIT: **n.** lacuna; **a.** PITTED: lacunal; lacunar

PITCH (*tar*), *of or like:* **a.** piceous

PITFALL: **n.** artifice; inveiglement; maelstrom; stratagem; subterfuge; temptation

PITH: **see** "heart" **and** "embodiment"; **a.** PITHY: (**see** "terse") aphoristic; apothegmatic; cogent; concentrated; epigrammatic(al); gnomic(al); laconic(al); sententious; vigorous

PITY: **n.** charity; commiseration; compassion; condolence; empathy; remorse; sympathy; **a.** PITIABLE: commiserable; squalid; **a.** PITIFUL: abject; commiserable; contemptible; despicable; lamentable; pathetic; squalid; touching; **a.** PITILESS: despiteful; dispiteous; impiteous; implacable; inexorable; malicious; merciless; relentless; revengeful; ruthless; unfeeling
appeal(ing) to: **adv. or n.** (*argumentum*) *ad misericordiam*
mock, person regarded w/: **n.** pilgarlic

PLACE(S): **n.** locale; locus; (**pl.** loci); status; situ(s); situation
cited or quoted, at: **adv.** *loco citato* (**abb.** *loc. cit.*)
in its: **adv.** *in situ*
in the first: **adv.** imprimis
in the proper or natural: **adv.** *in loco; in situ*
name: **n.** toponym; **a.** toponymic(al)
of torment or martyrdom: **n.** Golgotha; *via dolorosa*
out of: **a.** ill-timed; inappropriate; *mal à propos;* malapropos

PLAGUE: **n.** abomination; affliction; calamity; harassment; infestation; outbreak; pestilence: **a.** calamitous; pestilential; pestilentious

PLAIN: (see "clear" and "simple") **a.** candid; ingenious; literal; manifest; nondescript; perspicacious; transparent; unadorned; unalluring; unattractive; uncosmetized; undisguised; undramatic; unembellished; unembroidered; unobstructed; unprepossessing; unpretentious; unspectacular; unvariegated; unvarnished
in neatness: **adv.** *simplex munditiis*
in (plain) words or lang.: **adv.** *nudis verbis;* **a.** or **adv.** *en clair*

PLAN(S): **v.** calculate; cogitate; conspire; contemplate; contrive; ideate; preconceive; precogitate; prefigure; premeditate; scheme; **n.** conspiracy; formula; intrigue; preconception; project; regimen; schema; (**pl.** schemata); **a.** calculatory; formulaic; premeditative; schematic
abstract: **n.** architectonics
orderly: **n.** architectonics; cosmos; syntax; **a.** architectonic; syntactic(al)

PLANNED *progress:* **n.** conservation; husbandry; telesia; telesis

PLANT(S), *and animals, development of:* **n.** biology; **a.** biological
and animal life, regional: **n.** biota; flora and fauna
and domestic animals, science of propagation: **n.** thremmatology
and plant life, regional: **n.** flora
-eating: **a.** herbivorous; phytiverous; phytophagous; phytophilous; vegetarian
-eating animal: **n.** herbivore; (**pl.** herbivora); vegetarian
fond of: **a.** phytophilous
growing in solution: **n.** hydroponics
pert. to: **a.** botanical; herbaceous; herbal; phytologic(al)
science of distribution of: **n.** biogeography; phytogeography
specialist: **n.** botanist; herbologist; phytologist
study of: **n.** botany; herbology; phytology
worship of or undue fondness for: **n.** phytolatry

PLASTIC: (see "pliant") **a.** adaptable; creative; ductile; fictile; formative; governable; impressionable; labile; malleable; manageable; mutable; pluripotent; sculptural; **n.** PLASTICITY: creativity; ductility; elasticity; impressionability; malleability

PLATFORM: **n.** dais; *haut pas;* lectern; lyceum; podium; rostrum

PLAUSIBLE: (see "probable") **a.** colorable; credible; specious; **n.** PLAUSIBILITY: credibility
but not genuine: **a.** specious; **n.** speciosity

PLAY: (see "drama") **n.** *pièce de théâtre;* **n.pl.** PLAYERS: (see "actor(s)") *corps dramatique; dramatis personae*
subtle: **n.** artifice; finesse; maneuver; stratagem

PLAYFUL: (see "frolicsome") **a.** convivial; facetious; frivolous; impish; jocose; jocular; jovial; roguish; sportive; **n.** PLAYFULNESS: (see "banter") archness; jocosity; jocularity; joviality; roguery; roguishness; sportiveness

PLAYWRIGHT: **n.** dramatist; dramaturge; **a.** dramaturgic

PLEA: (see "entreaty") **n.** advocation; allegation; blandishment; contention; pretext; supplication; **n.** PLEADER: advocate; intercessor; paraclete; supplicant

PLEAD: see "beg"

PLEASANT: (see "pleasing") **a.** idyllic; **n.** PLEASANTNESS: amity; bonhom(m)ie; harmonization; harmony; **n.** PLEASANTRY: facetiosity; facetiousness; jocularity; *plaisanterie*
idleness: **n.** *dolce far niente*
in sound or tone: (see "harmonious") **a.** euphonic(al); euphonious; sonorous; **n.** euphony; harmonics; harmony
make: **v.** edulcorate

PLEASE: (see "satisfy") **v.** delectate; exhilarate; gratify; titillate; tit(t)ivate; **a.** *s'il vous plaît*
as you: **adv.** *al piacere*
hard to: **a.** captious; fastidious; hypercritical; implacable; inexorable; insatiable; meticulous; scrupulous; unappeasable
willingness or disposition to: **n.** amiability; complaisance; **a.** amiable; complaisant

PLEASING: (see "agreeable") **a.** amiable; comely; compatible; consonant; delectable; ecstatic; elysian; empyrean; felici-

tous; harmonious; idyllic; ingratiating; ingratiatory; palatable; prepossessing; **n.** harmonization; titillatation; tit(t)ivation
delusions or hallucinations: **n.** amenomania
for sake of: **adv.** *ad captandum*
in appearance: **a.** captivating; comely; enchanting; pellucid; personable; ravishing
to ear: **see** "harmonious"

PLEASURE(S): **n.** cakes and ale; delectation; diversion; fruition; inclination; oblectation; titil(l)ation; tit(t)ivation; **a.** PLEASURABLE: (**see** "pleasing") delectable; hedonistic(al); sybaritic(al)
and pain, rel. to either or both: **a.** algedonic
at: **adv.** *a beneplacito; ad arbitrium; ad lib(itum); al piacere; à volonté*
doctrine of: **n.** Cyreniacism hedonism; sybaritism; **a.** Cyrenaic; hedonistic(al); sybaritic(al); **n.** Cyrenaic; hedonist; Sybarite
enjoy those of the moment: **n.** *carpe diem;* **adv.** *carpe diem; in horam vivere*
everyone has his own: sua cuique voluptas
from being mistreated, hurt or dominated: **n.** algophilia; masochism; **a.** algophilic; masochistic; **n.** algophilist; masochist
given to: **a.** apolaustic; hedonic; hedonistic(al); sybaritic(al)
in administering physical or mental pain or cruelty: **n.** algophilia; sadism; **a.** algophilic; sadistic; **n.** algophilist; sadist
insensitiveness to: **n.** anesthesia; anhedonia; hypesthesia; hypnosis
one fond of: **n.** Cyrenaic epicure; hedonist; libertine; sybarite; tragalist; *viveur;* voluptuary
pert. to or to nature of: **a.** eudaemonic; eudemonia; hedonic(al)
sensual: **n.pl.** *voluptates corporis;* **a.** amatory; Anacreontic; convivial
small: **n.pl.** *menus plaisirs*
to each his own: çuique voluptas sui; sua cuique voluptas
with: **adv.** *avec plaisir*

PLEAT(ED): **v.** plicate; **a.** plicate(d)

PLEDGE: **v.** guarantee; hypothecate; (im)pignorate; plight; **n.** collateral; guarantee; hypothecation; (im)pignoration; surety; **a.** impignorative
as security: **v.** hypothecate
for performance: **n.** collateral; recognizance
living: **n.** *vivum vadium*
of love: **n.** betrothal; *gage d'amour;* plight

PLENTY: (**see** "abundance") **n.** affluence; amplitude; copiousness; copiosity; opulence; plen(t)itude; plethora; profusion; repletion; spate; **a.** PLENTIFUL: (**see** "abundant") abounding; ample; copious; cornucopian; exuberant; opulent; plentitudinous; plenteous; plethoric; replete; superabundant
horn of: **n.** *corne d'abondance;* cornucopia; **a.** cornucopian

PLIANT: (**see** "plastic") **a.** adaptable; amenable; ductile; fictile; flexible; governable; malleable; manageable; susceptible; tractable; yielding

PLIGHT: (**see** "predicament") **n.** dilemma; *mauvais pas;* quandary

PLOT: (**see** "conspiracy") **n.** cabal; conspiration; intrigue; junta; machination; scenario; stratagem; **a.** cabalistic; conspirative; conspiratorial; **n.** conspirator
secretly: **v.** conspire; machinate; **n.** cabal; conspiration; machination

PLUCK: **v.** velicate; **n.** determination; resolution; vellication
person with: **n.** Trojan

PLUG: **v.** occlude; **n.** embolus; occlusion; pledget; tamp(i)on

PLUMP: **a.** corpulent; distended; portly; rotund; **n.** corpulency; portliness; rotundity

PLUNDER: **v.** depredate; despoil; maraud; pillage; ransack; spoliate; **n.** depredation; (de)spoiliation; plunderage; rapine

POCKETBOOK, *appeal(ing) to the:* **n.** or **adv.** *(argumentum) ad crumenam*

POEM: **see** "poetry"
birthday: **n.** genethliacon
bucolic: **n.** eclogue; idyll; pastoral
initial letters in alphabetical order: **n.** abecedarius
medieval love: **n.** madrigal

POET, *distinguished:* **n.** laureate
is born, not made: poëta nascitur, non fit

poor or inferior: **n.** balladmonger; poetaster; versemonger
would-be: **n.** *poète manqué*

POETIC(AL): **a.** idealized; lyric; Pegasean; poematic
inspiration: **n.** pegasus
license: **n.** *licentia vatum*
quality or expression: **n.** poeticality
rage: **n.** *furor poeticus*

POETRY: **see** "verse"
art of: **n.** *ars poetica;* metrification; versification
dabbling in: **n.** balladmongering; poetastering; poetastery
muse of: **n.** Calliope (*epic*); Erato (*amatory and lyric*)
pert. to: **a.** bardic; lyric; melic; metrical; poetical
pert. to art of: **a.** Parnassian
second-rate: **n.** crambo

POINT(S): (**see** "gist") **n.** characteristic; locality; *locus;* (**pl.** *loci*); proposition; thesis
-by-point: **a.** alphabetical; categoric(al); seriatim
fine (*as distinction*): **n.** nuance; quiddity; subtlety; tenuosity
having or rel. to two: **a.** bipunctate; bipunct(u)al
highest or farthest: **n.** apogee; solstice; ultima Thule
lowest: **n.** nadir; perigee
pert. to: **a.** apical; cacuminal; cacuminous
to the: **adv.** *ad rem*
vantage: **see** "vantage point"

POINTED: **a.** aciculate(d); acuminate; apicular; apiculated; epigrammatic; incisive; poignant; pungent; spicate; spicigerous; stimulating; stimulative; zestful

POINTLESS: **a.** hebetudinous; impertinent; incongruous; irrelevant; obtuse; **n.** POINTLESSNESS: hebetude; ineffectuality; irrelevancy

POISE: **v.** balance; librate; stabilize; **n.** adroitness; aplomb; bearing; carriage; composure; dexterity; equilibrium; equipoise; imperturbability; libration; nonchalance; perpendicularity; posture; *savoir-faire; sang-froid;* self-possession; serenity; tranquility; **a.** libratory

POISON: **v.** corrupt; pollute; toxify; **n.** (**see** "pollution") bane; malignancy; pestilence; pestilency; toxicity; toxin; venenation; venom; virulence; **a.** POISONOUS: (**see** "deadly") baneful; deleterious; loathsome; malevolent; malignant; mortal; nauseating; (ob)noxious; pernicious; septic; toxiferous; venomous; viperous; virulent
antidote against: **n.** or **a.** alexipharmic; prophylaxis; **n.** mithridate; mithridatum; prophylaxis

POLISHED: (**see** "polite") **a.** cavalier; courteous; couth; cultivated; diplomatic; elegant; politic; refined; *soigné(e)*; suave; tactful; urbane; **n.** POLISH: artistry; consummation; courtliness; diplomacy; elegance; finesse; gloss; luster; preciosity; refinement; suavity; urbanity
affectedly: **a.** *précieuse; précieux;* **n.** preciosity
brilliantly: **a.** vernicose
literary style: **a.** Addisonian

POLITENESS: (**see** "polish") **n.** affability; civility; comity; complaisance; courtesy; courtliness; decorum; deferentiality; diplomacy; *prévenance;* suaveness; suavity; urbanity; **a.** POLITE: (**see** "courteous" **and** "polished") affable; cavalier; ceremonial; Chesterfieldian; complaisant; courtly; decorous; deferential; diplomatic; gracious; politic; sophisticated; suave; tactful
esp. if excessive: **n.** decorousness; politesse
expression of: **n.** euphemism
formal and cultivated: **n.** diplomacy; politesse
lack of: **n.** angularity; incivility; inurbanity; rusticity; uncourtliness

POLITICAL *boss w/ military following:* **n.** caudillo
favor: **n.** nepotism; patronage
party, aristocratic, or supporting authority: **n.** Ghibelline(s)
opposing authority: **n.** Guelf(s); (or Guelph[s])
organization: **n.** polity
power or authority; **n.** temporality
stumping or electioneering: **n.** hustings
to make: **v.** politici(ali)ze; **n.** politicalization; politicization

POLITICIAN: **n.** courtier; statesman
petty or contemptible: **n.** politicaster; **a.** unstatesmanlike

POLITICS, *bring within realm of:* **v.** politici(ali)ze; **n.** politicalization; politicization
discuss or discourse upon: **v.** politicize; **n.** politicization
power: **n.** *machtpolitik*
practical: **n.** *realpolitik*

POLLUTION: (**see** "poison") **n.** adulteration; contamination; corruption; defilement; desecration; impurity; profanation; uncleanliness

POMPOUS: (**see** "bombastic") **a.** consequential; fatuous; fustian; grandiose; imposing; magisterial; ostentatious; pretentious; supercilious; theatrical; turgid; **n.** POMP: *coup de théâtre;* grandeur; magnificence; pomposity; pretense; ostentation; ritual; vainglory
as of speech or writing(s): **a.** bombastic; grandiloquent; orotund; rubescent; **n.** grandiloquence; orotundity; pomposity; rubescence
excessively: **n.** pomposity; **v.** pontificate
official or person: (**see under** "person") **n.** panjandrum

PONDER: **v.** deliberate; (ex)cogitate; meditate; perpend; ruminate; **n.** cogitation; rumination; **a.** cogitative; meditative; ruminative

PONDS, *thriving in:* **a.** tychopotamic

POOR: **a.** bankrupt; despicable; destitute; hardscrabble; humble; impecunious; impoverished; inadequate; indigent; insolvent; meager; moneyless; necessitous; portionless; poverty-stricken; resourceless; shoddy; squalid; straitened; undesirable; unfavorable; **n.** (**see** "poverty") immiserization; impecuniosity; impecunity; impoverishment; indigence; indigency; mendicancy; pauperization
act of making: **n.** immiserization; impoverishment; pauperization; **v.** pauperize
devil or wretch: **n.** *pauvre diable*
in midst of great wealth: magna inter opes inops
to make: **v.** depauperate; impoverish; pauperize

POORLY *conceived:* **a.** malentendu
constructed, as lit. work: **a.** incondite

POPE, *pert. to:* **a.** episcopal; papal; pontifical

POPULACE, *appeal(ing) to the:* **n. or adv.** *(argumentum) ad populum*

POPULAR: (**see** "prevalent") **a.** accepted; approved; demotic; enchorial; exoteric; fashionable; modish; plebeian; prevailing; prevalent; proletarian; vulgar
favor: **n.** *aura popularis*

POPULATION(S) *area of greatest density:* **n.** ecumene
science or study of: **n.** demography; larithmics

POPULOUS: **a.** multitudinous

PORCH, *for carriages:* **n.** *porte cochère*

PORNOGRAPHY: **n.pl.** curiosa; erotica; esoterica; facetiae

PORTEND: (**see** "foretell") **v.** augur; auspicate; presage; **a.** auspicatory; foreboding; presageful: **n.** (**see** "omen") presentiment

PORTION: (**see** "amount" **and** "part") **n.** inheritance; quantum; (**pl.** quanta); quota

PORTRAY: **v.** delineate; depict; represent

POSE: **v.** attitudinize; baffle; **n.** (**see** "posture" **and** "staginess") affectation; attitude; attitudinization; mannerism; masquerade; theatricality
for effect: **v.** attitudinize; **n.** attitudinarian; *poseur;* (**fem.** *poseuse*)
in dancing: **n.** plastique

POSITION: (**see** "office") **n.** attitude; employment; *métier;* posture; ubiety; vocation
awareness or sense of: **n.** kinesthesia; orientation; proprioception; **a.** kinesthetic; proprioceptive
favorable: **n.** coign (of vantage)
having same relative: **a.** homologous; **n.** homologue

POSITIVE: **a.** absolute; affirmative; arbitrary; categorical; concrete; decisive; definitive; dogmatic; emphatic; indisputable; opinionated; philodoxic(al); peremptory; self-assured; substantive; thetic(al); unconditional; unequivocal; **n.** absolute; concretum; unconditionality

POSSIBILITY: **n.** contingency; dynamis; eventuality; feasibility; potentia; potential(ity); practicability; virtuality
to actuality: **adv.** *a posse ad esse*

POSSIBLE: **a.** achievable; conceivable; executable; implicit; *in posse;* latent; potential; practicable; practical; promising; superable; surmountable; undeveloped; **adv.** *in posse;* peradventure; potentially
to make: **v.** possibilitate

POSTCARD *collector:* **n.** deltiologist; **n.** deltiology

POSTER: **n.** affiche; broadside; bulletin; placard

POSTERIOR: **see** "behind"; **adv.** POSTERIORLY: cauded; posteriad

POSTPONE: **v.** defer; forbear; procrastinate; prorogue; protract; respite; **n.** POSTPONEMENT: (**see** "delay") **n.** deferment; procrastination; prorogation; respite
in law: **v.** continue; **n.** continuance

POSTURE: (**see** "pose") **n.** attitude; attudination
erect: **n.** orthograde; orthostatic

POTATOES, *served or prepared w/* **a.** parmentier; *parmentière*

POTENT: (**see** "strong") **a.** cogent; convincing; dynamic; puissant

POTENTIAL: **see** "possible"; **adv.** POTENTIALLY: *in posse; prima facie*

POUCH, *shaped like:* **a.** bursiculate; bursiform; saccate; scrotiform

POULTICE: **n.** fomentation

POUND: **v.** malleate; **n.** malleation

POUR *out:* **v.** disembogue

POVERTY: **n.** dearth; destitution; impecuniosity; inadequacy; indigence; mendicancy; paucity; pauperism; penury; privation; *res angusta domi;* scarcity; squalor; tenuity

POWDERY: **a.** friable; pulverous; pulverulent

POWER: (**see** "authority" **and** "rule") **n.** ascendency; capacity; cogency; control; domain; dominion; *dynamis;* dynamism; faculty; influence; potency; potentiality; prerogative; puissance; regency; superiority; supremacy
behind scenes: **n.** *éminence grise;* gray eminence
beyond permissive: **adv.** ultra licitum; ultra vires
creative or decisive (as institution, idea or person): **n.** demiurge; **a.** demiurgeous; demiurgic
full discretionary: **n.** *carte blanche;* plenipotentiary; **a.** plenary; plenipotent(ial); plenipotentiary
in acting or attempting to act: **n.** nisus
of office, etc.: **n.** attribution; jurisdiction; **a.** attributive; jurisdictional; jurisdictive
range or limit of: **n.** jurisdiction
supernatural, or of supposed divine origin: **n.** charism(a); **a.** charismatic
supreme or regal: **n.** diadem; imperium; sovereignty
to command admiration or esteem: **n.** prestige; **a.** prestigious
to do many things: **a.** multipotent; omnipotent; **n.** omnipotence; omnipotency
tyrannical: **n.** Moloch
unlimited: (**see** "full discretionary" **above**) **n.** absolutism; authoritarian(ism); omnipotence; omnipotency; **a.** authoritarian; omnipotent; plutocratic; tyrannical; tyrannous
within permitted: **adv.** intra vires

POWERFUL: (**see** "strong") **a.** almighty; authoritarian; cogent; dominant; dynamic; forceful; forte; Herculean; influential; leonine; (multi)potent; plutocratic; prepotent; puissant; substantious; tyrannical; tyrannous
all-: **see** "almighty"
group: **n.** powerhouse
in battle or arms: **a.** armipotent
make more: **v.** augment; potentiate
person: **n.** Croesus; leviathan; mogul; plutocrat; potentate; tycoon

POWERLESS: (**see** "helpless") **a.** *brutum fulmen;* impotent; impuissant; nugatory; sterile; **n.** POWERLESSNESS: impotency; impuissance; sterility

PRACTICAL: **a.** banausic; empirical; existential; feasible; functional; materialistic; practicable; pragmatic(al); profi-

cient; unromantic; unsentimental; utile; utilitarian
person: **n.** materialist; practician; pragmatist; utilitarian
thinker: **n.** Aristotelian; **n.** Aristotelianism; **a.** Aristotelian

PRACTICE, *correctness of:* **n.** orthopraxy
distinguished fr. theory: **n.** praxis
makes perfect: fit fabricando faber

PRAISE: **v.** adulate; applaud; approbate; celebrate; commend(ate); compliment; emblazon; extol; hosanna; laureate; lionize; paen; pean; rhapsodize; **n.** accolade; acclamation; adulation; approbation; ascription; blandishment; elegy; emblazonment; encomium; eulogy; hosanna; laudation; lionization; panegyric; plaudit; rhapsody; (**pl.** *baise-mains*); **a.** PRAISING: see "eulogistic"
be to God: laus Deo
deserved: **see** "praiseworthy"
eager or hungry for: **a.** esurient; **n.** captation; esurience
excessive or offensive: **n.** fulsomeness; panegyric; **a.** fulsome; panegryic(al)
expression of: **n.** approbation; commendation; plaudit; **a.** approbative; commendative; commendatory
high: **n**: dithyramb; encomium; eulogium; eulogy; extol(l)ment; panegyric; **v.** eulogize; panegyrize; **a.** commendative; commendatory; complimentary; encomiastic; eulogistic; panegyrical
hymn of: **n.** canticle; doxology; magnificat; paen; pean; *te deum;* theody
one who (praises): **n.** encomiast; eulogist; extoller; laudator; laureate; panegyrist; rhapsodist
shout of: **n.** hallelujah; hosanna
to God: **n.** ascription; doxology; *laus Deo*
with: **a.** or **adv.** *cum laude*
with great or high: **a.** or **adv.** *magna cum laude*
with greatest or highest: **a.** or **adv.** *summa cum laude*

PRAISEWORTHY: **a.** approbatory; commendable; commendatory: complimentary; credible; creditable; encomiastic(al); estimable; eulogistic(al); exemplary; honorific; laudable; laudative; laudatory; meritorious; panegyric(al); (super)eminent; **n.** PRAISEWORTHINESS: commendability; creditability; estimability; exemplarity; laudability
not: **a.** illaudable

PRANK(S): (**see** "frolic") **n.** caper; capriccio; dido; *échappée;* escapade; *espièglerie;* marlock; vagary; whimsicality
comic: **n.** harlequinade
reckless: **n.** escapade

PRAY: **v.** beseech; entreat; implore; importune; invocate; invoke; solicit; supplicate
and work: ora et labora
for us: ora pro nobis

PRAYER: **n.** *absit omen;* adjuration; benediction; conjuration; entreaty; imploration; imprecation; invocation; litany; obsecration; orison; petition; solicitation; supplication; **a.** PRAYING (or PRAYERFUL): invocative; invocatory; precative; precatory; supplicatory
for mercy: **n.** Miserere

PREACHER: **see** "clergyman"

PRECAUTION, *from excessive:* **adv.** *ex abundante cautela*

PRECEDENT(S), *uphold:* **n.** *res adjudicata; stare decisis*

PRECIOUS: (**see** "valuable") **a.** alembicated

PRECISE: (**see** "exact") **a.** ceremonious; conscientious; definite; definitive; determinative; discriminating; explicit; fastidious; immaculate; impeccable; implicit; mathematical; meticulous; minute; minutious; minutose; orthodox; painstaking; punctilious; puritanical; rigorous; scrupulous; slavish; specific; unequivocal; **n.** PRECISION: ceremony; correctitude; definitude; exactitude; exactness: literality; minuteness; scrupulosity; veracity
person, esp. in morals or religion: **n.** precisian; sabbatarian
very: **a.** scrupulous; slavish

PRECONCEIVED *opinion:* **n.** ideation; *parti pris;* predilection; prejudice

PREDATORY: **a.** harpactophagous; predaceous; predacious; predative; rapacious; **n.** predacity; rapacity

PREDESTINATION: **n.** determinism; fatalism; foreknowledge; foreordination; necessarianism

PREDETERMINATION: **n.** *parti pris;* prejudgment; prejudication

PREDICAMENT: **(see** "perplexity") **n.** *cul-de-sac;* cruciality; (horns of a) dilemma; imbroglio; impasse; quandary; **a.** PREDICAMENTAL: dilemmatic; nonplussed

PREDICT: **(see** "foretell") **v.** adumbrate; forecast; presage; predicate; prognosticate; **a.** PREDICTABLE: calculable; prognosticable; **a.** PREDICTING **(or** PREDICTIVE): foreboding; haruspical; ominous; prognostic; prophetic; **n.** PREDICTION: forecast; haruspication; haruspicy; prognosis; prognostication; prophecy; vaticination; **n.** PREDICTOR: forecaster; haruspex; Nostradamus; prognosticator; soothsayer

on basis of known facts: **v.** triangulate; **n.** triangulation

PREDISPOSITION: **(see** "tendency") **n.** diathesis; inclination; predilection

to disease: **n.** diathesis

PREDOMINATE: **see** "prevail"

PREEMINENTLY: **adv.** *par excellence*

PREFACE: **(see** "introduction") **n.** *avant-propos;* exordium; foreword; isagoge; preamble; prelude; proem; programma; prolegomenon; **(pl.** prolegomena); prologue; prolusion; protasis; **a.** PREFACTORY: prefactorial; preliminary; prolegomenous; premonitory

literary: **n.** isagoge

PREFERENCE: **(see** "prejudice") **n.** alternative; antecedence; discrimination; inclination; precedence; predilection; predisposition; priority

PREGNANCY: **n.** fecundity; fetation; gravidation; gravidity; gestation; meaningfulness

vomiting of: **n.** *hyperemesis gravidarum*

PREGNANT: **a.** *enceinte;* fecund; germinal; gravid; meaningful; parous; significant; weighty

with ideas, etc.: **a.** tumefacient; tumescent

PREJUDGMENT: **see** "predetermination"

PREJUDICE: **(see** "preference") **n.** bigotry; insularism; insularity; jaundice; partiality; *parti pris;* predilection; prepossession; sectionalism; **a.** PREJUDICED: **(see** "biased" **and** "narrow") bigoted; determined; insular; insulated; partial; prejudicial

appeal(ing) to: **n. or adv.** (*argumentum*) *ad hominem*

without: **adv.** *sine praejudicio*

PRELIMINARY: **(see** "introductory") **a.** antecedent; imperative; indispensable; liminary; precedential; precursive; precursory; prefactory; prefatorial; premonitory; **n. see** "prerequisite"

discussion: **n.** pourparler

knowledge: **n.** praecognitum

matter: **n.** *avant-propos*

PRELUDE: **(see** "preface") **n.** overture; prolusion; **a.** prolusory

PREMATURE: **a.** anticipatory; inopportune; precipitate; precocious; prevenient; unseasonable; untimely

PREPARATORY: **(see** "introductory" **and** "preliminary") **a.** antecedent; prefatorial

instruction: **n.** propaedeutics; **a.** propaedeutic(al)

PREPARE: **(see** "make") **v.** admonish; caution; confect; counsel; facilitate; precondition; **n.** PREPARATION: concoction; conditioning; confection; purveyance

PREPARED: **(see** "ready") **a.** admonished; *en garde;* expugnatory; preconditioned

always: **n. or adv.** *semper paratus*

for all things (*or ready for anything*): *in omnia paratus*

for either event: in utrumque paratus

PREREQUISITE: **n.** condition precedent; essentiality; indispensability; postulate; *sine qua non;* **a. see** "preliminary"

PRESCRIBED: **a.** arbitrary; prescriptive; recommended; thetic(al)

PRESENT: **a.** contemporary; immediate; instant; **n. (see** "gratuity") *status quo;* temporality

all-: **(see under** "all") **a.** multipresent; omnipresent; ubiquitous

for the: **adv.** pro nunc

I am: **adv.** *ad sum*

time: **n.** nonce

PRESERVATION: (**see** "conservation") **n.** guardianship; immortalization; maintenance; perpetuation

PRESSING: (**see** "clamorous" **and** "urgent") **a.** critical; exigent; imminent; impending; imperative; important; insistent; poignant; threatening

PRESSURE: **n.** constraint; exaction; exigency; imminency; insistence; ponderosity

PRESTIGE: **n.** ascendency; authority; cachet; influence; reputation; repute; (super)eminence; **a.** prestigious; reputable
having great: (**see** "eminent") **a.** illustrious; influential; prestigious

PRESUME: (**see** "presuppose") **v.** anticipate; assume; postulate; **a.** PRESUMED: (**see** "probable") circumstantial; presumable; presumptive: **n.** PRESUMPTION: arrogance; audacity; circumstantiality; effrontery; expectation: *outrecuidance*

PRESUMPTUOUS: (**see** "pretentious") **a.** arrogant; audacious; Icarian; imperious; impertinent; insolent; overweening
person: **n.** jackanapes

PRESUPPOSE: (**see** "presume") **v.** assume; posit; postulate; **n.** PRESUPPOSITION: postulate; postulation; prolepsis

PRETEND: **v.** beseem; counterfeit; dissemble; simulate; **a.** PRETENDED: (**see** "affected") affectional; barmecidal; beseeming; hypocritical; ostensible; ostensive; quasi; self-styled; simulated; so-called; *soi-disant*
to be sick: **v.** malinger; **n.** malingering; pathomimesis; **n.** malingerer

PRETENDER: **n.** affecter; charlatan; claimant; counterfeit; deceiver; hypocrite; imposter; mountebank; *poseur;* (**fem.** *poseuse*); pretendant; quacksalver; Tartuf(f)e; *tricheur;* (**fem.** *tricheuse*)
to knowledge or scholarship: **n.** sciolist; **a.** sciolistic; sciolous; **n.** sciolism

PRETENSE: (**see** "pomp") **n.** affectation; (dis)simulation; fabrication; hypocrisy; persiflage; postiche; pretention; pretex; semblance; simulacrum; subterfuge
almost transparent: **n.** charade

PRETENTIOUS: (**see** "showy") **a.** affectational; ambitious; bombastic; faustian; ostentatious; pharisaical; pompous; self-important; sonorous; **n.** PRETENTIOUSNESS: blague; bombast; flummery; humbug; ostentation; pomposity
official: **n.** panjandrum

PREVAIL: (**see** "conquer") **v.** actuate; (pre)dominate; preponderate; **n.** PREVALENCE: ascendency; circulation; currency; predominance; predomination; regnance; regnancy; **a.** PREVAILING: (**see** "popular") ascendant; current; demotic; enchorial; epidemic; indigenous; (pre)dominant; prevalent; regnal; regnant; victorious

PREVENT: **v.** anticipate; circumvent; forestall; intercept; obviate; preclude; restrain; **n.** PREVENTION: alexeteric, circumvention; prevent(at)ive; prophylactic; prophylaxis; **a.** PREVENTING: circumventive; preventative; preventive; prophylactic

PREVIOUS: **a.** antecedent; anterior; preceding; premature
condition: **n.** precedent; *status quo ante*

PREYING *or living on other animals:* (**see** "predatory") **a.** predaceous; predacious; predative; rapacious; **n.** predacity; predation; predatoriness; predatism; rapaciousness; rapacity; **n.** predator

PRICE, *at any or regardless of:* **adv.** *à tout prix; coûte que coûte*

PRICELESS: (**see** "costly") **a.** impayable; incalculable; inestimable; invaluable; matchless

PRICKLY: (**see** "spinous" **and** "spiny") **a.** acanthoid; acanthous; echinate; horrent; muricate

PRIDE: **n.** *amour propre;* arrogance; conceit; ego(t)ism; *esprit de corps;* exaltation; haughtiness; hauteur; hubris; pomposity; self-esteem; self-exaltation; vainglory; vanity; **a.** PRIDEFUL: (**see** "haughty") fastuous; **n.** PRIDEFULNESS: **see** "self-importance"
disdainful: **n.** haughtiness; hauteur; hubris
of group or organization: **n.** *esprit de corps*
overweening: **n.** hubris

PRIEST: **n.** cleric; ecclesiastic; hierophant; **n.** PRIESTHOOD: clericality; eccliasticism; priestianity (*usu.* disparagingly); sacerdocy; **a.** PRIESTLY: Aaronic; ecclesiastic; hieratical; hierophantic; levitical; sacertot(ic)al
functions of: **n.** clericature; priestcraft; (**pl.** spiritualities)

PRIM: **see** "prissy"; **n.** PRIMNESS: decorousness; preciosity; priggishness; sanctimony; squeamishness

PRIMARY: (**see** "basic") **a.** constitutional; fundamental; idiopathic; primitive

PRIME *of life:* **n.** *fleur de l'âge; les belles années*

PRIMER: **n.** abecedarium; (**pl.** abecedaria); hornbook

PRIMITIVE: **a.** aboriginal; antiquated; archaic; autochthonal; autochthonic; autochthonous; elemental; fundamental; indigenous; native; prehistoric; primeval; primogenial; primordial; rudimentary; **n.** aboriginal; aborigine; primitiveness; primitivism; primitivity
people, study of: **n.** agriology

PRINCIPAL: **see** "chief"

PRINCIPLE(S): **n.** *alpha and omega;* axiom; canon; doctrine; foundation; philosophy; principium; (**pl.** principia); (quint)essence; theorem; theory
basic: **n.** doctrine; fundament; postulate; tenet
having high: **a.** magnanimous; rectitudinous; righteous
statement of: **n.** canon; constitution; decalogue; declaration; *Magna C(h)arta*
system of: **n.** organon
vital: **n.** *anima bruta; anima mundi; élan vital*

PRINCIPLED, *overly:* **a.** rectitudinous; religiose; sanctimonious

PRINTED *on both sides of paper:* **a.** opisthographic(al)
on one side only: **a.** anopisthographic

PRIOR: (**see** "preliminary") **a.** antecedent; anterior; preceding; precursory

PRIORITY: **n.** antecedence; anteriority; precedence; preference; preeminence; preferment; prerogative; primacy; seniority; superiority; supremacy
having: **a.** antecedaneous; precedent(ial); preferential

PRISON: **n.** bastil(l)e; limbo; **n.** PRISONER: *detenu;* (**fem.** *detenué*)

PRISSY: (**see** "affected") **a.** demure; fastidious; priggish; prudish; squeamish; schoolteacherish

PRIVACY: **n.** hermitage; isolation; penetralia; sanctuary; secrecy; seclusion; solitude
place of utmost: **n.** *sanctum sanctorum*

PRIVATE: **a.** auricular; confidential; covert; delitescent; esoteric; personal; privy; restricted; sequestered; **adv.** PRIVATELY: *à deux; à huis clos; à la derobée;* backstage; confidentially; covertly; *entre nous; inter nos;* privatim; privily
in: (**see** "secretly") **adv.** *à deux; à huis clos;* covertly; *entre nous; in camerâ; inter nos; in petto; sub rosa*
knowledge: **n.** privity; (**pl.** esoterica)
state of being: **n.** insularity; interiority
to make: **v.** interiorize; **n.** interiorization

PRIVATION: (**see** "poverty") **n.** deprivation; destitution; hardship; penury; squalor
causing: **a.** privative

PRIVILEGE: **n.** dispensation; franchise; immunity; license; patent; prerogative; **a.** PRIVILEGED: immune; prerogative
prior or exclusive: **n.** franchise; immunity; precedence; prerogative

PRIZE, *highest or first:* **n.** *cordon bleu; grand prix*
pert. to winner of: **a.** laureate

PROBABLE: **a.** apparent; circumstantial; credible; ostensible; plausible; presumable; presumptive; *prima facie;* promising; verisimilar

PROBATION, *period or state of:* **n.** novitiate; postulancy; **a.** probationary

PROBATIONER: **n.** acousmatic; novice; novitiate; recruit; trainee

PROBING: **a.** inquisitorial

PROBLEM: (**see** "difficulty") **n.** bugbear; enigma; perplexity; proposition
many-sided: **n.** hydra

PROCEDURE: (**see** "method") **n.** accouterment; approach; method(ology); *modus operandi;* protocol; technique
code of, or of conduct: **n.** protocol

PROCEEDING: **n.** *démarche;* maneuver; negotiation; transaction

PROCLAIM: **v.** announce; annunciate; asseverate; manifest; nuncupate; predicate; promulgate; **n.** PROCLAMATION: **see** "edict"

PROCLIVITY: **see** "inclination"

PRODIGY: **see** "child, gifted"

PRODUCE: **v.** accomplish; beget; engender; fabricate; generate; manufacture; originate; procreate; propagate; **a.** PRODUCING: generative; procreant; procreative
abundantly: (**see** "fruitful") **a.** feracious
at point or in process of (producing): **a.** aborning; in production; parturient
live beings: **a.** proligerous; viviparous; **n.** viviparity; viviparousness

PRODUCED *by human skill or effort:* **a.** (arti) factitious; **n.** artifact; (**pl.** *fructus industriales*)
by natural methods: **n.pl.** *fructus naturales*
capable of being: **a.** manufacturable; producible; productible

PRODUCT(S): **n.** composition; consequence; manifestation; performance; progeny
man-made or industrial: **n.pl.** *fructus industriales;* **a.** (arti) factitious
natural: **n.pl.** *fructus naturales*

PRODUCTIVE: **a.** causative; constructive; creative; exuberant; fructiferous; fructuous; generative; imaginative; originative; procreative; profitable; uberous; **n.** PRODUCTIVENESS: creativity; fecundity; productivity; prolificity; uberty

PROFANE: (**see** "irreverent") **v.** blaspheme; desecrate; pollute; **a.** blasphemous; impious; mundane; sacrilegious; secular; sulfurous; sulphurous; temporal; **n.** PROFANITY: blasphemy; desecration; profanation; sacrilege

PROFESSION: **see** "work"

PROFESSIONAL *jealousy:* **n.** *jalousie de métier*

PROFICIENCY: (**see** "ability" **and** "perfection") **n.** accomplishment; adeptness; competence; competency; dexterity; expertise; expertness; mastery; virtuosity; **a.** PROFICIENT: accomplished; adept; *au fait;* consummate; dextrous; masterly; skillful

PROFILE: (**see** "outline") **n.** configuration; silhouette

PROFIT: (**see** "gain") **n.** increment; ophelimity; **a.** PROFITABLE: expedient; fructiferous; fructuous; fruitful; lucrative; remunerative

PROFLIGATE: **see** "lewd"

PROFUSE: (**see** "lavish") **a.** abundant; bountiful; copious; exuberant; prodigal; rampant; replete; superabundant; **n.** PROFUSION: (**see** "abundance") affluence; copiosity; extravagance; lavishness; opulence; plethora; prodigality; sumptuosity

PROGRAM: **n.** agendum; (**pl.** agenda); catalog(ue); exhibition; prospectus; schedule; syllabus; (**pl.** syllabi)

PROGRESS: **n.** evolution; movement; progression; progressivism
planned: **see** "planned"

PROGRESSIVE: (**see** "modern") **a.** categoric(al); consecutive; sequential; serial; successive

PROHIBIT: (**see** "ban") **v.** enjoin; inhibit; interdict; preclude; taboo; **n.** PROHIBITION: forbiddance; inhibition; injunction; interdiction; interdictum; outlawry; preclusion; proscription; **a.** PROHIBITIVE: inhibitory; interdictive; interdictory; proscriptive; verboten

PROJECTING: **a.** beetling; conspicuous; gibbous; prominent; protuberant; salient; **v.** PROJECT: extrapolate; **n.** enterprise; extrapolation; protuberance

abnormally: **a.** prognathous
part: **n.** ramus; (pl. rami)

PROLIFIC: (**see** "fertile" **and** "fruitful") **a.** fecund; philoprogenitive; propagative; reproductive; **n.** PROLIFICITY: fecundity; philoprogeneity
to make: **v.** prolificate

PROLOGUE: **see** "introduction"

PROLONG: **v.** lengthen; postpone; prorogue; protract; **a.** PROLONGED: profuse; protracted; protractive; prolix; repetitious; sostenente; sostenuto; sostinente; sustaining; **n.** PROLONGATION: prolixity; prorogation; sustentation; sustention

PROMINENCE: (**see** "superiority") **n.** celebrity; conspicuity; conspicuousness; eminence; prestige; protuberance; salience; saliency; **a.** PROMINENT: (**see** "eminent" **and** "notable") aquiline; blatant; celebrated; conspicuous; notorious; protuberant; salient; stellar

PROMISE: **v.** or **n.** covenant; pledge; plight
for promise: **n.** mutuality; *quid pro quo;* reciprocity
land of (promised land): **n.** Canaan

PROMOTION: (**see** "advancement") **n.** advertising; enhancement; preferment; **n.** PROMOTER: abettor; entrepreneur; (**fem:** entrepreneuse); encourager; impressario

PROMPT: **v.** actuate; animate; encourage; **a.** celeritous; expeditious; mercurial; punctual; telegraphic; **n.** PROMPTNESS: (**see** "speed") alacrity; celerity; expedition; promptitude; punctuality

PRONGS, *having two:* **a.** bidentate; bidigitate(d); **n.** bidigitation

PRONOUNCEMENT: **see** "edict"

PRONUNCIATION: (**see** "speech") **n.** articulation
bad **n.** cacoepy; cacology; **a.** cacoepistic
correct: **n.** orthoepy; phonology; **a.** orthoepic(al); orthoepistic; **n.** orthoepist
distinct, as in separation of syllables: **n.** incisiveness; syllabification; **a.** syllabic
standard, also study of: **n.** orthoepy; **a.** orthoepic(al); orthoepistic; **n.** orthoepist

PRONOUNCING *clearly:* **a.** enunciative; incisive; **n.** incisiveness; syllabification; **v.** syllabicate; syllabify

PROOF: **n.** attestation; certification; corroboration; demonstration; documentation; evidence; verification
burden of: **n.** *onus (probandi)*
capable of: **a.** apodictic(al); demonstrable; **n.** demonstrability
incapable of: **a.** undemonstrable; unverifiable

PROOFREAD: **v.** collate; **n.** authentication; collation

PROPAGANDA: **n.** agitprop

PROPER: (**see** "suitable") **a.** accepted; appropriate; à propos; *au fait;* comely; *comme il faut;* condign; conventional; decorous; felicitous; kosher; lawful; legitimate; licit; opportune; orthodox; seemly
stickler for what is: **n.** proprietarian; rigorist
what is considered: **see** "proprieties"

PROPERTIED *class:* **n.** proprietariat; **a.** proprietarian

PROPERTY: (**see** "attribute") **n.** essence; estate; resource(s); substance
given for support: **n.** ap(p)anage
inherited fr. father: **n.** patrimony; **a.** patrimonial
personal: **n.** chattels; personalty; (**pl.** personalia)
transfer of title: **v.** bequeath; convey; demise; devise; **n.** conveyance

PROPHECY: **n.** divination; foretelling; haruspication; omen; portent; prediction; prognostication; pythonism; **a.** **see** "foretelling"

PROPHESY: (**see** "foretell") **v.** auspicate; hariolate; prognosticate; vaticinate
art of (prophesying): **n.** or **a.** mantic

PROPHET: **n.** augur; Deborah; haruspex; mantic; Nostradamus; oracle; predictor; prognosticator; soothsayer; vaticinator
of misfortune or disaster: **n.** Cassandra; Jeremiah; **a.** Cassandran

PROPHETIC(AL): **a.** adumbrated; anticipative; apocalyptic(al); augural; cabalistic; divinatory; fatidic(al); incantatory; interpretive; ominous; oracular; phylacteric; portentious; presageful; prognosticative; pythonic; revelatory; sibylline; talismatic

PROPORTION: **n.** commensurability; commensuration; harmony; percentage; ration; symmetry; **a.** PROPORTIONATE: aliquot; commensurable; commensurate; corresponding

PROPOSITION: (**see** "assumption") **n.** hypothesis; philospheme; postulate; postulatum; (**pl.** *postulata*)
assumed for argument: **n.** *obligatum:* (**pl.** *obligata*)

PROPRIETIES, *social:* **n.pl.** *agrémen(t)s;* amenities; conventionalities; decora; *(les) convenances;* urbanities
stickler for: **n.** proprietarian; rigorist

PROPRIETY: **n.** *agrémen(t)s;* amenity, appropriateness; apropository; decorum; *bienséance;* grace; pertinence; pertinency; relevance; relevancy; suitability; **a.** appropriate; à propos; decorous; pertinent; relevant
departure or deviation fr.: **n.** aberrance; aberrant; aberration; **a.** aberrant; aberrational; aberrative
strict adherence to: **n.** correctitude; rigorism; scrupulosity; **n.** proprietarian; rigorist

PROSAIC: **a.** commonplace; down-to-earth; humdrum; jejune; literal(istic); matter-of-fact; monotonous; prolix; *terre à terre;* terrestrial; unimaginative; unleavened; **n.** prosaism

PROSCRIBE: **see** "ban"

PROSE, *writer of:* **n.** prosaist; prosateur

PROSPECT: (**see** "outlook") **n.** anticipation; expectation; foresight; futurity; panorama; perspective; prognosis; purview; vision; vista

PROSPERITY: **n.** *bonne fortune;* **a.** PROSPEROUS: (**see** "flourishing") affluent; auspicious; halcyon; propitious
has many friends: felicitas multos habet amicos
opposite of: **n.** illth

PROSTITUTE: **n.** courtesan; debauchee; demimondaine; demimonde; doxy; *fille de joie;* harlot; hetria; huzzy; *nymphe du pavé; petite dame;* quean; strumpet; trollop
higher rank: **n.** courtesan; courtezan
lover of (prostitutes): **n.** philopornist
of or rel. to, or having traits of: **a.** meretricious
part-time: **n.** grisette

PROSTITUTION: **n.** corruption; debasement; harlotry; promiscuity
of talents: **n.** venality

PROSTRATION: **n.** abashment; collapse; prosternation; stupefaction; submissiveness

PROTECTION: **n.** aegis; armament; auspice(s); bastion; bulwark; custody; guardianship; indemnity; palladium; patronage; preservation; prophylactic; prophylaxis; redoubt; sanctuary; tutelage; umbrella; **a.** PROTECTIVE: custodial; maternal(istic); paternal(istic); preservative; prophylactic; sheltering; tutelary; tutorial; **n.** PROTECTOR: (**see** "champion") chaperone; custodian; guardian; guarantor
means of: **n.** armament; muniment

PROTEST: (**see** "complain") **v.** deprecate; expostulate; inveigh; oppugn; remonstrate; **n.** (**see** "complaint") protestation; remonstrance; remonstration; a. remonstrative
one who makes: **n.** complainant; oppugner; protestant; remonstrator

PROTUBERANCE: **n.** gibbosity; protuberancy; protrusion; salience; saliency; **a.** PROTUBERANT: bulbous; conspicuous; gibbose; gibbous; obtrusive; prominent; salient

PROUD: **a.** arrogant; bombastic; contemptuous; disdainful; ego(t)istical; elated; exultant; haughty; hubristic; imperious; orgilous; orgulous; overweening; presumptuous; prideful; scornful; supercilious; **n. see** "pride"
boastfully: **a.** hubristic; vainglorious

PROVED (or PROVEN): **see** "established"; **v.** PROVE: circumstantiate; confirm; demonstrate; establish; manifest; verify; **a.** PROVING: confirmative; confirmatory; demonstrative

able to be: **a.** apodictic(al); indisputable
something which is (proved): **n.** probatum; (pl. probata)
that which was to be: quod erat demonstrandum (abb. q.e.d.)
unable to be: **a.** anapodictic

PROVERB(S): (see "maxim") **n.** apothegm; gnome; parable; **a.** apothegmatic(al); gnomic(al)
student of: **n.** par(o)emiologist
study of: **n.** paroemiology
writer of: **n.** paremiographer; paroemiographer

PROVIDE: see "prepare"

PROVIDENCE, *with favoring:* **adv.** *benigno numine*

PROVISION(S) *for journey or travel:* **n.** viaticum; (pl. viatica)

PROVISIONAL: **a.** *ad hoc;* circumstantial; conditional; contingent; interim; temporary; tentative

PROVOKE: (see "aggravate") **v.** exacerbate; excite; perturb; pique; quicken; stimulate

PROWL *lecherously:* **n.** or **v.** caterwaul

PRUDENCE: **n.** calculation; canniness; cautiousness; circumspection; discretion; forethought; frugality; judiciousness; moderation; providence; restraint; sophrosyne; temperance; vigilance; **a.** PRUDENT: see "careful"

PRUDISH: (see "prissy") **a.** lily-white; nice-Nellie; priggish; puribund; squeamish; PRUDERY: Comstockery; Grundyism; priggishness; puribundity; squeamishness

PRYING: **a.** curious; inquisitorial
observer: **n.** quidnunc; scopophiliac; *voyeur;* **a.** scopophilic; voyeuristic

PSYCHIC: see "mental" and "supernatural"

PUBERTY, not having reached: **n.** impuberty; **a.** impubic; prepubertal
of or happening at: **a.** hebetic; pubertal; pubescent
rites at attaining: see under "adulthood"

PUBIC *hair:* **n.** byssus; escutcheon
hair, site of: **n.** *mons veneris* (fem.) pubic triangle

PUBLIC: (see "popular") **a.** exoteric; **n.** commonalty; community; populace; population
belonging to the: **a.** *publici juris*
declaration or report: **n.** manifesto; white paper
for good of the: **adv.** *pro bono publico*
in: **a.** or **adv.** *coram populo; coram publico*
office, mania for holding: **n.** empleomania
officer: **n.** functionnaire
speaking, rel. to: **a.** demegoric
use, seize for: see under "seize"

PUBLICATION: (see "disclosure") **n.** divulgation; proclamation; promulgation

PUBLICITY: **n.** ballyhoo; dissemination; exploitation; promulgation; propaganda

PUBLICIZE (or PUBLISH): **v.** circulate; delate; disseminate; exploit; herald; nuncupate; proclaim; promote; promulgate; pronunciate; ventilate

PUBLISHED *after author's death:* **a.** posthumous

PULP: **n.** cellulose; magma; **a.** PULPY: macerated; magmatic; pultaceous

PULSATE: **v.** oscillate; palpitate; pulse; vibrate; **a.** PULSATIVE: palpitant; pulsatile; pulsatory; throbbing; **n.** PULSATION: ictus; oscillation; palmus; palpitation; undulation

PULVERIZE: **v.** annihilate; comminute; contriturate; demolish; disintegrate; levigate; triturate; **n.** PULVERIZATION: comminution; trituration

PUN: **n.** adnomination; assonance; calembour; equivoke; equivoque; *jeu de mots;* paradigm; paronomasia; *turlupinade*

PUNISH: **v.** admonish; castigate; chasten; chastize; discipline; flagellate; penalize; retaliate; **a.** PUNISHING: castigatory; corrective; disciplinary; expiatory; flagellant; penal; penitentiary; punitive; retaliatory; retributory; retributive; vindicative; vindicatory
by fine: **v.** amerce; **n.** amercement

PUNISHMENT: **n.** admonition; amercement; castigation; chastenment; chastisement; correction; discipline; expiation; Nemesis; penalty; penance; punition; purgatory; retaliation; retribution; vindication
enforcer of: **n.** disciplinarian; martinet; Nemesis; rigorist
freedom from: **n.** immunity; impunity
just: **n.** comeuppance; Nemesis
lessening of: **n.** commutation; leniency; mitigation; **v.** commute; mitigate; reprieve
liability to: **n.** penality; **a.** penalizable
not subject to or capable of: **a.** immune; indisciplinable; **n.** immunity; indiscipline
pert. to or having nature of: **a.** castigatory; disciplinal; disciplinary; disciplinatory; punitive; punitory; retributive; vindicatory
self, pert. to: **a.** intropunitive; self-condemnatory
strong and severe: **n.** *peine forte et dure*
study of: **n.** penology; **a.** penological; **n.** penologist
voluntary, as token of repentence: **n.** penance; **a.** penitential

PUNNING, *act or practice of:* **n.** adnomination; paronomasia

PUPIL: **n.** abecedarian; alphabetarian; apostle; catechumen; disciple; neophyte; novice; probationer; *protégé,* (**fem.** *protégée*); scholar
pert. to: **a.** abecedarian; apostolic; catechumenal; catechumenical; scholarly; scholastic

PURCHASES, *insane desire to make:* **n.** oniomania; **n.** oniomaniac

PURE: **a.** absolute; (arch)angelic; artless; chaste; cherubic; classic(al); crystalline; devout; guileless; hermetic(al); immaculate; imputrescible; incorrupt(ed); incorruptible; innocent; intemerate; inviolable; inviolate; *pur et simple;* seraphic; sheer; spotless; sterile; sublime; unadulterated; unalloyed; uncorrupted; uncorruptible; undefiled; unmixed; unsoiled; unstained; unsullied; untainted; untouched; upright; vestal; virgin
unqualifiedly: **a.** archangelic; *pur et simple;* simon-pure

PURGE: **v.** absterge; defecate; deterge; eliminate; **n.** abstersion; catharsis; cathartic; laxative; purgation; purgative

PURIFICATION: **n.** ablution; abreaction; alembication; catharsis; defecation; depuration; epuration; lustration; purgation; **a.** PURIFICATORY: expiatory; purgatorial
by ceremony: **n.** lustration; **a.** lustral; **v.** lustrate

PURIFY: **v.** alembicate; chasten; defecate; depurate; edulcorate; epurate; exorcise; lustrate
by washing: **v.** elutriate; **n.** elutriation
something which (purifies): **n.** purificant

PURITY: **n.** chastity; cleanliness; continence; immaculacy; incorruptibility; inviolability; sacredness; sanctity; sanctitude; virtue
exaggerated: (**see** "religious, overly") **n.** Comstockery; pudency; pudibundity; pudicity; puritanism; **a.** PURITANICAL: lily-white; priggish; prudish; puribund; sanctimonious
those who claim or profess: **n.** (the) *unco guid*

PURPLE, *clad in:* **a.** porporate
to become or make: **v.** empurple; **a.** empurpled

PURPLISH: **a.** porphyrous; purpureal; purpurean; purpurescent; purpureous; purpurine

PURPOSE: (**see** "destiny" and "intention") **n.** ambition; aspiration; *causa finalis;* design; determination; function; intendment; philosophy; purport; resolution; significance
aside from the: **adv.** *hors de propos*
for what?: **adv.** *cui bono?*
fulfilled and no longer valid: **adv.** *functus officio*
having many: **a.** multiphasic; multipurpose; multivious
without definite: **see** "purposeless"

PURPOSEFUL: (**see** "intentional") **a.** directional; functional; purposive; teleological; telic

PURPOSELESS: **a.** aimless; amorphous; dysteleological; meaningless; purportless; random; undirected; unpremeditated

PURSE, *appeal(ing) to the:* **n.** or **adv.** (*argumentum*) *ad crumenam*

PURSUIT: (see "quest") **n.** activity; *métier;* occupation; ploy; prosecution; **a.** persequent

PUS: **n.** suppuration; **a.** suppurative
discharge: **v.** maturate; suppurate
of, like or containing: **a.** puriform; purulent; suppurative; **n.** maturation; purulence; purulency

PUSHER: **n.** arrivst(e); parvenu; **n.** arrivism

PUSHING: **a.** aggressive; arrogant; bumptious; presumptuous

PUZZLE: **see** "bewilder" **and** "mystery"
key to the: **n.** *le mot de l'enigme*

PUZZLING: **a.** ambiguous; ambivalent; bewildering; cabalistic; cryptic; enigmatic(al); equivocal; impenetrable; incomprehensible; inexplicable; inscrutable; mysterious; occult; paradoxical; perplexing; sphinxlike; undecipherable; unfathomable

PYRAMID, *pert. to or having shape of:* **a.** pyramidal; **n.** ziggurat

Q

QUACK: (**see** "pretender") **n.** Cagliostro; charlatan; empiric; humbug; imposter; medicaster; mountebank; quacksalver

QUAINT: (**see** "odd") **a.** antique; bizarre; eccentric; exotic; grotesque; *outré;* rococo; singular; whimsical; **n. see** "oddity" **and** "peculiarity"

QUALIFY: **v.** capacitate; habilitate; **n.** QUALIFICATION: (**see** "capacity") capacitation; expertise; expertness; habilitation; hability; virtuosity; **a.** QUALIFIED: (**see** "capable") accomplished; certified; competent; conditional; consummate; eligible; licensed; registered; restricted; **a.** QUALIFYING: (**see** "limiting") adjectival; adjective; qualificatory

QUALITY: (**see** "attribute") **n.** character(istic); property; resonance; timbre
having different (qualities): **a.** heterogeneous; heteroousian; heterousian; **n.** heterogeneity
something of superior: **n.** *ne plus supra; ne plus ultra;* nonesuch; nonpareil; supernaculum

QUANTITY, *having to do with:* **a.** quantitative; **n.** amplitude; magnitude; quantum; (**pl.** quanta)
large: **n.** hecatomb; legion; multitude; spate
very small in: **a.** diminutive; homeopathic; miniscular; miniscule; minuscule

QUARREL: (**see** "breach") **n.** altercation; *démêlé;* dissention; embroglio; fracas; melee; ruction; wrangle
lover's: **n.pl.** *amatium irae*
noisily: **v.** or **n.** caterwaul;**n.** ruction
riotous: **n.** donnybrook

QUARRELSOME: **a.** *acariâtre;* argumentative; bellicose; belligerent; boisterous; cantankerous; choleric; combative; contentious; discordant; disputable; disputatious; dissentient; dissentious; dissident; fractious; gladiatorial; perverse; pugnacious; querulous; refractory; ructious; termagant(ish); turbulent; **n.** QUARRELSOMENESS: *acariâtre;* bellicosity; belligerency; pugnacity; turbulence

QUEER: **see** "odd"

QUEST: **n.** desideratum; emprise; expedition; (Holy) grail; inquisition; odyssey; perlustration; perscrutation; pursuit; reconnaissance; reconnoiter; safari; venture

QUESTION: **v.** catechize; inquisit; **n.** QUESTIONER: inquisitor
and answer method of discussion: **n.** dialectics; **a.** dialectic(al)
of instruction: **n.** catechesis; catechism; **v.** catechize; **a.** catechetic(al); catechistic; Socratean; Socratic
begging the: **n.** *petitio principii*
beyond: **a.** impregnable; indubitable; invulnerable; undoubtable; unquestionable
bringing into: **n.** impugnment; **v.** impugn
handbook of (questions): **n.** catechism
in rhetoric, as when speaker asks question to answer it: **n.** prosopopoeia; rhetorical question; sermocination
not open to: (**see** "beyond" above) **a.** axiomatic; incontestable; incontrovertible; indisputable; indubitable; unassailable; undoubted; **n.** matter of breviary
open to: **see** "questionable"
subject to. **a.** impugnable

QUESTIONABLE: (**see** "doubtful" **and** "vague") **a.** ambiguous; contentious; controversial; controvertible; cryptic; debatable; disputable; disputatious; disreputable; dubious; dubitable; equivocal; hypothetical; indeterminate; obscure; occult; paradoxical; polemical; problematical; provisional; shady; suspicious; uncertain; unreliable; unsafe
something which is: **n.** ambiguity; equivocality; equivocation
state of being: **n.** ambiguity; dubiosity; equivocality; equivocacy; equivocity

QUESTIONING, *close:* **n.** catechesis; catechism; catechization; inquisition; **v.** catechize; **a.** catechistic(al); inquisitorial
to bring forth ideas or memories: **n.** maieutics; **a.** maietuic(al); Socratic

QUIBBLE: **v.** bicker; carp; cavil; equivocate; **a.** QUIBBLING: captious; carping; causistic; sophistical; sophomoric; specious; **n.** chicanery; equivocation; scrupulosity; sophistry; speciosity

QUIBBLER: **n.** *advocatus diaboli* (devil's advocate); carper; caviler; equivocator

QUICK: **a.** animated; celeritous; expeditious; facile; impetuous; instantaneous; mercurial; nimble; telegraphic; **adv.** *tout de suite*
-tempered: (**see** "contentious" **and** "fiery") **a.** choleric; iracund; irascible
-witted: **a.** astucious; astute; mercurial; perspicacious; scintillescent

QUICKNESS: **n.** alacrity; celerity; expedition; facilitation; facility; instantaneity
mental: **n.** acumen; astucity; nous; perspicacity; sagacity

QUIET: (**see** "calm") **a.** dormant; pacific; quiescent; secluded; tranquil; **v.** allay; pacify; repress; tranquilize; **n.** QUIET (**or** QUIETNESS): dormancy; quiescence; quietude; repose; tranquility
that which produces: **n.** nepenthe; opiate; sedative; tranquilizer

QUIT: **see** "resign"

QUIVER: (**see** "throb") **n.** motitation

QUOTATIONS, *disjointed:* **n.pl.** *disjecta membra*

R

RABBIT: **n.** coney; cuniculus; hare; lagomorph

RABBLE: **n.** canaille; commonalty; demos; *faex populi; hoi polloi;* horde; *ignoble vulgus; lumpen proletariat;* populace; *profanum vulgus;* proletariat; masses; multitude; rifraff; varletry **a.** lumpen; plebeian; proletarian; proletariat(e)
-rouser: **n.** demagogue; ochlocrat; **a.** demogogic(al); ochlocratic
wretched: **n.pl.** *miserabile vulgus*

RACE(S): (**see** "people") **n.** genus; paternity; pedigree; phylum; sept
as a center: **a.** ethnocentric; **n.** ethnocentrism
human: **see** "man" **and** "mankind"
mixed: **n.** hybrid(ization); **a.** hybrid; **v.** hybridize
mixing of: **n.** hybridization; mestization; miscegenation
pert. to: **a.** ethnic; ethnologic
segregation: **n.** apartheid
study of: **n.** anthropology; ethnology; raciology; **a.** anthropologic(al); ethnologic(al);
of degeneration: **n.** dysgenics
of distribution: **n.** anthropogeography; ethnogeography
of origin and development: **n.** anthropogenesis; anthropogeny; **a.** anthropogenetic
of primitive: **n.** agriology

RACIAL: **a.** cultural; ethnic(al); gentilic; phyletic; phylogen(et)ic; tribal
extermination: **n.** genocide; **a.** genocidal
history (plant or animal): **n.** phylogensis; phylogeny; **a.** phylogen(et)ic

RADIANT: (**see** "brilliant") **a.** auroral; aurorean; blithe; divergent; ecstatic; lambent; luminous; resplendent; scintillescent; **n.** RADIANCE: effulgency; resplendency; scintillation; **v.** RADIATE: diffuse; disseminate; effulge

RADICAL: (**see** "rebel") **n.** firebrand; Jacobin; revolutionary; sansculotte; septembrist; ultraist; Young Turk; **a.** drastic; extreme; heretical; heterodox; Jacobinic; revolutionary; sansculottic; sansculottish; thoroughgoing; unconventional; unorthodox
to uphold (radical) principles: **v.** sansculottize

RADICALISM: **n.** heresy; heterodoxy; Jacobinism; radicality; sansculotterie; sansculottism; ultraism

RAGE: (**see** "anger") **n.** dudgeon; fashion; fervor; frenzy; enthusiasm; paroxysm; pique; **a.** RAGING: (**see** "violent") berserk; blustering; cyclonic; frenzied; fulminating; furibund; infuriated; maniac(al); paroxysmal; rampant
being in sudden: **a.** fulminating; fulminous; **v.** fulminate
poetic: **n.** *furor poeticus*

RAGGED *person:* **n.** ragamuffin; tatterdemalion

RAID: **v.** maraud; **n.** foray; incursion; inroad; **a.** incursionary

RAILLERY: (**see** "mockery") **n.** asteism; badinage; persiflage; pleasantry

RAIN: **v.** precipitate; **n.** precipitate; precipitation; **a.** pluvian; pluvious
abundant: **n.** pluviosity; **a.** pluviose
ga(u)ge: **n.** udometer
pert. to: **a.** pluvial; pluvian; pluvious
study of: **n.** ombrology
thriving in: **a.** ombrophilous

RAINBOW, *resembling:* **a.** iridian

RAISE: **v.** aggrandize; elevate; enhance; ennoble; escalate; exalt; extol; intensify; levitate; sublimate; transcend; **n.** advancement; elevation; enhancement; ennoble-

ment; escalation; promotion; transcendency
tending to: **a.** elevatory; transcendent

RAKE: **n.** debauchee; lecher; libertine; lothario; profligate; rakehell; *roué;* **a.** libertine; profligate; rakehell

RAMBLE: (**see** "wander") **v.** meander; perambulate; peregrinate; **n.** perambulation; peregrination; ploy; **a.** RAMBLING: circuitous; desultory; devious; discursive; meandering; parenthetical; perambulatory; peregrine; peripatetic; **n.** meandering; perambulation; peregrination
alone: **a.** or **n.** solivagant
in speech, thought or writing: **n.** circumbendibus; circumlocution; **n.pl.** circumambages; **a.** circumambagious

RANDOM: **a.** desultory; fortuitous; haphazard; indiscriminate; purposeless; stochastic
at: **adv.** *à l'abandon; à tort et à travers;* stochastically

RANGE: (**see** "outlook" **and** "prospect") **n.** calendar; catalog(ue); category; compass; diapason; excursion; gamut; gradation; incidence; jurisdiction; latitude; lexicon; orbit; purview; spectrum; **a.** categoric(al); jurisdictional; latitudinal; latitudinous
continuous: **n.** spectrum
of sight or understanding: **n.** panorama; purview

RANK: (**see** "grade") **n.** array; distinction; formation; precedence; prestige; rating; **a.** exuberant; flagrant; indecent; luxuriant; luxurious; rampant; rancid
equal for all: **n.** pantisocracy
equal in: **see** "equal"
lowering in: **a.** *declassé;* declensional; declinitory; **n.** declension; declination; subordination; **v.** declass; subordinate
of highest: **n.** top-drawer; top-flight
of lower: **a.** *déclassé* (**fem.** *déclassée*); junior; puisne; subaltern(ate); subordinate; **n.** juniority; subordinate
on acct. of or respect for: **adv.** *propter honoris respectum*
people of: (**see** "elite") **n.pl.** *gens de condition;* **n.** aristocratism; patriciate; (**pl.** aristoi)
superior in: **n.** antecedence; precedence; seniority; **a.** antecedent; precedent; superordinate

RAPID: (**see** "quick") **a.** agile; cursory; desultory; expeditious; meteoric; superficial
gallop or dash, in a: **n.** or **a.** tantivy

RAPIDLY *shifting:* **a.** kaleidoscopic; oscillatory; phantasmagoric(al)

RAPTURE: **n.** ecstasy; elation; enthusiasm; euphoria; exaltation; paroxysm; raptus; transport; **a.** RAPTUROUS: (**see** "elated") delirious; ecstatic; frenzied; orgiastic; paroxysmal; **v.** ecstasiate; ecstasize
frenzied: **n.** delirium; orgasm; paroxysm
greatest: **n.** seventh heaven
state of spiritual: **n.** raptus

RARE: **a.** estimable; exotic; incomparable; infrequent; novel; paranormal; *recherché;* supernacular; tenuous; uncommon; unexampled; unique; unparalleled; unprecedented; **n.** RARENESS: attenuation; rarefaction; subtilization; tenuity

RARITY: **n.** anomaly; extravaganza; infrequency; phenomenality; prodigality; prodigy; *rara avis;* scarcity; tenuity; *tulipe noir*
extreme: **n.** *cygne noir*

RASCAL: (**see** "rogue") **n.** miscreant; rakehell; rapscallion; reprobate; ribald; scalawag; scaramouche; villain; **a.** RASCALLY: villainous
conduct of: **n.** rascality; scalawaggery

RASH: (**see** "reckless") **a.** (ad)venturous; audacious; *écervelé;* hare-brained; headstrong; heady; Icarian; ill-advised; impetuous; imprudent; impulsive; inconsiderate; madcap; precipitate; presumptuous; temerarious; unadvised; **n.** RASHNESS: assumption; audacity; effrontery; impetuosity; presumption; temerity

RATE: (**see** "classify") **n.** incidence; proportion; velocity
at equal: **a.** or **adv.** *pari passu*

RATIFICATION, *formal, as by seal:* **n.** obsignation

RATIFY: **see** "affirm"

RATING: **see** "rank"

RATION: **see** "apportion"

RATIONAL: **a.** Apollonian; Apollon(ist)ic; Cartesian; cognitive; consequential; defensible; intellective; intellectual; intelligent; judicious; philosophical; reasonable; restrained; sapient; sensible; tenable

RATTLE: **v.** agitate; crepitate; discompose; disconcert; **n.** crepitation; **a.** crepitant

RAVAGE: **v.** denudate; deplumate; depauperate; deracinate; despoil; devastate; extirpate; impoverish; pillage; spoliate; **n.** denudation; deplumation; depradation; deracination; despoilment; despoliation; devastation; rapine; spoliation

RAVE: **v.** fulminate; **a.** RAVING: beserk; delirious; frenzied; fulminating; maniac(al)

RAVEN, *like or pert. to:* **a.** corvine

RAVENOUS: (**see** "gluttonous") *a.* lupine; rapacious; voracious

RAVISH: **see** "defile"

RAW: **a.** inclement; undigested; unevaluated; unprocessed; unseasoned
as to food: **a.** *au naturel*
flesh, eating of: **n.** omophagia; **a.** omophagic; omophagous

REACTIONARY: **see** "conservative"

REACTIVATE: (**see** "revive") **v.** recrudesce; revivify; **a.** recrudescent; revivescent; **n.** REACTIVATION: recrudescence; recrudescency; resuscitation; revivification

REACTOR: **n.** activator; catalyst; **a.** catalytic

READ *and write, able to:* **a.** literate; **n.** literacy
inability to: **n.** alexia; illiteracy

READABLE: **a.** comprehensible; decipherable; legible; scrutable; understandable

READING *beforehand, or a previous:* **n.** pr(a)election
or having read everything: **a.** omniligent; omnivorous
reversal of words, etc. in: **n.** strephosymbolia
systematic or habitual: **n.** frequentation

READY: **a.** available; compliant; convenient; dextrous; *en garde;* expectant; expeditious; facile; operational; opportune; preconditioned; prepared; resourceful; unhesitating; **n.** READINESS: alacrity; aptitude; facility; promptitude
for anything: **adv.** *in omnia paratus*
for attack: **a.** *en garde;* expugnatory; operational

REAL: (**see** "actual") **a.** authentic; *bona fide;* definitive; demonstrable; inherent; intrinsic; legitimate; objective; official; postival; substantive; veritable; **a.** REALISTIC: (**see** "practical") Cartesian; unromantic; unsentimental
assume to be or treat as: **v.** hypostatise; hypostatize

REALITY: **n.** actuality; entity; existent; objectivity; verity
appearing to have: **a.** verisimilar; verisimilous; **n.** verisimilitude; verisimility
doctrine of no: **n.** nihilism; **a.** nihilistic
escape fr. by fantasy: **n.** autism; escapism; identification; **a.** autistic; escapist
having, after existence of particulars: **a.** *post rem; post res*
before existence of particulars: **a.** *ante rem; ante res*
regard as: **v.** hypostatise; hypostatize
science dealing w/ nature of: **n.** ontology; **n.** ontologist; **a.** ontological

REALLY!: **int.** *ma foi!*

REALM: **see** "region"

REAR: **v.** construct; elevate; originate; produce; **n.** (**see** "rump") posterior
in the: **adv.** or **a.** *en arrière;* **a.** posterior

REARRANGE: **v.** permutate; refurbish; **n.** REARRANGEMENT: permutation; refurbishment

REASON: (**see** "think") **v.** expostulate; intellectualize; ratiocinate; rationalize; **n.** (**see** "reasoning") argument; intellect; intuition; justification; noesis; nous; ratiocination; rationale; rationality; understanding
against: **v.** oppugn; **n.** oppugnation; **a.** alogical; argumentative; disputatious
all the more: *raison de plus*

appeal to: **n.** argumentation; argumentum
by a stronger: **a.** *a fortiori*
by formal logic: **v.** ratiocinate; **a.** ratiocinative; **n.** ratiocination
creature of: **n.** *ens rationis*
falsely: **v.** paralogize; **a.** paralogistic; specious; **n.** paralogism; speciosity
for being or existing: **n.** *raison d'être*
life governed by: **n.** eudaemonia; sophrosyne; **a.** eudaemonic(al)
of state (diplomatic): **n.** *raison d'état*
"pure": (**see** "innate intelligence") **n.** noesis
with: **v.** expostulate; **n.** expostulation

REASONABLE: (**see** "rational") **a.** acceptable; defensible; judicious; justifiable; legitimate; moderate; rationalistic; tenable; **n.** justifiability; legitimacy; rationality
part: **n.** *pars rationabilis*

REASONER: **n.** dialectitian; dialectologist; logician; ratiocinator; rationalist

REASONING: (**see** "argument") **n.** argumentation; dialectics; intellection; ratiocination; **a.** ratiocinative
contrary to logic: (**see under** "logic") **n.** paralogism; **a.** paralogistic
deductive: **n.** syllogism; synthesis; **a.** *a priori;* aprioristic; intuitive; syllogistic(al)
equivocal or specious: **see** "subtle, etc." **below**
from general to particular: **see** "deductive" **above**
from particular to general: **see** "inductive" **below**
in a circle: **n.** *circulus in probando*
inductive: **n.** empiricism; epigogue; **a.** *a posteriori;* aposterioristic; empirical
intuitive: **n.** *a priori;* apriority; **a.** aprioristic
irrational: **n.** alogism; **a.** alogistic
logical or sophisticated: **n.** ergotism
mode of: **n.** *modus ponens; modus tollens*
presumptive: **see** "deductive" **above**
subtle, tricky or specious: **n.** casuistry; sophism; sophistry; syllogism; **a.** casuistic
w/o exam. or analysis: **a.** or **adv.** *a priori;* **a.** aprioristic; intuitive; presumptive

REBEL: (**see** "radical") **n.** anarch(ist); dissident; frondeur; insurgent; malcontent; mutineer; sansculotte; septembrist; **v. see** "oppose"

REBELLION: **n.** contumacy; insurrection; mutiny; putsch; sedition; **a.** REBELLIOUS: (**see** "stubborn") anarchic(al); disaffected; fractious; insurgent; insurrectionary; malcontent; mutinous; perverse; refractory; seditious
one who stirs up: **n.** firebrand; incendiary

REBIRTH: (**see** "revival") **n.** reincarnation; renascence; renaissance; revivification
of soul (doctrine): **n.** metempsychosis; reincarnation; transmigration
something which undergoes: **n.** phoenix

REBORN: **a.** redivivus; regenerated; reincarnated; renascent; revivified

REBOUND: **v.** carom; recoil; reecho; resile; repercuss; reverberate; richochet; **n.** carom; resilience; resiliency; richochet; **a.** resilient; reverberative
on the: **adv.** *à rebours*

REBUKE: **v.** admonish; animadvert; berate; castigate; objurgate; reprehend; reprimand; reprove; vituperate; **n.** admonishment; animadversion; castigation; objurgation; reproof; **a.** REBUKING: admonishing; admonitory; castigatory; objugatury; reprehensive
deserved: **n.** comeuppance; deserts

RECALL: **v.** recollect; reminisce; **n.** (**see** "recollection') reminiscence; **a.** reminiscent(ial)

RECANT: **see** "renounce"

RECEDE: **v.** countermarch; depreciate; dwindle; regress; retrocede; retrograde; **n. see** "recession"

RECEIVE: (**see** "admit") acquire; entertain; intromit
willingness to: **n.** receptivity; sentience; sentiency; susceptibility; **a.** receptive; susceptible

RECEIVER: **n.** bailee; conservator; donee; receptionist; receptor; **a.** or **n.** recipient

RECEIVING: **a.** recipient; **n.** reception; recipience; recipiency
within, act of: **n.** admittance; intromission; introsusception; intussusception

RECENT: (see "new") **a.** advanced; contemporary; modern(e); neoteric

RECEPTION: **n.** acceptance; admission; collation; conversazione; intromission; reaction; soiree

RECEPTIVE: **a.** acceptant; susceptible; susceptive; **n.** receptivity; susceptibility

RECESS: **n.** armistice; continuance; *entr'acte;* hiatus; interim; intermission; respite

RECESSION: **n.** abatement; declension; decrescence; diminution; retreat; retrocession; withdrawal

RECIPROCAL: see "mutual"

RECKLESS: (see "bold") **a.** audacious; foolhardy; harum-scarum; heedless; hotspur; Icarian; improvident; imprudent; incautious; irresponsible; precipitate; prodigal; *sans attention;* scatterbrain; temerarious; **n.** RECKLESSNESS: audacity; daredeviltry; improvidence; imprudence; prodigality; temerariousness; temerity

courage: **n.** bravado; derring-do

RECLINING: **n.** accumbency; anaclysis; decubation; decubitus; decumbency; recumbency; reclination; **a.** decumbent; recumbent

RECLUSE: **n.** anchoret; anchorite; ascetic; cenobite; eremite; solitudinarian

esp. religious: **n.** anchorite; eremite; Essene; **a.** anchoristic; cloistered; eremitic(al)

RECOGNITION: **n.** acknowledgment; apperception; discernment; identification; salutation; **a.** apperceptionistic; identificatory; recognitive; recognitory

RECOGNIZED, *capable of being:* **a.** cognoscible; cognoscitive; (re)cognizable; **n.** identifiability; recognizability

incapable of being: **a.** incognito; incognizable; incognoscible; indiscernible; **n.** incognoscibility; indiscernibility

RECOIL: (see "rebound") **v.** reecho; reverberate; richochet; **n.** reverberation; richochet

RECOLLECTION: **n.** anamensis; memoir; remembrance; reminiscence; **a.** reminiscent(ial)

RECOMPENSE: **v.** compensate; reimburse; remunerate; requite; **n.** (see "salary") compensation; emolument; guerdon; indemnification; indemnity; quittance; reimbursement; remuneration; requital; retribution

RECONCILE: (see "appease") **v.** harmonize; propitiate; (re)conciliate; syncretize; synchronize; **a.** RECONCILIATORY: conciliatory; syncretistic; **n.** RECONCILIATION: (see "harmony") (e)irenicon; rapprochment; reconcilement; syncretism

having power or tendency to: **a.** henotic; irenic; reconcilable; (re)conciliatory; **n.** reconcilability

RECORD(S): **v.** enscroll; **n.** agendum; (pl. agenda); archive; calendar; chronicle; compendium; dossier; lexicon; transcript(ion)

study of to determine authenticity, meaning, etc.: **n.** philology

written, of facts or proceedings: **n.** *procès-verbal;* (pl. *procès-verbaux*)

RECOVER, *as loss or health:* **v.** recup(erate); retrieve

unable to: **a.** irretrievable; irreversible; irrevocable

RECOVERY: **n.** reacquisition; recoverance; recuperation; retrieval; retrievement

period of: **n.** convalescence; puerperium; recuperation; **a.** convalescent; recuperative

RECREATION: see "entertainment"

RECUR: **v.** perseverate; reappear: (re)iterate; **n.** RECURRENCE: periodicity; perseveration; recurrency; (re)iteration; **a.** RECURRING: perennial; periodic; (re)iterative; revenant

tune, phrase, etc. which (recurs): **n.** leitmotif; leitmotiv

RED, *becoming:* **a.** rubescent; **n.** rubescence; **v.** empurple

-haired, **a.** hirsutorfous; rufous; xanthous; **n.** pyrrhotism

-handed, caught: **adv.** (in) *flagrante delicto*
paint with: **v.** miniate; rubify; rubricate

REDDISH (or REDDENED): **a.** (e)rubescent; incarmined; incarnadine; rubicund; rubious; rufescent; rutilant; **n.** REDDISHNESS: (e)rubescence; rubicundity; rufosity
glow, having: **a.** rubescent; rutilant
-yellow: **a.** fulvous; xanthous

REDNESS *of skin:* **n.** erythema; hyperemia; rubefaction; **a.** erythematous; hyperemic; rubescent; rubicund

REDUCE: **see** "lessen"
by half: (**see** "halved") **v.** bisect; dimidiate; **a.** bisected; dimidiate; **n.** dimidiation

REDUCTION: (**see** "lessening") **n.** abridgement; conquest; declension; decrement; demotion; depreciation; diminution; minimization; mitigation; subjugation
to absurdity: **n.** *reductio ad absurdum*
argument by this method: **n.** apagoge; **a.** apagogic(al)
to lower level: **n.** denigration; minimization; pejoration; plebification; vulgarization; **v.** denigrate; minify; minimize; pejorate; plebeianize; vulgarize

REDUNDANCY: **n.** circumlocution; copiosity; macrology; overabundance; periphrasis; pleonasm; profusion; prolixity; superabundance; supererogation; superfluity; tautology; verbiage; verboseness; verbosity; **a.** REDUNDANT: *de trop;* exuberant; immaterial; pleonastic; prolix; superabundant; supererogative; supererogatory; superfluous; tautological; tautologous; verbose

RE-ECHO: **v.** reverberate; **a.** reverberant; reverberative; reverberatory; **n.** reverberation

REED, *of or like:* **a.** arundinaceous

REESTABLISHMENT: (**see** "restoration") **n.** apocatastasis; reacquisition; recuperation
of friendship or relation: **n.** rapprochement

REFERABLE: **a.** ascribable; assignable; attributable; imputable; pertinent; referential; **adv.** anent; *in re*

REFERENCE(S): **n.** bibliography; testimonial (s); **n.pl.** compendia
book: (**see** "manual") **n.** *index rerum;* promptuary; *vade mecum*
exact: **n.** chapter and verse
for: **adv.** *ad referendum*
used for: **a.** referential

REFINE: **v.** alembicate; chasten; civilize; cultivate; debarbarize; defecate; depurate; educate; elevate; expurgate; rarefy; spiritualize; subtilize
something which (refines) or transmutes: **n.** alembic

REFINED: (**see** "polished") **a.** alembicated; cultivated; fastidious; *recherché*
extremely or affectedly: **a.** *précieuse; précieux;* **n.** preciosity

REFINEMENT: (**see** "elegance" **and** "polish") **n.** alembication; artistry; civilization; cultivation; discrimination; finesse; gentility; humanization; perfectionment; rarefaction; subtlety
characterized by exquisite: **a.** spirituel(le)
lacking in: **a.** gauche; incondite; maladroit; unpolished; **n.** gaucherie
over-: **n.** alembication; preciosity; **a.** *précieuse; précieux*

REFLECT: (**see** "re-echo" **and** "rebound") **v.** contemplate; deliberate; (ex)cogitate; ideate; mirror; perpend; philosophize; ponder; ratiocinate; ruminate; **n.** REFLECTION: (**see** "thought") aspersion; cogitation; consideration; ideation; imputation; meditation; perpension; ratiocination; **a.** REFLECTIVE: (**see** "meditative") cogitative; deliberative; ratiocinative; ruminant
light or sound: **v.** reverberate; **a.** reverberative; reverberatory; **n.** reverberation

REFLECTED *light, pert. to:* **a.** catoptric(al)

REFORM: **v.** chasten; convert; rectify; remodel; **n.** REFORMATION: conversion; emendation; redemption; renovation
capable of: (**see** "correctible") **a.** corrigible; docile; reformable; tractable; **n.** corrigibility; docility; tractability

REFRESHMENT(S): **n.** collation; reanimation; recreation; regeneration; reinvigoration; revivification; stimulation; **v.** REFRESH: recreate; refocillate; rein-

vigorate; replenish; revivify; **a.** REFRESHING: fragrant; heartening; oasitic
place of: **n.** oasis; **a.** oasitic

REFUGE: **see** "sanctuary"

REFUND: **v.** reimburse; restitute; **n.** reimbursement; restitution

REFUSAL: **n.** abnegation; declension; declination; denegation; disclaimer; rejection; **a.** declensional; declinatory; **v.** REFUSE: decline; reject; renege; **n.** debris; detritus; offal; offscouring(s); (**pl.** (d)ejecta; rejecta; (r)ejectamenta)

REFUTATION: **n.** confutation; disproof; elenchus; **a.** REFUTING: anatreptic; elenc(h)tic; refutative
incapable of: **a.** irrefrangable; irrefrangible; irrefutable

REGAL: (**see** "kingly") **a.** imperial; imposing
female, pert. to: **a.** junoesque; statuesque

REGARD: (**see** "admiration") **n.** estimation; *estime*

REGENERATION, *as of tissue:* **n.** neogenesis; **a.** neogenetic

REGION(S): (**see** "kingdom") **n.** domain; dominion; environment; hemisphere; jurisdiction; locale; milieu; purlieu; realm; terrain
description of: **n.** periegesis
native to, or occurring in several: **n.** polydemic

REGRESS: **v.** recidivate; retrograde; retrogress; **n.** REGRESSION: recidivation; retrogression; retrogradation; **a.** recidivous; retrograde; retrogressive

REGRET: (**see** "bewail") **v.** deplore; lament; repine; **n.** attrition; compassion; compunction; contrition; lamentation; penitence; qualm; remorse; scruple; **a.** REGRETFUL: compunctious; contrite; deplorable; deprecative; lamentable; penitent; remorseful; repining; rueful; **a.** REGRETTABLE: **see** "deplorable"
without: **a.** impenitent; **n.** impenitence

REGULAR: (**see** "authorized") **a.** methodical; metronomic(al); official; orderly; orthodox; rhythmic(al), symmetrical; synchronous; **n.** REGULARITY: periodicity; synchroneity

REGULATE: **see** "guide"

REGULATED, *capable of being:* **a.** modificative; modificatory; modulatory; normative; **n.** modificability; modulability

REGULATION: **see** "rule"

REGULATOR: **see** "controller"

REHASH: **a.** or **n.** *réchauffé;* **v.** refurbish; renovate; summarize

REJECT: **v.** abjure; decline; dismiss; forsake; forswear; ostracize; repudiate; **a.** REJECTING: rejectable; rejectaneous; rejectitious; renunciatory
incapable of being (rejected): **a.** irrecusable

REJECTION: **n.** abdication; banishment; denigation; disavowal; disclaimer; disclamation; ostracism; relegation; repudiation; renunciation
not subject to: **a.** irrecusable
of customary beliefs: **n.** nihilism; **a.** nihilistic

REJOICING: **n.** exuberation; exultation; festivity; jubilation; **a.** carnivalesque; exuberant; exultant; jubilant

RELAPSE: **v.** backslide; recidivate; retrocess; retrogress; **n.** declination; palindromia; recidivation; recidivism; regression; retrocession; **a.** palindromic; recidivant; recidivous; regressive; retrocessive

RELATE: **see** "tell"

RELATED: (**see** "akin") **a.** affiiliated; analogous; ancillary; applicable; apposite; auxiliary; cognate; congeneric; congenerous; consanguineous; correlative; germane; leagued; material; pertinent; satellite
by family or blood: **a.** or **n.** agnate; cognate; **a.** cognatic; consanguineous
closely: **a.** affinitive; **n.** affinity
naturally: **a.** correlate; **n.** correlation
on mother's side: **a.** or **n.** cognate; **a.** matrilateral; matrilineal; matrilinear; **n.** cognatus; (**pl.** cognati); matrilineage
thru male: **n.** agnate; agnation; **a.** ag-

natic; patrilineal; patrilinear; **n.** patrilineage

RELATION: **n.** agnate; cognate; congener; connection; kindred; kinsman; narration; pertinence
standing in same: **a.** homonymous

RELATIONSHIP: **n.** affinity; agnation; cognation; consanguinity; kinship; liaison; relativity
blood: **n.** cognate; (**pl.** cognati); cognatus; consanguinity; syngenesis; **a.** cognate; consanguineous
close spacial: **n.** juxtaposition; **a.** juxtapositional

RELATIVE: **see** "applicable" **and** "relation"

RELAXATION: (**see** "entertainment") **n.** abatement; cessation; detachment; *détente;* disengagement; diversion; laxation; recreation; remission; repose
carefree: **n.** *dolce far niente;* **a.** *dégagé*

RELEVANT: **a.** *ad rem;* applicable; apposite; appropriate; apropos; cognate; competent; congruous; germane; pertinent; material; **n.** RELEVANCE: applicability; aproposity; homogeneity; relevance; materiality
not: **a.** *à propos de rien;* impertinent; inappropriate; irrelevant

RELIABLE: **see** "dependable"; **n.** RELIABILITY: authenticity; credence; dependability; trustworthiness

RELIEF: **n.** alleviation; assuagement; *bon secours;* deliverance; succor
incapable of: **a.** implacable; intractable; **n.** implacability; intractability
that which brings: **n.** alleviant; anesthetic; antidote; nepenthe; opiate; palliative

RELIEVE: (**see** "ease") **a.** alleviate; assuage; deliver; diminish; lessen; mitigate; succor; unburden

RELIEVED, *not, or not capable of being:* (**see** "incurable") **a.** implacable; intractable; unassuaged; unmitigated

RELIGION(S): **n.** clericalism; creed; denomination; devoutness; faith; persuasion; sanctity; sect; theology
asst. in ceremonies: **n.** acolyte
belief in established: **n.** orthodoxy; **a.** orthodox
believer in all: **n.** omnist
bitterness or controversy over: **n.** *odium theologicum*
disbeliever in: (**see** "disbeliever") **n.** freethinker; latitudinarian
excessive devotion to: **n.** ecclesiolatry; religiosity; theomania; theopathy
indifference or apathy to: **n.** adiaphoria; adiaphorism; agnosticism; **a.** adiaphoric; adiaphorous; agnostic; **n. or a.** Laodicean; **n.** adiaphorist; agnostic
knowledge or beliefs of: **n.** hierology
lukewarm in: **n. or a.** Laodicean
pert. to: **a.** clerical; ecclesiastic(al); hierarchic(al)
practice, correctness of: **n.** orthopraxy
reconciliation or union of conflicting beliefs: **n.** syncretism; **a.** syncretic; syncretistic; **v.** syncretize

RELIGIOUS: **a.** benedictional; devout; orthodox; pious; sanctified; spiritual
elite: **n.pl.** *perfecti*
overly: **a.** pietistic(al); religiose; sacrosanct; sanctimonious; theopathetic; **n.** ecclesiolatry; piosity; religiosity; sanctimony; theomania; theopathy
not: (**see** "ungodly") **a.** heathenish; impious; laic(al); pagan; secular; worldly

RELINQUISH: **see** "renounce"
capable of being (relinquished): **a.** abdicable

RELISH: **n.** appetite; gratification; gusto; inclination; savor; zest

RELUCTANT: (**see** "indisposed") **a.** averse; recalcitrant; unwilling; **adv.** *à contre coeur*

REMAINS: (**see** "sediment") **n.** *caput mortuum;* magma; residue; residuum; vestige; vestigium; (**pl.** debris; detritus; remnants; residua; vestigia); **n.** REMAINDER: remnant; residual; (**pl.** residua); residue; residuum; **a.** residual; residuary; vestigial
worthless: **n.** *caput mortuum*

REMAKING, *as lit, or mus. work:* **n.** rifacimento

REMARK(S): **see** "expression"
commonplace or trite: **n.** bromide;

cliche; platitude; **a.** banal; bromidic; platitudinal; platitudinous
concluding: (**see** "farewell") **n.** envoi; valediction
derogatory: **n.** aspersion; innuendo; insinuation
foolish: **see under** "foolish"
gratuitous: **n.** *gratis dictum;* (**pl.** *dicta*)
idle: **n.** insipidity; vaporing(s)
incidental: **n.** interjection; *obiter dictum;* parenthesis; (**pl.** parentheses); **a.** parenthetical
sharp, rude or cutting: **n.** causticity; mordacity; spinosity
shrewd: **n.** sagacity; witticism
side or offhand, as by judge: **n.** (*obiter*) *dictum*

REMEDIAL: **a.** curative; lenitive; medicamentive; panacean; remediable; reparable; restorative; salubrious; salutary; salutiferous; sanable; sanatory; therapeutic(al)

REMEDY: **n.** antidote; corrective; elixir; embrocation; medicament; nostrum; panacea; palliative; pharmacon; prescription; reparation; restorative; specific; therapeutic(s); therapy
act or process of (remedying): **n.** remediation
capable of: **see** "remedial"
favorite or quack: **n.** catholicon; elixir; nostrum; panacea; placebo
incapable of: **a.** intractable; irremediable; irreparable; uncorrectable
secret: **n.** arcanum; elixir
useful in several diseases, etc.: **n.** polychrest; **a.** polychrestic
worse than disease: aegrescit mendendo; aegrescitque mendendo

REMEMBERING: **n.** anamnesis; reminiscence; **a.** anamnestic; reminiscent(ial); **v.** REMEMBER: recall; recollect; reminisce; **a.** REMEMBERED: commemorated; memoried; memorized
not worth: **a.** unmemorable
things worth: **n.pl.** memorabilia

REMEMBRANCE: (**see** "reminder") **n.** commendation; memento; memorial; reminiscence; souvenir; token
in everlasting: **adv.** *memoria in aeterna*
prayer: **n.** anamnesis

REMINDER: **n.** amulet; memento; memorandum; phylactery; remembrancer

REMINISCENCE(S): (**see** "remembrance") **n.** anamnesis; feuilleton; **a.** anamnestic
noteworthy: **n.pl.** memorabilia

REMISSION: **n.** delinquency; deliverance; dereliction; forgiveness; misfeasance; pardon; relaxation; **a.** REMISS: delinquent; derelict; dilatory; inattentive; misfeasant; neglectful; negligent
gradual, as fever: **n.** lysis

REMORSE: **n.** compunction; contrition; penitence; repentance; self-reproach; **a.** REMORSEFUL: (**see** "regretful") contrite; penitent; repentant

REMOTE: (**see** "isolated") **a.** alien; antipodean; distant; forane; inaccessible; segregated; separated; secluded; tramontane; transmontane; ultramundane; ultimate
control: **n.** *actio ad distans*
more: **a.** ulterior
place or thing: **n.** ultima Thule

REMOVE: **v.** abstract; depose; dislodge; eliminate; eradicate; resect; sequester; supersede; transfer; **n.** REMOVAL: ablation; abstraction; deprivation; elimination; eradication; expurgation; separation; sequestration; supersedence; supersedure; supersession; transference
by cutting: **v.** ablate; excide; excise; extirpate; resect
by shelling or husking: **v.** enucleate; **n.** enucleation
parts of book: **v.** bowdlerize; expurgate; **n.** bowdlerization; emasculation; expurgation

RENEW: (**see** "renovate") **v.** reawaken; reestablish; refurbish; reinvigorate; restore

RENOUNCE: **v.** abandon; abjure; abrogate; apostatize; disclaim; forswear; recant; renunicate; repudiate; rescind; retract; **a.** RENUNCIATORY: abjuratory; **n.** RENUNCIATION: abjuration; abnegation; abrogation; apostasy; disclaimer; recantation; recission; repudiation

RENOVATE: (**see** "renew") **v.** recondition; refurbish; regenerate; repristinate; **n.** RENOVATION: refurbishment; regeneration; repristination

REPAIR: (**see** "renovate") **n.** reconditioning; renovation; reparation; restoration
capable of: **see** "remedial"

REPARATION: (see "restoration") **n.** atonement; indemnification; propiation; recompense; requital; restitution; retribution
honorable: **n.** *amende honorable*

REPAY: **v.** compensate; reciprocate; recompense; refund; remunerate; requite; retaliate

REPEAL: (see "cancel") **v.** abrogate; rescind; revoke; **n.** abrogation; recision; rescission; revocation; **a.** rescissory; revocatory

REPEAT: see under "repetition"

REPENTANCE: **n.** contrition; penitence; remorse; **a.** REPENTANT: contrite; penitent; remorseful
not (repentant): **a.** or **n.** impenitent

REPETITION: **n.** alliteration; anaphora; battology; ingemination; perseverance; reduplication; reiteration; replication; reproduction; verbigeration; **v.** REPEAT: battologize; ingeminate; perseverate; recapitulate; redouble; reduplicate; (re)iterate; replicate; **n.** REPEATER: recidivist; repetent; **a.** REPEATING: alliterative; battological; frequentive; reduplicative; (re)iterative; repetitious; replicate; **a.** REPETITIOUS: alliterational; alliterative; echoic; frequentive; imitative; monotonous; perseverant; (re)iterative; repetitional; repetitive; stereotyped; stereotypical
in outline: **n.** recapitulation; summarization; **v.** recapitulate; summarize
mania for: **n.** cataphasia; echololia; onomatomania; verbigeration
needless, in diff. words: **n.** pleonasm; redundancy; tautology; **a.** pleonastic; tautologic(al); tautologous; **v.** tautologize
of actions of others (pathological): **n.** echomimia; echopraxia
of letters or words, unintentional: **n.** dittography
of same sound(s): **n.** tautophony; **a.** tautophonic; tautophonous
of word in sentence: **n.** anadiplosis
of words, senseless: **n.** echolalia; onomatomania; verbigeration; verbomania
of words, unnecessarily: **n.** battology; **a.** battological; **v.** battologize
of words or sentences, endlessly or meaninglessly: **n.** verbigeration; **v.** verbigerate
sound or phrase at beg. of each sentence: **n.** anaphora
stress by: **v.** ingeminate; **n.** ingemination
tedious: **n.** verbigeration; **a.** repetitious; repetitive

REPLACE: **v.** substitute; **a.** substitutionary; substitutive; **n.** see "removal"

REPLY: (see "answer") **v.** rejoin; replicate; *réplique;* resound; **n.** rejoinder; repartee; replication; reverberation
clever or witty: **n.** repartee
in writing: **n.** rescription; **a.** rescriptive
please: repondez s'il vous plaît (**abb.** R.S.V.P.)

REPORT: **n.** account; cahier; character; communiqué; fame; narration; reputation; repute; **a.** reportorial

REPOSE: (see "sleep") **n.** composure; *dolce far niente; en famille;* (re)laxation; (re)quiescence; respite; tranquility

REPRESENTATIVE: **n.** ambassador; champion; delegate; deputy; diplomat; representant; specimen; substitute; surrogate; **a.** emblematic(al); symbolic(al); typical; typifying; **v.** REPRESENT: delineate; depict; emblematize; exemplify; personate; portray; symbolize; typify
confidential: **n.** *alter ego*

REPRIMAND: see "rebuke"

REPROACH: (see "scold") **v.** chasten; reprimand; **n.** accusation; *bar sinister;* castigation; discredit; disgrace; ignominy; opprobrium; rebuke; reprehension; reproof
above: **a.** inviolable; inviolate; invulnerable; sacrosanct; unassailable

REPRODUCTION: **n.** counterpart; duplicate; duplication; ectype; gestation; reconstruction; regeneration; **a.** REPRODUCTIVE: gestational; gestative; progenitive; **n.** reproductivity
by bringing forth live beings: **n.** parturition; viviparity; **a.** parturient; viviparous
by budding: **n.** gemmation; protogenesis
by cross-fertilization: **n.** allogamy; **a.** allogamous
by eggs: see under "egg"
by union of male and female: **n.** amphig-

ony; gamogenesis; syngamy; syngenesis; **a.** amphigonous; gamogenetic; syngamic; syngamous; syngenetic

of original: **n.** duplicate; ectype; **a.** ectypal

period of: **n.** gestation; **a.** gestational

pert. to: **a.** reproductive; seminal

science of: **n.** genesiology

sexless: **n.** abiogenesis; accrementation; agamogenesis; autogenesis; fission; gemmation; parthenogenesis; protogenesis; **a.** abiogenetic; autogenetic; gemmative

sexual: **see** "by union of male and female" **above**

w/o male: **n.** parthenogenesis; **a.** parthenogenetic

REPROVE: **see** "rebuke" **and** "reproach"; **a.** REPROVING: admonitory; castigatory; chastening

REPTILE(S): (**see** "snake") **n.** amphibian; groveling; ophidian

pert. to: **a.** ophidian; reptant; reptilian; serpentiform; serpentine

resembling: **a.** ophidian; reptilian; reptiloid; serpentiform

specialist in study of: **n.** herpetologist; ophiologist

study of: **n.** herpetology; ophiology; **a.** herpetologic(al)

REPUDIATION: **n.** disaffirmance; disaffirmation; disclamation; reunuciation; **a.** REPUDIATIVE: disclamatory; renunciative; **v.** REPUDIATE: abjure; abrogate; disaffirm; disavow; disclaim; renunciate

REPUGNANT: (**see** "hateful") **a.** incompatible; inconsistent; loathsome; objectionable; repulsive

REPULSIVE: (**see** "hateful") **a.** abominable; despicable; fulsome; grisly; repugnant; sordid; squalid; unsavory; **n.** REPULSIVITY: despicability; repugnancy; squalidity; squalor

REPUTATION: (**see** "fame") **n.** character; distinction; estimation; odor; renown; prestige; **a.** REPUTABLE: (**see** "famous" **and** "respectable") prestigious

injury to: **n.** aspersion; calumny; defamation; libel; slander; vilification; **a.** defamatory; libelous; slanderous

of slightly respectable: **a.** subreputable

person(s) of doubtful: (**see** "rascal") **n.** rapscallion; villain; (**fem.** courtesan; demimondaine)

REPUTE: **see** "reputation"

REQUEST: (**see** "pray") **v.** importune; **n.** application; requisition; rogation; solicitation; supplication

expressing a: **a.** requisitorial; supplicatory

REQUIRED: (**see** "imperative") **a.** coercive; compelling; compulsory; deontic; *de rigueur;* essential; indispensable; mandatory; obligatory; (pre)requisite; **n.** REQUIREMENT: condition precedent; essentiality; indispensibility; precondition; (pre)requisite; prius; *sine qua non*

by fashion, etiquette, or custom: **a.** *de règle; de rigueur*

do more than: **v.** supererogate; **a.** supererogative; supererogatory; **n.** supererogation

RESCUE: (**see** "aid") **v.** emancipate; liberate; redeem; **n.** deliverance; emancipation; liberation; redemption

one who (rescues) fr. tyranny and injustice: **n.** pimpernel

to the!: **int.** *au secours!*

RESEMBLANCE: **n.** affinity; analogy; approximation; assonance; counterpart; equivalence; facsimile; image; parallelism; parity; representation; similarity; simile; similitude; simulacrum; uniformity; verisimilitude; verisimility

lack of: **n.** dissimilitude; heterogeneity

partial: **n.** analogy; homology; **a.** analogical; analogous; homologous

RESENTMENT: (**see** "anger") **n.** animosity; dudgeon; indignation; irascibility; jaundice; pique; prejudice; vexation; umbrage; **a.** RESENTFUL: belligerent; umbrageous

RESERVATION: **see** "condition"

RESERVED: **a.** apathetic; detached; distant; egocentric; incommunicable; incommunicative; indrawn; phlegmatic(al); phlegmatous; restrained; retarded; retentive; reticent; taciturn; unapproachable; uncommunicative; undemonstrative; unsociable; withdrawn; **n.** RESERVE: apathy; detachment; forbearance; restraint; retardation; reticence; self-control; self-restraint; taciturnity; unsociability

RESIDE, *or establish residence:* **v.** domicile; domiciliate; **n.** domiciliation

RESIDENT: **a.** denizen; domicile; *habitué;* inhabitant; inhabitress; occupant; **a.** RESIDENTIARY: immanent; indwelling; residential; **n.** RESIDENCE: inhabitance; inhabitancy; inhabitation; occupancy
of place of birth: **(see "native") n.** sedens; **(pl.** sedentes)

RESIDENTIAL *section, fashionable:* **n.** Belgravia; **a.** Belgravian

RESIDUE: **see** "remains"

RESIGNATION: **n.** abandonment; abdication; acquittance; defeatism; disaffiliation; disassociation; humility; obedience; obeisance; passivity; relinquishment; renunciation; retirement; submission; **v.** RESIGN: abdicate; disaffiliate; disassociate

RESIST: **see** "fight"; **a.** RESISTANT: **(see** "stubborn") incompliant; recalcitrant
capacity to: **n.** resistance; resistivity

RESISTANCE, *point or place of least:* **n.** *locus minoris resistentiae*

RESONANT: **a.** orotund; plangent; sonorant; son(or)iferous; sonorous; tympanic; vibrant; **n.** RESONANCE: orotundity; plangency; sonority

RESORT, *last:* **n.** *dernier ressort; pis aller; ultima ratio*

RESOURCE: **n.** expediency; expedient; makeshift; stratagem

RESPECT: **(see** "honor") **v.** admire; esteem; **n.** approbation; deference; deferentiality; devotion; devoir; fealty; homage; izzat; obeisance; obsequiousness; obsequity; prestige; veneration; **(pl.** *baisemains*)
act of: **n.** devoir; genuflection; obeisance; obsequity
as a token of: **a. or adv.** *honoris causa*
deserving of: **(see** "praiseworthy") **a.** estimable; venerable
expressive of: **a.** commendatory; complimentary; deferential; reverential; venerative
showing: **(see** "respectful") **a.** honorific

RESPECTABLE (or RESPECTED): **(see** "honorable") **a.** creditable; estimable; presentable; prestigious; reputable; venerable; **n.** RESPECTABILITY: creditability; estimability; reputability; prestige
not: **a.** disreputable
persons doubtfully: **see under** "reputation"

RESPECTFUL: **a.** amenable; decorous; deferent(ial); dutiful; obeisant; reputable; reverential; tractable
not: **see** "sassy"

RESPONSE: **(see** "answer") **n.** antiphon; reaction; retort; reverberation; **a.** RESPONSIVE: amenable; antiphonal; reactive; sensible; tractable
heightened: **n.** hyperesthesia; **a.** hyperesthetic

RESPONSIBLE: **a.** accountable; amenable; answerable; (re)liable; solvent; trustworthy; **n.** RESPONSIBILITY: accountability; amenability; obligation; onus; (re)liability; solvency; trustworthiness

REST: **(see** "repose" **and** "sleep") **n.** immobility; immobilization; **a.** RESTING: dormant; inactive; incumbent; latent; quiescent; sessile
at: **adv.** *in situ;* **a.** dormant; latent; quiescent; sessile; **n.** dormancy; tranquility
in peace: **adv.** *requiescat in pace* **(abb.** R.I.P.)
place or state of: **n.** Canaan; nirvana
recurring period of: **n.** diastole; **a.** diastolic; sabbatical
something to induce: **n.** anesthesia; anesthetic; opiate; sedative; tranquilizer

RESTITUTION: **(see** "restoration") **n.** apocatastasis; indemnification; indemnity; reparation; reinstatement

RESTLESS: **a.** agitato; anxious; disobedient; erethic; fitful; obstinate; rebellious; restive; riotous; spasmodic; unceasing; **n.** RESTLESSNESS: **(see** "uneasiness") agitation; disquietude; dyspathy; dysphoria; inquietude

RESTORATION: **n.** instauration; reanimation; reconstruction; redemption; reestablishment; refurbishment; rehabilitation; reimbursement; reinstitution; reinvigoration; rejuvenation; rejuvanescence; reparation; repristination; restitution; resurgence; resurgency; resuscitation; revitalization; revivescence; revivification; **v.** RESTORE: reanimate; reawaken; reconstruct; rehabilitate; reinstate; reinstitute; reinvigorate; rejuvenate; repristinate; restitute; resuscitate; revivify; **a.** RESTORED: reconditioned; redivivus; refurbished; reinvigorated; rejuvenated

capable of: **a.** reparable; restitutive; resuscitative; **n.** revivability; revivescent

of harmony or concord: **n.** rapprochement

of or to previous status: **n.** *restitutio in integrum; status quo (ante)*

something which undergoes: **n.** phoenix

RESTORATIVE: **see** "cure," "curable," **and** "remedy"

RESTORING: **a.** analeptic; invigorating; rejuvenating; rejuvenescent; resuscitative; roborant; tonic

RESTRAINT: (**see** "prudence") **n.** circumspection; coertion; confinement; constraint; discipline; durance; duress; embargo; hindrance; inhibition; interdiction; manacle; monopoly; repression; restriction; retention; sanction; shackle; **v.** RESTRAIN: circumscribe; constrain; demarcate; discipline; enslave; fetter; hamper; inhibit; manacle; repress; restrict; shackle; **a.** RESTRAINED (or RESTRAINING): Apollonian; Apollonic; Apollonistic; circumscribed; disciplined; harmonious; inhibitory; rational; restrictive; retentive; unemancipated

place of: **n.** limbo

revolt against or defiance of: **n.** titanism

RESTRICT: (**see** "restrain") **v.** delimit(ate); fetter; hamper; circumscribe; discipline

RESTRICTED *in outlook:* **a.** cloisteral; cloistered; insulated; parochial; provincial; truncated

in scope: **a.** abbreviated; abridged; circumscribed; circumscriptive; parochial; peninsular; provincial; truncated

RESTRICTION: (**see** "restraint") **n.** circumspection; coercion; (de)limitation; immanence; sanction

under: **adv.** *sub modo*

RESULT: **see** "consequence"

complex operation or sequence: **n.** denouement

justifies deed: exitus acta probat

RÉSUMÉ: **n.** abridgement; abstract; compendium; epitome; recapitulation; summary; syllabus; synopsis

RETAINER(S), *body of:* **n.** adherents; claque; clique; cortege; minions; retinue

loyal or hired: **see** "mercenary"

RETALIATION, *law of:* **n.** *lex talionis*

RETALIATORY *maneuver:* **n.** repartee; ripost(e)

RETARDED: **a.** impeded; inhibited; repressed; **v. see** "delay"

RETENTIVENESS: **n.** retentivity; tenacity

RETICENT: **a.** brachysyllabic; laconic; reserved; taciturn

RETIRED: (**see** "inactive") **a.** cloisteral; cloistered; emeritus; otiose; reserved; sequestered; withdrawn; **adv.** *en retraite; hors de combat;* **a.** RETIRING: **see** "shy" **and** "humble"; **v.** RETIRE: retreat; withdraw; **n.** RETIREMENT: insularity; otiosity; *otium cum dignitate;* sedentation

and no longer having power: **n.** or **a.** cidevant; emeritus

but retaining rank and title: **a.** or **n.** emeritus

for age or infirmity: **n.** invalidation; superannuation; **a.** superannuated

RETRACE: **v.** perseverate; recall; recollect; reiterate; reminisce

RETRACTION: **n.** disavowal; recantation; withdrawal

formal, or poem or song about: **n.** palinode

RETREAT: (**see** "sanctuary") **n.** asylum; hermitage; recession; redoubt; retrocession; withdrawal

disorganized: **n.** *sauve qui peut*

in: **adv.** *en retraite*

RETRIBUTION: (**see** "punishment") **n.** nemesis

also one who inflicts: **n.** nemesis
goddess of: **n.** Nemesis

RETROACTIVE: **a.** or **adv.** *ex post facto; nunc pro tunc*

RETURN(S): **v.** reciprocate; recompense; requite; **a.** reciprocative; **n.** reciprocation; reciprocity; recursion; restoration
give or do in: **v.** reciprocate; requite; **n.** reciprocation; requital
in: **adv.** *en revanche*
injury for injury, like for like, etc.: **v.** retaliate; **a.** retaliatory; retributory; **n.** retaliation; retribution
order to: **v.** or **n.** remand
person who, after long absence: **n.** Enoch Arden; prodigal (son); revenant; Rip van Winkle
to former cond. or situation: **n.** reparation; restitution; *status quo ante*
to previous place or cond.: **n.** apocatastasis; *status quo ante*

REUNITING, *act of:* **n.** reunition

REVEAL: **v.** disburden; disclose; divulge; evince; manifest; unmask; **a.** REVELATORY (or REVEALING): epiphanic; heuristic; revelative; **n.** REVELATION: disclosure; divulgence; epiphany; revealment

REVEL: (see "carouse") **v.** roister; royster; wassail; **a.** REVELROUS: (see "gay") roistering; roisterous; **n.** REVELRY: conviviality; ecstasy; saturnalia; wassail

REVELATION: **n.** apocalypse; disclosure; divulgence; *exposé;* oracle; revealment; **a.** REVELATIVE: apocalyptic; epiphanic; revelatory
psychic: **n.** (the) numinous

REVENGE: **v.** requite; retaliate; **n.** nemesis; requital; retaliation; retribution; *revanche;* vengeance; vindication; vindicativeness; **a.** REVENGEFUL: punitive; retaliative; retaliatory; retributive; retributory; *revanchist;* vindicative; viperish; vituperative

REVERE: (see "honor") **v.** esteem; reverence; venerate; worship; **n.** REVERENCE: veneration; **a.** REVERENT: (see "religious") reverential

REVERSAL: **n.** about-face; bouleversement; *culbuter;* inversion; metathesis; mutation; transposition; *volte-face;* **adv.** conversely; *vice versa*
of opinions, attitude, etc.: **n.** *volte-face*
of words, letters, etc. as in reading: **n.** strephosymbolia; **a.** strephosymbolic
sudden or unexpected: **n.** anticlimax; bathos; peripet(e)ia; peripety; **a.** anticlimactic(al); bathetic

REVERSION *to primitive type:* **n.** atavism; mutation; **a.** atavistic

REVIEW: see "survey"

REVISE: **v.** rearrange; redact; renovate; **a.** REVISIONAL: revisionary; **n.** REVISION: recension; redaction

REVISER *of manuscripts:* **n.** diaskeuast; redactor

REVIVE: **v.** reanimate; reawaken; refocillate; reinspirit; reinvigorate; repristinate; resurge; resuscitate; (re)vivify; revitalize; vivificate; **a.** REVIVING: redivivus; renascent; revivescent; **n.** REVIVAL: anabiosis; recrudescence; renaissance; renascence; repristination; restoration; resurrection; (re)vivification; risorgimento

REVOKE: **v.** abrogate; countermand; nullify; recant; rescind; vitiate; withdraw; **n.** REVOCATION: counteraction; countermand; nullification; recantation; recission; repeal; reversal; vitiation; withdrawal

REVOLTING: (see "disgusting") **a.** bilious; choleric; despicable; fulsome; irascible; loathsome; nauseating; noisome; offensive; repugnant; repulsive; revellent; revulsive

REVOLUTION (or REVOLT): (see "riot") **n.** anarchy; *coup d'état;* insubordination; insurgency; insurrection; sedition; **a.** REVOLUTIONARY: see "radical"

REVOLVE: **v.** circumduct; circumgyrate; vertiginate; **n.** circumduction; circumgyration; **a.** vertiginous

REWARD: **v.** guerdon; recompense; remunerate; requite; **n.** guerdon; honorarium; indemnity; recompense; requital; retribution

REWORD *and shorten:* **v.** or **n.** paraphrase; **a.** paraphrastic(al)

RHETORIC, *master or teacher of:* **n.** rhetor(ician)

RHETORICAL: (**see** "bombastic") **a.** Ciceronian; declamatory; Demosthenean; Demosthenic; eloquent; epideictic; forensic; grandiloquent; rubescent
flourish: **n.** circumgyration

RHINOCEROS: **n.** pachyderm

RHYTHM: **n.** cadence; ictus; melody; meter; periodicity; **a.** RHYTHMIC(AL); cadenced; cadential
abnormal or faulty: **n.** ar(r)hythmia; asynchronism; cacophony; dysrhythmia; **a.** ar(r)hythmic(al); asynchronous; cacophonic; cacophonous; immetrical; unmetrical
absence of: **n.** ar(r)hythmia; arrhythmicity

RICE, *feeding on:* **a.** oryzivorous

RICH: **a.** abundant; affluent; daedalian; daedal(ic); lavish; lucull(i)an; luxuriant; luxurious; opulent; plentiful; redolent; resourceful; sumptuous
govt. by: **n.** plutocracy
man: **n.** Croesus; *homme de fortune;* nabob
newly: **n.** *nouveau riche; parvenu; roturier*
person of plebeian origin: **n.** *roturier*

RICHES: (**see** "wealth") **n.** abundance; affluence; fortune; luxuriance; opulence; sumptuosity
as object of worship, or personified: **n.** mammon
embarrassment of: **n.** *embarras de richesses*
worship or undue love of: **n.** plutolatry; plutomania

RICKETY: (**see** "flimsy") **a.** rachitic; tenuous; tremulous

RID: (**see** "free") **v.** delete; disabuse; disencumber; eradicate; extricate; purge; relinquish; unburden
as a burden: **v.** disencumber; extricate
of mistake or error: **v.** disabuse

RIDDLE: **n.** ambiguity; charade; conundrum; enigma; intricacy; labyrinth; paradox; perplexity; quandary; rebus; sphinx; **a.** enigmatic(al)
key to: **n.** *le mot de l'enigme*

RIDGE: **n.** ruga; (**pl.** rugae); rugosity; RIDGED: corrugated; rugose

RIDICULE: **v.** deride; lampoon; satirize; **n.** asteism; derision; irony; lampoon; pasquinade; raillery; ridiculosity; satire; **a.** derisible; derisive; satirical

RIDICULOUS: **a.** bizarre; derisible; derisive; eccentric; extravagant; farcical; grotesque; ludicrous; *outré;* preposterous; risible
make: **v.** stultify; **n.** ridiculosity; stultification
perfectly: **adv.** *d'un ridicule achevé*

RIDING *academy:* **n.** *haute école;* manège

RIG: **v.** manipulate

RIGHT: **n.** appanage; franchise; immunity; perquisite; prerogative; **a.** (*see* "appropriate") dextral; equitable; legitimate; orthodox
-angled: **a.** orthogonal
as a matter of: **a.** or **adv.** *ex debito justitiae*
away: **adv.** *tout de suite*
by what?: **adv.** *quo jure?*
deviation or departure fr.: **n.** aberration; aberrance; **a.** aberrational; aberrative; aberrant
for the purpose: (**see** "timely") **a.** advantageous; opportune
hand: **n.** major hand; *mano destra*
-handedness: **n.** dextrality
of elder or superior: **n.** *droit et* (**or** *du*) *seigneur;* primogeniture
of first night (*of feudal lord to deflower bride*): **n.** *droit et* (**or** *du*) *seigneur; jus prima noctis*
prior or exclusive: **a.** or **n.** prerogative; **n.** seniority
strict legal: **n.** *strictum jus; summum jus*
to or on the (*right*): **a.** dexter; dextral; droite; **adv.** dextrad

RIGHTEOUS: **a.** equitable; magnanimous; principled; rectitudinous; upright; **n.** RIGHTEOUSNESS: **n.** dharma; probity; rectitude; uprightness
overly: **a.** religiose; sanctimonious; **n.** religiosity; sanctimoniousness; sanctimony; scrupulosity

RIGID: (see "strict") **a.** austere; immalleable; inclement; inelastic; inexorable; inflexible; rigorous; scrupulous; stringent; unshakable; unyielding; **n.** RIGIDITY: austerity; inclemency; inflexibility; rigidification; rigorism; severity; strenuosity

RIGOR: **n.** ardor; austerity; inclemency; rigidity; scrupulosity; severity; strenuosity; **a.** RIGOROUS: (see "harsh") asperous; austere; drastic; inclement; inexorable; peremptory; Procrustean; strenuous

RIND: (see "skin") **n.** integument

RING: **v.** circumnavigate; encircle; surround; **n.** annulation; encirclement; sonority; tintinnabulation; **a.** RINGED: annular; annulate; annulose; circumferential
  of or like: **a.** annular; armillary
  -shaped: **a.** annular; cingular; circinate

RINGING *or jingling sound, as of bells:* **n.** tintinnabulation; **a.** tintinnabular(y); tintinnabulous

RIOT: (see "revolution") *émeute;* pandemonium; turmoil; welter

RIOTOUS: **a.** abundant; agitated; exuberant; incendiary; inflammatory; mutinous; pandemoniac(al); profuse; seditious; tumultary; tumultuous; turbulent; ungovernable; unmanageable; unrestrained; unsubmissive
  affair: **n.** *attroupement;* donny-brook; insurrection; pandemonium; riotry

RIPEN: see "develop"

RISE: (see "advance") **n.** ascension; escalation
  in air: **v.** levitate; **n.** levitation
  tendency to: **n.** assurgency; **a.** ascensive; ascentional; assurgent

RISING, *as of sun or moon:* **a.** ortive

RISK: see "peril"; **a.** RISKY: (see "dangerous") explosive; hazardous; jeopardous; ominous; parlous; precarious; venturesome; **n.** RISKINESS: jeopardy; perilousness; precariousness

RISQUÉ: **a.** off-color; salacious; scabrous

RITUAL (or RITE): **n.** ceremonialism; ceremony; formality; procedure; protocol; liturgy; **a.** RITUALISTIC: ceremonious; ceremonial; **v.** ritualize
  on attaining adulthood: see under "adulthood"
  quality: **n.** rituality

RIVAL: **v.** emulate; **a.** antagonistic; competing; competitive; contesting; rivalrous; **n.** antagonist; competitor; opponent

RIVER(S), *adapted to life in:* **a.** autopotamic
  bank(s), of or pert. to: **a.** riparian; riparious
  bet. or enclosed by: **a.** interamnian; mesopotamian; **n.** mesopotamia
  description of: **n.** potamography; **a.** potamographic
  going up to spawn: **a.** anadromous
  in Hell: **n.** Acheron; Styx
  pert. to: **a.** potamic
  study of: **n.** potamology; **a.** potamological; **n.** potamologist

RIVIERA, *French:* **n.** *Côte d'Azur*

ROAD(S), *having many:* **a.** multivious
  main or principal: **n.** *camino real;* turnpike
  painful or difficult: **n.** *via doloroso*
  pert. to: **a.** viatic(al)

ROAMING: (see "roving") **a.** discursive; itinerant; meandering; migratory; nomadic; (per)ambulatory; peripatetic; prodigal; vagrant; vagarious

ROB: **v.** burglarize; depredate; despoil; plunder; rifle; spoliate; **a.** ROBBING: larcenous; predaceous; predacious; predatory; **n.** ROBBERY: burglary; depredation; (de)spoliation; larceny; pillage; piracy; predacity

ROBUST: **a.** athletic; brawny; lusty; muscular; robustious; robustuous; stalwart; virile; **n.** ROBUSTNESS: lustihood; lustiness; robusticity
  rudely: **a.** boisterous; robustious; robustuous

ROCK(S), *composed or inscribed on:* **a.** rupestral; rupestrian
  inhabiting or growing among: **a.** petricolous; saxicolous; saxigenous
  living among, inhabiting or growing on:

a. rupicoline; rupicolous
of or like: **a.** petrous
study or science of: **n.** geology; petrology; **a.** geologic(al); petrologic; **n.** geologist; petrologist

ROD, *appeal(ing) to the:* **adv.** or **n.** *(argumentum) ad baculum*
divining by: **n.** dowsing; rhabdomancy
pert. to punishment w/: **a.** baculin
-shaped: **a.** baculiform

ROGUE: **n.** caitiff; gamin; (**fem.** gamine); knave; malefactor; miscreant; picaro(on); rapscallion; renegade; reprobate; ribald; scant-o-grace; scalawag; scapegrace; scaramouche; scoundrel; vagabond; *vaurien;* **a.** ROGUISH: arch; *espiègle;* mischievous; picaresque; puckish; unprincipled; waggish; **n.** ROGUISHNESS: *espièglerie;* gaminerie; rascality; roguery; scalawaggery; waggishness
pert. to: **a.** picaresque; roguish; **n.** roguery

ROILY: **a.** turbid; turbulent; **n.** turbidity; turbulence

ROLLING: **a.** lurching; resounding; reverberating; undulant; undulate(d); undulating
inward: **a.** involuted; **n.** involution

ROMANTIC: (**see** "idealistic") **a.** cavalier; chimerical; enticing; exotic; fanciful; glamorous; imaginative; melodramatic; picturesque; quixotic; Romanesque; sentimental; unrealistic; utopian; visionary
episode: **n.** idyll
style: **a.** or **n.** Gothic

ROOF, *shaped like:* **a.** tectiform

ROOFLESS: **a.** *alfresco;* homeless; hypaethral; upaithric

ROOMY: **a.** ample; baronial; capacious; cavernous; commodious

ROOT *out:* **v.** deracinate; eradicate; exterminate; extirpate; **n.** deracination; extirpation
out, inability to: **a.** ineradicable; inextirpable

ROOTED *deeply:* **a.** chronic; confirmed; ingrained; inveterate; radicated

ROPE *walker:* **n.** funambulist

ROSTER: **n.** agendum; (**pl.** agenda); catalog(ue); register; rota

ROSY: **a.** auroral; aurorean; blooming; *couleur de rose;* optimistic; radiant; rosaceous; roseate; sanguine

ROT: **v.** corrupt: decay; decompose; degenerate; deteriorate; putrefy; putresce; **n.** corruption; degeneration; gangrene; mortification; necrosis; putrescence; **a.** ROTTING (or ROTTEN); abominable; carious; decomposed; fetid; necrotic; putrefied; putrescent; termitic
incapable of (rotting): **a.** imputrescible; **n.** imputrescibility
pert. to: **a.** putrefactive; saprogenic; saprogeneous

ROTATE: **v.** alternate; circulate; circumduct; (circum)gyrate; circumvolve; oscillate; pirouette; revolve; vertiginate; **a.** ROTATING: gyrating; rotary; vertiginous
around axis: **v.** circumduct; circumgyrate; **n.** circumduction; circumgyration

ROUGH: **a.** asperate; asperous; boisterous; hispidulous; hispidulate; inclement; robust(i)ous; scabrous; tartarly; unpolished; **n.** ROUGHNESS: asperity; hispidity; inclemency; robusticity; scabrousness
(bold): **a.** harageous; robust(i)ous
(bristly): **a.** hispid; **n.** hispidity

ROUND: (**see** "circular") **a.** annular; convex; cylindrical; gibbose; gibbous; globular; orbicular; rotund; spherical; spheroid(al); spheriform; **n.** ROUNDNESS: circularity; globosity; orbicularity; rotundity; spheroidicity

ROUNDABOUT: (**see** "devious") **a.** ambagious; ambient; anfractuous; circuitous; labyrinthian; labyrinthine; serpentine; **n.** anfractuosity; circuity; circumbendibus; circumlocution: indirection
in expression or writing: **n.** circularity; *circuitous verborum;* circumbendibus; circumlocution; periphrasis; **a.** circumlocutious; circumlocutory; periphrastic

ROUSE: **see** "incite"

ROUT: **n.** debacle; *sauve qui peut*

ROUTE, *painful or difficult:* **n.** *via dolorosa*

ROUTINE: (**see** "habit") **a.** administrative; customary; formal; functional; mechanical; ordinary; perfunctory; periodic; *pro forma;* usual
one who insists on: **n.** routineer

ROVING: (**see** "roaming") **a.** ambulatory; arrant; desultory; digressive; discursive; itinerant; migratory; nomadic; peregrine; Peripatetic; vagrant; **n.** ambulation; nomadism; peregrination; peregrinism; peregrinity; vagrancy

ROYAL: (**see** "kingly") **a.** basilic(al)
possessing (royal) privileges: **a.** palatine
symbol of (royalty) : **n.** diadem

RUBBISH: (**see** "debris") **n.** detritus; offal; scoria; (**pl.** scoriae); trumpery; (**pl.** (r)ejectamenta)

RUDDY: **a.** rubescent; rubicund; rufescent; **n.** rubefaction; rubescence; rufescence

RUDE: (**see** "abrupt," "bold" **and** "uncouth") **a.** abusive; awkward; barbarous; contumelious; dedecorous; discourteous; disrespectful; impudent; indecorous; inurbane; unceremonious; uncourtly; ungracious; unmannered; **n.** RUDENESS: barbarism; contumely; disrespect; impudence; incivility

RUDIMENTARY: **a.** abecedarian; abecedary; abortive; contingent; elementary; embryonic; fragmental; germinal; imperfect(ed); inchoate; inchoative; incipient; incomplete; nascent; potential; undeveloped; vestigial

RUIN: (**see** "decay") **n.** annihilation; bankruptcy; catastrophe; collapse; dilapidation; havoc; labefaction; perdition; undoing; **a.** RUINED: *flambé;* hopeless; kaput; perdue; **a.** RUINOUS: baneful; cataclysmic(al); catastrophic(al); damnatory; destructive; disastrous; malignant; pernicious
sudden and great: **n.** cataclysm; catastrophe; holocaust; **a.** cataclysmic(al); catastrophic(al)

RUINS: (**see** "rubbish") **n.** debris; détritus

RULE(S): **v.** administer; determine; govern; predominate; preponderate; **n.** administration; authority; criterion; (**pl.** criteria); covenant; discipline; dominion; imperative; method(ology); precedent; precept; predomination; principle; protocol; regency; regime; regimen; *règlement;* regnancy; regula; reign; technique; theorem
absolute: **n.** tyrannis; tyranny; **v.** tyrannize; **a.** tyrannic(al); tyrannous
according to: **a.** consuetudinary; conventional; *de rigueur; de règle;* programmatic; ritualistic; **adv.** *ad amussim; ad usum; ex more; secundum artem; secundum regulam*
according to the: **adv.** *selon les règles*
basic set of: **n.** constitution; decalogue; *Magna C(h)arta*
by pedantic system, as school, etc.: **n.** pedantocracy; **n.** pedantocrat
conforming to: (**see** *"according to"* **above**) **a.** conventional; exemplary; orthodox; **n.** conventionality; normalcy; normality; orthodoxy
equally by all: **n.** pantisocracy; **a.** pantisocratic(al)
individual: **n.** autocracy; monarchy; monocracy
joint: **n.** condominium; synarchy; **a.** condominate
of majority: **n.** arithmocracy
rel. or pert. to: **a.** administrative; normative; reglementary; regulatory
strict enforcer of: **n.** disciplinarian; martinet; precisian; rigorist; sabbatarian
subject to another's **a.** heteronomous; **n.** heteronomy
system of: **n.** discipline; organon
undivided: **n.** monocracy

RULER: (**see** "king") **n.** dictator; potentate
almighty: **n.** pantocrator

RULING: **a.** administrative; current; determinative; executive; precedential; predominant; predominating; regnal; regnant; reigning; **n. see** "decision"

RUMINANT: **n.** bovine; (**pl.** bovidae); **a.** bovine; bovid; meditative

RUMINATE: **see** "think"

RUMOR: **n.** canard; hearsay; notoriety; roorback; scuttlebutt

noisy: **n.** *fama clamosa*
vague: **n.** *on-dit*

RUMP: **n.** *derrière;* gluteus; podex; posterior; **a.** pygal

RUN-*down:* **a.** depleted; dilapidated; exhausted; squalid; tatterdemalian

RUNNING: **a.** continuous; cursive; linear
adapted to: **a.** cursorial
in opp. direction(s): **a.** countercourant; countercurrent

RURAL: (**see** "pastoral") **a.** agrarian; agrestic; Arcadian; bucolic; campestral; churlish; countrified; geoponic; georgic; idyllic; peasant; provincial; rustic; sylvan; villatic
feature, characteristic, etc.: **n.** pastorality; peasantry; provincialism; rurality; rusticism; rusticity

RUSH, *overwhelming:* **n.** avalanche; spate; **a.** Gaderine; precipitous

RUSHING: **a.** impetuous; precipitate; precipitous; torrential; **n.** exigency; impetuosity; precipitation
precipitously forward: **a.** Gaderine

RUST-*colored:* **a.** aeruginous; ferruginous; rubiginous
on copper or brass, accumulation of: **n.** aerugo; patina; verdigris

RUSTIC: (**see** "rural") **n.** bumpkin; hayseed; peasant; yokel
characteristic(s), as speech, habit or custom: **n.** provincialism; rurality; rusticism; rusticity

RUSTLING: **see** "murmuring"

RUTHLESS: **a.** barbaric; pitiless; Procrustean; relentless; revengeful; savage; unsparing

S

SABBATH, *act of keeping:* **n.** sabbatization; **v.** sabbatize
pert. to: **a.** dominical; sabbatarian
strict observance of: **n.** sabbatism; **a.** sabbatarian
one who advocates: **n.** sabbatarian

SACRED: (**see** "divine") **a.** consecrated; dedicated; hallowed; inviolable; inviolate; numinous; sacramental; sacramentary; sacrosanct; sainted; sanctified; **n.** SACREDNESS: sacramentality; (sacro)-sanctity; sanctification; sanctitude
thing(s) considered, as relic: **n.** halidom(e); (**pl.** sacramentalia)

SACRIFICE: **v.** immolate; **n.** deprivation; immolation; oblation; sacrification
anything regarded as great: **n.** moloch
of many: **n.** hecatomb
offer as: **v.** immolate; **n.** immolation; sacrification
pert. to: **a.** sacrificatory; sacrificial
ritual slaughter for: **n.** mactation
something offered as: **n.** oblation; sacrification

SACRILEGE: **n.** blasphemy; desecration; profanation; **a.** SACRILEGIOUS: blasphemous; hypocritical; impious; irreverent; profane

SAD: (**see** "sorrowful") **a.** dejected; *désolé;* despondent; disconsolate; distressing; doleful; dolent(e); dolentissimo; dolorific; doloroso; dolorous; elegaic; forlorn; funereal; funebr(i)ous; inconsolable; lachrymal; lachrymatory; lachrymose; lamentable; lamented; lugubrious; melancholic; melancholious; melancholy; morbid; mournful; pathetic; pensoroso; plaintive; sepulchral; somber; sombrous; triste; unfestive; wretched; **n.** SADNESS: dejection; depression; dreariment; forlornity; gloominess; languishment; lugubrosity; melancholia; melancholy; *tristesse;* (**pl.** doldrums; lachrymals; megrims)
person (man): **n.** *il pensioroso*
story or complaint: **n.** jeremiad; lamentation; (**pl.** pathetics)

SAFE: (**see** "certain") **a.** impregnable; invulnerable; unassailable; unconquerable

SAFEGUARD: (**see** "protection") **n.** palladium

SAFETY: **n.** *anchora salutis; ex abundanti cautela;* refuge; sanctuary
place of: **see** "stronghold"

SAGE: **n.** Nestor; philosopher; pundit; savant; Solomon; **a.** (**see** "wise") acuminous; discerning; judicious; Nestorian; perspicacious; profound; prudent; sagacious; sapient; Solomonic

SAILOR(S): **n.** matelot; (**pl.** *gens de mer*)

SAINTLY: (**see** "sacred") **a.** angelic; beatific; pietistic; seraphic
person: **n.** seraph; zaddik

SAINTS *and angels, homage to:* **n.** dulia
catalog(ue) of, or lives of: **n.** hagiography; hagiology; **n.** hagiographer; hagiographist; **a.** hagiographic(al)
reverence for or worship of: **n.** dulia; hagiolatry; hierolatry

SALARY: (**see** "recompense") **n.** compensation; emolument; honorarium; remuneration; stipend(ium); **a.** remunerative; stipendiary

SALE: **n.** vendition; **a.** SALABLE: marketable; mercenary; merchantable; venal; vendible

SALIVA, *excessive flow of:* **n.** ptyalism; salivation

SALLOW: **a.** etiolated; icteric; ischemic; jaundiced

SALT, *containing or producing:* **a.** saliferous; saline; **n.** salinity
with grain of: **adv.** *cum grano salis*

SALUTE: **v.** congratulate; **n.** allocution; salutation; **a.** salutatory
with rifles (mil.): **n.** *feu de joie*

SALVATION: **n.** absolution; atonement; deliverance; extrication; liberation; manumission; nirvana; preservation; redemption; regeneration; reprieve
anchor of (or of safety): **n.** *anchora salutis*
pert. to: **a.** soterial; soteriological; **n.** soteriology

SALVE: **n.** cerate; inunction; ointment; unction; unguent

SAME: (**see** "alike") **a.** adequate; commensurate; congruent; equiponderant; equipotent; equipotential; equivalent; identical; isonomous; synonymous; tantamount; **n.** SAMENESS: (**see** "equality") analogy; congruency; equiponderation; equivalence; identicality; parity
always the: **adv.** *semper idem* (**fem.** *eadem*)
condition, in: **adv.** *in statu quo;* **n.** *status quo*
nature or quality: **a.** cognate; consubstantial; homogeneous; **n.** consubstantiality; homogeneity
place, in the: **adv.** *ibidem* (**abb.** *ibid.*)
race, class, genus, etc.: **n.** congener; **a.** congeneric; congenerous
the: **adv.** *idem* (**abb.** *id*)
time, occurring at: (**see** "occurring") **a.** coexisting; contemporaneous; isochronous; synchronic(al); synchronous; **adv.** or **a.** *pari passu;* **n.** coetaneity; concurrency; contemporaneity; simultaneity; simultaneousness; synchroneity; synchronicity; synchrony; unanimity

SAMPLE: (**see** "pattern") archetype; *beau idéal;* exemplar; exemplification; microcosm; prototype; replica; specimen

SANCTION: **v.** approbate; countenance; encourage; ratify; vouchsafe; **n.** approbation; countenance; dispensation; imprimatur; indulgence; ratification; suffrage; sufferance; **a.** SANCTIONED: authorized; conventional; legitimate; institutive; official; orthodox
sign or mark of: **n.** cachet; hallmark; imprimatur

SANCTITY: **n.** godliness; inviolability; sacredness; saintliness
appearance of: **n.** odor of sanctity; piosity; religiosity; sanctimoniousness; sanctimony; **a.** holier-than-thou; Pecksniffian; pharisaic(al); pietistic(al); religiose; sanctimonious; self-righteous
persons who profess strict: **n.pl.** (the) *unco guid*

SANCTUARY: **n.** adytum; *anchora salutis; anchora spei;* asylum; haven; hospice; oasis; penetral(e); sanctum; *sanctum sanctorum;* **a.** oasitic
(as inner room): **n.** adytum; sanctum; *sanctum sanctorum*
shelter by: **v.** sanctuarize

SAND, *growing in:* **a.** ammophilous
living or burrowing in: **a.** arenicolous
of or like (sandy): **a.** acervulus; arenaceous; sabulous

SANE: (**see** "legally competent") **a.** competent; *compos mentis;* logical; lucid; *mens sana;* rational; **n.** SANITY: competence; lucidity; rationality

SANITARY: **a.** hygienic; sterile
act or process of making: **n.** sanification; sterilization; **v.** autoclave; sanify; sanitize; sterilize

SARCASM: (**see** "satire") **n.** aspersion; cynicism; derision; invective; irony; **a.** SARCASTIC: (**see** "abusive") acidulous; acrimonious; Archilochian; caustic; cynical; incisive; ironical; mordant; mordacious; sardonic; satiric(al); sulfurous; sulphurous; trenchant; virulent; vitriolic

SARDONIC: **see** "cynical"
grin: **n.** *risus sardonicus*

SASSY (or SAUCY): (**see** "abusive") **a.** contemptuous; contumelious; despicable; disdainful; impertinent; impudent; insolent; irreverent; malapert; officious; **n.** SASSINESS (or SAUCINESS): contemptibility; contumely; impertinence; impudence; insolence; procacity; protervity

SATAN, *get thee hence!:* **int.** *apage Satanas!*

SATIRE: **n.** cynicism; diatribe; irony; lampoon; pasquinade; philippic; sarcasm; sardonicism; Sotadic
good-natured: **n.** raillery
marked by coarse and extravagant: **a.**

Pantagruelian; **n.** Pantagruelism
one who engages in: **n.** *farceur;* (**fem.** *farceuse*); Pantagruelist; railleur; satirist
usu. w/ political implications: **n.** pasquinade

SATIRIC(AL): (**see** "sarcastic") **a.** ironic(al); Juvenalian; sardonic(al); Swiftian
coarsely: **a.** hudibrastic

SATIRIST: **n.** *farceur;* (**fem.** *farceuse*); Pantagruelist; railleur; sillographer

SATISFACTION: **n.** atonement; complacency; contentment; gratification; indemnification; oblectation; reconciliation; repletion; restitution; satiability; satiation; satiety; **v.** SATISFY: (**see** "please") appease; atone; convince; fulfill; gratify; indemnify; reconcile; satiate
capable of: **a.** satiable
hard to: (**see under** "please") **a.** insatiable
incapable of: **a.** implacable; inexorable; insatiable; unappeasable; **n.** insatiability

SATURATION: **n.** impregnation; interpenetration; permeation; satiation; satiety; surfeit; **v.** SATURATE: imbue; impregnate; infuse; interpenetrate; permeate; pervade
liquid: **n.** imbibition

SAUCY: **see** "sassy"

SAVAGE: (**see** "wild") **a.** barbarous; feral; ferocious; heathenish; inhuman; pagan; relentless; uncivilized; untamed; **n.** barbarian; primitive; **n.** SAVAGENESS: barbarity; ferity; primitivity

SAVIO(U)R: **n.** benefactor; deliverer; emancipator; liberator; Messiah; redeemer; **a.** messianic

SAVORY: (**see** "appetizing") **a.** ambrosial; delectable; edifying; flavorous; gustable; gustatory; nectareous; palatable; piquant; savorous; toothsome

SAWDUST, *resembling:* **a.** scobicular; scobiform

SAW-EDGED: **a.** denticulate; serrate(d) serrulate(d)

SAYING: (**see** "maxim") **n.** dictum; saw; witticism
clever: **n.** *bijouterie; bon mot;* epigram; witticism
gratuitous: **n.** *gratis dictum; obiter dictum*
it goes w/o: **adv.** *il va sans dire*
that goes w/o: **adv.** *cela va sans dire*
trite or commonplace: **n.** banality; bromide; cliché; platitude; shibboleth; stereotype; **a.** banal; bromidic; hackneyed; platitudinal; stereotyped; stereotypical
wise or witty: (**see** "witticism") **n.** apothegm; gnome; maxim; **a.** apothegmatic(al); gnomic(al); sentient

SCABBY: **a.** desquamative; scabrous; *n.* scabrousness

SCALE: **n.** despumation; desquamation; diapason; exfoliation; furfuration; gamut; incrustation; lamina; proportion; ramentum; **n.** SCALINESS: scabrousness; squamation; squamosity; **a.** SCALY: paleiform; scabrous; squamous
off (peel): **v.** desquamate; exfoliate; **a.** desquamative; exfoliative

SCAMP: (**see** "rogue") **n.** *mauvais sujet* (black sheep); *polisson;* rapscallion; scalawag; scaramouche

SCANDAL: **n.** aspersion; defamation; infamy; obloquy
current: **n.** *fama clamosa*

SCANDALOUS: **a.** atrocious; disreputable; flagitious; flagrant; heinous; infamous; malodorous; notorious; outrageous; villainous
details (report, history, biography, etc. which stresses): **n.** *chronique scandaleuse*

SCANTY: **a.** exiguous; infinitesimal; parsimonious; **n.** SCANTINESS: (**see** "scarcity") exiguity; frugality; parcity; paucity; stringency

SCAR: **v.** cicatrize; disfigure; scarify; **n.** cicatrix; cicatrization; ulosis

SCARCITY: **n.** dearth; deficiency; exiguity; famine; inadequacy; insufficiency; parcity; paucity; rareness; rarity; stringency; uncommonness

SCARE: **v.** affright; agrise; cow; intimidate; panic; petrify; terrorize

SCARECROW: **n.** bugaboo; *homme de paille;* ragamuffin; tatterdemalian; **a.** tatterdemalian

SCATHING: (**see** "sarcastic") **a.** caustic; corrosive; mordant; sulfurous; sulphurous; truculent; virulent; vitriolic; vituperative; **n.** causticity; corrosiveness; mordancy; vituperation

SCATTER: (**see** "spread") **v.** decentralize; derange; dispel; disperse; disseminate; dissipate; diverge; diversify; intersperse; promulgate; **a.** SCATTERED: discrete; disunited; infrequent; interspersed; isolated; sporadic; vagrant; **n.** SCATTERING: diaspora; diffusion; disbursion; dispersion; dissemination; distribution; promulgation; scatteration; sporadicity

SCENE, *changing or complex, as in a dream:* **n.** phantasmagoria; phantasmagory; **a.** kaleidoscopic; phantasmagoric(al)
unlimited: **n.** panorama; **a.** panoramic

SCENT: **n.** aroma; aura; bouquet; cachet; effluvium; (**pl.** effluvia); essence; fragrance; redolence; **a.** SCENTED: aromatic; fragrant; odiferous; odorous; perfumed; pungent; redolent

SCHEDULE: **n.** agendum; (**pl.** agenda); curriculum; inventory; program(me); prospectus; regime; tariff

SCHEME: (**see** "plot") **v.** contemplate; contrive; machinate; premeditate; **n.** cabal; cadre; hypothesis; machination; stratagem; strategy; **a.** (**see** "shrewd") schematic; stratagematic
abstract: **n.** architectonics; hypothesis
as with evil intent: **v.** machinate; **n.** machination

SCHOLAR: (**see** "person of letters") **n.** academician; academist; literato; *literatus;* (**pl.** *literati*); pedant; philomath; pundit; savant
universal: **n.** polyhistor; polymath

SCHOLARLY: (**see** "learned") **a.** academic; erudite; philomathic(al); scholastic; **n.** SCHOLARLINESS (**or** SCHOLARSHIP): erudition
person: (**see** "scholar") **n.** littérateur; (**pl.** intelligentsia; literati)

SCHOOL, *graduate of:* **n.** alumnus; (**pl.** alumni)
leader of (as painters, writers, etc.): **n.** *chef d'école;* coryphaeus; dean
life or environment: **n.** academia
one's own: **n.** *alma mater*
pert. to: **a.** academic; scholastic(al); collegiate; **n.** scholasticism

SCHOOLFELLOW: **n.** condisciple

SCIENTIFIC *club:* **n.** athena(e)um

SCOFFER: **n.** Abderite

SCOLD: (**see** "censure") **v.** berate; castigate; excoriate; lambaste; objurgate; upbraid; vilify; vituperate; **a.** SCOLDING: castigatory; termagant(ish); vituperative

SCOPE: **n.** ambit; compass; comprehensiveness; diapason; gamut; jurisdiction; latitude; lexicon; panorama; purview; spectrum; **a.** SCOPIC: comprehensive; jurisdictional; latitudinal; latitudinous; panoramic

SCORCHED, *or discolored as if by scorching:* **a.** ustulate

SCORN: (**see** "contempt") **n.** asteism; contumely; derision; disdain; opprobrium; **a.** SCORNFUL: contemptuous; derisible; derisive; despicable; disdainful; haughty; supercilious
meriting: **a.** contemptible; despicable; disdainful; opprobrious

SCORNFULNESS: **n.** arrogance; condescension; contemptibility; derision; despicability; disdain; hauteur

SCOTSMAN: **n.** Caledonian

SCOUNDREL: (**see** "rogue") **n.** knave; miscreant; rapscallion; reprobate; varlet

SCOUT: **v.** explore; reconnoiter; **n.** exploration; reconnoiter; reconnaissance

SCOUTING *party:* **n.** reconnaissance

SCRAPE: (**see** "predicament") **n.** dilemma; *mauvais pas;* quandary

SCRATCH: **v.** abrade; cicatrize; scarify; score; obliterate; **n.** abradant; cicatrix; cicatrization

SCREAM: **v.** caterwaul; protest; vociferate; **n.** caterwaul; clamor; protestation; vociferation; **a.** SCREAMING: clamorous; stentorian; vociferous

SCRIBBLING: **n.** cacography; griffonage; hieroglyphic(s); *pattes de mouche*
on walls, etc.: **n.** graffito; (**pl.** graffiti)

SCRIBE: **n.** amanuensis; scrivner

SCRUPLE: (**see** "peculiarity") **n.** compunction; hesitation; penitence; qualm; scrupulosity; suspicion; **a.** SCRUPULOUS: (**see** "precise") compunctious; conscientious; fastidious; meticulous; painstaking; precise; punctilious; rabbinic(al); **n.** SCRUPULOUSNESS: meticulosity; punctiliousness; scrupulosity

SCULPTURED *human figure or face, fantastic, as in architectural support:* **n.** antic; caryatid; telamon

SCUM: **n.** despumation; desquamation; offscouring(s)

SEA(S), *beyond the:* **a.** *outre mer;* transmarine; transmarinus; ultramarine
inhabiting, or floating on open: **a.** pelagic
living in: **a.** maricolous
living in or pert. to deep: **a.** bathybic; bathypelagic; bathysmal; benthopelagic
open, or freedom of the: **n.** *mare liberum*
pert. to: **a.** marine; maritime; naval; oceanic; thalassic
pert. to open: **a.** oceanic; pelagic
study of: **n.** oceanography; thalassography
the high: **n.** *altum mare*

SEAL *of approval:* **n.** cachet; imprimatur
under: **adv.** *sub pede sigilli*

SEAM: **n.** cicatrix; cicatrization; commisure; juncture; raphe; suture; synchrondrosis

SEAMAN: **n.** matelot; (**pl.** *gens de mer*)

SEARCH: **v.** expiscate; explore; investigate; perlustrate; scrutinize; **n.** expiscation; exploration; inquiry; inquisition; perlustration; reconnaissance; safari; scrutiny; **a.** SEARCHING: expiscatory; inquisitive; inquisitorial; inquisitory; scrutinous; **n.** SEARCHER: disquisitor; inquisitor; investigator; querist; researcher

SEASHORE, *pert. to:* **a.** littoral

SEASICKNESS: **n.** *mal de mer;* naupathia; *nausea marina; nausea navalis*

SEASON: **see** "accustom"; **a.** SEASONABLE: (**see** "timely") auspicious; convenient; expedient; opportune; propitious
out of: **n.** *hors de saison*

SEATED: **see** "sitting"

SECEDER(S): **n.** Adullamite; cave of Adullam; schismatic; schismatist; secessionist

SECLUDE: (**see** "hide") **v.** cache; isolate; protect; secrete; sequester; **a.** SECLUDED: ascetic; cloisteral; cloistered; deserted; desolate; enisled; hermitic; isolated; monastic; seclusive; secreted; sequestered; unfrequented; withdrawn; **n.** SECLUSION: detachment; isolation; retirement; sequestration; solitude
oneself: **v.** immure; **n.** immurement

SECOND *in order* (*as brightness of star*): **a.** *beta*
person, use of in speaking: **n.** tuism
son, right of inheritance: **n.** secundogeniture
to none: **a.** *nulli secondus*

SECONDARY: **a.** accessorial; accessory; ancillary; auxiliary; collateral; consequential; derivational; derivative; epiphenomenal; subaltern(ate); subordinate; subservient; subsidiary; substandard; tangential; tributary

SECRET(S): (**see** "hidden") **a.** abstruse; acroamatic; *à huis clos;* apocryphal; arcane; auricular; cabalistic; clandestine; concealed; confidential; covert; cryptic(al); cryptogenic; epoptic; enigmatic(al); esoteric; furtive; hugger-mugger; mysterious; occult; privy; recondite; sibylline; stealthy; surreptitious; undivulged; unrevealed; veiled; **n.** arcanum; (**pl.** arcana; apocrypha; esoterica); **adv.** SECRETLY: *à huis clos; en sourdine; à porte close;* confidentially; covertly; *in camera; in pectore; in petto; januis clausis; sub rosa; sub silento;* **n.** SECRECY: clandestinity; confidentiality
agent: **n.** *agent provocateur*
agreement: **n.** cabal; collusion; **a.** cabalistic; collusive; collusory

bet. two persons: **n.** privity; **a.** privy
court, deliberative body or proceedings: **n.** star chamber; **a.** star-chamber
doctrine(s): **n.** cabalism; **n.pl.** cabala; **a.** cabalistic
extremely: **a.** super secret; top-drawer
in: **see** "secretly"
love affair: **n.** amour; intrigue; liaison
matter(s): **n.** cabal; (**pl.** cabala); **a.** cabalistic
meeting: **n.** assignation; conclave; rendezvous; tryst
name: **n.** cryptonym; **a.** cryptonymous
not: **a.** exoteric; manifest; notorious; patent
place: **n.** adytum; penetrale; rendezvous; *sanctum sanctorum;* tryst
plot: **n.** cabal; (**pl.** cabala); conspiracy; intrigue; machination; **a.** cabalistic; conspiratorial; conspirative
political association: **n.** Carbonari
religious rights: **n.pl.** Eleusinian mysteries
society: **n.** Mafia
state (secrets): **n.pl.** *arcana imperii*
teachings or things: **n.pl.** acroamata; acroamatics; acousmatics; arcana; cabalas; esoterica; **a.** acroamatic; cabalistic
thing(s) kept: **n.** penetrale; (**pl.** penetralia)
ultimate: **n.** *arcanum arcanorum*
ways of action: **n.** ambage(s)

SECT, *narrow-minded attachment to:* **n.** sectarianism

SECTIONAL: **a.** disjunctive; multipartite; provincial; provisional

SECULAR: **a.** civil; laic; mundane; nonclerical; profane; **n.** secularity; **v.** SECULARIZE: temporalize

SECURE: **a.** *à couvert;* dependable; impregnable; inalienable; inviolable; invulnerable; trustworthy; **n.** SECURITY: confidence; guaranty; impregnability; inalienability; invulnerability; pledge; protection; stability

SEDENTARY: **a.** sedent; sessile

SEDIMENT: (**see** "remains") **n.** alluvium; deposit; hypostasis; precipitate; recrement; residuum; sedimentation; scoria; (**pl.** scoriae)

SEDUCE: (**see** "allure") **v.** corrupt; debauch; entice; **a.** SEDUCTIVE: **see** "alluring"; **n.** SEDUCTION: debauchery; debauchment; seducement

SEDUCER, *female;* **n.** Circe; seductress; succubus; vampire

SEE: **v.** ascertain; comprehend; descry; discern; perceive; understand
and believe: vide et crede
we shall: nous verrons

SEED(S), *feeding on:* **a.** granivorous; seminivorous
of, containing or like: **a.** seminal

SEEKING: **a.** appetent; **n.** appetency; desideration

SEEMING: **a.** apparent; ostensible; ostensive; quasi; semblable; virtual
to be true or real: **a.** verisimilar; **n.** verisimilitude; versimility

SEEMLY: (**see** "proper") **a.** appropriate; comely; decorous; handsome

SEGREGATE: (**see** "isolate") **v.** ghettoize; **a.** SEGREGATED: **see** "isolated"; **n.** SEGREGATION: **see** "isolation"
capable of being (segregated): **a.** segregable; segregative

SEIZE: **v.** afflict; appropriate; arrogate; commandeer; confiscate; preempt; sequester; **n.** SEIZURE: confiscation; manucapture; orgasm; paroxysm; preemption; **a.** SEIZING: confiscatory
by public authority: **v.** appropriate; confiscate; sequester; **n.** *eminent domain;* impressment; sequestration

SELECTED *from various authors:* **n.** anthology; chrestomathy; (**pl.** analecta)
from various sources: **n.** eclecticism; **a.** eclectic
passages: **n.pl.** analecta; analects; collectanea

SELECTIVE: **a.** eclectic; discriminative; **n.** SELECTIVITY; discrimination; eclecticism

SELF: **n.** ego; psyche
-assured: **a.** confident; sophomoric
-centered (or self-conceited): **a.** autotheistic; egocentric; egocentristic(al); ego(t)istic(al); individualistic; introversive; **n.** (**see** "selfishness") autism; ego-

centricity; ego(t)ism; iotacism; *outrecuidance;* solipsism

-condemnatory: **a.** compunctious; intropunitive; penitent; remorseful; self-accusatory

-consciousness: **n.** apperception; **a.** apperceptionistic

-contained: **a.** autonomous

-contradictory: **a.** antinomic; paradoxical; **n.** paradox

-control: (**see** "calmness" **and** "poise") **n.** abnegation; abstinence; aplomb; ascesis; asceticism; automat(i)on; continence; perpendicularity; temperance; **a.** ascetic; automatic; automatous; mechanical; self-contained; temperate

defense, in: **adv.** *se defendendo*

-denial: **n.** abnegation; abstinence; ascesis; asceticism; humility; self-abnegation; **a.** abstemious; abstentious; abstinent; ascetic; monastic

-derived or originated, quality of: **n.** aseitas; aseity

-educated, one who is: **n.** autodidact; **a.** autodidactic

-evident: **a.** aphoristic; axiomatic; hypothetico-deductive; indubitable; manifest; patent; postulational; prima facie; *res ipsa loquitur*

examination: **n.** introspection

excessive interest in: **n.** egocentrism; narcissism; **a.** autotheistic; egocentristic(al); narcissistic; narcistic

-existent entity: **n.** substantive

-generated: **a.** autogenic; autogenous; endogenous

-governed: **a.** autonomic; autonomous

-gratification: **n.** onanism; sybartism

-humiliation: **n.** abnegation; ascesis; asceticism; **v.** abnegate

identification w/ another (self): **n.** empathy; escapism; identification; **a.** empath(et)ic; escapist; heteropathic

-importance: **n.** conceit; consequentiality; illuminism; pomposity; pursiness; **a.** arrogant; assertive; assertoric; autotheistic; consequential; insufferable; pompous; pontifical; pretentious; pursey

air of: **n.** consequentiality; flatulence; pomposity; pontificality; pursiness

-important person: **n.** bashaw; bigwig; megalomaniac; panjandrum; pasha; philodox

-inclusive: **adv.** *per se;* **n.** perseity

-indulgent: **a.** apolaustic; gluttonous; hedonistic; intemperate; sybaritic

interest in: (**see** "self-centered" **above**) **n.** introversion

-knowledge: **n.** autognosis; **a.** autognostic

-love: (**see** "selfishness") **n.** *amour de soi;* amour; autophilia; egocentricity; egocentrism; narcissism; **a.** egocentric; narcissan; narcissistic; narcistic; **n.** autophiliac; egocentrist; narcissist

manifestation of (self): **n.** heautophany

-originated or derived: **n.** aseity; **a.** autogenic; autogenous; endogenous

other, or another (self): **n.** *alter ego;* alteregoism; *alter idem;* **a.** alteregoistic

-possession: (**see** "calmness" **and** "poise") **n.** perpendicularity

-respect: **n.** *amour-propre*

-restraint: **n.** abnegation; abstinence; continence; moderation; sobriety; sophrosyne; temperance; **a.** abstemious; abstentious; abstinent; continent; temperate

-righteous: **a.** hypocritical; pharisaic(al); pietistic(al); rectitudinous; sanctimonious; **n. see** "hypocrisy"

-satisfied: **a.** complacent; vainglorious

second (self): **see** "other" **above**

-seeker: **n.** cormorant; hedonist; sybarite; sycophant

-styled: **a.** *soi-disant*

-sufficiency: **n.** aseitas; aseity; confidence; perseity; resourcefulness; smugness

-taught, one who is: **n.** autodidact; **a.** autodidactic

theory that nothing exists or is real but the (self): **n.** solipsism

-tormenter: **n.** heautontimorumenos

-worship: **n.** autotheism; **a.** autotheistic(al)

SELFHOOD: **n.** individualization; ipseity· personality; proprium

SELFISH: (**see** "self-centered") **a.** *aleni appetens;* asocial; egocentric(al); ego(t)istic(al); gluttonous; intemperate; narcissan; narcis(sis)tic; self-serving; **n.** SELFISHNESS: (**see** "self-love") asociality; autism; *après nous* (or *moi*) *le déluge;* egocentricity; egoism; hedonism; introversion; iotacism; *outrecuidance;* selfhood; self-satisfaction; solipsism

interests, appeal(ing) to: **n. or adv.** *(argumentum) ad hominem*

person: **n.** egocentric; egocentrist; ego(t)ist; hedonist; iotacist; misanthropist; narcissist; solipsist; sycophant

SELLING *or buying of church office or preferment:* **n.** simony

SEND *back:* **v.** or **a.** remand

SENILE: (**see** "aged") **a.** anecdotal; caducous; decrepit; senescent; superannuated; venerable; **n.** SENILITY: (anec)dotage; anility; caducity; senescence; superannuation
study of the: **n.** geriatrics; nostology

SENIOR *member:* **n.** dean; doyen; (**fem.** doyenne)
state of being: **n.** precedence; precedency; seniority

SENIORITY: **see** "priority"

SENSATION: **n.** esthesia; perception; phenomenality; sensibility
concomitant: **n.** syn(a)esthesia; **a.** synesthetic; **n.** synesthete
conveying: **a.** sensiferous
distorted or abnormal: **n.** paralgesia; **a.** paralgesic
having: **a.** sensate
lacking: **a.** inanimate; insensate; insentient
loss or reduction of: **n.** anesthesia; hypalgesia; **a.** anesthetic; hypalgesic
producing: **a.** sensific; sensiferous

SENSATIONAL: **a.** arresting; extraordinary; melodramatic; phenomenal; sensationary; spectacular

SENSE(S), *as of word or phrase:* **n.** connotation; denotation; intendment; purport; signification
common: **n.** *bon sens;* prudence; sophrosyne
in a bad: **adv.** *sensu malo*
in proper: **adv.** *in sano sensu*
involving more than one: **a.** synesthetic
muscular (as movement): **n.** kinesthesia; proprioception; **a.** kinesthetic; proprioceptive
perceptible to the: **a.** sensate; sensible
perception or apprehension: **n.** Anschauung
pert. to: **a.** sensorial; sensory; sensual sensuous
remote from common: **a.** stratospheric(al)
transcending: **a.** supersensory; supersensual

SENSED, *what is:* **n.pl.** sensibilia

SENSELESS: (**see** "nonsensical" **and** "pointless") **a.** fatuous; insensate; irrational; irrelevant
talk: **n.** Choctaw; galimatias; gallimaufry; gibberish; jargon; stultiloquence; **a.** stultiloquent(ial)

SENSIBLE: (**see** "aware") **a.** cognizant; conscious; judicious; perspicacious; philosophic(al); politic; prudent; rational; sagacious; sapient

SENSITIVE: **a.** allergic; fastidious; hyperesthetic; impressible; impressionable; leiodermatous; sentient; susceptible
highly, as skin or to pain: **a.** hyperalgesic; hyperesthesic; **n.** hyperalgesia; hyperesthesia
low (sensitivity): **n.** hypesthesia; **a.** hypesthetic; insensitivity

SENSUAL: (**see** "sensuous") **a.** Apician; carnal; epicurean; epithumetic; irreligious; lurid; materialistic; scabrous; sensualistic; sultry; sybaritic; *voluptuaire;* voluptuary; *voluptueux;* voluptuous; **n.** SENSUALITY: carnality; concupiscence; sensualism; sensuosity; sensuousness; sybaritism; *volupté* voluptuosity; voluptuousness; worldliness
appetite: **n.** concupiscence; **a.** concupiscent; concupiscible
pleasures: **n.pl.** *voluptates corporis*

SENSUOUS: **a.** anacreontic; Bacchic; Dionysian; epicurean; faustian; hedonic; hedonistic; orgiastic; sensualistic; sybaritic(al); voluptuous; **n. see** "sensuality"
person: **n.** epicure; hedonist; libertine; sybarite; voluptuary; voluptueux

SENTENCE, *ambiguous:* **n.** amphibology; **a.** amphibiological; amphibolous
breaking of thought in: **n.** aposiopesis; **a.** aposiopetic
change in structure before completion: **n.** anacoluthon; (**pl.** anacoluthia)
construction or structure, science of: **n.** syntax
contrast of thoughts in: **n.** antithesis; **a.** antithetic(al)
reading same backward as forward: **n.** palindrome
reversal or inversion of regular order: **n.** anastrophe
stopping in middle of: **n.** abscission
violation of structure in: **n.** anacoluthon; **a.** anacoluthic

SENTIMENTAL: **a.** bathetic; maudlin; mawkish; (melo)dramatic; romantic; **n.** SENTIMENTALISM: bathos; maudlin-

ism; mawkishness; romanticism
song: **n.** strephonade
value: **n.** *pretium affectionis*
weakly: **a.** cloying; conciliatory; insipid; maudlin; mawkish; namby-pamby; nauseating; wishy-washy

SEPARATE: (**see** "divide") **v.** abstract; compartmentalize; demarcate; departmentalize; disassociate; disaffiliate; discriminate; dissect; dislocate; dissociate; divaricate; diverge; exclude; fractionalize; ghettoize; isolate; segregate; sequester; sunder; **a.** SEPARATE(D): (**see** "distinct") compartmentalized; departmentalized; detached; discrete; disengaged; distinguished; individual; secluded; solitary; unaffiliated; unassociated; **n.** SEPARATENESS: detachment; disjointure; disjunction; distinctness; individuality; sejunction; severality; **a.** SEPARATING: (**see** "divisive") centrifugal; demarcative; disjunctive; dissociative; schismatic(al)
for special purpose: **v.** sequester; **n.** sequestration
from environment: **v.** deracinate; **n.** deracination
into parts: **v.** atomize; disjoin(t); dissect; divaricate; subdivide; **n.** disjunction; divarication
portions: **n.pl.** *disjecta membra*
unable to: **a.** indiscerptible; indissociable; indissoluble; indivisible; inextricable; infractible; inseparable; inseverable; inviolable

SEPARATION: (**see** "parting") **n.** demarcation; detachment; diremption; disarticulation; discerption; discharge; disjointure; disjunction; disjunctivity; dissociation; distinction; divarication; divergence; divorcement; estrangement; resignation; schism; seclusion; segregation; sejunction; sequestration
of substances: **n.** dialysis; dissolution; **a.** dialytic
violent: **n.** divulsion

SEQUENCE: (**see** "series") **n.** concatenation; consecution; sequacity; succession
in: **a.** alphabetical; categorical; chronological; consecutive; *en suite;* numerical; ordinal; sequacious; sequential; **n.** concatenation; sequacity; seriality
in continuous: **n.** spectrum
regular: **n.** causality

SERENE: (**see** "calm") **a.** halcyon; limpid; tranquil; unperturbed; **n.** SERENITY: (**see** "composure") equanimity; imperturbability; imperturbation; limpidity; *sang-froid;* tranquility

SERF: **n.** *ascriptus glebae;* colonus; helot; peon; villein; **n.** SERFDOM: bondage; helotism; helotry; peonage; servitude; subjection; thralldom

SERIAL: (**see** "sequence") **a.** chronologic(al); **adv.** *seriatim;* **n.** seriality
novel in form of: **n.** feuilleton

SERIES, *arrange in:* **v.** alphabetize; categorize; concatenate; hierarchize; serialize; stratify; **n.** alphabetization; categorization; concatenation; hierarchization; seriality; stratification
continuing, of scenes or events: **n.** feuilleton; panorama; phantasmagoria
in a: **see under** "sequence"
of miseries, disasters, marital exploits, etc.: **n.** iliad; *via doloroso*
unite in: (**see** "arrange in" **above**) **a. or v.** concatenate; **n.** concatenation

SERIOUSNESS: **n.** gravity; sedateness; seriosity; sobriety; solemnity; **a.** SERIOUS: consequential; critical; formidable; earnest; emphatic; grievous; humorless; momentous; sedate; *sérieux;* serioso; significant; unmirthful; **adv.** *au sérieux*
in all: **adv.** *au grand sérieux*
lack of: (**see** "frivolity") **n.** levity

SERMON: **n.** discourse; dissertation; exhortation; homily; lecture; preachment; **a.** homiletic; sermonic
knowledge or study of (sermons): **n.** homiletics; sermonology

SERRATED: **a.** denticulated

SERVANT(S): (**see** "serf") **n.** menial; servitor; servitress; **a.** menial; servitorial

SERVILE: (**see** "compliant") **a.** abject; cringing; deferential; fawning; imitative; menial; obsequious; parasitical; sequacious; servient; slavish; subordinate; subservient; sycophantic; toadyish; tractable; **n.** SERVILITY: deference; obsequiousness; obsequity; subservience:; subserviency; sycophancy; toadyism

SERVITUDE: **see** "serfdom"

SET: (see "clique") **n.** battery; series
against: **v.** contrapose; **n.** contraposition
apart: (see "separate") **v.** demarcate; discriminate; enisle; segregate; sequester; **a.** demarcative; **n.** demarcation; sequestration
in a: **a.** *en suite*
in place or position: **v.** posit
right: **v.** disabuse

SETTING: (see "environment") **n.** locale; milieu; *mise-en-scène*

SETTLE: **v.** colonize; determine; establish; liquidate; resolve
as bet. contestants: **v.** intercede; interpose; mediate

SETTLED: (see "stable") **a.** immutable; liquidated; *res judicata;* sedentary; sessile; steadfast; unswerving
in habits, practices, prejudices, etc.: **a.** inveterate; **n.** sedentation
that which can be: **a.** resoluble; **n.** resolubility

SETTLEMENT: **n.** accommodation; adaptation; colonization; compromise; disposition; habitation; harmonization; installation; liquidation; reconciliation; sedentation; understanding
final: **n.** liquidation; quietus

SEVEN: **n.** hebdomad; heptad; septenary
composed of, or occurring every 7 days: **a.** hebdomadal; **n.** hebdomad
consisting of or including, 7-fold or 7-times as great: **a.** septuple; **n.** septuplicate
lasting or occurring every 7 years: **a.** septennial; **n.** septennium
ruling body of: **n.** septemvirate; **a.** septemviral
the number, group of, or consisting of 7: **n.** hebdomad; heptad; septenary; **a.** hebdomadal; septenary; septennium
years, period of: **n.** septennate; septennium; **a.** septennial

SEVENTY, *or bet. 70 and 80:* **a.** septuagenary; **n.** septuagenarian

SEVER: **v.** disarticulate; disengage; dissociate; divorce; **n.** SEVERANCE: disarticulation; disengagement; dissociation; dissolution; divorcement

SEVERAL, *comb. of into whole:* **n.** polysynthesis

SEVERE: (see "harsh") **a.** arduous; ascetic; atrocious; austere; crucial; exacting; flagrant; heinous; grievous; inclement; inexorable; inflexible; lamentable; obdurate; rigorous; stringent; tyrannical; uncharitable; unrelenting; vehement; **n.** SEVERITY: austerity; harshness; inclemency; rigor; stringency; vehemence
inhumanly: **a.** Draconian; Procrustean
state of becoming progressively: **n.** ingravescence; **a.** ingravescent

SEX: **n.** gender
attraction to either: **n.** amphigenous; bisexual; **n.** amphieroticism; bisexuality
double or doubtful: **n.** androgyny; hermaphrodite; **a.** androgynous; hermaphroditic
indicating neither, or common to both: **a.** epicene
male and fem. as different individuals: **n.** dioecism; **a.** dioecious
male and fem. in one: **n.** androgyne; androgyneity; androgyny; hermaphrodite; hermaphroditism; monoecism; monoecy; **a.** androgynous; hermaphroditic; mon(o)ecious
organs: **n.pl.** externalia; genitalia; pudenda; naturalia
female: **n.** *vulva;* (pl. muliebria); pudenda
male: **n.** see "male generative organ"
pert. to both: **a.** ambisexual; ambosexual; androgynous; bisexual; epicene
pert. to or having desire for opp.: **a.** or **n.** hetersexual; **n.** alleroti(ci)sm; heteroti(ci)sm
pert. to or having desire for same: **a.** or **n.** homosexual; uranist; urning; **n.** homoeroti(ci)sm; homosexuality; uranism; **a.** homoerotic
state or period of development when child becomes interested in opp.: **n.** altrigenderism

SEXINESS: **n.** erotogenicity; ero(to)geneity; erotogenesis; voluptuousness; voluptuosity

SEXLESS: **a.** asexual; castrate(d); neuter; **n.** asexuality; asexualization

SEXUAL *activity, abstinence fr.:* **n.** chastity; continence; **a.** chaste; continent; virginal
craving, excessive or unreasonable: **n.** erogeneity; erotogenesis; erotomania

female: **n.** andromania; nymphomania; **n.** nymphomaniac
male: **n.** gynecomania; satyriasis
desire: **n.** *ardor veneris;* erogeneity; ero(to)genesis; erotogeneity; erogeny; eroti(ci)sm; **a.** erogenic; erogenous
abnormal: **(see** "craving" **above) n.** aidiomantia; aphrodisia; erotomania; erotopathy; **a.** aphrodisiac
arousing or increasing, or drug or agent to increase: **n. or a.** aphrodisiac; **n.** erotogenesis
inclination or capacity: **n.** lustihood; potency
intercourse: **n.** carnal knowledge; coition; coitus; copulation; concubitus; pareunia; venery
inability to perform: **n.** impotence; impotency; *impotentia coeundi*
interest in others: **n.** alleroti(ci)sm; heteroti(ci)sm; **n. or a.** heterosexual
in same (*sex*): **n.** homosexuality; uranism; **n. or a.** homosexual; uranist; urning
in self: **n.** autoeroti(ci)sm; onanism
love, inclined or pert. to: **a.** amative; amatory; amorous; passionate
matters, abnormal preoccupation w/: **n.** erogeneity; eroticism; erotomania
organs: **see under** "sex"
perversion: **n.** homosexuality; uranism; **n.** homosexual; uranist; urning
pleasure by hurting or mistreating: **n.** algolagnia; sadism; **a.** sadistic; **n.** sadist
fr. receiving pain or mistreatment: **n.** algolagnia; masochism; **a.** masochistic
fr. watching: **n.** scopophilia; voyeurism; **a.** scopophilic; voyeuristic; **n.** scopophiliac; voyeur
pleasures, indulging in: **n.** venery; **a.** venereal
practices, preference for unusual; **n.** paraphilia; paraphiliac
reproduction: **(see under** "reproduction") **a.** syngamic
urge (*instinct*): **n.** libido; passion

SEXUALLY *stimulating:* **a.** aphrodisiac; ero(to)genic; erogenous; erotic; **n.** aphrodisiac; erogenesis; erogeneity; erotogenesis; erotogenicity
books, pictures, etc.: **n.pl.** *erotica;* facetiae; pornography

SEXY: **(see** "sexiness") **a.** bawdy; erogenous; erotic; voluptuary

SHABBY: **(see** "contemptible" **and** "untidy") **a.** despicable; deteriorated; dilapidated; dishonorable; paltry; sordid; squalid; tatterdemalian; threadbare; unfair; **n.** SHABBINESS: squalidity

SHACKLED: **see** "restrained"

SHADE: **v.** inumbrate; **n.** adumbration; obscurity; nuance; (pen)umbra; protection; umbrage; umbrella; **a. see** "shady"
of difference in tone, color or meaning: **n.** nuance
thriving in: **a.** sciophilous

SHADOW: **v.** adumbrate; inumbrate; **n.** adumbration; aura; (pen)umbra; umbrage
-boxing: **n.** sciamachy
dispelling: **a.** scialytic
having or casting a long: **a.** macroscian
projecting: **n.** skiagraphy
veiled in, or use in painting: **n.** chiaroscuro; sfumato; tenebrism

SHADOWY: **a.** adumbral; fleeting; imaginary; penumbral; tenebrous; unsubstantial
area: **n.** penumbra; twilight zone

SHADY: **(see** "suspicious") **a.** devious; disreputable; dubious; *louche;* penumbral; questionable; uncertain; unethical; unreliable
(*giving shade*): **a.** adumbral; umbrageous; umbriferous
place: **n.** frescade

SHAGGY: **a.** hirsutal; hirsute; unkempt; **n.** hirsutism

SHAKESPEARE, *supporting of as author of plays:* **n. or a.** Stratfordian
worship of or undue fondness for: **n.** bardolatry; **n.** bardolatrist

SHAKING: **a.** quavering; tremorous; tremulous; **n.** quaver; tremblement; tremor; tremulation

SHALLOW: **(see** "artificial") **a.** cursory; frivolous; inane; incondite; magazinish; sophomoric; specious; superficial; tenuous; trifling; trivial; **n.** SHALLOWNESS: **(see** "emptiness") inanity; speciosity; superficiality; tenuosity; triviality

SHAM: **v.** counterfeit; simulate; travesty; **a. (see** "bogus") adulterated; apocryphal; artificial; Brummagem; dissimulative; factitious; postiche; pseudo; simulated; spurious; **n.** affectation; deceitfulness; decep-

tion; dissemblance; dissimulation; hypocrisy; imposture; legerdemain; pretense; simulacrum; travesty
fight: **n.** sciamachy

SHAME: (**see** "disgrace") **v.** abash; discomfit; disconcert; discountenance; dishonor; **n.** abashment; chagrin; discomfiture; dishonor; ignominy; infamy; humiliation; mortification; opprobrium; reproach; stigma; **a.** SHAMEFUL: (**see** "disgraceful") degrading; ignominious; indecent; infamous; inglorious; outrageous; **a.** SHAMELESS: (**see** "brazen") arrant; degrading; immodest; outrageous; unabashed; unblushing; unmitigated; **a. or adv.** *sans pudeur* **n.** SHAMELESSNESS: (**see** "brass") immodesty; impudicity
false: **n.** *malus pudor; mauvaise honte;* prudery
feeling of: **n.** abashment; embarrassment
for (shame!): **int.** *fi!; pro(h) pudor!* (or) *fi donc!*

SHAPE: (**see** "form" **and** "outline") **n.** configuration; conformation; construction; profile; silhouette; **a.** SHAPELESS: amorphous; heterogeneous; misshapen; **a.** SHAPELY: curvaceous; sculpturesque; statuesque; symmetrical; **a.** SHAPING: determinative; formative
having a single, or but one: **a.** monomorphic; monomorphous
having similar or identical: **a.** homeomorphic; isomorphic

SHARE: **v.** apportion; partake; participate
incapable of being (shared): **a.** impartible; imparticipable
indefinite: **n.** moiety

SHARP, *as biting to smell or taste:* **a.** acrid; piquant; poignant; pungent
-cornered: **a.** angular; angulous; **a.** angularity
remark: **n.** mordacity; sarcasm; spinosity
-sighted: **a.** hawkeyed; lyncean

SHAVING: **n.** pogonotomy

SHED, *as skin:* **v.** desquamate; exfoliate; exuviate; slough; **a.** SHEDDING: desquamative; exfoliative; **n.** desquamation; ecdysis; exfoliation; exuviation

SHEDDING, *as leaves:* **a.** deciduate; deciduous; exfoliative

SHEEN: **n.** brightness; brilliance; fluorescence; fulguration; glossiness; illumination; luminosity; luster; nitidity; phosphorescence; radiance; refulgence; refulgency; scintillation

SHEER: **a.** absolute; diaphanous; precipitous; utter; unmitigated; unmixed
assertion: **n.** *gratis dictum*

SHEET, *roll or compress in:* **v.** laminate

SHELL, *of turtle, etc.:* **n.** carapace
out, remove by: **v.** enucleate; **n.** enucleation

SHELTER: **v.** embosom; **n.** asylum; coverture; protection; retreat; sanctuary; sanctum; **a.** see "secure"
temporary: **n.** bivouac

SHEPHERDESS: **n.** Amaryllis

SHERIFF'S *deputies:* **n.** posse (comitatus)

SHIELD: (**see** "shelter") **n.** aegis; escutcheon
of Zeus or Athena: **n.** (a)egis
shaped like: **a.** clypeate; clypeiform; scutate

SHIFT, *as in disease:* **v.** metastasize; **n.** metabasis; metastasis; **a.** metastatic

SHIFTING: **a.** inefficient; vagabond; vagrant
person: **n.** prodigal; vagabond; (**pl.** flotsam and jetsam)

SHIFTY: (**see** "unreliable") **a.** elusive; evasive; fickle; lubricious; oleaginous; resourceful; unstable; **n.** lubricity; **a.** SHIFTLESS: **see** "idle" **and** "lazy"

SHIN: **n.** antecnemion; cnemis; tibia

SHINING: **a.** effulgent; lucent; lustrous; nitid; phosphorescent; radiant; refulgent; resplendent; rutilant; splendorous; **v.** SHINE: effulge; irradiate; phosphoresce; rutilate; scintillate; **n.** see "sheen"
most brightly: **a.** prefulgent; **n.** prefulgence; prefulgency

SHIP(S), *pert. to:* **a.** nautical; naval
shaped like or resembling: **a.** navicular
wreckage from: **n.** flotsam and jetsam

SHIRK: **v.** malinger; **n.** SHIRKER: *embusqué;* malingerer

SHOCKED, *easily:* **a.** squeamish; **n.** squeamishness

SHOCKING: (**see** "deplorable" **and** "vulgar") **a.** appalling; dedecorous; degrading; humiliating; *infra dignitatem;* opprobrious; percussive

SHODDY: **see** "cheap"

SHOEMAKER, *let not the . . . leave his last: ultra crepidam ne sutor*

SHOOT, *as of plant:* **n.** (s)cion

SHORE, *region along:* **n.** or **a.** littoral

SHORT (or SHORTENED): (**see** "abrupt" **and** "terse") **a.** abbreviated; compendious; curtailed; decurtate; diminished; diminutive; ephemeral; expeditious; fugitive; inadequate; instantaneous; insufficient; momentaneous; summary; transitory; truncated
in: **adv.** basically; essentially; fundamentally
lit. or mus. piece: **n.** morceau
-lived: **a.** deciduous; ephemeral; transient; transitory; **n.** ephemerid; ephemeron; transient
-sighted: **a.** astigmatic; myopic; purblind; strabismic; **n.** astigmatism; brachymetropia; myopia; strabismus
syllables, rel to or composed of: **a** brachysyllabic; **n.** brachysyllabicism
-winded: **a.** dyspn(o)eic; pursy; **n.** dyspn(o)ea; pursiness

SHORTCOMING: (**see** "defect") **n.** deficiency; dereliction; foible; imperfection; remission

SHORTEN, *as a word:* **v.** abbreviate, abridge; apocopate; elide; syncopate; **n.** abbreviation; aph(a)eresis; apocopation; elision; syncopation

SHORTENING: (**see** "abridgement") **n.** abbreviation; apocopation; curtailment; retrenchment; truncation
as of lit. work: **n.** abridgement; epitome; *résumé;* synopsis

SHOUT: (**see** "scream") **v.** vociferate; **n.** vociferation; **a.** vociferous
of multitude or many: **n.** conclamation; **a.** conclamant
of praise: **n.** hallelujah; hosanna
or thunder forth denunciations: **v.** fulminate; **n.** fulmination; **a.** fulminous
together w/ joy: **v.** conjubilate; **n.** conjubilation; **a.** conjubilant

SHOW: **see** "demonstrate"
gorgeous or ornate: **n.** extravaganza; floridity; ostentation; pageantry; pomposity; pontificality; pretentiousness
serving to: **a.** demonstrative; revelatory

SHOWY: (**see** "ornate") **a.** actorish; actressy; agonistic; baronial; baroque; bedizened; blatant; Brummagem; carnivalesque; circusy; claptrap; clinquant; dramatic(al); dramaturgic(al); extravagant; fastuous; flamboyant; garish; grandiloquent; grandiose; orgillous; orgulous; orotund; ostentatious; pretentious; prismatic; rococo; sonorous; specious; splendid; splendorous; theatrical; thespian; tessellated; **n.** SHOWINESS: (**see** "gaudiness") acrobatics; acrobatism; affectation; attitudinization; blatancy; cabotinage; floridity; histrionism; orotundity; ostentation; pageantry; pomposity; pontificality; Sardoodledom; speciosity; theatricality; trumpery
and elaborate in style: **a.** rhetoric(al); rococo; rubescent
but worthless: **n.** trumpery
something which is: **n.** bric-a-brac; furbelow; trumpery
to make: **v.** gaudify; glamorize; theatricalize

SHREWD: **a.** acuminous; artful; astute; calculating; canny; circumspect; diplomatic; discerning; heady; parlous; penetrating; perspicacious; politic; reflective; sagacious; stratagematic; suave; **n.** SHREWDNESS: acumen; callidity; canniness; comprehension; discrimination; perspicacity; sagacity

SHRILL: **a.** calliopean; penetrating; strident; stridulous; **n.** SHRILLNESS: stridor; stridulation

SHRINE: **n.** adytum; mausoleum; reliquary; sanctorium; sanctuary; *sanctum sanctorum*

SHRINK: **v.** atrophy; contract; diminish; recoil; retract; telescope: **a.** **see** "shrunken" *ability or tendency to:* **n.** contractibility; contractility

SHROUD: **n.** cerement; winding-sheet

SHRUB(S): **n.** arboret; boscage; foliage; **a.** arboresque; frutescent
pert. to art of trimming and shaping: **a.** topiary
trimmed and shaped: **n.** topiary

SHRUNKEN: **a.** atrophic; atrophied; wizened

SHUDDER: **n.** frisson; quake; tremor; tremulation; vibration

SHUN: (**see** "avoid") **v.** disdain; eschew; evade; **n.** avoidance; eschewal; evasion

SHY: (**see** "bashful") **a.** cautious; circumspect; constrained; daphnean; demure; diffident; distrustful; pavid; modest; reclusive; shamefaced; solitary; suspicious; timorous; verecund; unassuming; **n.** SHYNESS: bashfulness; coyness; diffidence; timidity; verecundity
away from: **v.** or **n.** demur

SICK (or SICKLY): (**see** "diseased") **a.** *à la mort;* aeger; amort; cachetic; chagrined; disgusted; indisposed; infirm; maladive; morbific; morbose; queasy; unhealthy; unwholesome; valetudinarian; valetudinary; wretched; **a.** SICKEN: deteriorate; nauseate
as result of intemperance: **n.** crapulence; **a.** crapulent; crapulous
man's dream: **n.** *aegri somnia*
near point of dying: **a.** *in articulo mortis;* in extremis; fey; moribund
pretend to be: **v.** malinger; **n.** malingerer; malingering; pathomimesis

SICKENING: **a.** cloying; insipid; mawkish; nauseating; nauseous
to point of being: **adv.** *ad nauseam*

SICKLE, *shaped like:* **a.** falciform

SICKNESS: **see** "disease"
sudden fit of: **n.** paroxysm; qualm; seizure

SIDE, *affecting or appearing on same:* **a.** homolateral; ipsilateral; unilateral
-by-side: (**see** "parallel") **adv.** paradromic; *pari passu*
to set or place: **v.** collocate; juxtapose; **n.** collocation; juxtaposition; **a.** juxtapositional
having many (sides): **a.** multilateral; multiphasic; polygonal
hear the other: audi alteram partem
on opposite: **a.** contralateral; heteronymous; oppositious; **adv.** *ex adverso; ex adversum*
pert. to both (sides): **a.** ambilateral; bilateral; bipartisan; bipartite
to many: **a.** multilateral; multiphasic; polygonal
to one: **a.** homolateral; homonymous; ipsilateral; unilateral

SIGH: **v.** suspirate; **n.** suspiration; **a.** suspirous

SIGHT: **see** "vision"
at first: **adv.** *d'abord; au premier abord;* **a.** *prima facie*

SIGN(S): (**see** "warning") **n.** adumbration; augury; criterion; divination; emblem; escutcheon; gesture; indication; indicia; indicium; manifestation; portent; signum; symptom; vestige; **a.** augural; emblematic; indicial; portentous; signific; symptomatic
advance or warning: **n.** adumbration; harbinger; symptom
behold the: ecce signum
by this (sign) thou wilt conquer: in hoc signo vinces
language: **n.** dactylology; *lingua franca*
of disease: **n.** semeiotics; stigma; (**pl.** stigmata); symptom(atology); syndrome; **a.** emblematic; pathognominic(al); semeiotic; symptomatic(al)
study of: **n.** semantics; semasiology; sem(e)iology; symptomatology; **n.** semeiologist

SIGNATURE: **n.** autograph; signum; **a.** autographic(al)
flourish at end of: **n.** paraph
made for another: **n.** allograph
without: **a.** anonymous; pseudonymous

SIGNIFICANT: **see** "important"

SILENCE: **n.** inarticulation; muteness; obmutescence; quiescence; quietude; taciturnity; tranquility
gives consent: chi tace acconsenti; qui tacet consentit
under or in: **adv.** *sub rosa; sub silento*

SILENT: **a.** brachysyllabic; inarticulate; inaudible; incommunicable; incomunicative; laconic; quiescent; reserved; retentive; reticent; silentious; speechless; tacit; taciturn; tranquil; uncommunicative; **adv.** *nil decit*
actor: **n.** pantomimist; *persona muta*
becoming or keeping: **n.** muteness; obmutescence; reticence; taciturnity; **a.** obmutescent; reticent; taciturn
habitually: **a.** reticent; silentious; taciturn
keep (silent) and be counted a philosopher: sile, et philosophus esto
singing or speaking (moving lips): **n.** mussitation

SILKY: **a.** sericeous

SILLY: (**see** "foolish") **a.** anserine; anserous; asinine; fatuous; inane; frivolous; preposterous; puerile; ridiculous; vertiginous; **n.** SILLINESS: (**see** "absurdity") asininity; fatuity; frivolity; inanition; inanity; *niaiserie;* puerility; ridiculosity
person: **n.** Abderite; flibbertigibbet; goose; nincompoop; simpleton

SILVER, *like or pert. to:* **a.** argentine; argentous
ore-bearing: **a.** argentiferous

SIMILAR: (**see** "comparable") **a.** analogical; analogous; congruent; duplicate; equivalent; homogenous; homologous; homonymous; parallel; semblable; synonymous
in a (similar) case: **adv.** *in pari materia*
in function but diff. in structure: **a.** analogical; **n.** analogue
in structure and function: **a.** homologous
something which is: **n.** analog(ue); duplicate; homolog(ue); parallel

SIMPLE: (**see** "easy") **a.** artless; asinine; candid; credulous; fatuous; guileless; humble; idyllic; ignorant; incomplex; incomplicate; inelaborate; ingenuous; naïve; non-pontifical; primitive; unadorned; uncomplicated; uncompounded; unembellished; unillusioned; unsophisticated; untutored; unvarnished
(*easy to understand*): **a.** limpid; pellucid; translucent
elegance, of: **adv.** *simplex munditiis*
(*foolish*): **a.** anserine; asinine; fatuous
person: **see** "simpleton"

SIMPLETON: **n.** Abderite; *bon enfant;* goose; nincompoop

SIMPLICITY: **n.** artlessness; austerity; clarity; guilelessness; humility; ingenuousness; intelligibility; *naïveté;* primitivity
elegant in: **adv.** *simplex munditiis*
natural or childlike: **n.** artlessness; guilelessness; humility; *naïveté;* unsophistication
rustic: **a.** bucolic; idyllic; pastoral; Theocritean

SIMPLIFY: **v.** clarify; informalize; streamline
over-: **a.** simplistic; **n.** simplism

SIMULATED: (**see** "artificial" **and** "assumed") **a.** counterfeit; derivative; factitious; imitated; **v.** SIMULATE: **see** "counterfeit"

SIMULTANEOUS: **see** "at same time"

SIN: **v.** transgress; **n.** delict; depravity; immorality; iniquity; misdemeanor; peccancy; transgression; wickedness
capable of or liable to: **a.** peccable; **n.** peccability
forgiveness of: **n.** absolution; **a.** absolutory
minor or petty: **n.** peccadillo; veniality
not capable of or liable to: (**see** "sinless"): **a.** impeccable
that which may be forgiven: **a.** venial

SINCERE: (**see** "innocent") **a.** artless; *bona fide;* candid; genuine; guileless; heartfelt; ingenuous; unaffected; unfeigned; wholehearted; **adv.** *ex animo;* **n.** SINCERITY: *bona fides; bonne foi;* candor; innocence; integrity; probity; veracity

SINFUL: (**see** "wicked") **a.** culpable; depraved; flagitious; heinous; iniquitous; nefarious; piacular; unregenerate(d); unrepentant
beings to obtain blessedness, doctrine: **n.** apocatastasis

SING: **v. or n.** descant

SINGER: **n.** cantor; chanteur; (**fem.** chanteuse); descanter
cabaret: **n.** chansonnier

SINGING, *at pleasure:* **adv.** *a capriccio*
coach: **n.** repititeur
florid: **n.pl.** melismatics; **n.** coloratura; obbligato
pert. to: **a.** canorous; cantabile; cantatory; melodious
suitable for: **a.** lyric; melic; melodic
the same old song: cantilenam enadem canis
w/o music: **adv.** *a capella*
w/o music and solo: **a.** monophonic; monophonous
w/o sound, as in moving lips (pretended): **n.** mussitation

SINGLE: **a.** azygous; celibate; discrete; individual; particular; separate; solitary; unique; unwedded
state of being: **n.** celibacy

SINGULAR: **see** "odd"; **n.** SINGULARITY: (**see** "peculiarity") haecceity; individuality; particularity; specificity

SINK *or swim: aut vincere aut mori*

SINLESS: (**see** "innocent") **a.** immaculate; impeccable; impeccant; inculpable; **n.** SINLESSNESS: immaculacy; impeccability; impeccancy

SINNING, *capable of:* **n.** peccability

SISTER (*or brother*), *pert. to:* **a.** or **n.** sibling
pert. to (sister only): **a.** sibling; sisterly; sororial

SITTING: **a.** sedent(ary); situated; **adv.** *in situ*

SITUATION: **n.** (con)juncture; predicament; locality; status
bad: (**see** "predicament") **n.** *mauvais pas*
perplexed or awkward: **n.** dilemma; plight; predicament; quandary; **a.** dilemmatic; predicamental

SIX-*fold:* **a.** sextuple
group of: **n.** hexad; **a.** hexadic; senary; sextuple
months, pert. to or occurring every: **a.** semestral; **n.** semester
-sided or angled figure: **n.** hexagon; **a.** hexagonal; sexagonal; sexangular
times as much or folded or duplicated 6 times: **a.** or **v.** sextuple
years, lasting, coming every, or 6-year event, etc.: **n.** or **a.** sex(t)ennial

SIXTY, *pert. to number:* **a.** sexagenary
years, being bet. 60 or 70 or pert. to such person or period: **n.** or **a.** sexagenarian

SIZE: **n.** amplitude; caliber; dimension; enormity; magnitude; volume
person or thing of great: **n.** gargantua; titan

SKELETON, *like:* **a.** cadaverous; skeletonic
organization: **n.** cadre; nucleus

SKEPTICAL: **a.** aporetic; *cum grano salis;* dissident; distrustful; dubious; dubitable; incredulous; negativistic; negatory; Pyrrhonian; Pyrrhonic; recusant; **n.** SKEPTIC: (**see** "disbeliever") agnostic; apikores (or apikoros); (**pl.** apikorsim); aporetic; giaor; latitudinarian; nullifidian; pyrrhonist; zetetic; **n.** SKEPTICISM: (**see** "doubt") agnosticism; dogmatism; dubiety; dubiosity; dubitation; incredulity; negativism; negativity; Pyrrhonism; skepsis

SKETCH: (**see** "outline") **n.** adumbration; *aperçu;* compendium; delineation; portrayal; **a.** SKETCHY: adumbral; diagrammatic(al); superficial
short literary: **n.** feuilleton; vignette

SKILL(S): (**see** "art") **n.** adeptness; adroitness; (ambi)dexterity; aptitude; artifice; competence; efficiency; expertise; expertness; hability; ingeniosity; ingenuity; inventiveness; *savoir-faire;* technique; virtuosity; **a.** SKILLED: **see** "expert"
expert or specialized: **n.** expertise; virtuosos; virtuosity
in part. occupation or field: **n.** armamentarium; expertise; repertoire; repertory; technique(s); virtuosity
special or mysterious surrounding a calling, etc.: **n.** mystique; virtuosity

SKILLFUL: **a.** accomplished; adept; adroit; (ambi)dextrous; consummate; daedalian; daedal(ic); facile; habile; ingenious; inventive; masterful; masterly; proficient; scient(al); subtle; versatile; **n.** SKILLFULNESS: **n.** accomplishment; adeptness; adroitness; consumma-

tion; dexterity; expertise; proficiency; virtuosity
feat: **n.** legerdemain; *passe-passe;* prestidigitation; *tour de force*
in statecraft: **a.** politic

SKIM: **v.** despumate

SKIN: **n.** cutis; epidermis; integument; pelage
bluish discoloration of: **n.** cyanosis; ecchymosis; purpura; **a.** cyanotic; ecchymotic; purpureal; purpureous
flabby: **n.** *cutis pendula*
having brown or blackish: **a.** melanous
having dark or swarthy: **a.** melanochrous
of animal (hairy) : **n.** pelage
pert. to: **a.** cutaneous; cuticular; (epi)-dermal; integumental
redness of: **n.** erythema; **a.** erythematic; erythemic; erythematous
shedding of: **n.** desquamation; ecdysis; exfoliation; exuviation; **v.** exuviate; molt
tenderness of: **n.** hyperalgesia; hyperesthesia; **a.** hyperalgesic; hyperesthesic
thick, having: **a.** pachydermatous; pachydermic; **n.** callosity; pachydermia
thin, having: **a.** leptodermous

SKINNY: **a.** cadaverous; malnourished; skeletonic; tabescent; **n.** SKINNINESS: **see** "malnutrition"

SKIRMISH: **n.** engagement; recontre; tilt; tournament; velitation

SKIRTING: **a.** circumferential; peripheral

SKULL, *openings or soft parts in infant's:* **n.** fontanel(le)
thick: **n.** pachycephalia; pachycephaly; **a.** pachycephalous

SKY: (**see** "atmosphere") **n.** empyrean; firmament; welkin
-blue: **a.** cerulean
of, from or being in the: **a.** celestial; empyreal; firmamental; supernal
open to the: **a.** alfresco; hypaethral; upaithric

SLACK *period, as in business:* **n.pl.** depression; doldrums; recession

SLACKER: **see** "shirker"; **n.** SLACK(ENING): abatement; detente; moderation; (re)laxation; retardation

SLACKNESS *toward duty:* **n.** laches; misfeasance

SLANDER: **v.** calumniate; defame; denigrate; derogate; disparage; malign; revile; traduce; vilify; vituperate; **n.** aspersion; calumniation; calumny; *coup de bec;* execration; libel; malediction; traducement; traduction

SLANDEROUS: **a.** calumnial; calumnious; defamatory; libelous; vilifying
report: **n.** calumniation; *chronique scandaleuse; fama clamosa*

SLANG: **n.** argot; cant; colloquialism; dialect; jargon; Koine; lingo; *lingua franca;* patois; vulgarism

SLAUGHTER, *great or wholesale:* **n.** aceldama; armageddon; hecatomb; holocaust

SLAUGHTERHOUSE: **n.** abattoir

SLAVE(S): (**see** "serf") **n.** mancipium; **n.** SLAVERY: helotism; helotry; peonage; servitude; subjection; thraldom; vassalage
female: **n.** odalisk; odalisque
recently freed: **n.pl.** *hesterni quirites*
willing and devoted: **n.** *âme damnée*

SLEEP: **n.** dormancy; hibernation; hypnosis; quiescence; repose; slumber; somnolence
abnormal or disordered: **n.** somnipathy
deity of: **n.** Hypnos; Morpheus; Somnus
drug or agent for: **n.** hypnotic; narcotic; opiate; soporific
during day: **n.** diurnation
inducing or causing: **a.** dormitive; hypnotic; lethargic; somnifacient; somniferous; somnorific; soporiferous; soporific; **n.** hypnotic; hypnotoxin; morpheus; narcotic; opiate; soporific
study of: **n.** hypnology
talker in: **n.** somniloquist
talking in, also words said: **n.** somniloquy
uncontrollable desire for: **n.** narcolepsy; **a.** narcoleptic
unnaturally deep: **n.** coma; sopor; stupor; **a.** comatose; soporous; stuporous
walker in: **n.** noctambulist; somnambule; somnambulist
walking in: **n.** noctambulation; somnambulation; **a.** noctambulistic; noctambulous; somnambulant; somnambulistic; somnambulous

SLEEPING: (**see** "asleep"): **a.** comatose; dormant; latent; quiescent; **a.** SLEEPLESS: insomnious; **n.** SLEEPLESSNESS: insomnia; insomnolence; insomnolency; **a.** SLEEPY: comatose; hypnotic; lethargic; phlegmatic; oscitant; somnolent; soporiferous; soporific

SLENDER: **a.** acicular; aciculate(d); gracile; lissome; lithe(some); *soigné(e)*; svelt(e); tenuous; **n.** SLENDERNESS: gracility; lissomness; lithesomness; tenuity

SLIGHT: **v.** disparage; disregard; disrespect; **n.** denigration; detraction; disparagement; **a.** cursory; imperceptible; inconsiderable; insignificant; nominal; paltry; superficial; trivial
importance or value, thing of: **n.** bagatelle; nihility; *peu de chose;* triviality; (**pl.** inconsequentia; trivia)
-of-hand: (**see** "magic") **n.** conjuration; escamotage; legerdemain; prestidigitation; manipulation; **n.** conjurer; conjuror; prestidigitator

SLIM: **see** "slender"

SLIMY: **a.** glutinous; offensive; mucilaginous; oleaginous; saponaceous; unctuous; viscid; viscous

SLIP: **see** "relapse"
of memory: **n.** *lapsus memoriae*
of the pen: **n.** *lapsus calami*
of the tongue: **n.** *lapsus linguae;* parapraxia

SLIPPERY: (**see** "slimy") **a.** elusive; lubricious; treacherous; unreliable; **n.** SLIPPERINESS: lubricity; unctuosity

SLOGAN: **n.** catchword; maxim; password; shibboleth; watchword

SLOPE: **n.** acclivity; declension; declination; declivity; gradient; inclination; **a.** SLOPING: acclivitous; declensional; declinatory; declivitous; oblique
downward: **n.** declivity; **a.** declivitous
of a mountain, or general of a country: **n.** inclination; versant
steep: **n.** perpendicularity; **a.** perpendicular; precipitous
upward: **n.** acclivity; **a.** acclivitous

SLOPPY: (**see** "slovenly") **a.** dishevel(l)ed; effusive; gushing; tatterdemalian; unkempt; **n.** SLOPPINESS: dishevelment

SLOTH: (**see** "inaction") **n.** acedia; adynamia; inertia; lassitude; lethargy; otiosity; slothfulness; sluggishness; supinity; torpidity

SLOVENLY: (**see** "sloppy" **and** "untidy") **a.** raunchy; slatternly; unkempt

SLOW: **v.** decelerate; slacken; **a.** (**see** "sluggish") apathetic; bovine; comatose; deliberate; dilatory; languescent; languid; languorous; lentago; lentissimo; lethargic; listless; lumbering; phlegmatic; tedious; torpid; unenergetic; unprogressive; **adv.** lentado; lentamente; lentissimo; **n.** SLOWNESS: (**see** "sloth") inertia; lassitude; lethargy; log(g)iness; retardation; tediosity; torpidity
cautiously: **n.** cunctation
in perceiving or understanding: **a.** purblind
moderately: **adv.** andante
(*plodding*): **a.** elephantine
very: **adv.** lentissimo
-witted: **a.** adenoid(al); cretinous; lumbering; moronic; stolid; **n.** moron; nincompoop

SLUGGISH: (**see** "slow") **a.** adynamic; apathetic; indolent; inert; languescent; languorous; lethargic; listless; slothful; stagnant; supine; tardigrade; torpid; **n.** SLUGGISHNESS: (**see** "slowness") inertia; lethargy; listlessness; log(g)iness; torpidity

SLUMP: **n.** depression; doldrum(s); repression

SLUR: (**see** "slander") **v.** asperse; denigrate; disparage; **n.** aspersion; calumny; defamation; denigration; disparagement; innuendo; insinuation; vilification
as omission of letter or vowel: **v.** elide; **n.** elision

SLY: (**see** "sneaky" **and** "stealthy") **a.** artful; cunning; diplomatic; duplicitous; furtive; guileful; hugger-mugger; ingenuous; insidious; roguish; *rusé(e)*; serpentine; sinuous; strategic; subtle; **adv.** *en tapinois*
on the: **see** "secretly"

SMALL: (**see** "little") **a.** diminutive; inappreciable; infinitesimal; insignificant;

lilliputian; microscopic; miniature; minikin; miniscular; miniscule; minute; petite; ultramicroscopic; **n.** SMALLNESS: (**see** "insignificance") infinitesimality; minitude; parvanimity; parvitude
amount or portion: **n.** modicum; moiety
as to space: **a.** hampering; incommodious
compared to expectation: **a.** subnominal; suboptional
in body: **a.** microsomatic; microsomatous
in viewpoint: **see** "narrow-minded"
indefinitely or insignificantly: **a.** atomic; inappreciable; infinitesimal; microscopic; **n.** infinitesimality
matter: **n.** nihility; *peu de chose*
-minded: **a.** liliputian; parvanimitous; **n.** parvanimity
number: **n.** dearth; paucity
quantity: **n.** iota
scale, on a: **a.** miniscular; miniscule; **adv.** *in petto*
very, or very small thing: **n.** lilliputian; miniscule; parvitude; **a.** atomic; infinitesimal; microscopic; miniscular; miniscule; minute; submicroscopic; ultramicroscopic

SMALLER *than required:* **a.** subminimal; suboptimal

SMART: (**see** "intelligent") **a.** adroit; astute; natty; *soigné(e)*; spruce; svelt(e)

SMELL: (**see** "scent") **n.** aroma; atmosphere; aura; bouquet; effluvium; (**pl.** effluvia); olfaction; osmesis; osphresis; redolence
absence or loss of: **n.** anosmia
having delicate sense of: **n.** hyperosmia; macrosmatic; nasute
offensive (**see** "stinking") **a.** mephitic; noisome; noxious; pestilential
perceiving by: **n.** olfaction; osmesis
pert. to sense of: **a.** olfactory; osphretic
stimulating to sense of: **a.** osmagogue

SMILE, *sardonic:* **n.** *risus sardonicus*
wearing or offered with a: **a.** subrident

SMILING: **a.** subrident; subrisive

SMOOTH: (**see** "easy") **v.** edulcorate; facilitate; palliate; polish; tranquilize; **a.** amiable; courteous; frictionless; glabrate; glabrescent; glabrous; levigate; oleaginous; saponaceous; unctuous; uninterrupted; velutinous; **adv.** *sans à coups;* **n.** SMOOTHNESS: lubricity; polish; saponaceousness; unctuosity
as in music: **a.** dolce; dolcissimo; legato
like marble: **a.** marmoreal; marmorean
-skinned: **a.** glabrous; leiodermatous
(*sweet-sounding*): **a.** mellifluent; mellifluous; mellisonant; melodic; sonorous
-talking: **a.** mellifluent; mellifluous; oleaginous; sonorous; unctuous

SMUG: **a.** bourgeoise; complacent; egocentric; pedantic; pretentious; priggish; self-inflated; self-satisfied; **n.** SMUGNESS: complacency; egocentricity; pedanticism; self-satisfaction

SNAKE(S): (**see** "reptile") **n.** groveling; ophidian; reptilian; serpent
in the grass: **n.** *anguis in herbâ*
like in form or motion: **a.** anguiform; anguinal; anguine(ous); ophidian; reptilian; serpentiform; serpentine; sinuous
poisonous: **n.pl.** thantophidia
study of: **n.** herpetology; ophiology; **n.** herpetologist; ophiologist
worship of or undue fondness for: **n.** ophiolatry

SNAP (*easy job*): **n.** sinecure; *un (bon) fromage*

SNARE: (**see** "trick") **n.** cajolement; enticement; inveiglement; pitfall

SNEAKY: (**see** "sly") **a.** cowardly; duplicitous; furtive; Janus-faced; ophidian; perfidious; reptilian; serpentine; sinuous; stealthy; treacherous; two-faced

SNEERING: **a.** cynical; derisive; ironical; sarcastic; sardonic; **n.** cynicism; derision; irony; sarcasm; sardonism

SNEEZE: **n.** sternutation; **a.** ptarmic(al), sternutative; sternutatory
something which causes: **n.** ptarmic

SNOB: **n.** arriviste; *nouveau riche;* parvenu; pedant; **n.** SNOBBERY (or SNOBBISHNESS) arrogance; *chichi;* hauteur; haughtiness; pedantry; **a.** SNOBBISH: *chichi;* haughty; pedantic

SNORE: **n.** rhonchus; stertor; **a.** rhonchial stertorous

SNOUT: **see** "nose"

SNOW, *pert. to or growing in or under:* **a.** nival; niveous
situated or occurring under: **a.** subnivean

SNOWY: **a.** niveous

SO-*called:* **a.** pretended; quasi; *soi-disant*
much the better: **adv.** *tant mieux*
much the worse: **adv.** *tant pis*

SOAKING, *soften by:* **v.** macerate; **n.** maceration

SOAP, *convert into:* **v.** saponify; **n.** saponification
resembling: **a.** saponaceous

SOBER: (**see** "calm") **a.** abstemious; abstentious; ascetic; continent; dispassionate; moderate; self-controlled; temperate; **n.** SOBERNESS: ascesis; asceticism; continence; temperance

SOCIABLE: **a.** affable; amadelphous; companionable; convivial; hospitable; gregarious; jovial: **n.** SOCIABILITY: affability; conviviality; cordiality; gregariousness; joviality; sociality

SOCIAL *circle or set:* **n.** clique; coterie
error or blunder: (**see** "impropriety") **n.** *faux pas; gaffe;* solecism
proprieties: **see** "proprieties"
propriety, strict observance of: **n.** correctitude; scrupulosity
register: **n.** *libro d'oro*
sympathy: **n.** philia
usage(s), etc.: **n.** *agrémens;* (**pl.** *agréments*); amenities; convenances; *savoir vivre;* (the) proprieties
person who prescribes rules or is authority on: **n.** *arbiter elegantiarum* (*or elegantiae*)
sanctioned by: **a.** conventional; **n.** conventionality

SOCIALIZATION, *process of:* **n.** acculturation; **a.** acculturational; acculturative

SOCIETY: (**see** "association") **n.** companionship; ethnos; monde; **a.** societal; sociogenic
betterment of by improving health conds., etc.: **n.** meliorism
dangerous to: **a.** pernicious; pestiferous; pestilent(ial)
fear of or aversion to: **n.** anthropophobia; apanthropia; apanthropy
high, fashionable or refined: **n.** *beau(x) monde(s); bon ton; haut monde; grand monde*
observance of usages of fashionable: **n.** *savoir vivre*
religious or charitable: **n.** confraternity; confraternization; **a.** eleemosynary
world of fashionable: **n.** *le beau monde; (le) monde*

SOCRATIC *method of questioning:* **n.** maieutics; Socraticism; Socratic induction; **a.** maieutic(al)

SOFT, *very (mus.)*: **a.** pianissimo

SOFTENING: **a.** emollient; emulsive; lenitive; mitigatory; **v.** SOFTEN: assuage; edulcorate; intenerate; palliate; macerate; mitigate; mollify
by soaking: **n.** maceration; **v.** macerate
or tending to soften: **a.** mollescent; **n.** mollescence

SOIL, *bound to, one who is:* **n.** *adscriptus glebae*
management: **n.** agronomics; agronomy; **n.** agronomist
of or arising fr. the: **a.** telluric; terrestrial
of or pert. to science of: **a.** pedologic(al)
pert. to or affected by: **a.** edaphic
son of the: **n.** *fillius terrae*
study of: **n.** *agrology;* pedology; **n.** agrologist

SOLDIERLY: **a.** heroic; martial; military

SOLEMN: (**see** "formal") **a.** awe-inspiring; ceremonial; ceremonious; dispassionate; funereal; imposing; impressive; memorable; momentous; ritualistic; sedate; sermonic; somber; **n.** SOLEMNITY: ceremony; reverence; sedateness

SOLICITOUS: (**see** "diligent") **a.** assiduous; **n.** assiduity; solicitude

SOLID: (**see** "compact") **a.** concentrated; massive; monolithic; ponderable; substantial; unanimous
process of making or state of being: **n.** calculus; concretion; concretization; gelation; solidification; **a.** concretionary

SOLITARY: (**see** "secluded") **a.** desolate; hermitic; individual; isolated; ivory-towered; reclusive; sequestered; solitudinarian

SOLO *voice w/o accompaniment:* **a.** monophonic; monophonous

SOLUTION: **n.** dénouement; explanation
artificial or strained, or out of ordinary: **n.** *deus ex machinâ*
capable of: **a.** resoluble; **n.** resolubility
to riddle or puzzle: **n.** *le mot de l'enigme*

SOMETIME: **a.** erstwhile; formerly; occasional; quondam

SOMEWHAT: **adv.** *un peu*

SON *or daughter:* **n.** or **a.** sibling
pert. to: **a.** filial; sibling

SONG(S): **n.** aria; arietta; canticle; canzona; canzone; chanson; descant; lyric; madrigal; melisma; rondo; roundelay
collection of: **n.** chansonnier; repertoire
cradle: **n.** berceuse
light and graceful: **n.** canzonet
-like: **a.** ariose; canorous; cantabile; lyric; melic
morning: **n.** aubade
of praise: **n.** anthem; canticle; doxology; hymn; magnificat; paen; *te deum*
pert. to: **a.** lyric; melic
sentimental: **n.** strephonade
swan: **n.** *chant du cygne*
w/ alternation of voices: **n.** antiphony; **a.** antiphonal; antiphonic
-writing: **n.** melopoeia; **a.** melopoe(t)ic

SONGFUL: **a.** lyric(al); melodic; **n.** lyricism

SOOT, *of or like:* **a.** fuliginous; **n.** fuliginosity

SOOTHING: (**see** "bland") **a.** anodynic; anodynous; anodyne; antiphlogistic; assuasive; calmative; conciliatory; conciliative; demulcent; dulcent; emollient; hesychastic; lenitive; mitigatory; nepenthean; palliative; placative; placatory; sedative; tranquilizing; **n.** assuagement; conciliation; lenity; placation; **v.** SOOTHE: (**see** "appease") allay; alleviate; assuage; conciliate; pacify; palliate; placate; mollify; reconcile; tranquilize
agent or drug to (soothe): **n.** antiphlogistic; balm of Gilead; calmative; demulcent; emollient; nepenthe; opiate; placebo; tranquilizer; unction

SOOTHSAYER: (**see** "prophet") **n.** auspex; Chaldean; diviner; haruspex; prognosticator; pythonist; **a.** divinatory; haruspical; prognosticative

SOP: (**see** "bribe") **n.** concession; placebo

SOPHISTICATED: **a.** alembicated; *blasé;* knowledg(e)able; knowing; precocious; subtle; world-weary

SORCERY: (**see** "magic") **n.** conjuration; diablerie; diabolism; enchantment; exorcism; incantation; necromancy; sortilege; thaumaturgy; theurgy; witchcraft; **n.** SORCERER: alchemist; conjurer; conjuror; haruspex; necromancer; sortileger; thaumaturge; thaumaturgist; warlock

SORE: **n.** affliction; lesion
bed-: **n.** decubitus (ulcer)
excretion(s) from: **n.** acatharsia; maturation; purulence; purulency; **a.** purulent
water discharge: **n.** ichor; serum

SORROW: **n.** commiseration; compassion; compunction; dolor; lamentation; penitence; remorse; sympathy; *tristesse;* **a.** SORROWFUL: (**see** "sad") commiserable; compassionate; contrite; *désolé;* doleful; dolent(e); dolentissimo; doloroso; dolorous; lamentable; lamented; mournful; penitent; pitiable; plaintive; rueful
causing: **a.** luctiferous
forgetfulness of, drug or agent for: **n.** euphoriant; nepenthe; **a.** euphoric; nepenthean

SORRY: **a.** contemptible; contrite; despicable; insignificant; lamentable; mournful; paltry; penitent; regretful
not: **a.** impenitent

SORT: **v.** alphabetize; arrange; catalogue; categorize; classify; collate; collocate; compartmentalize; concinnate; dispose; distribute; orchestrate; segregate; systematize; tabulate; **n.** character; disposition; quality

SO-SO: **a.** intermediate; mediocre; middling; passable; tolerable; **adv.** *comme ci comme ça; couci-couci;* tolerable; **n.** mediocrity

SOUL(S): **n.** pneuma; psyche; quint(essence)
divine: **n.** *anima divina*
of the world: **n.** *anima mundi*
one who denies that exists in space: **n.** nullibist; nullifidian
the brute: **n.** *anima bruta*
transmigration of, theory: **n.** metempsychosis; reincarnation; transmigration
world of the: **n.** pneuma

SOUND(S), *confusion of:* (see "confusion") **n.** Babelism; Babelization; **v.** Babelize
harsh or discordant: **n.** cacophony; discordance; dissonance; **a.** cacophonic; cacophonous; discordant; disharmonious; dissonant; immelodious; ineuphonious; strident; unharmonious
loud and piercing: **a.** calliopean
mania for repeating: **n.** echolalia; onomatomania; verbigeration
mind in sound body: mens sana in corpore sano
mind, not of: **a.** incompetent; *non compos (mentis)*
mind, of: **a.** competent; *compos mentis*
morbid fear of: **n.** phonophobia
multiplication of, as echo: **n.** polyphony; reverberation; **a.** echoic; polyphonic; polyphonous
outburst of: **n.** diapason
pert. to: **a.** acoustic; phonetic; sonant; sonic; **n.** phonology; sonics
pert. to single or single sound path: **a.** monophonic; monophonous
producing: **a.** articulate; phonetic; sonant; soniferous; sonorant; sonorous; **n.** articulation; sonification
ringing or jingling as of bells: **n.** tintinnabulation; **a.** tintinnabular(y)
sameness of: **n.** homophony; monotony; **a.** homophonic; homophonous; monotonous; unisonous
science of: **n.** acoustics; phonetics; phonology; sonics
seeming to come fr. elsewhere: **a.** ventriloquistic; ventrilquous
similarity of: **n.** assonance; homeophony; **a.** homeophonic; homeophonous
word derived fr.: **n.** echoic (word); onomatope; onomatopoeia; **a.** echoic; onomatopoeic

SOUNDNESS: **n.** integrality; integrity; levelheadedness; solidarity; solidity; solvency

SOUR: **v.** acidify; ferment; **a.** (see "acid") acerb(ic); acetose; acidulent; acidulous; cynical; embittered; infestive; mirthless; querulous; vinegary; **n.** SOURNESS: acerbity; acidification; infestivity; mirthlessness
-tempered: **a.** acidulent; acidulous; austere; morose

SOURCE(S): (see "origin") **n.** bibliography; derivation; etiology; fountain(head); genesis; incipience; provenance; provenience; wellspring
and origin: **n.** *fons et origo*
consisting of a: **a.** seminal
from another: **a.** or **adv.** *aliunde*
having many, or more than one: **a.** polygenetic; polyphyletic
of information: **n.** bibliography

SOUTHERN (or SOUTHERLY): **a.** austral; meridional; **n.** meridionality

SOUVENIR: **n.** bibelot; keepsake; memento; recollection; remembrance

SOVEREIGNTY: **n.** authority; autonomy; dominion; empery; independence; jurisdiction
emblems, insignia or prerogatives of: **n.** regalia; regality
joint: **n.** condominium

SPACE: **n.** capacity; expanse; firmament; hiatus; interstice; interval; lacuna; **a.** SPATIAL: hiatal; spacial
filled with matter: **n.** plenum; **a.** gravid; plenum
for life, growth, activity, etc.: **n.** lebensraum
lacking: **a.** incapacious
navigation: **n.** astrogation
pert. to, happening or existing in: **a.** hiatal; lacunal; lacunar; spacial; spatial
state of being located in, or of being spatial: **n.** spatiality; ubiety
vacant: **n.** vacuum

SPACIOUS: **a.** barcnial; capacious; cavernous; commodious; comprehensive; copious; expansive; scopious; voluminous

SPANGLED: **a.** caparisoned; clinquant

SPARK (or SPARKLE): **v.** coruscate; scintillate; **n.** coruscation; scintilla(tion); **a.** rutilant; scintillesce(nt)

SPASM: **n.** agitation; clonicity; clonus; convulsion; orgasm; paroxysm; seizure; tetany; throe; tonus; **a.** SPASMODIC(AL): clonic; convulsive; intermittent; paroxysmal; spasmatic; spastic

SPEAK: (**see** "talk") **v.** articulate; converse; enunciate; intonate; labialize; phonate; pronounce; utter; verbalize; vocalize; **n. see** "speech"
at length: (**see** "wordliness") **v.** harangue; perorate
disinclined to: (**see** "reserved") **a.** incommunicative; inconversable; laconic; obmutescent; retentive; reticent; taciturn
emphatically: **a.** lexical; **n.** lexicality
extravagantly: **v.** rhapsodize
indistinctly or disconnected: **v.** maunder
in flowing or rhetorical lang.: **v.** (per)orate; rhapsodize; **n.** (per)oration
in short syllables: **a.** brachysyllabic; monosyllabic; telegraphic
unable to: (**see** "muteness") **a.** aphonetic; aphonic; inarticulate

SPEAKER: (**see** "orator") **n.** annunciator; chairman; collucator; *conférencier;* conversationalist
elegant: **n.** rhetorician

SPEAKING: (**see** "speech") **n.** articulation; enunciation; phonation; vocalization
at length: **see** "wordiness"
indirect or roundabout: **n.** circumambage(s); circumlocution; periphrasis; **a.** circuitous; circumlocutory; periphrastic
mania for: **n.** *furor loquendi*
pert. to: **a.** elocutionary; enunciative; exophasic; phonetic; vocal
public, pert. to: **a.** demegoric; oratori(c)al; **n.** elocution
thru closed or partly-closed teeth: **n.** dentiloquy
thru nose: **v.** nasalize; **n.** nasality
to self (inaudible): **n.** endophasia
unbounded, fondness for: **n.** *studium immane loquendi*
way of: **n.** *façon de parler*
with heavy stress: **a.** labial; lexical

SPECIALIZED *skill:* **n.** expertise; technique; virtuosity

SPECIALTY: **n.** forte; *métier;* particularity

SPECIFIC: **a.** categorical; definitive; determinative; explicit; express; peculiar; specificative; unequivocal
purpose, for a: **adv.** *ad hoc; pro tempore*
quality or state of being: **n.** specificality; specification; specificity

SPECIOUS *reasoning:* **n.** casuistry; sophism; sophistry; speciosity; syllogism; **a.** casuistical; sophistical; syllogistic(al)

SPECTACLE: **n.** drama; exhibition; extravaganza; pageant(ry); spectacular

SPECULATE: **v.** conjecture; hypothesize; philosophize; surmise; theorize; **n.** SPECULATION: conjecture; hypothesis; surmise; theoretics
in psychological terms or ideas: **v.** psychologize

SPEECH: (**see** "language," "speaking," and "talk") **n.** allocution; articulation; colloquy; confabulation; conversation; declamation; dialogue; diction; discourse; disquisition; (e)locution; enunciation; exophasia; glottology; harangue; linguistics; oration; parlance; peroration; phonation; phraseology; pronunciation; recitation; recitative; vocalization
artificial, affected or excessive eloquence of: **n.** bombast; euphuism; grandiloquence; **a.** bombastic; declamatory; euphuistic(al); rhetorical; rubescent
authoritative: **n.** allocution; (ex)hortation; **a.** (ex)hortative; (ex)hortatory
boastful: **n.** kompology; rodomontade
brevity of: **see under** "brevity"
common or informal: (**see under** "language") **n.** colloquialism; patois; vernacular; vulgate
conciseness of: (**see under** "brevity") **n.** brachylogy; syllabification
defects, pert. to: **a.** phoniatric
disordered: **n.** idoglossia; idiolalia; lalopathy; pararthria
eloquent: **see** "grandiose" **below**
empty, stilted, etc.: **n.** balderdash; flatulence; gasconade; kompology
exactness in: **n.** incisiveness; syllabification
figure of: **n.** apostrophe; hyperbole; metaphor; metonymy; litotes; simile; synecdoche; tralatition; trope; **a.** synecdochic(al); tropological
use of: **n.** tropology; **a.** tropological
flowery or rhetorical: **n.** peroration; **v.** perorate
fluency of: **n.** *copia verborum;* eloquence; facundity; grandiloquence; loquaciousness; loquacity; mellifluence

fondness for: **n.** *stadium immane loquendi*
foolish: **see under** "language"
grandiose: (**see** "bombast") **n.** grandiloquence; magniloquence; rubescence; **a.** grandiloquent; magniloquent; mercurial; rubescent
high-flown or pompous: (**see** "bombast") **n.** altiloquence; grandiloquence; grandiosity; kompology; pomposity; **a.** altiloquent; grandiloquent; pompous
honeyed: **a.** mellifluent; mellifluous; mellisonant
illiterate or substandard: **n.** Choctaw; vulgate; **a.** grammarless
imitative: **n.** onomatopoea; **a.** echoic; mimetic; onomatopoe(t)ic
indirect or roundabout: **see under** "speaking"
internal or inaudible (to self): **n.** endophasia
lightness or gaiety of: **n.** levity
local or individual: **n.** colloquialism; patois; provincialism; vernacular; villagism; **a.** colloquial; idiomatic; vernacular
long, monopolizing conversations: **n.** monologue
long, w/ little sense: **n.** macrology; pleonasm; **a.** pleonastic
loss of power of: **n.** aphonia; obmutescence; **a.** aphonic; obmutescent
mania for: **n.** *furor loquendi*
nonsense: (**see** "foolish" **under** "language") **n.** Choctaw; gibberish; jabberwock(y); jargon
pause in: **n.** hiatus
pert. to: **a.** glottologic(al); linguistic; lingual; phonetic
rambling: **a.** peripatetic
rustic: **n.** ruralism; rusticism; **a.** ruralistic
solo: **n.** monologue; soliloquy
specialist in: **n.** glottologist; linguist; phoneticist
study of: **n.** glottology; linguistics; phonetics; phonology
substandard, use of: **see under** "language"
that puts one asleep: **n.** *discours assoupissant*
thru body motions, signs, etc.: **n.pl.** kinesics; **n.** *lingua franca;* **a.** *kinesic*
to self: **n.** endophasia; soliloquy
uncontrolled in: **a.** rampageous; rampant; **n.** *furor loquendi;* onomatomania; verbomania
unintelligible: **see** "jargon"
uttered or vocalized: **n.** *exophasia*
vocalized: **n.** exophasia; **a.** exophasic
warning or advisory w/ authority: **n.** allocution
windiness or emptiness of: (**see** "empty" **above**): **n.** bombast; flatulence

SPEED (or SPEEDINESS): (**see** "haste") **n.** acceleration; alacrity; *aussitôt dit, aussitôt fait;* celerity; deftness; dispatch; expedition; promptitude; velocity; **a.** SPEEDY: (**see** "fast") adept; alacritous; celeritous; expeditious; expeditive; posthaste; velocious
at full or breakneck: **adv.** *à corps perdu; à toute allure;* Gaderine; precipitous
reduce: **v.** decelerate; **n.** deceleration

SPELL, *magic:* (**see** "charm") **n.** conjuration; enchantment; evocation; incantation

SPELLING *correct or as subject or style or way of:* **n.** orthography
diff. from current way: **n.** heterography
in letters or characters of another lang.: **n.** metagraphy; transliteration; **v.** transliterate; **a.** transliterative

SPHERE: **n.** domain; dominion; jurisdiction; *métier;* milieu; province; purview; spheroid; theater; **a.** SPHERICAL: cylindrical; discoid; globate; globose; globular; orbicular; (o)rotund; spheriform; spheroidal; spheroidical
form of: **n.** sphericity; spheroidicity; **a.** spheroidal

SPIKED: **a.** spicate; spicigerous

SPINE: **n.** acantha; chine; rachis; spicule; spinosity; vertebra
near or beside the: **a.** juxtaspinal; paraspinal
pert. to: **a.** spondylic; vertebral

SPINELESS: (**see** "spiritless") **a.** invertebrate; **n.** invertebracy

SPINY (or SPINOUS): (**see** "prickly") **a.** acanthaceous; acanthological; acanthous; acicular; aciculate(d); spicose; spicular; spiculate; spiculiferous; spiculose; spinose

SPIRAL: (**see** "coiled") **a.** cochleate; (con)voluted; helical; helicoid(al); volute; whorled; **n.** convolution; helix; spirality; volute

SPIRIT(S): **(see** "ghost" **and** "soul") **n.** animus; ardor; *brio;* character; courage; *élan; esprit; esprit de corps;* mettle; nous; phantasm(ata); pneuma; vigor; vivacity; (pl. lemures)
evil: **n.** cacod(a)emon
guiding: **n.** muse; numen
high: **n.** animation; ebullience; enthusiasm; euphoria; exhilaration; exuberance; intoxication; invigoration; optimism; **a.** ebullient; euphoric; exuberant; flamboyant; heady; intoxicated
low in: **(see** "sad") **a.** vaporish; **n.pl.** doldrums; megrims
of a place or locality: **n.** *genius loci*
of natural objects(s) or phenomena, belief: **n.** numen
of the time: **n.** zeitgeist
presiding: **n.** numen
with: **(see** "spirited") **adv.** *con spirito*
world of the: **n.** pneuma

SPIRITED: **(see** "brisk") **a.** animated; assiduous; energetic; enterprising; forceful; mettlesome; spiritful; vigorous; vivacious; zealous; zestful; **adv.** *avec ardeur; con anima; con brio; con spirito;* **n.** SPIRITEDNESS: **see** "briskness"

SPIRITLESS: **a.** adenoid(al); amort; apathetic; arenaceous; dejected; depressed; desiccated; dispirited; exanimate; feckless; inanimate; invertebrate; lackadaisical; lackluster; languescent; languorous; lethargic; listless; pusillanimous; unenthusiastic

SPIRITUAL: **a.** angelic; celestial; ethereal; incorporeal; intellectual; psychic(al); religious; supermundane; supernatural; supersensible; supersensory; supersensual; **n.** SPIRITUALITY: ethereality; incorporeality; incorporeity; interiority
ideals, pert. to: **a.** anagogic(al)
make: **v.** apotheosize; canonize; celestialize; deify; etherealize; spiritualize; **n.** apotheosis; deification; spiritualization
rapture, state of: **n.** raptus
torpor or apathy: **n.** acedia

SPITE, *out of:* **adv.** *par dépit*

SPITEFUL: **(see** "abusive") **a.** dispiteous; malevolent; malicious; malignant; rancorous; splenetic(al); venomous; vindicative; **n.** SPITEFULNESS: malevolence; maliciousness; malignancy; venom; venosity

SPLENDID: **a.** aurelian; bravissimo; effulgent; gorgeous; lustrous; magnificent; opulent; refulgent; splendaceous; splendacious; splendiferous; sublime; sumptuous; superb; **n.** SPLENDOR: *éclat;* effulgence; luster; magnificence; pomp; sublimity; sumptuosity; sumptuousness

SPLIT: **a.** bifid; bifurcate(d); bipartite; bipartisan; bisected; cleft; cloven; dichotomous; dimidate; schismatic(al); **n.** bifurcation; cleavage; divarication; dichotomy; dissidence; disunion; diversity; fission; fracture; **adv.** *à cheval*
(burst open): **v.** dehise; **n.** dehiscence; **a.** dehiscent
on issues: **adv.** *à cheval*
-personality: **n.** schizophrenia; **a.** schizophrenic; **n.** schizoid; schizophrene; schizophreni(a)c

SPOIL: **v.** corrupt: defile; pervert; putrefy; putresce; vitiate; **n.** pillage
not subject to (spoiling): **a.** imputrescible

SPOKEN: **see** "oral"
word cannot be recalled: nescit vox missa reverti

SPOKESMAN: **n.** advocate; chairman; hierophant; prolocutor; protagonist

SPONGING: **a.** parasitic(al); predatory; sycophantic; **n.** commensalism; parasitism; predation; symbiont; symbiosis

SPONSORSHIP: **(see** "protection") **n.** (a)egis; auspice(s); guardianship; patronage; protectorship; tutelage

SPONTANEOUS: **(see** "natural" **and** "off-hand") **a.** automatic; impulsive; indigenous; unpremeditated; **n.** impulsivity; spontaneity
generation: **n.** abiogenesis; autogenesis; **a.** abiogenetic(al)
not: **(see** "artificial") **a.** factitious
origin, of: **a.** idiogenetic; idiopathic; **n.** idiogenesis
state of being: **n.** automaticity; automatism; impusivity; spontaneitv

SPORT: **n.** *bon vivant;* diversion; divertissement; mutation; recreation; **a.** divertive; recreational; sportful; sportive

SPOT: **n.** macula(tion) macule; stigma

SPOTLESS: (**see** "clean") **a.** blameless; immaculate; irreproachable; unblemished; unsullied; untarnished

SPOTTED: **a.** maculate; macular; maculose; mottled; piebald; punctate(d); puncticular; punctiform; sullied; tarnished; variegated; **n.** maculation; puncticulation; variegation
like a leopard: **a.** pardine

SPRAY: **v.** atomize; nebulize

SPREAD: (**see** "radiate" **and** "scatter") **v.** circulate; diffuse; dilate; disperse; disseminate; diversify; (inter)penetrate; (ir)radiate; proliferate; promulgate; propagate; publish
out or branch: **v.** decentralize; divaricate; **n.** decentralization; divarication; proliferation; ramification

SPREADING: **a.** expanded; patulous; serpiginous; **n.** circulation; diaspora; diffusion; dispersion; dissemination; diversification; diversity; irradiation; proliferation; promulgation; propagation
in all directions: **a.** radial; radiating
(*standing open*): **a.** patulous; **n.** patulousness

SPREE: **n.** bacchanal; bender; brannigan; orgy

SPRIGHTLY: (**see** "gay") **a.** animated; balletic; blithe(ful); effervescent; exuberant; frolicsome; jaunty; perky; roguish; spirited; sportive; vivacious; zestful; **n.** SPRIGHTLINESS: (**see** "gaiety") *allégresse;* buoyancy; exuberance; lightheartedness; vivacity; zest

SPRING(TIME): **n.** *le printemps;* primavera; **a.** primaveral; vernal
beginning of: **n.** vernal equinox

SPROUT: **v.** burgeon; germinate; pullulate; **a.** burgeoning; pullulant; **n.** burgeoning; pullulation

SPRUCE: *up:* **v.** tit(t)ivate; **n.** tit(t)ivation

SPUR: (**see** "stimulus") **n.** calcar; calcarium; **v.** see "stimulate"

SPURIOUS: (**see** "counterfeit") **a.** adulterine; apocryphal; inauthentic; meretricious; pinchback; specious
argument: **n.** casuistry; philosophism; pilpul; sophism; sophistry; speciosity; **a.** casuistic; sophistical; specious
as of writing(s): **n.pl.** apocrypha; pseudepigrapha; **a.** apocryphal; pseudepigraphic(al); pseudepigraphous

SQUABBLE: **see** "controversy"

SQUALID: **a.** contemptible; feculent; ordurous; scabrous; sordid; **n.** scabrousness; squalidity

SQUEAKY: **a.** strident; stridulate; stridulous

SQUEAMISH: (**see** "prissy" **a.** fastidious; hypercritical; nauseated; sanctimonious; scrupulous

SQUINT: **n.** esotropia; exotropia; *louchement;* strabismus; **a.** SQUINTING: louche; strabismic

STAB: **v.** impale; lancinate

STABILITY: **n.** constancy; equilibrium; permanence; permanency; *status quo;* steadfastness; steadiness; **a.** STABLE: (**see** "steady") immutable; inexpungable; irreversible; irrevocable
internal, social or psychological (*or tending to maintain*): **n.** homeostasis

STAFF *officers:* **n.** cadre

STAGE, *front part of:* **n.** proscenium
manager: **n.** impresario; regisseur
setting: **n.** *mise-en-scène*
trick: **n.** *jeu de theâtre;* legerdemain; prestidigitation; *tour de force*

STAGED: (**see** "showy") **a.** contrived; histrionic; manipulated; (melo)dramatic; operated; theatric(al); **n.** STAGINESS: (**see** "showiness") melodrama; sardoodledom; theatricality
situation or effect(s): **n.** acrobatics; cabotinage; *deus ex machinâ;* histrionics; histrionism; melodramatics; sardoodledom; theatricality; theatrics

STAGGER: **v.** titubate; welter; **n.** titubation; **a.** titubant

STAGNATION: **n.** quiescence; sluggishness; stasis; torpidity; torpor

STAGY: **see** "showy"

STAIN: **n.** *bar sinister;* macula(tion); stigma; tarnish
without: **adv.** *sans tache;* **a.** immaculate; virtuous

STALE: (**see** "dull") **a.** banal; commonplace; hackneyed; jejune; stereotyped; threadbare; trite; vapid; **n.** banality; jejunity; vapidity
become by lapse of time: **v.** obsolesce; superannuate; **n.** obsolescence; superannuation

STAMP *collecting or collector:* **n.** philately; **n.** philatelist; **a.** philatelic

STAND *by decided cases:* **n.** precedent; *res adjudicata; stare decisis*

STANDARD(S): **n.** *beau idéal;* canon; criterion; (**pl** criteria); emblem; gauge; gonfalon; modality; touchstone; yardstick; **a.** (**see** "uniform") classic; emblematic; prime; recognized; typical
accepted: **n.pl.** canons of propriety; civilities; convenances; conventions; criteria; (the) amenities; (the) proprieties
below normal: **a.** raunchy; subnormal; suboptimal
conforming to: (**see** "proper") **a.** canonical; consuetudinary; conventional; *de rigueur; en règle;* ethical; exemplary; orthodox; sanctioned; traditional
for distinguishing: **n.** criterion; (**pl.** criteria); differentia(e); differentiation
not conforming to: **see** "improper"

STANDARDIZE: **v.** calibrate; gauge; **n.** calibration

STANDING: (**see** "status") **n.** antecedence; perpendicular; precedence; prestige; statant; stature; status; vertical

STAR(S): **n.** asterisk; *étoile;* luminary; pentacle; **a.** STARRY: (**see** "visionary") astral; sidereal; stellar; stellate
as symbol of Judaism: **n.** Magen (or Morgen) David; Shield of David; Star of David
covered w/ or resembling: **a.** stellar; stellate; stelliform
group or patch of: **n.** asterism; constellation; galaxy; nebula; **a.** asterismal; constellational; constellatory
having: **a.** astiferous
one fond of (star) lore: **n.** astrophile
pert. to or like: **a.** asterial; astral; stellar; stellate; stelliform
set among or turn into: **v.** stellify; **n.** instellation: stellification
study of: **n.** astronomy; uranology
to the, thru difficulties: ad astra per aspera
worship of: **n.** astrolatry

STARCHY: **a.** amyloid; farinaceous

STARLINGS, *flock of:* **n.** murmuration

START: **see** "begin"

STARTING *point:* **n.** commencement; *terminus (ad quem)*

STARTLING: **a.** awe-inspiring; bizarre; electrifying; galvanic

STATE: **n.** body politic; civitas; commonalty; commonweal(th); dilemma; plight; posture; predicament; situation; status; (the) *res publica*
economic planning and control: **n.** *dirigisme*
highly centralized, advocacy of: **n.** statolatry
lack of planning and control by: **n.** *laissez faire;* laissez-faireism
secrets: **n.pl.** *arcana imperli*
worship of the: **n.** *statolatry*

STATELY: (**see** "dignified") **a.** august; baronial; ceremonious; courtly; eminent; haughty; imposing; magnificent; majestic; marmoreal; palatial; pompous; Praxitelean; regal; sculpturesque; statuesque; togated; unapproachable
esp. if exaggerated: **a.** pompous; pontifical; portentous
female, pert. to: **a.** Junoesque

STATEMENT: **n.** allegation; assertion; asseveration; constantation; declaration; dictum; presentation; profession; recital; recitation; verbality; **a.** assertative; assertoric; assertorial
dogmatic, or w/o confirmation: **n.** dixit
gratuitous: **n.** *gratis dictum; obiter dictum*
positive: **n.** asseveration; **v.** asseverate; aver

STATESMAN: **n.** *homme d'état*

STATUE, *like:* **a.** Junoesque; marmoreal; Praxitelean; sculpturesque; statuesque

STATUS: **n.** posture; prestige; recognition; situation; standing; stature
high: **n.** cachet; eminence; prestige; **a.** eminent; illustrious; prestigious
inferior in: **a.** subalternate
lowering of: **v.** denigrate; minimize; pejorate; plebify; vulgarize; **n.** declension; degradation; demotion; denigration; pejoration; plebification; vulgarization; **a.** *déclassé;* declensional; declinatory; denigratory; pejorative

STEADY (or STEADFAST): (**see** "constant," "cool" and "firm") **a.** continual; dependable; disciplined; equable; immutable; incessant; irreversible; irrevocable; persistent; reliable; resolute; undeviating; unfaltering; unflinching; unhesitating; uninterrupted; unremittant; unremitting; **n.** **see** "stability"
(*stable*): **a.** equable; stabile; **v.** stabilize; **n.** equability; equanimity; stability

STEAL: **v.** abstract; burglarize; defalcate; embezzle; extort; extract; filch; misapply; misappropriate; peculate; pilfer; purloin; **n.** STEALING: abstraction; defalcation; embezzlement; extraction; larceny; misappropriation; peculation; **a.** burglarious; larcenous; thieving; thievish
abnormal impulse to: **n.** kleptomania; **n.** kleptomaniac; **a.** kleptomaniac(al)
lit. work, etc.: **v.** plagiarize; **n.** piracy; plagiarism; **a** plagiaristic; **n.** plagiarist
one who (steals): **n.** burglar; defalcator; embezzler; larcenist; peculator

STEALTHY: **a.** cabalistic; clandestine; duplicitous; furtive; Machiavellian; secretive; serpentine; sinuous; surreptitious; **adv.** *à la dérobée; en tapinois*

STEEP: **a.** acclivitous; arduous; declivitous; exorbitant; perpendicular; precipitous

STEMLESS: **a.** acaulescent; acauline; **n.** acaulescence

STENCH: (**see** "stink") **n.** mephitis; **a.** malodorous; mephitic; noisome; noxious

STEP(S): **n.** *démarche;* echelon; maneuver; plateau
by: **adv.** *per gradus*
first: **n.** *le premier pas*
w/o intermediary (by single bound): **adv.** or **a.** *per saltum*

STERN: (**see** "severe" **and** "strict") **a.** (a)stringent; austere; exacting; inexorable; inflexible; inhospitable; resolute; rigorous; scrupulous; uncompromising; uninviting

STEW: **n.** olla podrida; potpourri; ragout

STICK: **v.** (ag)glutinate; adhere; cohere; conglutinate; **n.** agglutination; conglutination; **n.** STICKINESS: glutinosity; tenacity; viscosity; **a.** STICKING (or STICKY) adherent; adherescent; adhesive; agglutinant; glutinous; mucilaginous; tenacious; viscid; viscous; **n.** adherence; agglutination; conglutination

"STICKS" (*back country*): **n.** hinterland; **n.** or **a.** up-country

STICK-TO-ITIVENESS: **n.** importunity; perseverance; pertinacity; steadfastness; tenacity

STIFF: **see** "inflexible"

STIFFENED, *as a joint:* **a.** ankylosed; ankylotic; **n.** ankylosis

STIGMA: (**see** "disgrace") **n.** *bar sinister*

STILL: **a.** dormant; halcyon; immobile; impassive; inactive; inarticulate; inoperative; obmutescent; quiescent; silentious; stationary; tranquil; unperturbed; **n.** STILLNESS: immobility; lifelessness; quiescence; quietude; serenity; tranquility
standing (still): **a.** languishing; **v.** languish; **n.** languishment

STIMULATION: (**see** "incentive" **and** "incitement") **n.** piquancy; provocation; refreshment; (re)invigoration; stimulant; titillation; tit(t)ivation; **v.** STIMULATE: animate; foment; incite; innervate; inspirit; instigate; provoke; titillate; tit(t)ivate; **a.** STIMULATING (or STIMULATIVE): (**see** "brisk") accelerative; animating; aspirational; catalytic; galvanic; heartening; incisive; inspirational; inspiriting; piquant; poignant; promptive; provocative; psychogogic; pungent; stimulogenous; titillating; tit(t)ivating
developing as a consequence of: **a.** stimulatory; stimulogenous

STIMULATOR: **n.** accelerant; accentuator; agitator; catalyst; catalytic; flagellant;

gadfly; incendiary; precipitator; propulsor; synergist

STIMULUS: **n.** catalyst; catalytic; fillip; incendiary; incentive; provocation

STINGING: **a.** acrimonious; caustic; incisive; mordant; penetrating; piquant; poignant

STINGY: **a.** avaricious; cheeseparing; curmudgeonly; extortionate; miserly; niggardly; parsimonious; penny-pinching; penurious; tight-fisted; ungenerous; **n.** STINGINESS: avarice; parsimony; penury

STINK: **n.** effluvium; (**pl.** effluvia); fetor; mephitis; nidor; putridity; stench; **a.** STINKING: effluvial; fetid; fulsome; graveolent; malodorant; malodorous; mephitic; nidorous; noisome; (ob)noxious; pestilent(ial); putrid; undeodorized

STIR: **see** "incite" **and** "stimulate"

STOCK, *single ancestral, of or developed fr.:* **a.** monophyletic

STOIC(AL): **a.** dispassionate; impassive; imperturbable; indifferent; philosophic(al); phlegmatic; resolute; spartanic; stolid; undemonstrative; Zenonian

STOLID: (**see** "stubborn") **a.** anserine; asinine; bovine; brutish; **n.** STOLIDITY: asininity; bovinity; impassiveness; imperturbation; indifference; phlegm

STOOP-SHOULDERED: **a.** gibbose; gibbous; kyphotic; **n.** gibbosity; gibbousness; kyphosis

STONE(S), *consisting of or pert. to one:* **a.** monolithic

leave no (stone) unturned: omnem movere lapidem

pelt w/ or kill by: **v.** lapidate; **n.** lapidation

precious, cutter or polisher of: **n.** lapidarist

precious, pert. to: **a.** lapidary

rel. to: **a.** lapideous; lithic; petrous

rolling gathers no moss: saxum volutum non obducitur musco

turn into: **v.** calcify; lapidify; lithify; petrify; **n.** calcification; lapidification; petrification; **a.** petrescent; petrefactive

STOP: (**see** "discontinue") **v.** arrest; cease; checkmate; circumvent; thwart; **n.** STOPPAGE: armistice; cessation; obstruction; obturation; oppilation; stasis

cause to: **v.** arrest; surcease

for a time: **v.** intermit; **n.** armistice; hiatus; intermission

up: **v.** obstruct; occlude; oppilate; **n.** obturation; occlusion; oppilation

STOPPING: **a.** cessative; oppilative; **n.** arrestation; arrestment; quiescence

in middle of sentence: **n.** abscission

STORAGE *place:* **n.** ambry; argosy; arsenal; cache; depository; entrepot; larder; magazine; repertorium; repertory; repository; storehouse

STORE: **v.** accumulate; cache; secrete; **n.** accumulation; budget; repertoire; repository

up: **v.** thesaurize; **n.** thesaurization

STOREHOUSE: **see** "storage place"

STORK, *pert. to the:* **a.** pelargic

STORM: **v.** besiege; bombard; fulminate; **n.** agitation; disturbance; monsoon; tempest; turbulence; vortex; **a.** STORMY: cyclonic; fulminous; inclement; passionate; procellous; tempestical; tempestuous; turbulent; **n.** STORMINESS: inclemency; tempestivity; tempestuousness; turbulence; turbulency

STORY: **n.** anecdote; chronicle; epic; falsehood; lexicon; narration; narrative; romance; saga

add fictitious details to: **v.** confabulate; embellish; fantasticate; **n.** confabulation; embellishment

continued, or in installments: **n.** feuilleton

doleful: **n.** jeremiad; lamentation

false and scandalous, as in politics: **n.** canard; roorback

long: **n.** epic (*poem*); heroic (*poem*); iliad

of house, chief: **n.** *bel étage*

old: **n.** *crambe repetita*

scandalous: **n.** *chronique scandaleuse;* roorback

several in one: **n.** polymythy

teller of (stories): **n.** narrator; (ra)-conteur; (**fem.** (re)conteuse)

STOUT: (**see** "obese") **a.** corpulent; courageous; forceful; hearty; implacable;

liparous; lusty; orbicular; plentitudinous; plethoric; portly; powerful; pursy; replete; resolute; robust; rotund; valiant; vigorous; **n.** STOUTNESS: corpulence; embonpoint; firmness; fortitude; plethora; ponderosity; portliness; pursiness; robusticity

STRADDLE (or STRADDLING), *as line or issue:* **adv.** *à cheval*

STRAIGHT: (**see** "straightforward): **a.** direct; undiluted; uninterrupted; unmixed; unmodified; perpendicular; vertical; **n.** perpendicularity; verticality

STRAIGHT LINE, *bring into:* **v.** collimate; **n.** collimation
lying in: **a.** collinear

STRAIGHTFORWARD: (**see** "simple") **a.** artless; candid; clear-cut; ingenuous; naïve; outspoken; precise; undeviating; **n.** candidness; ingenuosity; ingenuousness; probity; rectitude; scrupulosity

STRAINED: **see** "far-fetched"

STRANGE: (**see** "unusual") **a.** alien; anomalous; atypic(al); bizarre; eccentric; exceptional; exotic; extraordinary; fantastic; foreign; glamorous; grotesque; outlandish; *outré;* picturesque; preternatural; singular; tramontane; unaccountable; unaccustomed; uncanny; unfamiliar; unfrequented; unique
hater of anything (strange) or new: **see under** "new"
something which is: **see** "curiosity"

STRANGENESS: **n.** bizzarerie; grotesquerie

STRANGER(S): **n.** auslander; foreigner; inconnu; *novus homo;* outlander; tramontane
entertainment of: **n.** xenodochy
fear of: **n.** xenophobia
hatred of: **n.** misoxeny; xenophobia; **n.** misoxene; xenophobe

STRAW, *like or resembling (straw-colored)*: **a.** stramineous
-man: **n.** *homme de paille*

STRAYING: (**see** "deviation") **n.** divagation; divergence; **v.** STRAY: deviate; digress; divagate; divaricate; meander; **n.** maverick; straggler; waif
fr. truth or correct course: **n.** aberrance; aberrancy; aberration; **n.** aberrant; **a.** aberrational; aberrative; aberrant

STREAKED: **a.** linear(istic); lineate; **n.** lineation

STREAM(S), *adapted to life in:* **a.** autopotamic
lying bet. two: **a.** interfluvial; **n.** mesopotamia

STRENGTH: (**see** "strong") **n.** brawn; concentration; doughtiness; durability; fortitude; intensity; lustihood; permanency; potency; robusticity; stamina; sthenia; strenuosity; vigor; virility; vitality
bodily: **n.** brawn; lustihood; physique; robusticity; thews
established in position of: **a.** castellated; ensconced; fortified
from on high: vigueur de dessus
loss or lessening of: **n.** adynamia; asthenia; **a.** adynamic; asthenic
of or by own: **adv.** *(ex) propria vigore*
place of: **see** "stronghold"
pregnant with: **a.** Dionysian

STRENGTHEN: (**see** "support") **v.** anneal; augment; buttress; confirm; corroborate; encourage; enhance; fortify; hearten; intensify; invigorate; lace; reinforce; sustain; **a.** STRENGTHENING: (**see** "bracing") corroborative; corroboratory; roborant
as character, conduct, etc.: **v.** chasten; **n.** chastenment

STRENUOUS: **a.** arduous; Herculean; onerous; rigorous; vigorous; **n.** strenuosity

STRESS: **v.** accent(uate); emphasize; **n.** **see** "accent" **and** "pressure"
period of great: **n.** convulsion
physical or mental: **n.** trauma(tism); **a.** traumatic; **v.** traumatize

STRETCHING, *as when drowsy or on awakening:* **n.** pandiculation

STRICT: (**see** "stern") **a.** austere; conscientious; Draconian; inclement; inexorable; inquisitorial; intransigent; obdurate; onerous; orthodox; pharisaical; precise; puritanical; rigorist(ic); rigorous; ruth-

less; scrupulous; Spartanic; stringent; tyrannical; uncompromising; unsparing; unyielding; **n.** STRICTNESS: austerity; correctitude; intransige(a)nce; obduracy; preciseness; precisianism; puritanism; rigidity; rigorism; scrupulosity; stringency; tyranny
enforcer of discipline or rules: **n.** ascetic; disciplinarian; martinet; Pharisee; *precisian;* rigorist
extremely: **a.** rhadamanthine; rigoristic
in customs, religion or morality: **a.** puritanic(al); sabbatarian; **n.** precisian; precisionist; rigorist; sabbatarian
in living: **a.** ascetic; cenobitic(al); **n.** asceticism; ascesis; ascetic; cenobite
person who is rigidly: **n.** disciplinarian; martinet; Pharisee; precisian; rigorist; ritualist; sabbatarian

STRIDE: **see** "step"
with a giant's: **adv.** *à pas de géant*

STRIFE: (**see** "fight") **n.** *concours;* contention; dissension; warfare
breeds strife: lis litem generat
excuse or cause for: **n.** *casus belli*
one fond of: **n.** stormy petrel
one who stirs up: **n.** incendiary; mutineer

STRIKING: **a.** conspicuous; eminent; extraordinary; impressive; noticeable; notorious; percussive; prominent; remarkable; salient

STRIP: **v.** decorticate; defoliate; denudate; denude; deplume; disembellish; dismantle; divest; ransack; **a.** STRIPPING: denudative; **n.** decortication; denudation; desquamation; dismantlement; divestiture; ecdysis; excoriation; exfoliation
as of leaves: **v.** defoliate; **n.** defoliation; **a.** defoliative
or peel, as of skin: **v.** desquamate; excoriate; **n.** desquamation; excoriation

STRIPED: **see** "streaked"

STRIPTEASER: **n.** ecdysiast; stripteuse

STRIVING: **a.** conative; **n.** conation; conatus; **v.** STRIVE: contend; contest; endeavor
creatively: **a.** Dionysian

STROKE: **n.** coup; ictus
finishing: **n.** *coup de grâce*
master: **n.** *coup de maître; tour de force*
of apoplexy: **n.** cerebral accident (or insult)
result of: **n.** hemiplegia
of state: **n.** *coup d'état*

STROLL: **v.** perambulate; promenade; **n.** deambulation; perambulation; promenade; **a.** circumforaneous; deambulatory; perambulatory; promenading

STRONG: **a.** Achillean; adamantine; Atalantean; brawny; castellated; cogent; Cyclopean; Dionysian; doughty; emphatic; Herculean; impregnable; indomitable; invincible; potent; puissant; robust(ious); Samsonesque; Samsonian; stalwart; sthenic; tenacious; urgent; vigorous
man: **n.** gladiator; Hercules; Samson
point, person's: **n.** forte
right of the (strongest): **n.** *le droit du plus fort*

STRONGHOLD: **n.** bastion; blockhouse; breastwork; citadel; fastness; Gibraltar; redan; redoubt

STRUCTURE: **n.** anatomy; architecture; cadre; configuration; conformation; fabrication; lineament; organization; skeleton; texture; **a.** STRUCTURAL: constitutional; edificial; skeletonic
having similar or identical: **a.** homologous; isomorphic; isomorphous
of irregular or unusual: **a.** heteromorphic; heteromorphous; **n.** heteromorphosis
or position, having same relative: **a.** homologous

STRUGGLE: (**see** "fight") **n.** agon; colluctation; contention; endeavor; warfare; **a.** agonistic; contending; contentious

STUB, *check or receipt:* **n.** counterfoil

STUBBORN: (**see** "obstinate") **a.** absonant; adamant(ine); cantankerous; contemptuous; contumacious; contumelious; crotchety; defiant; determined; disdainful; disobedient; dogged; *entêté;* fractious; implacable; incompliant; indocile; indurate; indurative; inductible; inexorable; inflexible; insubordinate; intractable; intransigent; inveterate; irreconcilable; monolithic; mulish; oppositious; persistent; pertinacious; perverse; pervicacious; pigheaded; preemptory; rebellious; re-

calcitrant; refractory; renitent; resistant; restive; stiff-necked; tenacious; unalterable; uncompromising; unreconcilable; unreconstructed; unregenerate(d); unrepentant; unswerving; untoward; willful; **n.** STUBBORNNESS: (**see** "obstinacy") adamancy; contumely; crotchiness; determination; incompliance; incompliancy; intractability; intransigeance; noncompliance; obduracy; persistency; pertinacity; pigheadedness; recalcitrance
person: **n.** intransigeant; recalcitrant

STUDENT: (**see** "pupil") **n.** disciple; scholar; scholastic; undergraduate
fellow-: **n.** condisciple

STUDIO, *artist's:* **n.** atelier

STUDY: (**see** "ponder") **v.** lucubrate; **n.** abstraction; concentration; contemplation; investigation; lucubration; meditation; reflection
fondness for: **n.** *attachement à l'étude*
place for: **n.** atelier; phrontistery

STUFF, *ever the same old:* **n.** *cantilenam enadem canis; crambe repetita*

STUFFED: **a.** copious; replete; sated; satiated; surfeited; **n.** copiosity; satiety

STUN: **v.** flabbergast; paralyze; perplex; stupefy; **n.** stupefaction; **n.** torporific

STUNT, *special or spectacular:* **n.** acrobatics; derring-do; forte; prestidigitation; *tour de force*

STUPID: **a.** Abderian; anserine; anserous; asinine; baboonish; Boeotian; bovine; brutish; crass; doltish; fatuous; hebetate; idiotic; imperceptive; inane; loutish; oafish; obtuse; opaque; oscitant; moronic; purblind; unimaginative; vacuous; **a.** STUPIDITY: absurdity; baboonery; *balourdise; bêtise;* crassitude; fatuity; hebetation; hebetude; impercipience; inanity; insipience; moronity; obtusity; oscitancy; stupidness
cause to appear: **v.** stultify; stultification
person: **n.** Abderite; Boeotian; Juke; nincompoop

STUPOR: **n.** asphyxia; catalepsy; coma; hypnosis; insensibility; lethargy; narcosis; stupefaction; torpor; **a.** STUPOROUS: cataleptic; comatose; hypnotic; lethargic; stupefactive

STURDY (**see** "strong") **a.** lusty; roborant; robust(ious); stalwart; yeomanly

STY (*eye*): **n.** hordeolum

STYLE: **see** "fashion"
high-flown: **n.** *un style ampoulé*
imposing or impressive in: **see** "pretentious" **and** "showy"
literary: **see under** "literary"
passing out of: **a.** archaic; *démodé; fin-de-siècle;* obsolescent; *passé*

STYLISH: **a.** *à la mode; bon ton;* fashionable; jaunty; modish; *recherché;* *soigné(e)*; well-groomed; **n.** STYLISHNESS: *bon ton; dernier cri;* fashionableness
elegantly: **a.** *soigné;* (**fem.** *soignée*)

SUAVITY: **n.** amenity; diplomacy; unctuosity; urbanity; **a.** SUAVE: (**see** "oily") diplomatic; gracious; modish; oleaginous; politic; unctuous; urbane
lack of: **n.** angularity; barbarism; insuavity; inurbanity; rusticity

SUBDUE: **v.** conquer; overwhelm; quash; subjugate; surmount; vanquish

SUBJECT(S): **v.** enthral(l); **n.** liege; propositus; *protégé;* subordinate; **a.** accountable; susceptible
dealing w/ wide range of: **a.** polygraphic
foreign to the: **see under** "foreign"
on the same, or w/ single: **a.** monographic; **adv.** *in pari materia*

SUBJECTIVE: **a.** emotional; intellectual; pectoral; psychic; psychological; psychosomatic

SUBLIME: (**see** "supreme") **a.** eminent; empyreal; exalted; magnanimous; magnificent; majestic; transcendent; **n.** SUBLIMITY: eminence; exaltation; magnanimity; magnificence; majesty
to ridiculous: **n.** bathos; anticlimax; **a.** bathetic; anticlimactic(al)

SUBMISSIVE: (**see** "subservient") **a.** amenable; deferential; genuflectory; humble; menial; obedient; penitent; slavish; tractable; yielding; **n.** SUBMISSIVENESS: acquiescence; amenability; deferentiality; genuflection; genuflexion; inertia; obsequiousness; obsequity; servility; tractability
overly: **a.** cringing; deferential; fawn-

ing; humble; menial; obsequious; servile; slavish

SUBNORMAL: **a.** subminimal; suboptional; substandard

SUBORDINATE: (**see** "assistant") **n.** ancilla(ry); auxiliary; minion; parergon; *protégé;* satellite; subaltern(ant); subalternation; subalternity; subordination; subserviency; **a.** SUBORDINATE(D): ancillary; auxiliary; satellite; satellitic; secondary; servile; subalternate; submissive; subservient; tangential
loyal or hired: **see** "mercenary"
official: **n.** satrap
something which is: **n.** ancilla; parergon; (pl. parerga)

SUBSEQUENT: **see** "after"

SUBSERVIENT: (**see** "submissive") **a.** menial; ministerial; obeisant; subalternate; subordinate; subsidiary; truckling; unemancipated

SUBSIDIARY: (**see** "accessory") **a.** derivitive; segmental; segmentary; succursal; supplemental; tangential; tributary; **n.** assistant; tributary

SUBSTANCE: **n.** corporality; corporeity; essence; materiality; resource(s); substantia
give (substance) or substantive character to: **v.** substantify; **n.** substantification
having some (substance) or essence: **a.** coessential; consubstantial; **n.** consubstantiality
in the (substance) of the matter: **adv.** *in medias res*
lacking: (**see** "unreal") **a.** disembodied; insubstantial; **n.** disembodiment; insubstantiality
pert. to or having to do w/: **a.** hypostatic(al)

SUBSTANTIAL: **a.** abundant; corporeal; essential; formidable; fundamental; material; plenteous; plentiful; ponderable; substantious; **n.** SUBSTANTIALITY; corporeality; corporeity; materiality; physicality

SUBSTITUTE: **v.** commute; exchange; **n.** commutation; expedient; *faute de mieux;* Hobson's choice; *quid pro quo;* understudy; **a.** SUBSTITUTED: substitutional; substitutionary; substitutive; succedaneous; **n.** SUBSTITUTION: exchange; surrogation; vicariousness
for another: **n.** *locum tenems;* succedaneum; surrogate

SUBTLE: **a.** alembicated; crafty; elusive; imperceptible; ingenious; insidious; intangible; skillful; sophisticated; wily

SUBURB(S): **n.** *banlieue(x)*; environ(s); *faubourg;* purlieu(s); suburbia
being in, or pert. to: **a.** suburbicarian
social life, manners, customs, etc. of: **n.** suburbia

SUCCESS, *accidental:* **n.** *succès de circonstance*
brilliant: **n.** éclat
due to scandalous conduct or by conn. w/ scandal: **n.** *succès de scandale*
extraordinary: **n.** *succès fou*
indifferent: **n.** *succès d'estime*

SUCCESSION: **n.** alternance; alternation; consecution; progression; sequacity; sequence; subsequence; **a.** SUCCESSIVE: alphabetical; categorical; consecutive; hereditary; repetitive; sequacious; seriate; (sub)sequential; succedent

SUCH *is life:* **adv.** *sic eunt fata hominum*

SUCKING: **a.** paratrophic
adapted for: **a.** suctorial
period of in young: **n.** lactation

SUDDEN: (**see** "abrupt") **a.** imminent; precipitate; subitaneous; **adv.** *à l'improviste*
change, movement or development: **n.** saltation
disappearance of symptoms: **n.** delitescence
stroke, political: **n.** *coup d'état*
utterance: **n.** ejaculation; exclamation; interjection

SUFFER: **v.** agonize; allow; brook; endure; experience; languish; permit; tolerate

SUFFERING: **n.** agony; languishment; resignation; tribulation
incapable of: **a.** impassible; **n.** impassibility
penitential: **n.** satispassion

place or state of: (see "hell") **n.** Gethsemane; inferno; purgatory
relieving or lessening: **v.** alleviate; palliate; **a.** alleviatory; palliatory
voluntary, as token of repentence: **n.** penance; satispassion

SUFFICIENT: (see "adequate") **a.** commensurate; equipollent; equiponderant; resourceful; **n.** SUFFICIENCY: see "adequacy"
to make: **v.** adequate; **a.** adequative; **n.** adequation; *quantum sufficit* (**abb.** q.s.)

SUFFOCATE: **v.** asphyxiate; **n.** asphyxiation

SUGAR, *producing or containing:* **a.** sacchariferous; saccharogenic

SUGGESTION: **n.** connotation; implication; innuendo; insinuation; insinuendo; overtone; **v.** SUGGEST: adumbrate; allude; connote; insinuate; intimate; prompt; **a.** SUGGESTIVE: connotative; insinuative; meaningful; provocative; reminiscent; *risqué;* seminal; significant
false: **n.** *suggestio falsi*
(trace): **n.** *soupçon*
used to influence another: **n.** heterosuggestion

SUICIDE: **n.** *felo-de-se*
mania for: **n.** thantomania

SUITABLE: (see "pertinent" and "proper") **a.** adequate; appropriate; apropos; comely; comportable; condign; congruent; congruous; consonant; convenient; creditable; decorous; expedient; felicitous; idoneous; opportune; plausible; semblable; **n.** SUITABILITY: (see "fitness") appropriateness; apropository; creditability; expediency; idoneity; plausibility; propriety
not: (see "improper") **adv.** *à propos de rien*

SULLEN: (see "stubborn") **a.** irascible; melancholy; morose; peevish; saturnine; splenetic; unsociable; **n.** SULLENNESS: (see "moody condition") irascibility; melancholy; moodiness; morosity; saturninity

SULTRY, *as of air:* **a.** miasmic; sulfurous; sulphurous

SUM: **n.** aggregate; complement; epitome; quantity; recapituation; result(ant); substance; summation
up: **v.** recapitulate; summarize; **a.** recapitulative; recapitulatory; summatory; **n.** recapitulation; summation

SUMMARIZE: **v.** epitomize; recapitulate; synopsize; **a.** recapitulative; recapitulatory; summarizable; summative; **n.** SUMMARY: abbreviation; abridgement; breviary; breviate; compendium; conspectus; epitome; pandect; *précis;* prospectus; recapitulation; *résumé;* schema; summarization; summation; syllabus; synopsis; truncation

SUMMER, *spend the:* **v.** estivate; **n.** estivation

SUMMIT: (see "acme") **n.** apogee; climax; consummation; crown; culmination; meridian; pinnacle; zenith

SUMMON: **v.** convene; convoke; muster; **n.** SUMMONING: convocation; evocation; invocation; muster

SUN, *at greatest distance fr. equator:* **n.** solstice (*Dec. and June*)
crosses equator: **n.** autumnal equinox (**Sept.**); vernal equinox (**Mar.**)
fear of or of sunlight: **n.** heliophobia
nothing new under: **n.** *nihil sub sole novi*
point most distant from: **n.** aphelion
point nearest to: **n.** perihelion
-stroke: **n.** calenture; *coup de soleil;* heliosis; siriasis
worship of: **n.** heliolatry

SUNBATHE: **v. or n.** apricate

SUNDAY: see "sabbath"

SUNLIGHT, *one sensitive to:* **n.** heliophobe; photophobe; **a.** heliophobic; photophobic; heliophobia; photophobia
treatment by: **n.** heliotherapy

SUNRISE (*or sunset*) *glow:* **n.** alpenglow
song: **n.** aubade

SUPERFICIAL: (see "shallow") **a.** casual; cursory; desultory; incondite; sophomoric; specious; tenuous; **n.** SUPERFICIALITY: inanity; speciosity; tenuosity; triviality
appearance: **n.** externality; (**pl.** superficies)
knowledge: **n.** sciolism; **a.** sciolistic; **n.** sciolist

SUPERFLUOUS: (see "extravagant") **a.** *de trop;* nonessential; prodigal; profuse; recrementious; recrementitious; redundant; superabundant; supernumerary; supererogatory; **n.** SUPERFLUITY: extravagance; prodigality; superabundance; supererogation; superfluity; superflux
do what is: pisces natare docere (to teach fishes to swim)

SUPERIOR: **a.** haughty; magisterial; magistratical; meritorious; palmy; paramount; predominant; preeminent; prepotent; supercilious; supereminent; supernal; supernatural; superordinary; superordinate; unsurpassed; **n.** see "superiority"
in rank: **n.** antecedence; precedence; seniority; unsurpassed; **a.** antecedent; precedent; superordinate
manner, in or w/ a: **a.** or **adv.** *de haut en bas;* **a.** supercilious
that which is: **n.** magnifico; *ne plus supra; ne plus ultra;* supereminence; supernaculum
to be: **v.** predominate; preponderate; **a.** paramount; predominant; supernal

SUPERIORITY: **n.** conspicuity; haughtiness; meliority; (pre)eminence; predominance; predomination; preponderance; preponderation; prominence; superciliousness; transcendence; worthiness
in race, culture, group, etc., belief in: **n.** chauvinism; ethnocentrism; sociocentrism
personal, belief or claim of intellectual or cultural: **n.** illuminism; illuminist

SUPERLATIVE: (see "choice" and "supreme") **a.** consummate; exaggerated; excessive; incomparable; peerless; pluperfect; prepotent; transcendent; **n.** supereminence; supernaculum

SUPERNATURAL: **a.** extraphysical; ex-extrasensory; hyperphysical; incorporeal; metaphysical; miracular; miraculous; numinous; paraphysical; parapsychological; preternatural; psychic; superhuman; supermundane; transcendent(al); **n.** extraphysicality; incorporeality; incorporeity; supermundanity; transcendentality; transcendence
effects, etc.: **n.** phantasmagoria; **a.** phantasmagoric(al)
power, claimed: **n.** charism(a); **a.** charismatic
semi-: **a.** metempirical
study of the: **n.** metaphysics; parapsychology

SUPERSEDE: see "remove"

SUPERVISE: **v.** chaperone; invigilate; proctor; scrutinize; survey; **a.** SUPERVISORY: supervisorial; surveillant; **n.** SUPERVISOR: chaperone; director; proctor; superintendent; surveillant; **n.** SUPERVISION: chaperonage; invigilation; oversight; proctorship; superintendence; surveillance

SUPPLE: **a.** complacent; compliant; gracile; lissom(e); lithe(some); obsequious; submissive; **n.** SUPPLENESS: gracility; lissomeness

SUPPLEMENT: **n.** addendum; (**pl.** addenda); additament; postscript; **a.** SUPPLEMENTAL or SUPPLEMENTARY): (see "contributory") accessorial; accessory; addititious; adjuvant; adjunctive; adminicular; adscititious; ancillary; auxiliary; complemental; complementary; corollary; corroborative; succenturiate; supervenient; tangential
containing things passed over: **n.** paralipomena
containing data as basis for critical study: **n.** *apparatus criticus*

SUPPLICATION: (see "prayer") **n.** entreaty; obsecration; petition; rogation; solicitation

SUPPLY (or SUPPLIES), *abundant:* (see "abundance") **n.** affluence; copiosity; reservoir; spate
as for troops: **n.pl.** armamentaria; impedimenta; *matériel*
for journey or trip: **n.** viaticum

SUPPORT: **v.** abet; advocate; bolster; buttress; champion; corroborate; countenance; espouse; maintain; patronize; sanction; **n.** (see "assistance") abetment; adminicle; advocacy; alimentation; auxiliary; clientele; corroboration; patronage; sponsorship; sustentation; sustention; **a.** SUPPORTIVE (or SUPPORTING): adminicular; alimentative; auxiliary; corroborative; corroboratory; sustenacular; sustentative; tangential
for cause, etc.: **n.** advocacy; espousal; **v.** advocate; espouse
serving to: **a.** sustentacular

SUPPORTER: (see "follower") **n.** abettor; adherent; advocate; aficionado; (**fem.** aficionada); cohort; colleague; constituent; patron; votary
of unrighteous cause or course: **n.** *advocatus diaboli*

SUPPOSE: **v.** conceive; conjecture; divine; postulate; presume; speculate; surmise; theorize; **a.** SUPPOSED: academic; alleged; conjectural; deemed; hypothetical; presumptive; putative; reputed; suppositional; suppositi(ti)ous; suppositive; theoretic(al); **adv.** *ex hypothesi*

SUPPOSITION: **n.** assumption; conception; conjecturality; conjecture; divination; hypothesis; postulation; postulatum; speculation; surmise; theory
based on: **a.** hypothetical; supposititious; theoretic(al)
logical: **n.** hypothesis; philosophy; theory

SUPPRESS: **v.** annihilate; extinguish; inhibit; overpower; overwhelm; quash; quell; repress; subdue; **a.** SUPPRESSIVE: inhibitory; **n.** SUPPRESSION: inhibition; repression

SUPPRESSED *emotions, relief of by talking:* **n.** abreaction; catharsis

SUPREMACY: **n.** ascendancy; ascendency;; domination; dominion; eminence; precedence; preeminence; preeminency; preponderance; primacy; priority; sovereignty; suzerainty

SUPREME: (see "sublime") **a.** celestial; crucial; eminent; *hors concours;* inimitable; incomparable; matchless; nonpareil; olympian; outstanding; palmy; paramount; peerless; predominant; preeminent; preponderant; *sans pareil;* stellar; signal; significant; supereminent; superlative; sovereign; transcendent; vital
Being: **n.** *Ens Entium*
homage: **n.** latria
jurisdiction: **n.** *jus gladii* (right of the sword)

SURE: (see "certain") **a.** authentic; enduring; indubitable; ineluctable; inevitable; secure; unfaltering; **adv.** *à coup sûr;* **n.** SURENESS: (see "certainty") indubitability; ineluctability; inevitability

SURETY: **n.** adpromissor; assurance; certainty; guaranty; recognizance

SURFACE: **n.** exterior(ity); facet; periphery; veneer
feature(s): **n.** lineament(s); mien; topography
floating on the: **a.** supernatant
outer: **n.** externality; periphery; superficies

SURGICAL *removal:* **n.** ablation; abscission; enucleation; resection; **v.** ablate; abscise; enucleate; excise; resect
union, two hollow parts: **n.** anastomosis; **a.** anastomotic

SURLY: (see "sullen") **a.** acrimonious; boorish; churlish; crabbed; haughty; morose; sullen
person: **n.** curmudgeon

SURMISE: (see "suppose") **v.** conjecture; deduce; extrapolate; hypothesize; imagine; infer; theorize; **n.** conjecture; deduction; extrapolation; hypothesis; inference; peradventure; presumption; suspicion

SURNAME: **n.** cognomen(ation); *nom de famille;* patronym(ic); **a.** patronymic; surnominal

SURPASS: **v.** eclipse; preponderate; outstrip; overstep; surmount; transcend; **n.** preponderance; **a.** SURPASSING: excelling; preponderating; transcendent

SURPRISE: (see "astonish") **v.** amaze; astound; electrify; **a.** see "baffle"
attack or move: **n.** *coup d'état; coup de main*

SURRENDER: **v.** abandon; abnegate; capitulate; relinquish; **n.** abandonment; capitulation; cessation; compliance; dedition; resignation; **a.** capitulatory
one who does: **n.** capitulant; capitulator

SURROUNDING(S): **n.** alentours; ambient; circumfusion; circumjacencies; circumvention; confines; entourage; environment; environs; milieu; *mise-en-scène;* periphery; **a.** circumambient; circumferential; circumjacent; circumvallate; encapsulated; encompassing
in strange: **a.** *dépaysé*
space or area: **n.** environment; externality; periphery; (pl. environs)

SURVEY: **v.** appraise; estimate; evaluate; perlustrate; **n.** conspectus; examination; perlustration; prospectus; recension; reconnaissance; scrutiny; surveillance
comprehensive: **n.** panorama; **a.** panoramic

SURVIVAL: **n.** continuation; survivance
from another period: **n.** relict
incapable of: **a.** inviable; **n.** inviability

SURVIVE *or perish: aut vincere aut mori*

SUSCEPTIBLE: (**see** "sensitive") **a.** impressible; prone; tendentious; **n.** SUSCEPTIBILITY: impressibility; impressionability; predilection; sensitivity; tendentiousness

SUSPEND: **v.** adjourn; discontinue; intermit; interrupt; postpone; pretermit
indefinitely: **n.** *sine die*

SUSPENSION: **n.** abeyance; abeyancy; armistice; cessation; intermission; moratorium; pendulosity; pretermission
of activity or payment: **n.** armistice; moratorium

SUSPICIOUS: **a.** accusatory; distrustful; dubious; equivocal; incredulous; incriminatory; *louche;* querulant; querulent(ial); questionable; umbrageous; **n.** dubiety; incredulity; skepticism
person, pathologically: **n.** paranoi(a)c; paranoid; **a.** paranoid

SUSTAIN: **see** "support" **and** "prolong"; **n.** SUSTENANCE: (**see** "food") aliment(ation); nutriment; refreshments; **n.** SUSTENTION: maintenance; sustentation; **a.** SUSTAINING: sustentative; sustenacular

SWAGGER: **v.** hector; swashbuckle; **n.** arrogance; bravado; cockiness; fanfaronade; flamboyance; gasconade; panache; rodomontade; **n.** SWAGGERER: braggadocio; bravado; gasconade; rodomontade; swashbuckler; **a.** SWAGGERING: jaunty; swashbuckling

SWALLOWING, *act of:* **n.** deglutition; ingurgitation

SWAMP: **v.** deluge; engulf; inundate; overwhelm; **n.** morass; quagmire; slough; **a.** SWAMPY: deluginous; fenny; paludal; paludous; palustral; uliginose
living or growing in (swamps): **a.** palustrine; uliginous

SWAN, *curved like neck of:* **a.** cygneous
song: **n.** *chant du cygne*

SWASTIKA: **n.** gammadion; gammation; hakenkreuz; tetraskelion; (**pl.** tetraskelia **or** tetraskelions)

SWAY: (**see** "hang **and** "influence") **n.** ascendency; dominance; dominion; oscillation; sovereignty
ability to: **n.** puissance

SWEAR: (**see** "curse") **v.** adjure; affirm; anathematize; asseverate; depone; depose; pledge; testify
falsely: **v.** perjure; **n.** perjury

SWEARING: **n.** adjuration; affirmation; asseveration; blasphemy; deposition; profanity; testimony
together: **n.** conjuration

SWEAT: **see** "perspire"

SWEEPING: **see** "absolute"

SWEET, *as innocent:* **a.** cherubic; engaging; personable; winsome
soft, as music: **a.** dolce; dolcissimo
soothing: **a.** dulcet
sugary: **a.** honeyed; nectareous; saccharine; treacly

SWEETHEART: **n.** *bonne amie;* chéri(e); dulcinea; inamorato; (**fem.** inamorata); valentine
country: **n.** amaryllis

SWEETNESS: **n.** amiability; saccharinity

SWELL: **v.** dilate; distend; inflate; intumesce; protrude; tumefy; **a.** **see** "swollen"

SWELLING: **n.** inflation; (in)tumescence; nodosity; protuberance; protuberation; tumefaction; tumidity; turgescence; turgor; undulation; **a.** nodal; nodose; nodular; overweening; tumefactive; (in)-tumescent; turgescent
as music: **n.** crescendo; undulation; **a.** undulatory; undulous
in volume: **a.** or **n.** crescendo

subsidence of: **n.** detumescence; deturgescence; **a.** detumescent; deturgescent

SWIFT: **a.** celeritous; expeditious; mercurial; meteoric; precipitous; quicksilver; summary; telegraphic; **n.** SWIFTNESS: acceleration; alacrity; celerity; expedition

SWIMMER, *girl or woman:* **n.** naiad
male or female: **n.** natator

SWIMMING: **a.** natant; natatory; **n.** natation
pert. to or adapted for: **a.** natatorial; natatory
pool, esp. inside: **n.** natatorium

SWINDLE: **see** "cheat"; **n.** SWINDLER: charlatan; *chevalier d'industrie;* cozener; embezzler; imposter; mountebank; quacksalver

SWINE, *pert. to:* **a.** porcine; suoid; swinish

SWING: **v.** fluctuate; oscillate; pendulate; suspend; undulate; **a.** fluctuating; oscillating; pedant; pendular; pendulous; undulating; **n.** SWINGING: oscillation; pendulation; pendulosity; undulation

SWOLLEN: **a.** bulbous; distended; dropsical; edematous; gravid; hypertrophied; incrassate; (in)tumescent; pompous; protuberant; tumefacient; tumefactive; tumid; turgescent; turgid

SWORD: **n.** cutlass; estoc; foil; rapier; saber
right of the: **n.** *jus gladii*
streamer or ribbon for: **n.** cicisbeo
trust not to a boy: ne puero gladium

SYLLABLE(S), *dropping of first:* **n.** aphaereasis; aph(a)eresis
dropping of last: **n.** apocopation; apocope; **v.** apocopate
dropping one or more sounds or letters from middle of word: **n.** syncope
having more than two: **a.** polysyllabic(al)
having one: **a.** monosyllabic(al)
last but one: **n.** penult(ima); **a.** penultimate
last but two: **n.** antepenult(ima); **a.** penultimate
short, pert. to or composed of: **a.** brachysyllabic(al)
to form or divide into: **v.** syllabify; **n.** syllabification
word of many: **n.** plurisyllable; polysyllable; sesquipedalian

SYMBOL(S): **n.** attribute; emblem; ensign; ideogram; logogram; **v.** SYMBOLIZE: allegorize; emblematize; typify; **n.** SYMBOLIZATION: typification
inspiring devotion: **n.** oriflamme
magical: **n.** pentacle; pentagram
mysterious: **n.** or **a.** hieroglyphic; **n.** mystique
science of: **n.** symbolics; symbology
used as word, as %: **n.** ideogram; logogram; **a.** ideogrammatic; ideogram(m)ic; logogrammatic
worship of: **n.** symbololatry

SYMBOLIC(AL): **a.** allegorical; emblematic(al); hieroglyphic; figurative; metaphoric(al); pathognomonic; representative; schematic
banner or standard: **n.** labrum
invested w/ (symbolical) significance: **a.** fetichistic

SYMPATHETIC: **(see** "kind") **a.** altruistic; compassionate; condolatory; congenial; empathetic; infectious; Samaritan; simpatico
relationship: **n.** empathy; *en rapport*

SYMPATHY: **n.** altropathy; altruism; benevolence; clemency; commiseration; compassion; condolence; empathy; tendresse
feeling of: **n.** compassion; empathy; identification; pathos; simpatico
in: **(see** "sympathetic") **a.** empath(et)ic; *en rapport*
lack of: **n.** antipathy; dyspathy; **a.** unsympathetic

SYMPHONY, *small or w/ fewer instruments:* **n.** sinfonietta

SYMPTOM(S): **(see** "clew") criterion; **(pl.** criteria); indication
comb. of, characteristic of disease or condition: **n.** syndrome
decline of, in disease: **n.** catastasis; lysis
pert. to: **a.** diagnostic; pathognomonic; semeiotic; symptomatic
sudden disappearance of: **n.** crisis; delitescence
warning: **n.** prodrome; **a.** prodromal

SYNONYMS, *express variously by means of:* **v.** synonymize; **n.** synonymization
list or study of: **n.** synonymicon; synonymics; synonymy
pert. to: **a.** synonymatic; synonymic; synonymous

SYNOPSIS: (**see** "summary") **n.** abridgement; epitome; **v.** SYNOPSIZE: (**see** "abbreviate") epitomize

SYSTEM: (**see** "organization") **n.** arrangement; economy; network; organism; regime(n); syntax
complete and orderly: **n.** cosmos

SYSTEMATIC: **a.** cosmic; methodical; orderly; regular; symmetrical; taxonomic(al)
in arrangement or construction: **a.** architectonic; **n.** regime(n)

T

TABLE *companion:* **n.** commensal
good talker at (table philosopher): **n.** deipnosophist
pert. to or happening at: **a.** mensal
talks, collection of: **n.** ana

TABOO (or TABU): **n.** convention; embargo; interdiction; prohibition; proscription; restraint; superstition; **a.** contraband; ineffable; inviolate; prohibited; proscribed; proscriptive

TACT: **n.** acumen; address; aptness; delicacy; delicatesse; diplomacy; discrimination; discernment; discretion; finesse; perspicacity; poise; prudence; refinement; *savoir-faire;* sensitivity; **a.** TACTFUL: adroit; consummate; diplomatic; discriminating; fitting; perspicacious; prudent; sensitive; suave

TACTLESS: **a.** gauche; impolite; impolitic; inapt; inconsiderate; indiscreet; inept; maladroit; undiplomatic; untactful; **n.** TACTLESSNESS: gaucheness; indiscretion; ineptitude; maladroitness
act: **n.** gaucherie; indiscretion; ineptitude

TAIL: **n.** cauda; caudal appendage
having or pert. to: **a.** caudal; caudate
having long: **a.** macrurous
having short: **a.** brevicaudate
remove: **v.** decaudate
shaped like: **a.** caudiform
toward the: **a.** caudad

TAILLESS: **a.** acaudal; acaudate; anurous; ecaudate

TAILOR(S), *master:* **n.** *maestro-sastre*
pert. to or to work of: **a.** sartorial

TAINT: **v.** contaminate; corrupt; debase; defile; deprave; pollute; tarnish; **n.** blemish; cloud; contamination; corruption; defilement; macula(tion); pollution; reproach; vitiation

TAKE *by force:* **v.** accroach; appropriate; assume; confiscate; sequester; usurp; **n.** appropriation; confiscation; sequestration; usurpation; **a.** confiscatory; usurpative; usurpatory
by govt. action: **v.** appropriate; commandeer; confiscate; preempt; sequester; **n.** eminent domain; preemption; sequestration; **a.** confiscatory; preemptive
for one's own: (**see** "steal") **v.** appropriate; embezzle; purloin; spheterize

TALE, *folk:* **n.** fabula; (**pl.** fabulae)
unbelievable: **n.** Munchausenism

TALENT(S): **n.** accomplishment(s); adeptness; adroitness; aptitude; capacity; dexterity; endowment; expertise; genius; hability; ingeniosity; inventiveness; virtuosity
comic: **n.** *vis comica*
divine or supernatural: **n.** charism(a); **a.** charismatic

TALK: (**see** "speak" **and** "speech") **n.** articulation; babblement; colloquy; communication; confabulation; conversation; descant; discourse; discussion; lecture; palaver; parlance; **v.** articulate; communicate; confabulate; converse; descant; discourse; palaver
and nothing else: vox et praeterea nihil
boasting or blustering: **n.** bravado; gasconade; kompology
by use of hands: **v.** gesticulate; **n.** dactylology; gesticulation; **a.** gesticulatory
by use of one syllable: **n.** monosyllabicity; monosyllabism; **a.** monosyllabic(al)
clever: **n.** asteism; banter; persiflage; witticism
familiarly together: **v.** confabulate; **n.** confabulation
idle: **n.** *caquet*
inclined or liking to: (**see** "talkative") **a.** conversable; conversant
indirect: **n.** ambage; circumlocution; **a.** ambagious; circuitous; circumlocutory
informal, light: **n.** badinage; bavardage; causerie

informally: **v.** confabulate; **n.** confabulation
in sleep: (**see under** "sleep") **n.** somniloquy; **n.** somniloquist
intimate or private bet. two: **n.** *tête-à-tête*
loud: **see under** "loud"
mania for (talking): **n.** *furor loquenti*
meaningless or nonsense: **n.** Choctaw; galimatias; gibberish; stultiloquence; stultiloquy
meeting for: **n.** conversazione
not liking to: (**see** "silent") **a.** laconic; reticent; tactiturn; trenchant; **n.** obmutescent; reticence; tactiturnity
pert. to: **a.** colloquial; conversational; discursive
relieving emotions by: **n.** abreaction; catharsis; **a.** abreactive; cathartic
senseless or silly: **see** "meaningless" **above**
"small": **n.** asteism; badinage; causerie; persiflage
together: **v.** confabulate; **n.** confabulation; powwow
to oneself: **n.** monologue; soliloquy
inaudible: **n.** endophasia
use of hands in (talking): **see** "by use of hands" **above**

TALKATIVE: (**see** "wordy") **a.** articulate; babblative; communicative; conversable; discursive; fluent; garrulous; logorrheic; (multi)loquacious; multiloquent; verbose; vocative; vociferous; voluble
person: **n.** blatherskite; popinjay

TALKATIVENESS: **n.** *flux de bouche* (**or** *paroles*); garrulity; garrulousness; loquaciousness; loquacity; multiloquence; volubility
abnormal: **n.** *flux de bouche* (or *paroles*); *furor loquenti;* logomania; logorrhea; verbomania

TALKER: **n.** colloquist; confabulator; conversationalist
fluent or witty: **n.** causeur; (**fem.** causeuse); raconteur; (**fem.** raconteuse)

TALL: **a.** altitudinous; statuesque; towering

TAME(D): **a.** amenable; benign(ant); cultivated; docile; domestic(ated); *domitae naturae;* tractable; **n.** TAMENESS: complaisance; docility; domesticality; domesticity; tractability; tractableness

TAMPER: **v.** manipulate; **a.** manipulable; manipulatory

TAN, *light:* **a.** *café au lait*

TANGIBLE: **see** "material"

TAPERING: **a.** acuminate; lanceolar; lanceolate(d)

TAR, *of or like:* **a.** piceous

TARDY: (**see** "slow") **a.** comatose; dilatory; lethargic; procrastinative; remiss

TARNISH: (**see** "darken") **n.** debasement; deterioration
on bronze or copper: **n.** aerugo; patina; verdigris

TASK: **n.** assignment; devoir; enterprise; onus; undertaking
insurmountable: **n.** pile Pelion on Ossa; **a.** Sisyphean
onerous, unpleasant or unavoidable: **n.** *corvée*

TASKMASTER, *cruel:* (**see** "disciplinarian") **n.** Simon Legree

TASTE: (**see** "appetite") **n.** degustation; inclination; penchant; predilection; preference; sapidity; **v.** degustate; **a.** TASTELESS: banal; inartistic; insipid; uninteresting; unleavened; unsavory; vapid; **n.** TASTELESSNESS: insipidity; **a.** TASTY (**or** TASTEFUL); (**see** "appetizing") (a)esthetic(al); artistic; discriminating
abnormal or perverted: **n.** allotriogeustia; allotriophagia; allotriophagy; geophagy; parageusia; pica
act or sense of. **n.** (de)gustation; **a.** gustatory
agreeable: **see** "appetizing"
bad: **n.** cacogeusia; *mauvais goût;* parageusia; **a.** egregious; execrable
blunting of: **n.** hypogeusia
everyone to own: chacun à son goût; de gustibus non est disputandum
increased sense of: **n.** hypergeusia; hypergeusesthesia
judge or arbiter of good: **n.** *arbiter elegantiae* (or *elegantarum*)
no accounting for: **see** "everyone to own" **above**
showing good: **a.** (a)esthetic(al); discriminating; **n.** (a)esthetics

person of low: **n.** groundling
pert. to: **a.** gustatory
pleasing to: **see** "appetizing"
testing by: **v.** degustate; **n.** degustation

TATTLETALE: **n.** quidnunc

TAUGHT, *capable of being:* **see** "teachable"

TAVERN: **see** "inn"

TAWDRY: **see** "cheap"

TAWNY: **a.** *café au lait;* fulvous

TAX, *poll:* **n.** capitation; **a.** capitation; *per capita*

TEACH: **v.** discipline; disseminate; educate; enlighten; exhort; exposit; expound; inculcate; indoctrinate; tutor; **a.** TEACHABLE: disciplined; docible; docile; educa(ta)ble; governable; instructible; manipul(at)able; tractable; **n.** docility; tractability
he who (teaches) learns: qui docet discit
not (teachable): **a.** indocile; intractable; uneduca(ta)ble; unteachable
things which injure (teach): quae nocent docent

TEACHER(S): **n.** didact; didacticist; docent; doctor; educator; guru; instructor; maestro; mentor; pedagog(ue); preceptor; scholastic
chief (headmaster): **n.** archididascalos; archididasculus; **a.** archididascalian; archididascaline
not on regular faculty: **n.** docent
pert. to or to teaching: **a.** didactic(al); educational; instructional; instructorial; pedagogic(al); preceptorial; professorial; propaedeutic(al); sermonic; tutelary; tutorial
who rules strictly: **n.** disciplinarian; pedantocrat; *precisian;* rigorist

TEACHING(S): **n.** didacticism; didactics; instruction; pedagogics; pedagogism; pedagogy; propaedeutics; tuition; tutelage
bad or perverse: **n.** cacodoxy; heterodoxy
college or univ.: **n.** professordom; professoriat(e)
pert. to: **see under** "teacher"
secret or abstruse: **n.pl.** acousmata; acroamatics; arcana; esoterica
theory or art of: **n.** didacticism; paedeutics; pedagogy
we learn by: docendo discimus

TEAR: **v.** dilacerate; disarticulate; discerp; disjoin; dismember; lacerate; lancinate; laniate; rupture; **n.** disarticulation; discerption; dismemberment; divulsion; laceration; rupture

TEARFUL: **a.** lachrymal; lachrymatory; lachrymose; maudlin; mawkish

TEARS, *burst into:* **n.** *fondre en larmes*

TEDIOUS: **see** "tiresome"
passage, as in a book, play or music: **n.** longueur

TEEM: **v.** burgeon; pullulate; **n.** burgeoning; pullulation

TEETH, *gnashing of (involuntary):* **n.** bruxomania
having: **a.** dentate; denticulate(d); denticular; dentulous
having large: **a.** macrodont;
having small: **a.** denticulate(d)
not having: **a.** edentate; edentulate; edentulous
speaking thru closed or partly closed: **n.** dentiloquy

TELL: **v.** acquaint; annunciate; articulate; asseverate; communicate; disclose; divulge; enunciate; narrate; unbosom
shudder to: horresco referens
too horrible to: **adv.** *horribile dictu*
wonderful to: **adv.** *mirable dictu*

TEMPER, *sharpness of:* **n.** acerbity; asperity; **a.** acerbic; asperous; vinegary

TEMPERAMENT: (**see** "humor") **n.** constitution; crasis; disposition; personality; propensity; **a.** TEMPERAMENTAL: capricious; mercurial; quicksilver; volatile; **n.** mercurality; quicksilver; volatility
steady in: **a.** equable; equanimous; phlegmatic; undemonstrative; **n.** composure; equability; equanimity; phlegm; *sang-froid*

TEMPERANCE: **n.** abnegation; mediocrity; moderation; restraint; self-control; sobriety; sophrosyne
a virtue is: est modus in rebus

TEMPERATE: (**see** "calm") **a.** abstemious; Apollonian; Apollon(ist)ic; continent; moderate; self-controlled; sober; **n.**

TEMPERATENESS: abstention; abstinence; moderation; sobriety

TEMPERATURE, *abnormally high body:* **n.** hyperpyrexia
having equality of: **a.** isothermal; synthermal

TEMPORARY: (**see** "fleeting") **a.** *ad hoc; ad interim;* conditional; deciduous; ephemeral; ephemerous; episodic(al); evanescent; impermanent; interm(istic); mundane; provisional; temporal; tentative; topical; transient; transitory; transitional; **adv.** *ad hoc; ad interim; pro tem(pore)*; **n.** TEMPORARINESS: ephemerality; impermanence; impermanency; temporality; topicality
agreement: **n.** *modus vivendi*
delay: **n.** armistice; continuance; moratorium

TEMPTATION: **n.** allurement; enticement; seduction; **v.** TEMPT: allure; entice; persuade; provoke; seduce; **a.** TEMPTING: enticing; provocative; seductive; sirenic(al)
susceptible to: **a.** gullible; peccable; seducible

TEN *persons, group of:* **n.** decemvir(ate)
-sided: **a.** decagonal; **n.** decagon
-thousand: **n.** millennium; myriad
years, occurring every: **a. or n.** decennial
period of: **n.** decade; decennary; decenniad; decennium; **a.** decennial

TENACIOUS: (**see** "stubborn") **a.** adhesive; cohesive; obstinate; retentive; viscous
of purpose: **n.** tenacity; *tenax propositi*

TENDENCY: **n.** conatus; direction; disposition; inclination; nisus; predilection; (pre)disposition; proclivity; propensity; susceptibility; temperament; **a.** tendentious
congenital or constitutional: **n.** diathesis; innate; predisposition; propensity
natural: **n.** conatus; diathesis; nisus
to act in opp. ways or directions: **n.** ambitendency; ambivalence; **a.** ambivalent

TENDER: (**see** "merciful") **a.** affectionate; benevolent; clement; compassionate; hyperalgesic; solicitous; sympathetic; **adv.** *amoroso; con amore*
feeling: (**see** "sympathy") **n.** empathy; tendresse
to make: (**see** "soften") **v.** intenerate; tenderize

TENDERNESS, *as of skin:* **n.** hyperalgesia; hyperesthesia; **a.** hyperalgesic; hyperesthetic

TENDING *in favor of point of view:* (**see** "prejudiced") **a.** tendential; tendentious; **n.** predilection

TENSE: **a.** frenetic; hectic; high-strung, tonic

TENSION, *pert. to or characterized by:* **a.** tonic; **n.** tonicity
state of: **n.** fanteeg; fantigue; tautness; tonicity

TENTH *anniversary:* **n.** decennial
kill every (tenth): **v.** decimate; **n.** decimation

TERM(S): (**see** "name") **n.** condition; duration; semester; tenure
idea w/o exact: **n.** anonym(e)
in express: **adv.** *expressis verbis*
list of: **see under** "word"
technical, science of defining: **n.** orismology; **a.** orismological

TERMINAL (**or** TERMINATION): (**see** "conclusion" **and** "ending") **a.** ultimate

TERMINOLOGY: **n.** nomenclature; orismology; **a.** TERMINOLOGICAL: orismological

TERRIBLE: **a.** apocalytic(al); appalling; awesome; formidable; ghastly; horrific; portentious; redoubtable

TERRITORY: **n.** demesne; dominion; empire; imperium; jurisdiction; terrain; terrene; topography
necessary for expansion, etc.: **n.** lebensraum
not claimed by any nation: **n.** *terra nullius*
within a territory: **n.** enclave; *imperium in imperio*

TERROR: **n.** apprehension; *bête noir;* bugbear; consternation; scourge; **v.** TERRIFY: affright; agrise; appal(l); petrify; **a.** TERRIFYING: Gorgonian; gorgonesque; hideous

TERSE: (see "concise") **a.** abbreviated; aphoristic; axiomatic; brachysyllabic; compact; compendious; epigrammatic(al); laconic(al); poignant; pointed; postulational; sententious; succinct; tacitean; telegrammatic; telegraphic; trenchant
as in speaking: **a.** brachysyllabic; laconic(al); monoyllablic; succinct; **n.** monosyllabicity; monosyllabism

TEST(S): **n.** analysis; audition; criterion; (**pl.** criteria); norm; **a.** analytical
of ability, imposed on inexperienced or ignorant: **n.** *pons asinorum*
serving to: **a.** exploratory; probative; probatory; substantiating

TESTICLES, *removal of:* **see** "castrate"

TESTIFY: (**see** "swear") **v.** affirm; depone; depose; **n.** TESTIMONY: allegation; attestation; declaration; deposition; evidence

THANK *you:* **n.** *danke schön; gracias; merci*

THANKLESS: **see** "ungrateful"

THANKS *to God:* **n.** *Deo gratias*

THANKSGIVING, *hymn of:* **n.** doxology; magnificat; *te deum*

THAT *is:* **adv.** *id est* (**abb.** *i.e.*)
is to say: **adv.** *c'est-à-dire*

THAT'S *war:* **adv.** *c'est la guerre*

THAW: **v.** deliquesce; **n.** deliquescence; **a.** deliquescent

THEATRE, *art of the:* **n.pl.** dramatics; histrionics; theatricals; theatrics

THEATRICAL: (**see** "showy") **a.** artificial; dramaturgic(al); histrionic; (melo)dramatic; meretricious; operatic; pompous; stag(e)y; thespian
hit: **n.** *coup de theâtre*
situation or effect: **n.pl.** histrionics; (melo)dramatics; theatricalities; theatrics; **n.** cabotinage; histrionism; sardoodledom; theatricality

THEFT: **see** "stealing"
literary: **n.** piracy; plagiarism; **v.** plagiarize; **a.** piratical; plagiaristic

THEME, *dominant recurring:* **n.** leitmotif; leitmotiv
having but one dominant: **a.** monothematic
underlying, or symbolic meaning: **n.** mythos; (**pl.** mythoi)

THEMSELVES, *among or between:* **a.** or **adv.** *inter se*

THEORETIC(AL): (**see** "academic") **a.** conjectural; contemplative; fictitious; hypothetical; impractical; platonic; postulatory; presumptive; putative; quodlibetic(al); speculative; supposititious; suppositional; **adv.** *ex hypothesi;* **n.** THEORIST: doctrinaire; dogmatist; idealogist; idealogue; theoretician; theorician; visionary; **v.** THEORIZE: hypothesize; philosophize; postulate; speculate; **n.** THEORY: conjecture; doctrine; dogma; fundament; hypothesis; philosopheme; (pre)supposition; postulate; postulatum; speculation; surmise; (**pl.** postulata; theoretics)

THEY *say:* **adv.** *on-dit*

THICK: (**see** "stupid") **a.** coagulated; consolidated; inspissate(d)
-skinned: **a.** callous; insensate; insensitive; pachydermatous

THICKET: **n.** boscage; chaparral; coppice; copse; covert

THIEF: **n.** burglar; depredator; embezzler; felon; larcener; larcenist; peculator; picaroon; pilferer; **a.** THIEVISH: burglarious; furtive; larcenous; mercurial; stealthy
opportunity makes the: occasio facit furem

THIGH, *pert. to:* **a.** crural

THIN: **a.** attenuated; cadaverous; emaciated; macilent; malnourished; skeletal; skeletonic; tenuous; **n.** THINNESS: macilency; malnourishment; malnutrition; tenuity
watery: **a.** ichorous

THING(S), *among other:* **adv.** *inter alia*
belonging to no one: **n.** *res nullius*
concerning all: de omnibus rebus
done: **n.** *fait accompli; res geste*

regard as a: **v.** hypostatize; materialize; reify; **n.** hypostatization; reification
speaks for itself: **n.** *res ipsa loquitur*
to do (customary): **adv.** *de rigueur; en règle*
worthless: **n.** ambsace; flummadiddle; nihility

THINK: **v.** cerebrate; conceive; conceptualize; conjecture; contemplate; deliberate; (ex)cogitate; hypothesize; ideate; intellectualize; lucubrate; meditate; opine; ponder; rationalize; reflect; ruminate; speculate; **n. see** "thought"
beforehand: **v.** precogitate; premeditate; **a.** precognitive; premeditative
carefully: **v.** excogitate; **n.** excogitation
I (think) therefore I am: cogito ergo sum
inability to: **a.** incogitable; incogitative
that which does: **n.** *res cogitans*

THINKABLE: **a.** cogitable

THINKER: **n.** contemplater; philosopher; speculator; theorist

THINKING: (**see** "thought") **a.** cogitative; conceptualistic; contemplative; meditative; ruminant; ruminative
contrary to logic: **a.** alogical; dereistic; **n.** alogism; dereism
fallacy in: **n.** idolum; (**pl.** idola); illogicality; paradoxicality; *petitio principii*
due to human factors, as lang.: **n.pl.** idols of the forum; idols of the market
due to peculiarities and prejudices: **n.pl.** idols of the cave
false form of: **n.** idolum
place for: **n.** phrontistery
practical: **a.** Aristotelian; **n.** Aristotelianism
way of: **n.** ideology; philosophy

THINNER: **n.** solvent

THIRD, *also in rank, order or formation:* **a.** tertiary
day, every, or occurring every: **a.** tertian
party of ambiguous status: **n.** *tertium quid*

THIRST, *intense or excessive:* **n.** anadipsia; dipsomania; polydipsia

THIRTEEN, *morbid fear of number:* **n.** triadaidekaphobia

THORNY: **see** "spiny"

THOROUGHGOING: **see** "absolute" **and** "out-and-out"

THOROUGH(LY): **a.** complete; consummate; perscrutative; **adv.** *à fond; au pied de la lettre*

THOUGHT: (**see** "think") **n.** cerebration; cogitation; conception; conceptualization; consideration; contemplation; deliberation; ideation; intellection; lucubration; meditation; mentation; perception; ponderation; recollection; reflection; rumination; sentiment; speculation; supposition
absence or want of: **n.** incogitancy; **a.** incogitant; incogitative; unmindful
being lost in: (**see** "daydream") **n.** reverie
creative, capacity for: **n.** ideaphoria
expressed in lit. form: **n.** *pensée*
having appearance of deep: **a.** cogitabund
in deep: **a.** cogitabund; meditative; pensive
lost in: **a.** abstracted; bemused; **n.** abstraction; bemusement; reverie
one given to lofty: **a.** or **n.** altitudinarian
process of: (**see** "mental activity") **n.** mentation
"pure": **n.** noesis; **a.** noetic
rel. to: **a.** cogitative; contemplative; dianoetic; intellectual; meditative; ruminative
science or fundamental laws of: **n.** stoichiology
system or rules of: **n.** organon
transference of (claimed): **n.** telepathy; **a.** mentiferous; telepathic

THOUGHTFUL: (**see** "wise") **a.** calculative; circumspect; cogitative; considerate; contemplative; deliberative; engrossed; heedful; introspective; meditative; mindful; penetrating; pensive; philosophic(al); provident; prudent; reflective; sagacious; speculative; studious

THOUGHTLESS: **a.** abstracted; frivolous; hoity-toity; heedless; improvident; imprudent; inattentive; incogitable; incogitant; incogitative; inconsiderate; indeliberate; insensate; unmindful: **n.** THOUGHTLESSNESS: frivolity; improvidence; imprudence; incogitability;

incogitance; incogitancy
act: étourderie; impropriety

THOUSAND, *or thousand years or anniversary:* **n.** chiliad; millennial; millenniary; millennium; **a.** millenarian; millenary
years, pert. to: **a.** chiliadal; chiliastic; millenarian; millennial
years, period of: **n.** chiliad; millenary; millennium

THOUSANDTH: **n. or a.** millesimal

THRASH: **v.** flog; flourish; lambaste; vanquish

THREAD, *like a:* **a.** capillaceous; capilliform; filamentous; filar
of a novel, tune, etc.: **n.** leitmotif; leitmotiv
suspended by, or strung upon a: **a.** filipendulous

THREADBARE: **a.** banal; deteriorated; hackneyed; jejune; stale; stereotyped; tatterdemalion; trite; vapid; **n.** banality; jejunity; vapidity

THREAT: **n.** anathema; commination; denunciation; minacity; sword of Damocles; **v.** THREATEN: comminate; hector; menace; portend
by way of: **a. or adv.** *in terrorem*
empty: **n.** *brutum fulmen*

THREATENING: (**see** "pressing") **a.** comminatory; denunciatory; fateful; imminent; inauspicious; menacing; minacious; minatorial; minatory; ominous; prognostic; portentous; sinister
evil or harm: **a.** apocalyptic(al); ominous; portentous; sinister; sinistrous
force: **n.** Four Horsemen (of the Apocalypse)

THREE: **see** "third"
bet. or shared by: **adv.** *à trois*
consisting of or based on: **a.** ternate; ternary
corners or angles, having: **a.** triangular; trigonal; trigonous
-fold: **a.** ternary; trinal; trinary; trinitarian; triple; **n. or v.** triplicate; **n.** triplication
group or set of: **n.** ternion; triad; trilogy; trinity; trio; triplet; triplicity
household of, one the lover of one of spouses: **n.** *ménage à trois*
hundred, anniv. or celebration: **n.** tercentenary; **a.** tercentenary; tercentennial
liberal arts: **n.** trivium
parts, divide into or having: **a.** trichotomic; trichotomous; tripartite; **n.** trichotomy; tripartition; triplex; **v.** trisect
-sided: **a.** pyramidal; triangular; trilateral
years, celebration or event, or period of: **n.** triennium
happening every or lasting: **a.** triennial

THRESHOLD, *as of consciousness, pert. to:* **a.** liminal
at the: **adv.** *in limine*
below the: **a.** subliminal

THRIFT: **n.** conservation; economy; frugality; husbandry; parcity; providence; prudence; **a.** THRIFTY: frugal; provident; prudent; **a.** THRIFTLESS: (**see** "wasteful") improvident; imprudent; lavish; prodigal; **n.** improvidence; imprudence; prodigality

THRILL: **n.** enthrallment; frisson

THRIVE: **see** "flourish"

THROAT: **n.** gorge
"lump in": **n.** *globus hystericus*

THROB: **v.** oscillate; palpitate; pulsate; undulate; **n.** ictus; oscillation; palmus; palpitation; pulsation; undulation; **a.** palpitant; pulsatile; pulsating; pulsatory

THRONG: **see** "multitude"

THROUGH *right and wrong: per fas et nefas*

THROUGHOUT: **adv.** completely; passim

"THROWBACK": **n.** atavism; mutation; **a.** atavistic

THRUST: **n.** intrusion
verbal: **n.** repartee; ripost(e); *touché*

THRUSTING *away:* **n.** abstrusion

THUMB, *lacking a:* **a.** epollicate
or its equivalent: **n.** pollex

THUNDER *and lightning, of or like:* **a.** fulmin(e)ous; tonitruant; sulfureous; sulphureous
fear of: **n.** tonitruphobia

THUNDERING: **a.** foudroyant; fulminating; fulmin(e)ous; thunderous; tonitruant; tonitruous

THUS: **adv.** sic
ever to tyrants (motto of Va.): sic semper tyrannis
go to the fates of men: sic enut fata hominum
passes the glory of the world: sic transit gloria mundi

THYROID *deficiency:* **n.** hypothyroidism; cretinism; myxedema

TICKET: **n.** *carte d'entrée;* voucher

TICKLE: **v.** provoke; stimulate; titillate; tit(t)ivate; **n.** titillation; tit(t)ivation

TIDBIT: **n.** *bonne bouche;* kickshaw; morceau; morsel

TIDY: **(see** "neat") **a.** *soigné(e)*; spruce; **n.** nattiness

TIE: **n.** ligation; ligature; linchpin; nexus; stalemate

TIME(S), *arranged in order of:* **a.** calendric(al); chronological; **n.** chronology
at same: **see under** "same"
at the right: **adv.** *dextro tempore*
at this or at present: **adv.** *hoc tempore; in praesenti*
behind the: **(see** "old-fashioned") **a. or n.** ultraconservative
being: **n.** nonce
for the: **adv.** *ad hoc; pro tempore*
beyond: **a.** supertemporal
computing by tree rings: **n.** dendrochronology
duration, position or extension in: **n.** temporality
error of: **see** "chronological error"
extending over long period of: **a.** longitudinal; **n.** perpetuity
flies: **n.** *hora fugit; tempus fugit*
from olden: **adv.** *ab antiquo*
gone by: **n.pl.** *tempi passati*
lasting for long or indefinite: **a.** *ad infinitum;* aeonial; aeonian; aeonic
measuring of: **n.** chronometry
method of reckoning and measuring: **n.** chrononomy
occurring at same: **see** "occurring" **and** "same"
one must yield to the: tempori parendum
parley so as to gain: **v.** temporize; **n.** temporization
person or thing out of, or of historical order: **n.** anachronism; **a.** anachronistic
place in definite (time)relation: **v.** temporalize
reveals the truth: veritatem dies asperit
uncovers all things: tempus omnia revelat
unlimited: **n.** infinity; perpetuity; timelessness

TIMELESS: **(see** "everlasting") **a.** dateless; eternal; in perpetuity; intemporal; interminable; **n.** TIMELESSNESS: indefinitude; infinity; perpetuality; perpetuity

TIMELY: **a.** advantageous; apposite; appropriate; auspicious; expedient; opportune; propitious; providential; relevant; seasonable; tempestive

TIMEPIECE(S): **n:** chronometer; horologue; sundial
dealer in: **n.** horologist
description of, or art of making: **n.** horo(lo)graphy; horology
water: **n.** clepsydra

TIMES, *one must yield to the: tempori parendum*

TIMID: **a.** cowardly; craven; effeminate; humble; irresolute; pavid; pusillanimous; timorous; tremulous; **n.** TIMIDITY: inferiority complex; pusillanimity
make: **see** "intimidate"

TIN, *containing:* **a.** stanniferous
pert. to: **a.** stannic; stannous

TINGE: **v.** affect; imbue; impregnate; tincture; **n. see** "shade"

TINGLE: **v.** stimulate; **n.** frisson

TINSEL: **n. or a.** clinquant

TINY: **see** "small"

TIP: **n.** baksheesh; douceur; gratuity; insinuation; lagniappe; perquisite; pourboire; terminus; trinkgeld

TIPPLER, *fellow:* **n.** compotator

TIRADE: **n.** fulmination; invective; philippic

TIRED: **see** "fatigued"

TIRELESS: **a.** indefatigable; sustained; unflagging; **n.** indefatigability

TIRESOME: (**see** "dull") **a.** bromidic; exhausting; monotonous; tedious; **n.** TIRESOMENESS: exhaustion; monotony

TITLE: (**see** "name") **n.** appellation; appellative; denomination; designation; honorific; ownership; rubric
act of calling or addressing by: **n.** compellation
bearing the, or in title only: **a.** titular(y); **n.** titularity
evidence which defends: **n.** muniment
transfer of: **v.** abalienate; convey; **n.** abalienation; conveyance

TO *be rather than to seem: esse quam videri*
be sure: **adv.** *bien entendu*
this extent: **adv.** *quod hoc*

TOASTMASTER: **n.** *arbiter bibendi;* ceremoniarius; officiator

TOBACCO *smoke, hater of:* **n.** misocapnist; **a.** misocapnic

TODAY *king, tomorrow nothing: aujourd'hui roi, demain rien*

TOE (or finger): **n.** dactyl; digit; phalanx
like: **a.** digiform; digit; phalanx
major or large: **n.** hallux

TOGETHER: **adv.** (con)jointly; mutually; *pari passu;* reciprocally; *tête-à-tête; vis-à-vis*
all: (**see** "unanimous") **adv.** *en banc; en masse;* holus-bolus
belonging or going: **a.** companionate
coming: **n.** concourse; concursion; confluence; congress(ion); rapprochement; unanimity
done or existing: (**see** "at same time") **a.** conjoined; conjoint; unanimous; unisonant; unisonous

TOGETHERNESS: **n.** concentricity; cooperation; mutuality; omneity; oneness; simultaneity; solidarity; unanimity

TOIL: **v.** or **n.** travail
unending, pert. to: **a.** Sisyphean

TOKEN: **see** "symbol"

TOLERANT: (**see** "peaceable") **a.** agnostic(al); benign(ant); benevolent; broadminded; enduring; forbearing; indulgent; latitudinarian; magnanimous; placable; submissive; tractable; undogmatic; **n.** TOLERANCE (or TOLERATION): allowance; benevolence; fortitude; habituation; indulgence; *laissez faire;* latitudinarianism; license; magnanimity; stamina; sufferance

TOMB: **see** "grave"
empty, as monument: **n.** cenotaph

TOMBOY. **n.** gamine; *garçon manqué;* hoyden; **a.** TOMBOYISH: gamine; hoydenish

TONE: **n.** accent; pitch; resiliency; timbre; tonicity; tonus
high and thin (mus.): **a.** sfogato
lack of muscular: **n.** hypokinesia; myasthenia; myatonia
quality of: **n.** timbre; tonality
vary in: **v.** modulate; **n.** modulability

TONGUE: (**see** "language") **n.** glossa; (**pl.** glossae)
pert. to or produced by, as certain sounds: **a.** glossal; lingual
shaped like: **a.** linguiform; lingulate
slip of the: **n.** *lapsus linguae*
speaking in unknown (tongues): **n.** glossolalia

TONIC: **n.** catalyst; fillip; roborant; **a.** bracing; invigorating; refreshing; roborant

TOO *much, or too many:* **a.** *de trop;* excessive; redundant; replete; superabundant; supererogatory; supernumerary

TOOLS, *ability to use:* **a.** chrestic
and materials necessary to work: **n.** armentarium; (**pl.** armamentaria); *matériel*
of another, willing and devoted: (**see** "mercenary") **n.** *âme damnée;* minion

TOOTH-*shaped:* **a.** dentate; denticulate(d); dentiform; serrate(d)

TOP: (**see** "apex") **n.** apogee; climax; consummation; crown; culmination; maximum; meridian; pinnacle; summit; zenith
pert. to: **a.** apical; cacuminal; cacuminous; climactic; consummate; meridian

TOPIC(S): **n.** gambit; theme (**pl.** themata); **a.** TOPICAL: current; thematic; timely
index of: **n.** *index rerum*

TORMENT: **v.** afflict; agonize; dragoon; excruciate; harrow; lacerate; persecute; plague; tantalize; **n.** affliction; agony; calamity; distress; (ex)cruciation; plague; persecution; purgatory; scourge; visitation
place or state of: (**see** "hell") **n.** golgotha; inferno

TORPID: **a.** apathetic; comatose; dormant; hypnotic; lackadaisical; lethargic; phlegmatic(al); pococurante, nonchalant; somnolent; stolid

TORTOISE: **n. or a.** chelonian; **n.** terrapin
pert. to or resembling: **a.** chelonian; testudinal; testudinarious
shell: **n.** carapace

TORTURE: **see** "torment"

TORTUOUS: **see** "devious"

TOSS *about:* **v. or n.** welter

TOTAL: (**see** "all" **and** "sum") **a.** absolute; out-and-out; summatory; thoroughgoing; utter; **adv.** *in toto; tout à fait;* **n.** aggregate; recapitulation; summarization; **n.** TOTALITY: entirety; integrality; omneity; mutuality; unanimity; universality
expression, as of work of art: **n.** *tout ensemble*

TOTTER: **see** "stagger"

TOUCH: **n.** (**see** "touching") modicum; palpation; scintilla; smattering; *soupçon;* tincture; trace; vestige
closely: **v.** impinge; osculate; **a.** osculant; **n.** impingement
diminished sense of: **n.** hypesthesia; **a.** hypesthetic
do not: noli me tangere
examine by: **v.** palpate; **n.** palpation
increased sense of: **n.** hyperesthesia; **a.** hyperesthetic
loss of power to recognize by: **n.** astereognosis
not perceivable by: **a.** impalpable
perceivable by or pert. to: **a.** palpable; tactic; tactile; tactual; tangible; **n.** palpability; tactility
up: **v.** adorn; embellish; ornament; refurbish

TOUCHING: **a.** attingent; concerning; co(n)terminous; contiguous; pathetic; tactual; tangent(ial); **n.** contact; contingence; continuity; palpation; tactation; taction; tangency
light on subject: **a.** lambent; tangential

TOUCHY: **a.** choleric; irascible; precarious

TOUGH: (**see** "stubborn") **a.** aggressive; crustaceous; forceful; hardy; inured; rowdyish; ruffianly; tenacious; threatening; **n.** TOUGHNESS: hardihood; tenacity

TOUR: **n.** circuit; excursion; expedition; itineration; peregrination; pilgrimage; promenade; safari

TOWERING: **see** "tall"

TOWN (*or city*): **n.** municipality
citizen of: **n.** burgher; oppidan; urbanite
officers: **n.pl.** *corps de ville*
pert. to: **a.** municipal; oppidan; urban(istic)

TOWNSMAN: **n.** burgher; oppidan; urbanite
characteristic of: **a.** bourgeois; urbanistic

TOY: **v.** philander; **n.** bauble; geegaw; kickshaw; knick-knack

TRACE: **v.** delineate; **n.** (**see** "touch") scintilla; vestige; vestigium; (**pl.** vestigia) **a.** delineative; vestigial
as of vestigial organ or part, or mark or sign of something that once existed: **n.** vestige; vestigium; **a.** vestigial

TRADE: **v.** barter; negotiate; traffic; **n.** clientele; commerce; commutation; merchandise; *métier;* occupation; patronage; profession; transaction

TRADITION: **n.** convention; custom; folklore; **a.** TRADITIONAL: (**see** "conventional") ancestral; characteristic; customary; legendary; orthodox(ical); prescriptive; tralatitious; unwritten; venerated; veteran
breaker of: **n.** iconoclast; **a.** iconoclastic
worship or veneration of, pert. to: **a.** filiopietistic

TRAGEDY, *muse of:* **n.** Melpomene
pert. to or characteristic of: **a.** calamitous; cothurnal; tragic(al)

TRAGIC(AL): **a.** calamitous; deplorable; lamentable; woeful
make: **v.** tragedize

TRAIT: (**see** "peculiarity") **n.** h(a)ecceitas; h(a)ecceity; particularity

TRAITOR: **n.** apostate; Judas (Iscariot); Modred; renegade; tergiversator; turncoat; **a.** TRAITOROUS: (**see** "treacherous") faithless; iscariotic(al); perfidious; treasonable

TRANCE: **n.** coma; hypnosis; stupor
of joy: **n.** ecstasy; raptus

TRANSFORM: **v.** convert; metamorphose; renovate; transfigure; transmogrify; transmutate; transmute; **a.** TRANSFORMATIVE; permutative; metamorphic; metamorphous; transmutative; **n.** TRANSFORMATION: conversion; metamorphosis; permutation; renovation; transfiguration; transmogrification; transmutation

TRANSIENT: (**see** "fleeting") **a.** deciduous; ephemeral; ephemerous; evanescent; fugitive; impermanent; momentary; preterient; temporary; transitory; **n.** TRANSIENCY: ephemerality; evanescence; fugacity; temporality; transitoriness

TRANSIENTS: **n.pl.** flotsam and jetsam

TRANSITORY: (**see** "transient") **a.** evanescent; transitional
quality: **see** "transiency"

TRANSLATE *in letters or characters of another lang.:* **v.** transliterate; **n.** metagraphy; transliteration
loosely: **v.** or **n.** paraphrase; **a.** paraphrastic(al)

TRANSLATION: **n.** conversion; rendition; transformation; transition; transmutation

TRANSMIGRATION: **n.** metempsychosis; reincarnation

TRANSMISSION: **n.** conductance; conduction; conveyance

TRANSPARENT: **a.** amorphous; crystalline; diaphanous; hyaline; intelligible; limpid; luminous; pellucid; perspicacious; translucent; transpicuous; vitreous; vitrescent; **n.** TRANSPARENCY: (**see** "clearness") crystallinity; diaphaneity; limpidity; perspicacity; translucence; translucency; transpicuity; vitrescence
made so by wetting: **a.** hydrophanous

TRANSPLANTED *fr. native land or environment:* **a.** heterochthonous

TRANSPOSITION *of letters, words, etc., as in reading or writing:* **n.** metathesis; strephosymbolia

TRAP: **v.** incarcerate; **n.** incarceration; inveiglement; pitfall

TRASH: (**see** "refuse") **n.** balderdash; debris; detritus; fatras; flummaddidle; (pl. dejecta; (r)ejectamanta): **a.** TRASHY: **see** "cheap"

TRAVEL: (**see** "tour") **v.** itinerate; journey; peregrinate; safari; traverse; **n.** excursion; expedition; itineration; peregrination; pilgrimage; safari
daily or regular: **v.** commute; **n.** commutation
expenses, also provisions: **n.** viaticum
urge to: **n.** wanderlust

TRAVELER(S): **n.** itinerant; peregrinator; viator; wayfarer
on particular quest: **n.** argonaut
refuge for: (**see** "inn") **n.** caravansary; hospice; hostelry; xenodochium

TRAVELING: **a.** ambulatory; discursive; errant; itinerant; locomotive; nomadic; perambulatory; peripatetic; portable
companion: **n.** *compagnon de voyage*

TREACHERY: (**see** "treason") **n.** duplicity; fides Punica (or Punica fides) (Punic faith); perfidy; *tracasserie;* triplicity; **a.** TREACHEROUS: arrant; duplicitous; faithless; infamous; insidious; iscariotic(al); malignant; perfidious; Punic; rascally; traitorous; unscrupulous; venomous; viperish

TREASON: **n.** betrayal; duplicity; *lese majesty;* perfidy; prodition; treachery

TREASURE, *hidden:* **n.** cache
up: **v.** thesaurize; **n.** thesaurization

TREASURER: **n.** bursar; chamberlain; exchequer; quaestor

TREAT: **v.** administer; negotiate; regale; **n.** (see "delicacy") *bonne bouche*
difficult to (cure): **a.** intractable; irremediable; irreparable; refractory

TREATISE: see "essay"
comprehensive: **n.** catholicon; encyclopedia
covering entire subject. **n.** pandect
explanatory: **n.** exegesis; **a.** exegetic(al)
formal: **n.** disquisition
further explanatory: **n.** epexegesis; **a.** epexegetic(al)
on single subject: **n.** monograph
rudimentary or basic: **n.** abecedarium; (pl. abecedaria); hornbook; primer

TREATMENT: (see "remedy") **n.** medicament(s); medication; therapeusis; therapeutics; therapy; **a.** therapeutic(al)
grows worse w/ the: **adv:** *aegrescitque mendendo*
one who administers: **n.** therapist
science of: **n.** iatreusiology; iatrics; therapeutics; therapy

TREE(S), *culture of:* **n.** arboriculture; silviculture; sylviculture
feeding on: **a.** dendrophagous
growth or grove of: **n.** arboretum; boscage; copse
like or pert. to: **a.** arboraceous; arboreal; arbor(e)ous; arborescent; arboresque; arboriform; dendriform; dendroid
living in or on: **a.** arboreal; dendrophagous; dendrophilous
place where grown: **n.** arboretum
rings, computing time by: **n.** dendrochronology
shaped like or resembling: **a.** arboriform; dendriform; dendroid
study of: **n.** dendrology; silvics; silviculture; sylvics; **n.** dendrologist

TREMBLE: (see "throb") **v.** agitate; quaver; quiver; tremulate; vibrate; **a.** TREMBLING: quavering, tremorous; tremulous; **n.** agitation; tremblement; tremor; tremulation

TRENCH, *shallow:* **n.** scorbicula

TRESPASS: **v.** encroach; impinge; infringe; invade; **n.** encroachment; impingement; infringement; misfeasance; transgression; **n.** TRESPASSER: encroacher; misfeasor; transgressor

TRIAL: **n.** affliction; calvary; *crucis experimentum;* demonstration; endeavor; experiment; ordeal; tribulation; visitation
-and-error method: **n.** empiricism; **a.** empiric; experimental; factual; observational
by ordeal: **n.** *dei judicium*
liable for or subject to: **a.** justiciable
pert. to: **a.** empiric(al); judiciary

TRIANGULAR: **a.** deltoid(al); pyramidal

TRIBE, *as a center:* **n.** ethnocentrism; **a.** ethnocentric
life of: **n.** tribalism
subdivision of: **n.** clan; phratry; **a.** phratric

TRIBUTE: see "praise"

TRICK: (see "artifice") **v.** cajole; cozen; defraud; inveigle; manipulate; victimize; **n.** expedient; maneuver; manipulation; prestidigitation; stratagem; subterfuge; **n.** TRICKERY: (see "deception") artifice; charlatanry; chicanery; cozenage; defraudation; duplicity; escamotage; finesse; fourberie; hanky-panky; hocus-pocus; inveiglement; legerdemain; maneuver; mountebankery; pettifoggery; phonus-bolonus; prestidigitation; roguishness; skullduggery; stratagem; subterfuge; subtlety; wile; **a.** TRICKY: (see "dishonest") artful; captious; circuitous; disingenuous; duplicitous; ingenious; ingenuous; insidious; intricate; stratagemic(al); subtle; tortuous; unreliable
skillful: see under "skillful"

TRIFLE(S): (see "nothingness") **n.** bagatelle; bauble; flotsam and jetsam; flummadiddle; folderol; geegaw; inconsequence; inconsequentia; kickshaw; nihility; *nugae (canorae)*; particle; *peu de*

chose; quelque-chose; triviality
silly: **n.** *niaiserie*
very great in: maximus in minimus

TRIFLER: **n.** boulevardier; *flaneur;* (**fem.** *flaneuse*)

TRIFLING: (**see** "trivial") **a.** banal; commonplace; contemptible; decipient; frivolous; hackneyed; immoment(ous); inconsequential; insignificant; namby-pamby; negligible; nugacious; nugatory; paltry; pettifogging; picayune; picayunish; puerile; ridiculous; trivial; wishy-washy; **n.** TRIFLINGNESS: desipience; desipiency; negligibility; triviality
point or particular: **n.** minutia; (**pl.** minutiae); nugacity; quiddity; subtlety; triviality; (**pl.** inconsequentia; trivia)

TRINKET(S): **n.** bagatelle; bauble; bibelot; bijou(terie); geegaw; kickshaw; *objet d'art; peu de chose; quelque-chose*

TRIP: (**see** "travel") **n.** expedition; peregrination; safari
record or outline of: **n.** itinerary

TRIPLE: **v.** triplicate; **a.** ternate; ternary; threefold; treble; trichotomus; trinal; trine; trinitarian

TRITE: (**see** "commonplace") **a.** banal; bromidic; hackneyed; pedestrian; platitudinous; stereotyped; stereotypical; threadbare; **n.** TRITENESS: banality; bathos; pedestrianism
saying: (**see under** "saying") **n.** banality; bromide; *cliché;* platitude; stereotype

TRIUMPH: **see** "conquest"

TRIUMPHANT: **a.** elated; exultant; jubilant; triumphal; victorious

TRIVIAL: (**see** "petty" **and** "trifling") **a.** inconsequential; inconsiderable; mediocre; nugacious; **n.** TRIVIALITY: banality; inconsequenticality; insignificality; nugacity; (**pl.** inconsequentia; marginalia; minutiae; trivia)

TROOPS, *science of moving, supplying and quartering:* **n.** logistics; **a.** logistic(al)

TROUBLE(S): **v.** discommode; perplex; **n.** adversity; annoyance; chagrin; coil; encumbrance; hindrance; obstruction; perplexity; uneasiness; vexation; **a.** TROUBLED: agitated; solicitous; stormy; troublous; turbulent; vexatious
harbinger of, or one fond of: **n.** stormy petrel
not worth the: non est tanti
prolific source of: **n.** Pandora's box

TROUBLESOME: (**see** "inconvenient") **a.** arduous; boisterous; discommodious; distressing; disturbing; Herculean; infestive; laborious; lamentable; obstreperous; pestiferous; pestilent(ial); recalcitrant; refractory; turbulent; unruly; vexatious
person: **n.** *enfant terrible;* stormy petrel

TRUE: (**see** "truth") **a.** accurate; inherent; intrinsic; legitimate; official; orthodox; unassailable; unfeigned; veracious; veritable
accept as: **v.** nostrificate; **n.** fideism
considered as (*not denied or proved otherwise*): **a. or adv.** *pro confesso*
necessarily: **a.** apodictic(al); indisputable

TRUISM: (**see** "maxim") **n.** axiom; banality; bromide; *cliché;* platitude; postulate

TRUST: (**see** "confidence") **n.** assurance; credence; dependence; reliance; monopoly
betrayal of: **n.** duplicity; perfidy; traitorism; **a.** duplicitous; perfidious; traitorous
breach of: **n.** *trahison des clercs*
implicit: **n.** *uberrima fides*
not overmuch to appearance: nimium ne credi colori
not the face: ne fronti credi

TRUSTWORTHY: **see** "dependable"

TRUTH: (**see** "certainty") **n.** accuracy; actuality; certitude; fidelity; precision; probity; veracity; verisimilitude; verity; (**pl.** verities); *vraisemblance;* **a.** TRUTHFUL: accurate; candid; sincere; trustworthy; veracious; veridical; **n.** TRUTHFULNESS: accuracy; veracity; vericacity; veridicality
according to: **adv.** *secundum veritatem*
conquers: veritas vincit
conquers all things: vincit omnia veritas
denial of any basis for: **n.** nihilism; **a.** nihilistic
departing fr.. **a** (ab)errant; aberrational; aberrative; **n.** aberrance; abberation; inveracity

engenders hatred: veritas odium parit
eternal (truths): **n.pl.** (the) eternities; (the) verities
having appearance of: **a.** verisimilar; verisimilous; **n.** verisimilarity; verisimilitude
in: **adv.** *en vérité*
in wine (when intoxicated): *in vino veritas*
lover of: **n.** philalethist
naked: **n.** *nuda veritas*
nothing is so lovely as: rien n'est plus beau que le vrai
of or pert. to: **a.** alethic; gnomic; veracious
suppression of: **n.** *suppressio veri*
w/o fear: vérité sans peur

TRY: (see "endeavor") **v.** essay; **a.** TRYING: annoying; arduous; exacting; irritating; rigorous; strenuous
anything once: ein mal, kein mal

TUBERCULOSIS, *pulmonary:* **n.** phthisis; **a.** phthisic(al); tubercular; tuberculous

TUFTED: **a.** cespitose; comose

TUMOR: see "growth"

TUMULT: (see "commotion") **n.** agitation; Babelism; bouleversement; brouhaha; disturbance; paroxysm; rabblement; *Sturm und Drang;* welter; **a.** TUMULTUOUS: see "turbulent"

TUNE: **v.** syntonize; **n.** intonation; melisma; sonance; syntonization; **a.** TUNEFUL: (see "melodious") chantant
in: **a.** assonant; *d'accord; en rapport;* harmonious; homophonous; melodious; rhythmic(al); symphonious; syntonic; syntonous; unisonant
out of: **a.** absonant; asynchronistic; asynchronous; cacophonous; discordant; disharmonious; dissonant; inharmonious; unharmonious

TURBULENT: (see "noisy") **a.** termagant; tumultuous

TURMOIL: (see "commotion" **and** "tumult") **n.** *Sturm und Drang*

TURN: (see "rotate") v. gyrate; pirouette; slue

TURNING: **n.** about-face; flexure; gyration; reversal; *volte-face;* **a.** flexuous; serpentine
aside: **n.** declination; deflection; deviation; divergence; ricochet; veering; **a.** declinatory; divergent
involved or marked by: **a.** rotary; vertiginous
point: **n.** climax; crisis; fulcrum

TURNED *up, as a nose:* **a.** retroussé; **n.** *nez retroussé*

TURTLE: **n.** or **a.** chelonian
shell: **n.** carapace

TWELFTH: **a.** duodecimal

TWELVE, *based on number:* **a.** duodenary
occurring once in 12 years: **a.** duodecennial
pert. to: **a.** duodecimal; duodenary

TWILIGHT: **n.** crepuscule
pert. to or appearing at: **a.** crepuscular, vespertilian; vespertine

TWIN(S): **n.** *alter ego;* counterpart; sibling(s); **a.** binary; didymous; dioscuric; duplicate; dyadic; gemel; jumelle; parallel
-like: **a.** bigeminal
product of one ovum: **n.** or **a.** enzymotic; identical; monovular
product of two ova: **n.** or **a.** biovular; dizygotic; fraternal

TWINKLING: **a.** scintillating; scintillescent; **n.** scintillization; **v.** TWINKLE: scintillate
of an eye: **n.** *clin d'oeil*

TWIRL (or TWIST): **v.** contort; gyrate; gnarl; intort; vertiginate; **n.** convolution; sinuosity; tortuosity; twistification; **a.** (con)volute; intorted; meandering serpentine; sinuous; tortile; tortuous; vertiginous

TWITCH: **v.** vellicate; **n.** fasciculation; tic; vellication

TWO, *between:* **a.** *à deux*
consisting of: **a.** duel(istic)
conversation by: **n.** duologue
divide into: **v.** bifurcate; bisect; dichotomize; halve; **a.** bifurcate(d); bipartient; bipartisan; bipartite; bisected; dichotomic; dichotomous; distichous; **n.** bifurcation; dichotomy; diremption
-faced: (see "double-dealing") **a.** duplicitous; Janus-faced; Janus-like

-fold: **a.** bigeminal; binal; binary; bipartisan; bipartite; didymous; duplicate(d); twifold; **n.** duality; duplexity; duplicity

govt. by: **n.** diarchy; diumvirate; duumvirate; dyarchy

having (two) lives, natures, positions, qualities, etc.: **a.** amphibian; amphibious

having (two) shapes or bodies: **a.** twiformed

heads better than one: due teste valgano più che una sola; nemo solus satis sapit

-hoofed: **a.** bifid; bisulcate; **n.** bifidity

-hundred-and-fiftieth anniversary: **a.** or **n.** sestertio-centennial

insanity of (two, as hus. and wife): **n.** *folie à deux*

parties, shared by: **a.** bilateral; bipartisan; bipartite; **n.** bipartisanism; bipartisanship

parts, divided into or having: **see** "divide into" **above**

position held jointly by: **n.** diumvirate; duumvirate; **n.** duumvir

-sided: **a.** bilateral; bipartisan; syngal(l)agmatic; **n.** bilaterality; duality

-toned or colored: **a.** dichromatic

units regarded as one: **n.** dyad; **a.** dyadic

TYPE: (**see** "model") **n.** description; exemplar; exemplum; ilk; kidney; nature; representation; species; stripe

conforming to: **see** "rule" **and** "typical"

perfect: **n.** *beau idéal; ne plus supra*

to act as: **v.** exemplify; typify; **n.** exemplification; typification

TYPICAL: **a.** classic; emblematic; exemplary; prefigurative; quintessential; symbolic(al); typic; **n.** TYPICALITY: exemplarity; quintessentiality; typification

TYRANNY: **n.** absolutism; autocracy; despotism; oppression; **a.** TYRANNOUS: **see** "oppressive"

TYRANT(S): (**see** "dictator") **n.** autocrat; commissar; despot; martinet

petty: **n.** martinet; satrap

thus ever to (motto of Va.): sic semper tyrannis

U

UGLY: (**see** "unappealing") **a.** inaesthetic; unbeauteous; uncomely; uncosmeticised
something which is: **n.** hideosity
to make: **v.** plebify; uglify; **n.** plebification; uglification

ULTERIOR: **a.** latent; remote
motive: **n.** *arrière pensée*

UNABRIDGED: **a.** comprehensive; cyclopedic(al); *in extenso;* unexpurgated

UNAFRAID: (**see** "bold") **a.** unapprehensive

UNADULTERATED: (**see** "pure") **a.** simon-pure

UNALTERABLE: **see** "unchangeable"

UNANIMOUS: **a.** concordant; consentient; harmonious; unisonant; unisonous; **adv.** UNANIMOUSLY: *nemine contradicente* (**abb.** nem con.); *nemine dissentiente; una voce; unanime;* **n.** UNANIMITY: concordance; consension; consentience; harmony

UNAPPEALING: (**see** "ugly") **a.** impersonable; inaesthetic; insipid; somber; subfusc(ous); unbeauteous

UNAPPEASABLE: **see** "appeased, incapable of being"

UNATTACHED: (**see** "isolated") **a.** celibate; discrete; uncommitted.
to any party or faction: **n.** or **a.** maverick; recalcitrant

UNATTAINABLE *goal, seemingly or nearly so:* **n.** ultima Thule

UNATTEMPTED: (**see** "untried") **a.** unessayed; untested

UNATTRACTIVE: **see** "unappealing"

UNAUTHORIZED: (**see** "unofficial") **a.** apocryphal; contraband; counterfeit; illegal; proscriptive; spurious; unapproved; unauthoritative; unsanctioned

UNAVOIDABLE: (**see** "certain") **a.** accidental; indubitable; inevitable; unpremeditated
accident: **n.** act of God; *casus fortitus; force majeure; vis major*

UNAWARE: **a.** incognizant; nescient; oblivious; unconscious; **n.** UNAWARENESS: incognizance; incognoscibility

UNBALANCE: **n.** astasia; disequilibration; disequilibrium; imbalance; instability

UNBEARABLE: **see** "unendurable"

UNBEATABLE: (**see** "unconquerable") **a.** invincible; unexcelled; unsurpassable

UNBECOMING: **a.** demeritorious; dishonorable; disreputable; immodest; impertinent; improper; inappropriate; incongruous; indecent; indecorous; unseemly; unsuitable; untoward

UNBELIEVABLE: **a.** improbable; incredible; incredulous; preposterous; prodigious; **adv.** *ab absurdo;* **n.** incredibility

UNBELIEVER: (**see** "disbeliever" **and** "heretic") **n.** atheist; latitudinarian; miscreant; nihilist; skeptic; **a.** UNBELIEVING: aporetic; heretical; heterodox; incredulous; skeptical; unorthodox

UNBEND: **v.** condescend; slacken; vouchsafe
on occasion, to: desipere in loco

UNBRANDED: **a.** or **n.** maverick

UNBREAKABLE: **a.** adamant(ine); immarcescible (or immarcessible); immutable; imperishable; indestructible; infrangible; inviolable; inviolate; invulnerable; irrefragable

UNBRIDLED: **(see** "unrestrained") **a.** crapulous; incontinent; intemperate; rampageous; rampant; unchecked; ungoverned

UNBROKEN: **a.** contiguous; continuous; intact; inviolate(d); uninterrupted; unsubsided; unsubdued; untamed; **n.** contiguity; continuity

series or succession: **n.** continuity; continuum

UNCALLED *for:* **(see** "unbecoming") **a.** gratuitous; impertinent; inappropriate; indecorous; unmerited; unnecessary; unseemly; **n.** impertinency; impropriety; indecorousness; indecorum; unseemliness

UNCERTAIN: **(see** "vague") **a.** *ambigendi locus;* ambiguous; ambivalent; amphibolic; contingent; dubious; dubitable; enigmatical; equivocal; flickering; impredictable; improbable; inconclusive; indefinite; indefinitive; irregular; nebulous; penumbral; precarious; problematic(al); questionable; unformalized; unmathematical; vacillary; variable; visionary

middle ground: **n.** penumbra

UNCERTAINTY: **(see** "doubt") **n.** ambiguity; ambivalence; dubiety; dubiosity; dubitation; fluctuation; incertitude; indefinability; indefinitude; indetermination; inexactitude; precariousness; skepticism

of meaning: **n.** ambiguity; amphibologism; **a.** ambiguous; amphibolic(al); amphibolous

of occurrence: **n.** contingency; fortuitousness; fortuity; **a.** contingent; fortuitous

state of being in: **n.** (horns of a) dilemma; predicament; quandary; **a.** dilemmatic; predicamental

state of, as to whether thing is true: **n.** dubiosity; *non liquet*

UNCHANGEABLE: **(see** "absolute", "fixed" **and** "stubborn") **a.** adamant(ine); immutable; implacable; imprescriptible; inalienable; incommutable; inconvertible; indomitable; inexorable; intractable; invariable; irreversible; irrevocable; monolithic; permanent; unalterable; **a.** UNCHANGED: intact; pristine; sedentary; sessile; static; stationary; unaltered; unexpurgated; unretouched; **n.** staticism; *status quo*

UNCHANGING: **(see** "fixed" **and** "eternal") **a.** changeless; consistent; constant; immarcescible; indomitable; intractable; invariable; static

UNCHECKED: **(see** "unrestrained") **a.** unextirpated

UNCIVILIZED: **a.** barbaric; barbarous; discourteous; *ferae naturae;* feral; Gothic; inhuman; primitive; savage; uncultivated; uncultured; **n.** barbarity; ferity; inhumanity; primitivity

UNCLASSIFIABLE: **a.** acategorical; amorphous; heterogeneous

UNCLE, *pert. to maternal:* **a.** avunculocal

pert. to or like: **a.** avuncular; **n.** avuncularity

UNCLEANLINESS: **n.** acatharsia; feculence; immundity; maculacy; squalor; **a** UNCLEAN: **(see** "dirty" **and** "filthy") excrementious; immund; impure; maculate(d); putrid

abnormal attraction to: **n.** mysophilia

abnormal fear of or distaste for: **n** mysophobia

UNCLEAR: **see** "ambiguous" **and** "vague

UNCOMMON: **(see** "rare") **a.** exceptional; outstanding; *recherché*

UNCOMMUNICATIVE: **a.** laconic; obmutescent; reserved; reticent; tactiturn; **n.** obmutescence; reticence; taciturnity

UNCOMPLIMENTARY: **a.** antagonistic derogatory; disparaging; dyslogistic

UNCOMPROMISING: **a.** inflexible; intractable; intransigent; recalcitrant; unyielding; **n.** intransigence; recalcitrance

UNCONCERN: **(see** "apathy" **and** "indifference") **n.** insouciance; nonchalance; **a.** UNCONCERNED: **(see** "apathetic" **and** "calm") indifferent; insouciant; lackadaisical; phlegmatic; pococurante; unsolicitous

UNCONDITIONAL: **(see** "absolute") **a** plenary; **n.** unconditionality

UNCONFORMING: *see* "unconventional"

UNCONGENIAL: **a.** asocial; discordant; incompatible; incongruous; inharmonious;

ungregarious; unsociable; **n.** UNCONGENIALITY: asocialism; asociality; incompatibility; unsociability

UNCONQUERABLE: **a.** Achillean; impregnable; indefeasible; indomitable; inexpugnable; insurmountable; intractable; invincible; invulnerable; irrepressible; undefeatable; unsurpassable; unswerving; unyielding; **n.** UNCONQUERABILITY: impregnability; indomitability; inexpugnability; invincibility; invulnerability

UNCONSCIOUS: **(see** "unaware") **a.** comatose; insensible; **n.** UNCONSCIOUSNESS: coma; insensibility; narcosis

UNCONTROLLED: **(see** "unbridled" **and** "unrestrained") **a.** irrepressible; rampant; unbounded; unchecked; ungoverned; **n.** rampancy; unrestraint

UNCONVENTIONAL: **a.** Bohemian; *dégagé;* eccentric; heretical; heterodox; *outré;* uncultured; unorthodox; **n.** UNCONVENTIONALITY: Bohemianism; heterodoxy; unorthodoxy
action or behavior: **n.** heresy; heterodoxy; solecism; transgression
person: **see under** "person"

UNCOOKED: **adv.** *au naturel*

UNCOUTH: **(see** "rude") **a.** agrestic; baboonish; barbarous; clownish; incondite; indecorous; plebeian; provincial; rustic; unbeseeming; unchivalrous; uncourtly; uncultivated; **n.** babbittry; baboonery; indecorum; rusticity

UNCOVERED: **see** "naked"
(*unroofed*): **a.** *al fresco;* hypaethral; upaithric

UNCULTIVATED: **see** "uncouth"

UNDAMAGED: **(see** "whole") **a.** unscarred; unscathed

UNDAUNTED: **a.** undiscouraged; undismayed

UNDECEIVE: **v.** disabuse

UNDECIDED: **a.** abeyant; ambivalent; inconstant; irresolute; pendant; pendent; pending; under advisement; undetermined; unresolved; unsettled; vacillating; volatile; wavering

UNDEFILED: **(see** "pure") **a.** immaculate; intemerate; inviolate; uncorrupted; unpolluted; unstained; untainted

UNDEMONSTRABLE (**or** UNDEMONSTRATIVE): **(see** "indifferent") **a.** anapodictic; apathetic; laconic(al); nonchalant; phlegmatic; phlegmatous; reserved; restrained; stoic(al); stolid

UNDENIABLE: **a.** incontestable; incontrovertible; indisputable; indubitable; unquestionable; **n.** indisputability; indubitability

UNDER: **adv.** inferior; nether; subalternate; subjacent; subordinate; substrative
state of being: **n.** inferior; infraposition; subalternity; subordination
to place (*under or beneath*): **v.** infrapose; infraposition

UNDERGROUND: **a.** submundane; subterranean; subterrestrial
pert. to: **a.** chthonian; subterranean

UNDERHAND: **a.** chicane; clandestine; devious; disingenuous; duplicitous; furtive; huggermugger; Machiavellian; oblique; sinister; stealthy; surreptitious; wily; **n.** UNDERHANDEDNESS: chicanery; clandestinity; duplicity; sinisterity; stealth; surreption

UNDERLYING: **a.** fundamental; implicit; subjacent; substantive; substratal; substrative; subtending; **n. see** "base"

UNDERSTAND, *ability to:* **n.** acumen; comprehensibility; impenetrability; perspicacity
difficult to: **a.** abstruse; impalpable; impenetrable; inscrutable; obscure; opaque; recondite; tenebrific; tenebrous; tenuous; unfathomable; **n.** abstrusity; impenetrability; opacity; tenebrosity; **(pl.** impalpables)
easy to: **a.** limpid; perspicacious; translucent
one who does: **n.** appercipient

UNDERSTANDABLE: **see** "clear"

UNDERSTANDING: **(see** "insight" **and** "reason") **n.** apperception; apprehension;

discernment; empathy; entente; implication; intelligence; intuition; perception; perspicacity; signification; **a.** apperceptive; appercipient; empathetic; empathic; intuitive; sympathetic
beyond ordinary: **a.** abstruse; arcane; cabalistic; recondite; profound; **n.** abstruseness; abstrusity; profundity
exercising or implying: **a.** intelligential
friendly: **n.** *entente cordiale*
lack of: **n.** anoesia; anoesis; incomprehensibility; incomprehension; **a.** anoetic
science or study of: **n.** noology
slow in: (**see** "stupid") **a.** astigmatic(al); pedestrian; purblind
where not specifically expressed: **n.** subaudition; subintelligitur

UNDERSTATEMENT: **n.** litotes; meiosis

UNDERSTOOD: **a.** assumed; connotative; implicate; implicit; implied; tacit
by intuition: **a.** intuitive; noumenal; **n.** noumenon
capable of being: (**see** "clear") **a.** comprehensive; exoteric; intelligible; limpid; **n.** comprehensibility; intelligibility
condemn what is not: damnat quoa ɴon intelligunt
not capable of being: (**see** "vague") **a.** impenetrable; incomprehensible; inde·ipherable; inscrutable; undecipherable; unfathomable; unintelligible
well: **adv.** *bien entendu*

UNDERTONE, *in an:* **a.** or **adv.** *sotto voce*

UNDERVALUE: **v.** depreciate, misprize

UNDERWORLD, *pert. to.* **a.** chthonian; plutonian; plutonic; subterranean

UNDESERVED (**or** UNDESERVING: (**see** "unworthy") **a.** unearned; unjustified; unmerited; unwarranted

UNDESIRABLE: **a.** egregious; flagrant, inappropriate; inexpedient; inopportune; objectionable; unenviable
highly: **a.** cancerous; leprous; malignant; sarcomatous; scabrous

UNDETERMINED: **see** "unfathomed"

UNDEVELOPED: (**see** "crude") **a.** embryonic; immature; incipient; latent; nascent; primitive; primordial; quiescent; rudimentary; vestigial

UNDIGNIFIED: **a.** *infra dignitatem* (**abb.** infra dig.)

UNDIPLOMATIC: **see** "tactless"

UNDISCIPLINED: (**see** "aimless" **and** "unrestrained") **a.** haphazard; tumultuary

UNDISCOURAGED: **see** "undaunted"

UNDISCLOSED *thought or intention:* **n.** *arrière pensée*

UNDIVIDED: (**see** "whole") **a.** impartible; imparticipable; impartite

UNDOING: (**see** "ruin") **n.** defeasance; destruction; labefaction

ᑎNDOUBTED: **see** "unquestionable"

UNDRESSED, *partly:* **a.** deshabille; dishabille; *en déshabillé*

UNDULY: **adv.** excessively; overweening

UNDYING: (**see** "permanent") **a.** amaranthine; immarcescible; immarcessible; immortal; immutable; indestructible; perpetual

UNEARTHLY: (**see** "heavenly") **a.** miraculous; preternatural; supernatural; unworldly

UNEASINESS: (**see** "anxiety") **n.** agitation; compunction; disquiet(ude); dyspathy; dysphoria; inquietude; instability; malaise; penitence; queasiness; remorse; restlessness; scruple; **a.** UNEASY: (**see** "restless") dysphoric; erethic; **adv.** *gêné*
mental: **n.** psychalgia
physical: **n.** dysphoria; malaise

UNEDUCATED: **see** "ignorant" **and** "illiterate"

UNEMOTIONAL: **see** "calm'

UNEMPLOYED: **see** "idle"

UNENDURABLE: **a.** insufferable; insupportable; intolerable; unbearable; unbrookable; **a.** UNENDURING: (**see** "transient") caducous; deciduous; ephemeral; transitory

UNENFORCEABLE *agreement or pact:* **n.** *nudum pactum*

UNENLIGHTENED: (**see** "ignorant") **a.** benighted; uninformed; uninstructed

UNEQUAL: (**see** "unjust") **a.** disparate; disproportionate; dissimilar; inadequate; incommensurate; inegalitarian; inequalitarian; inequitable; irregular; variable

UNEQUALED: **a.** incommensurable; incomparable; matchless; *ne plus ultra;* nonpareil; peerless; transcendent; unparagoned; unparalleled; unprecedented; unrivaled; unsurpassed; untranscended; **n.** UNEQUALITY: **see** "inequality"
or unrivaled: **a.** or **adv.** *hors concours*
person or thing which is: **n.** *ne plus ultra;* nonesuch; nonpareil; paragon

UNESSENTIAL: (**see** "nonessential") **a.** dispensable; supererogatory; unimportant
small decorative: **n.** grace note

UNEVEN: (**see** "erratic") **a.** asperate; asperous; asymmetric(al); disparate; dissymetric(al); inadequate; inequitable; irregular; spasmodic; unsymmetric(al)

UNEXPECTED: (**see** "accidental" **and** "sudden") **a.** supervenient; unannounced; unanticipated; unforeseen; unheralded

UNEXPLAINED: **a.** inscrutable; insoluble; irresolute; unresolved

UNEXPLORED: **a.** uncharted; undetermined; unfathomed; uninvestigated; unplumbed
territory or field of knowledge: **n.** *terra incognita*

UNEXPRESSED: **a.** implicit; implied; inarticulate; tacit; unspoken; unuttered

UNFADING: (**see** "permanent" **and** "undying") **a.** amaranthine; immarcescible; immortal

UNFAIR: **a.** disproportionate; excessive; inequitable; prejudiced

UNFAITHFULNESS: **n.** apostasy; disloyalty; improbity; infidelity; perfidy; treachery

UNFAMILIAR: (**see** "strange") **a.** exotic; inconversant; unaccustomed; uncanny

UNFATHOMED: **a.** immense; undetermined; unsounded

UNFAVORABLE: (**see** "undesirable") **a.** derogatory; detrimental; disadvantageous; dyslogistic; ill-omened; inauspicious; inclement; ominous; portentous; sinister; sinistrous; unpropitious

UNFEELING: (**see** "stoical") a. analgesic; apathetic; impassible; impenitent; impervious; impiteous; implacable; incompassionate; indurate; indurative; insensate; insentient; insensitive; obdurate; unaffectionate; uncompassionate; unemotional; unresponsive; unsusceptible; **n.** (**see** "callousness") insensibility

UNFERMENTED: **a.** azymous

UNFIT: (**see** "improper" **and** "unsuitable") **a.** unexemplary
to be mentioned: (**see** "unspeakable") **a.** nefandous

UNFITNESS, *total and absurd:* **n.** *asinus ad lyram* (ass at the lyre)

UNFORGIVABLE: **a.** inexcusable; inexpiable; irremissible; unpardonable

UNFORGIVING: **a.** impenitent; implacable; relentless

UNFORESEEABLE: (**see** "unexpected") **a.** incalculable

UNFORTUNATE: **a.** calamitous; deplorable; hapless; infelicitous; inopportune; lamentable; unpropitious; unsuitable; unsuccessful; untoward
it's most: **adv.** *c'est un grand malheur*

UNFRIENDLY: (**see** "hostile") **a.** asocial; disaffected; frosty; inhospitable; inimical; uncongenial; unfavorable; ungregarious; unsympathetic; **n.** inhospitality

UNFRUITFUL: **see** "barren"

UNGAINLY: **a.** angulous; **n.** angularity; ungainliness

UNGODLY: **a.** blasphemous; desecrating; heathenish; impious; irreligious; pagan; profane; sacrilegious; unholy; **n.** UNGODLINESS: blasphemy; impiety; irreligiosity
to make: **v.** heathenize; paganize; vulgarize

UNGRATEFUL: **a.** thankless; ungracious

UNHAPPINESS: (**see** "sadness") **n.** anhedonia; dysphoria; infelicity; melancholy; misfortune; wretchedness; **a.** UNHAPPY: (**see** "mournful") anhedonic; disconsolate; dysphoric; infelicitous; melancholy; miserable; unfortunate; wretched
chronic: **n.** anhedonia
productive of: **a.** infelicific

UNHARMONIOUS: (**see** "disharmonious") **a.** cacophonic; cacophonous; discordant; disputatious; dissentient; dissentious; dissident; dissonant

UNHEALTHY (**or** UNHEALTHFUL): (**see** "unwholesome") **a.** inimical; insalubrious; insalutary; insanitary; morbid; noxious; pathological; pernicious; septic; **n.** insalubrity; morbidity

UNHOLY: (**see** "ungodly" **and** "wicked") **a.** unconsecrated; unhallowed

UNHONORED: **a.** unacknowledged; unesteemed; unlaureated; unrespected; unsung

UNIDENTIFIED: **a.** incognito; (**fem.** incognita); unrecognized

UNIFIED: **see** "united"; **a.** UNIFYING: afferent; cementatory; centralizing; centripetal; consolidating; integrative

UNIFORM: (**see** "comparable") **a.** consistent; constant; equable; equiform; harmonious; homogenous; invariable; isogenous; monolithic; symmetrical; synonymous; unanimous; unchanging; undifferentiated; **n.** UNIFORMITY: equability; equanimity; homogeneity; isogeny; monolithism; monotony; (re)semblance; similitude; unanimity
as dress or clothing: **n.** panoply

UNIMAGINATIVE: (**see** "prosaic") **a.** frigid; insipid; monotonous; pedantic; pedestrian; pointless; practical; unleavened

UNIMPORTANT: (**see** "trifling" and "trivial") **a.** dispensable; inconsequential; insignificant; insubstantial; irrelevant; minor-league; unessential; unimpressive; **n.** UNIMPORTANCE: **see** "insignificance"
matter, or unnecessary details: **n.** minutia; (pl. inconsequentia; inconsequentialities; infinitesimalities; minutiae; trivia(lities)
matters, being interested in: **a.** finical; meticulous; minutiose; minutious; picayune; picayunish; rabbinic(al)

UNINSPIRED: (**see** "dull") **a.** pedestrian; prosaic

UNINTELLIGENT: **see** "stupid"; **a.** UNINTELLIGIBLE: abstruse; incomprehensible; unfathomable

UNINTENTIONAL: (**see** "accidental") **a.** inadvertent; unpremeditated; **n.** inadvertence; inadvertency

UNINTERESTED: **a.** apathetic; inattentive; incurious; indifferent; lackadaisic(al); languid; languorous

UNINTERESTING: (**see** "dull") **a.** banal; bromidic; commonplace; immature; insipid; jejune; prosaic(al); sterile; vapid: **n.** banality; insipidity; jejunity; sterility; vapidity

UNION: (**see** "unite") **n.** accouplement; agglutination; alliance; amalgamation; anastomosis; association; coadunation; coalescence; coalition; colligation; (con)federation; confluence; conjugation; conjunction; (con)juncture; consolidation; consortion; fusion; integration; lamination; *rapprochement;* suture; syncretism; synchrondrosis; synoecism; unanimity; unition
in strength: **adv.** *juncta juvant; vis unita fortior*
of blood vessels or channels: **n.** anastomosis; **a.** anastomotic
of cells or parts: **n.** coalescence; concrescence
of govt. or territory: **n.** anschluss
political or economic: **n.** anschluss

UNIQUE: (**see** "rare") **a.** eccentric; exceptional; nonpareil; *sui generis;* uncommon; unequaled; unexampled; unprecedented; **n.** UNIQUENESS: phoenixity; unicity; uniquity
person or thing: **n.** nonpareil; nonesuch; *rara avis;* uniquity
pert. to, involving or dealing w/ the: **a.** idiographic

UNISON, *being in:* **a.** unanimous; unisonant; unisonous; **n.** unanimity

UNIT: **n.** entity; existent; monad; **a.** UNITARY: integrative; monadic; monadological; monistic

UNITE: **(see** "union") **v.** agglutinate; amalgamate; associate; centralize; coadunate; coagment; colligate; (con)catenate; concur; conjugate; consolidate; cooperate; federate; incorporate; inosculate; laminate; recapitulate; syncretize; synoecize
by adhesion: **v. or a.** conglutinate; **n.** conglutination
having power or tendency to: **a.** henotic; irenic
one who (unites) : **n.** concatenator; integrationist; syncretist

UNITED: **a.** amalgamative; coadunate; coadunative; conjugate; conjugative; integrated; syncretic; syncretistic
in fellowship: **a.** consociate; integrative
in opn. or view: **a.** concordant; consentaneous; consentient; harmonious; unanimous; **adv.** *una voce;* **n.** concordance; consentience; harmony; solidarity; totality; unanimity; unification

UNITY: **n.** allness; harmony; integration; omneity; oneness; singleness; solidarity; syncretism; totality; unanimity; unification
of opn., purpose, feeling, etc.: **see under** "united"

UNIVERSAL. **a.** catholic; cosmopolitan; ecumenical; encyclopedical; epidemic; (macro)cosmic; pandemic; panharmonic; peregrine; transcendental; **n.** UNIVERSALITY: catholicity
language: **n.** Esperanto; pasigraphy
principle: **n.** logos
solvent: **n.** menstruum
solvent, supposed (in alchemy) : **n.** alkahest; **a.** alkahestic
wisdom or knowledge: **n.** pansophism; pansophy; **a.** pansophic(al)

UNIVERSE: **n.** cosmos; firmament; macrocosm(os) ; **a.** (macro)cosmic
as orderly system, or pert. to: **n.** cosmos **· a.** cosmic
on small scale: **n.** microcosm; **a.** microcosmic(al)
science or study of: **n.** cosmography; cosmology; universology; **a.** cosmologic(al)
theory of origin: **n.** cosmogeny; cosmogony; **a.** cosmogenetic
worship of: **n.** cosmolatry; cosmotheism; pantheism

UNJUST: **a.** inequal; inequitable; unequal; unwarranted; wrongful

UNJUSTIFIED: **a.** gratuitous; iniquitous; injudicious; unwarranted

UNKIND: **(see** "cruel") **a.** *désobligeant;* disobliging; disgracious; inconsiderate; ungracious; ungrateful; **n.** UNKINDNESS: inconsideration; ingratitude; ungratefulness

UNKNOWABLE: **a.** imponderable; **(pl.** imponderabilia) ; incogitable; incomprehensible
object, as soul: **n.** noumenon; **a.** noumenal

UNKNOWN: **a.** imponderable; **(pl.** imponderabilia) ; incalculable; inglorious; uncharted
cause, per. to: **a.** agnogenic; idiopathic
everything (unknown) is thought to be magnificent: omne ignotum pro magnifico
origin, of: **a.** cryptogenic; idiopathic; phanterogen(et)ic
person: **(see** "stranger") **n.** inconnu
place: **n.** Weissnichtwo
the: **n.** *l'inconnu;* **(pl.** imponderabilia; imponderables)

UNLADYLIKE: **a.** gamine; hoydenish; tomboyish
behavior: **n.** gaminerie; hoydenism; rowdyism; tomboyishness

UNLAWFUL: **(see** "illegal") **a.** *bar sinister;* illegitimate; illicit; irregular; malfeasant
act: **(see** "crime") **n.** malfeasance; misdemeanor

UNLEAVENED: **a.** azymous; banal; pedestrian; tedious; trite; unimaginative

UNLIKE: **(see** "dissimilar") **a.** anomalous; antipathic; disparate; heterogeneous; incongruous; **n.** UNLIKENESS: disparity; heterogeneity; incongruity

UNLIKELY: **(see** "doubtful") **a.** dubious; dubitable; implausible; improbable; incredible; **n.** dubiety; dubiousness; implausibility; improbability; unlikelihood

UNLIMITED: (see "free" **and** "vast") **a.** boundless; immeasurable; immeasurate; imponderable; infinite; innumerable; plenipotent(ial); plenipotentiary; unconfined; unimpeded; untrammeled
power to transact business: **a.** plenipotent(ial)
time: **n.** boundlessness; infinity; perpetuity

UNLOAD: (**see** "rid") **v.** disburden; disencumber; disgorge

UNLUCKY: (**see** "disastrous") **a.** hapless; ill-omened; ill-starred; inauspicious; infaust; inopportune; unfortunate; unpropitious; untoward
day: **n.** *dies infastus* (**or** *infaustus*); (**pl.** *nefasti dies*)

UNMANAGEABLE: (**see** "stubborn" **and** "unruly") **a.** recalcitrant; **n.** recalcitrance

UNMARRIED: **a.** celebate; **n.** celibacy; celibate
born of (unmarried) woman: **a.** parthenic; parthenian; **n.** *bar sinister*

UNMERCIFUL: **see** "merciless"

UNMERITED: **a.** indign; undeserved; unearned

UNMINDFUL: (**see** "careless") **a.** abstracted; forgetful; inattentive; neglectful; oblivious; ungrateful

UNMISTAKABLE: (**see** "clear") **a.** decisive; definitive; manifest; obvious; patent

UNMIXABLE: **a.** immiscible; incompatible; **n.** immiscibility; incompatibility

UNMOVABLE: (**see** "stubborn") **a.** apathetic; inexorable; obstinate; recalcitrant; resolute; unbudgeable

UNMUSICAL: **a.** arrhythmic(al); cacophonic; cacophonous; discordant; inharmonious; unharmonious; **n.** cacophony, discordance

UNNAMED: **a.** anonymous; incognito; innominate; pseudonymous; undubbed; unidentified; unspecified; **n.** anonymity; pseudonymity

UNNECESSARY: **a.** gratuitous; inessential; needless; **n.** inessentiality
to make: **v.** obviate; **n.** obviation

UNOBSERVANT: **a.** astigmatic; inattentive; incurious

UNOFFICIAL: **a.** contraband; intormal; officious; offstage; unauthorized; unorthodox

UNORIGINAL: (**see** "counterfeit") **a.** derivative; unimaginative

UNORTHODOX: (**see** "radical") **a.** heretical; heterodox; unconventional; **n.** UNORTHODOXY: heterodoxy; unconventionality
labeling as: **n.** mark of the beast

UNPAIRED: **a.** azygous; unmatched

UNPARALLELED: (**see** "exceptional") **a.** epochal; nonpareil; unequaled; unsurpassed

UNPARDONABLE: **a.** inexcusable; inexpiable; irremissible; unforgivable

UNPIERCED: **a.** imperforate; intact; unpenetrated

UNPLEASING (**or** UNPLEASANT) (*see* "disagreeable") **a.** bilious; plutonian; plutonic; unpalatable; **n.** UNPLEASANTNESS: (**see** "disagreement") disamenity

UNPOLISHED: (**see** "coarse" **and** "uncouth") **a.** agrestic; gauche; inurbane; uncivilized; unrefined

UNPREDICTABLE. (**see** "erratic") **a.** ambivalent; capricious; chameleonic; fickle; incalculable; vagarious

UNPREJUDICED: **a.** cosmopolitan; equitable; impartial; unbiased

UNPREMEDITATED: (**see** "accidental") **a.** *a brevi manu;* extemporaneous; headlong; impromptu; undesigned; unintentional

UNPREPAREDNESS, *in state of:* **n.** *illotis manibus*

UNPROFITABLE: **a.** frustaneous; infructuous; inutile; sterile; unremunerative; unrewarding; **n.** inutility

UNPROVED: **a.** undocumented; unestablished; unsubstantiated
theory, proposition, etc.: **n.** hypothesis, theorem

UNPUBLISHED *material:* **n.** ineditum; (pl. inedita)

UNPUNISHED: **a.** unatoned; unchastened; unchastised; unexpiated

UNQUALIFIED: (**see** "absolute" **and** "incompetent" **a.** disbarred; disqualified; plenary; ineligible; unreserved; unrestricted

UNQUESTIONABLE: (**see** "certain") **a.** implicit; indisputable; indubitable; undisputable; **n.** indubitability

UNREAL(ISTIC): **a.** affected; artificial; barmecidal; baroque; chimerical; delusive; disembodied; fantastic; fictitious; grotesque; histrionic; illusive; illusory; illusional; imaginary; impalpable; imperceptible; incorporeal; insubstantial; intangible; (melo) dramatic, paper-mache; *papier-mâché;* phantasmagoric(al); phantasmal; phantom; platonic; staged; unsubstantial; Utopian; visionary; **a. or n.** Gothic; **n.** UNREALISM: aeriality; ideality; unsubstantiality

UNREASONABLE: (**see** "illogical" **and** "stubborn") **a.** absonant; fatuous; inappropriate; incongruous; inordinate; irrational; paralogical; paralogistic; preposterous; unconscionable; **n.** UNREASONABLENESS: illogicality; incoherence; irrationality; unsoundness

UNREASONED. **see** "thinking"

UNREFINED: (**see** "coarse") **a.** barbaric earthy; inelegant; troglodytic

UNRELATED: **a.** accidental; arbitrary; discrete; disjointed; dissociate(d); extraneous; extrinsic; heterogenous; impertinent; inapplicable; inapposite; incidental; intercalary; irrelevant; parenthetical; tangential

UNRELIABLE: (**see** "tricky") **a.** contradictuous; duplicitous; feckless; shiftless; unconscionable; undependable; unprincipled; unscrupulous; untrustworthy; villainous; **n.** UNRELIABILITY: duplicity; unconscionability; unscrupulosity

UNRESERVED: **see** "unrestrained"

UNRESPECTABLE: **see** "disrespectable"

UNREST: **see** "disquiet"

UNRESTRAINED: (**see** "free," "lawless" **and** "uncontrolled") **a.** bizarre; exaggerated; extravagant; flamboyant; immoderate; impertinent; incontinent; indiscriminate; inordinate; intemperate; limitless; *outré;* prodigal; promiscuous; rampant; spontaneous; tumultuary; uncontrolled; uncurbed; undampened; undisciplined; unlicensed; unreserved; wanton; **adv.** *abandonnement; con abbandono; con alcuna licenza*

UNRESTRICTED: (**see** "open" **and** "unrestrained") **a.** plenary; plenipotent(ial)

UNREVEALED: (**see** "hidden") **adv.** *in pectore; in petto*

UNREWARDING: **see** "unprofitable"

UNRIVALED: **a.** incomparable; peerless; nonpareil; unparalleled

UNRULY: (**see** "stubborn") **a.** boisterous; headstrong; intractable; mutinous; obstinate; rampageous; rampant; recalcitrant; recusant; refractory; turbulent; unbridled; undisciplined; ungovernable; wanton; willful

UNSAID: **see** "unspoken"

UNSATISFIED: **a.** insatiated; unfulfilled
desire: **n.** insatiability; insatiety

UNSEASONABLE: (**see** "untimely") **a.** inexpedient; inopportune; **adv.** malapropos

UNSEEMLY: (**see** "unbecoming") **a.** inappropriate; indecent; indecorous; solecistic; unbecoming; unseasonable
something which is: **n.** barbarism; impropriety; solecism

UNSELFISH: (see "generous") **a.** altruistic; charitable; chivalrous; magnanimous; philanthropic; **n.** UNSELFISHNESS: (see "generosity") altropathy; altruism; magnanimity; philanthropy

UNSETTLED: **a.** abeyant; deranged; erratic; itinerant; pendant; pendent; nomadic; unstable; vagrant; **n.** instability; itinerancy; vagrancy

UNSHAKABLE: (see "firm") **a.** adamant; impregnable; inflexible

UNSIGNED: **a.** anonymous; pseudonymous; unidentified

UNSKILLFUL: (see "inexperienced") **a.** amateurish; gauche; inapt; inept; maladroit; unartful; **n.** UNSKILLFULNESS: gaucherie; inaptitude; maladroitness

UNSOCIABLE: **a.** antisocial; asocial; detached; discordant; incompatible; inharmonious; inhospitable; insociable; moronic; reserved; solitary; solitudinarian; troglodytic; uncompanionable; uncongenial; ungregarious; withdrawn; **n.** UNSOCIABILITY: see "reserve"

UNSOLVABLE: **a.** inextricable; inscrutable; insoluble; unexcogitable

UNSPARING: **a.** inexorable; procrustean; profuse; relentless; ruthless; **adv.** *à outrance*

UNSPEAKABLE: **a.** execrable; ineffable; indescribable; indicible; inenarrable; inexpressible; nefandous; unmentionable; unutterable; utterless; **adv.** *horrible dictu;* **n.** ineffability

UNSPOKEN: **a.** inarticulate; obmutescent; tacit; unarticulated; uncommunicated; unexpressed; unsaid; unuttered; unverbalized

UNSTABLE: (see "unsteady") **a.** astatic; ataxic; fickle; inconstant; labile; mercurial; mutable; protean; titubant; vacillating; variable, vertiginous; volatile; voluable; **n.** astasis; astaticism; ataxia; lability; volatility; volubility

UNSTOPPABLE: **a.** inextinguishable; insatiable; unextinguishable; unquenchable

UNSUBSTANTIAL: (see "unreal") **a.** aerial; diaphanous; ethereal; filigree; imaginary; shadowy; visionary; **n.** UNSUBSTANTIALITY: aeriality; diaphaneity; ethereality; shadowiness

UNSUCCESSFUL: **a.** *manqué*

UNSUITABLE (or UNSUITED): (see "untimely") **a.** *à propos de rien;* discordant; impertinent; inapplicable; inappropriate; inapt; incompatible; incongruent; incongruous; inept; infelicitous; inharmonious; unbecoming; unmeet; unseemly; **n.** UNSUITABILITY: inaptitude; inconcinnity; incongruity; infelicity; maladroitness; maladjustment; misalliance

UNSUPPORTED: **a.** unbuttressed; undocumented

UNSURPASSED: **see** "unequaled"

UNSYMPATHETIC: **a.** ill-disposed

UNTAMED: (see "wild") **a.** barbarous; *ferae naturae;* feral; rambunctious; unfettered; unsubdued; **n.** barbarity; ferity; ferocity

UNTEACHABLE: **a.** indocile; intractable; **n.** indocility; intractability

UNTHINKABLE: (see "unspeakable") **a.** extraordinary; incogitable; inconceivable; incredible; unimaginable

UNTHINKING: **a.** heedless; inattentive, incogitant; inconsiderate; unmindful; unmotivated; unphilosophic(al); **n.** incogitability

UNTIDY: **a.** dishevel(l)ed; slovenly; tatterdemalian; unfastidious; unkempt; **n.** UNTIDINESS: dishevelment

or confused place: **n.** Bedlam; mare's nest

UNTIMELY: **a.** inappropriate; inauspicious; inconvenient; inexpedient; inopportune; intempestive; premature; unfavorable; unpropitious; unpunctual; unseasonable

UNTIRING: **a.** everlasting; indefatigable; sustained; tireless; unflagging; unwearying; **n.** indefatigability

UNTOLD: **a.** boundless; immeasurable; incalculable; innumerable; unrevealed

UNTOUCHABLE: **a.** inviolable; invulnerable; sacrosanct; **n.** inviolability; invulnerability; sacrosanctity

UNTRAINED: **a.** illiterate; nescient; uncultivated; uneducated; untutored

UNTRIED: (**see** "unattempted") **a.** callow; immature; inexperienced; unexpert; unfledged

UNTRUE: **a.** disloyal; fabulous; fictitious; mendacious; mythological; spurious; supposititious; unfaithful; **n.** UNTRUTHFUL: **see** "false" **and** "truth, departing from"; **n.** UNTRUTHFULNESS: dishonesty; inaccuracy; inveracity; mendacity

though characteristic or appropriate: **a.** *ben trovato*

UNTRUSTWORTHY: (**see** "dishonest" **and** "uncertain") **a.** disingenuous

UNUNITED: **a.** disarticulated; disassembled; discrete; disunited

UNUSABLE: (**see** "useless") **a.** afunctionable; afunctional; inutile; **n.** inutility

UNUSUAL: (**see** "odd" **and** "strange") **a.** anomalistic; anomalous; bizarre; exceptional; exotic; extraordinary; fantastic; grotesque; irregular; *outré;* paranormal; peculiar; phenomenal; *recherché;* remarkable; singular

experience: **n.** escapade

person: **n.** *rara avis*

structurally: **a.** ectopic; heteromorphic, heteromorphous; **n.** heteromorphosis

thing: **n.** extravaganza; *rara avis;* unusuality

UNUTTERABLE: (**see** "unspeakable") **a.** indescribable; ineffable; inexpressible

UNVARYING: (**see** "dull") **a.** constant; monotonous; unchanging; uniform

UNWANTED: **a.** *de trop;* nonessential, superfluous; undesirable

UNWARLIKE: **see** "peaceful"

UNWELCOME: **a.** *de trop; non grata;* unacceptable

person: **n.** *persona non grata*

UNWHOLESOME: (**see** "unhealthy") **a.** deleterious; inimical; insalubrious; malignant; morbid; pathological; pernicious

UNWIELDLY: (**see** "bulky") **a.** awkward; cumbrous; cumbersome; elephantine; hippopotamian; hippopotamic; ponderous; ungainly

UNWILLING: (**see** "indisposed" **and** "involuntary") **a.** a(d)verse; reluctant; **n.** UNWILLINGNESS: aversion; disinclination; nolition; repugnance; reluctance; reluctancy; reluctation

or willing: **adv.** *nolens volens*

UNWISE: (**see** "senseless") **a.** ill-advised; impolitic; imprudent; indiscreet; inexpedient; injudicious; untimely

UNWORTHY: (**see** "base" **and** "undeserving") **a.** indign; inglorious; derogatory; despicable; unmeet; worthless

UNWRITTEN: **a.** customary; nuncupative; tacit; traditional

law: **n.** *jus commune; lex non scripta*

UNYIELDING: (**see** "rigid" **and** "stubborn") **a.** adamant(ine); immalleable; impregnable; indomitable; inductile; inflexible; intractable; obstinate; perseverant; persistent; pertinacious; recalcitrant; resolute; tenacious; unalterable; unassailable; uncompromising; unshakable

UPHEAVAL: **n.** cataclysm; convulsion; labefaction; orogeny; overthrow; **a.** cataclysmal; cataclysmic(al)

UPKEEP: **n.** maintenance; sustentation; **a.** sustentative

UPLIFTING: **a.** inspirational; inspirative, inspiriting; instigative

UPPISH: **see** "proud"

UPRIGHT: **a.** chivalrous; conscientious; honorable; perpendicular; punctilious; rectitudinous; scrupulous; vertical; **n.** UPRIGHTNESS: integrity; perpendicularity; probity; rectitude; scrupulosity; verticality

UPRISING: **n.** *coup d'état;* insurgence; insurgency; insurrection; mutiny
tending to: **a.** insurgescence; mutinous

UPROAR: (**see** "clamor") **n.** Babelism; Bedlam; brouhaha; callithump; furore; hubbub; pandemonium
great: **n.** charivari; conclamation; pandemonium; tintamar(re); **a.** callithumpian; pandemoniac(al)

UPROOT: **v.** deracinate; eradicate; exterminate; extirpate; **n.** deracination; extirpation; **a.** UPROOTED: (**see** "displaced"); lumpen

UPSET: **v.** capsize; discompose; disconcert; disparage; overthrow; overturn; subvert; **n.** bouleversement

UPSIDE *down:* **a.** *sens dessus dessous;* topsy-turvy; **n.** topsy-turvydom; topsy-turviness

UPSTART: **n.** *arrivist(e); hesterni quirites;* Johnny-come-lately; *novus homo; nouveau riche; parvenu;* pip-squeak
social: **n.** *arrivist(e); parvenu*

UP-TO-DATE: **see** "modern"

UPWARD, *moving or tending:* **a.** anabatic; ascensional; ascensive; assurgent; **n.** assurgency; escalation

URGE: **see** "beseech"

URGENCY: **n.** criticality; exigency; imminence; importunity; instancy; **a.** URGENT: compelling; critical; exigent; imminent; impending; imperative; imperious; importunate; insentient; menacing momentous; necessitous; persistent; poignant; solicitous; straitened; vehement; vital

URINATE: **v.** micturate; void; **n.** miction; micturition

USABLE: (**see** "practical") **a.** feasible; functional; instrumental; practicable; utile
not: **see** "useless"

USAGE(S): **n.** consuetude custom, mores; prescription; tradition; utility; **a.** consuetudinal; traditional
according to: **adv.** consuetudinally; customarily; *secundum usum*
fashionable, observance of: **n.** *savoir vivre*

USE(S): **n.** applicability; application; deployment; disposition; employment; exercitation; utility; utilization
something having many: **n.** polychresty
to own advantage: **n.** embezzlement; exploitation; (mis)appropriation
unethical: **n.** exploitation
up: **v.** deplete; impoverish; **n.** impoverishment

USEFUL: **a.** advantageous; beneficial; efficacious; expedient; feasible; functional; materialistic; opportune; practicable; remunerative; utilitarian; yeoman; **n.** USEFULNESS: efficacy; feasibility; functionality; practicability; utility
things, learning of: **n.** chrestomathy; **a.** chrestomathic(al)

USELESS: **a.** afunctional; futile; ineffectual; inefficacious; inefficient; inutile; nugatory; otiose; unavailing; unserviceable; **n.** USELESSNESS: *hors de combat;* ineffectuality; inutility; otiosity

USER: **a.** beneficiary; consumer

USUAL: **a.** accustomed; commonplace; conventional; customary; habitual; ordinary; prevalent; prevailing; traditional; wonted; **n.** USUALNESS: conventionality; prevalence; tradition
as: **adv.** *à l'ordinaire; comme à l'ordinaire; comme d'ordinaire*

UTILITY: **see** "usefulness"

UTMOST *degree:* **n.** fare-thee-well; fare-you-well; uttermost
extent: **adv.** *à fond*
to the: **adv.** *à outrance*

UTTER: (**see** "speak") **v.** articulate; phonate; pronounce; **a.** (**see** "complete") consummate; incarnate; peremptory; pluperfect; sheer; unqualified; unspeakable; uttermost; **n.** UTTERANCE: articulation; descant; expression; observation

UTTERED, *capable of being:* **a.** effable

V

VACANT: (**see** "void") untenanted; vacuous

VACILLATING: **see** "wavering"

VAGABOND: (**see** "rogue") **n.** Bohemian; gypsy; nomad; truant; wastrel; **a.** VAGABONDISH: Bohemian; nomadic; picaresque

VAGRANT: (**see** "roving") **a.** circumforaneous; itinerant; peregrine; peripatetic; **n.** (**see** "vagabond") itinerant; peregrine; Peripatetic; (**pl.** flotsam and jetsam)

VAGUE: (**see** "abstract" **and** "indecisive") **a.** acategorical; aerial; ambiguous; amorphous; amphibolic; amphibological; cryptic; doubtful; dubious; dubitable; elusive; equivocal; illogical; imprecise; inconcrete; indefinable; indefinite; indescribable; indeterminate; indistinct; insubstantial; intangible; nubilous; obscure; sibylline; unexplicit; vaporous; **adv.** *in nubibus;* **n.** VAGUENESS: dubiety; dubiosity; insubstantiality; vaporosity

suggestion: (**see** "trace") **n.** nuance; *soupçon;* umbrage

VAIN: **a.** abortive; dogmatic; ego(t)istical; flatulent; fruitless; frustaneous; hubristic; nugatory; officious; ostentatious; otiose; pedantic; pompous; pragmatic(al); pretentious; vainglorious; **n. see** "vanity"

person: **n.** coxcomb; dandiprat; dogmatist; jackanapes; macaroni; popinjay

threat: **n.** *fulmen brutum*

VALIANT: (**see** "bold" **and** "brave") **a.** chivalric; chivalrous; intrepid; noteworthy; stout-hearted; valorous; *n. see* "valor"

VALIDITY, *accept or give full to:* **v.** nostrificate; **n.** nostrification

without: **a.** null and void; *nullius juris*

VALOR: **n.** arete; chivalry; gallantry; intrepidity; **a. see** "valiant"

VALUABLE: **a.** classic; (in)estimable; meritorious; priceless; treasured

VALUE(S), *according to:* **adv.** *ad valorem*

based on or involving intrinsic or fundamental: **a.** axiological

based on sentiment or whim: **n.** *pretium affectionis*

having same relative in position or structure: **a.** analogous; homologous

least possible: **n.** ambsace; nihility; triviality; (**pl.** trivia)

lowering in: **see under** "lower"

making moral obligations dependent on: **a.** axiological

of little or slight, thing of: **n.** ambsace; bagatelle; continental; *corpus vile;* (**pl.** *corpus villa*); nihil(ity); *sou markee*

of no: **a.** fustian

theory or study of: **n.** axiology; **a.** axiological

VALUELESS: **see** "worthless"

VAMPIRE: **n.** Dracula; extortioner; lamia; sorceress; succubus

VANISHING: (**see** "fleeting") **a.** diaphanous; ephemeral; ethereal; evanescent; unsubstantial; **n.** diaphaneity; ethereality; evanescence; unsubstantiality

VANITY: **n.** *amour-propre;* arrogance; ego(t)ism; flatulence; hollowness; hubris; ostentation; otiosity; pomposity; vainglory

all is: omnia vanitas

of vanities: **n.** *vanitas vanitatum*

VANTAGE *point:* **n.** coign (of vantage); *pou sto*

VAPOR: **see** "cloud"

changing readily to: **a.** volatile; **n.** volatility

disagreeable: **n.** effluvium; (**pl.** effluvia); miasma; **a.** effluvial; miasmic

heavy, as from swamps: **n.** miasma; **a.** miasmatic; miasmic

VARIABLE: (**see** "changeable") **a.** alterable: (am)bivalent; capricious; chamele-

onic; fickle; inconstant; irresolute; mercurial; mutable; quicksilver; vagrant
exceedingly: **a.** protean

VARIATION: **n.** alternation; diversification; modification; (per)mutation; variance
allowed fr. standard: **n.** tolerance
in form: **n.** multiformity; mutation; polymorph; sport; **a.** allotropic; polymorphic; polymorphous
slight: **n.** nuance

VARIED: **a.** diversified; manifold; mosaic; multifarious; multiform
quality or state: **n.** heterogeneity; miscellaneity

VARIEGATED: **a.** chimeral; diversified; heterogeneous; iridescent; kaleidoscopic; mosaic; motley; parti-colored; opalescent; prismatic; tessellate(d); **n.** VARIEGATION: diversification; heterogeneity; iridescence; mosaic; tessellation

VARIETIES, *composed of or containing all:* **a.** omnigenous
of all: **a.** heterogeneous; omnifarious

VARIETY: **n.** assortment; diversification; diversity; genre; genus; heterogeneity; medley; melange; multifariousness; multiformity; stock; strain; versatility
having infinite or great: **a.** kaleidoscopic
of great: **a.** heterogeneous; manifold; multifarious; multiple; multiplex; multiplicitous; protean

VARIOUS *parts, in (of a book)*: **adv.** *passim*
sources, drawn or derived from: **a.** eclectic; variorum
things: **n.pl.** miscellanea; varia

VARY: **see** "diversify"; **a.** VARYING: **see** "unstable"

VAST: (**see** "huge") **a.** boundless; colossal; comprehensive; cosmic; cyclopean; elephantine; Gargantuan; grandiose; herculean; immeasurable; imponderable; infinite; magnitudinous; titanic; unlimited; **n.** VASTITUDE: collosality; comprehensiveness; immeasurability; immensity; indefinitude; infinitude; magnitude; vastity

VAULT: **n.** concameration; fornix; **a.** concamerated

VEGETABLES, *cultivation and marketing of:* **n.** olericulture
garden: **n.** potagerie(s)

VEGETATION, *feeding on:* **a.** herbivorous; phytophagous; vegetarian; **n.** herbivore: (pl. herbivora); vegetarian
goddess of: **n.** Ceres; Flora
of or characteristic of growing: **a.** verdant; verdurous; **n.** verdancy

VEILED: (*in shadow*): **n.** chiaroscuro; sfumato; tenbrism; **a.** penumbral; tenebrous

VELVETY: **a.** velutinous

VENAL: **see** "mercenary"

VENERABLE: (**see** "ancient") **a.** patriarchal; respected; reverential

VENEREAL: **a.** aphrodisiac; Cytherean

VENGEANCE: **n.** Nemesis; reprisal; retaliation; retribution
goddess of: **n.** Fury; Nemesis
inflictor of: **n.** Nemesis

VENT: **n.** aperture; orifice; **a.** orificial

VENTURE: **n.** enterprise; jeopardy; speculation; **a.** VENTURESOME: **see** "adventurous"

VENUS, *votary of, or pert. to:* **a.** or **n.** Cytherean

VERB, *change into:* **v.** verbify; **n.** verification

VERBAL: (**see** "oral") **adv.** *ore tenus*
description: **see under** "description"
statement or formulation: **n.** verbality
thrust: **n.** repartee; ripost(e)

VERIFIED: (**see** "established") **a.** documented
capable of being: **a.** confirmable; verifiable; verificatory; **n.** verificability

VERSATILE: **a.** ambidextrous; inconstant; polygraphic; **n.** VERSATILITY: ambidexterity

VERSE: (**see** "poetry") **n.** metrification; versification
obscene piece of: **n.** ithyphallic

witty, light or ironic: **n.** limerick; *vers de société*

VERTICAL: (**see** "erect") **a.** perpendicular; **n.** VERTICALITY: perpendicularity

VERY *good or well:* **adv.** *très bien*
great in trifles: maximus in minimus
nature of the case, by the: **adv.** *ipso facto*
words, the: **n.** *ipissima verba*

VETERAN: **n.** grognard; oldster; patriarch; stager; **a. see** "venerable"

VEX: (**see** "annoy") **v.** afflict; pique; **n.** VEXATION: affliction; chagrin; displeasure; impatience; irritation; mortification; pique; **a.** VEXATIOUS: (**see** "annoying") afflictive; choleric; disordered; impatient; pestilent; petulant; restive

VIBRATE: **v.** oscillate; palpitate; quaver; tremulate; undulate; **a.** VIBRATORY: oscillant; tremulant; tremulous; undulant; undulatory

VICE: **see** "wickedness"

VICIOUS: (**see** "wicked") **a.** egregious; feral; flagitious; flagrant; iniquitous; villainous; **n.** VICIOUSNESS: barbarity; egregiousness; ferity; flagitiousness; flagrancy; iniquity; villainy

VICTORY: (**see** "conquest" **and** "defeat") **n.** achievement; ascendancy; mastery; prevailment; subjugation; supremacy; triumph
at great loss or sacrifice: **n.** Cadmean (victory); Pyrrhic (victory)
celebrating: **a.** epinician
hymn or ode in honor of: **n.** epinicion; **a.** epicinian
in name only: **see** "at great loss" **above**
sign of (vee): **n.** bidigitation

VIEW: (**see** "opinion" **and** "outlook") **n.** panorama; perspective; perspectivity; prospect; scrutiny; survey; vista
affording a general: **a.** panoramic; synoptic
or survey, quick: **n.** *coup d'oeil*
unlimited: **n.** panorama; **a.** panoptic; panoramic

VIEWPOINT: (**see** "scope") **n.** frame of reference

VIGILANT: (**see** "aware") **a.** Cerberean; circumspect; watchful

VIGOR: **n.** ardor; *élan;* gusto; impetuosity; lustiness; stamina; tonicity; verve; vivacity; zest; **a.** VIGOROUS: (**see** "bracing") animated; *con spirito;* cyclonic(al); dynamic(al); energetic; flourishing; forceful; puissant; spirited; strenuous; torrential; vehement; virile; **adv.** *con anima; con brio; con spirito*
deprive of: **v.** debilitate; devitalize; emasculate; enervate; **n.** enervation
given to great: **a.** cyclonic(al); dynamic; robustious; **n.** dynamism; robusticity
lacking in: **see under** "vitality"

VILE: (**see** "bad" **and** "wicked") **a.** abominable; contemptible; degenerate; despicable; egregious; flagitious; flagrant; infamous; ignominious; odious; profligate; putrid; sordid; vicious; vulturine; vulturous; **n.** (**see** "abuse") VILENESS: abomination; despicability; putridity

VILIFY: **see** "slander"

VILLAGE: **n.** microcosm; settlement; **a.** microcosmic(al); villagic; villageous

VILLAIN: (**see** "rogue" **and** "traitor") **n.** miscreant; profligate; rapscallion; **n.** VILLAINY: miscreancy; wickedness; **a.** VILLAINOUS: miscreant; rapscallion; unconscionable; unprincipled; unscrupulous

VINDICATION: **n.** compurgation; exoneration; justification; revenge; substantiation; **v.** VINDICATE: absolve; exculpate; exonerate; justify; substantiate

VINEGAR, *like:* **a.** acetous; acidulant; acidulous; vinegary

VIOLATE: (**see** "defile") **v.** contravene; desecrate; impinge; transgress; **a.** VIOLATIVE: transgressive; violational; **n.** VIOLATION: contravention; desecration; encroachment; impingement; infraction; infringement; misdeed; profanation; ravishment; transgression; trespass
not capable of (violation): **a.** inviolable; invulnerable; irrefrangable; irrefrangible

VIOLENT: (**see** "raging") **a.** impetuous; maniac(al); rampant; tempestuous; torrential; turbulent; vehement; **n.** VIO-

LENCE: barbarity; ferocity; fervor; fury; impetuosity; impetuousness; mania; passion; rampancy; tempestuousness; turbulency; vehemence

VIOLIN, *resembling in outline:* **a.** pandurate; panduriform

VIRGIN(S): **n.** *virgio intacta;* **a.** undefiled; unspoiled; unsullied; untapped
demi- or "technical": **n.** demi-vierge
for, and for boys: virginibus puerisque
pert. or belonging to: **a.** parthenian; parthenic
worship of: **n.** parthenolatry

VIRGINITY, *deprive of:* **v.** devirginate; devirginize; **n.** devirgination; **n.** devirginator

VIRTUE: **n.** arete; chastity; dharma; fidelity; integrity; morality; probity; rectitude; sanctity; uprightness; **a.** VIRTUOUS: exemplary; meritorious; rectitudinous; righteous; seraphic; virginal
false assumption of: **n.** hypocrisy; piosity; religiosity; **a.** hypocritical; religiose
four cardinal (virtues): **n.** fortitude; justice; prudence; temperance
goddess of: **n.** Fides
honor is reward of: virtutis praemium
is strongest shield: aegis fortissima virtus
rejoices in trial: gaudet tentamine virus
"science of": **n.** aretaics

VIRULENCE, *lessening of:* **n.** abatement; attenuation

VISIBLE: **a.** apparent; discernible; manifest; obvious; patent; perceptible; **adv.** *à vue; d'oeil; ad oculos*
to naked eye: **a.** macroscopic; **adv.** *nudis oculis*

VISION: **(see** "prospect") **n.** apparition; discernment; foresight; hallucination; illusion; percipience; perception; perspicacity
acuteness of: **see** "keenness of" **below**
blurred: **n.** astigmatism; **a.** astigmatic(al)
defective: **n.** amblyopia
double: **n.** diplopia; **a.** diplopic
fallacy in: **n.** fantasy; illusion; mirage; phantasm(agory); phantom; poltergeist; specter; wraith; **a.** phantasmagoric(al); spectral
faulty: **see** "blurred" **above**
keenness of: **n.** *acuité visuelle;* oxyblepsia; visual acuity; **a.** lynx-eyed
universal (all-seeing): **n.** omnividence

VISIONARY: **a.** aerial; airy-fairy; chimerical; doctrinaire; dogmatic(al); dreamy; idealistic; impractical; irresponsible; ivory-tower; laputan; notional; platonic; platonistic; poetic(al); quixotic(al); romantic; starry-eyed; theoretical; translunary; unsubstantial; Utopian; **n.** (see "dreamer") doctrinaire; dogmatist; enthusiast; ideologist; ideologue; theorist

VISIT: **n.** sojourn(ment); visitation
esp. brief or temp.: **v.** sojourn; **n.** sojournment; **n.** sojourner

VISITING *card:* **n.** *carte de visite*
often or habitually: **n.** frequentation; habituation; **v.** frequent; habituate

VISITOR: **n.** sojourner; visitant

VISUALIZE: **(see** "imagine") **v.** envision; foresee; perceive

VITAL: **(see** "important") **a.** animated; energetic; fatal; fundamental; indispensable; mortal; pivotal
force: **n.** *anima bruta; anima mundi; élan vital*
statistics, science of: **n.** demography

VITALITY: **see** *"vigor"*
drain of: **v.** desiccate; devitalize; enervate
lack of: **n.** abiotrophy; adynamia; **a.** abiotrophic; adynamic; desiccated

VIVID: **a.** eidetic; picturesque; piquant; poignant; trenchant

VOCALIZE: **v.** articulate; enunciate; phonate; pronounce; **n.** VOCALIZATION: articulation; enunciation; phonation; **a.** **see** "voiced"

VOCATIONAL: **a.** banausic; employmental; materialistic; professional

VOICE, *clearness or distinctness of:* **n.** lamphrophonia
characteristic of: **n.** timbre
deep, heavy bass: **n.** *basso profundo*
effeminate: **a.** gynecophonous
high: **n.** *haute voix*

in a clear and distinct: **see under** "pronunciation"
in a low: **a. or adv.** *sotto voce*
loss of: **n.** aphonia; obmutescence
of God: **n.** *vox Dei*
of one crying in wilderness: vox clamantis in deserto
of the people: **n.** *vox populi* **(abb.** vox pop.)
secret: **n.** *vox clandestina*
with one: **adv.** *una voce*

VOICED: **a.** articulated; enunciated; phonated; phonetic; sonant; sonic; vocalized

VOCIFEROUS: **see** "loud"

VOID: **(see** "null") **a.** nugatory; *nullis juris;* vacuous; **n.** vacuum
make: **v.** abrogate; delete; negate; nullify; quash; repeal

VOLUME: **(see** "capacity") **n.** amplitude; loudness; magnitude; **a.** VOLUMINOUS: **(see** "huge") bouffant(e); multitudinous

VOLUPTUOUS: **see** "sensuous"

VOMIT: **v.** disgorge; regurgitate; **n.** disgorgement; emesis; regurgitation

VOMITING: **n.** (hyper)emesis; **a.** emetic; regurgitating
drug or agent for: **n.** emetic
of pregnancy: **n.** hyperemesis; *hyperemesis gravidarum*

VOTE: (or VOTING) : **n.** franchise; plebiscite (or plebescite); referendum; suffrage; **a.** plebiscitary; plebiscitic: **n.** VOTER(S): constituency; constituent

VOW: **n.** profession
of chastity: **n.** *votum castitatis*
pert. to or consecrated by: **a.** votary

VOWEL, *having more than one:* **a.** plurivocalic
immediately preceding a: **a.** antevocalic; prevocalic

VULGAR: **(see** "common" **and** "lewd") **a.** earthy; Falstaffian; Hogarthian; ignoble; irreverent; obscene; plebeian; Rabelaisian; ribald(rous); scurrile; scurrilous; sordid; unrefined; **n.** VULGARITY: commonness; pleb(e)ianism; ribaldry; scurrility; vulgarization
person: **see under** "person"
to make: **v.** heathenize; paganize; plebeianize; vulgarize

VULTURE, *of or characteristic of:* **a.** vulturine; vulturous

W

WAG: see "wit"

WAGE: **n.** compensation; emolument; honorarium; remuneration; stipend(ium); **a.** stipendiary
earner(s) **n.** bourgeois; proletarian; proletariat; **a.** bourgeois; proletarian

WAGGISH: (see "humorous") **a.** espiegle; frolicsome; **n.** WAGGISHNESS: *espieglerie;* roguery; roguishness

WAIL: **v.** caterwaul; deplore; lament; ululate; **n.** caterwaul; lamentation; ululation; **a.** WAILING: plangorous; ululant

WAIST, *having slender:* **a.** waspish

WAITER, *head:* **n.** *maître d'hôtel*

WALK: **v.** pedestrianize; (per)ambulate; peregrinate; traverse; **n.** promenade; peregrination
about and around: **v.** circumambulate; deambulate; promenade; **n.** circumambulation; deambulation; promenade; **a.** circumambulatory; deambulatory; perambulatory
inability to fr. muscular incoordination: **n.** astasia-abasia; astasis; ataxia
thru, around or about: **v.** perambulate; **a.** perambulatory; **n.** perambulation

WALKING: **a.** ambulant; *à pied;* (de)ambulatory; itinerant; pedestrian; Peripatetic; **n.** deambulation; (per)ambulation; peregrination; peripateticism
adapted for: **a.** gressorial
alone: **n.** or **a.** solivagant
fr. place to place: **n.** or **a.** itinerant; Peripatetic
in sleep: see under "sleep"
pert. to ability for: **a** ambulatorial
upright or vertical: **n.** or **a.** orthograde; orthostatic; plantigrade
w/ body horizontal, as most animals: **a.** pronograde

WALL *in:* **v.** immure; **n.** immurement
pert. to: **a.** mural; parietal

WALLOW(ING): **v.** flounder; welter; **n.** volutation

WAND, *divination by:* **n.** rhabdomancy

WANDER: **v.** circumambulate; deviate; divagate; expatiate; itinerate; meander; perambulate; peregrinate; **n.** circumambulation; divagation; itineration; perambulation; peregrination
aimlessly or idly: **v.** meander; **n.** meandering
at leisure; **v.** circumambulate; **a.** circumambulatory; **n.** circumambulation
tendency to: **n.** itinerancy; peregrinism; peregrinity
urge to: **n.** dromomania; wanderlust

WANDERER: **n.** itinerant; Odysseus; peregrinator; peregrine; vagabond
solitary: **n.** or **a.** solivagant

WANDERING: (see "straying") **a.** circumambulatory; errant; erring; itinerant; meandering; migratory; nomadic; Odyssean; Peripatetic; vagabond(ish); vagarious; vagrant; **n.** circumambulation; divagation; errantry; expatiation; fugitivity; odyssey; peregrination; peregrinity; vagabondage; vagabondism
alone: **a.** solivagant
extended, incl. intellectual, etc.: **n.** odyssey; **a.** Odyssean; peregrinate
fr, place to place: **a.** circumforaneous; itinerant; Odyssean; peregrinic; vagrant
intellectual or spiritual: **n.** odyssey; **a.** Odyssean
one topic to another: **a.** desultory; digressive; discursive; pleonastic

WANING: **a.** decrescent; declinatory; **n.** (see "recession") abatement; declension; declination; decrescence; diminution

WANT: (see "need") **v.** desiderate; necessitate; require; **n.** dearth; deficiency; desideratum; destitution; exigency; indigence; (pl. desiderata; desideria); **a.** WANTING: deficient; desiderative; destitute; lacking; necessitous

WANTON: see "lustful" and "extravagant"

WAR(S) (or WARFARE): **n.** hostility
after the: **a.** postbellum
before the (as Civil): **a.** antebellum
between: **a.** interbella; interbellum
deadly or lethal: **n.** *bellum lethale*
doctrine opposed to: **n.** pacifism; **a.** pacifistic
during the: **adv.** *flagrante bello*
equipment for: **n.** *apparatus belli;* armamentarium; (pl. armamentaria); armament(s); *matériel*
excuse or cause for: **n.** *casus belli*
hating of: **a.** misopolemical
-horse: **n.** *cheval de bataille*
laws are silent in time of: silent legis inter arma
paper (war): **n.** *guerre de plume*
stratagem of: **n.** *ruse de guerre*
such is, or that is: **adv.** *c'est la guerre*
to the death: **n.** *guerre à mort; guerre à outrance*
widespread or annihilative: **n.** armageddon; holocaust

WAREHOUSE: (see "storage place") **n.** *entrepôt*

WARINESS: see "prudence"

WARLIKE: (see "hostile") **a.** agonistic; amazonian; armigerous; bellicose; belligerent; disputatious; martial; militant; oppugnant; Spartan(ic) unpacific

WARM: **a.** ardent; calid; enthusiastic; **a.** WARMING: calefacient; calefactory; calescent; **n.** calefaction; calescence
-blooded: **a.** endothermic
growing: **a.** incalescent
-up: **n.** prologue; prolusion; **a.** prolusory

WARMED-*over:* **n.** or **a.** *réchauffé*
-over cabbage (old story): **n.** *crambe repetita*

WARMTH: (see "heat") **n.** ardency; ardor; calor; cordiality; fervor; hospitality; graciosity; graciousness; empressement; passion; temperature
excess: **n.** empressement; hyperpyrexia
producing or promoting: **a.** euthermic
sense or sensation of: **n.** thalposis; **a.** thalpotic

WARNING: **n.** (ad)monition; augury; caveat; (ex)hortation; homily; omen; premonition; presentiment; tocsin; **a.** (ad)monitorial; (ad)monitory; (ex)hortative; (ex)hortatory; homiletic; ominous; premonitory; **v.** WARN: admonish; caution; counsel; exhort; precondition; sermonize
against touching or interference: **n.** *noli me tangere*
as a (or by way of): **adv.** *in terrorem*
of death: **n.** *memento mori*
serving as a: **a.** deterrent; (ex)hortative; (ex)hortatory; monitory; sematic
symptom: **n.** prodrome; **a.** pathognomonic(al); prodromal

WART: **n.** ecphyma; excrescence; papilloma; verruca vulgaris
resembling: **a.** verrucose; verrucous

WASHING: **n.** ablution; lavage; lavation; **a.** ablutionary; **v.** WASH: (see "clean") deterge; erode; mundify
religious ceremonial: **n.** ablution; lavabo; maundy; nipter

WASTE(S): **v.** despoil; devastate; dissipate; emaciate; exhaust; pillage; **n.** debris; decrement; depreciation; detritus; dilapidation; diminution; dross; excrement; prodigality; recrement; scoria; sordor; wilderness; (pl. (d)ejecta; egesta; excreta; rejecta[menta])
away, as by fasting or disease: **v.** atrophy; macerate; **a.** atrophic; atrophied; emaciated; tabescent; **n.** atrophy; emaciation; tabefaction; tabescence
giving off: **a.** depurant; emunctory; excretory
pert. to: **a.** excremental; excrementious; recrementitious
products: **n.** carrion; offal; offscourings
to lay: **v.** denudate; depauperate; depredate; deracinate; despoil; pillage

WASTEFUL: **a.** extravagant; improvident; imprudent; lavish; prodigal; profligate; thriftless; **n.** WASTEFULNESS: extravagance; improvidence; lavishness; prodigality; profligacy; superfluity
person: **n.** prodigal; profligate; spendthrift; wastrel

WATCH: **v.** chaperone; invigilate; proctor; supervise; survey; **n.** chaperonage; invigilation; scrutiny; surveillance; **a.** WATCHFUL: (see "aware") alert; Cerberean; surveillant; vigilant; wide-awake
on the: **adv.** *aux aguets*

WATCHER **n.** Cerberus; chaperone; custodian; surveillant; watchdog
sexual: **n.** scopophiliac; *voyeur*

WATCHMAKER *or repairman:* **n.** horologist; **n.** horology

WATCHWORD: **see** "password"

WATER(S), *absorbing:* **a.** bibulous; hydrophilic; hygroscopic; osmotic; **n.** bibulosity; deliquescence; osmosis
animal that sheds: **n.** hydrophobe
being in shallow: **a.** adlittoral
containing (*watery*): **a.** hydrated; hydrous; ichorous; serous
conveying or supplying: **a.** aquiferous
cultivating plants, etc. in: **n.** aquiculture; hydroponics
destitute of, or not containing: **a.** anhydrous; desiccated
living in fresh: **a.** helolimnic
living in, or on land: **a.** amphibious; **n.** amphibian
moving, living or active in: **a.** lotic
needing minimal amt. of: **a.** xerophilous
nymph: **n.** naiad
of the world: **n.** seven seas
one adverse to: **n.** hydrophobe
pure: **n.** *aqua pura*
rel. to: **a.** aquatic
still, rel. to or living in: **a.** lentic
swimming or floating in or on: **a.** natant; natatory
thriving in both flowing and still: **a.** eupotamic
in flowing only: **a.** autopotamic
in salt (*water*): **a.** halophilic
in stagnant: **a.** stagnicolous
in still only: **a.** tychopotamic
to remove: **v.** dehydrate; desiccate; distil; evaporate; inspissate; sublimate
treatment by: **n.** balneotherapy; balneotherapeutics; hydrotherapy
under: **a.** subaqueous; submarine; suboceanic
without: **a.** anhydrous; dehydrated; desiccated; inspissated; sublimated

WATERPROOF: **a.** repellant

WATERY: **a.** humid; hydrated; hydrous; ichorous; serous; **n.** WATERINESS: aquosity; humectation; humidity

WAVE(S): **v.** brandish; oscillate; undulate; **a.** **see** "wavy"
sound of breaking: **n.** plangency; **a.** plangent

WAVER(ING): **v.** fluctuate; hesitate; oscillate; vacillate; **n.** indecision; irresolution; oscillation; vacillation; **a.** ambivalent; desultory; fitful; inconclusive; indecisive; intermittent; irresolute; pendulous; spasmodic; vacillating

WAVY (or WAVING): **a.** flexuating; flexuous; ondoyant; oundy; undulating; undulant

WAX, *ear:* **n.** cerumen; **a.** ceruminous
producing: **a.** ceriferous

WAY(S), *having many:* **a.** multivious
in his own: more suo
of life or living: **n.** *modus vivendi*
on the: **adv.** *chemin faisant*
painful or sorrowful: **n.** *via dolorosa*

WAYLAY: **v.** ambush; **n.** ambuscade; ambush(ment)

WAYWARD *act or tendency:* **n.** caprice; capriciousness; erraticism; peccadillo; venality

WEAK (or WEAKENED): **a.** adynamic; anile; asthenic; attenuated; debilitated; decrepit; devitalized; effete; enervated; enfeebled; etiolated; feckless; fragile; impotent; impuissant; ineffective; infirm; invertebrate; irresolute; maladive; milk-and-water; phthisic(al); sapless; unfortified; unsupported; vacillating; valetudinarian; vulnerable; wavering; wishy-washy
of mind: **n. or adv.** *impos animi;* **n.** imbecility
morally: **a.** maladive
person: **see under** "person"
point. **n.** Achilles' heel; *locus minoris resistentiae;* vulnerability

WEAKEN: **v.** attenuate; debilitate; denude; denudate; devitalize; disable; emasculate; enervate; enfeeble; exhaust; incapacitate; undermine; unman; unnerve

WEAKENING: **a.** debilitating; devitalizing; enervating; **n.** attenuation
as of moral principles or civil authority; **n.** labefaction
gradual: **n.** attrition; erosion

WEAKNESS: (see "defect") **n.** adynamia, asthenia; atony; attenuation; cowardice; cowardliness; debilitation; debility; decrepitude; devitalization; effeminacy; enervation; *faiblesse;* foible; hypodynamia; imbecility; impotence; impuissance; inability; inanition; incapacity; languor; languishment; lassitude; marasmus; pusillanimity; tenuity; vulnerability
body: **n.** adynamia; asthenia; **a.** adynamic; asthenic
muscular: **n.** hypokinesia; hypokinesis; myasthenia; **a.** myasthenic
of mind: **see under** "weak"
point or place of: **n.** Achilles' heel; *locus minoris resistentiae;* vulnerability
small, as of character: **n.** foible

WEALTH: **n.** abundance; affluence; luxuriance; luxury; opulence; profusion; prosperity; substance
as evil or personified: **n.** mammon
delusions of, or mad pursuit of: **n.** plutomania
devoted to: **a.** mammonish; **n.** mammonist
of, pert. to, or occupied in gaining: **a.** chrematistic
opposite of: **n.** illth; poverty
place or source of great: **n.** bonanza; El Dorado
study of: **n.** chrematistics
theory of as measured in money: **n.** chrematistics
worship of: **n.** plutolatory; plutomania

WEALTHY: (see "rich") **a.** abundant; affluent; luxuriant; luxurious; opulent; profuse
person: **n.** Croesus; leviathan; plutocrat; tycoon
person who favors the: **n.** plutogogue; **n.** plutogogery

WEANING: **n.** ablactation

WEAR *and tear:* **n.** attrition; detrition; erosion

WEARINESS: (see "fatigue") **n.** boredom; ennui; languishment; lassitude; lethargy; monotony; tedium; **adv.** *ad nauseam*
of life: **n.** *taedium vitae*

WEATHER *conditions, pert. to:* **a.** meteorologic(al); synoptic(al)
forecasting: **n.** aeromancy; meteorology; prognostication; **a.** synoptic(al)
harshness of: **n.** asperity; inclemency; **a.** inclement
science of: **n.** climatology; meteorology; **a.** meteorologic(al)
study of effects on living beings: **n.** biometeorology; **a.** biometeorologic(al)

WEDDING: **see** "marriage"
pert. to: **a.** epithalmic(al); hymeneal; nuptial
song or poem: **n.** epithalamion; epithalamium; prothalamion; hymenal

WEDGE-*shaped:* **a.** cuneate; cuneatic; cuneiform

WEEK: **n.** hebdomad; **a.** hebdomadal

WEEP: **see** "cry"

WEIGH *in the mind:* **n.** perpension; **v.** perpend
well the end: **adv.** *avise la fin*

WEIGHED, *capable of being:* **a.** ponderable
not capable of being: **a.** imponderable

WEIGHT: **n.** avoirdupois; consequence; gravity; importance; influence; ponderance; ponderosity; prestige
greater in: **a.** preponderant; **n.** preponderance
having little: **a.** imponderable
loss of: **see** "emaciation"
of equal: **a.** equiponderant; isonomous
pert. to or estimated in terms of: **a.** ponderal

WEIGHTY: **a.** burdensome; corpulent; cumbersome; cumbrous; gravid; grievous; important; influential; momentous; onerous; ponderable; ponderous; significant; solemn; **n.** WEIGHTINESS: ponderability; ponderosity

WEIRD: **a.** bizarre; cabalistic; eerie; eldri(t)ch; grotesque; incantatory; mysterious; supernatural; talismanic; uncanny; unearthly; **n.** bizarrerie; grotesquerie

WELCOME: **n.** *accueil; bienvenue;* salutation; **a.** delectable; felicitous; salutatory; salutiferous
one who is: **n.** *persona grata; persona gratissimo;* (**pl.** *personae gratissimae*)
one who is not: **n.** *persona non grata*

WELFARE, *harmful to, or to society:* **a.** *contra bonos mores*

WELL *and good:* **adv.** *à la bonne heure*
-being: **n.** eudaemonia; euphoria; **a.** eudaemonic(al); euphoric; euphorious
feeling of: **n.** euphoria
-bred or mannered: **a.** *bien elevé(e)*
done!: **adv.** *à la bonne heure;* bravissimo; bravo
groomed: **a.** modish; *soigné* (**fem.** *soignée*)
-known: **a.** celebrated; classic; eminent; proverbial; notorious

WELL, *as source of water, pert. to:* **a.** phreatic

WELSH *singing festival:* **n.** eisteddfod

WEST: **n.** or **a.** Occident

WESTERN: **a.** Hesperian; Occidental
inhabitant: **n.** Hesperian; Occidental

WETNESS: **n.** aquosity; humectation; humidity

WETTING, *made transparent by:* **a.** hydrophanous

WHALE(S), *pert. to:* **a.** cetacean; cetaceous; **n.** cetacean

WHAT *will be, will be: che sarà sarà*

WHEAT, *of or like:* **a.** farinaceous; frumentaceous

WHEEDLE: **v.** cajole; flatter; **n.** cajolery; cajolement

WHEEL(S), *of or pert. to:* **a.** rotal; rotary

WHEN *all is said and done: en fin de compte*

WHERE (*mentioned*) *above:* **adv.** *ubi supra* (**abb.** u.s.)

WHERENESS: **n.** ubiety

WHICH *is.* **adv.** *quod est* (**abb.** q.e.)
see: **adv.** *quod vide* (**abb.** q.v.)

WHILE, *not worth:* **adv.** *non est tanti*

WHIM(S): **n.** bizarrerie; caprice; chimera; eccentricity; fancy; fantasque; haecceity; idiosyncrasy; megrim(s); oddity; peculiarity; quiddity; quirk; singularity; vagary; whimsicality; **a.** WHIMSICAL. capricious; captious; crotchety; fanciful fantastic; impish; notional; puckish; roguish; vagarious; **n.** WHIMSICALNESS: caprice; chimera; puckishness; roguery; vagary; whimsicality

WHIP: **v.** castigate; chastise; flagellate; fustigate

WHIRL: **v.** pirouette; vertiginate; **a.** vertiginous; **n.** bustle; commotion

WHIRLPOOL: **n.** charybdis; gurge; maelstrom; riptide; vortex; **a.** vertiginous
large and violent: **n.** maelstrom

WHISKEY: **n.** *spiritus frumenti*

WHISPER: **v.** siffilate; **n.** sussurus; *vox clandestina;* **a.** WHISPERING: **see** "murmuring"
in a: **a.** or **adv.** *sotto voce*

WHISTLE: **v.** siffle; **n.** siffleur

WHITE, *from heat:* **a.** candent; candescent; **n.** candescence
like marble: **a.** marmoreal
turning: **a.** albescent; canescent; etiolated; **n.** canescence; etiolation

WHO *goes there?:* **n.** *qui va là?; qui vive?*
guards the guards?: **n.** *quis custodiet ipsos custodes?*

WHOLE: (**see** "entire") **n.** integer; integral; solidium; totality; **a.** *en bloc; en masse;* impartite; intact; maiden; unbroken; undivided; unimpaired; unmarred; unmotivated; **adv.** WHOLLY: *de fond; de haut en bas; en comble;* **n.** WHOLENESS: (**see** "totality") integrality; integrity
affording a gen. view of: **a.** panoramic; synoptic
as a: **adv.** *en masse; in toto*
form into a: **v.** synthesize; **n.** synthesis

WHOLESOME: **a.** beneficial; curative; healthful; remedial; restorative; salubrious; salutary; salutiferous; **n.** WHOLESOMENESS: salubrity; salutariness

WHOOPING *cough:* **n.** pertussis; **a.** pertussal

WICKED: (**see** "base" **and** "evil") **a.** abhorrent; abominable; atrocious; Babylonian; devilish; diabolic(al); dissolute; execrable; flagitious; flagrant; ghoulish; heinous; hellish; infamous; iniquitous; intractable; licentious; malignant; Mephistophelian; nefarious; nefast; notorious; odious; piacular; sacrilegious; satanic; saturnine; scandalous; vicious; villainous; viperish; viperous; **n.** WICKEDNESS: (**see** "evil") abomination; Belial; diablerie; enormity; flagitiousness; infamy; iniquity; rascality; sinfulness; turpitude
no rest for the: nemo malus felix
(*not pious*): **a.** blasphemous; impious; irreligious; profane; sacrilegious
person: **n.** Beelzebub; caitiff; Mephistopheles

WIDE: (**see** "intensive") **a.** expansive; extensive; illimitable; magnitudinous; **n. see** "width"
in range of knowledge: **a.** bibliognostic; cyclopedic; omniscient; pansophic(al)
open: **a.** distended; patulous
-spread: **a.** catholic; epidemic; far-reaching; peregrine; peregrinic; predominant; prevalent; regnal; regnant; universal; **n.** catholicity; ecumenicity; prevalence; regnancy; universality

WIDOW: **n.** relict

WIDTH: **n.** amplitude; comprehension; expansiveness; expansivity; fullness; liberality; magnitude; spaciousness

WIFE: (**see** "wives") **n.** consort; *femme couverte;* spouse; *ux(or)*
dear: **n.** *cara sposa*
doting or fond of, or submissive to: **a.** uxorious; **n.** uxoriousness
faithful: **n.** Penelope
having but one at a time: **n.** monogamy; monogyny; **a.** monogamous; monogynous
two or more at a time: **n.** polygamy; polygyny **a.** polygamous; polygynous
located or centered around family of the: **a.** matrilocal
murder of by hus.: **n.** uxorcide
of, befitting or characteristic of: **a.** uxerial

WILD: (**see** "reckless") **a.** barbaric; barbarous; beserk; boisterous; brutal; corybantic; dissolute; extravagant; fantastic; feral, heathenish; impassioned; inordinate, insane; licentious; maniac(al); pagan; riotous; savage; tempestuous; turbulent; uncivilized; uncultivated; undisciplined; undomesticated; ungovernable; unruly; unsubdued; untamed; **n.** WILDNESS: barbarity; ferity; mania; turbulence; wilderness
by nature: **a.** *ferae naturae*
emotionally: **a.** berserk; corybantic; dithyrambic; frantic; frenetic(al); frenzied; hysterical; impassioned; insane; maniac(al); phrenetic(al)
(*growing in fields, etc.*): **a.** agrestic
nature, having: **a.** *ferae naturae*

WILE: (**see** "whimsicality") **n.** artifice; machination; stratagem

WILL: **v.** bequeath; demise; devise; **n.** determination; disposition; inclination; intention; resolution; testament; volition
act or exercise of: **n.** volition; **a.** volitional
adverse action of: **n.** nolition
against one's (will) or consent: **adv.** *in invitum*
at: **adv.** *a capriccio; ad arbitrium; à discrétion*
freedom of (doctrine): **n.** libertarianism; **a. or n.** libertarian
having made none, or not disposed by: **a.** intestate
-power, loss of: **n.** abulia
with good: **adv.** *de bonne volonté*

WILLING: (**see** "compliant") **a.** acceptant; acquiescent; amenable; voluntary; **adv.** WILLINGLY: *de bonne grâce; de bonne volonté; ex animo*
and able: **adv.** *volens et potens*
or unwilling: **adv.** *nolens volens*

WILLINGNESS: **n.** amenability; tractability
to receive: **n.** receptivity; **a.** receptive

WILLY-NILLY: **a.** *nolens volens;* **adv.** *bon gré; mal gré; nolens volens*

WILY: **see** "cunning"

WIND(S), *fertilized by:* **a.** anemophilous
measuring velocity: **n.** anemography; anemology; anemometry
puff of: **n.** flatus
sound of: **a.** aeolian; aeolic
study of: **n.** anemology; **n.** anemologist
treatise on: **n.** anemography; anemology

WIND(ING): (see "devious") v. intort; meander; undulate; wreathe; a. anfractuous; circuitous; flexuous; meandering; meandrous; serpentine; sinuate; sinuous; tortuous; n. anfractuosity; flexuosity; intorsion; sinuation; torsion
path, course or action: n. anfractuosity; sinuosity

WINDOW(S): n. aperture; fenestration; (pl. fenestra)
situated bet.: a. interfenestral
throwing or being thrown thru: n. defenestration

WINE, *god of:* n. Bacchus
lover or connoisseur of: n. oenophile; oenophilist
of or pert. to: a. vinic; vinous
maker of, or merchant: n. vinter
pert. to making: a. oenopoetic
science of, or of making: n. (o)enology
steward: n. sommelier
truth in (in intoxication): n. *in vino veritas*

WINEBIBBER: n. oenophilist

WING(S), *having:* a. aliferous
having two: a. bipentate; dipterous
pert. to or resembling: a. pteric
-shaped: a. aliform

WINK: v. nictate; nictitate; n. nictitation

WINTER, *pert. to (wintery):* a. boreal; brumal; heimal; hibernal
spend the, or become dormant in: v. hibernate; n. hibernation; a. hibernatant

WISDOM: n. acumen; discernment; discretion; discrimination; judgment; judicality; knowledge; perspicacity; prudence; rationality; sagacity; sageness; sanity; sapience; sapiency; subtlety
divine: n. Sophia; a. Sophian
goddess of: n. Minerva
hater of: n. misosopher; misosophist; n. misosophy
human: n. anthroposophy; a. anthroposophic(al)
marked by great: a. Nestorian; Solomonian; Solomonic
pert. to or having great: a. sagacious; sapient(ial); sophistic(al)
rel. to a. paladian

WISE: (see "sage") a. acuminous; cognizant: circumspect; discerning; discreet; discriminating; equitable; erudite; judgmatic(al); judicious; Nestorian; oracular; orphic; perspicacious; politic; profound; sagacious; sapient(ial); Solomonian; Solomonic
and pithy: a. aphoristic; apothegmatic; gnomic(al); gnomonic; n. see "witticism"
moderation: n. continence; prudence; sophrosyne
no one sufficiently by himself: nemo solus satis sapit
person: (see "intellectual") n. Nestor(ian); patriarch; sage; Solomon
saying: see "maxim" and "witticism"

WISECRACKING *spirit:* n. gaminerie

WISH *or desire, expressing:* a. benedictive; optative; precative
slight: n. velleity

WIT(S): n. acumen; alertness; coruscation; drollery; facetiosity; facetiousness; irony; jocularity; *nugae canorae;* persiflage; repartee; *sal Atticus;* sarcasm; whimsicality; n. Aristophanes; *bel esprit; causeur; farceur;* (fem. *farceuse*); *homme d'esprit; persifleur*
biting: n. causticity; mordacity; sarcasm; spinosity
display flashes of: v. coruscate; n. coruscation; pyrotechnics
end, at his: au bout de son latin
light: n. badinage; bavardage; causerie; repartee
sallies or flashes of: n.pl. coruscations; *feux d'artifice;* pyrotechnics

WITCH: n. Circe; enchantress; lamia; necromancer; pythoness; sibyl; sorceress; vampire; n. WITCHCRAFT: necromancy; sorcery; n. necromancer; sorcerer

WITCHES, *midnight assembly of:* n. sabbat

WITH *all one's might:* adv. *à toute force*
certainty: adv. *à coup sûr*
equal pace: a. or adv. *pari passu*
grain of salt: adv. *cum grano salis*
great praise: adv. *magna cum laude*
greatest praise or highest honors; adv. *summa cum laude*
honor(s) or praise: adv. *cum laude*
many others: cum multis allis
one voice; adv. una voce; unisonal; unisonous
pleasure: adv. *avec plaisir*
running pen: adv. *currente calamo*

WITHDRAW: **v.** abjure; recede; relinquish; retract; retreat; revoke; subduct; **n.** WITHDRAWAL: detachment; insularity; retraction; revocation; revulsion; subduction; **a.** WITHDRAWN: **see** "secluded"

WITHER: **v.** atrophy; decline; paralyze; senesce; wizen; **n.** WITHERING: annihilation; devastation; senescence; tabescence

WITHIN, *from or existing:* **adv.** *ab intra;* **a.** autogenous; endogenous; indwelling
originating or developing fr.: **a.** autogenous; endogenous; esoteric

WITHOUT *a day (being set)*: **a. or adv.** *sine die*
care or worry: **adv.** *sans souci; sine cura;* **a.** *dégagé*
definite plan or method: **a.** desultory
delay: **adv.** *sine mora; tout de suite*
doubt: **adv.** assuredly; indisputably; indubitable; *sans doute; sine dubio;* undoubtedly
embarrassment or constraint: **adv.** *sans gene;* unconstrainedly
envy: **adv.** *sine invidia*
equal: **adv.** *sans pareil*
fail: **adv.** *à coup sûr*
from: **adv.** *ab extra;* **a.** advenient; adventitious; exogeneous; extraneous; extrinsic
hatred: **adv.** *sine odio*
issue: **adv.** *sine prole*
prejudice: **adv.** *sine praejudicio*
this: **adv.** *abseque hoc*

WITHSTAND: **v.** brook; contest; endure; oppose; resist

WITNESS, *call to:* **v.** obtest; **n.** obtestation
in: **adv.** *in testimonium*

WITTICISM: (**see** "maxim") **n.** aphorism; apothegm; bijouterie; *bon mot;* coruscation; epigram; *jeu d'esprit; jeu de mots;* jocosity; *mot pour rire;* truism; *turlupinade;* (**pl.** *facetiae*)

WITTY: **a.** Aristophanic; epigrammatic(al); facetious; jocose; jocular; laconic; mercurial; scintillescent; scintillating; **n.** WITTINESS: facetiosity; jocosity; *plaisanterie*
person: **see under** "wit"
sprightly: **a.** spirituel(le)
to be: **v.** coruscate; scintillate
writer: **n.** epigrammatist; satirist
writing(s): **n.pl.** *facetiae*

WIVES: **see** "wife"
having but one, or having more than one: **see under** "wife"
or husband(s), having two or more at same time: **n.** polygamy; **a.** polygamous

WIZARD: **see** "magician"

WOE: **n.** affliction; anguish; dolor; heartache; tribulation
tale of: **n.** jeremiad; lamentation; threnode; threnody; **a.** lamentable; threnodic
to the conquered: vae victis

WOLF-*like:* **a.** lupine
mental cond. or belief that person has turned into: **n.** loup-garou; lycanthropy; werewolf; **n.** lycanthrope

WOMAN (**or** WOMEN): (**see** "lady") **n.** femineity; feminity; womankind
abnormal fear of: **n.** gynephobia
adviser or companion: **n.** Egeria
apartment for: **n.** gynaeceum; seraglio; thalamus; zenana
bold, brazen, impudent or immoral: **n.** quean
club for: **n.** sorority; sorosis
enchanting: **n.** charmeuse; Circe; enchantress; *femme fatale;* sorceress
exclusion from public: **n.** purdah
"fallen": **n.** *femme perdue*
fascinating: **see** "seductive" **below**
fashionable: **n.** *femme du monde;* mondaine; sophisticate
flighty or silly: **n.** flibbertigibbet
fond of: **a.** philogynous; **n.** philogyny; **n.** philogynist
frenzied, raving or distressed: **n.** maenad; **a.** maenadic
frivolous, young: **n.** coquette; soubrette
govt. by: **n.** gynarchy; gynecocracy; matriarchy
hater, hatred or distrust of: **n.** misogyne; misogynist; **n.** misogynism; misogyny; **a.** misogynic; misogynous
having borne more than one child: **n.** multipara; **a.** multiparous
having borne no child: **n.** nullipara; **a.** nonparous; nulliparous
head of house: **n.** chatelaine; materfamilias; matriarch; **a.** matriarchal
idealization or worship of: **n.** Mariol-

atry; philogyny; **a.** Mariolatrous; philogenous
ill-tempered: **n.** shrew; termagant; virago; vixen; Xanthippe; **a.** shrewish; termagantish; viraginous; vixenish
Jewish, attaining age 13, also rite: **n.** *bat(h)* **or** *bas mitzvah*
kept: **n.** demimondaine
learned and literary, esp. if pedantic and undomestic: **n.** bluestocking; *femme savante*
little: **n.** microgyne; *petite dame*
look for the: **adv.** *cherchez la femme*
loud: **n.** rounceval; shrew; termagant; virago
love or fondness for. **n.** philogyny; **n.** philogynist
lover of married: **n.** cicisbeo
married: **n.** *femme couverte*
masculine-like: **n.** Amazon; amazonism; hermaphrodite; hermaphroditism; gynander; gynandry; **a.** amazonian; gynandrous; hermaphroditic; mannish; unwomanish
of erudition: **n.** *femme savante*
of fashionable society: **see** "fashionable" **above**
of high rank: **n.** *grande dame*
of loose morals: **n.** nymph; nymphet (young)
of questionable reputation: **n.** coquette; courtesan; demimondaine; demimonde; quean
of the house(hold): **see** "head of house" **above**
of the street: (**see** "prostitute") **n.** *nymphe du pavé*
of the world: **n.** *femme du monde;* mondaine; sophisticate
old and imposing, or dominant: **n.** dowager; matriarch
old or cantankerous: **n.** beldam(e); crone; gammer; grimalkin; harridan
old, state of being: **n.** anility; **a.** anile
pregnant for first time, or borne but one child: **n.** primipara; **a.** primiparous
pure and chaste: **n.** vestal (virgin)
raging: **n.** beldam(e); shrew; virago
rel. to or characteristic of: **a.** distaff; muliebral; **n.** muliebriety
rooms or apts. for: **see** "apartment for" **above**
scolding: **see** "loud" **above**
seductive: **n.** charmeuse; Circe; enchantress; *femme fatale;* intrig(u)ante; Lorelei; siren; sorceress; succubus
separate quarters: **see** "apartment for" **above**
separation or exclusion of: **n.** purdah
shameless: **n.** huzzy; Jezebel; quean; trollop
small: **see** "little" **above**
society: **see** "fashionable" **above**
stately old: **n.** dowager; matriarch
treacherous: **n.** Delilah
unmarried: **n.** *femme seule*
untidy or slovenly: **n.** gorgon; grimalkin; slattern; trollop
young, inexperienced and unworldly: **n.** ingenue; soubrette
if flighty or silly: **n.** flibbertigibbet
wise: **n.** *femme savante*
worldly or sophisticated: **n.** bluestocking; *femme du monde; flaneuse;* mondaine; sophisticate
worship of: **see** "idealization" **above**

WOMANHOOD: **n.** feminality; femineity; femininity; muliebrity; (**pl.** feminie)
goddess of: **n.** Juno
Jewish, attaining age 13: **see under** "woman"

WONDER *at nothing: nil admirari*

WONDERFUL: **a.** admirable; astonishing; astounding; extraordinary; ineffable; marvelous; miraculous; mirific; phenomenal; stupendous; surprising; wondrous
to see: **adv.** *mirabile visu*
to tell: **adv.** *mirabile dictu*

WONDERS, *year of:* **n.** *annus mirabilis*

WOOD(S), *inhabiting:* **a.** nemoral; silvicolous
pert. to: **a.** ligneous; nemoral; sylvan; sylvatic; sylvestran
resembling: **a.** ligneous; lignescent; xyloid

WOODED: **a.** arboraceous; arboreal; arboreous; arborescent; **a.** WOODY: ligneous; lignescent; xyloid
place: **n.** arboretum

WOOLLY: **a.** flocculent; lanate; laniferous; lanigerous

WORD(S): (**see** "name") **n.** lexicon; thesaurus; vocabulary
abundant flow of: (**see** "wordiness") **n.** affluence; *copia verborum;* facundity; loquaciousness; loquacity
adaption of foreign to English: **v.** anglicise; anglicize; **n.** anglicization
addition of letter(s) to: **n.** prosthesis
agreeable or inoffensive in lieu of harsh or indelicate: **n.** euphemism; **a.** euphemistic(al); **v.** euphemize.

ambiguous use of: **n.** amphibolism; amphibology; verbal fallacy

arbitrary or capricious coinage of; **n.** logodaedaly

at a loss for: **a.** nonplussed

backward same as forward: **n.** palindrome

-blindness: **n.** alexia

blunder: **see** "mischance or misuse" below

-book: **n.** calepin; dictionary; glossary; gradus; lexicon; nomenclature; onomasticon; synonymicon; terminology; thesaurus; vocabulary

burning (words): **n.** *ardentia verba*

choice or pattern of: **n.** diction; phraseology

coinage of, arbitrary: **n.** logodaedaly

compound, separation of: **n.** tmesis

consisting of one: **a.** monepic

contradictory or incongruous in effect (as "kind cruelty"): **n.** oxymoron

defining, art or practice of: **n.** lexicography; **a.** lexicographic

degeneration in meaning of: **n.** bastardization; corruption; pejoration

derivation: **n.** etymology; lexicology; provenance; semantics

derived fr. another in another lang.: **n.** paronym; **a.** paronymous

derived fr. sound(s): **n.** onomatope; onomatopoea; **a.** echoic; onomatopoeic(t)ic

disparaging one for usual, also word so used: **n.** dysphemism

dispute over or about: **n.** logomachy

distortion of sense of, also one who does: (**see** "punning") **n.** verbicide

drop first letter or syllable of: **n.** aph(a)eresis

drop last letter or syllable of: **n.** apocopation; apocope; elision; **a.** apocopate; elide

drop middle or internal letter or sound: **n.** syncope

empty or idle: **n.pl.** *paroles en l'air*

enough: **n.** *satis verborum*

exact or appropriate (the right): **n.** *mot juste*

excess use of: **see** "wordiness"

expert: **n.** etymologist; lexicographer; morphologist; philologist; phonemicist; semanticist

expressing a definite image or idea: **n.** semanteme

few, in a: **adv.** *en abrégé; paucis verbis*

for a symbol, as %: **n.** logogram

-for-word: **a.** *ad verbum;* literal(istic); *literatim; mot à mot;* textual; unvarnished; *verbatim; verbatim et literatim*

-for-word-and-letter-for-letter: **a.** *verbatim et literatim*

formed for an occasion: **n.** nonce (word)

formed fr. first letters, as A.W.O.L.: **n.** acronym; **a.** acronymic

formed fr. word in another lang.: **n.** paronym; **a.** paronymous

foul: **n.pl.** *gros mot*

four-letter: **n.** tetragram

game: **n.** anagrams; logomachy

having few syllables: **a.** brachysyllabic

having many syllables: **a.** polysyllabic(al); sesquipedalian(istic)

having more than one meaning: **n.** polysemant; **a.** polysemantic; polysemous

having one meaning only: **a.** or **n.** univocal

history or course of development of: **n.** phylogenesis; phylogeny; **n.** phylogenist

honeyed: **n.pl.** *paroles mielleuses;* **a.** **see** "honeyed"

idea w/ no exact (word) for: **n.** anonym(e)

idle: **see** "empty" **above**

imitative of sound(s): **see** "derived fr. sound(s)" **above**

in a few: **adv.** *en abrégé; paucis verbis*

in express: **adv.** *expressis verbis*

in plain: **adv.** *nudis verbis;* **a.** or **adv.** *en clair*

in so many: **adv.** *(in) totidem verbis*

in these (or in the same): **adv.** *in haec verba*

index of: **n.** *index verborum*

last syllable of: **n.** ultima

last syllable but one: **n.** penult; penultima(te); **a.** penultimate

last syllable but two: **n.** antepenult; **a.** antepenultimate

list of: **n.** lexicon; nomenclature; onomasticon; synonymicon; terminology; vocabulary

literal meaning acc. to origin: **n.** etymon

long: **n.** polysyllable; sesquipedalian; (**pl.** *sesquipedalia verba*) **a.** multisyllabic· polysyllabic(al); sesquipedalian(istic)

use of: **n.** polysyllabism; sesquipedalianism: sesquipedality

loss of one or more sounds in middle in pronouncing: **n.** syncope; **a.** syncopal

loss of ability to remember: **n.** aphasia; **a.** aphasic

loss of vowel at beginning: **n.** aphesis

loss of vowel or letter at end: **n.** apocopation; apocope; **v.** apocopate

made for the time or occasion: **n.** nonce (word)
mania for repeating certain: **n.** echolalia; onomatomania; verbomania
meaning: **n.** etymology
study of: **n.** semantics; semasiology; semology; significs
where changed for worse: **see** "degeneration" **above**
mischoice or misuse of: **n.** cacology; catachresis; impropriety; malaprop(ism); solecism; spoonerism; **a.** catachrestic(al); **n.** malaprop; spoonerism
new, or new meaning for old: **n.** neologism; neoterism; **v.** neologize; **a.** neological; neologistic
next to last syllable: **n.** penult; penultima(te) **a.** penultimate
obsession w/: **n.** onomatomania; verbo-onomatomania; verbomania; **n.** verbo-onomatomaniac; verbomaniac
of honor: **n.** *parole d'honneur*
of many syllables: **a.** multisyllabic; polysyllabic
of mouth: **adv.** *ore tenus; viva voce*
of one syllable: **n.** monosyllable; **a.** monosyllabic(al)
of opposite meaning: **n.** antonym; **a.** antonymous
omission of sound in: **n.** apocopation; elision; haplology; **v.** apocopate; elide
opp. or diff. fr. meaning for emphasis: **n.** trope; tropology; **a.** tropologic(al)
opp. to meaning as in humor: **n.** antiphrasis; **a.** antiphrastic
parting: (**see** "farewell") **n.** envoi; valediction
pass-, watch-, or catchword: **n.** shibboleth
pert. to: **a.** lexical; verbal; vocabular
pert. to meaning: **a.** semasiological; semantic(al)
play on: (**see** "pun") **n.** equivoque; *jeu de mots*
pretentious use of recondite: **n.** lexiphanicism; **a.** lexiphanic
pronounced alike but spelled diff.: **n.** homophone (*as sea and see*)
pronounced alike and spelled same: **n.** homograph; homonym (*as pool, a game; and pool, water*)
reading same backward as forward: **n.** palindrome
repeat endlessly and meaninglessly: **v.** verbigerate; **n.** echolalia; verbigeration
repetition for emphasis or effect: **n.** alliteration; iteration; ploce
repetition of, in sentence: **n.** anadiplosis
repetition, senseless: **n** cataphasia; echolalia; onomatomania; verbigeration
repetition, unnecessary: **n.** battolology; **a.** battological; **v.** battologize
ridiculous misuse of: **n.** malapropism
same backward as forward: **n.** palindrome
same pronunciation as another but diff. meaning: **n.** homonym
same spelling as another but diff. meaning and pronunciation: **n.** heteronym
science of origin and development: **n.** etymology; onomastics; onomatology; phylogeny; **a.** etymological; onomasiologic(al)
senseless repetition or meaningless jumble of: **n.** Babelism; cataphasia; echolalia; onomatomania; verbigeration
sentence expressed by a: **n.** polysynthesism; **a.** holophrastic
serving to fill out sentence or line: **n.** expletive
sharp: **n.pl.** *paroles aigres;* **n.** mordacity; spinosity
spell or represent in letters or characters of another lang.: **v.** transliterate; **n.** metography; transliteration
spoken (word) cannot be recalled: nescit vox missa reverti
student of: **see** "expert" **above**
study of: **n.** etymology; semantics; semasiology; semology; significs
study of form and structure of: **n.** morphology; phonetics
study of origin and development: **see** "science" **above**
substandard: **n.** barbarism; bastardization; colloquialism; patois
symbol used to represent, as %: **n.** ideogram; logogram; **a.** ideogrammatic; ideogram(m)ic; logogrammatic
the right: **n.** *mot juste*
the very: **n.** *ipsissima verba*
to a: **adv.** *ad verbum*
to blows: **adv.** *a verbis ad verba*
to wise is sufficient: verbum sapient satis est (**abb.** *verbum sap.*)
transposition of, or of letters in: **n.** metathesis; strephosymbolia
transposition of sounds: **n.** spoonerism; **v.** spoonerize
unacceptable use of: **see** "misuse of" **above**
unconscious use of other than intended: **n.** heterophemy; *lapsus linguae*
uncontrollable obsession for: **see** "obsession with" **above**
unsound reasoning by ambiguous use of: amphibologism; amphibology; verbal fallacy

use of equivocal or ambiguous: **n.** amphibologism; amphibilogy; officialese; parsiology
of long: **see under** "long" **above**
of many where few would do: **n.** circumlocution; periphrasis; **a.** periphrastic
of too many: **see** "wordiness" **and** "wordy"
of wrong for context: **n.** catachresis; **a.** catachrestic(al)
opp. to meaning as in humor: **n.** antiphrasis; **a.** antiphrastic
opp. to or diff. fr. meaning for emphasis: **n.** trope; tropology; **a.** tropologic(al)
worship of: **n.** grammatolatry
written: **n.pl.** *literae scriptae*

WORDBOOK: **see under** "word"
in specialized field: **n.** nomenclature; onomasticon

WORDINESS: **n.** affluence; catalogia; circumlocution; *copia verborum;* diffusion; fecundity; garrulity; logorrhea; loquacity; loquaciousness; macrology; officialese; periphrasis; pleonasm; prolixity; redundancy; tautology; verbality; verbiage; verbalism; verbigeration; verbomania; verbosity voluminosity

WORDY (**see** "talkative") **a.** circumlocutious; circumlocutory; copious; diffuse, garrulous; logorrheic; palaverous; pleonastic; profuse; prolix; protracted; redundant; repetitious; tautological; verbose

WORK: **n.** accomplishment; employment; exertion; *métier;* moil; occupation; production; profession
able to do any kind of: **a.** panurgic
additional: **n.** supererogation; **a.** supererogatory
as musical or literary: **n.** oeuvre; opus
major: **n.** *chef d'oeuvre; magnus opus; meisterwerk; pièce de résistance*
minor: **n.** opuscule; opusculum
fear of or aversion to: **n.** ergasiophobia; ergophobia
love of or great desire to: **n.** ergasiomania; ergomania; ergophilia
-over: **see** "rehash"
pert. to: **a.** employmental; industrial; occupational; vocative; vocational
subordinate or accessory: **n.** parergon; (**pl.** parerga)

WORKED-*over:* **n.** or **a.** *réchauffé;* **a.** refurbished; renovated

WORKING *class:* **n.** proletarian; proletariat; **a.** proletarian
hard and steady: **a.** sedulous; **n.** sedulity

WORKMANSHIP: (**see** "skill") **n.** artisanship; artistry; craftsmanship; expertise; virtuosity

WORKSHOP: **n.** atelier

WORLD: (**see** "earth") **n.** creation; humanity; macrocosm; mankind; sphere
against the (in defiance of opn.): **a.** or **adv.** *contra mundum*
all the: **adv.** *tout le monde*
ancient or primeval: **n.** foreworld
before creation of: **a.** antemundane; premundane
belief that tends to become better: **n.** meliorism
citizen of: **n.** cosmopolitan; cosmopolite; *homme du monde*
-creating: **a.** cosmopoietic
denying reality of temporal: **a.** acosmic; **n.** acosmism
end of: **n.** götterdämmerung
extending or lying beyond the: **a.** extramundane; transmundane
fashionable: **n.** *le beau monde; (le) monde*
in its entirety: **n.** macrocosm; **a.** macrocosmic
learned, the: **n.** *le monde savant*
little: **n.** microcosm; **a.** microcosmic(al)
lower, of or rel. to: **a.** chthonian; plutonian; plutonic; subterranean
man of the: **n.** boulevardier; cosmopolitan; cosmopolite; *homme du monde*
of the dead: **n.** netherworld
of this: **see** "worldly"
on small scale: **n.** microcosm; **a.** microcosmic(al)
out of this, or not of this: **a.** extramundane; extraterrestrial; supermundane; transmundane
pert. to: **a.** cosmic; cosmopolitan, global; mundane; planetary; subcelestial; terrestrial; universal
private: **n.** autocosm; **a.** autocosmic
transcending the: **a.** extramundane; supermundane; supernatural; transmundane
under-: **n.** or **a.** chthonian; subterranean; subterrestrial; **n.** subterrene
view or outlook: **n.** weltanschauung
vital force: **n.** *anima mundi; élan vital*

way of the: **n.** *l'usage du monde*
-weariness: **n.** ennui; **a.** *fin-de-siècle*
-wide: **a.** cosmopolitan; ecumenic(al); global; pandemic; peregrinic; planetary; terrestrial; universal(ized); **n.** ecumenic ity; pandemia; universality
wishes to be fooled: mundus vult decepi
within this: **a.** intramundane

WORLDLY: **(see** "sensuous") **a.** carnal; fashionable; global; hedonic; intramundane; laic; lustful; luxurious; mondain(e); mortal; mundane; profane; secular; sensual; sensuous; sophisticated; subastral; subcelestial; sublunary; temporal; terrene; terrestrial; uncelestial; universal; unspiritual; **n.** WORLDLINESS: carnality; mundacity; mundanity; secularism; secularity; sensuality; temporality; universality
activities or troubles: **n.** coil; moil; **(pl.** temporalities)
not: **see** "heavenly" **and** "unearthly"

WORM-*eaten:* **a.** vermiculate; vermoulu
infested w/ (worms): **a.** verminous; **n.** verminosis
resembling: **a.** vermicular; vermiculate; vermiform

WORN *by constant use:* **a.** hackneyed; stereotyped; threadbare; trite; vapid; **n.** attrition; erosion
-out: **a.** decrepit; dilapidated; effete; **n.** decrepitude; dilapidation

WORRY: **(see** "annoyance") **v.** disconcert; harass; importune; tantalize; torment; **n.** complication; fantod(s); harassment; nightmare; vexation; **a.** WORRYING: **(see** "concerned") apprehensive; disconcerted; distressed; perplexed

WORSE, *so much the:* **adv.** *tant pis*
state of becoming progressively: **n.** ingravescence; **a.** ingravescent
to make: **v.** bastardize; denigrate; disimprove; exacerbate; minify; pejorate; tragedize; **a.** denigrative; exacerbative; pejorative; **n.** denigration; disimprovement; exacerbation; pejoration
to worse, from: **adv.** *de pis en pis*

WORSEN: **v.** decline degenerate; deteriorate; exacerbate, retrograde; retrogress; **a.** WORSENING exacerbative; retrogressive; retrograde, **n.** declination; deterioration, exacerbation; retrogression

WORSHIP: **v.** adore; adulate; observe; venerate; **n.** adoration; adulation; devotion; dulia; hierurgy; homage; liturgy; observation; veneration; **n.** WORSHIPER: adulator; congregant; devotee
due to God alone: **n.** latria
erotic, as of articles of female clothing: **n.** fetichism; **a.** fetichistic
of ancestors: **n.** ancestor cult; manism; **a.** filopietistic; manistic
of Bible: **n.** Bibliolatry
of books: **n.** bibliolatry; bibliomania; **a.** bibliolatrous; **n.** bibliolater; bibliomaniac
of church or church matters: **n.** ecclesiolatry
of dead: **n.** necrolatry; **a.** necrolatrous
of devil(s): **n.** demonolatry; **n.** diabolist
of dogs: **n.** cynolatry; **n.** cynolatrist
of foreign or unsanctioned gods: **n.** allotheism
of idols: **n.** iconolatry; idolatry
of letters or words: **n.** grammatolatry
of man: **n.** anthropolatry
of many gods: **n.** polytheism
of money: **n.** amor nummi; mammonism; plutolatry; plutomania
of nature or natural forces: **n.** pantheism; physiolatry; priapism; **a.** pantheistic; physiolatrous; **n.** pantheist; physiolater
of obscenity: **n.** aischrolatreia
of old, or what is old: **n.** archeolatry; archai(ci)sm
of one god: **n.** henotheism; monolatry; monotheism; **a.** monolatrous; monotheistic(al)
of religion: **n.** ecclesiolatry
of riches: **see** "of money" **above**
of saints or sacred things: **(see** "saints") **n.** hierolatry
of self: **n.** autotheism; **a.** auththeistic(al)
of Shakespeare and/or his works: **n.** bardolatry
of snakes: **n.** ophiolatry
of spirits of deceased: **see** "of ancestors" **above**
of state or govt.: **n.** statolatry
of sun: **n.** heliolatry
of symbols: **n.** symbololatry
of virgin(s): **n.** Mariolatry; parthenolatry
of wealth: **see** "of money" **above**
of woman or women: **n.** Mariolatry; philogyny
of words or letters: **n.** grammatolatry
place of: **n.** adoratory

religious, pert. to: **a.** hierurgical; liturgical; ritualistic; rubrical

WORST, *at the:* **adv.** *au pis aller*
govt. by (worst) men: **n.** kakistocracy

WORTH: **n.** appreciation; estimation; excellence; integrity; importance; merit; morality; nobleness; rectitude; sincerity; stability; usefulness
man of: **n.** *homme de bien;* (**pl.** *gens de condition*)

WORTHLESS: **a.** contemptible; despicable; fustian; impotent; incompetent; ineffectual; insignificant; inutile; nugatory; paltry; profligate; stramineous; unproductive; valueless; **n.** WORTHLESSNESS: floccinaucinihilipilification
object: **n.** ambsace; nihil(ity)
part of anything: (**see** "waste") **n.** *caput mortuum;* dross; recrement; scoria
person: **see** "rogue"
thing: (**see** "waste") **n.** ambsace; *corpus vile;* (**pl.** *corpus villa*); flummadiddle; nihil(ity); (**pl.** flotsam and jetsam)

WORTHY: **a.** chivalrous; commendable; condign; creditable; estimable; exemplary; heroic; honorable; laudable; meritorious
of note: **adv.** *notatu dignum*

WOUND: (**see** "sore") **v.** lacerate; traumatize; **n.** contusion; laceration; lesion; trauma(tism); traumatization; vulnus; **a.** traumatic; vulnerary
incurable: **n.** *immedicable vulnus*

WRANGLE: (**see** "argue") **v.** ergotize

WRATH: (**see** "anger") **n.** animosity; exasperation; indignation; resentment; **a.** WRATHFUL: (**see** "angry") Achillean
day of: **n.** *dies irae*

WREATHE: **v.** intort; **a.** intorted

WRECKAGE, *ship's:* **n.pl.** flotsam and jetsam

WRETCHED: (**see** "deplorable") **a.** abominable; abysmal; calamitous; contemptible; damnable; despicable; detestable; execrable; lamentable; miserable; odious; paltry; squalid

WRINKLE: **n.** corrugation; rugosity; **a.** corrugated; rugate; rugose

WRITE *extravagantly:* **v.** rhapsodize
having strong desire to: **a.** scripturient: **n.** *cacoëthes scribendi; furor scribendi*

WRITER: (**see** "author") **n.** communicator; contributor; correspondent; essayist; litterateur; novelist; prosaist; prosateur; satirist; **a.** contributorial
bearing name of: **a.** onomatous; onymous
complete works of: **n.pl.** *opera omnia*
elegant: **n.** belletrist; bellelettrist; rhetorician; **a.** Addisonian; bellet(t)ristic; Ovidian; rhetorical
insignificant anonymous: **n.** anonymuncule
man using woman's name: **n.** pseudogyny
modern: **n.** neoteric
not bearing name of: **a.** anonymous; pseudonymous
of prose: **n.** prosaist; prosateur
of satires: **n.** satirist; sillographer
professional: **n.** litterateur
witty: **n.** epigrammatist; satirist; sillographer
woman using man's name: **n.** pseudandry

WRITER'S *cramp.* **n** chirospasm

WRITING(S): **n.** *belles lettres;* communication; literature; scrivening(s)
abstruse: **n.pl.** esoterica; esoterics; hermetics; **n.** hermeti(ci)sm
ancient: **a.** or **n.** cuneiform; hieroglyphic(s)
at length: **see** "wordiness"
collection of: **n.** *corpus;* (**pl.** collectanea; corpora); syntagm(a)
of varied: **n.** miscellanea; variorum
conversational style: **n.** causerie; journalese
disputatious or controversial: **n.** polemic(s); **a.** polemic(al)
doubtful authenticity: **n.pl.** apocrypha; **a.** apocryphal
erased, found beneath later writing: **n.** or **a.** palimpsest
excess refinement in: **n.** literaryism
false and spurious: **n.pl.** anagignoskomena; apocrypha; pseudepigraph(a); pseudograph(a); **a.** apocryphal; pseudepigraphic(al); pseudepigraphous
falsely attributed to Biblical characters: **n.pl.** pseudepigrapha
fine: **n.pl.** *belles lettres,* **a.** bellet(t)ristic
hand: **see** "handwriting"
high-flown or pompous. (**see** 'bom-

bast") **n** fustian; gasconade; grandiloquence; grandiosity; lexiphanticism; pomposity; **a.** bombastic; fustian; grandiloquent; rubescent

made for another: **n.** allograph

mania for: **n.** *cacoëthes scribendi; furor scribendi*

newspaper or magazine style of: **n.** journalese; **a.** magazinish

obscene: **n.** *erotica; esoterica; facetiae;* ithyphallic (verse); pornography

of early church fathers, or of any church, cult or system: **n.pl.** patristics; **a.** patristic

of words not having certain letters: **n.** lipogram

omission in, inadvertent, as of letter or syllable: **n.** lipography; **a.** lipogrammatic; **n.** lipogrammatism

on both sides of paper: **a.** opisthographic

on one side of paper: **a.** anopisthographic

on many subjects, or wide range of: **a.** polygraphic; **n.** polygraph

on single subject: **a.** monographic; **n.** monograph

on walls, etc.: **n.** graffito; (**pl.** graffiti)

ornate and artificial style: **n.** gongorism; mandarinism; rubescence

overly recondite, derivative, or artificial: **a.** alexandrian

pert. to: **a.** bellet(t)ristic; epistolary; graphic; scriptory; scriptorial; textual

picture: **n.pl.** curiologics; hieroglyphics

praising something, exaltedly: **n.** dithyramb

pretentious: **see** "high-flown" **above**

reply in: **n.** rescription; **a.** rescriptive

ribald or coarsely witty: **n.pl.** *facetiae*, **a** Rabelaisian

style of: **see under** "literary"

superficial or shallow, pert. to: **a.** magazinish

systematic collection of: **n.** syntagm(a)

vividness in: **a.** Addisonian; Ovidian

witty or clever: (**see** "witticism") **n.** *jeu d'esprit;* (**pl.** *facetiae*)

WRITTEN **above: a.** superscribed; **n.** antescript; superscription

afterwards: **n.** postscript (**abb.** p.s.)

as: **adv.** *ad lit(t)eram;* sic

before or above: **n.** antescript; superscription; **a.** superscribed

in handwriting of author: **n.** holograph; **a.** holographic(al); onomastic

minutely: **a.** micrographic

on both back and front: **a.** opisthographic

on one side only: **a.** anopisthographic

WRONG: **n.** delict; delinquency; iniquity; malefaction; malfeasance; misdemeanor; misfeasance; transgression; turpitude; venality; villainy; violation; **a.** erroneous; immoral; inappropriate; inequitable; venal; villainous

avenger of: **a.** Nemesis; retributor; *vindex injuriae*

because prohibited or unlawful: **adv.** or **n.** *malum prohibitum*

civil: **n.** tort

in itself or inherently: **adv.** or **n.** *malum in se*

of or by reason of a: **adv.** or **a.** *ex delicto*

-side-out: **adv.** *à rebours*

way: **adv.** *à rebours*

WRONGFUL: **see** "unjust"

Y

YAWN: **v.** dehise; oscitate; **n.** dehiscence; oscitance; oscitation; **a.** YAWNING: cavernous; gaping; oscitant; patulous

YEAR, *great:* **n.** *annus magnus*
in the course of the (years): **adv.** *volventibus annis*
of relief for travel, education, etc.: **n.** sabbatical; Shemittah; **a.** sabbatical
of wonders: **n.** *annus mirabilis*
school: **n.** *année scolaire*

YEARLY: **see** "annual"

YEARN(ING) **see** "long" **and** "desire"

YELLOW(ISH): **a.** flavescent; flavous; fulvid; fulvous; luteous; lutescent; xanthic; xanthous

YESTERDAY, *pert. to:* **a.** hesternal

YIELDING: **a.** adaptable; amenable; capitulatory; (com)pliant; ductile; malleable; plastic; submissive; susceptible; tractable; **n.** capitulation; cession; complaisance; compliance; resignation; submission; succumbence; succumbency; surrender; **v.** YIELD: capitulate; submit; succumb; surrender
in judgment or opn.: **n.** deference; **a.** deferential

YOUNG: (**see** "youthful") **a.** adolescent; immature; impubic; inconabular; inexperienced; juvenile; puisne; vernal
bearing or bringing forth living: **a.** parturient; proligerous; viviparous; **n.** parturition; viviparity
bringing forth by eggs: **a.** oviparous; ovoviparous; **n.** oviparity; ovoviparity
bringing forth, or about to: **a.** aborning; parturient; **n.** parturition
lit. works designed for: **n.pl.** juvenilia
made by (writings, drawings, scratchings, etc.): **n.pl.** juvenilia
man: **n.** ephebe; ephebus; (**pl.** ephebi); yo(u)nker; **a.** ephebic
people, rich and fashionable ("gilded youth"): **n.pl.** *jeunesse dorée*
person: **n.** juvenile; minor; adolescent
state of being: **n.** adolescence; juniority; juvenescence; minority; nonage; puberty
to make again: **v.** reinvigorate; rejuvenate; rejuvenesce; **n.** reinvigoration; rejuvenation; rejuvenescence; renaissance; **a.** rejuvenescent
woman: **n.** ingénue; soubrette
actress who plays this part: **n.** ingénue
unsophisticated: **n.** debutant(e); ingénue
writings, drawings, scratchings, etc. of: **n.pl.** juvenilia

YOUNGER: **a.** junior; puisne; **n.** cadet; puisne
status of being: **n.** juniority, minority

YOUTH, *gawky:* **n.** hobbledehoy (**or** hobbletehoy)
"gilded:" **n.pl.** *jeunesse dorée*
goddess of: **n.** Hebe
period of: **n.** adolescence; juniority; *bel âge;* minority; nonage; puberty

YOUTHFUL: (**see** "young") **a.** adolescent; callow; hebetic; juvenile; maiden(ly); nealogic; neanic; puerile; vernal; virginal
growing: **v.** juvenesce; **a.** juvenescent; **n.** juvenescence
state of being: **n.** juvenescence

Z

ZEAL: **n.** ardor; assiduity; calenture; devotion; diligence; eagerness; enthusiasm; fanaticism; fervidity; fervor; fidelity; gusto; intensity; loyalty; passion; rabidity; sedulity; vehemence; verve; vigor; zest

excess of: **n.** fanaticism; zealotry

ZEALOUS: **a.** animated; ardent; assiduous; devoted; diligent; eager; evangelistic; fanatic(al); fervent; fervid; impassioned; intense; perfervid; rabid; sedulous; vehement; vivacious; zestful; **n.** animation; ardency; assiduity; devotion; diligence; eagerness; evangelism; vivacity; zest; zestfulness

ZENITH: **see** "acme"

ZEST: **see** "vigor" **and** "zeal"